Derivatives and Portfolio Management

CFA® PROGRAM CURRICULUM • VOLUME 6

LEVEL II
2007

PEARSON

Custom Publishing

Printed in the United States of America

10 9 8 7 6 5 4 3 2 1

ISBN 0-536-17614-0

2005160781

BK/JS

Please visit our web site at *www.pearsoncustom.com*

PEARSON CUSTOM PUBLISHING
75 Arlington Street, Suite 300, Boston, MA 02116
A Pearson Education Company

CONTENTS

45/8 4
5½ 5½ — 1/8
5½ 21¾6 — 1/8
20⅝ 21³/₁₆ — 7/8
17⅜ 18⅛ +
6½ 6½ —
7¼ 15/16 31/32 —
15/16
9/16 9/16
19/32
7¹⁵/₁₆ 7¹³/₁₆ 7¹⁵/₁₆
2⅝ 2¹¹/₃₂ 2½ +
2¾ 2¼ 2¼
6⅛ 12¹/₁₆ 11⅜ 11¾ +
87 33¾ 33 33⅛ —
25⅝ 24⁹/₁₆ 25⅜ +
833 12 11⅝ 11⅞ +
16 10½ 10½ 10½ —
78 15⅞ 15¹³/₁₆ 15⅜ —
4508 9¹/₁₆ 8¼ 8⅞ +
430 11¼ 10⅛ 10½
4⅜ 4⅞

HOW TO USE THE CFA PROGRAM CURRICULUM

Congratulations on passing LI of the Chartered Financial Analyst (CFA®) Program. This exciting and rewarding program of study reflects your desire to become a serious investment professional. You are participating in a program noted for its requirement of ethics and breadth of knowledge, skills, and abilities.

The credential you seek is respected around the world as a mark of accomplishment and dedication, and each level of the program represents a distinct achievement in professional development. Successful completion of the program is rewarded with membership in a prestigious global community of investment professionals. CFA charterholders are dedicated to life-long learning and maintaining currency with the ever-changing dynamics of a challenging profession.

Curriculum Development

The CFA Program curriculum is grounded in the practice of the investment profession. CFA Institute regularly conducts a practice analysis survey of investment professionals around the world to determine the knowledge, skills, and abilities that are relevant to the profession. The survey results define the Candidate Body of Knowledge (CBOK™), an inventory of knowledge and responsibilities expected of the investment management professional at the level of a new CFA charterholder. The survey also determines how much emphasis each of the major topic areas receives on the CFA examinations.

A committee made up of practicing charterholders, in conjunction with CFA Institute staff, designs the CFA Program curriculum to deliver the CBOK to candidates. The examinations, also written by practicing charterholders, are designed for you to demonstrate mastery of the CBOK as set forth in the CFA Program curriculum. As you structure your personal study program, you should emphasize mastery of the CBOK and the practical application of that knowledge. For more information on the practice analysis, CBOK, and development of the CFA Program curriculum, please visit www.cfainstitute.org/course.

Organization

The 2007 Level II CFA Program curriculum is organized into 10 topic areas. Each topic area begins with a topic level learning outcome that summarizes the broad objective of the material to follow and indicates the depth of knowledge expected. Each topic area is then divided into one or more study sessions, each devoted to a sub-topic (or group of sub-topics) within that topic area. The 2007 Level II curriculum is organized into 18 study sessions. Each study session begins with a purpose statement defining the content structure and objective of that session. Finally, each study session is further divided into reading assignments. *The outline on the inside front cover of each volume should further illustrate this important hierarchy.*

The reading assignments are the basis for all examination questions. The readings are selected or developed specifically to teach candidates the CBOK. Readings are drawn from textbook chapters, professional journal articles, research analyst reports, CFA Program-commissioned content, and cases. Many readings include problems and solutions as well as appendices to help you learn.

Reading-specific Learning Outcome Statements (LOS) are listed in the study session opener page as well as prior to each reading. Reading-specific LOS indicate what you should be able to accomplish after studying the reading. It is important, however, not to interpret LOS narrowly by focusing on a few key sentences in a reading. Readings, particularly CFA Program-commissioned readings, provide context for the learning outcome and enable you to apply a principle or concept in a variety of scenarios. Thus, you should use the LOS to guide and focus your study, as each examination question is based explicitly on one or more LOS. We encourage you to thoroughly review how to properly use LOS and the list and descriptions of commonly used LOS command words at www.cfainstitute.org/toolkit. The command words signal the depth of learning you are expected to achieve from the reading.

Features for 2007

▶ **Required vs. Optional segments** - Several reading assignments use only a portion of the original source textbook chapter or journal article. In order to allow you to read the assignment within its full context, however, we have reprinted the entire chapter or article in the curriculum. When an optional segment begins, you will see an icon. A vertical solid bar in the outside margin will continue until the optional segment ends, symbolized by another icon. Unless the material is specifically noted as optional, you should assume it is required. Keep in mind that the optional material is provided strictly for your convenience and will not be tested. *You should rely on the required segments and the reading-specific LOS in preparing for the examination.*

▶ **Problems/Solutions** - When appropriate, we have developed and assigned problems after readings to demonstrate practical application and reinforce understanding of the concepts presented. The solutions to the problems are provided in an appendix at the back of each volume. Candidates should consider all problems and solutions required material as your ability to solve these problems will prepare you for exam questions.

▶ **Margins** - We have inserted wide margins throughout each volume to allow for easier note taking.

▶ **Two-color format** - To enrich the visual appeal and clarity of the exhibits, tables, and required vs. optional treatments, we have printed the curriculum in two-color format.

▶ **Six- volume structure** - To improve the portability of the curriculum, we have spread the material over six volumes.

▶ **Glossary and Index** - For your convenience, we have printed a comprehensive glossary and index in each volume. Throughout the curriculum, a **bolded blue** word in a reading denotes a glossary term.

Designing your personal study program:

Create a schedule - An orderly, systematic approach to preparation is critical to successful completion of the examination. You should dedicate a consistent block of time every week to reading and studying. Complete all reading assignments and the associated problems and solutions in each study session. Review the LOS both before and after you study each reading to ensure that you have mastered the applicable content and can complete the action(s) specified. Upon

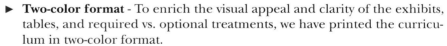

completion of each study session, review the session's purpose statement and confirm that you thoroughly understand the subject matter. When you complete a topic area, review the topic level learning outcome and verify that you have mastered the objectives.

CFA Institute estimates that you will need to devote a minimum of 10-15 hours per week for 18 weeks to study the assigned readings. Allow a minimum of one week for each study session spread over several days, with completion scheduled for at least 30-45 days prior to the examination. This schedule will allow you to spend the final four to six weeks before the examination reviewing the assigned material and taking multiple on-line sample examinations. At CFA Institute, we believe that candidates need to commit to a *minimum* of 250 hours reading and reviewing the curriculum and taking online sample exams to master the material. This recommendation, however, may substantially underestimate the hours needed for appropriate exam preparation depending on individual circumstances and academic background.

You will undoubtedly adjust your study time to conform to your own strengths and weaknesses and academic background, and you will probably spend more time on some study sessions than on others. You should allow ample time for both in-depth study of all topic areas and additional concentration on those topic areas for which you feel least prepared.

Candidate Preparation Toolkit - We have created the online toolkit to provide a single comprehensive location for resources and guidance for candidate preparation. In addition to in-depth information on study program planning, the CFA Program curriculum, and the online sample exams, the toolkit also contains curriculum errata, printable study session outlines, sample exam questions, and more. We encourage you to use the toolkit as your central preparation resource during your tenure as a candidate. Visit the toolkit at www.cfainstitute.org/toolkit.

Online Sample Exams - After completing your study of the assigned curriculum, use the CFA Institute online sample exams to measure your knowledge of the topics and improve your exam-taking skills. After each question, you will receive immediate feedback noting the correct response and indicating the assigned curriculum for further study. The sample exams are designed by the same people who create the actual CFA exams, and reflect the question formats, topics, and level of difficulty of the actual CFA examinations, in a timed environment. Aggregate data indicate that the CFA examination pass rate was higher among candidates who took one or more online sample examinations than for candidates who did not take the online sample exams. For more information on the online sample exams, please visit www.cfainstitute.org/toolkit.

Review Programs - After you enroll in the CFA Program, you may receive numerous solicitations for preparatory courses and review materials. Although preparatory courses and notes may be helpful to some candidates, you should view these resources as *supplements to the assigned CFA Program curriculum*. The CFA exams reference *only* the 2007 CFA Institute assigned curriculum; no preparatory course or review course materials are consulted or referenced.

Furthermore, CFA Institute does not endorse, promote, review, or warrant the accuracy of the products or services offered by preparatory organizations. CFA Institute does not verify or endorse the pass rates or other claims made by these organizations.

Feedback

At CFA Institute, we are committed to delivering a comprehensive and rigorous curriculum for the development of competent, ethically grounded investment professionals. We rely on candidate and member feedback as we work to incorporate content, design, and packaging improvements. You can be assured that we will continue to listen to your suggestions. Please send any comments or feedback to curriculum@cfainstitute.org. Ongoing improvements in the curriculum will help you prepare for success on the upcoming examinations, and for a lifetime of learning as a serious investment professional.

ANALYSIS OF DERIVATIVE INVESTMENTS

TOPIC LEVEL LEARNING OUTCOME

The candidate should be able to value futures, forwards, options, and
swaps, and demonstrate how they may be used in various strategies.

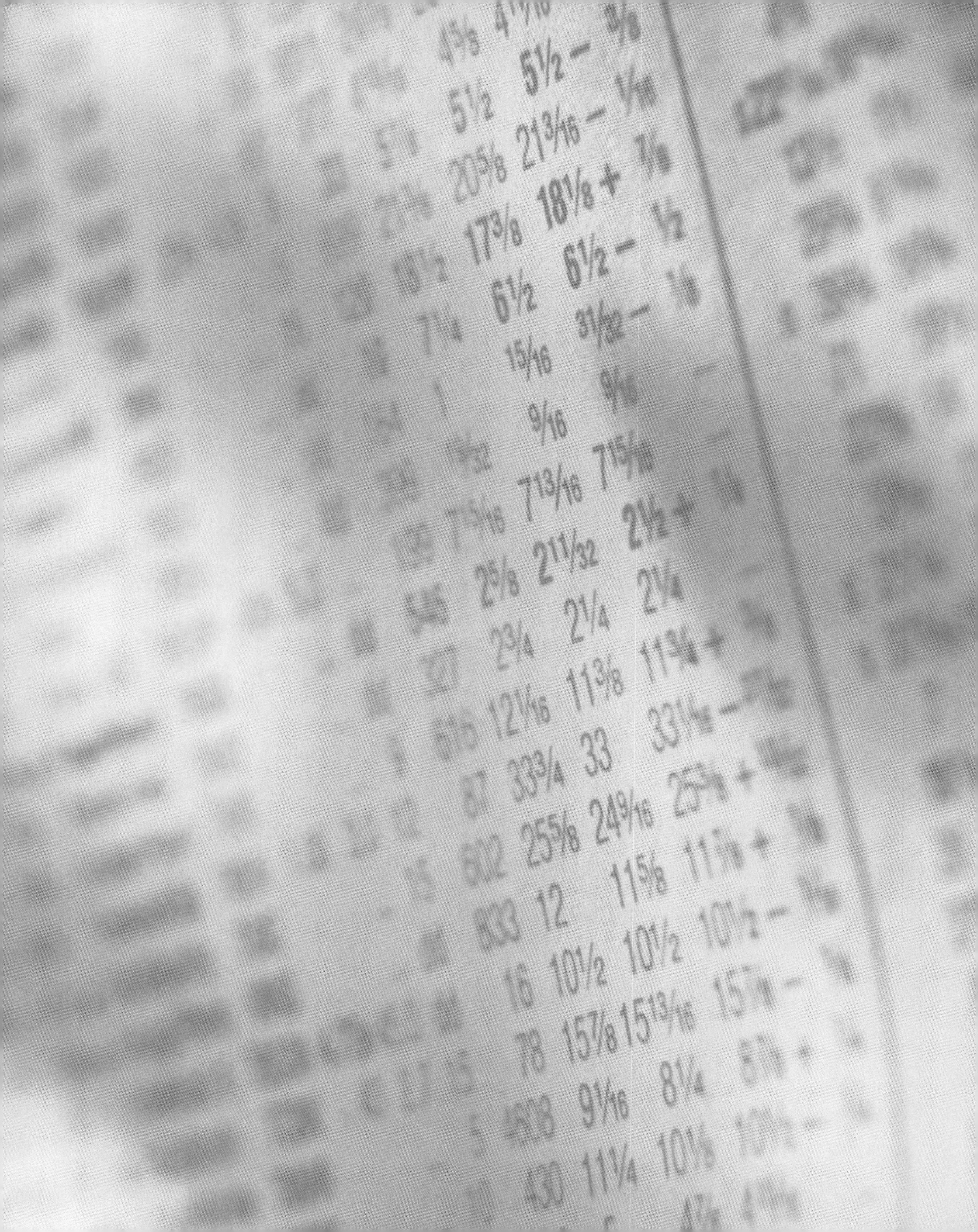

4⅝ 4¹¹/₁₆

5½ 5½ – ⅜

5½ 21³/₁₆ – ⁵/₁₆

20⅝ 21³/₁₆

17⅜ 18⅛ + ⅞

18½

6½ 6½ – ½

7¼ 31/32 – ⅛

15/16 9/16

1 9/16

9/16

13/32 7¹⁵/₁₆

7¹⁵/₁₆ 7¹³/₁₆ 7¹⁵/₁₆

2⅝ 2¹¹/₃₂ 2½ +

2¾ 2¼ 2¼

12¹/₁₆ 11⅜ 11¾ +

33¾ 33 33¼ –

602 25⅝ 24⁹/₁₆ 25⅝ +

833 12 11⅝ 11⅝ +

16 10½ 10½ 10½ –

78 15⅞ 15¹³/₁₆ 15⅞ –

4608 9¹/₁₆ 8¼ 8⅛ +

430 11¼ 10⅛

STUDY SESSION 16
DERIVATIVE INVESTMENTS:
Forwards and Futures

READING ASSIGNMENTS

Reading 64   Forward Markets and Contracts
Reading 65   Futures Markets and Contracts

This study session looks at derivative investments and markets and focuses on the concepts of derivative pricing and valuation and credit risk evaluation. To assist in determining the relative cost/benefit of using derivative instruments or investments with embedded derivatives, it is essential to know and understand the factors that affect valuation. This study session addresses interest rate, equity, and currency forwards and futures.

LEARNING OUTCOMES

Reading 64: Forward Markets and Contracts
The candidate should be able to:

a. explain how the value of a forward contract is determined at initiation, during the life of the contract, and at expiration;

b. distinguish an off-market forward contract from the more standard type of forward contract;

c. calculate and interpret the price and the value of an equity forward contract, given the different possible patterns of dividend payments;

d. calculate and interpret the price and the value of 1) a forward contract on a fixed income security, 2) a forward rate agreement (FRA), and 3) a forward contract on a currency;

e. evaluate credit risk in a forward contract and how market value is a measure of the credit risk to a party in a forward contract.

Reading 65: Futures Markets and Contracts

The candidate should be able to:

a. describe the difficulties in determining the price of Eurodollar futures and creating a pure arbitrage opportunity;

b. explain why the futures price must converge to the spot price at expiration;

c. explain how to determine the value of a futures contract;

d. explain how forward and futures prices differ;

e. identify the different types of monetary and non-monetary benefits and costs associated with holding the underlying asset, and explain how they affect the futures price; illustrate with backwardation and contango;

f. discuss whether futures prices equal expected spot prices;

g. describe and illustrate how to price Treasury bond futures, stock index futures, and currency futures.

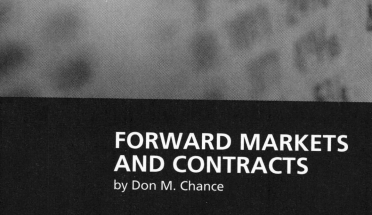

FORWARD MARKETS AND CONTRACTS
by Don M. Chance

LEARNING OUTCOMES

The candidate should be able to:

a. explain how the value of a forward contract is determined at initiation, during the life of the contract, and at expiration;

b. distinguish an off-market forward contract from the more standard type of forward contract;

c. calculate and interpret the price and the value of an equity forward contract, given the different possible patterns of dividend payments;

d. calculate and interpret the price and the value of 1) a forward contract on a fixed income security, 2) a forward rate agreement (FRA), and 3) a forward contract on a currency;

e. evaluate credit risk in a forward contract and how market value is a measure of the credit risk to a party in a forward contract.

INTRODUCTION 1

OPTIONAL SEGMENT
BEGINS

Recall the definition of a forward contract: *A forward contract is an agreement between two parties in which one party, the buyer, agrees to buy from the other party, the seller, an underlying asset or other derivative, at a future date at a price established at the start of the contract.* Therefore, it is a commitment by two parties to engage in a transaction at a later date with the price set in advance. The buyer is often called the **long** and the seller is often called the **short**.[1] Although any two parties can agree on such a contract, in this book we are interested only in forward contracts that involve large corporations, financial institutions, nonprofit organizations, or governments.

---

[1]The derivatives industry often uses nouns, verbs, adjectives, and adverbs as parts of speech other than what they are. Hence, words like *long* and *short* are used not as adjectives but as nouns.

As an example, a pension fund manager, anticipating the receipt of cash at a future date, might enter into a commitment to purchase a stock portfolio at a later date at a price agreed on today. By doing so, the manager's position is unaffected by any changes in the value of the stock portfolio between today and the date of the actual investment in the stock portfolio. In this sense, the manager is hedged against an increase in stock prices until the cash is received and invested. The disadvantage of such a transaction is that the manager is also hedged against any decreases in stock prices. If stock prices fall between the time the commitment is established and the time the cash is received, the manager will regret having entered into the forward contract because the stock could have been acquired at a lower price. But that is the nature of a forward contract hedge: It locks in a price.

An important feature of a forward contract is that neither party pays any money at the start. The parties might require some collateral to minimize the risk of default, but we shall ignore this point. So keep in mind this very important aspect of forward contracts: *No money changes hands at the start.*

1.1 Delivery and Settlement of a Forward Contract

When a forward contract expires, there are two possible arrangements that can be used to settle the obligations of the parties. A deliverable forward contract stipulates that the long will pay the agreed-upon price to the short, who in turn will deliver the underlying asset to the long, a process called **delivery**. An alternative procedure, called **cash settlement**, permits the long and short to pay the net cash value of the position on the delivery date. For example, suppose two parties agree to a forward contract to deliver a zero-coupon bond at a price of $98 per $100 par. At the contract's expiration, suppose the underlying zero-coupon bond is selling at a price of $98.25. The long is due to receive from the short an asset worth $98.25, for which a payment to the short of $98.00 is required. In a cash-settled forward contract, the short simply pays the long $0.25. If the zero-coupon bond were selling for $97.50, the long would pay the short $0.50. Delivery of a zero-coupon bond is not a difficult thing to do, however, and cash-settled contracts are more commonly used in situations where delivery is impractical.[2] For example, if the underlying is the Russell 3000 Index, the short would have to deliver to the long a portfolio containing each of the Russell 3000 stocks proportionate to its weighting in the index. Consequently, cash settlement is much more practical. Cash-settled forward contracts are sometimes called **NDFs**, for **nondeliverable forwards**, although this term is used predominately with respect to foreign exchange forwards.

1.2 Default Risk and Forward Contracts

An important characteristic of forward contracts is that they are subject to default. Regardless of whether the contract is for delivery or cash settlement, the potential exists for a party to default. In the zero-coupon bond example above,

---

[2]Be aware, however, that the choice of delivery or cash settlement is not an option available at expiration. It is negotiated between the parties at the start.

the long might be unable to pay the $98 or the short might be unable to buy the zero-coupon bond and make delivery of the bond to the long. Generally speaking, however, forward contracts are structured so that only the party owing the greater amount can default. In other words, if the short is obligated to deliver a zero-coupon bond selling for more than $98, then the long would not be obligated to make payment unless the short makes delivery. Likewise, in a cash settled contract, only one party—the one owing the greater amount—can default. We discuss the nature of this credit risk in the following section and in Section 5 after we have determined how to value forward contracts.

1.3 Termination of a Forward Contract

Let us note that a forward contract is nearly always constructed with the idea that the participants will hold on to their positions until the contract expires and either engage in delivery of the asset or settle the cash equivalent, as required in the specific contract. The possibility exists, however, that at least one of the participants might wish to terminate the position prior to expiration. For example, suppose a party goes long, meaning that she agrees to buy the asset at the expiration date at the price agreed on at the start, but she subsequently decides to terminate the contract before expiration. We shall assume that the contract calls for delivery rather than cash settlement at expiration.

To see the details of the contract termination, suppose it is part of the way through the life of the contract, and the long decides that she no longer wishes to buy the asset at expiration. She can then re-enter the market and create a new forward contract expiring at the same time as the original forward contract, taking the position of the seller instead. Because of price changes in the market during the period since the original contract was created, this new contract would likely have a different price at which she would have to commit to sell. She would then be long a contract to buy the asset at expiration at one price and short a contract to sell the asset at expiration at a different price. It should be apparent that she has no further exposure to the price of the asset.

For example, suppose she is long to buy at $40 and short to deliver at $42. Depending on the characteristics of the contract, one of several possibilities could occur at expiration. Everything could go as planned—the party holding the short position of the contract on which she is long at $40 delivers the asset to her, and she pays him $40. She then delivers the asset to the party who is long the contract on which she is short at $42. That party pays her $42. She nets $2. The transaction is over.

There is always a possibility that her counterparty on the long contract could default. She is still obligated to deliver the asset on the short contract, for which she will receive $42. But if her counterparty on the long contract defaults, she has to buy the asset in the market and could suffer a significant loss. There is also a possibility that the counterparty on her short contract could fail to pay her the $42. Of course, she would then not deliver the asset but would be exposed to the risk of changes in the asset's price. This type of problem illustrates the credit risk in a forward contract. We shall cover credit risk in more detail in Section 5 of this reading.

To avoid the credit risk, when she re-enters the market to go short the forward contract, she could contact the same counterparty with whom she engaged in the long forward contract. They could agree to cancel both contracts. Because she would be owed $2 at expiration, cancellation of the contract would result in the counterparty paying her the present value of $2. This termination or offset of the original forward position is clearly desirable for both counterparties because it eliminates the credit risk.[3] It is always possible, however, that she might receive a better price from another counterparty. If that price is sufficiently attractive and she does not perceive the credit risk to be too high, she may choose to deal with the other counterparty and leave the credit risk in the picture.

2 THE STRUCTURE OF GLOBAL FORWARD MARKETS

The global market for forward contracts is part of a vast network of financial institutions that make markets in these instruments as well as in other related derivatives, such as swaps and options. Some dealers specialize in certain markets and contracts, such as forward contracts on the euro or forward contracts on Japanese equity products. These dealers are mainly large global banking institutions, but many large non-banking institutions, such as Goldman Sachs and Merrill Lynch, are also big players in this market.

Dealers engage in transactions with two types of parties: end users and other dealers. An end user is typically a corporation, nonprofit organization, or government.[4] An end user is generally a party with a risk management problem that is searching for a dealer to provide it with a financial transaction to solve that problem. Although the problem could simply be that the party wants to take a position in anticipation of a market move, more commonly the end user has a risk it wants to reduce or eliminate.

As an example, Hoffman-LaRoche, the large Swiss pharmaceutical company, sells its products globally. Anticipating the receipt of a large amount of cash in U.S. dollars and worried about a decrease in the value of the dollar relative to the Swiss franc, it could buy a forward contract to sell the dollar and buy Swiss francs. It might seek out a dealer such as UBS Warburg, the investment firm affiliated with the large Swiss bank UBS, or it might approach any of the other large multinational banks with which it does business. Or it might end up dealing with a non-bank entity, like Merrill Lynch. Assume that Hoffman-LaRoche enters into this contract with UBS Warburg. Hoffman-LaRoche is the end user; UBS Warburg is the dealer.

Transactions in forward contracts typically are conducted over the phone. Each dealer has a quote desk, whose phone number is well known to the major participants in the market. If a party wishes to conduct a transaction, it simply phones the dealer for a quote. The dealer stands ready to take either side of the transaction, quoting a bid and an ask price or rate. The bid is the price at which the dealer is willing to pay for the future purchase of the asset, and the ask is the price at which the dealer is willing to sell. When a dealer engages in a forward transaction, it has then taken on risk from the other party. For example, in the aforementioned transaction of Hoffman-LaRoche and UBS Warburg, by entering into the contract, UBS Warburg takes on a risk that Hoffman-LaRoche has eliminated. Specifically, UBS Warburg has now committed to buying dollars and selling Swiss francs at a future date. Thus, UBS Warburg is effectively long the dollar and stands to gain from a strengthening dollar/weakening Swiss franc.

---

[3] This statement is made under the assumption that the parties do not want the credit risk. Credit risk, like other risks, however, can be a risk that some parties want because of the potential for earning attractive returns by using their expertise in measuring the actual credit risk relative to the credit risk as perceived by the market. In addition, credit risk offers diversification benefits.

[4] The U.S. government does not transact in forward contracts or other derivatives, but some foreign governments and central banks do. Within the United States, however, some state and local governments do engage in forward contracts and other derivatives.

Typically dealers do not want to hold this exposure. Rather, they find another party to offset the exposure with another derivative or spot transaction. Thus, UBS Warburg is a wholesaler of risk—buying it, selling it, and trying to earn a profit off the spread between its buying price and selling price.

One might reasonably wonder why Hoffman-LaRoche could not avoid the cost of dealing with UBS Warburg. In some cases, it might be able to. It might be aware of another party with the exact opposite needs, but such a situation is rare. The market for financial products such as forward contracts is made up of wholesalers of risk management products who use their technical expertise, their vast network of contacts, and their access to critical financial market information to provide a more efficient means for end users to engage in such risk management transactions.

Dealers such as UBS Warburg lay off the risk they do not wish to assume by transacting with other dealers and potentially other end users. If they do this carefully, quickly, and at accurate prices, they can earn a profit from this market-making activity. One should not get the impression, however, that market making is a highly profitable activity. The competition is fierce, which keeps bid–ask spreads very low and makes it difficult to earn much money on a given transaction. Indeed, many market makers do not make much money on individual transactions—they typically make a small amount of money on each transaction and do a large number of transactions. They may even lose money on some standard transactions, hoping to make up losses on more-complicated, nonstandard transactions, which occur less frequently but have higher bid–ask spreads.

Risk magazine conducts annual surveys to identify the top dealers in various derivative products. Exhibit 64-1 presents the results of those surveys for two of the forward products we cover here, currency and interest rate forwards. Interest rate forwards are called forward rate agreements (FRAs). In the next section, we shall study the different types of forward contracts and note that there are some others not covered in the *Risk* surveys.

One of these surveys was sent to banks and investment banks that are active dealers in over-the-counter derivatives. The other survey was sent to end users. The tabulations are based on respondents' simple rankings of who they think are the best dealers. Although the identities of the specific dealer firms are not critical, it is interesting and helpful to be aware of the major players in these types of contracts. Most of the world's leading global financial institutions are listed, but many other big names are not. It is also interesting to observe that the perceptions of the users of these dealer firms' services differ somewhat from the dealers' self-perceptions. Be aware, however, that the rankings change, sometimes drastically, each year.

TYPES OF FORWARD CONTRACTS

3

In this section, we examine the types of forward contracts that fall within the scope of this reading. By the word "types," we mean the underlying asset groups on which these forward contracts are created. Because the CFA Program focuses on the asset management industry, our primary interest is in equity, interest rate and fixed-income, and currency forwards.

3.1 Equity Forwards

An **equity forward** is a contract calling for the purchase of an individual stock, a stock portfolio, or a stock index at a later date. For the most part, the differences

EXHIBIT 64-1	*Risk* Magazine Surveys of Banks, Investment Banks, and Corporate End Users to Determine the Top Three Dealers in Currency and Interest Rate Forwards

	Respondents	
Currencies	**Banks and Investment Banks**	**Corporate End Users**
Currency Forwards		
$/€	UBS Warburg	Citigroup
	Deutsche Bank	Royal Bank of Scotland
	JP Morgan Chase	JP Morgan Chase/Bank of America
$/¥	UBS Warburg	Citigroup
	Citigroup	Bank of America
	JP Morgan Chase	JP Morgan Chase/UBS Warburg
$/£	UBS Warburg	Royal Bank of Scotland
	Royal Bank of Scotland	Citigroup
	Hong Kong Shanghai Banking Corporation	UBS Warburg
$/SF	UBS Warburg	UBS Warburg
	Credit Suisse First Boston	Citigroup
	BNP Paribas	Credit Suisse First Boston
Interest Rate Forwards (FRAs)		
$	JP Morgan Chase	JP Morgan Chase
	Bank of America	Royal Bank of Scotland
	Deutsche Bank	Bank of America
€	Deutsche Bank	Royal Bank of Scotland
	Intesa BCI	JP Morgan Chase
	Royal Bank of Scotland	Deutsche Bank
¥	Mizuho Securities	Citigroup
	JP Morgan Chase	Merrill Lynch
	BNP Paribas	Hong Kong Shanghai Banking Corporation
£	Royal Bank of Scotland	Royal Bank of Scotland
	Commerzbank	Bank of America/ING Barings
	Deutsche Bank	
SF	Credit Suisse First Boston	UBS Warburg
	UBS Warburg	Credit Suisse First Boston
	Deutsche Bank	Citigroup/ING Barings

Note: $ = US dollar, € = euro, ¥ = Japanese yen, £ = U.K. pound sterling, SF = Swiss franc.

Source: Risk, September 2002, pp. 30–67 for banks and investment banking dealer respondents, and June 2002, pp. 24–34 for end user respondents. The end user survey provides responses from corporations and asset managers. The above results are for corporate respondents only.

in types of equity forward contracts are only slight, depending on whether the contract is on an individual stock, a portfolio of stocks, or a stock index.

3.1.1 Forward Contracts on Individual Stocks

Consider an asset manager responsible for the portfolio of a high-net-worth individual. As is sometimes the case, such portfolios may be concentrated in a small number of stocks, sometimes stocks that have been in the family for years. In many cases, the individual may be part of the founding family of a particular company. Let us say that the stock is called Gregorian Industries, Inc., or GII, and the client is so heavily invested in this stock that her portfolio is not diversified. The client notifies the portfolio manager of her need for $2 million in cash in six months. This cash can be raised by selling 16,000 shares at the current price of $125 per share. Thus, the risk exposure concerns the market value of $2 million of stock. For whatever reason, it is considered best not to sell the stock any earlier than necessary. The portfolio manager realizes that a forward contract to sell GII in six months will accomplish the client's desired objective. The manager contacts a forward contract dealer and obtains a quote of $128.13 as the price at which a forward contract to sell the stock in six months could be constructed.[5] In other words, the portfolio manager could enter into a contract to sell the stock to the dealer in six months at $128.13. We assume that this contract is deliverable, meaning that when the sale is actually made, the shares will be delivered to the dealer. Assuming that the client has some flexibility in the amount of money needed, let us say that the contract is signed for the sale of 15,600 shares at $128.13, which will raise $1,998,828. Of course when the contract expires, the stock could be selling for any price. The client can gain or lose on the transaction. If the stock rises to a price above $128.13 during the six-month period, the client will still have to deliver the stock for $128.13. But if the price falls, the client will still get $128.13 per share for the stock.

3.1.2 Forward Contracts on Stock Portfolios

Because modern portfolio theory and good common sense dictate that investors should hold diversified portfolios, it is reasonable to assume that forward contracts on specific stock portfolios would be useful. Suppose a pension fund manager knows that in three months he will need to sell about $20 million of stock to make payments to retirees. The manager has analyzed the portfolio and determined the precise identities of the stocks he wants to sell and the number of shares of each that he would like to sell. Thus the manager has designated a specific subportfolio to be sold. The problem is that the prices of these stocks in three months are uncertain. The manager can, however, lock in the sale prices by entering into a forward contract to sell the portfolio. This can be done one of two ways.

The manager can enter into a forward contract on each stock that he wants to sell. Alternatively, he can enter into a forward contract on the overall portfolio. The first way would be more costly, as each contract would incur administrative costs, whereas the second way would incur only one set of costs.[6] Assume that the manager chooses the second method. He provides a list of the stocks and

---

[5]In Section 4, we shall learn how to calculate forward prices such as this one.

[6]Ignoring those costs, there would be no difference in doing forward contracts on individual stocks or a single forward contract on a portfolio. Because of the non-linearity of their payoffs, this is not true for options. A portfolio of options is not the same as an option on a portfolio, but a portfolio of forward contracts is the same as a forward contract on a portfolio, ignoring the aforementioned costs.

number of shares of each he wishes to sell to the dealer and obtains a quote. The dealer gives him a quote of $20,200,000. So, in three months, the manager will sell the stock to the dealer and receive $20,200,000. The transaction can be structured to call for either actual delivery or cash settlement, but in either case, the client will effectively receive $20,200,000 for the stock.[7]

3.1.3 Forward Contracts on Stock Indices

Many equity forward contracts are based on a stock index. For example, consider a U.K. asset manager who wants to protect the value of her portfolio that is a Financial Times Stock Exchange 100 index fund, or who wants to eliminate a risk for which the FTSE 100 Index is a sufficiently accurate representation of the risk she wishes to eliminate. For example, the manager may be anticipating the sale of a number of U.K. blue chip shares at a future date. The manager could, as in our stock portfolio example, take a specific portfolio of stocks to a forward contract dealer and obtain a forward contract on that portfolio. She realizes, however, that a forward contract on a widely accepted benchmark would result in a better price quote, because the dealer can more easily hedge the risk with other transactions. Moreover, the manager is not even sure which stocks she will still be holding at the later date. She simply knows that she will sell a certain amount of stock at a later date and believes that the FTSE 100 is representative of the stock that she will sell. The manager is concerned with the systematic risk associated with the U.K. stock market, and accordingly, she decides that selling a forward contract on the FTSE 100 would be a good way to manage the risk.

Assume that the portfolio manager decides to protect £15,000,000 of stock. The dealer quotes a price of £6,000 on a forward contract covering £15,000,000. We assume that the contract will be cash settled because such index contracts are nearly always done that way. When the contract expiration date arrives, let us say that the index is at £5,925—a decrease of 1.25 percent from the forward price. Because the manager is short the contract and its price went down, the transaction makes money. But how much did it make on a notional principal of £15,000,000?

The index declined by 1.25 percent. Thus, the transaction should make $0.0125 \times £15,000,000 = £187,500$. In other words, the dealer would have to pay £187,500 in cash. If the portfolio were a FTSE 100 index fund, then it would be viewed as a portfolio initially worth £15,000,000 that declined by 1.25 percent, a loss of £187,500. The forward contract offsets this loss. Of course, in reality, the portfolio is not an index fund and such a hedge is not perfect, but as noted above, there are sometimes reasons for preferring that the forward contract be based on an index.

3.1.4 The Effect of Dividends

It is important to note the effect of dividends in equity forward contracts. Any equity portfolio nearly always has at least a few stocks that pay dividends, and it is inconceivable that any well-known equity index would not have some component

---

[7] If, for example, the stock is worth $20,500,000 and the transaction calls for delivery, the manager will transfer the stocks to the dealer and receive $20,200,000. The client effectively takes an opportunity loss of $300,000. If the transaction is structured as a cash settlement, the client will pay the dealer $300,000. The client would then sell the stock in the market, receiving $20,500,000 and netting $20,200,000 after settling the forward contract with the dealer. Similarly, if the stock is selling for less than the amount guaranteed by the forward contract, the client will deliver the stock and receive $20,200,000 or, if the transaction is cash settled, the client will sell the stock in the market and receive a cash payment from the dealer, making the effective sale price still $20,200,000.

stocks that pay dividends. Equity forward contracts typically have payoffs based only on the price of the equity, value of the portfolio, or level of the index. They do not ordinarily pay off any dividends paid by the component stocks. An exception, however, is that some equity forwards on stock indices are based on total return indices. For example, there are two versions of the well-known S&P 500 Index. One represents only the market value of the stocks. The other, called the S&P 500 Total Return Index, is structured so that daily dividends paid by the stocks are reinvested in additional units of the index, as though it were a portfolio. In this manner, the rate of return on the index, and the payoff of any forward contract based on it, reflects the payment and reinvestment of dividends into the underlying index. Although this feature might appear attractive, it is not necessarily of much importance in risk management problems. The variability of prices is so much greater than the variability of dividends that managing price risk is considered much more important than worrying about the uncertainty of dividends.

In summary, equity forwards can be based on individual stocks, specific stock portfolios, or stock indices. Moreover, these underlying equities often pay dividends, which can affect forward contracts on equities. Let us now look at bond and interest rate forward contracts.

3.2 Bond and Interest Rate Forward Contracts

Forward contracts on bonds are similar to forward contracts on interest rates, but the two are different instruments. Forward contracts on bonds, in fact, are no more difficult to understand than those on equities. Drawing on our experience of Section 3.1, we simply extend the notion of a forward contract on an individual stock, a specific stock portfolio, or a stock index to that of a forward contract on an individual bond, a specific bond portfolio, or a bond index.[8]

3.2.1 Forward Contracts on Individual Bonds and Bond Portfolios

Although a forward contract on a bond and one on a stock are similar, some basic differences nonetheless exist between the two. For example, the bond may pay a coupon, which corresponds somewhat to the dividend that a stock might pay. But unlike a stock, a bond matures, and a forward contract on a bond must expire prior to the bond's maturity date. In addition, bonds often have many special features such as calls and convertibility. Finally, we should note that unlike a stock, a bond carries the risk of default. A forward contract written on a bond must contain a provision to recognize how default is defined, what it means for the bond to default, and how default would affect the parties to the contract.

In addition to forward contracts on individual bonds, there are also forward contracts on portfolios of bonds as well as on bond indices. The technical distinctions between forward contracts on individual bonds and collections of bonds, however, are relatively minor.

The primary bonds for which we shall consider forward contracts are default-free zero-coupon bonds, typically called Treasury bills or T-bills in the United States, which serve as a proxy for the risk-free rate.[9] In a forward contract

---

[8]It may be useful to review Chapters 1 and 3 of *Fixed Income Analysis for the Chartered Financial Analyst Program* by Frank J. Fabozzi, New Hope, PA: Frank J. Fabozzi Associates (2000).

[9]A government-issued zero-coupon bond is typically used as a proxy for a risk-free asset because it is assumed to be free of default risk. It can be purchased and held to maturity, thereby eliminating any market value risk, and it has no reinvestment risk because it has no coupons. If the bond is liquidated before maturity, however, some market value risk exists in addition to the risk associated with reinvesting the market price.

on a T-bill, one party agrees to buy the T-bill at a later date, prior to the bill's maturity, at a price agreed on today. T-bills are typically sold at a discount from par value and the price is quoted in terms of the discount rate. Thus, if a 180-day T-bill is selling at a discount of 4 percent, its price per $1 par will be $1 − 0.04(180/360) = $0.98. The use of 360 days is the convention in calculating the discount. So the bill will sell for $0.98. If purchased and held to maturity, it will pay off $1. This procedure means that the interest is deducted from the face value in advance, which is called **discount interest**.

The T-bill is usually traded by quoting the discount rate, not the price. It is understood that the discount rate can be easily converted to the price by the above procedure. A forward contract might be constructed that would call for delivery of a 90-day T-bill in 60 days. Such a contract might sell for $0.9895, which would imply a discount rate of 4.2 percent because $1 − 0.042(90/360) = $0.9895. Later in this reading, we shall see how forward prices of T-bills are derived.

In addition to forward contracts on zero-coupon bonds/T-bills, we shall consider forward contracts on default-free coupon-bearing bonds, also called Treasury bonds in the United States. These instruments pay interest, typically in semiannual installments, and can sell for more (less) than par value if the yield is lower (higher) than the coupon rate. Prices are typically quoted without the interest that has accrued since the last coupon date, but with a few exceptions, we shall always work with the **full price**—that is, the price including accrued interest. Prices are often quoted by stating the yield. Forward contracts call for delivery of such a bond at a date prior to the bond's maturity, for which the long pays the short the agreed-upon price.

3.2.2 Forward Contracts on Interest Rates: Forward Rate Agreements

So far in Section 3.2 we have discussed forward contracts on actual fixed-income securities. Fixed-income security prices are driven by interest rates. A more common type of forward contract is the interest rate forward contract, more commonly called a **forward rate agreement** or **FRA**. Before we can begin to understand FRAs, however, we must examine the instruments on which they are based.

There is a large global market for time deposits in various currencies issued by large creditworthy banks. This market is primarily centered in London but also exists elsewhere, though not in the United States. The primary time deposit instrument is called the **Eurodollar**, which is a dollar deposited outside the Unites States. Banks borrow dollars from other banks by issuing Eurodollar time deposits, which are essentially short-term unsecured loans. In London, the rate on such dollar loans is called the London Interbank Rate. Although there are rates for both borrowing and lending, in the financial markets the lending rate, called the **London Interbank Offer Rate** or **LIBOR**, is more commonly used in derivative contracts. LIBOR is the rate at which London banks lend dollars to other London banks. Even though it represents a loan outside of the United States, LIBOR is considered to be the best representative rate on a dollar borrowed by a private, i.e., nongovernmental, high-quality borrower. It should be noted, however, that the London market includes many branches of banks from outside the United Kingdom, and these banks are also active participants in the **Eurodollar market**.

A Eurodollar time deposit is structured as follows. Let us say a London bank such as NatWest needs to borrow $10 million for 30 days. It obtains a quote from the Royal Bank of Scotland for a rate of 5.25 percent. Thus, 30-day LIBOR is 5.25 percent. If NatWest takes the deal, it will owe $10,000,000 × [1 + 0.0525 (30/360)] = $10,043,750 in 30 days. Note that, like the Treasury bill market, the convention in the Eurodollar market is to prorate the quoted interest rate over 360 days. In contrast to the Treasury bill market, the interest is not deducted from the principal. Rather, it is added on to the face value, a procedure appropriately called **add-on interest**. The market for Eurodollar time deposits is quite large, and the rates on these instruments are assembled by a central organization and quoted in financial newspapers. The British Bankers Association publishes a semi-official Eurodollar rate, compiled from an average of the quotes of London banks.

The U.S. dollar is not the only instrument for which such time deposits exist. Eurosterling, for example, trades in Tokyo, and Euroyen trades in London. You may be wondering about Euroeuro. Actually, there is no such entity as Euroeuro, at least not by that name. The Eurodollar instrument described here has nothing to do with the European currency known as the euro. Eurodollars, Euroyen, Eurosterling, etc. have been around longer than the euro currency and, despite the confusion, have retained their nomenclature. An analogous instrument does exist, however—a euro-denominated loan in which one bank borrows euros from another. Trading in euros and euro deposits occurs in most major world cities, and two similar rates on such euro deposits are commonly quoted. One, called EuroLIBOR, is compiled in London by the British Bankers Association, and the other, called **Euribor, is** compiled in Frankfurt and published by the European Central Bank. Euribor is more widely used and is the rate we shall refer to in this book.

Now let us return to the world of FRAs. FRAs are contracts in which the underlying is neither a bond nor a Eurodollar or Euribor deposit but simply an interest payment made in dollars, Euribor, or any other currency at a rate appropriate for that currency. Our primary focus will be on dollar LIBOR and Euribor, so we shall henceforth adopt the terminology LIBOR to represent dollar LIBOR and Euribor to represent the euro deposit rate.

Because the mechanics of FRAs are the same for all currencies, for illustrative purposes we shall use LIBOR. Consider an FRA expiring in 90 days for which the underlying is 180-day LIBOR. Suppose the dealer quotes this instrument at a rate of 5.5 percent. Suppose the end user goes long and the dealer goes short. The end user is essentially long the rate and will benefit if rates increase. The dealer is essentially short the rate and will benefit if rates decrease. The contract covers a given notional principal, which we shall assume is $10 million.

The contract stipulates that at expiration, the parties identify the rate on new 180-day LIBOR time deposits. This rate is called 180-day LIBOR. It is, thus, the underlying rate on which the contract is based. Suppose that at expiration in 90 days, the rate on 180-day LIBOR is 6 percent. That 6 percent interest will be paid 180 days later. Therefore, the present value of a Eurodollar time deposit at that point in time would be

$$\frac{\$10,000,000}{1 + 0.06\left(\dfrac{180}{360}\right)}$$

At expiration, then, the end user, the party going long the FRA in our example, receives the following payment from the dealer, which is the party going short:

$$\$10,000,000\left[\frac{(0.06 - 0.055)\left(\dfrac{180}{360}\right)}{1 + 0.06\left(\dfrac{180}{360}\right)}\right] = \$24,272$$

If the underlying rate is less than 5.5 percent, the payment is calculated based on the difference between the 5.5 percent rate and the underlying rate and is paid by the long to the short. It is important to note that even though the contract expires in 90 days, the rate is on a 180-day LIBOR instrument; therefore, the rate calculation adjusts by the factor 180/360. The fact that 90 days have elapsed at expiration is not relevant to the calculation of the payoff.

Before presenting the general formula, let us review the calculations in the numerator and denominator. In the numerator, we see that the contract is obviously paying the difference between the actual rate that exists in the market on the contract expiration date and the agreed-upon rate, adjusted for the fact that the rate applies to a 180-day instrument, multiplied by the notional principal. The divisor appears because when Eurodollar rates are quoted in the market, they are based on the assumption that the rate applies to an instrument that accrues interest at that rate with the interest paid a certain number of days (here 180) later. When participants determine this rate in the London Eurodollar market, it is understood to apply to a Eurodollar time deposit that begins now and matures 180 days later. So the interest on an actual Eurodollar deposit would not be paid until 180 days later. Thus, it is necessary to adjust the FRA payoff to reflect the fact that the rate implies a payment that would occur 180 days later on a standard **Eurodollar deposit**. This adjustment is easily done by simply discounting the payment at the current LIBOR, which here is 6 percent, prorated over 180 days. These conventions are also followed in the market for FRAs with other underlying rates.

In general, the FRA payoff formula (from the perspective of the party going long) is

$$\text{Notional principal} \left[\frac{\left(\begin{array}{c} \text{Underlying rate at expiration} \\ - \text{ Forward contract rate} \end{array} \right)\left(\dfrac{\text{Days in underlying rate}}{360} \right)}{1 + \text{Underlying rate at expiration}\left(\dfrac{\text{Days in underlying rate}}{360} \right)} \right]$$

where *forward contract rate* represents the rate the two parties agree will be paid and *days in underlying rate* refers to the number of days to maturity of the instrument on which the underlying rate is based.

One somewhat confusing feature of FRAs is the fact that they mature in a certain number of days and are based on a rate that applies to an instrument maturing in a certain number of days measured from the maturity of the FRA. Thus, there are two day figures associated with each contract. Our example was a 90-day contract on 180-day LIBOR. To avoid confusion, the FRA markets use a special type of terminology that converts the number of days to months. Specifically, our example FRA is referred to as a 3 × 9, reflecting the fact that the contract expires in three months and that six months later, or nine months from the contract initiation date, the interest is paid on the underlying Eurodollar time deposit on whose rate the contract is based.[10]

FRAs are available in the market for a variety of maturities that are considered somewhat standard. Exhibit 64-2 presents the most common maturities. Most dealers follow the convention that contracts should expire in a given number of exact months and should be on the most commonly traded Eurodollar rates such as 30-day LIBOR, 60-day LIBOR, 90-day LIBOR, 180-day LIBOR, and so on. If a party wants a contract expiring in 37 days on 122-day LIBOR, it would be considered an exception to the standard, but most dealers would be willing to make a market in such an instrument. Such nonstandard instruments are called *off the run*. Of course, FRAs are available in all of the leading currencies.

---

[10] The notation "3 × 9" is pronounced "three by nine."

EXHIBIT 64-2	FRA Descriptive Notation and Interpretation	
Notation	**Contract Expires in**	**Underlying Rate**
1 × 3	1 month	60-day LIBOR
1 × 4	1 month	90-day LIBOR
1 × 7	1 month	180-day LIBOR
3 × 6	3 months	90-day LIBOR
3 × 9	3 months	180-day LIBOR
6 × 12	6 months	180-day LIBOR
12 × 18	12 months	180-day LIBOR

Note: This list is not exhaustive and represents only the most commonly traded FRAs.

The FRA market is large, but not as large as the swaps market. It is important, however, to understand FRAs before trying to understand swaps. As we will show in Reading 67, a swap is a special combination of FRAs. But let us now turn to another large forward market, the market for currency forwards.

3.3 Currency Forward Contracts

Spurred by the relaxation of government controls over the exchange rates of most major currencies in the early 1970s, a currency forward market developed and grew extremely large. Currency forwards are widely used by banks and corporations to manage foreign exchange risk. For example, suppose Microsoft has a European subsidiary that expects to send it €12 million in three months. When Microsoft receives the euros, it will then convert them to dollars. Thus, Microsoft is essentially long euros because it will have to sell euros, or equivalently, it is short dollars because it will have to buy dollars. A currency forward contract is especially useful in this situation, because it enables Microsoft to lock in the rate at which it will sell euros and buy dollars in three months. It can do this by going short the forward contract, meaning that it goes short the euro and long the dollar. This arrangement serves to offset its otherwise long-euro, short-dollar position. In other words, it needs a forward contract to sell euros and buy dollars.

For example, say Microsoft goes to JP Morgan Chase and asks for a quote on a currency forward for €12 million in three months. JP Morgan Chase quotes a rate of $0.925, which would enable Microsoft to sell euros and buy dollars at a rate of $0.925 in three months. Under this contract, Microsoft would know it could convert its €12 million to 12,000,000 × $0.925 = $11,100,000. The contract would also stipulate whether it will settle in cash or will call for Microsoft to actually deliver the euros to the dealer and be paid $11,100,000. This simplified example is a currency forward hedge.

Now let us say that three months later, the spot rate for euros is $0.920. Microsoft is quite pleased that it locked in a rate of $0.925. It simply delivers the euros and receives $11,100,000 at an exchange rate of $0.925.[11] Had rates risen,

---

[11]Had the contract been structured to settle in cash, the dealer would have paid Microsoft 12,000,000 × ($0.925 − $0.920) = $60,000. Microsoft would have converted the euros to dollars at the current spot exchange rate of $0.920, receiving 12,000,000 × $0.920 = $11,040,000. Adding the $60,000 payment from the dealer, Microsoft would have received $11,100,000, an effective rate of $0.925.

however, Microsoft would still have had to deliver the euros and accept a rate of $0.925.

A few variations of currency forward contracts exist, but most of them are somewhat specialized and beyond the objectives of this reading. Let us now take a very brief look at a few other types of forward contracts.

3.4 Other Types of Forward Contracts

Although we focus primarily on the financial derivatives used by asset managers, we should mention here some of the other types. Commodity forwards—in which the underlying asset is oil, a precious metal, or some other commodity—are widely used. In addition, the derivatives industry has created forward contracts and other derivatives on various sources of energy (electricity, gas, etc.) and even weather, in which the underlying is a measure of the temperature or the amount of disaster damage from hurricanes, earthquakes, or tornados.

Many of these instruments are particularly difficult to understand, price, and trade. Nonetheless, through the use of derivatives and indirect investments, such as hedge funds, they can be useful for managing risk and investing in general. They are not, however, our focus.

In the examples and illustrations used above, we have made reference to certain prices. Determining appropriate prices and fair values of financial instruments is a central objective of much of the process of asset management. Accordingly, pricing and valuation occupies a major portion of the CFA Program. As such, we turn our attention to the pricing and valuation of forward contracts.

4   PRICING AND VALUATION OF FORWARD CONTRACTS

Before getting into the actual mechanics of pricing and valuation, the astute reader might wonder whether we are being a bit redundant. Are pricing and valuation not the same thing?

An equity analyst often finds that a stock is priced at more or less than its fair market value and uses this conclusion as the basis for a buy or sell recommendation.[12] In an efficient market, the price of a stock would always equal its value or the price would quickly converge to the value. Thus, for all practical purposes, pricing and valuation would be the same thing. In general, when we speak of the value and price of an *asset*, we are referring to what that asset is worth and what it sells for. With respect to certain *derivatives*, however, value and price take on slightly different meanings.

So let us begin by defining value: *Value is what you can sell something for or what you must pay to acquire something.* This applies to stocks, bonds, derivatives, and used cars.[13] Accordingly, *valuation is the process of determining the value of an asset or service.* Pricing is a related but different concept; let us explore what we mean by pricing a forward contract.

---

[12]From your study of equity analysis, you should recall that we often use the discounted cash flow model, sometimes combined with the capital asset pricing model, to determine the fair market value of a stock.

[13]Be careful. You may think the "value" of a certain used car is $5,000, but if no one will give you that price, it can hardly be called the value.

A forward **contract price** is the fixed price or rate at which the transaction scheduled to occur at expiration will take place. This price is agreed to on the contract initiation date and is commonly called the **forward price** or **forward rate**. Pricing means to determine the forward price or forward rate. Valuation, however, means to determine the amount of money that one would need to pay or would expect to receive to engage in the transaction. Alternatively, if one already held a position, valuation would mean to determine the amount of money one would either have to pay or expect to receive in order to get out of the position. Let us look at a generic example.

4.1 Generic Pricing and Valuation of a Forward Contract

Because derivative contracts have finite lives, it is important to carefully specify the time frame in which we are operating. We denote time in the following manner: Today is identified as time 0. The expiration date is time T. Time t is an arbitrary time between today and the expiration. Usually when we refer to "today," we are referring to the date on which the contract is created. Later we shall move forward to time t and time T, which will then be "today."

The price of the underlying asset in the spot market is denoted as S_0 at time 0, S_t at time t, and S_T at time T. The forward contract price, established when the contract is initiated at time 0, is $F(0,T)$. This notation indicates that $F(0,T)$ is the price of a forward contract initiated at time 0 and expiring at time T. The value of the forward contract is $V_0(0,T)$. This notation indicates that $V_0(0,T)$ is the value at time 0 of a forward contract initiated at time 0 and expiring at time T. In this reading, subscripts always indicate that we are at a specific point in time.

We have several objectives in this analysis. First, we want to determine the forward price $F(0,T)$. We also want to determine the forward contract value today, denoted $V_0(0,T)$, the value at a point during the life of the contract such as time t, denoted $V_t(0,T)$, and the value at expiration, denoted $V_T(0,T)$. Valuation is somewhat easier to grasp from the perspective of the party holding the long position, so we shall take that point of view in this example. Once that value is determined, the value to the short is obtained by simply changing the sign.

If we are at expiration, we would observe the **spot price** as S_T. The long holds a position to buy the asset at the already agreed-upon price of $F(0,T)$. Thus, the value of the forward contract at expiration should be obvious: $S_T - F(0,T)$. If the value at expiration does not equal this amount, then an arbitrage profit can be easily made. For example, suppose the forward price established at the initiation of the contract, $F(0,T)$, is \$20. Now at expiration, the spot price, S_T, is \$23. The contract value must be \$3. If it were more than \$3, then the long would be able to sell the contract to someone for more than \$3—someone would be paying the long more than \$3 to obtain the obligation of buying a \$23 asset for \$20. Obviously, no one would do that. If the value were less than \$3, the long would have to be willing to sell for less than \$3 the obligation of buying a \$23 asset for \$20. Obviously, the long would not do that. Thus, we state that the value at expiration of a forward contract established at time 0 is

$$V_T(0,T) = S_T - F(0,T)$$

(64-1)

Note that the value of a forward contract can also be interpreted as its profit, the difference between what the long pays for the underlying asset, F(0,T), and what the long receives, the asset price S_T. Of course, we have still not explained how F(0,T) is determined, but the above equation gives the value of the contract at expiration, at which time F(0,T) would certainly be known because it was agreed on at the initiation date of the contract.

Now let us back up to the time when the contract was originated. Consider a contract that expires in one year. Suppose that the underlying asset is worth $100 and that the forward price is $108. We do not know if $108 is the correct forward price; we will simply try it and see.

Suppose we buy the asset for $100 and sell the forward contract for $108. We hold the position until expiration. We assume that there are no direct costs associated with buying or holding the asset, but we must recognize that we lose interest on the $100 tied up in the asset. Assume that the interest rate is 5 percent.

Recall that no money changes hands at the start with a forward contract. Consequently, the $100 invested in the asset is the full outlay. At the end of the year, the forward contract expires and we deliver the asset, receiving $108 for it—not bad at all. At a 5 percent interest rate, we lose only $5 in interest on the $100 tied up in the asset. We receive $108 for the asset regardless of its price at expiration. We can view $108 − $105 = $3 as a risk-free profit, which more than covered the cost. In fact, if we had also borrowed the $100 at 5 percent, we could have done this transaction without putting up any money of our own. We would have more than covered the interest on the borrowed funds and netted a $3 risk-free profit. This profit is essentially free money—there is no cost and no risk. Thus, it is an arbitrage profit. We would certainly want to execute any transaction that would generate an arbitrage profit.

In the market, the forces of arbitrage would then prevail. Other market participants would execute this transaction as well. Although it is possible that the spot price would bear some of the adjustment, in this reading we shall always let the derivative price make the full adjustment. Consequently, the derivative price would have to come down to $105.

If the forward price were below $105, we could also earn an arbitrage profit, although it would be a little more difficult because the asset would have to be sold short. Suppose the forward price is $103. If the asset were a financial asset, we could borrow it and sell it short. We would receive $100 for it and invest that $100 at the 5 percent rate. We would simultaneously buy a forward contract. At expiration, we would take delivery of the asset paying $103 and then deliver it to the party from whom we borrowed it. The short position is now covered, and we still have the $100 invested plus 5 percent interest on it. This transaction offers a clear arbitrage profit of $2. Again, the forces of arbitrage would cause other market participants to undertake the transaction, which would push the forward price up to $105.

If short selling is not permitted, too difficult, or too costly, a market participant who already owns the asset could sell it, invest the $100 at 5 percent, and buy a forward contract. At expiration, he would pay $103 and take delivery on the forward contract, which would return him to his original position of owning the asset. He would now, however, receive not only the stock but also 5 percent interest on $100. Again, the forces of arbitrage would make this transaction attractive to other parties who held the asset, provided they could afford to part with it for the necessary period of time.[14]

---

[14] In other words, a party holding the asset must be willing to part with it for the length of time it would take for the forces of arbitrage to bring the price back in line, thereby allowing the party to capture the risk-free profit and return the party to its original state of holding the asset. The period of time required for the price to adjust should be very short if the market is relatively efficient.

Going back to the situation in which the forward contract price was $103, an arbitrage profit could, however, be eliminated if the party going long the forward contract were required to pay some money up front. For example, suppose the party going long the forward contract paid the party going short $1.9048. Then the party going long would lose $1.9048 plus interest on this amount. Notice that $1.9048 compounded at 5 percent interest equals precisely $2, which not surprisingly is the amount of the arbitrage profit.

Thus, if the forward price were $103, the value of the contract would be $1.9048. With T = 1, this value equals

$$V_0(0,T) = V_0(0,1) = \$100 - \$103/1.05 = \$1.9048$$

Therefore, to enter into this contract at this forward price, one party must pay another. Because the value is positive, it must be paid by the party going long the forward contract to the party going short. Parties going long must pay positive values; parties going short pay negative values.[15]

If the forward price were $108, the value would be

$$V_0(0,T) = \$100 - \$108/1.05 = -\$2.8571$$

In this case, the value is negative and would have to be paid from the short to the long. Doing so would eliminate the arbitrage profit that the short would have otherwise been able to make, given the forward price of $108.

Arbitrage profits can be eliminated with an up-front payment from long to short or vice versa that is consistent with the forward price the parties select. The parties could simply negotiate a forward price, and any resulting market value could be paid from one party to the other. *It is customary, however, in the forward market for the initial value to be set to zero.* This convention eliminates the necessity of either party making a payment to the other and results in a direct and simple determination of the forward price. Specifically, setting $V_0(0,T) = 0$ and letting r represent the interest rate,

$$V_0(0,T) = S_0 - F(0,T)/(1 + r) = 0$$

which means that $F(0,T) = S_0(1 + r)$. In our example, $F(0,T) = \$100(1.05) = \$105$, which is the forward price that eliminates the arbitrage profit.

Our forward price formula can be interpreted as saying that the forward price is the spot price compounded at the risk-free interest rate. In our example, we had an annual interest rate of r and one year to expiration. With today being time 0 and expiration being time T, the time $T - 0 = T$ is the number of years to expiration of the forward contract. Then we more generally write the forward price as

$$F(0,T) = S_0(1 + r)^T \qquad \textbf{(64-2)}$$

Again, this result is consistent with the custom that no money changes hands at the start of a forward contract, meaning that the value of a forward contract at its start is zero.

Exhibit 64-3 summarizes the process of pricing a forward contract. At time 0, we buy the asset and sell a forward contract for a total outlay of the spot price of the asset.[16] Over the life of the contract, we hold the asset and forgo interest on

---

[15]For example, when a stock is purchased, its value, which is always positive, is paid from the long to the short. This is true for any asset.

[16]Remember that in a forward contract, neither party pays anything for the forward contract at the start.

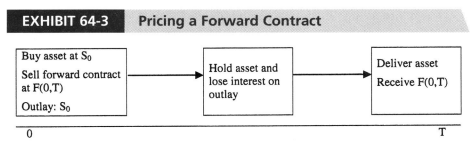

EXHIBIT 64-3   **Pricing a Forward Contract**

| Buy asset at S_0
Sell forward contract at $F(0,T)$
Outlay: S_0 | → | Hold asset and lose interest on outlay | → | Deliver asset
Receive $F(0,T)$ |

0   T

The transaction is risk free and should be equivalent to investing S_0 dollars in a risk-free asset that pays $F(0,T)$ at time T. Thus, the amount received at T must be the future value of the initial outlay invested at the risk-free rate. For this equality to hold, the forward price must be given as

$$F(0,T) = S_0(1 + r)^T$$

Example: The spot price is $72.50, the risk-free rate is 8.25 percent, and the contract is for five years. The forward price would be

$$F(0,T) = F(0,5) = 72.50(1.0825)^5 = 107.76$$

the money. At expiration, we deliver the asset and receive the forward price for a payoff of $F(0,T)$. The overall transaction is risk free and equivalent to investing the spot price of the asset in a risk-free bond that pays $F(0,T)$ at time T. Therefore, the payoff at T must be the future value of the spot price invested at the risk-free rate. This equality can be true only if the forward price is the spot price compounded at the risk-free rate over the life of the asset.

A contract in which the initial value is intentionally set at a nonzero value is called an **off-market FRA**. In such a contract, the forward price is set arbitrarily in the process of negotiation between the two parties. Given the chosen forward price, the contract will have a nonzero value. As noted above, if the value is positive, the long pays that amount up front to the short. If it is negative, the short pays that amount up front to the long. Although off-market FRAs are not common, we shall use them in Reading 67 when studying swaps.

Now suppose we are at a time t, which is a point during the life of the contract. We may want to know the value of the forward contract for several reasons. For one, it makes good business sense to know the monetary value of an obligation to do something at a later date. Also, accounting rules require that a company mark its derivatives to their current market values and report the effects of those values in income statements and balance sheets. In addition, the market value can be used as a gauge of the credit exposure. Finally, the market value can be used to determine how much money one party can pay the other to terminate the contract.

Let us start by assuming that we established a long forward contract at time 0 at the price $F(0,T)$. Of course, its value at time 0 was zero. But now it is time t, and we want to know its new value, $V_t(0,T)$. Let us consider what it means to hold the position of being long at time t a forward contract established at time 0 at the price $F(0,T)$ and expiring at time T:

We will have to pay $F(0,T)$ dollars at T.
We will receive the underlying asset, which will be worth S_T, at T.

At least part of the value will clearly be the present value of a payment of $F(0,T)$, or in other words, $-F(0,T)/(1 + r)^{T - t}$. The other part of the contract value comes from the fact that we have a claim on the asset's value at T. We do not know what S_T (the asset value at T) will be, but we do know that the market tells us its present value is S_t, the current asset price. *By definition, an asset's value today is the present value of its future value.*[17] Thus we can easily value our forward contract at time t during the life of the contract:

$$V_t(0,T) = S_t - F(0,T)/(1 + r)^{(T-t)}$$

(64-3)

Consider our earlier example in which we entered into a one-year forward contract to buy the asset at $105. Now assume it is three months later and the price of the asset is $102. With $t = 0.25$ and $T = 1$, the value of the contract would be

$$V_t(0,T) = V_{0.25}(0,1) = \$102 - \$105/(1.05)^{0.75} = \$0.7728$$

Again, why is this the value? The contract provides the long with a claim on the asset at expiration. That claim is currently worth the current asset value of $102. That claim also obligates the long to pay $105 at expiration, which has a present value of $\$105/(1.05)^{0.75} = \$101.2272$. Thus, the long position has a value of $102 − $101.2272 = $0.7728.

As noted above, this market value may well affect the income statement and balance sheet. In addition, it gives an idea of the contract's credit exposure, a topic we have touched on and will cover in more detail in Section 5. Finally, we noted earlier that a party could re-enter the market and offset the contract by paying the counterparty or having the counterparty pay him a cash amount. This cash amount is the market value as calculated here.[18]

Exhibit 64-4 summarizes how we value a forward contract. If we went long a forward contract at time 0 and we are now at time t prior to expiration, we hold a claim on the asset at expiration and are obligated to pay the forward price at expiration. The claim on the asset is worth its current price; the obligation to pay the forward price at expiration is worth the negative of its present value. Thus, the value of the forward contract is the current spot price minus the forward price discounted from expiration back to the present.

Therefore, we have seen that the forward contract value is zero today: the asset price minus the present value of the forward price at a time prior to expiration, and the asset price minus the forward price at expiration. It may be helpful to note that in general, we can always say that *the forward contract value is the asset price minus the present value of the exercise price*, because given $V_t(0,T) = S_t - F(0,T)/(1 + r)^{(T - t)}$:

If $t = 0$, $V_t(0,T) = V_0(0,T) = S_0 - F(0,T)/(1 + r)^T = 0$
because $F(0,T) = S_0(1 + r)^T$

If $t = T$, $V_t(0,T) = V_T(0,T) = S_T - F(0,T)/(1 + r)^0 = S_T - F(0,T)$

The formulas for pricing and valuation of a forward contract are summarized in Exhibit 64-5.

---

[17]This statement is true for any type of asset or financial instrument. It always holds by definition.

[18]If the market value is positive, the value of the asset exceeds the present value of what the long promises to pay. Thus, it makes sense that the short must pay the long. If the market value is negative, then the present value of what the long promises to pay exceeds the value of the asset. Then, it makes sense that the long must pay the short.

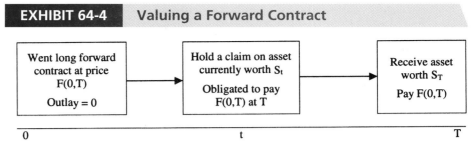

EXHIBIT 64-4   Valuing a Forward Contract

| Went long forward contract at price F(0,T) Outlay = 0 | → | Hold a claim on asset currently worth S_t Obligated to pay F(0,T) at T | → | Receive asset worth S_T Pay F(0,T) |

0   t   T

The value of the forward contract at t must be the value of what it will produce at T:

$$V_t(0,T) = S_t - F(0,T)/(1 + r)^{(T - t)}$$

Example: A two-year forward contract was established with a price of $62.25. Now, a year and a half later (t = 1.5), the spot price is $71.19 and the risk-free rate is 7 percent. The value of the forward contract is

$$V_t(0,T) = V_{1.5}(0,2) = 71.19 - 62.25/(1.07)^{0.5} = 11.01$$

EXHIBIT 64-5   Pricing and Valuation Formulas for a Forward Contract

Today = time 0
Arbitrary point during the contract's life = time t
Expiration = time T

Value of a forward contract at any time t:

$$V_t(0,T) = S_t - F(0,T)/(1 + r)^{(T - t)}$$

Value of a forward contract at expiration (t = T):

$$V_T(0,T) = S_T - F(0,T)$$

Value of a forward contract at initiation (t = 0):

$$V_0(0,T) = S_0 - F(0,T)/(1 + r)^T$$

Customarily, no money changes hands at initiation so $V_0(0,T)$ is set equal to zero. Thus,

$$F(0,T) = S_0(1 + r)^T$$

Practice Problem 1

An investor holds title to an asset worth €125.72. To raise money for an unrelated purpose, the investor plans to sell the asset in nine months. The investor is concerned about uncertainty in the price of the asset at that time. The investor learns about the advantages of using forward contracts to manage this risk and enters into such a contract to sell the asset in nine months. The risk-free interest rate is 5.625 percent.

A. Determine the appropriate price the investor could receive in nine months by means of the forward contract.

B. Suppose the counterparty to the forward contract is willing to engage in such a contract at a forward price of €140. Explain what type of transaction the investor could execute to take advantage of the situation. Calculate the rate of return (annualized), and explain why the transaction is attractive.

C. Suppose the forward contract is entered into at the price you computed in Part A. Two months later, the price of the asset is €118.875. The investor would like to evaluate her position with respect to any gain or loss accrued on the forward contract. Determine the market value of the forward contract at this point in time from the perspective of the investor in Part A.

D. Determine the value of the forward contract at expiration assuming the contract is entered into at the price you computed in Part A and the price of the underlying asset is €123.50 at expiration. Explain how the investor did on the overall position of both the asset and the forward contract in terms of the rate of return.

▶ **Solution to A.** $T = 9/12 = 0.75$
$$S_0 = 125.72$$
$$r = 0.05625$$

$$F(0,T) = 125.72(1.05625)^{0.75} = 130.99$$

▶ **Solution to B.** As found in Part A, the forward contract should be selling at €130.99, but it is selling for €140. Consequently, it is overpriced—and an overpriced contract should be sold. Because the investor holds the asset, she will be hedged by selling the forward contract. Consequently, her asset, worth €125.72 when the forward contract is sold, will be delivered in nine months and she will receive €140 for it. The rate of return will be

$$\left(\frac{140}{125.72}\right) - 1 = 0.1136$$

This risk-free return of 11.36 percent for nine months is clearly in excess of the 5.625 percent annual rate. In fact, a rate of 11.36 percent for nine months annualizes to

$$(1.1136)^{12/9} - 1 = 0.1543$$

An annual risk-free rate of 15.43 percent is clearly preferred over the actual risk-free rate of 5.625 percent. The position is not only hedged but also earns an arbitrage profit.

▶ **Solution to C.** $t = 2/12$

$$T - t = 9/12 - 2/12 = 7/12$$
$$S_t = 118.875$$
$$F(0,T) = 130.99$$

$$V_t(0,T) = V_{2/12}(0,9/12) = 118.875 - 130.99/(1.05625)^{7/12} = -8.0$$

The contract has a negative value. Note, however, that in this form, the answer applies to the holder of the long position. This investor is short. Thus, the value to the investor in this problem is positive 8.0.

▶ **Solution to D.** $S_T = 123.50$

$$V_T(0,T) = V_{9/12}(0,9/12) = 123.50 - 130.99 = -7.49$$

This amount is the value to the long. This investor is short, so the value is a positive 7.49. The investor incurred a loss on the asset of $125.72 - 123.50 = 2.22$. Combined with the gain on the forward contract, the net gain is $7.49 - 2.22 = 5.27$. A gain of 5.27 on an asset worth 125.72 when the transaction was initiated represents a return of $5.27/125.72 = 4.19$ percent. When annualized, the rate of return equals

$$(1.0419)^{12/9} - 1 = 0.05625$$

It should come as no surprise that this number is the annual risk-free rate. The transaction was executed at the no-arbitrage forward price of €130.99. Thus, it would be impossible to earn a return higher or lower than the risk-free rate.

In our examples, there were no costs or cash flows associated with holding the underlying assets. In the specific examples below for equity derivatives, fixed-income and interest rate derivatives, and currency derivatives, we present cases in which cash flows on the underlying asset will slightly alter our results. We shall ignore any costs of holding assets. Such costs are primarily associated with commodities, an asset class we do not address in this reading.

4.2 Pricing and Valuation of Equity Forward Contracts

Equity forward contracts are priced and valued much like the generic contract described above, with one important additional feature. Many stocks pay dividends, and the effects of these dividends must be incorporated into the pricing and valuation process. Our concern is with the dividends that occur over the life of the forward contract, but not with those that may come after the contract ends. Following standard procedure, we assume that these dividends are known or are a constant percentage of the stock price.

We begin with the idea of a forward contract on either a single stock, a portfolio of stocks, or an index in which dividends are to be paid during the life of the contract. Using the time notation that today is time 0, expiration is time T, and there is an arbitrary time t during its life when we need to value the contract, assume that dividends can be paid at various times during the life of the contract between t and T.[19]

In the examples that follow, we shall calculate present and future values of this stream of dividends over the life of the forward contract. Given a series of these dividends of $D_1, D_2, \ldots D_n$, whose values are known, that occur at times $t_1, t_2, \ldots t_n$, the present value will be defined as PV(D,0,T) and computed as

$$PV(D,0,T) = \sum_{i=1}^{n} \frac{D_i}{(1+r)^{t_i}}$$

The future value will be defined as FV(D,0,T) and computed as

$$FV(D,0,T) = \sum_{i=1}^{n} D_i(1+r)^{T-t_i}$$

Recall that the forward price is established by eliminating any opportunity to arbitrage from establishing a forward contract without making any cash outlay today, as is customary with forward contracts. We found that the forward price is the spot price compounded at the risk-free interest rate. To include dividends, we adjust our formula slightly to

$$F(0,T) = [S_0 - PV(D,0,T)](1+r)^T \qquad \text{(64-4)}$$

In other words, we simply subtract the present value of the dividends from the stock price. Note that the dividends reduce the forward price, a reflection of the fact that holders of long positions in forward contracts do not benefit from dividends in comparison to holders of long positions in the underlying stock.

For example, consider a stock priced at $40, which pays a dividend of $3 in 50 days. The risk-free rate is 6 percent. A forward contract expiring in six months (T = 0.5) would have a price of

$$F(0,T) = F(0,0.5) = [\$40 - \$3/(1.06)^{50/365}](1.06)^{0.5} = \$38.12$$

If the stock had more than one dividend, we would simply subtract the present value of all dividends over the life of the contract from the stock price, as in the following example.

The risk-free rate is 4 percent. The forward contract expires in 300 days and is on a stock currently priced at $35, which pays quarterly dividends according to the following schedule:

Days to Ex-Dividend Date	Dividend
10	$0.45
102	$0.45
193	$0.45
283	$0.45

[19]Given the way dividends are typically paid, the right to the dividend leaves the stock on the ex-dividend date, which is prior to the payment date. To precisely incorporate this feature, either the dividend payment date should be the ex-dividend date or the dividend should be the present value at the ex-dividend date of the dividend to be paid at a later date. We shall ignore this point here and assume that it would be taken care of in practice.

The present value of the dividends is found as follows:

$$PV(D,0,T) = \$0.45/(1.04)^{10/365} + \$0.45/(1.04)^{102/365} \\ + \$0.45/(1.04)^{193/365} + \$0.45/(1.04)^{283/365} = \$1.77$$

The time to expiration is T = 300/365. Therefore, the forward price equals

$$F(0,T) = F(0,300/365) = (\$35 - \$1.77)(1.04)^{300/365} = \$34.32$$

Another approach to incorporating the dividends is to use the future value of the dividends. With this forward contract expiring in 300 days, the first dividend is reinvested for 290 days, the second for 198 days, the third for 107 days, and the fourth for 17 days. Thus,

$$FV(D,0,T) = \$0.45(1.04)^{290/365} + \$0.45(1.04)^{198/365} \\ + \$0.45(1.04)^{107/365} + \$0.45(1.04)^{17/365} = \$1.83$$

To obtain the forward price, we compound the stock value to expiration and subtract the future value of the dividends. Thus, the forward price would be

$$F(0,T) = S_0(1 + r)^T - FV(D,0,T) \qquad \text{(64-5)}$$

This formula will give the same answer as the one using the present value of the dividends, as shown below:

$$F(0,300/365) = \$35(1.04)^{300/365} - \$1.83 = \$34.32$$

An alternative way to incorporate dividends is to express them as a fixed percentage of the stock price. The more common version of this formulation is to assume that the stock, portfolio, or index pays dividends continuously at a rate of δ^c. By specifying the dividends in this manner, we are allowing the dividends to be uncertain and completely determined by the stock price at the time the dividends are being paid. In this case, the stock is constantly paying a dividend at the rate δ^c. In Reading 65, we will again discuss how to incorporate dividends.

Because we pay dividends continuously, for consistency we must also compound the interest continuously. The continuously compounded equivalent of the discrete risk-free rate r will be denoted r^c and is found as $r^c = \ln(1 + r)$.[20] The future value of \$1 at time T is $\exp(r^c T)$. Then the forward price is given as

$$F(0,T) = (S_0 e^{-\delta^c T}) e^{r^c T} \qquad \text{(64-6)}$$

The term in parentheses, the stock price discounted at the dividend yield rate, is equivalent to the stock price minus the present value of the dividends. This value

---

[20] The notation "ln" stands for natural logarithm. A logarithm is the power to which its base must be raised to equal a given number. The base of the natural logarithm system is e, approximately 2.71828. With an interest rate of r = 0.06, we would have $r^c = \ln(1.06) = 0.058$. Then $e^{0.058} = 1.06$ is called the exponential function and often written as $\exp(0.058) = 1.06$. The future value factor is thus $\exp(r^c)$. The present value factor is $1/\exp(r^c)$ or $\exp(-r^c)$. If the period is more or less than one year, we also multiply the rate by the number of years or fraction of a year—that is, $\exp(-r^c T)$ or $\exp(r^c T)$.

is then compounded at the risk-free rate over the life of the contract, just as we have done in the other versions.

Some people attach significance to whether the forward price is higher than the spot price. It is important to note that the forward price should not be interpreted as a forecast of the future price of the underlying. This misperception is common. If the forward price is higher than the spot price, it merely indicates that the effect of the risk-free rate is greater than the effect of the dividends. In fact, such is usually the case with equity forwards. Interest rates are usually greater than dividend yields.

As an example, consider a forward contract on France's CAC 40 Index. The index is at 5475, the continuously compounded dividend yield is 1.5 percent, and the continuously compounded risk-free interest rate is 4.625 percent. The contract life is two years. With $T = 2$, the contract price is, therefore,

$$F(0,T) = F(0,2) = (5475 \times e^{-0.015(2)})e^{0.04625(2)} = 5828.11$$

This specification involving a continuous dividend yield is commonly used when the underlying is a portfolio or stock index. If a single stock in the portfolio pays a dividend, then the portfolio or index can be viewed as paying a dividend. Given the diversity of dividend policies and ex-dividend dates, such an assumption is usually considered a reasonable approximation for stock portfolios or stock indices, but the assumption is not as appropriate for individual stocks. No general agreement exists on the most appropriate approach, and you must become comfortable with all of them. To obtain the appropriate forward price, the most important point to remember is that one way or another, the analysis must incorporate the dividend component of the stock price, portfolio value, or index level. If the contract is not trading at the correct price, then it is mispriced and arbitrage, as described in the generic forward contract pricing section, will force an alignment between the market forward price and the theoretical forward price.

Recall that the value of a forward contract is the asset price minus the forward price discounted back from the expiration date. Regardless of how the dividend is specified or even whether the underlying stock, portfolio, or index pays dividends, the valuation formulas for a forward contract on a stock differ only in that the stock price is adjusted by removing the present value of the remaining dividends:

$$V_t(0,T) = S_t - PV(D,t,T) - F(0,T)/(1 + r)^{(T-t)} \qquad \textbf{(64-7)}$$

where we now note that the dividends are only those paid after time t. If we are using continuous compounding,

$$V_t(0,T) = S_t e^{-\delta^c(T-t)} - F(0,T)e^{-r^c(T-t)} \qquad \textbf{(64-8)}$$

At the contract initiation date, $t = 0$ and $V_0(0,T)$ is set to zero because no cash changes hands. At expiration, $t = T$ and no dividends remain, so the valuation formula reduces to $S_T - F(0,T)$.

The formulas for pricing and valuation of equity forward contracts are summarized in Exhibit 64-6.

EXHIBIT 64-6	Pricing and Valuation Formulas for Equity Forward Contracts

Forward price = (Stock price − Present value of dividends over life of contract) × $(1 + r)^T$

or (Stock price) × $(1 + r)^T$ − Future value of dividends over life of contract

Discrete dividends over the life of the contract:

$$F(0,T) = [S_0 - PV(D,0,T)](1 + r)^T \text{ or } S_0(1 + r)^T - FV(D,0,T)$$

Continuous dividends at the rate δ^c:

$$F(0,T) = (S_0 e^{-\delta^c T}) e^{r^c T}$$

Value of forward contract:

$$V_t(0,T) = S_t - PV(D,t,T) - F(0,T)/(1 + r)^{(T - t)}$$

or

$$V_t(0,T) = S_t e^{-\delta^c(T - t)} - F(0,T) e^{-r^c(T - t)}$$

Practice Problem 2

An asset manager anticipates the receipt of funds in 200 days, which he will use to purchase a particular stock. The stock he has in mind is currently selling for $62.50 and will pay a $0.75 dividend in 50 days and another $0.75 dividend in 140 days. The risk-free rate is 4.2 percent. The manager decides to commit to a future purchase of the stock by going long a forward contract on the stock.

A. At what price would the manager commit to purchase the stock in 200 days through a forward contract?

B. Suppose the manager enters into the contract at the price you found in Part A. Now, 75 days later, the stock price is $55.75. Determine the value of the forward contract at this point.

C. It is now the expiration day, and the stock price is $58.50. Determine the value of the forward contract at this time.

$S_0 = \$62.50$
$T = 200/365$
$D_1 = \$0.75, t_1 = 50/365$
$D_2 = \$0.75, t_2 = 140/365$
$r = 0.042$

▶ **Solution to A.** First find the present value of the dividends:

$$\$0.75/(1.042)^{50/365} + \$0.75/(1.042)^{140/365} = \$1.48$$

Then find the forward price:

$$F(0,T) = F(0,200/365) = (\$62.50 - \$1.48)(1.042)^{200/365} = \$62.41$$

▶ **Solution to B.** We must now find the present value of the dividends 75 days after the contract begins. The first dividend has already been paid, so it is not relevant. Because only one remains, the second dividend is now the "first" dividend. It will be paid in 65 days. Thus, $t_1 - t = 65/365$. The present value of this dividend is $\$0.75/(1.042)^{65/365} = \$0.74$. The other information is

$$t = 75/365$$
$$T - t = (200 - 75)/365 = 125/365$$
$$S_t = \$55.75$$

The value of the contract is, therefore,

$$V_t(0,T) = V_{75/365}(0,200/365) = (\$55.75 - \$0.74) - \$62.41/(1.042)^{125/365} = -\$6.53$$

Thus, the contract has a negative value.

▶ **Solution to C.** $S_T = \$58.50$

The value of the contract is

$$V_{200/365}(0,200/365) = V_T(0,T) = \$58.50 - \$62.41 = -\$3.91$$

Thus, the contract expires with a value of negative $3.91.

4.3 Pricing and Valuation of Fixed-Income and Interest Rate Forward Contracts

Forward contracts on fixed-income securities are priced and valued in a virtually identical manner to their equity counterparts. We can use the above formulas if S_t represents the bond price at time t and D_i represents a coupon paid at time t_i. We denote B^c as a coupon bond and then use notation to draw attention to those coupons that must be included in the forward contract pricing calculations. We will let $B_t^c(T + Y)$ represent the bond price at time t, T is the expiration date of the forward contract, Y is the remaining maturity of the bond on the forward contract expiration, and $(T + Y)$ is the time to maturity of the bond at the time the forward contract is initiated. Consider a bond with n coupons to occur before its maturity date. Converting our formula for a forward contract on a stock into that for a forward contract on a bond and letting

CI be the coupon interest over a specified period of time, we have a forward price of

$$F(0,T) = \left[B_0^c(T + Y) - PV(CI,0,T)\right](1 + r)^T \qquad \textbf{(64-9)}$$

where $PV(CI,0,T)$ is the present value of the coupon interest over the life of the forward contract. Alternatively, the forward price can be obtained as

$$F(0,T) = \left[B_0^c(T + Y)\right](1 + r)^T - FV(CI,0,T) \qquad \textbf{(64-10)}$$

where $FV(CI,0,T)$ is the future value of the coupon interest over the life of the forward contract.

The value of the forward contract at time t would be

$$V_t(0,T) = B_t^c(T + Y) - PV(CI,t,T) - F(0,T)/(1 + r)^{(T-t)} \qquad \textbf{(64-11)}$$

at time t; note that the relevant coupons are only those remaining as of time t until expiration of the forward contract. As in the case for stock, this formula will reduce to the appropriate values at time 0 and at expiration. For example, at expiration, no coupons would remain, $t = T$, and $V_T(0,T) = B_T^c(T + Y) - F(0,T)$. At time $t = 0$, the contract is being initiated and has a zero value, which leads to the formula for $F(0,T)$ above.

Consider a bond with semiannual coupons. The bond has a current maturity of 583 days and pays four coupons, each six months apart. The next coupon occurs in 37 days, followed by coupons in 219 days, 401 days, and 583 days, at which time the principal is repaid. Suppose that the bond price, which includes accrued interest, is $984.45 for a $1,000 par, 4 percent coupon bond. The coupon rate implies that each coupon is $20. The risk-free interest rate is 5.75 percent. Assume that the forward contract expires in 310 days. Thus, $T = 310$, $T + Y = 583$, and $Y = 273$, meaning that the bond has 273 days remaining after the forward contract expires. Note that only the first two coupons occur during the life of the forward contract.

The present value of the coupons is

$$\$20/(1.0575)^{37/365} + \$20/(1.0575)^{219/365} = \$39.23$$

The forward price if the contract is initiated now is

$$F(0,T) = (\$984.45 - \$39.23)(1.0575)^{310/365} = \$991.18$$

Thus, we assume that we shall be able to enter into this contract to buy the bond in 310 days at the price of $991.18.

Now assume it is 15 days later and the new bond price is $973.14. Let the risk-free interest rate now be 6.75 percent. The present value of the remaining coupons is

$$\$20/(1.0675)^{22/365} + \$20/(1.0675)^{204/365} = \$39.20$$

The value of the forward contract is thus

$$\$973.14 - \$39.20 - \$991.19/(1.0675)^{295/365} = -\$6.28$$

The contract has gone from a zero value at the start to a negative value, primarily as a result of the decrease in the price of the underlying bond.

EXHIBIT 64-7	Pricing and Valuation Formulas for Fixed Income Forward Contracts

Forward price = (Bond price − Present value of coupons over life of contract) $(1 + r)^T$ or (Bond price)$(1 + r)^T$ − Future value of coupons over life of contract

Price of forward contract on bond with coupons CI:

$$F(0,T) = [B_0{}^c(T + Y) - PV(CI,0,T)](1 + r)^T$$

$$\text{or } [B_0{}^c(T + Y)](1 + r)^T - FV(CI,0,T)$$

Value of forward contract on bond with coupons CI:

$$V_t(0,T) = B_t{}^c(T + Y) - PV(CI,t,T) - F(0,T)/(1 + r)^{(T - t)}$$

If the bond is a zero-coupon bond/T-bill, we can perform the same analysis as above, but we simply let the coupons equal zero.

Exhibit 64-7 summarizes the formulas for the pricing and valuation of forward contracts on fixed-income securities.

Practice Problem 3

An investor purchased a bond when it was originally issued with a maturity of five years. The bond pays semiannual coupons of $50. It is now 150 days into the life of the bond. The investor wants to sell the bond the day after its fourth coupon. The first coupon occurs 181 days after issue, the second 365 days, the third 547 days, and the fourth 730 days. At this point (150 days into the life of the bond), the price is $1,010.25. The bond prices quoted here include accrued interest.

A. At what price could the owner enter into a forward contract to sell the bond on the day after its fourth coupon? Note that the owner would receive that fourth coupon. The risk-free rate is currently 8 percent.

B. Now move forward 365 days. The new risk-free interest rate is 7 percent and the new price of the bond is $1,025.375. The counterparty to the forward contract believes that it has received a gain on the position. Determine the value of the forward contract and the gain or loss to the counterparty at this time. Note that we have now introduced a new risk-free rate, because interest rates can obviously change over the life of the bond and any calculations of the forward contract value must reflect this fact. The new risk-free rate is used instead of the old rate in the valuation formula.

▶ **Solution to A.** First we must find the present value of the four coupons over the life of the forward contract. At the 150th day of the life of the bond, the coupons occur 31 days from now, 215 days from now, 397 days from now, and 580 days from now. Keep in mind that we need consider only the first four coupons because the owner will sell the bond on the day after the fourth coupon. The present value of the coupons is

$$\$50/(1.08)^{31/365} + \$50/(1.08)^{215/365} + \$50/(1.08)^{397/365}$$
$$+ \$50/(1.08)^{580/365} = \$187.69$$

Because we want the forward contract to expire one day after the fourth coupon, it expires in $731 - 150 = 581$ days. Thus, $T = 581/365$.

$$F(0,T) = F(0,581/365) = (\$1,010.25 - \$187.69)(1.08)^{581/365} = \$929.76$$

▶ **Solution to B.** It is now 365 days later—the 515th day of the bond's life. There are two coupons to go, one occurring in $547 - 515 = 32$ days and the other in $730 - 515 = 215$ days. The present value of the coupons is now

$$\$50/(1.07)^{32/365} + \$50/(1.07)^{215/365} = \$97.75$$

To address the value of the forward contract and the gain or loss to the counterparty, note that $731 - 515 = 216$ days now remain until the contract's expiration. Because the bondholder would sell the forward contract to hedge the future sale price of the bond, the bondholder's counterparty to the forward contract would hold a long position. The value of the forward contract is the current spot price minus the present value of the coupons minus the present value of the forward price:

$$\$1,025.375 - \$97.75 - \$929.76/(1.07)^{216/365} = \$34.36$$

Because the contract was initiated with a zero value at the start and the counterparty is long the contract, the value of $34.36 represents a gain to the counterparty.

Now let us look at the pricing and valuation of FRAs. Previously we used the notations t and T to represent the time to a given date. The expressions t or T were, respectively, the number of days to time point t or T, each divided by 365. In the FRA market, contracts are created with specific day counts. We will use the letter h to refer to the day on which the FRA expires and the letter g to refer to an arbitrary day prior to expiration. Consider the time line shown below. We shall initiate an FRA on day 0. The FRA expires on day h. The rate underlying the FRA is the rate on an m-day Eurodollar deposit. Thus, there are h days from today until the FRA expiration and h + m days until the maturity date of the Eurodollar instrument on which the FRA rate is based. The date indicated by g will simply be a date during the life of the FRA at which we want to determine a value for the FRA.

Now let us specify some notation. We let $L_i(j)$ represent the rate on a j-day LIBOR deposit on an arbitrary day i, which falls somewhere in the above period from 0 to h, inclusive. Remember that this instrument is a j-day loan from one bank to another. For example, the bank borrowing \$1 on day i for j days will pay back the amount

$$\$1\left[1 + L_i(j)\left(\frac{j}{360}\right)\right]$$

in j days.

The rate for m-day LIBOR on day h, $L_h(m)$, will determine the payoff of the FRA. We denote the fixed rate on the FRA as FRA(0,h,m), which stands for the rate on an FRA established on day 0, expiring on day h, and based on m-day LIBOR. We shall use a \$1 notional principal for the FRA, which means that at expiration its payoff is

$$\frac{[L_h(m) - FRA(0,h,m)]\left(\frac{m}{360}\right)}{1 + L_h(m)\left(\frac{m}{360}\right)} \tag{64-12}$$

The numerator is the difference between the underlying LIBOR on the expiration day and the rate agreed on when the contract was initiated, multiplied by the adjustment factor m/360. Both of these rates are annual rates applied to a Eurodollar deposit of m days; hence, multiplying by m/360 is necessary. The denominator discounts the payoff by the m-day LIBOR in effect at the time of the payoff. As noted earlier, this adjustment is necessary because the rates in the numerator apply to Eurodollar deposits created on day h and paying off m days later. If the notional principal is anything other than \$1, we also must multiply the above payoff by the notional principal to determine the actual payoff.

To derive the formula for pricing an FRA, a specific arbitrage transaction involving Eurodollars and FRAs is required. We omit the details of this somewhat complex transaction, but the end result is that the FRA rate is given by the following formula:

$$FRA(0,h,m) = \left[\frac{1 + L_0(h + m)\left(\frac{h + m}{360}\right)}{1 + L_0(h)\left(\frac{h}{360}\right)} - 1\right]\left(\frac{360}{m}\right) \tag{64-13}$$

This somewhat awkward-looking formula is actually just the formula for a LIBOR forward rate, given the interest payment conventions in the FRA market. The numerator is the future value of a Eurodollar deposit of h + m days. The denominator is the future value of a shorter-term Eurodollar deposit of h days. This ratio is 1 plus a rate; subtracting 1 and multiplying by 360/m annualizes the rate.[21]

Consider a 3 × 9 FRA. This instrument expires in 90 days and is based on 180-day LIBOR. Thus, the Eurodollar deposit on which the underlying rate is

---

[21] To compare with the traditional method of calculating a forward rate, consider a two-year rate of 10 percent and a one-year rate of 9 percent. The forward rate is $[(1.10)^2/(1.09)] - 1 = 0.1101$. The numerator is the future value of the longer-term bond, and the denominator is the future value of the shorter-term bond. The ratio is 1 plus the rate. We do not need to annualize in this example, because the forward rate is on a one-year bond.

based begins in 90 days and matures in 270 days. Because we are on day 0, h = 90, m = 180, and h + m = 270. Let the current rates be

$$L_0(h) = L_0(90) = 0.056$$
$$L_0(h + m) = L_0(270) = 0.06$$

In other words, the 90-day rate is 5.6 percent, and the 270-day rate is 6 percent. With h = 90 and m = 180, using our formula for the FRA rate, we obtain

$$FRA(0,h,m) = FRA(0,90,180) = \left[\frac{1 + 0.06\left(\dfrac{270}{360}\right)}{1 + 0.056\left(\dfrac{90}{360}\right)} - 1 \right]\left(\frac{360}{180}\right) = 0.0611$$

So to enter into an FRA on day 0, the rate would be 6.11 percent.[22]

As noted, the initial outlay for entering the forward contract is zero. Thus, the initial value is zero. Later during the life of the contract, its value will rise above or fall below zero. Now let us determine the value of an FRA during its life. Specifically, we use the notation $V_g(0,h,m)$ to represent the value of an FRA on day g, prior to expiration, which was established on day 0, expires on day h, and is based on m-day LIBOR. Omitting the derivation, the value of the FRA will be

$$V_g(0,h,m) = \frac{1}{1 + L_g(h - g)\left(\dfrac{h - g}{360}\right)} - \frac{1 + FRA(0,h,m)\left(\dfrac{m}{360}\right)}{1 + L_g(h + m - g)\left(\dfrac{h + m - g}{360}\right)} \qquad \textbf{(64-14)}$$

This formula looks complicated, but the ideas behind it are actually quite simple. Recall that we are at day g. The first term on the right-hand side is the present value of $1 received at day h. The second term is the present value of 1 plus the FRA rate to be received on day h + m, the maturity date of the underlying Eurodollar time deposit.

Assume that we go long the FRA, and it is 25 days later. We need to assign a value to the FRA. First note that g = 25, h − g = 90 − 25 = 65, and h + m − g = 90 + 180 − 25 = 245. In other words, we are 25 days into the contract, 65 days remain until expiration, and 245 days remain until the maturity of the Eurodollar deposit on which the underlying LIBOR is based. First we need information about the new term structure. Let

$$L_g(h - g) = L_{25}(65) = 0.059$$
$$L_g(h + m - g) = L_{25}(245) = 0.065$$

We now use the formula for the value of the FRA to obtain

$$V_g(0,h,m) = V_{25}(0,90,180) = \frac{1}{1 + 0.059\left(\dfrac{65}{360}\right)} - \frac{1 + 0.0611\left(\dfrac{180}{360}\right)}{1 + 0.065\left(\dfrac{245}{360}\right)} = 0.0026$$

Thus, we went long this FRA on day 0. Then 25 days later, the term structure changes to the rates used here and the FRA has a value of $0.0026 per $1

---

[22] It is worthwhile to point out again that this rate is the forward rate in the LIBOR term structure.

EXHIBIT 64-8	Pricing and Valuation Formulas for Interest Rate Forward Contracts (FRAs)

Forward price (rate):

$$FRA(0,h,m) = \left[\frac{1 + L_0(h + m)\left(\dfrac{h + m}{360}\right)}{1 + L_0(h)\left(\dfrac{h}{360}\right)} - 1 \right]\left(\frac{360}{m}\right)$$

Value of FRA on day g:

$$V_g(0,h,m) = \frac{1}{1 + L_g(h - g)\left(\dfrac{h - g}{360}\right)} - \frac{1 + FRA(0,h,m)\left(\dfrac{m}{360}\right)}{1 + L_g(h + m - g)\left(\dfrac{h + m - g}{360}\right)}$$

notional principal. If the notional principal is any amount other than $1, we multiply the notional principal by $0.0026 to obtain the full market value of the FRA.

We summarize the FRA formulas in Exhibit 64-8. We have now looked at the pricing and valuation of equity, fixed-income, and interest rate forward contracts. One of the most widely used types of forward contracts is the currency forward. The pricing and valuation of currency forwards is remarkably similar to that of equity forwards.

Practice Problem 4

A corporate treasurer needs to hedge the risk of the interest rate on a future transaction. The risk is associated with the rate on 180-day Euribor in 30 days. The relevant term structure of Euribor is given as follows:

30-day Euribor	5.75%
210-day Euribor	6.15%

A. State the terminology used to identify the FRA in which the manager is interested.

B. Determine the rate that the company would get on an FRA expiring in 30 days on 180-day Euribor.

C. Suppose the manager went long this FRA. Now, 20 days later, interest rates have moved significantly downward to the following:

10-day Euribor	5.45%
190-day Euribor	5.95%

The manager would like to know where the company stands on this FRA transaction. Determine the market value of the FRA for a €20 million notional principal.

D. On the expiration day, 180-day Euribor is 5.72 percent. Determine the payment made to or by the company to settle the FRA contract.

► **Solution to A.** This transaction would be identified as a 1×7 FRA.

► **Solution to B.** Here the notation would be $h = 30$, $m = 180$, $h + m = 210$. Then

$$FRA(0,h,m) = FRA(0,30,180) = \left[\frac{1 + 0.0615\left(\dfrac{210}{360}\right)}{1 + 0.0575\left(\dfrac{30}{360}\right)} - 1 \right]\left(\frac{360}{180}\right) = 0.0619$$

► **Solution to C.** Here $g = 20$, $h - g = 30 - 20 = 10$, $h + m - g = 30 + 180 - 20 = 190$. The value of the FRA for a €1 notional principal would be

$$V_g(0,h,m) = V_{20}(0,30,180) = \frac{1}{1 + 0.0545\left(\dfrac{10}{360}\right)} - \frac{1 + 0.0619\left(\dfrac{180}{360}\right)}{1 + 0.0595\left(\dfrac{190}{360}\right)} = -0.0011$$

Thus, for a notional principal of €20 million, the value would be €20,000,000(−0.0011) = −€22,000.

► **Solution to D.** At expiration, the payoff is

$$\frac{[L_h(m) - FRA(0,h,m)]\left(\dfrac{m}{360}\right)}{1 + L_h(m)\left(\dfrac{m}{360}\right)} = \frac{(0.0572 - 0.0619)\left(\dfrac{180}{360}\right)}{1 + 0.0572\left(\dfrac{180}{360}\right)} = -0.0023$$

For a notional principal of €20 million, the payoff would then be €20,000,000(−0.0023) = −€46,000. Thus, €46,000 would be paid by the company, because it is long and the final rate was lower than the FRA rate.

4.4 Pricing and Valuation of Currency Forward Contracts

Foreign currency derivative transactions as well as spot transactions must be handled with care. The exchange rate can be quoted in terms of units of the domestic currency per unit of foreign currency, or units of the foreign currency per unit of the domestic currency. In this reading, we shall always quote exchange rates in terms of units of the domestic currency per unit of the foreign currency, which is also called a direct quote. This approach is in keeping with the way in which other underlying assets are quoted. For example, from the perspective of a U.S. investor, a stock that sells for $50 is quoted in units of the domestic currency per unit (share) of stock. Likewise, if the euro exchange rate is quoted as $0.90, then the euro sells for $0.90 per unit, which is one euro. Alternatively, we could quote that $1 sells for 1/$0.90 = €1.1111—that is, €1.1111 per $1; in this case, units of foreign currency per one unit of domestic currency from the perspective of a U.S. investor. In fact, this type of quote is commonly used and is called an indirect quote. Taking that approach, however, we would quote the stock price as $1/\$50 = 0.02$ shares per \$1, a very unusual and awkward way to quote a stock price.

By taking the approach of quoting prices in terms of units of the domestic currency per unit of foreign currency, we facilitate a comparison of currencies and their derivatives with equities and their derivatives—a topic we have already covered. For example, we have previously discussed the case of a stock selling for S_0, which represents units of the domestic currency per share of stock. Likewise, we shall treat the currency as having an exchange rate of S_0, meaning that it is selling for S_0. We also need the foreign interest rate, denoted as r^f, and the domestic interest rate, denoted as r.[23]

Consider the following transactions executed today (time 0), assuming a contract expiration date of T:

Take $S_0/(1 + r^f)^T$ units of the domestic currency and convert it to $1/(1 + r^f)^T$ units of the foreign currency.[24]

Sell a forward contract to deliver one unit of the foreign currency at the rate $F(0,T)$ expiring at time T.

Hold the position until time T. The $1/(1 + r^f)^T$ units of foreign currency will accrue interest at the rate r^f and grow to one unit of the currency at T as follows:

$$\left(\frac{1}{1 + r^f}\right)^T (1 + r^f)^T = 1$$

Thus, at expiration we shall have one unit of the foreign currency, which is then delivered to the holder of the long forward contract, who pays the amount $F(0,T)$. This amount was known at the start of the transaction. Because the risk has been hedged away, the exchange rate at expiration is irrelevant. Hence, this transaction is risk-free. Accordingly, the present value of $F(0,T)$, found by discounting at the domestic risk-free interest rate, must equal the initial outlay of $S_0/(1 + r^f)^T$. Setting these amounts equal and solving for $F(0,T)$ gives

$$F(0,T) = \left[\frac{S_0}{(1 + r^f)^T}\right](1 + r)^T \qquad \textbf{(64-15)}$$

The term in brackets is the spot exchange rate discounted by the foreign interest rate. This term is then compounded at the domestic interest rate to the expiration day.[25]

Recall that in pricing equity forwards, we always reduced the stock price by the present value of the dividends and then compounded the resulting value to the expiration date. We can view currencies in the same way. The stock makes

---

[23] We do not use a superscript "d" for the domestic rate, because in all previous examples we have used r to denote the interest rate in the home country of the investor.

[24] In other words, if one unit of the foreign currency costs S_0, then $S_0/(1 + r^f)^T$ units of the domestic currency would, therefore, buy $1/(1 + r^f)^T$ units of the foreign currency.

[25] It is also common to see the above Equation 64-15 written inversely, with the spot rate divided by the domestic interest factor and compounded by the foreign interest factor. This variation would be appropriate if the spot and forward rates were quoted in terms of units of the foreign currency per unit of domestic currency (indirect quotes). As we mentioned earlier, however, it is easier to think of a currency as just another asset, which naturally should have its price quoted in units of the domestic currency per unit of the asset or foreign currency.

cash payments that happen to be called dividends; the currency makes cash payments that happen to be called interest. Although the time pattern of how a stock pays dividends is quite different from the time pattern of how interest accrues, the general idea is the same. After reducing the spot price or rate by any cash flows over the life of the contract, the resulting value is then compounded at the risk-free rate to the expiration day.

The formula we have obtained here is simply a variation of the formula used for other types of forward contracts. In international financial markets, however, this formula has acquired its own name: **interest rate parity** (sometimes called covered interest rate parity). It expresses the equivalence, or parity, of spot and forward exchange rates, after adjusting for differences in the interest rates in the two countries. One implication of interest rate parity is that the forward rate will exceed (be less than) the spot rate if the domestic interest rate exceeds (is less than) the foreign interest rate. With a direct quote, if the forward rate exceeds (is less than) the spot rate, the foreign currency is said to be selling at a premium (discount). One should not, on the basis of this information, conclude that a currency selling at a premium is expected to increase or one selling at a discount is expected to decrease. A forward premium or discount is merely an implication of the relationship between interest rates in the two countries. More information would be required to make any assumptions about the outlook for the exchange rate.

If the forward rate in the market does not equal the forward rate given by interest rate parity, then an arbitrage transaction can be executed. Indeed, a similar relationship is true for any of the forward rates we have studied. In the foreign exchange markets, however, this arbitrage transaction has its own name: **covered interest arbitrage**. If the forward rate in the market is higher than the rate given by interest rate parity, then the forward rate is too high. When the price of an asset or derivative is too high, it should be sold. Thus, a trader would 1) sell the forward contract at the market rate, 2) buy $1/(1 + r^f)^T$ units of the foreign currency, 3) hold the position, earning interest on the currency, and 4) at maturity of the forward contract deliver the currency and be paid the forward rate. This arbitrage transaction would earn a return in excess of the domestic risk-free rate without any risk. If the forward rate is less than the rate given by the formula, the trader does the opposite, selling the foreign currency and buying a forward contract, in a similar manner. The combined actions of many traders undertaking this transaction will bring the forward price in the market in line with the forward price given by the model.

In Equation 64-15, both interest rates were annual rates with discrete compounding. In dealing with equities, we sometimes assume that the dividend payments are made continuously. Similarly, we could also assume that interest is compounded continuously. If that is the case, let r^{fc} be the continuously compounded foreign interest rate, defined as $r^{fc} = \ln(1 + r^f)$, and as before, let r^c be the continuously compounded domestic interest rate. Then the forward price is given by the same formula, with appropriately adjusted symbols, as we obtained when working with equity derivatives:

$$F(0,T) = (S_0 e^{-r^{fc}T}) e^{r^cT} \tag{64-16}$$

Now consider how we might value a foreign currency forward contract at some point in time during its life. In fact, we already know how: We simply apply to foreign currency forward contracts what we know about the valuation of equity forwards during the contract's life. Recall that the value of an equity forward is the stock price minus the present value of the dividends over the remaining life of the contract minus the present value of the forward price over the remaining life of the contract. An analogous formula for a currency forward gives us

$$V_t(0,T) = \frac{S_t}{(1 + r^f)^{(T-t)}} - \frac{F(0,T)}{(1 + r)^{(T-t)}} \qquad \textbf{(64-17)}$$

In other words, we take the current exchange rate at time t, S_t, discount it by the foreign interest rate over the remaining life of the contract, and subtract the forward price discounted by the domestic interest rate over the remaining life of the contract. Under the assumption that we are using continuous compounding and discounting, the formula would be

$$V_t(0,T) = (S_t e^{-r^{fc}(T-t)}) - F(0,T) e^{-r^c(T-t)} \qquad \textbf{(64-18)}$$

For example, suppose the domestic currency is the U.S. dollar and the foreign currency is the Swiss franc. Let the spot exchange rate be $0.5987, the U.S. interest rate be 5.5 percent, and the Swiss interest rate be 4.75 percent. We assume these interest rates are fixed and will not change over the life of the forward contract. We also assume that these rates are based on annual compounding and are not quoted as LIBOR-type rates. Thus, we compound using formulas like $(1 + r)^T$, where T is the number of years and r is the annual rate.[26]

Assuming the forward contract has a maturity of 180 days, we have T = 180/365. Using the above formula for the forward rate, we find that the forward price should be

$$F(0,T) = F(0,180/365) = \left[\frac{\$0.5987}{(1.0475)^{180/365}} \right] (1.055)^{180/365} = \$0.6008$$

Thus, if we entered into a forward contract, it would call for us to purchase (if long) or sell (if short) one Swiss franc in 180 days at a price of $0.6008.

Suppose we go long this forward contract. It is now 40 days later, or 140 days until expiration. The spot rate is now $0.65. As assumed above, the interest rates are fixed. With t = 40/365 and T − t = 140/365, the value of our long position is

$$V_t(0,T) = V_{40/365}(0,180/365) = \frac{\$0.6500}{(1.0475)^{140/365}} - \frac{\$0.6008}{(1.055)^{140/365}} = \$0.0499$$

So the contract value is $0.0499 per Swiss franc. If the notional principal were more than one Swiss franc, we would simply multiply the notional principal by $0.0499.

If we were working with continuously compounded rates, we would have $r^c = \ln(1.055) = 0.0535$ and $r^{fc} = \ln(1.0475) = 0.0464$. Then the forward price would be $F(0,T) = F(0,180/365) = (0.5987 e^{-0.0464(180/365)}) e^{0.0535(180/365)} = 0.6008$, and the value 40 days later would be $V_{40/365}(0,180/365) = 0.65 e^{-0.0464(140/365)} - 0.6008 e^{-0.0535(140/365)} = 0.0499$. These are the same results we obtained working with discrete rates.

Exhibit 64-9 summarizes the formulas for pricing and valuation of currency forward contracts.

---

[26] If these were LIBOR-style rates, the interest would be calculated using the factor 1 + [Rate(Days/360)].

EXHIBIT 64-9	Pricing and Valuation Formulas for Currency Forward Contracts

Forward price (rate) = (Spot price discounted by foreign interest rate) compounded at domestic interest rate:

Discrete interest: $F(0,T) = \left[\dfrac{S_0}{(1 + r^f)^T}\right](1 + r)^T$

Continuous interest: $F(0,T) = (S_0 e^{-r^{fc}T}) e^{r^c T}$

Value of forward contract:

Discrete interest: $V_t(0,T) = \left[\dfrac{S_t}{(1 + r^f)^{(T-t)}}\right] - \dfrac{F(0,T)}{(1 + r)^{(T-t)}}$

Continuous interest: $V_t(0,T) = [S_t e^{-r^{fc}(T-t)}] - F(0,T) e^{-r^c(T-t)}$

Note: The exchange rate is quoted in units of domestic currency per unit of foreign currency.

Practice Problem 5

The spot rate for British pounds is $1.76. The U.S. risk-free rate is 5.1 percent, and the U.K. risk-free rate is 6.2 percent; both are compounded annually. One-year forward contracts are currently quoted at a rate of $1.75.

A. Identify a strategy with which a trader can earn a profit at no risk by engaging in a forward contract, regardless of her view of the pound's likely movements. Carefully describe the transactions the trader would make. Show the rate of return that would be earned from this transaction. Assume the trader's domestic currency is U.S. dollars.

B. Suppose the trader simply shorts the forward contract. It is now one month later. Assume interest rates are the same, but the spot rate is now $1.72. What is the gain or loss to the counterparty on the trade?

C. At expiration, the pound is at $1.69. What is the value of the forward contract to the short at expiration?

▶ **Solution to A.** The following information is given:

$S_0 = \$1.76$
$r = 0.051$
$r^f = 0.062$
$T = 1.0$

The forward price should be

$$F(0,T) = \left(\frac{\$1.76}{1.062}\right)(1.051) = \$1.7418$$

With the forward contract selling at $1.75, it is slightly overpriced. Thus, the trader should be able to buy the currency and sell a forward contract to earn a return in excess of the risk-free rate at no risk. The specific transactions are as follows:

▶ Take $1.76/(1.062) = $1.6573. Use it to buy 1/1.062 = £0.9416.

▶ Sell a forward contract to deliver £1.00 in one year at the price of $1.75.

▶ Hold the position for one year, collecting interest at the U.K. risk-free rate of 6.2 percent. The £0.9416 will grow to (0.9416)(1.062) = £1.00.

▶ At expiration, deliver the pound and receive $1.75. This is a return of

$$\frac{1.75}{1.6573} - 1 = 0.0559$$

A risk-free return of 5.59 percent is better than the U.S. risk-free rate of 5.1 percent, a result of the fact that the forward contract is overpriced.

▶ **Solution to B.** We now need the value of the forward contract to the counterparty, who went long at $1.75. The inputs are

$$t = 1/12$$
$$S_t = \$1.72$$
$$T - t = 11/12$$
$$F(0,T) = \$1.75$$

The value of the forward contract to the long is

$$V_t(0,T) = \frac{1.72}{(1.062)^{11/12}} - \frac{1.75}{(1.051)^{11/12}} = -0.0443$$

which is a loss of $0.0443 to the long and a gain of $0.0443 to the short.

▶ **Solution to C.** The pound is worth $1.69 at expiration. Thus, the value to the long is

$$V_T(0,T) = 1.69 - 1.75 = -0.06$$

and the value to the short is +$0.06. Note the minus sign in the equation $V_T(0,T) = -0.06$. The value to the long is always the spot value at expiration minus the original forward price. The short will be required to deliver the foreign currency and receive $1.75, which is $0.06 more than market value of the pound. The contract's value to the short is thus $0.06, which is the negative of its value to the long.

We have now seen how to determine the price and value of equity, fixed-income and interest rate, and currency forward contracts. We observed that the price is determined such that no arbitrage opportunities exist for either the long or the short. We have found that the value of a forward contract is the amount we would pay or receive to enter or exit the contract. Because no money changes hands up front, the value of a forward contract when initiated is zero. The value at expiration is determined by the difference between the spot price or rate at expiration and the forward contract price or rate. The value prior to expiration can also be determined and is the present value of the claim at expiration.

Determining the value of a forward contract is important for several reasons. One, however, is particularly important: Forward contracts contain the very real possibility that one of the parties might default. By knowing the market value, one can determine the amount of money at risk if a counterparty defaults. Let us now look at how credit risk enters into a forward contract.

5　CREDIT RISK AND FORWARD CONTRACTS

To illustrate how credit risk affects a forward contract, consider the currency forward contract example we just finished in the previous section. It concerns a contract that expires in 180 days in which the long will pay a forward rate of $0.6008 for each Swiss franc to be received at expiration. Assume that the contract covers 10 million Swiss francs. Let us look at the problem from the point of view of the holder of the long position and the credit risk faced by this party.

Assume it is the contract expiration day and the spot rate for Swiss francs is $0.62. The long is due to receive 10 million Swiss francs and pay $0.6008 per Swiss franc, or $6,008,000 in total. Now suppose that perhaps because of bankruptcy or insolvency, the short cannot come up with the $6,200,000 that it would take to purchase the Swiss francs on the open market at the prevailing spot rate.[27] In order to obtain the Swiss francs, the long would have to buy them in the open market. Doing so would incur an additional cost of $6,200,000 − $6,008,000 = $192,000, which can be viewed as the credit risk at the point of expiration when the spot rate is $0.62. Not surprisingly, this amount is also the market value of the contract at this point.

This risk is an immediate risk faced at expiration. Prior to expiration, the long faces a potential risk that the short will default. If the long wanted to gauge the potential exposure, he would calculate the current market value. In the example we used in which the long is now 40 days into the life of the contract, the market value to the long is $0.0499 per Swiss franc. Hence, the long's exposure would be 10,000,000($0.0499) = $499,000. Although no payments are due at this point, $499,000 is the market value of the claim on the payment at expiration. Using an estimate of the probability that the short would default, the long can gauge the expected credit loss from the transaction by multiplying that probability by $499,000.

The market value of a forward contract reflects the current value of the claim at expiration, given existing market conditions. If the Swiss franc rises significantly, the market value will increase along with it, thereby exposing the long to the potential for even greater losses. Many participants in derivatives markets estimate this potential loss by running simulations that attempt to reflect the potential market value of the contract along with the probability of the counterparty defaulting.

We have viewed credit risk from the viewpoint of the long, but what about the short's perspective? In the case in which we went to expiration and the short owed the long the greater amount, the short faces no credit risk. In the case prior to expiration in which the contract's market value was positive, the value of the future claim was greater to the long than to the short. Hence, the short still did not face any credit risk.

---

[27] Even if the short already holds the Swiss franc, she might be declaring bankruptcy or otherwise unable to pay debts such that the forward contract claim is combined with the claims of all of the short's other creditors.

The short would face credit risk, however, if circumstances were such that the value of the transaction were negative to the long, which would make the value to the short positive. In that case, the scenario discussed previously in this section would apply from the short's perspective.

There are various methods of managing the credit risk of various types of derivatives transactions. At this point, however, it will be helpful to specifically examine one particular method. Let us go back to the long currency forward contract that had a market value of $499,000. As it stands at this time, the holder of the long position has a claim on the holder of the short position that is worth $499,000. Suppose the two parties had agreed when they entered into the transaction that in 40 days, the party owing the greater amount to the other would pay the amount owed and the contract would be repriced at the new forward rate. Now on the 40th day, the short would pay the long $499,000. Recalling that the U.S. interest rate was 5.5 percent and the Swiss interest rate was 4.75 percent, the contract, which now has 140 days to go (T = 140/365), would then be repriced to the rate

$$F(0,T) = F(0,140/365) = \left[\frac{\$0.65}{(1.0475)^{140/365}} \right] (1.055)^{140/365} = \$0.6518$$

In other words, from this point, the contract has a new rate of $0.6518. The long now agrees to pay $0.6518 for the currency from the short in 140 days.

What the two parties have done is called **marking to market**. They have settled up the amount owed and marked the contract to its current market rate. If the parties agree in advance, a forward contract can be marked to market at whatever dates the parties feel are appropriate. Marking to market keeps one party from becoming too deeply indebted to the other without paying up. At the dates when the contract is marked to market, the parties restructure the contract so that it remains in force but with an updated price.

Forward contracts and swaps are sometimes marked to market to mitigate credit risk. In Reading 65, we shall examine futures contracts. A distinguishing characteristic of futures contracts is that they are marked to market every day. In essence, they are forward contracts that are marked to market and repriced daily to reduce the credit risk.

THE ROLE OF FORWARD MARKETS   6

In this reading we have discussed many aspects of forward contracts and forward markets. We will conclude the reading with a brief discussion of the role that these markets play in our financial system. Although forward, futures, options, and swap markets serve similar purposes in our society, each market is unique. Otherwise, these markets would consolidate.

Forward markets may well be the least understood of the various derivative markets. In contrast to their cousins, futures contracts, forward contracts are a far less visible segment of the financial markets. Both forwards and futures serve a similar purpose: They provide a means in which a party can commit to the future purchase or sale of an asset at an agreed-upon price, without the necessity of paying any cash until the asset is actually purchased or sold. In contrast to futures contracts, forward contracts are private transactions, permitting the ultimate in customization. As long as a counterparty can be found, a party can structure the contract completely to its liking. Futures contracts are standardized and may not have the exact terms required by the party. In addition, futures contracts, with their daily marking to market, produce interim cash flows that can lead to imperfections in a hedge transaction designed not to hedge interim events but to hedge a specific event at a target horizon date. Forward markets also provide secrecy and have only a light degree of regulation. In general, forward markets serve a specialized clientele, specifically large corporations and institutions with specific target dates, underlying assets, and risks that they wish to take or reduce by committing to a transaction without paying cash at the start.

As Reading 67 will make clear, however, forward contracts are just miniature versions of swaps. A swap can be viewed as a series of forward contracts. Swaps are much more widely used than forward contracts, suggesting that parties that have specific risk management needs typically require the equivalent of a series of forward contracts. A swap contract consolidates a series of forward contracts into a single instrument at lower cost.

Forward contracts are the building blocks for constructing and understanding both swaps and futures. Swaps and futures are more widely used and better known, but forward contracts play a valuable role in helping us understand swaps and futures. Moreover, as noted, for some parties, forward contracts serve specific needs not met by other derivatives.

In Reading 65 we shall look at futures contracts. We shall demonstrate how similar they are to forward contracts, but the differences are important, and some of their benefits to society are slightly different and less obvious than those of forwards.

SUMMARY

▶ The holder of a long forward contract (the "long") is obligated to take delivery of the underlying asset and pay the forward price at expiration. The holder of a short forward contract (the "short") is obligated to deliver the underlying asset and accept payment of the forward price at expiration.

▶ At expiration, a forward contract can be terminated by having the short make delivery of the underlying asset to the long or having the long and short exchange the equivalent cash value. If the asset is worth more (less) than the forward price, the short (long) pays the long (short) the cash difference between the market price or rate and the price or rate agreed on in the contract.

▶ A party can terminate a forward contract prior to expiration by entering into an opposite transaction with the same or a different counterparty. It is possible to leave both the original and new transactions in place, thereby leaving both transactions subject to credit risk, or to have the two transactions cancel each other. In the latter case, the party owing the greater amount pays the market value to the other party, resulting in the elimination of the remaining credit risk. This elimination can be achieved, however, only if the counterparty to the second transaction is the same counterparty as in the first.

▶ A dealer is a financial institution that makes a market in forward contracts and other derivatives. A dealer stands ready to take either side of a transaction. An end user is a party that comes to a dealer needing a transaction, usually for the purpose of managing a particular risk.

▶ Equity forward contracts can be written on individual stocks, specific stock portfolios, or stock indices. Equity forward contract prices and values must take into account the fact that the underlying stock, portfolio, or index could pay dividends.

▶ Forward contracts on bonds can be based on zero-coupon bonds or on coupon bonds, as well as portfolios or indices based on zero-coupon bonds or coupon bonds. Zero-coupon bonds pay their return by discounting the face value, often using a 360-day year assumption. Forward contracts on bonds must expire before the bond's maturity. In addition, a forward contract on a bond can be affected by special features of bonds, such as callability and convertibility.

▶ Eurodollar time deposits are dollar loans made by one bank to another. Although the term "Eurodollars" refers to dollar-denominated loans, similar loans exist in other currencies. Eurodollar deposits accrue interest by adding it on to the principal, using a 360-day year assumption. The primary Eurodollar rate is called LIBOR.

▶ LIBOR stands for London Interbank Offer Rate, the rate at which London banks are willing to lend to other London banks. Euribor is the rate on a euro time deposit, a loan made by banks to other banks in Frankfurt in which the currency is the euro.

▶ An FRA is a forward contract in which one party, the long, agrees to pay a fixed interest payment at a future date and receive an interest payment at a rate to be determined at expiration. FRAs are described by a special notation. For example, a 3×6 FRA expires in three months; the underlying is a Eurodollar deposit that begins in three months and ends three months later, or six months from now.

▶ The payment of an FRA at expiration is based on the net difference between the underlying rate and the agreed-upon rate, adjusted by the notional principal and the number of days in the instrument on which the underlying rate is based. The payoff is also discounted, however, to reflect the fact that the underlying rate on which the instrument is based assumes that payment will occur at a later date.

▶ A currency forward contract is a commitment for one party, the long, to buy a currency at a fixed price from the other party, the short, at a specific date. The contract can be settled by actual delivery, or the two parties can choose to settle in cash on the expiration day.

▶ A forward contract is priced by assuming that the underlying asset is purchased, a forward contract is sold, and the position is held to expiration. Because the sale price of the asset is locked in as the forward price, the transaction is risk free and should earn the risk-free rate. The forward price is then obtained as the price that guarantees a return of the risk-free rate. If the forward price is too high or too low, an arbitrage profit in the form of a return in excess of the risk-free rate can be earned. The combined effects of all investors executing arbitrage transactions will force the forward price to converge to its arbitrage-free level.

▶ The value of a forward contract is determined by the fact that a long forward contract is a claim on the underlying asset and a commitment to pay the forward price at expiration. The value of a forward contract is, therefore, the current price of the asset less the present value of the forward price at expiration. Because no money changes hands at the start, the value of the forward contract today is zero. The value of a forward contract at expiration is the price of the underlying asset minus the forward price.

▶ Valuation of a forward contract is important because 1) it makes good business sense to know the values of future commitments, 2) accounting rules require that forward contracts be accounted for in income statements and balance sheets, 3) the value gives a good measure of the credit exposure, and 4) the value can be used to determine the amount of money one party would have to pay another party to terminate a position.

▶ An off-market forward contract is established with a nonzero value at the start. The contract will, therefore, have a positive or negative value and require a cash payment at the start. A positive value is paid by the long to the short; a negative value is paid by the short to the long. In an off-market forward contract, the forward price will not equal the price of the underlying asset compounded at the risk-free rate but rather will be set in the process of negotiation between the two parties.

▶ An equity forward contract is priced by taking the stock price, subtracting the present value of the dividends over the life of the contract, and then compounding this amount at the risk-free rate to the expiration date of the contract. The present value of the dividends can be found by assuming the dividends are risk-free and calculating their present value using the risk-free rate of interest. Or one can assume that dividends are paid at a constant continuously compounded rate and then discount the stock price by the exponential function using the continuously compounded dividend rate. Alternatively, an equity forward can be priced by compounding the stock price to the expiration date and then subtracting the future value of the dividends at the expiration date. The value of an equity forward contract is the stock price minus the present value of the dividends minus the present value of the forward price that will be paid at expiration.

► To price a fixed-income forward contract, take the bond price, subtract the present value of the coupons over the life of the contract, and compound this amount at the risk-free rate to the expiration date of the contract. The value of a fixed-income forward contract is the bond price minus the present value of the coupons minus the present value of the forward price that will be paid at expiration.

► The price of an FRA, which is actually a rate, is simply the forward rate embedded in the term structure of the FRA's underlying rate. The value of an FRA based on a Eurodollar deposit is the present value of $1 to be received at expiration minus the present value of $1 plus the FRA rate to be received at the maturity date of the Eurodollar deposit on which the FRA is based, with appropriate (days/360) adjustments.

► The price, which is actually an exchange rate, of a forward contract on a currency is the spot rate discounted at the foreign interest rate over the life of the contract and then compounded at the domestic interest rate to the expiration date of the contract. The value of a currency forward contract is the spot rate discounted at the foreign interest rate over the life of the contract minus the present value of the forward rate at expiration.

► Credit risk in a forward contract arises when the counterparty that owes the greater amount is unable to pay at expiration or declares bankruptcy prior to expiration. The market value of a forward contract is a measure of the net amount one party owes the other. Only one party, the one owing the lesser amount, faces credit risk at any given time. Because the market value can change from positive to negative, however, the other party has the potential for facing credit risk at a later date. Counterparties occasionally mark forward contracts to market, with one party paying the other the current market value; they then reprice the contract to the current market price or rate.

► Forward markets play an important role in society, providing a means by which a select clientele of parties can engage in customized, private, unregulated transactions that commit them to buying or selling an asset at a later date at an agreed-upon price without paying any cash at the start. Forward contracts also are a simplified version of both futures and swaps and, therefore, form a basis for understanding these other derivatives.

PROBLEMS FOR READING 64

1. Consider a security that sells for $1,000 today. A forward contract on this security that expires in one year is currently priced at $1,100. The annual rate of interest is 6.75 percent. Assume that this is an off-market forward contract.

A. Calculate the value of the forward contract today, $V_0(0,T)$.

B. Indicate whether payment is made by the long to the short or vice versa.

2. Assume that you own a security currently worth $500. You plan to sell it in two months. To hedge against a possible decline in price during the next two months, you enter into a forward contract to sell the security in two months. The risk-free rate is 3.5 percent.

A. Calculate the forward price on this contract.

B. Suppose the dealer offers to enter into a forward contract at $498. Indicate how you could earn an arbitrage profit.

C. After one month, the security sells for $490. Calculate the gain or loss to your position.

3. Consider an asset currently worth $100. An investor plans to sell it in one year and is concerned that the price may have fallen significantly by then. To hedge this risk, the investor enters into a forward contract to sell the asset in one year. Assume that the risk-free rate is 5 percent.

A. Calculate the appropriate price at which this investor can contract to sell the asset in one year.

B. Three months into the contract, the price of the asset is $90. Calculate the gain or loss that has accrued to the forward contract.

C. Assume that five months into the contract, the price of the asset is $107. Calculate the gain or loss on the forward contract.

D. Suppose that at expiration, the price of the asset is $98. Calculate the value of the forward contract at expiration. Also indicate the overall gain or loss to the investor on the whole transaction.

E. Now calculate the value of the forward contract at expiration assuming that at expiration, the price of the asset is $110. Indicate the overall gain or loss to the investor on the whole transaction. Is this amount more or less than the overall gain or loss from Part D?

4. A security is currently worth $225. An investor plans to purchase this asset in one year and is concerned that the price may have risen by then. To hedge this risk, the investor enters into a forward contract to buy the asset in one year. Assume that the risk-free rate is 4.75 percent.

A. Calculate the appropriate price at which this investor can contract to buy the asset in one year.

B. Four months into the contract, the price of the asset is $250. Calculate the gain or loss that has accrued to the forward contract.

C. Assume that eight months into the contract, the price of the asset is $200. Calculate the gain or loss on the forward contract.

D. Suppose that at expiration, the price of the asset is $190. Calculate the value of the forward contract at expiration. Also indicate the overall gain or loss to the investor on the whole transaction.

E. Now calculate the value of the forward contract at expiration assuming that at expiration, the price of the asset is $240. Indicate the overall gain or loss to the investor on the whole transaction. Is this amount more or less than the overall gain or loss from Part D?

5. Assume that a security is currently priced at $200. The risk-free rate is 5 percent.

    A. A dealer offers you a contract in which the forward price of the security with delivery in three months is $205. Explain the transactions you would undertake to take advantage of the situation.

    B. Suppose the dealer were to offer you a contract in which the forward price of the security with delivery in three months is $198. How would you take advantage of the situation?

6. Assume that you own a dividend-paying stock currently worth $150. You plan to sell the stock in 250 days. In order to hedge against a possible price decline, you wish to take a short position in a forward contract that expires in 250 days. The risk-free rate is 5.25 percent. Over the next 250 days, the stock will pay dividends according to the following schedule:

Days to Next Dividend	Dividends per Share
30	$1.25
120	$1.25
210	$1.25

    A. Calculate the forward price of a contract established today and expiring in 250 days.

    B. It is now 100 days since you entered the forward contract. The stock price is $115. Calculate the value of the forward contract at this point.

    C. At expiration, the price of the stock is $130. Calculate the value of the forward contract at expiration.

7. A portfolio manager expects to purchase a portfolio of stocks in 90 days. In order to hedge against a potential price increase over the next 90 days, she decides to take a long position on a 90-day forward contract on the S&P 500 stock index. The index is currently at 1145. The continuously compounded dividend yield is 1.75 percent. The discrete risk-free rate is 4.25 percent.

    A. Calculate the no-arbitrage forward price on this contract.

    B. It is now 28 days since the portfolio manager entered the forward contract. The index value is at 1225. Calculate the value of the forward contract 28 days into the contract.

    C. At expiration, the index value is 1235. Calculate the value of the forward contract.

8. An investor purchased a newly issued bond with a maturity of 10 years 200 days ago. The bond carries a coupon rate of 8 percent paid semiannually and has a face value of $1,000. The price of the bond with accrued interest is currently $1,146.92. The investor plans to sell the bond 365 days from now. The schedule of coupon payments over the first two years, from the date of purchase, is as follows:

Coupon	Days after Purchase	Amount
First	181	$40
Second	365	$40
Third	547	$40
Fourth	730	$40

A. Should the investor enter into a long or short forward contract to hedge his risk exposure? Calculate the no-arbitrage price at which the investor should enter the forward contract. Assume that the risk-free rate is 6 percent.

B. The forward contract is now 180 days old. Interest rates have fallen sharply, and the risk-free rate is 4 percent. The price of the bond with accrued interest is now $1,302.26. Determine the value of the forward contract now and indicate whether the investor has accrued a gain or loss on his position.

9. A corporate treasurer wishes to hedge against an increase in future borrowing costs due to a possible rise in short-term interest rates. She proposes to hedge against this risk by entering into a long 6 × 12 FRA. The current term structure for LIBOR is as follows:

Term	Interest Rate
30 day	5.10%
90 day	5.25%
180 day	5.70%
360 day	5.95%

A. Indicate when this 6 × 12 FRA expires and identify which term of the LIBOR this FRA is based on.

B. Calculate the rate the treasurer would receive on a 6 × 12 FRA.

Suppose the treasurer went long this FRA. Now, 45 days later, interest rates have risen and the LIBOR term structure is as follows:

Term	Interest Rate
135 day	5.90%
315 day	6.15%

C. Calculate the market value of this FRA based on a notional principal of $10,000,000.

D. At expiration, the 180-day LIBOR is 6.25 percent. Calculate the payoff on the FRA. Does the treasurer receive a payment or make a payment to the dealer?

10. A financial manager needs to hedge against a possible decrease in short term interest rates. He decides to hedge his risk exposure by going short on an FRA that expires in 90 days and is based on 90-day LIBOR. The current term structure for LIBOR is as follows:

Term	Interest Rate
30 day	5.83%
90 day	6.00%
180 day	6.14%
360 day	6.51%

A. Identify the type of FRA used by the financial manager using the appropriate terminology.

B. Calculate the rate the manager would receive on this FRA.

It is now 30 days since the manager took a short position in the FRA. Interest rates have shifted down, and the new term structure for LIBOR is as follows:

Term	Interest Rate
60 day	5.50%
150 day	5.62%

C. Calculate the market value of this FRA based on a notional principal of $15,000,000.

11. Consider a U.S.-based company that exports goods to Switzerland. The U.S. company expects to receive payment on a shipment of goods in three months. Because the payment will be in Swiss francs, the U.S. company wants to hedge against a decline in the value of the Swiss franc over the next three months. The U.S. risk-free rate is 2 percent, and the Swiss risk-free rate is 5 percent. Assume that interest rates are expected to remain fixed over the next six months. The current spot rate is $0.5974.

A. Indicate whether the U.S. company should use a long or short forward contract to hedge currency risk.

B. Calculate the no-arbitrage price at which the U.S. company could enter into a forward contract that expires in three months.

C. It is now 30 days since the U.S. company entered into the forward contract. The spot rate is $0.55. Interest rates are the same as before. Calculate the value of the U.S. company's forward position.

12. The euro currently trades at $1.0231. The dollar risk-free rate is 4 percent, and the euro risk-free rate is 5 percent. Six-month forward contracts are quoted at a rate of $1.0225. Indicate how you might earn a risk-free profit by engaging in a forward contract. Clearly outline the steps you undertake to earn this risk-free profit.

13. Suppose that you are a U.S.-based importer of goods from the United Kingdom. You expect the value of the pound to increase against the U.S. dollar over the next 30 days. You will be making payment on a shipment of imported goods in 30 days and want to hedge your currency exposure. The U.S. risk-free rate is 5.5 percent, and the U.K. risk-free rate is 4.5 percent. These rates are expected to remain unchanged over the next month. The current spot rate is $1.50.

A. Indicate whether you should use a long or short forward contract to hedge the currency risk.

B. Calculate the no-arbitrage price at which you could enter into a forward contract that expires in 30 days.

C. Move forward 10 days. The spot rate is $1.53. Interest rates are unchanged. Calculate the value of your forward position.

14. Consider the following: The U.S. risk-free rate is 6 percent, the Swiss risk-free rate is 4 percent, and the spot exchange rate between the United States and Switzerland is $0.6667.

  A. Calculate the continuously compounded U.S. and Swiss risk-free rates.

  B. Calculate the price at which you could enter into a forward contract that expires in 90 days.

  C. Calculate the value of the forward position 25 days into the contract. Assume that the spot rate is $0.65.

15. The Japanese yen currently trades at $0.00812. The U.S. risk-free rate is 4.5 percent, and the Japanese risk-free rate is 2.0 percent. Three-month forward contracts on the yen are quoted at $0.00813. Indicate how you might earn a risk-free profit by engaging in a forward contract. Outline your transactions.

FUTURES MARKETS AND CONTRACTS
by Don M. Chance

READING
65

LEARNING OUTCOMES

The candidate should be able to:

a. describe the difficulties in determining the price of Eurodollar futures and creating a pure arbitrage opportunity;

b. explain why the futures price must converge to the spot price at expiration;

c. explain how to determine the value of a futures contract;

d. explain how forward and futures prices differ;

e. identify the different types of monetary and non-monetary benefits and costs associated with holding the underlying asset, and explain how they affect the futures price; illustrate with backwardation and contango;

f. discuss whether futures prices equal expected spot prices;

g. describe and illustrate how to price Treasury bond futures, stock index futures, and currency futures.

INTRODUCTION   1

OPTIONAL SEGMENT BEGINS

In Reading 64, we focused on forward markets. Now we explore futures markets in a similar fashion. Although we shall see a clear similarity between forward and futures contracts, critical distinctions nonetheless exist between the two.

Like a forward contract, *a futures contract is an agreement between two parties in which one party, the buyer, agrees to buy from the other party, the seller, an underlying asset or other derivative, at a future date at a price agreed on today*. Unlike a forward contract, however, a futures contract is not a private and customized transaction but rather a public transaction that takes place on an organized futures exchange. In addition, a futures contract is standardized—the

Analysis of Derivatives for the CFA® Program, by Don M. Chance, Copyright © 2003 by Association for Investment Management and Research. Reprinted with permission.

exchange, rather than the individual parties, sets the terms and conditions, with the exception of price. As a result, futures contracts have a secondary market, meaning that previously created contracts can be traded. Also, parties to futures contracts are guaranteed against credit losses resulting from the counterparty's inability to pay. A clearinghouse provides this guarantee via a procedure in which it converts gains and losses that accrue on a daily basis into actual cash gains and losses. Futures contracts are regulated at the federal government level; as we noted in Reading 64, forward contracts are essentially unregulated. Futures contracts are created on organized trading facilities referred to as futures exchanges, whereas forward contracts are not created in any specific location but rather initiated between any two parties who wish to enter into such a contract. Finally, each futures exchange has a division or subsidiary called a **clearinghouse** that performs the specific responsibilities of paying and collecting daily gains and losses as well as guaranteeing to each party the performance of the other.

In a futures transaction, one party, the long, is the buyer and the other party, the short, is the seller. The buyer agrees to buy the underlying at a later date, the expiration, at a price agreed on at the start of the contract. The seller agrees to sell the underlying to the buyer at the expiration, at the price agreed on at the start of the contract. Every day, the futures contract trades in the market and its price changes in response to new information. Buyers benefit from price increases, and sellers benefit from price decreases. On the expiration day, the contract terminates and no further trading takes place. Then, either the buyer takes delivery of the underlying from the seller, or the two parties make an equivalent cash settlement. We shall explore each of these characteristics of futures contracts in more detail. First, however, it is important to take a brief look at how futures markets came into being.

1.1 A Brief History of Futures Markets

Although vestiges of futures markets appear in the Japanese rice markets of the 18th century and perhaps even earlier, the mid-1800s marked the first clear origins of modern futures markets. For example, in the United States in the 1840s, Chicago was becoming a major transportation and distribution center for agricultural commodities. Its central location and access to the Great Lakes gave Chicago a competitive advantage over other U.S. cities. Farmers from the Midwest would harvest their grain and take it to Chicago for sale. Grain production, however, is seasonal. As a result, grain prices would rise sharply just prior to the harvest but then plunge when the grain was brought to the market. Too much grain at one time and too little at another resulted in severe problems. Grain storage facilities in Chicago were inadequate to accommodate the oversupply. Some farmers even dumped their grain in the Chicago River because prices were so low that they could not afford to take their grain to another city to sell.

To address this problem, in 1848 a group of businessmen formed an organization later named the Chicago Board of Trade (CBOT) and created an arrangement called a "to-arrive" contract. These contracts permitted farmers to sell their grain before delivering it. In other words, farmers could harvest the grain and enter into a contract to deliver it at a much later date at a price already agreed on. This transaction allowed the farmer to hold the grain in storage at some other location besides Chicago. On the other side of these contracts were the businessmen who had formed the Chicago Board of Trade.

It soon became apparent that trading in these to-arrive contracts was more important and useful than trading in the grain itself. Soon the contracts began trading in a type of secondary market, which allowed buyers and sellers to discharge their obligations by passing them on, for a price, to other parties. With the addition of the clearinghouse in the 1920s, which provided a guarantee against default, modern futures markets firmly established their place in the financial world. It was left to other exchanges, such as today's Chicago Mercantile Exchange, the New York Mercantile Exchange, Eurex, and the London International Financial Futures Exchange, to develop and become, along with the Chicago Board of Trade, the global leaders in futures markets.

We shall now explore the important features of futures contracts in more detail.

1.2 Public Standardized Transactions

A private transaction is not generally reported in the news or to any price-reporting service. Forward contracts are private contracts. Just as in most legal contracts, the parties do not publicly report that they have engaged in a contract. In contrast, a futures transaction is reported to the futures exchange, the clearinghouse, and at least one regulatory agency. The price is recorded and available from price reporting services and even on the Internet.[1]

We noted that a futures transaction is not customized. Recall from Reading 64 that in a forward contract, the two parties establish all of the terms of the contract, including the identity of the underlying, the expiration date, and the manner in which the contract is settled (cash or actual delivery) as well as the price. The terms are customized to meet the needs of both parties. In a futures contract, the price is the only term established by the two parties; the exchange establishes all other terms. Moreover, the terms that are established by the exchange are standardized, meaning that the exchange selects a number of choices for underlyings, expiration dates, and a variety of other contract-specific items. These standardized terms are well known to all parties. If a party wishes to trade a futures contract, it must accept these terms. The only alternative would be to create a similar but customized contract on the forward market.

With respect to the underlying, for example, a given asset has a variety of specifications and grades. Consider a futures contract on U.S. Treasury bonds. There are many different Treasury bonds with a variety of characteristics. The futures exchange must decide which Treasury bond or group of bonds the contract covers. One of the most actively traded commodity futures contracts is oil, but there are many different types of oil.[2] To which type of oil does the contract apply? The exchange decides at the time it designs the contract.

The parties to a forward contract set its expiration at whatever date they want. For a futures contract, the exchange establishes a set of expiration dates. The first specification of the expiration is the month. An exchange might establish that a given futures contract expires only in the months of March, June, September, and December. The second specification determines how far the expirations go out into the future. For example, in January of a given year, there may be expirations

---

[1] The information reported to the general public does not disclose the identity of the parties to transactions but only that a transaction took place at a particular price.

[2] Some of the main types are Saudi Arabian light crude, Brent crude, and West Texas intermediate crude.

of March, June, September, and December. Expirations might also be available for March, June, September, and December of the following year, and perhaps some months of the year after that. The exchange decides which expiration months are appropriate for trading, based on which expirations they believe would be actively traded. Treasury bond futures have expirations going out only about a year. Eurodollar futures, however, have expirations that go out about 10 years[3] The third specification of the expiration is the specific day of expiration. Many, but not all, contracts expire some time during the third week of the expiration month.

The exchange determines a number of other contract characteristics, including the contract size. For example, one Eurodollar futures contract covers $1 million of a Eurodollar time deposit. One U.S. Treasury bond futures contract covers $100,000 face value of Treasury bonds. One futures contract on crude oil covers 1,000 barrels. The exchange also decides on the price quotation unit. For example, Treasury bond futures are quoted in points and 32nds of par of 100. Hence, you will see a price like 104 21/32, which means 104.65625. With a contract size of $100,000, the actual price is $104,656.25.

The exchange also determines what hours of the day trading takes place and at what physical location on the exchange the contract will be traded. Many futures exchanges have a trading floor, which contains octagonal-shaped pits. A contract is assigned to a certain pit. Traders enter the pits and express their willingness to buy and sell by calling out and/or indicating by hand signals their bids and offers. Some exchanges have electronic trading, which means that trading takes place on computer terminals, generally located in companies' offices. Some exchanges have both floor trading and electronic trading; some have only one or the other.

1.3 Homogenization and Liquidity

By creating contracts with generally accepted terms, the exchange standardizes the instrument. In contrast, forward contracts are quite heterogeneous because they are customized. Standardizing the instrument makes it more acceptable to a broader group of participants, with the advantage being that the instrument can then more easily trade in a type of secondary market. Indeed, the ability to sell a previously purchased contract or purchase a previously sold contract is one of the important features of futures contracts. A futures contract is therefore said to have liquidity in contrast to a forward contract, which does not generally trade after it has been created.[4] This ability to trade a previously opened contract allows participants in this market to offset the position before expiration, thereby obtaining exposure to price movements in the underlying without the actual requirement of holding the position to expiration. We shall discuss this characteristic further when we describe futures trading in Section 2.

1.4 The Clearinghouse, Daily Settlement, and Performance Guarantee

Another important distinction between futures and forwards is that the futures exchange guarantees to each party the performance of the other party, through a mechanism known as the clearinghouse. This guarantee means that if one

[3] You may be wondering why some Eurodollar futures contracts have such long expirations. Dealers in swaps and forward rate agreements use Eurodollar futures to hedge their positions. Many of those over-the-counter contracts have very long expirations.

[4] The notion of liquidity here is only that a market exists for futures contracts, but this does not imply a high degree of liquidity. There may be little trading in a given contract, and the bid–ask spread can be high. In contrast, some forward markets can be very liquid, allowing forward contracts to be offset, as described in Reading 64.

party makes money on the transaction, it does not have to worry about whether it will collect the money from the other party because the clearinghouse ensures it will be paid. In contrast, each party to a forward contract assumes the risk that the other party will default.

An important and distinguishing feature of futures contracts is that the gains and losses on each party's position are credited and charged on a daily basis. This procedure, called **daily settlement** or **marking to market**, essentially results in paper gains and losses being converted to cash gains and losses each day. It is also equivalent to terminating a contract at the end of each day and reopening it the next day at that **settlement price**. In some sense, a futures contract is like a strategy of opening up a forward contract, closing it one day later, opening up a new contract, closing it one day later, and continuing in that manner until expiration. The exact manner in which the daily settlement works will be covered in more detail later in Section 3.

1.5 Regulation

In most countries, futures contracts are regulated at the federal government level. State and regional laws may also apply. In the United States, the Commodity Futures Trading Commission regulates the futures market. In the United Kingdom, the Securities and Futures Authority regulates both the securities and futures markets.

Federal regulation of futures markets generally arises out of a concern to protect the general public and other futures market participants, as well as through a recognition that futures markets affect all financial markets and the economy. Regulations cover such matters as ensuring that prices are reported accurately and in a timely manner, that markets are not manipulated, that professionals who offer their services to the public are qualified and honest, and that disputes are resolved. In the United States, the government has delegated some of these responsibilities to an organization called the National Futures Association (NFA). An industry self-regulatory body, the NFA was created with the objective of having the industry regulate itself and reduce the federal government's burden.

FUTURES TRADING   2

In this section, we look more closely at how futures contracts are traded. As noted above, futures contracts trade on a futures exchange either in a pit or on a screen or electronic terminal.

We briefly mentioned pit trading, also known as floor-based trading, in Section 1.2. Pit trading is a very physical activity. Traders stand in the pit and shout out their orders in the form of prices they are willing to pay or accept. They also use hand signals to indicate their bids and offers.[5] They engage in transactions with other traders in the pits by simply agreeing on a price and number of contracts to trade. The activity is fast, furious, exciting, and stressful. The average pit trader is quite young, owing to the physical demands of the job and the toll it takes on body and mind. In recent years, more trading has come off of the exchange floor to electronic screens or terminals. In electronic or screen-based trading, exchange members enter their bids and offers into a computer system,

---

[5] Hand signals facilitate trading with someone who is too far away in the pit for verbal communication.

which then displays this information and allows a trader to consummate a trade electronically. In the United States, pit trading is dominant, owing to its long history and tradition. Exchange members who trade on the floor enjoy pit trading and have resisted heavily the advent of electronic trading. Nonetheless, the exchanges have had to respond to market demands to offer electronic trading. In the United States, both pit trading and electronic trading are used, but in other countries, electronic trading is beginning to drive pit trading out of business.[6]

A person who enters into a futures contract establishes either a long position or a short position. Similar to forward contracts, long positions are agreements to buy the underlying at the expiration at a price agreed on at the start. Short positions are agreements to sell the underlying at a future date at a price agreed on at the start. When the position is established, each party deposits a small amount of money, typically called the **margin**, with the clearinghouse. Then, as briefly described in Section 1.4, the contract is marked to market, whereby the gains are distributed to and the losses collected from each party. We cover this marking-to-market process in more detail in the next section. For now, however, we focus only on the opening and closing of the position.

A party that has opened a long position collects profits or incurs losses on a daily basis. At some point in the life of the contract prior to expiration, that party may wish to re-enter the market and close out the position. This process, called **offsetting**, is the same as selling a previously purchased stock or buying back a stock to close a short position. The holder of a long futures position simply goes back into the market and offers the identical contract for sale. The holder of a short position goes back into the market and offers to buy the identical contract. It should be noted that when a party offsets a position, it does not necessary do so with the same counterparty to the original contract. In fact, rarely would a contract be offset with the same counterparty. Because of the ability to offset, futures contracts are said to be fungible, which means that any futures contract with any counterparty can be offset by an equivalent futures contract with another counterparty. Fungibility is assured by the fact that the clearinghouse inserts itself in the middle of each contract and, therefore, becomes the counterparty to each party.

For example, suppose in early January a futures trader purchases an S&P 500 stock index futures contract expiring in March. Through 15 February, the trader has incurred some gains and losses from the daily settlement and decides that she wants to close the position out. She then goes back into the market and offers for sale the March S&P 500 futures. Once she finds a buyer to take the position, she has a long and short position in the same contract. The clearinghouse considers that she no longer has a position in that contract and has no remaining exposure, nor any obligation to make or take delivery at expiration. Had she initially gone short the March futures, she might re-enter the market in February offering to buy it. Once she finds a seller to take the opposite position, she becomes long and short the same contract and is considered to have offset the contract and therefore have no net position.

3   THE CLEARINGHOUSE, MARGINS, AND PRICE LIMITS

As briefly noted in the previous section, when a trader takes a long or short position in a futures, he must first deposit sufficient funds in a **margin account**. This amount of money is traditionally called the margin, a term derived from the

---

[6] For example, in France electronic trading was introduced while pit trading continued. Within two weeks, all of the volume had migrated to electronic trading and pit trading was terminated.

stock market practice in which an investor borrows a portion of the money required to purchase a certain amount of stock.

Margin in the stock market is quite different from margin in the futures market. In the stock market, "margin" means that a loan is made. The loan enables the investor to reduce the amount of his own money required to purchase the securities, thereby generating leverage or gearing, as it is sometimes known. If the stock goes up, the percentage gain to the investor is amplified. If the stock goes down, however, the percentage loss is also amplified. The borrowed money must eventually be repaid with interest. The margin percentage equals the market value of the stock minus the market value of the debt divided by the market value of the stock—in other words, the investor's own equity as a percentage of the value of the stock. For example, in the United States, regulations permit an investor to borrow up to 50 percent of the initial value of the stock. This percentage is called the initial margin requirement. On any day thereafter, the equity or percentage ownership in the account, measured as the market value of the securities minus the amount borrowed, can be less than 50 percent but must be at least a percentage known as the maintenance margin requirement. A typical **maintenance margin** requirement is 25 to 30 percent.

In the futures market, by contrast, the word **margin** is commonly used to describe the amount of money that must be put into an account by a party opening up a futures position, but the term is misleading. When a transaction is initiated, a futures trader puts up a certain amount of money to meet the **initial margin requirement**; however, the remaining money is not borrowed. The amount of money deposited is more like a down payment for the commitment to purchase the underlying at a later date. Alternatively, one can view this deposit as a form of good faith money, collateral, or a performance bond: The money helps ensure that the party fulfills his or her obligation.[7] Moreover, both the buyer and the seller of a futures contract must deposit margin.

In securities markets, margin requirements are normally set by federal regulators. In the United States, maintenance margin requirements are set by the securities exchanges and the NASD. In futures markets, margin requirements are set by the clearinghouses. In further contrast to margin practices in securities markets, futures margins are traditionally expressed in dollar terms and not as a percentage of the futures price. For ease of comparison, however, we often speak of the futures margin in terms of its relationship to the futures price. In futures markets, the initial margin requirement is typically much lower than the initial margin requirement in the stock market. In fact, futures margins are usually less than 10 percent of the futures price.[8] Futures clearinghouses set their margin requirements by studying historical price movements. They then establish minimum margin levels by taking into account normal price movements and the fact that accounts are marked to market daily. The clearinghouses thus collect and disburse margin money every day. Moreover, they are permitted to do so more often than daily, and on some occasions they have used that privilege. By carefully setting margin requirements and collecting margin money every day, clearinghouses are able to control the risk of default.

In spite of the differences in margin practices for futures and securities markets, the effect of leverage is similar for both. By putting up a small amount of money, the trader's gains and losses are magnified. Given the tremendously

---

[7] In fact, the Chicago Mercantile Exchange uses the term "performance bond" instead of "margin." Most other exchanges use the term "margin."

[8] For example, the margin requirement of the Eurodollar futures contract at the Chicago Mercantile Exchange has been less than one-tenth of one percent of the futures price. An exception to this requirement, however, is individual stock futures, which in the United States have margin requirements comparable to those of the stock market.

low margin requirements of futures markets, however, the magnitude of the leverage effect is much greater in futures markets. We shall see how this works as we examine the process of the daily settlement.

As previously noted, each day the clearinghouse conducts an activity known as the daily settlement, also called marking to market. This practice results in the conversion of gains and losses on paper into actual gains and losses. As margin account balances change, holders of futures positions must maintain balances above a level called the **maintenance margin requirement**. The maintenance margin requirement is lower than the initial margin requirement. On any day in which the amount of money in the margin account at the end of the day falls below the maintenance margin requirement, the trader must deposit sufficient funds to bring the balance back up to the initial margin requirement. Alternatively, the trader can simply close out the position but is responsible for any further losses incurred if the price changes before a closing transaction can be made.

To provide a fair mark-to-market process, the clearinghouse must designate the official price for determining daily gains and losses. This price is called the **settlement price** and represents an average of the final few trades of the day. It would appear that the closing price of the day would serve as the settlement price, but the closing price is a single value that can potentially be biased high or low or perhaps even manipulated by an unscrupulous trader. Hence, the clearinghouse takes an average of all trades during the closing period (as defined by each exchange).

Exhibit 65-1 provides an example of the marking-to-market process that occurs over a period of six trading days. We start with the assumption that the futures price is $100 when the transaction opens, the initial margin requirement is $5, and the maintenance margin requirement is $3. In Panel A, the trader takes a long position of 10 contracts on Day 0, depositing $50 ($5 times 10 contracts) as indicated in Column 3. At the end of the day, his ending balance is $50.[9] Although the trader can withdraw any funds in excess of the initial margin requirement, we shall assume that he does not do so.[10]

The ending balance on Day 0 is then carried forward to the beginning balance on Day 1. On Day 1, the futures price moves down to 99.20, as indicated in Column 4 of Panel A. The futures price change, Column 5, is $-0.80 (99.20 - 100)$. This amount is then multiplied by the number of contracts to obtain the number in Column 6 of $-0.80 \times 10 = -\$8$. The ending balance, Column 7, is the beginning balance plus the gain or loss. The ending balance on Day 1 of $42 is above the maintenance margin requirement of $30, so no funds need to be deposited on Day 2.

On Day 2 the settlement price goes down to $96. Based on a price decrease of $3.20 per contract and 10 contracts, the loss is $32, lowering the ending balance to $10. This amount is $20 below the maintenance margin requirement. Thus, the trader will get a **margin call** the following morning and must deposit $40 to bring the balance up to the initial margin level of $50. This deposit is shown in Column 3 on Day 3.

Here, we must emphasize two important points. First, additional margin that must be deposited is the amount sufficient to bring the ending balance up to the initial margin requirement, not the maintenance margin requirement.[11] This

---

[9] Technically, we are assuming that the position was opened at the settlement price on Day 0. If the position is opened earlier during the day, it would be marked to the settlement price at the end of the day.

[10] Virtually all professional traders are able to deposit interest-earning assets, although many other account holders are required to deposit cash. If the deposit earns interest, there is no opportunity cost and no obvious necessity to withdraw the money to invest elsewhere.

[11] In the stock market, one must deposit only the amount necessary to bring the balance up to the maintenance margin requirement.

EXHIBIT 65-1	Mark-to-Market Example

Initial futures price = $100, Initial margin requirement = $5, Maintenance margin requirement = $3

A. *Holder of Long Position of 10 Contracts*

Day (1)	Beginning Balance (2)	Funds Deposited (3)	Settlement Price (4)	Futures Price Change (5)	Gain/ Loss (6)	Ending Balance (7)
0	0	50	100.00			50
1	50	0	99.20	−0.80	−8	42
2	42	0	96.00	−3.20	−32	10
3	10	40	101.00	5.00	50	100
4	100	0	103.50	2.50	25	125
5	125	0	103.00	−0.50	−5	120
6	120	0	104.00	1.00	10	130

B. *Holder of Short Position of 10 Contracts*

Day (1)	Beginning Balance (2)	Funds Deposited (3)	Settlement Price (4)	Futures Price Change (5)	Gain/ Loss (6)	Ending Balance (7)
0	0	50	100.00			50
1	50	0	99.20	−0.80	8	58
2	58	0	96.00	−3.20	32	90
3	90	0	101.00	5.00	−50	40
4	40	0	103.50	2.50	−25	15
5	15	35	103.00	−0.50	5	55
6	55	0	104.00	1.00	−10	45

additional margin is called the **variation margin**. In addition, the amount that must be deposited the following day is determined regardless of the price change the following day, which might bring the ending balance well above the initial margin requirement, as it does here, or even well below the maintenance margin requirement. Thus, another margin call could occur. Also note that when the trader closes the position, the account is marked to market to the final price at which the transaction occurs, not the settlement price that day.

Over the six-day period, the trader in this example deposited $90. The account balance at the end of the sixth day is $130—nearly a 50 percent return over six days; not bad. But look at Panel B, which shows the position of a holder of 10 short contracts over that same period. Note that the short gains when prices decrease and loses when prices increase. Here the ending balance falls below the maintenance margin requirement on Day 4, and the short must deposit $35 on Day 5. At the end of Day 6, the short has deposited $85 and the balance is $45, a loss of $40 or nearly 50 percent, which is the same $40 the long made. Both cases illustrate the leverage effect that magnifies gains and losses.

When establishing a futures position, it is important to know the price level that would trigger a margin call. In this case, it does not matter how many contracts one has. The price change would need to fall for a long position (or rise for a short position) by the difference between the initial and maintenance margin requirements. In this example, the difference between the initial and maintenance margin requirements is $5 - $3 = $2. Thus, the price would need to fall from $100 to $98 for a long position (or rise from $100 to $102 for a short position) to trigger a margin call.

As described here, when a trader receives a margin call, he is required to deposit funds sufficient to bring the account balance back up to the initial margin level. Alternatively, the trader can choose to simply close out the position as soon as possible. For example, consider the position of the long at the end of the second day when the margin balance is $10. This amount is $20 below the maintenance level, and he is required to deposit $40 to bring the balance up to the initial margin level. If he would prefer not to deposit the additional funds, he can close out the position as soon as possible the following day. Suppose, however, that the price is moving quickly at the opening on Day 3. If the price falls from $96 to $95, he has lost $10 more, wiping out the margin account balance. In fact, if it fell any further, he would have a negative margin account balance. He is still responsible for these losses. Thus, the trader could lose more than the amount of money he has placed in the margin account. The total amount of money he could lose is limited to the price per contract at which he bought, $100, times the number of contracts, 10, or $1,000. Such a loss would occur if the price fell to zero, although this is not likely. This potential loss may not seem like a lot, but it is certainly large relative to the initial margin requirement of $50. For the holder of the short position, there is no upper limit on the price and the potential loss is theoretically infinite.

Practice Problem 1

Consider a futures contract in which the current futures price is $82. The initial margin requirement is $5, and the maintenance margin requirement is $2. You go long 20 contracts and meet all margin calls but do not withdraw any excess margin. Assume that on the first day, the contract is established at the settlement price, so there is no mark-to-market gain or loss on that day.

A. Complete the table below and provide an explanation of any funds deposited.

Day	Beginning Balance	Funds Deposited	Futures Price	Price Change	Gain/Loss	Ending Balance
0			82			
1			84			
2			78			
3			73			
4			79			
5			82			
6			84			

B.   Determine the price level that would trigger a margin call.

▶ **Solution to A.**

Day	Beginning Balance	Funds Deposited	Futures Price	Price Change	Gain/Loss	Ending Balance
0	0	100	82			100
1	100	0	84	2	40	140
2	140	0	78	−6	−120	20
3	20	80	73	−5	−100	0
4	0	100	79	6	120	220
5	220	0	82	3	60	280
6	280	0	84	2	40	320

On Day 0, you deposit $100 because the initial margin requirement is $5 per contract and you go long 20 contracts. At the end of Day 2, the balance is down to $20, which is $20 below the $40 maintenance margin requirement ($2 per contract times 20 contracts). You must deposit enough money to bring the balance up to the initial margin requirement of $100 ($5 per contract times 20 contracts). So on Day 3, you deposit $80. The price change on Day 3 causes a gain/loss of −$100, leaving you with a balance of $0 at the end of Day 3. On Day 4, you must deposit $100 to return the balance to the initial margin level.

▶ **Solution to B.** A price decrease to $79 would trigger a margin call. This calculation is based on the fact that the difference between the initial margin requirement and the maintenance margin requirement is $3. If the futures price starts at $82, it can fall by $3 to $79 before it triggers a margin call.

Some futures contracts impose limits on the price change that can occur from one day to the next. Appropriately, these are called **price limits**. These limits are usually set as an absolute change over the previous day. Using the example above, suppose the price limit was $4. This would mean that each day, no transaction could take place higher than the previous settlement price plus $4 or lower than the previous settlement price minus $4. So the next day's settlement price cannot go beyond the price limit and thus no transaction can take place beyond the limits.

If the price at which a transaction would be made exceeds the limits, then price essentially freezes at one of the limits, which is called a **limit move**. If the price is stuck at the upper limit, it is called **limit up**; if stuck at the lower limit, it is called **limit down**. If a transaction cannot take place because the price would be beyond the limits, this situation is called **locked limit**. By the end of the day, unless the price has moved back within the limits, the settlement price will then be at one of the limits. The following day, the new range of acceptable prices is based on the settlement price plus or minus limits. The exchanges have different rules that provide for expansion or contraction of price limits under some circumstances. In addition, not all contracts have price limits.

Finally, we note that the exchanges have the power to mark contracts to market whenever they deem it necessary. Thus, they can do so during the trading day rather than wait until the end of the day. They sometimes do so when abnormally large market moves occur.

The daily settlement procedure is designed to collect losses and distribute gains in such a manner that losses are paid before becoming large enough to impose a serious risk of default. Recall that the clearinghouse guarantees to each party that it need not worry about collecting from the counterparty. The clearinghouse essentially positions itself in the middle of each contract, becoming the short counterparty to the long and the long counterparty to the short. The clearinghouse collects funds from the parties incurring losses in this daily settlement procedure and distributes them to the parties incurring gains. By doing so each day, the clearinghouse ensures that losses cannot build up. Of course, this process offers no guarantee that counterparties will not default. Some defaults do occur, but the counterparty is defaulting to the clearinghouse, which has never failed to pay off the opposite party. In the unlikely event that the clearinghouse were unable to pay, it would turn to a reserve fund or to the exchange, or it would levy a tax on exchange members to cover losses.

4   DELIVERY AND CASH SETTLEMENT

As previously described, a futures trader can close out a position before expiration. If the trader holds a long position, she can simply enter into a position to go short the same futures contract. From the clearinghouse's perspective, the trader holds both a long and short position in the same contract. These positions are considered to offset and, therefore, there is no open position in place. Most futures contracts are offset before expiration. Those that remain in place are subject to either delivery or a final cash settlement. Here we explore this process, which determines how a futures contract, terminates at expiration.

When the exchange designs a futures contract, it specifies whether the contract will terminate with delivery or cash settlement. If the contract terminates in delivery, the clearinghouse selects a counterparty, usually the holder of the oldest long contract, to accept delivery. The holder of the short position then delivers the underlying to the holder of the long position, who pays the short the necessary cash for the underlying. Suppose, for example, that two days before expiration, a party goes long one futures contract at a price of $50. The following day (the day before expiration), the settlement price is $52. The trader's margin account in then marked to market by crediting it with a gain of $2. Then suppose that the next day the contract expires with the settlement price at $53. As the end of the trading day draws near, the trader has two choices. She can attempt to close out the position by selling the futures contract. The margin account would then be marked to market at the price at which she sells. If she sells close enough to the expiration, the price she sold at would be very close to the final settlement price of $53. Doing so would add $1 to her margin account balance.

The other choice is to leave the position open at the end of the trading day. Then she would have to take delivery. If that occurred, she would be required to take possession of the asset and pay the short the settlement price of the previous day. Doing so would be equivalent to paying $52 and receiving the asset. She could then sell the asset for its price of $53, netting a $1 gain, which is equivalent to the final $1 credited to her margin account if she had terminated the position at the settlement price of $53, as described above.[12]

---

[12] The reason she pays the settlement price of the previous day is because on the previous day when her account was marked to market, she essentially created a new futures position at a price of $52. Thus, she committed to purchase the asset at expiration, just one day later, at a price of $52. The next day when the contract expires, it is then appropriate that she buy the underlying for $52.

EXHIBIT 65-2 Closeout versus Physical Delivery versus Cash Settlement

Closeout:
Sell contract at 53
Mark to market profit/loss:
53 − 52 = 1

or

Physical Delivery:
Pay 52, receive asset worth 53

Mark to market profit/loss: 52 − 50 = 2

or

Cash Settlement:
Receive 53 − 52 = 1

Buy futures at 50: Pay nothing

2 days before expiration (futures price = 50) | 1 day before expiration (settlement price = 52) | Expiration (settlement price = 53)

An alternative settlement procedure, which we described in Reading 64 on forward contracts, is cash settlement. The exchange designates certain futures contracts as cash-settled contracts. If the contract used in this example were cash settled, then the trader would not need to close out the position close to the end of the expiration day. She could simply leave the position open. When the contract expires, her margin account would be marked to market for a gain on the final day of $1. Cash settlement contracts have some advantages over delivery contracts, particularly with respect to significant savings in transaction costs.[13]

Exhibit 65-2 illustrates the equivalence of these three forms of delivery. Note, however, that because of the transaction costs of delivery, parties clearly prefer a closeout or cash settlement over physical delivery, particularly when the underlying asset is a physical commodity.

Contracts designated for delivery have a variety of features that can complicate delivery. In most cases, delivery does not occur immediately after expiration but takes place over several days. In addition, many contracts permit the short to choose when delivery takes place. For many contracts, delivery can be made any business day of the month. The delivery period usually includes the days following the last trading day of the month, which is usually in the third week of the month.

In addition, the short often has other choices regarding delivery, a major one being exactly which underlying asset is delivered. For example, a futures contract on U.S. Treasury bonds trading at the Chicago Board of Trade permits the short to deliver any of a number of U.S. Treasury bonds.[14] The wheat futures contract at the Chicago Board of Trade permits delivery of any of several types of wheat. Futures contracts calling for physical delivery of commodities often permit delivery at different locations. A given commodity delivered to one location is not the same as that commodity delivered to another because of the costs

[13] Nonetheless, cash settlement has been somewhat controversial in the United States. If a contract is designated as cash settlement, it implies that the buyer of the contract never intended to actually take possession of the underlying asset. Some legislators and regulators feel that this design is against the spirit of the law, which views a futures contract as a commitment to buy the asset at a later date. Even though parties often offset futures contracts prior to expiration, the possibility of actual delivery is still present in contracts other than those settled by cash. This controversy, however, is relatively minor and has caused no serious problems or debates in recent years.

[14] We shall cover this feature in more detail in Sections 6.2 and 7.2.3.

OPTIONAL SEGMENT

involved in transporting the commodity. The short holds the sole right to make decisions about what, when, and where to deliver, and the right to make these decisions can be extremely valuable. The right to make a decision concerning these aspects of delivery is called a **delivery option**.

Some futures contracts that call for delivery require delivery of the actual asset, and some use only a book entry. For example, in this day and age, no one physically handles U.S. Treasury bonds in the form of pieces of paper. Bonds are transferred electronically over the Federal Reserve's wire system. Other contracts, such as oil or wheat, do actually involve the physical transfer of the asset. Physical delivery is more common when the underlying is a physical commodity, whereas **book entry** is more common when the underlying is a financial asset.

Futures market participants use one additional delivery procedure, which is called **exchange for physicals (EFP)**. In an EFP transaction, the long and short arrange an alternative delivery procedure. For example, the Chicago Board of Trade's wheat futures contracts require delivery on certain dates at certain locations either in Chicago or in a few other specified locations in the Midwest. If the long and short agree, they could effect delivery by having the short deliver the wheat to the long in, for example, Omaha. The two parties would then report to the Chicago Board of Trade that they had settled their contract outside of the exchange's normal delivery procedures, which would be satisfactory to the exchange.

5 FUTURES EXCHANGES

A futures exchange is a legal corporate entity whose shareholders are its members. The members own memberships, more commonly called **seats**. Exchange members have the privilege of executing transactions on the exchange. Each member acts as either a **floor trader** or a **broker**. Floor traders are typically called **locals**; brokers are typically called **futures commission merchants (FCMs)**. Locals are market makers, standing ready to buy and sell by quoting a bid and an ask price. They are the primary providers of liquidity to the market. FCMs execute transactions for other parties off the exchange.

The locals on the exchange floor typically trade according to one of several distinct styles. The most common is called scalping. A **scalper** offers to buy or sell futures contracts, holding the position for only a brief period of time, perhaps just seconds. Scalpers attempt to profit by buying at the bid price and selling at the higher ask price. A **day trader** holds a position open somewhat longer but closes all positions at the end of the day.[15] A **position trader** holds positions open overnight. Day traders and position traders are quite distinct from scalpers in that they attempt to profit from the anticipated direction of the market; scalpers are trying simply to buy at the bid and sell at the ask.

Recall that futures exchanges have trading either on the floor or off the floor on electronic terminals, or in some cases, both. As previously described, floor trading in the United States takes place in pits, which are octagonal, multitiered areas where floor traders stand and conduct transactions. Traders wear jackets of specific colors and badges to indicate such information as what type of trader (FCM or local) they are and whom they represent.[16] As noted, to indicate a willingness to trade, a trader shouts and uses a set of standard hand signals. A

---

[15] The term "day trader" has been around the futures market for a long time but has recently acquired a new meaning in the broader financial markets. The term is now used to describe individual investors who trade stocks, often over the Internet, during the day for a living or as a hobby. In fact, the term has even been used in a somewhat pejorative manner, in that day traders are often thought of as naïve investors speculating wildly with money they can ill afford to lose.

[16] For example, an FCM or local could be trading for himself or could represent a company.

EXHIBIT 65-3	The World's 20 Leading Futures Exchanges

Exchange and Location	Volume in 2001 (Number of Contracts)
Eurex (Germany and Switzerland)	435,141,707
Chicago Mercantile Exchange (United States)	315,971,885
Chicago Board of Trade (United States)	209,988,002
London International Financial Futures and Options Exchange (United Kingdom)	161,522,775
Bolsa de Mercadorias & Futuros (Brazil)	94,174,452
New York Mercantile Exchange (United States)	85,039,984
Tokyo Commodity Exchange (Japan)	56,538,245
London Metal Exchange (United Kingdom)	56,224,495
Paris Bourse SA (France)	42,042,673
Sydney Futures Exchange (Australia)	34,075,508
Korea Stock Exchange (Korea)	31,502,184
Singapore Exchange (Singapore)	30,606,546
Central Japan Commodity Exchange (Japan)	27,846,712
International Petroleum Exchange (United Kingdom)	26,098,207
OM Stockholm Exchange (Sweden)	23,408,198
Tokyo Grain Exchange (Japan)	22,707,808
New York Board of Trade (United States)	14,034,168
MEFF Renta Variable (Spain)	13,108,293
Tokyo Stock Exchange (Japan)	12,465,433
South African Futures Exchange (South Africa)	11,868,242

Source: Futures Industry, January/February 2002.

trade is consummated by two traders agreeing on a price and a number of contracts. These traders might not actually say anything to each other; they may simply use a combination of hand signals and/or eye contact to agree on a transaction. When a transaction is agreed on, the traders fill out small paper forms and turn them over to clerks, who then see that the transactions are entered into the system and reported.

Each trader is required to have an account at a clearing firm. The clearing firms are the actual members of the clearinghouse. The clearinghouse deals only with the clearing firms, which then deal with their individual and institutional customers.

In electronic trading, the principles remain essentially the same but the traders do not stand in the pits. In fact, they do not see each other at all. They sit at computer terminals, which enable them to see the bids and offers of other traders. Transactions are executed by the click of a computer mouse or an entry from a keyboard.

Exhibit 65-3 lists the world's 20 leading futures exchanges in 2001, ranked by trading volume. Trading volume can be a misleading measure of the size of a futures markets; nonetheless, it is the measure primarily used. The structure of global futures exchanges has changed considerably in recent years. Exchanges in the United States, primarily the Chicago Board of Trade and the Chicago Mercantile Exchange, were clearly the world leaders in the past. Note that the volume leader now, however, is Eurex, the combined German–Swiss exchange. Eurex has been so successful partly because of its decision to be an all-electronic futures exchange, whereas the Chicago exchanges are still primarily pit-trading exchanges. Note the popularity of futures trading in Japan; four of the 20 leading exchanges are Japanese.

6   TYPES OF FUTURES CONTRACTS

The different types of futures contracts are generally divided into two main groups: commodity futures and financial futures. Commodity futures cover traditional agricultural, metal, and petroleum products. Financial futures include stocks, bonds, and currencies. Exhibit 65-4 gives a broad overview of the most active types of futures contracts traded on global futures exchanges. These contracts are those covered by the *Wall Street Journal* on the date indicated.

Our primary focus in this book is on financial and currency futures contracts. Within the financials group, our main interest is on interest rate and bond futures, stock index futures, and currency futures. We may occasionally make reference to a commodity futures contract, but that will primarily be for illustrative purposes. In the following subsections, we introduce the primary contracts we shall focus on. These are U.S. contracts, but they resemble most types of futures contracts found on exchanges throughout the world. Full contract specifications for these and other contracts are available on the web sites of the futures exchanges, which are easy to locate with most Internet search engines.

6.1 Short-Term Interest Rate Futures Contracts

The primary short-term interest rate futures contracts are those on U.S. Treasury bills and Eurodollars on the Chicago Mercantile Exchange.

6.1.1 Treasury Bill Futures

The Treasury bill contract, launched in 1976, was the first interest rate futures contract. It is based on a 90-day U.S. Treasury bill, one of the most important U.S. government debt instruments (described in Reading 64, Section 3.2.1). The Treasury bill, or T-bill, is a discount instrument, meaning that its price equals the face value minus a discount representing interest. The discount equals the face value multiplied by the quoted rate times the days to maturity divided by 360. Thus, using the example from Reading 64, if a 180-day T-bill is selling at a discount of 4 percent, its price per $1 par is $1 - 0.04(180/360) = 0.98$. An investor who buys the bill and holds it to maturity would receive $1 at maturity, netting a gain of $0.02.

The futures contract is based on a 90-day $1,000,000 U.S. Treasury bill. Thus, on any given day, the contract trades with the understanding that a 90-day T-bill will be delivered at expiration. While the contract is trading, its price is quoted as 100 minus the rate quoted as a percent priced into the contract by the futures market. This value, 100 − Rate, is known as the IMM Index; IMM stands for **International Monetary Market**, a division of the Chicago Mercantile Exchange.

EXHIBIT 65-4 Most-Active Global Futures Contracts as Covered by the *Wall Street Journal*, 18 June 2002

Commodity Futures

Corn (CBOT)
Oats (CBOT)
Soybeans (CBOT)
Soybean Meal (CBOT)
Soybean Oil (CBOT)
Wheat (CBOT, KCBT, MGE)
Canola (WPG)
Barley (WPG)
Feeder Cattle (CME)
Live Cattle (CME)
Lean Hogs (CME)
Pork Bellies (CME)
Milk (CME)
Lumber (CME)
Cocoa (NYBOT)
Coffee (NYBOT)
World Sugar (NYBOT)
Domestic Sugar (NYBOT)
Cotton (NYBOT)

Financial Futures

Treasury Bonds (CBOT)
Treasury Notes (CBOT)
10-Year Agency Notes (CBOT)
10-Year Interest Rate Swaps (CBOT)
2-Year Agency Notes (CBOT)
5-Year Treasury Notes (CBOT)
2-Year Treasury Notes (CBOT)
Federal Funds (CBOT)
Municipal Bond Index (CBOT)
Treasury Bills (CME)
1-Month LIBOR (CME)
Eurodollar (CME)
Euroyen (CME, SGX)
Short Sterling (LIFFE)
Long Gilt (LIFFE)
3-Month Euribor (LIFFE)
3-Month Euroswiss (LIFFE)
Canadian Bankers Acceptance (ME)
10-Year Canadian Government Bond (ME)

Euro (CME)
Euro–Sterling (NYBOT)
Euro–U.S. Dollar (NYBOT)
Euro–Yen (NYBOT)
Dow Jones Industrial Average (CBOT)
Mini Dow Jones Industrial Average (CBOT)
S&P 500 Index (CME)
Mini S&P 500 Index (CME)
S&P Midcap 400 Index (CME)
Nikkei 225 (CME)
Nasdaq 100 Index (CME)
Mini Nasdaq Index (CME)
Goldman Sachs Commodity Index (CME)
Russell 1000 Index (CME)
Russell 2000 Index (CME)
NYSE Composite Index (NYBOT)
U.S. Dollar Index (NYBOT)
Share Price Index (SFE)
CAC 40 Stock Index (MATIF)

(Exhibit continued on next page …)

EXHIBIT 65-4   Most-Active Global Futures Contracts as Covered by the *Wall Street Journal*, 18 June 2002 (continued)

Commodity Futures	Financial Futures
Orange Juice (NYBOT)	10-Year Euro Notional Bond (MATIF)
Copper (NYMEX)	3-Month Euribor (MATIF)
Gold (NYMEX)	3-Year Commonwealth T-Bonds (SFE)
Platinum (NYMEX)	5-Year German Euro Government Bond (EUREX)
Palladium (NYMEX)	10-Year German Euro Government Bond (EUREX)
Silver (NYMEX)	2-Year German Euro Government Bond (EUREX)
Crude Oil (NYMEX)	Japanese Yen (CME)
No. 2 Heating Oil (NYMEX)	Canadian Dollar (CME)
Unleaded Gasoline (NYMEX)	British Pound (CME)
Natural Gas (NYMEX)	Swiss Franc (CME)
Brent Crude Oil (IPEX)	Australian Dollar (CME)
Gas Oil (IPEX)	Mexican Peso (CME)
	Xetra Dax (EUREX)
	FTSE 200 Index (LIFFE)
	Dow Jones Euro Stoxx 50 Index (EUREX)
	Dow Jones Stoxx 50 Index EUREX)

Exchange codes: CBOT (Chicago Board of Trade), CME (Chicago Mercantile Exchange), LIFFE (London International Financial Futures Exchange), WPG (Winnipeg Grain Exchange), EUREX (Eurex), NYBOT (New York Board of Trade), IPEX (International Petroleum Exchange), MATIF (Marché a Terme International de France), ME (Montreal Exchange), MGE (Minneapolis Grain Exchange), SFE (Sydney Futures Exchange), SGX (Singapore Exchange), KCBT (Kansas City Board of Trade), NYMEX (New York Mercantile Exchange).

Note: These are not the only global futures contracts but are those covered in the *Wall Street Journal* on the date given and represent the most active contracts at that time.

The IMM Index is a reported and publicly available price; however, it is not the actual futures price, which is

$$100 - (\text{Rate}/100)(90/360)$$

For example, suppose on a given day the rate priced into the contract is 6.25 percent. Then the quoted price will be $100 - 6.25 = 93.75$. The actual futures price would be

$$\$1{,}000{,}000[1 - 0.0625(90/360)] = \$984{,}375$$

Recall, however, that except for the small **margin deposit**, a futures transaction does not require any cash to be paid up front. As trading takes place, the rate fluctuates with market interest rates and the associated IMM Index price changes accordingly. The actual futures price, as calculated above, also fluctuates according to the above formula, but interestingly, that price is not very important. The same information can be captured more easily by referencing the IMM Index than by calculating the actual price.

Suppose, for example, that a trader had his account marked to market to the above price, 6.25 in terms of the rate, 93.75 in terms of the IMM Index, and $984,375 in terms of the actual futures price. Now suppose the rate goes to 6.50, an increase of 0.25 or 25 basis points. The IMM Index declines to 93.50, and the actual futures price drops to

$$\$1{,}000{,}000[1 - 0.065(90/360)] = \$983{,}750$$

Thus, the actual futures price decreased by $984,375 - \$983,750 = \$625$. A trader who is long would have a loss of $625; a trader who is short would have a gain of $625.

This $625 gain or loss can be arrived at more directly, however, by simply noting that each basis point move is equivalent to $25.[17] This special design of the contract makes it easy for floor traders to do the necessary arithmetic in their heads. For example, if floor traders observe the IMM Index move from 93.75 to 93.50, they immediately know that it has moved down 25 basis points and that 25 basis points times $25 per basis point is a loss of $625. The minimum tick size is one-half basis point or $12.50.

T-bill futures contracts have expirations of the current month, the next month, and the next four months of March, June, September, and December. Because of the small trading volume, however, only the closest expiration has much trading volume, and even that one is only lightly traded. T-bill futures expire specifically on the Monday of the week of the third Wednesday each month and settle in cash rather than physical delivery of the T-bill, as described in Section 4.

As important as Treasury bills are in U.S. financial markets, however, today this futures contract is barely active. The Eurodollar contract is considered much more important because it reflects the interest rate on a dollar borrowed by a high-quality private borrower. The rates on T-bills are considered too heavily influenced by U.S. government policies, budget deficits, government funding plans, politics, and Federal Reserve monetary policy. Although unquestionably Eurodollar rates are affected by those factors, market participants consider them much less directly influenced. But in spite of this relative inactivity, T-bill futures are useful instruments for illustrating certain principles of futures market

---

[17] Expressed mathematically, $\$1{,}000{,}000[0.0001(90/360)] = \$25$. In other words, any move in the last digit of the rate (a basis point) affects the actual futures price by $25.

pricing and trading. Accordingly, we shall use them on some occasions. For now, however, we turn to the Eurodollar futures contract.

6.1.2 Eurodollar Futures

Recall that in Reading 64, we devoted a good bit of effort to understanding Eurodollar forward contracts, known as FRAs. These contracts pay off based on LIBOR on a given day. The Eurodollar futures contract of the Chicago Mercantile Exchange is based on $1 million notional principal of 90-day Eurodollars. Specifically, the underlying is the rate on a 90-day dollar-denominated time deposit issued by a bank in London. As we described in Reading 64, this deposit is called a Eurodollar time deposit, and the rate is referred to as LIBOR (London Interbank Offer Rate). On a given day, the futures contract trades based on the understanding that at expiration, the official Eurodollar rate, as compiled by the British Bankers Association (BBA), will be the rate at which the final settlement of the contract is made. While the contract is trading, its price is quoted as 100 minus the rate priced into the contract by futures traders. Like its counterpart in the T-bill futures market, this value, 100 − Rate, is also known as the IMM Index.

As in the T-bill futures market, on a given day, if the rate priced into the contract is 5.25 percent, the quoted price will be $100 − 5.25 = 94.75$. With each contract based on $1 million notional principal of Eurodollars, the actual futures price is

$$\$1,000,000[1 - 0.0525(90/360)] = \$986,875$$

Like the T-bill contract, the actual futures price moves $25 for every basis point move in the rate or IMM Index price.

As with all futures contracts, the price fluctuates on a daily basis and margin accounts are marked to market according to the exchange's official settlement price. At expiration, the final settlement price is the official rate quoted on a 90-day Eurodollar time deposit by the BBA. That rate determines the final settlement. Eurodollar futures contracts do not permit actual delivery of a Eurodollar time deposit; rather, they settle in cash, as described in Section 4.

The Eurodollar futures contract is one of the most active in the world. Because its rate is based on LIBOR, it is widely used by dealers in swaps, FRAs, and interest rate options to hedge their positions taken in dollar-denominated over-the-counter interest rate derivatives. Such derivatives usually use LIBOR as the underlying rate.

It is important to note, however, that there is a critical distinction between the manner in which the interest calculation is built into the Eurodollar futures contract and the manner in which interest is imputed on actual Eurodollar time deposits. Recall from Reading 64 that when a bank borrows $1 million at a rate of 5 percent for 90 days, the amount it will owe in 90 days is

$$\$1,000,000[1 + 0.05(90/360)] = \$1,012,500$$

Interest on Eurodollar time deposits is computed on an add-on basis to the principal. As described in this section, however, it appears that in computing the futures price, interest is deducted from the principal so that a bank borrowing $1,000,000 at a rate of 5 percent would receive

$$\$1,000,000[1 - 0.05(90/360)] = \$987,500$$

and would pay back $1,000,000. This procedure is referred to as discount interest and is used in the T-bill market.

The discount interest computation associated with Eurodollar futures is merely a convenience contrived by the futures exchange to facilitate quoting prices in a manner already familiar to its traders, who were previously trading T-bill futures. This inconsistency between the ways in which Eurodollar futures and Eurodollar spot transactions are constructed causes some pricing problems, as we shall see in Section 7.2.2.

The minimum tick size for Eurodollar futures is 1 basis point or $25. The available expirations are the next two months plus March, June, September, and December. The expirations go out about 10 years, a reflection of their use by over-the-counter derivatives dealers to hedge their positions in long-term interest rate derivatives. Eurodollar futures expire on the second business day on which London banks are open before the third Wednesday of the month and terminate with a cash settlement.

6.2 Intermediate- and Long-Term Interest Rate Futures Contracts

In U.S. markets, the primary interest-rate-related instruments of **intermediate** and long maturities are U.S. Treasury notes and bonds. The U.S. government issues both instruments: Treasury notes have an original maturity of 2 to 10 years, and Treasury bonds have an original maturity of more than 10 years. Futures contracts on these instruments are very actively traded on the Chicago Board of Trade. For the most part, there are no real differences in the contract characteristics for Treasury note and Treasury bond futures; the underlying bonds differ slightly, but the futures contracts are qualitatively the same. We shall focus here on one of the most active instruments, the U.S. Treasury bond futures contract.

The contract is based on the delivery of a U.S. Treasury bond with any coupon but with a maturity of at least 15 years. If the deliverable bond is callable, it cannot be callable for at least 15 years from the delivery date.[18] These specifications mean that there are potentially a large number of deliverable bonds, which is exactly the way the Chicago Board of Trade, the Federal Reserve, and the U.S. Treasury want it. They do not want a potential run on a single issue that might distort prices. By having multiple deliverable issues, however, the contract must be structured with some fairly complicated procedures to adjust for the fact that the short can deliver whatever bond he chooses from among the eligible bonds. This choice gives the short a potentially valuable option and puts the long at a disadvantage. Moreover, it complicates pricing the contract, because the identity of the underlying bond is not clear. Although when referring to a futures contract on a 90-day Eurodollar time deposit we are relatively clear about the underlying instrument, a futures contract on a long-term Treasury bond does not allow us the same clarity.

To reduce the confusion, the exchange declares a standard or hypothetical version of the deliverable bond. This hypothetical deliverable bond has a 6 percent coupon. When a trader holding a short position at expiration delivers a bond with a coupon greater (less) than 6 percent, she receives an upward (a downward) adjustment to the price paid for the bond by the long. The adjustment is done by means of a device called the **conversion factor**. In brief, the conversion factor is the price of a $1.00 par bond with a coupon and maturity equal to those of the deliverable bond and a yield of 6 percent. Thus, if the short delivers a bond with a

---

[18] The U.S. government no longer issues callable bonds but has done so in the past.

coupon greater (less) than 6 percent, the conversion factor exceeds (is less than) 1.0.[19] The amount the long pays the short is the futures price at expiration multiplied by the conversion factor. Thus, delivery of a bond with coupon greater (less) than the standard amount, 6 percent, results in the short receiving an upward (a downward) adjustment to the amount received. A number of other technical considerations are also involved in determining the delivery price.[20]

The conversion factor system is designed to put all bonds on equal footing. Ideally, application of the conversion factor would result in the short finding no preference for delivery of any one bond over any other. That is not the case, however, because the complex relationships between bond prices cannot be reduced to a simple linear adjustment, such as the conversion factor method. As a result, some bonds are cheaper to deliver than others. When making the delivery decision, the short compares the cost of buying a given bond on the open market with the amount she would receive upon delivery of that bond. The former will always exceed the latter; otherwise, a clear arbitrage opportunity would be available. The most attractive bond for delivery would be the one in which the amount received for delivering the bond is largest relative to the amount paid on the open market for the bond. The bond that minimizes this loss is referred to as the **cheapest-to-deliver** bond.

At any time during the life of a Treasury bond futures contract, traders can identify the cheapest-to-deliver bond. Determining the amount received at delivery is straightforward; it equals the current futures price times the conversion factor for a given bond. To determine the amount the bond would cost at expiration, one calculates the forward price of the bond, positioned at the delivery date. Of course, this is just a forward computation; circumstances could change by the expiration date. But this forward calculation gives a picture of circumstances as they currently stand and identifies which bond is currently the cheapest to deliver. That bond is then considered the bond most likely to be delivered. Recall that one problem with this futures contract is that the identity of the underlying bond is unclear. Traders traditionally treat the cheapest to deliver as the bond that underlies the contract. As time passes and interest rates change, however, the cheapest-to-deliver bond can change. Thus, the bond underlying the futures contract can change, adding an element of uncertainty to the pricing and trading of this contract.

With this complexity associated with the U.S. Treasury bond futures contract, one might suspect that it is less actively traded. In fact, the opposite is true: Complexity creates extraordinary opportunities for gain for those who understand what is going on and can identify the cheapest bond to deliver.

The Chicago Board of Trade's U.S. Treasury bond futures contract covers $100,000 par value of U.S. Treasury bonds. The expiration months are March, June, September, and December. They expire on the seventh business day preceding the last business day of the month and call for actual delivery, through the Federal Reserve's wire system, of the Treasury bond. Prices are quoted in points and 32nds, meaning that you will see prices like 98 18/32, which equals 98.5625. For a contract covering $100,000 par value, for example, the price is $98,562.50. The minimum tick size is 1/32, which is $31.25.

In addition to the futures contract on the long-term government bond, there are also very similar futures contracts on intermediate-term government bonds. The Chicago Board of Trade's contracts on 2-, 5-, and 10-year Treasury notes are

---

[19] This statement is true regardless of the maturity of the deliverable bond. Any bond with a coupon in excess of its yield is worth more than its par value.

[20] For example, the actual procedure for delivery of U.S. Treasury bonds is a three-day process starting with the short notifying the exchange of intention to make delivery. Delivery actually occurs several days later. In addition, as is the custom in U.S. bond markets, the quoted price does not include the accrued interest. Accordingly, an adjustment must be made.

very actively traded and are almost identical to its long-term bond contract, except for the exact specification of the underlying instrument. Intermediate and long-term government bonds are important instruments in every country's financial markets. They give the best indication of the long-term default-free interest rate and are often viewed as a **benchmark bond** for various comparisons in financial markets.[21] Accordingly, futures contracts on such bonds play an important role in a country's financial markets and are almost always among the most actively traded contracts in futures markets around the world.

If the underlying instrument is not widely available and not actively traded, the viability of a futures contract on it becomes questionable. The reduction seen in U.S. government debt in the late 1990s has led to a reduction in the supply of intermediate and long-term government bonds, and some concern has arisen over this fact. In the United States, some efforts have been made to promote the long-term debt of Fannie Mae and Freddie Mac as substitute benchmark bonds.[22] It remains to be seen whether such efforts will be necessary and, if so, whether they will succeed.

6.3 Stock Index Futures Contracts

One of the most successful types of futures contracts of all time is the class of futures on stock indices. Probably the most successful has been the Chicago Mercantile Exchange's contract on the Standard and Poor's 500 Stock Index. Called the S&P 500 Stock Index futures, this contract premiered in 1982 and has benefited from the widespread acceptance of the S&P 500 Index as a stock market benchmark. The contract is quoted in terms of a price on the same order of magnitude as the S&P 500 itself. For example, if the S&P 500 Index is at 1183, a two-month futures contract might be quoted at a price of, say, 1187. We shall explain how to determine a stock index futures price in Section 7.3.

The contract implicitly contains a multiplier, which is (appropriately) multiplied by the quoted futures price to produce the actual futures price. The multiplier for the S&P 500 futures is $250. Thus, when you hear of a futures price of 1187, the actual price is 1187($250) = $296,750.

S&P 500 futures expirations are March, June, September, and December and go out about two years, although trading is active only in the nearest two to three expirations. With occasional exceptions, the contracts expire on the Thursday preceding the third Friday of the month. Given the impracticality of delivering a portfolio of the 500 stocks in the index combined according to their relative weights in the index, the contract is structured to provide for cash settlement at expiration.

The S&P 500 is not the only active stock index futures contract. In fact, the Chicago Mercantile Exchange has a smaller version of the S&P 500 contract,

[21] For example, the default risk of a corporate bond is often measured as the difference between the corporate bond yield and the yield on a Treasury bond or note of comparable maturity. Fixed rates on interest rate swaps are usually quoted as a spread over the rate on a Treasury bond or note of comparable maturity.

[22] Fannie Mae is the Federal National Mortgage Association, and Freddie Mac is the Federal Home Loan Mortgage Corporation. These institutions were formerly U.S. government agencies that issued debt to raise funds to buy and sell mortgages and mortgage-backed securities. These institutions are now publicly traded corporations but are considered to have extremely low default risk because of their critical importance in U.S. mortgage markets. It is believed that an implicit Federal government guarantee is associated with their debt. Nonetheless, it seems unlikely that the debt of these institutions could take over that of the U.S. government as a benchmark. The Chicago Board of Trade has offered futures contracts on the bonds of these organizations, but the contracts have not traded actively.

called the Mini S&P 500, which has a multiplier of $50 and trades only electronically. Other widely traded contracts in the United States are on the Dow Jones Industrials, the S&P **Midcap** 400, and the Nasdaq 100. Virtually every developed country has a stock index futures contract based on the leading equities of that country. Well-known stock index futures contracts around the world include the United Kingdom's FTSE 100 (pronounced "Footsic 100"), Japan's Nikkei 225, France's CAC 40, and Germany's DAX 30.

6.4 Currency Futures Contracts

In Reading 64, we described forward contracts on foreign currencies. There are also futures contracts on foreign currencies. Although the forward market for foreign currencies is much more widely used, the futures market is still quite active. In fact, currency futures were the first futures contracts not based on physical commodities. Thus, they are sometimes referred to as the first financial futures contracts, and their initial success paved the way for the later introduction of interest rate and stock index futures.

Compared with forward contracts on currencies, currency futures contracts are much smaller in size. In the United States, these contracts trade at the Chicago Mercantile Exchange with a small amount of trading at the New York Board of Trade. In addition there is some trading on exchanges outside the United States. The characteristics we describe below refer to the Chicago Mercantile Exchange's contract.

In the United States, the primary currencies on which trading occurs are the euro, Canadian dollar, Swiss franc, Japanese yen, British pound, Mexican peso, and Australian dollar. Each contract has a designated size and a quotation unit. For example, the euro contract covers €125,000 and is quoted in dollars per euro. A futures price such as $0.8555 is stated in dollars and converts to a contract price of

$$125,000(\$0.8555) = \$106,937.50$$

The Japanese yen futures price is structured somewhat differently. Because of the large number of yen per dollar, the contract covers ¥12,500,000 and is quoted without two zeroes that ordinarily precede the price. For example, a price might be stated as 0.8205, but this actually represents a price of 0.008205, which converts to a contract price of

$$12,500,000(0.008205) = \$102,562.50$$

Alternatively, a quoted price of 0.8205 can be viewed as $1/0.008205 = ¥121.88$ per dollar.

Currency futures contracts expire in the months of March, June, September, and December. The specific expiration is the second business day before the third Wednesday of the month. Currency futures contracts call for actual delivery, through book entry, of the underlying currency.

We have briefly examined the different types of futures contracts of interest to us. Of course there are a variety of similar instruments trading on futures exchanges around the world. Our purpose, however, is not to provide institutional details, which can be obtained at the web sites of the world's futures exchanges, but rather to enhance your understanding of the important principles necessary to function in the world of derivatives.

Until now we have made reference to prices of futures contracts. Accordingly, let us move forward and examine the pricing of futures contracts.

OPTIONAL SEGMENT
ENDS

PRICING AND VALUATION OF FUTURES CONTRACTS

7

In Reading 64, we devoted considerable effort to understanding the pricing and valuation of forward contracts. We first discussed the notion of what it means to *price* a forward contract in contrast to what it means to *value* a forward contract. Recall that pricing means to assign a fixed price or rate at which the underlying will be bought by the long and sold by the short at expiration. In assigning a forward price, we set the price such that the value of the contract is zero at the start. A zero-value contract means that the present value of the payments promised by each party to the other is the same, a result in keeping with the fact that neither party pays the other any money at the start. The value of the contract to the long is the present value of the payments promised by the short to the long minus the present value of the payments promised by the long to the short. Although the value is zero at the start, during the life of the contract, the value will fluctuate as market conditions change; the original forward contract price, however, stays the same.

In Reading 64, we presented numerous examples of how to apply the concept of pricing and valuation when dealing with forward contracts on stocks, bonds, currencies, and interest rates. To illustrate the concepts of pricing and valuation, we started with a generic forward contract. Accordingly, we do so here in the futures reading. We assume no transaction costs.

7.1 Generic Pricing and Valuation of a Futures Contract

As we did with forward contracts, we start by illustrating the time frame within which we are working:

Today is time 0. The expiration date of the futures contract is time T. Times $t - 1$ and t are arbitrary times between today and the expiration and are the points at which the contract will be marked to market. Thus, we can think of the three periods depicted above, 0 to $t - 1$, $t - 1$ to t, and t to T, as three distinct trading days with times $t - 1$, t, and T being the end of each of the three days.

The price of the underlying asset in the spot market is denoted as S_0 at time 0, S_{t-1} at time $t - 1$, S_t at time t, and S_T at time T. We denote the futures contract price at time 0 as $f_0(T)$. This notation indicates that $f_0(T)$ is the price of a futures contract at time 0 that expires at time T. Unlike forward contract prices, however, futures prices fluctuate in an open and competitive market. The marking-to-market process results in each futures contract being terminated every day and reinitiated. Thus, we not only have a futures price set at time 0 but we also have a new one at time $t - 1$, at time t, and at time T. In other words,

$f_0(T)$ = price of a futures contract at time 0 that expires at time T

$f_{t-1}(T)$ = price of a futures contract at time $t - 1$ that expires at time T

$f_t(T)$ = price of a futures contract at time t that expires at time T

$f_T(T)$ = price of a futures contract at time T that expires at time T

Note, however, that $f_{t-1}(T)$ and $f_t(T)$ are also the prices of contracts newly established at times $t - 1$ and t for delivery at time T. Futures contracts are homogeneous and fungible. Any contract for delivery of the underlying at T is equivalent to any other contract, regardless of when the contracts were created.[23]

The value of the futures contract is denoted as $v_0(T)$. This notation indicates that $v_0(T)$ is the value at time 0 of a futures contract expiring at time T. We are also interested in the values of the contract prior to expiration, such as at time t, denoted as $v_t(T)$, as well as the value of the contract at expiration, denoted as $v_T(T)$.[24]

7.1.1 The Futures Price at Expiration

Now suppose we are at time T. The spot price is S_T and the futures price is $f_T(T)$. To avoid an arbitrage opportunity, *the futures price must converge to the spot price at expiration:*

$$f_T(T) = S_T \qquad\qquad \text{(65-1)}$$

Consider what would happen if this were not the case. If $f_T(T) < S_T$, a trader could buy the futures contract, let it immediately expire, pay $f_T(T)$ to take delivery of the underlying, and receive an asset worth S_T. The trader would have paid $f_T(T)$ and received an asset worth S_T, which is greater, at no risk. If $f_T(T) > S_T$, the trader would go short the futures, buy the asset for S_T, make delivery, and receive $f_T(T)$ for the asset, for which he paid a lesser amount. Only if $f_T(T) = S_T$ does this arbitrage opportunity go away. Thus, the futures price must equal the spot price at expiration.

Another way to understand this point is to recall that by definition, a futures contract calls for the delivery of an asset at expiration at a price determined when the transaction is initiated. If expiration is right now, a futures transaction is equivalent to a spot transaction, so the futures price must equal the spot price.

7.1.2 Valuation of a Futures

Let us consider how to determine the value of a futures contract. We already agreed that because no money changes hands, the value of a forward contract at the initiation date is zero. For the same reason, *the value of a futures contract at the initiation date is zero.* Thus,

$$v_0(T) = 0 \qquad\qquad \text{(65-2)}$$

Now let us determine the value of the contract during its life. Suppose we are at the end of the second day, at time t. In our diagram above, this point would be

---

[23] As an analogy from the bond markets, consider a 9 percent coupon bond, originally issued with 10 years remaining. Three years later, that bond is a 9 percent seven-year bond. Consider a newly issued 9 percent coupon bond with seven years maturity and the same issuer. As long as the coupon dates are the same and all other terms are the same, these two bonds are fungible and are perfect substitutes for each other.

[24] It is important at this point to make some comments about notation. First, note that in Reading 64 we use an uppercase F and V for forward contracts; here we use lowercase f and v for futures contracts. Also we follow the pattern of using subscripts to indicate a price or value at a particular point in time. The arguments in parentheses refer to characteristics of a contract. Thus, in Reading 64 we described the price of a forward contract as $F(0,T)$ meaning the price of a forward contract initiated at time 0 and expiring at time T. This price does not fluctuate during the life of the contract. A futures contract, however, reprices on a daily basis. Its original time of initiation does not matter—it is reinitiated every day. Hence, futures prices are indicated by notation such as $f_0(T)$ and $f_t(T)$. We follow a similar pattern for value, using $V_0(0,T)$, $V_t(0,T)$, and $V_T(0,T)$ for forwards and $v_0(T)$, $v_t(T)$, and $v_T(T)$ for futures.

essentially at time t, but perhaps just an instant before it. So let us call it time $t-$. An instant later, we call the time point $t+$. In both cases, the futures price is $f_t(T)$. The contract was previously marked to market at the end of day $t-1$ to a price of $f_{t-1}(T)$. An instant later when the futures account is marked to market, the trader will receive a gain of $f_t(T) - f_{t-1}(T)$. We can reasonably ignore the present value difference of receiving this money an instant later. Let us now state more formally that the value of a futures contract is

$$v_{t-}(T) = f_t(T) - f_{t-1}(T) \text{ } an \text{ } instant \text{ } before \text{ } the \text{ } account \text{ } is \text{ } marked \text{ } to \text{ } market$$

$$v_{t+}(T) = 0 \text{ } as \text{ } soon \text{ } as \text{ } the \text{ } account \text{ } is \text{ } marked \text{ } to \text{ } market \hspace{2cm} \textbf{(65-3)}$$

Suppose, however, that the trader is at a time j during the second trading day, between $t-1$ and t. The accumulated gain or loss since the account was last marked to market is $f_j(T) - f_{t-1}(T)$. If the trader closes the position out, he would receive or be charged this amount at the end of the day. So the value at time j would be $f_j(T) - f_{t-1}(T)$ discounted back from the end of the day at time t until time j—that is, a fraction of a day. It is fairly routine to ignore this intraday interest. Thus, in general we say that *the value of a futures contract before it has been marked to market is the gain or loss accumulated since the account was last marked to market.*

So to recap, the value of a futures contract is the accumulated gain or loss since the last mark to market. The holder of a futures contract has a claim or liability on this amount. Once that claim is captured or the liability paid through the mark-to-market process, the contract is repriced to its current market price and the claim or liability goes back to a value of zero. Using these results, determining the value of a futures contract at expiration is easy. An instant before expiration, it is simply the accumulated profit since the last mark to market. At expiration, the value goes back to zero. With respect to the value of the futures, expiration is no different from any other day. Exhibit 65-5 summarizes the principles of valuation.

In Reading 64, we devoted considerable effort toward understanding how forward contracts are valued. When holding positions in forward contracts, we are forced to assign values to instruments that do not trade in an open market with widely disseminated prices. Thus, it is important that we understand how forward contracts are valued. When dealing with futures contracts, the process is considerably simplified. Because futures contracts are generally quite actively traded, there is a market with reliable prices that provides all of the information we need. For futures contracts, we see that the value is simply the observable price change since the last mark to market.

EXHIBIT 65-5	The Value of a Futures Contract Before and After Marking to Market

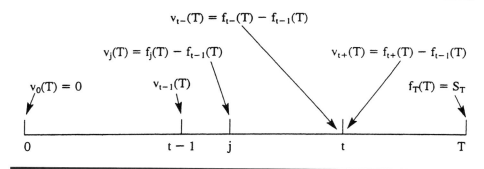

7.1.3 Forward and Futures Prices

For all financial instruments, it is important to be able to determine whether the price available in the market is an appropriate one. Hence, we engage in the process of "pricing" the financial instrument. A major objective of this reading is to determine the appropriate price of a futures contract. Given the similarity between futures and forward prices, however, we can benefit from studying forward contract pricing, which was covered in Reading 64. But first, we must look at the similarities and differences between forward and futures contracts.

Recall that futures contracts settle daily and are essentially free of default risk. Forward contracts settle only at expiration and are subject to default risk. Yet both types of contracts allow the party to purchase or sell the underlying asset at a price agreed on in advance. It seems intuitive that futures prices and forward prices would be relatively close to each other.

The issues involved in demonstrating the relationship between futures and forward prices are relatively technical and beyond the scope of this book. We can, however, take a brief and fairly nontechnical look at the question. First let us ignore the credit risk issue. We shall assume that the forward contract participants are prime credit risks. We focus only on the technical distinction caused by the daily marking to market.

The day before expiration, both the futures contract and the forward contract have one day to go. At expiration, they will both settle. These contracts are therefore the same. At any other time prior to expiration, futures and forward prices can be the same or different. If interest rates are constant or at least known, any effect of the addition or subtraction of funds from the marking-to-market process can be shown to be neutral. If interest rates are positively correlated with futures prices, traders with long positions will prefer futures over forwards, because they will generate gains when interest rates are going up, and traders can invest those gains for higher returns. Also, traders will incur losses when interest rates are going down and can borrow to cover those losses at lower rates. Because traders holding long positions prefer the marking to market of futures over forwards when futures prices are positively correlated with interest rates, futures will carry higher prices than forwards. Conversely, when futures prices are negatively correlated with interest rates, traders will prefer not to mark to market, so forward contracts will carry higher prices.

Because interest rates and fixed-income security prices move in opposite directions, interest rate futures are good examples of cases in which forward and futures prices should be inversely related. Alternatively, when inflation is high, interest rates are high and investors oftentimes put their money in such assets as gold. Thus, gold futures prices and interest rates would tend to be positively correlated. It would be difficult to identify a situation in which futures prices are not correlated with interest rates. Zero correlation is rare in the financial world, but we can say that when the correlation is low or close to zero, the difference between forward and futures prices would be very small.

At this introductory level of treatment, we shall make the simplifying assumption that futures prices and forward prices are the same. We do so by ignoring the effects of marking a futures contract to market. In practice, some significant issues arise related to the marking-to-market process, but they detract from our ability to understand the important concepts in pricing and trading futures and forwards.

Therefore, based on the equivalence we are assuming between futures and forwards, we can assume that the value of a futures contract at expiration, before marking to market, is

$$v_T(T) = f_T(T) - f_0(T) = S_T - f_0(T)$$

with the spot price substituted for the futures price at T, given what we know about their convergence.

7.1.4 Pricing Futures Contracts

Now let us proceed to the pricing of futures contracts. As we did with forward contracts, we consider the case of a generic underlying asset priced at $100. A futures contract calls for delivery of the underlying asset in one year at a price of $108. Let us see if $108 is the appropriate price for this futures contract.

Suppose we buy the asset for $100 and sell the futures contract. We hold the position until expiration. For right now, we assume no costs are involved in holding the asset. We do, however, lose interest on the $100 tied up in the asset for one year. We assume that this opportunity cost is at the risk-free interest rate of 5 percent.

Recall that no money changes hands at the start of a futures contract. Moreover, we can reasonably ignore the rather small margin deposit that would be required. In addition, margin deposits can generally be met by putting up interest-earning securities, so there is really no opportunity cost. As discussed in the previous section, we also will assume away the daily settlement procedure; in other words, the value of the futures contract paid out at expiration is the final futures price minus the original futures price. Because the final futures price converges to the spot price, the final payout is the spot price minus the original futures price.

So at the contract expiration, we are short the futures and must deliver the asset, which we own. We do so and receive the original futures price for it. So we receive $108 for an asset purchased a year ago at $100. At a 5 percent interest rate, we lose only $5 in interest, so our return in excess of the opportunity cost is 3 percent risk free. This risk-free return in excess of the risk-free rate is clearly attractive and would induce traders to buy the asset and sell the futures. This arbitrage activity would drive the futures price down until it reaches $105.

If the futures price falls below $105, say to $102, the opposite arbitrage would occur. The arbitrageur would buy the futures, but either we would need to be able to borrow the asset and sell it short, or investors who own the asset would have to be willing to sell it and buy the futures. They would receive the asset price of $100 and invest it at 5 percent interest. Then at expiration, those investors would get the asset back upon taking delivery, paying $102. This transaction would net a clear and risk-free profit of $3, consisting of interest of $5 minus a $2 loss from selling the asset at $100 and buying it back at $102. Again, through the buying of the futures and shorting of the asset, the forces of arbitrage would cause prices to realign to $105.

Some difficulties occur with selling short certain assets. Although the financial markets make short selling relatively easy, some commodities are not easy to sell short. In such a case, it is still possible for arbitrage to occur. If investors who already own the asset sell it and buy the futures, they can reap similar gains at no risk. Because our interest is in financial instruments, we shall ignore these commodity market issues and assume that short selling can be easily executed.[25]

If the market price is not equal to the price given by the model, it is important to note that regardless of the asset price at expiration, the above arbitrage guarantees a risk-free profit. That profit is known at the time the parties enter the transaction. Exhibit 65-6 summarizes and illustrates this point.

---

[25] Keep in mind that there are some restrictions on the short selling of financial instruments, such as uptick rules and margin requirements, but we will not concern ourselves with these impediments here.

EXHIBIT 65-6   The Risk-Free Nature of Long and Short Futures Arbitrage

Asset is priced at \$100, futures is priced at $f_0(T)$ and expires in one year. Interest rate over the life of the futures is 5 percent.

Time	Long Asset, Short Futures Arbitrage	Short Asset, Long Futures Arbitrage
Today (time 0)	Buy asset at \$100 Sell futures at $f_0(T)$	Sell short asset for \$100 Buy futures for $f_0(T)$
Expiration (time T)	Asset price is S_T Futures price converges to asset price Deliver asset Profit on asset after accounting for the 5 percent (\$5) interest lost from \$100 tied up in the investment in the asset: $S_T - 100 - 5$ Profit on futures: $f_0(T) - S_T$ Total profit: $f_0(T) - 100 - 5$	Asset price is S_T Futures price converges to asset price Take delivery of asset Profit on asset after accounting for the 5 percent (\$5) interest earned on the \$100 received from the short sale of the asset: $100 + 5 - S_T$ Profit on futures: $S_T - f_0(T)$ Total profit: $100 + 5 - f_0(T)$

Conclusion: The asset price at expiration has no effect on the profit captured at expiration for either transaction. The profit is known today. To eliminate arbitrage, the futures price today, $f_0(T)$, must equal $100 + 5 = \$105$.

The transactions we have described are identical to those using forward contracts. We did note with forward contracts, however, that one can enter into an off-market forward contract, having one party pay cash to another to settle any difference resulting from the contract not trading at its arbitrage-free value up front. In the futures market, this type of arrangement is not permitted; all contracts are entered into without any cash payments up front.

So in general, through the forces of arbitrage, we say that *the futures price is the spot price compounded at the risk-free rate*:

$$f_0(T) = S_0(1 + r)$$

It is important, however, to write this result in a form we are more likely to use. In the above form, we specify r as the interest rate over the life of the futures contract. In financial markets, however, interest rates are nearly always specified as annual rates. Therefore, to compound the asset price over the life of the futures, we let r equal an annual rate and specify the life of the futures as T years. Then the futures price is found as

$$f_0(T) = S_0(1 + r)^T \tag{65-4}$$

The futures price is the spot price compounded over the life of the contract, T years, at the annual risk-free rate, r. From this point on, we shall use this more general specification.

As an example, consider a futures contract that has a life of 182 days; the annual interest rate is 5 percent. Then T = 182/365 and r = 0.05. If the spot price is $100, the futures price would then be

$$f_0(T) = S_0(1 + r)^T$$
$$f_0(182/365) = 100(1.05)^{182/365}$$
$$= 102.46$$

If the futures is selling for more than $102.46, an arbitrageur can buy the asset for $100 and sell the futures for whatever its price is, hold the asset (losing interest on $100 at an annual rate of 5 percent) and deliver it to receive the futures price. The overall strategy will net a return in excess of 5 percent a year at no risk. If the futures is selling for less than $102.46, the arbitrageur can borrow the asset, sell it short, and buy the futures. She will earn interest on the funds obtained from the **short sale** and take delivery of the asset at the futures expiration, paying the original futures price. The overall transaction results in receiving $100 up front and paying back an amount less than the 5 percent risk-free rate, making the transaction like a loan that is paid back at less than the risk-free rate. If one could create such a loan, one could use it to raise funds and invest the funds at the risk-free rate to earn unlimited gains.

7.1.5 Pricing Futures Contracts When There Are Storage Costs

Except for opportunity costs, we have until now ignored any costs associated with holding the asset. In many asset markets, there are significant costs, other than the opportunity cost, to holding an asset. These costs are referred to as **storage costs** or **carrying costs** and are generally a function of the physical characteristics of the underlying asset. Some assets are easy to store; some are difficult. For example, assume the underlying is oil, which has significant storage costs but a very long storage life.[26] One would not expect to incur costs associated with a decrease in quality of the oil. Significant risks do exist, however, such as spillage, fire, or explosion. Some assets on which futures are based are at risk for damage. For example, cattle and pigs can become ill and die during storage. Grains are subject to pest damage and fire. All of these factors have the potential to produce significant storage costs, and protection such as insurance leads to higher storage costs for these assets. On the other hand, financial assets have virtually no storage costs. Of course, all assets have one significant storage cost, which is the opportunity cost of money tied up in the asset, but this effect is covered in the present value calculation.

It is reasonable to assume that the storage costs on an asset are a function of the quantity of the asset to be stored and the length of time in storage. Let us specify this cost with the variable FV(SC,0,T), which denotes the value at time T (expiration) of the storage costs (excluding opportunity costs) associated with holding the asset over the period 0 to T. By specifying these costs as of time T, we are accumulating the costs and compounding the interest thereon until the end of the storage period. We can reasonably assume that when storage is initiated, these costs are known.[27]

Revisiting the example we used previously, we would buy the asset at S_0, sell a futures contract at $f_0(T)$, store the asset and accumulate costs of FV(SC,0,T), and deliver the asset at expiration to receive the futures price. The total payoff is

---

[26] After all, oil has been stored by nature for millions of years.

[27] There may be reason to suggest that storage costs have an element of uncertainty in them, complicating the analysis.

$f_0(T) - FV(SC,0,T)$. This amount is risk free. To avoid an arbitrage opportunity, its present value should equal the initial outlay, S_0, required to establish the position. Thus,

$$[f_0(T) - FV(SC,0,T)]/(1 + r)^T = S_0$$

Solving for the futures price gives

$$f_0(T) = S_0(1 + r)^T + FV(SC,0,T)$$

(65-5)

This result says that *the futures price equals the spot price compounded over the life of the futures contract at the risk-free rate, plus the future value of the storage costs over the life of the contract.* In the previous example with no storage costs, we saw that the futures price was the spot price compounded at the risk-free rate. With storage costs, we must add the future value of the storage costs. The logic behind this adjustment should make sense. The futures price should be higher by enough to cover the storage costs when a trader buys the asset and sells a futures to create a risk-free position.[28]

Consider the following example. The spot price of the asset is \$50, the interest rate is 6.25 percent, the future value of the storage costs is \$1.35, and the futures expires in 15 months. Then $T = 15/12 = 1.25$. The futures price would, therefore, be

$$f_0(T) = S_0(1 + r)^T + FV(SC,0,T)$$
$$f_0(1.25) = 50(1.0625)^{1.25} + 1.35$$
$$= 55.29$$

If the futures is selling for more than \$55.29, the arbitrageur would buy the asset and sell the futures, holding the position until expiration, at which time he would deliver the asset and collect the futures price, earning a return that covers the 6.25 percent cost of the money and the storage costs of \$1.35. If the futures is selling for less than \$55.29, the arbitrageur would sell short the asset and buy the futures, reinvesting the proceeds from the short sale at 6.25 percent and saving the storage costs. The net effect would be to generate a cash inflow today plus the storage cost savings and a cash outflow at expiration that would replicate a loan with a rate less than the risk-free rate. Only if the futures sells for exactly \$55.29 do these arbitrage opportunities go away.

7.1.6 Pricing Futures Contracts When There Are Cash Flows on the Underlying Asset

In each case we have considered so far, the underlying asset did not generate any positive cash flows to the holder. For some assets, there will indeed be positive cash flows to the holder. Recall that in Reading 64, we examined the pricing and valuation of forward contracts on stocks and bonds and were forced to recognize that stocks pay dividends, bonds pay interest, and these cash flows affect the forward price. A similar concept applies here and does so in a symmetric manner to what we described in the previous section in which the asset incurs a cash cost.

---

[28] We did not cover assets that are storable at significant cost when we studied forward contracts because such contracts are less widely used for these assets. Nonetheless, the formula given here would apply for forward contracts as well, given our assumption of no credit risk on forward contracts.

As we saw in that section, a cash cost incurred from holding the asset increases the futures price. Thus, we might expect that cash generated from holding the asset would result in a lower futures price and, as we shall see in this section, that is indeed the case. But in the next section, we shall also see that it is even possible for an asset to generate nonmonetary benefits that must also be taken into account when pricing a futures contract on it.

Let us start by assuming that over the life of the futures contract, the asset generates positive cash flows of FV(CF,0,T). It is no coincidence that this notation is similar to the one we used in the previous section for the storage costs of the underlying asset over the life of the futures. Cash inflows and storage costs are just different sides of the same coin. We must remember, however, that FV(CF,0,T) represents a positive flow in this case. Now let us revisit our example.

We would buy the asset at S_0, sell a futures contract at $f_0(T)$, store the asset and generate positive cash flows of FV(CF,0,T), and deliver the asset at expiration, receiving the futures price. The total payoff is $f_0(T)$ + FV(CF,0,T). This amount is risk free and known at the start. To avoid an arbitrage opportunity, its present value should equal the initial outlay, S_0, required to establish the position. Thus,

$$[f_0(T) + FV(CF,0,T)]/(1 + r)^T = S_0$$

Solving for the futures price gives

$$f_0(T) = S_0(1 + r)^T - FV(CF,0,T) \qquad \textbf{(65-6)}$$

In the previous example that included storage costs, we saw that the futures price was the spot price compounded at the risk-free rate plus the future value of the storage costs. With positive cash flows, we must subtract the future value of these cash flows. The logic behind this adjustment should make sense. The futures price should be reduced by enough to account for the positive cash flows when a trader buys the asset and sells a futures to create a risk-free position. Otherwise, the trader would receive risk-free cash flows from the asset *and* the equivalent amount from the sale of the asset at the futures price. Reduction of the futures price by this amount avoids overcompensating the trader.

As noted, these cash flows can be in the form of dividends from a stock or coupon interest from a bond. When we specifically examine the pricing of bond and stock futures, we shall make this specification a little more precise and work an example.

7.1.7 *Pricing Futures Contracts When There Is a Convenience Yield*

Now consider the possibility that the asset might generate nonmonetary benefits that must also be taken into account. The notion of nonmonetary benefits that could affect futures prices might sound strange, but upon reflection, it makes perfect sense. For example, a house is a common and normally desirable investment made by individuals and families. The house generates no monetary benefits and incurs significant costs. As well as being a possible monetary investment if prices rise, the house generates some nonmonetary benefits in the form of serving as a place to live. These benefits are quite substantial; many people consider owning a residence preferable to renting, and people often sell their homes for monetary gains far less than any reasonable return on a risky asset. Clearly the notion of a nonmonetary benefit to owning an asset is one most people are familiar with.

In a futures contract on an asset with a nonmonetary gain, that gain must be taken into account. Suppose, for the purpose of understanding the effect of nonmonetary benefits on a futures contract, we create a hypothetical futures contract on a house. An individual purchases a house and sells a futures contract on it. We shall keep the arguments as simple as possible by ignoring the operating or carrying costs. What should be the futures price? If the futures is priced at the spot price plus the risk-free rate, as in the original case, the homeowner receives a guaranteed sale price, giving a return of the risk-free rate *and* the use of the home. This is clearly a good deal. Homeowners would be eager to sell futures contracts, leading to a decrease in the price of the futures. Thus, any nonmonetary benefits ought to be factored into the futures price and logically would lead to a lower futures price.

Of course, in the real world of standardized futures contracts, there are no futures contracts on houses. Nonetheless, there are futures contracts on assets that have nonmonetary benefits. Assets that are often in short supply, particularly those with seasonal and highly risky production processes, are commonly viewed as having such benefits. The nonmonetary benefits of these assets are referred to as the **convenience yield**. Formally, a convenience yield is the nonmonetary return offered by an asset when in short supply. When an asset is in short supply, its price tends to be high. Holders of the asset earn an implicit incremental return from having the asset on hand. This return enables them, as commercial enterprises, to avoid the cost and inconvenience of not having their primary product or resource input on hand. Because shortages are generally temporary, the spot price can be higher than the futures price, even when the asset incurs storage costs. If a trader buys the asset, sells a futures contract, and stores the asset, the return is risk free and will be sufficient to cover the storage costs and the opportunity cost of money, but it will be reduced by an amount reflecting the benefits of holding the asset during a period of shortage or any other nonmonetary benefits.

Now, let the notation $FV(CB,0,T)$ represent the future value of the costs of storage minus the benefits:

$$FV(CB,0,T) = \text{Costs of storage} - \text{Nonmonetary benefits (Convenience yield)}$$

where all terms are expressed in terms of their future value at time T and are considered to be known at time 0. If the costs exceed the benefits, $FV(CB,0,T)$ is a positive number.[29] We refer to $FV(CB,0,T)$ as the **cost of carry**.[30] The general futures pricing formula is

$$f_0(T) = S_0(1 + r)^T + FV(CB,0,T) \qquad \textbf{(65-7)}$$

The futures price is the spot price compounded at the risk-free rate plus the cost of carry. This model is often called the **cost-of-carry model**.

Consider an asset priced at \$75; the risk-free interest rate is 5.15 percent, the net of the storage costs, interest, and convenience yield is \$3.20, and the futures expires in nine months. Thus, $T = 9/12 = 0.75$. Then the futures price should be

$$f_0(T) = S_0(1 + r)^T + FV(CB,0,T)$$
$$f_0(0.75) = 75(1.0515)^{0.75} + 3.20$$
$$= 81.08$$

As we have always done, we assume that this price will prevail in the marketplace. If it does not, the forces of arbitrage will drive the market price to the

---

[29] In other words, $FV(CB,0,T)$ has to be positive to refer to it as a "cost."

[30] In some cases, such as in inventory storage, it is customary to include the opportunity cost in the definition of cost of carry; but we keep it separate in this text.

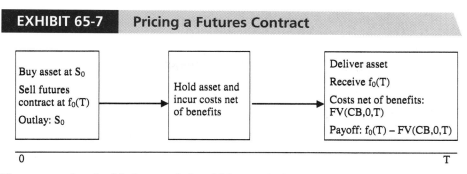

| EXHIBIT 65-7 | Pricing a Futures Contract |

The transaction is risk-free and should be equivalent to investing S_0 dollars in a risk-free asset that pays $f_0(T) - FV(CB,0,T)$ at time T. Therefore, the payoff at T must be the future value of the initial outlay invested at the risk-free rate. For this relationship to hold, the futures price must be given as

$$f_0(T) = S_0(1 + r)^T + FV(CB,0,T)$$

Example: An asset is selling for \$225. A futures contract expires in 150 days (T = 150/365 = 0.411). The risk-free rate is 7.5 percent, and the net cost of carry is \$5.75. The futures price will be

$$f_0(T) = f_0(0.411) = \$225(1.075)^{0.411} + \$5.75 = \$237.54$$

model price. If the futures price exceeds \$81.08, the arbitrageur can buy the asset and sell the futures to earn a risk-free return in excess of the risk-free rate. If the futures price is less than \$81.08, the arbitrageur can either sell the asset short or sell it if he already owns it, and then also buy the futures, creating a risk-free position equivalent to a loan that will cost less than the risk-free rate. The gains from both of these transactions will have accounted for any non-monetary benefits. This arbitrage activity will force the market price to converge to the model price.

The above equation is the most general form of the futures pricing formula we shall encounter. Exhibit 65-7 reviews and illustrates how we obtained this formula and provides another example.

Some variations of this general formula are occasionally seen. Sometimes the opportunity cost of interest is converted to dollars and imbedded in the cost of carry. Then we say that $f_0(T) = S_0 + FV(CB,0,T)$; the futures price is the spot price plus the cost of carry. This is a perfectly appropriate way to express the formula if the interest is imbedded in the cost of carry, but we shall not do so in this book.

Another variation of this formula is to specify the cost of carry in terms of a rate, such as y. Then we have $f_0(T) = S_0(1 + r)^T(1 + y)^T$. Again, this variation is certainly appropriate but is not the version we shall use.[31]

Note that when we get into the specifics of pricing certain types of futures contracts, we must fine-tune the formulas a little more. First, however, we explore some general characterizations of the relationship between futures and spot prices.

---

[31] Yet another variation of this formula is to use $(1 + r + y)^T$ as an approximation for $(1 + r)^T(1 + y)^T$. We do not, however, consider this expression an acceptable way to compute the futures price as it is an approximation of a formula that is simple enough to use without approximating.

Practice Problem 2

Consider an asset priced at $50. The risk-free interest rate is 8 percent, and a futures contract on the asset expires in 45 days. Answer the following, with questions A, B, C, and D independent of the others.

A. Find the appropriate futures price if the underlying asset has no storage costs, cash flows, or convenience yield.

B. Find the appropriate futures price if the future value of storage costs on the underlying asset at the futures expiration equals $2.25.

C. Find the appropriate futures price if the future value of positive cash flows on the underlying asset equals $0.75.

D. Find the appropriate futures price if the future value of the net overall cost of carry on the underlying asset equals $3.55.

E. Using Part D above, illustrate how an arbitrage transaction could be executed if the futures contract is trading at $60.

F. Using Part A above, determine the value of a long futures contract an instant before marking to market if the previous settlement price was $49.

▶ **Solution to A.** First determine that $T = 45/365 = 0.1233$. Then the futures price is

$$f_0(0.1233) = \$50(1.08)^{0.1233} = \$50.48$$

▶ **Solution to B.** Storage costs must be covered in the futures price, so we add them:

$$f_0(0.1233) = \$50(1.08)^{0.1233} + \$2.25 = \$52.73$$

▶ **Solution to C.** A positive cash flow, such as interest or dividends on the underlying, reduces the futures price:

$$f_0(0.1233) = \$50(1.08)^{0.1233} - \$0.75 = \$49.73$$

▶ **Solution to D.** The net overall cost of carry must be covered in the futures price, so we add it:

$$f_0(0.1233) = \$50(1.08)^{0.1233} + \$3.55 = \$54.03$$

▶ **Solution to E.** Follow these steps:
▶ Sell the futures at $60.
▶ Buy the asset at $50.
▶ Because the asset price compounded at the interest rate is $50.48, the interest forgone is $0.48. So the asset price is effectively $50.48 by the time of the futures expiration.
▶ Incur costs of $3.55.
▶ At expiration, deliver the asset and receive $60. The net investment in the asset is $50.48 + $3.55 = $54.03. If the asset is sold for $60, the net gain is $5.97.

▶ **Solution to F.** If the last settlement price was $49.00 and the price is now $50.48 (our answer in Part A), the value of a long futures contract equals the difference between these prices: $50.48 − $49.00 = $1.48.

7.1.8 Backwardation and Contango

Because the cost of carry, FV(CB,0,T), can be either positive or negative, the futures price can be greater or less than the spot price. Because the costs plus the interest tend to exceed the benefits, it is more common for the futures price to exceed the spot price, a situation called **contango**. In contrast, when the benefits exceed the costs plus the interest, the futures price will be less than the spot price, called **backwardation**. These terms are not particularly important in understanding the necessary concepts, but they are so commonly used that they are worthwhile to remember.

7.1.9 Futures Prices and Expected Spot Prices

An important concept when examining futures prices is the relationship between futures prices and expected spot prices. In order to fully understand the issue, let us first consider the relationship between spot prices and expected spot prices. Consider an asset with no risk, but which incurs carrying costs. At time 0, the holder of the asset purchases it with the certainty that she will cover her opportunity cost and carrying cost. Otherwise, she would not purchase the asset. Thus, the spot price at time 0 is the present value of the total of the spot price at time T less costs minus benefits:

$$S_0 = \frac{S_T - FV(CB,0,T)}{(1 + r)^T}$$

$$= \frac{S_T}{(1 + r)^T} - \frac{FV(CB,0,T)}{(1 + r)^T}$$

Because FV(CB,0,T) is the future value of the carrying cost, $FV(CB,0,T)/(1 + r)^T$ is the present value of the carrying cost. So on the one hand, we can say that the spot price is the future spot price minus the future value of the carrying cost, all discounted to the present. On the other hand, we can also say that the spot price is the discounted value of the future spot price minus the present value of the carrying cost.

If, however, the future price of the asset is uncertain, as it nearly always is, we must make some adjustments. For one, we do not know at time 0 what S_T will be. We must form an expectation, which we will denote as $E_0(S_T)$. But if we simply replace S_T above with $E_0(S_T)$ we would not be acting rationally. We would be paying a price today and expecting compensation only at the risk-free rate along with coverage of our carrying cost. Indeed, one of the most important and intuitive elements of all we know about finance is that risky assets require a risk premium. Let us denote this risk premium with the symbol, $\phi_0(S_T)$. It represents a discount off of the expected value that is imbedded in the current price, S_0. Specifically, the current price is now given as

$$S_0 = \frac{E_0(S_T) - FV(CB,0,T) - \phi_0(S_T)}{(1 + r)^T}$$

where we see that the risk premium lowers the current spot price. Intuitively, investors pay less for risky assets, all other things equal.

Until now, we have worked only with the spot price, but nothing we have said so far violates the rule of no arbitrage. Hence, our futures pricing formula, $f_0(T) = S_0(1 + r)^T + FV(CB,0,T)$, still applies. If we rearrange the futures pricing formula for FV(CB,0,T), substitute this result into the formula for S_0, and solve for the futures price, $f_0(T)$, we obtain $f_0(T) = E_0(S_T) - \phi_0(S_T)$. This equation says that the futures price equals the expected future spot price minus the risk premium.

An important conclusion to draw from this formula is that the futures price does not equal the expectation of the future spot price. The futures price would be biased on the low side. If one felt that the futures price were an unbiased predictor of the future spot price, $f_0(T) = E_0(S_T)$, one could expect on average to be able to predict the future spot price of oil by looking at the futures price of oil. But that is not likely to be the case.

The intuition behind this result is easy to see. We start with the assumption that all units of the asset must be held by someone. Holders of the asset incur the risk of its future selling price. If a holder of the asset wishes to transfer that risk by selling a futures contract, she must offer a futures contract for sale. But if the futures contract is offered at a price equal to the expected spot price, the buyer of the futures contract takes on the risk but expects to earn only a price equal to the price paid for the futures. Thus, the futures trader incurs the risk without an expected gain in the form of a risk premium. On the opposite side of the coin, the holder of the asset would have a risk-free position with an expected gain in excess of the risk-free rate. Clearly, the holder of the asset would not be able to do such a transaction. Thus, she must lower the price to a level sufficient to compensate the futures trader for the risk he is taking on. This process will lead to a futures price that equals the expected spot price minus the risk premium, as shown in the above equation. In effect, the risk premium transfers from the holder of the asset to the buyer of the futures contract.

In all fairness, however, we must acknowledge that this view is not without its opponents. Some consider the futures price an unbiased predictor of the future spot price. In such a case, the futures price would tend to overshoot and undershoot the future spot price but on average would be equal to it. For such a situation to exist would require the unreasonable assumption that there is no risk or that investors are risk neutral, meaning that they are indifferent to risk. There is, however, one other situation in which the risk premium could disappear or even turn negative. Suppose holders of the asset who want to hedge their holdings could find other parties who need to purchase the asset and who would like to hedge by going long. In that case, it should be possible for the two parties to consummate a futures transaction with the futures price equal to the expected spot price. In fact, if the parties going long exerted greater pressure than the parties going short, it might even be possible for the futures price to exceed the expected spot price.

When futures prices are lower than expected spot prices, the situation is called **normal backwardation**. When futures prices are higher than expected spot prices, it is called **normal contango**. Note the contrast with the terms backwardation and contango, which we encountered in Section 7.1.8. Backwardation means that the futures price is lower than the spot price; contango means that the futures price exceeds the spot price. Normal backwardation means that the futures price is lower than the expected spot price; normal contango means that the futures price exceeds the expected spot price.

Generally speaking, we should favor the notion that futures prices are biased predictors of future spot prices because of the transferal of the risk premium from holders of the asset to buyers of futures. Intuitively, this is the more likely case, but the other interpretations are possible. Fortunately, for our purposes, it is not critical to resolve the issue, but we do need to be aware of it.

7.2 Pricing Interest Rate Futures

We shall examine the pricing of three classes of interest rate futures contracts: Treasury bill futures, Eurodollar futures, and Treasury bond futures. In Section 6.1, we described the characteristics of these instruments and contracts. Now we look at their pricing, keeping in mind that we established the general foundations for pricing—the cost-of-carry model—in the previous section. Recall that in the cost-of-carry model, we buy the underlying asset, sell a futures contract, store the asset (which incurs costs and could generate benefits), and deliver the asset at expiration. To prevent arbitrage, the futures price is found in general as

Futures price = Spot price of underlying asset × Compounding factor
+ Costs net of monetary and nonmonetary benefits

When the underlying is a financial instrument, there will be no nonmonetary benefits and no costs other than the opportunity cost.

7.2.1 Pricing T-Bill Futures

Consider the following time line of our problem:

0	h	h + m
(today)	(expiration)	(maturity of underlying T-bill)

Time 0 is today, and time h is the expiration day of the futures contract. The T-bill underlying the contract is an m-day T-bill. Thus, when the futures expires, the T-bill is required to have m days to go before maturity. So from our perspective today, the underlying T-bill is an (h + m)-day T-bill.[32] As in Reading 64, for FRAs, h and m represent a particular number of days. In accordance with common practice, m is traditionally 90. We now introduce some necessary notation. First, where necessary, we use a simple expression, r, for the risk-free interest rate. But when pricing Treasury bill futures, we need a more flexible notation. Here we need the rates for T-bills maturing on day h and on day h + m. In addition, because interest rates can change from day 0 to day h, we need notation that distinguishes rates for different maturities and rates at different points in time.[33]

To find the spot price of the underlying asset, we need the discount rate on an (h + m)-day T-bill. Suppose we have

$$r_0^d(h), r_0^d(h + m) = \text{Discount rates in effect on day 0 of h-day}$$
$$\text{and } (h + m)\text{-day T-bills}$$

As described in Section 6, these are discount rates and convert to prices by the following formula: $B_0(j) = 1 - r_0^d(j)(j/360)$, where in this case j will either be h or h + m. Thus, the prices of h- and (h + m)-day spot T-bills on day 0 (assuming $1 face amounts) are

$$B_0(h) = 1 - r_0^d(h)\left(\frac{h}{360}\right)$$

$$B_0(h + m) = 1 - r_0^d(h + m)\left(\frac{h + m}{360}\right)$$

In other words, the h- or (h + m)-day discount rate is multiplied by the number of days in the life of the T-bill over 360 and subtracted from the face value of $1.

---

[32] It is common practice in the T-bill futures market to refer to the underlying as an m-day T-bill, but at time 0, the underlying must be an (h + m)-day T-bill in order for it to be an m-day T-bill at time h.

[33] When we assume that the interest rates are the same for all maturities and cannot change over time, which is considered acceptable when working with stock index and currency futures, we can use the simpler notation of r for the rate.

Now let us turn to the futures market. We define

$r_0^{df}(h)$ = implied discount rate on day 0 of futures contract expiring on day h, where the deliverable instrument is an m-day T-bill

$f_0(h)$ = price on day 0 of futures contract expiring on day h

The relationship between $r_0^{df}(h)$ and $f_0(h)$ is

$$f_0(h) = 1 - r_0^{df}(h)\left(\frac{m}{360}\right)$$

It is important to note that the futures price, not the implied discount rate, is the more important variable. Like any price, the futures price is determined in a market of buyers and sellers. Any rate is simply a way of transforming a price into a number that can be compared with rates on various other fixed-income instruments.[34] Do not think that a futures contract pays an interest rate. It is more appropriate to think of such a rate imbedded in a futures price as an *implied rate*, hence our use of the term *implied discount rate*. Although knowing this rate does not tell us any more than knowing the futures price, traders often refer to the futures contract in terms of the rate rather than the price.

Finally, let us note that at expiration, the futures price is the price of the underlying T-bill

$$f_h(h) = B_h(h + m)$$
$$= 1 - r_h^d(h + m)\left(\frac{m}{360}\right)$$

where $B_h(h + m)$ is the price on day h of the T-bill maturing on day h + m, and $r_h^d(h + m)$ is the discount rate on day h on the T-bill maturing on day h + m.

We now derive the futures price by constructing a risk-free portfolio that permits no arbitrage profits to be earned. This transaction is referred to as a cash-and-carry strategy, because the trader buys the asset in the cash (spot) market and carries (holds) it.

On day 0, we buy the (h + m)-day T-bill, investing $B_0(h + m)$. We simultaneously sell a futures contract at the price $f_0(h)$. On day h, we are required to deliver an m-day T-bill. The bill we purchased, which originally had h + m days to maturity, now has m days to maturity. We therefore deliver that bill and receive the original futures price. We can view this transaction as having paid $B_0(h + m)$ on day 0 and receiving $f_0(h)$. Because $f_0(h)$ is known on day 0, this transaction is risk free. It should thus earn the same return per dollar invested as would a T-bill purchased on day 0 that matures on day h. The return per dollar invested from the arbitrage transaction would be $f_0(h)/B_0(h + m)$, and the return per dollar invested in an h-day T-bill would be $1/B_0(h)$.[35] Consequently, we set these values equal:

---

[34] To further reinforce the notion that an interest rate is just a transformation of a price, consider a zero-coupon bond selling at $95 and using 360 days as a year. The price can be transformed into a rate in the manner of $1/0.95 - 1 = 0.0526$ or 5.26 percent. But using the convention of the Treasury bill market, the rate is expressed as a discount rate. Then $0.95 = 1 - $ Rate $\times (360/360)$, and the rate would be 0.05 or 5 percent. A price can be converted into a rate in a number of other ways, such as by assuming different compound periods. The price of any asset is determined in a market-clearing process. The rate is just a means of transforming the price so that interest rate instruments and their derivatives can be discussed in a more comparable manner.

[35] For example, if a one-year $1 face value T-bill is selling for $0.90, the return per dollar invested is $1/$0.90 = 1.1111$.

$$\frac{f_0(h)}{B_0(h + m)} = \frac{1}{B_0(h)}$$

Solving for the futures price, we obtain

$$f_0(h) = \frac{B_0(h + m)}{B_0(h)}$$

In other words, the futures price is the ratio of the longer-term bill price to the shorter-term bill price. This price is, in fact, the same as the forward price from the term structure. In fact, as we noted above, futures prices and forward prices will be equal under the assumptions we have made so far and will follow throughout this book.

Recall that we previously demonstrated that the futures price should equal the spot price plus the cost of carry. Yet the above formula looks nothing like this result. In fact, however, it is consistent with the cost-of-carry formula. First, the above formula can be written as

$$f_0(h) = B_0(h + m)\left[\frac{1}{B_0(h)}\right]$$

As noted above, the expression $1/B_0(h)$ can be identified as the return per dollar invested over h days, which simplifies to $[1 + r_0(h)]^{h/365}$, which is essentially a **compound interest** factor for h days at the rate $r_0(h)$. Note that h is the number of days, assuming 365 in a year. For the period ending at day h, the above formula becomes

$$f_0(h) = B_0(h + m)[1 + r_0(h)]^{h/365} \qquad \textbf{(65-8)}$$

and the futures price is seen to equal the spot price of the underlying compounded at the interest rate, which simply reflects the opportunity cost of the money tied up for h days.

Note that what we have been doing is deriving the appropriate price for a futures contract. In a market with no arbitrage opportunities, the actual futures price would be this theoretical price. Let us suppose for a moment, however, that the actual futures price is something else, say $f_0(h)^*$. The spot price is, of course, $B_0(h + m)$. Using these two numbers, we can infer the implied rate of return from a transaction involving the purchase of the T-bill and sale of the futures. We have

$$f_0(h)^* = B_0(h + m)[1 + r_0(h)^*]^{h/365}$$

where $r_0(h)^*$ is the implied rate of return. Solving for $r_0(h)^*$ we obtain

$$r_0(h)^* = \left[\frac{f_0(h)^*}{B_0(h + m)}\right]^{365/h} - 1 \qquad \textbf{(65-9)}$$

This rate of return, $r_0(h)^*$, has a special name, the **implied repo rate**. It is the rate of return from a cash-and-carry transaction that is implied by the futures price relative to the spot price. Traders who engage in such transactions often obtain the funds to do so in the repurchase agreement (repo) market. The implied repo rate tells the trader what rate of return to expect from the strategy. If the financing rate available in the repo market is less than the implied repo rate, the strategy is worthwhile and would generate an arbitrage profit. If the trader could lend in the repo market at greater than the implied repo rate, the appropriate strategy would be to reverse the transaction—selling the T-bill short and buying the futures—turning the strategy into a source of financing that would cost less than the rate at which the funds could be lent in the repo market.[36]

The implied repo rate is the rate of return implied by the strategy of buying the asset and selling the futures. As noted above, the futures price is often expressed in terms of an implied discount rate. Remember that the buyer of a futures contract is committing to buy a T-bill at the price $f_0(h)$. In the convention of pricing a T-bill by subtracting a discount rate from par value, the implied discount rate would be

$$r_0^{df}(h) = [1 - f_0(h)]\left(\frac{360}{m}\right)$$

(65-10)

We can also determine this implied discount rate from the discount rates on the h- and (h + m)-day T-bills as follows:[37]

$$r_0^{df}(h) = \left\{1 - \left[\frac{1 - r_0^d(h + m)\left(\dfrac{h + m}{360}\right)}{1 - r_0^d(h)\left(\dfrac{h}{360}\right)}\right]\right\}\left(\frac{360}{m}\right)$$

Now let us look at an example. We are interested in pricing a futures contract expiring in 30 days. A 30-day T-bill has a discount rate of 6 percent, and a 120-day T-bill has a discount rate of 6.6 percent. With h = 30 and h + m = 120, we have

$$r_0^d(h) = r_0^d(30) = 0.06$$
$$r_0^d(h + m) = r_0^d(120) = 0.066$$

The prices of these T-bills will, therefore, be

$$B_0(h) = 1 - r_0^d(h)\left(\frac{h}{360}\right)$$

$$B_0(30) = 1 - 0.06\left(\frac{30}{360}\right) = 0.9950$$

$$B_0(h + m) = 1 - r_0^d(h + m)\left(\frac{h + m}{360}\right)$$

$$B_0(120) = 1 - 0.066\left(\frac{120}{360}\right) = 0.9780$$

Using the formula we derived, we have the price of a futures expiring in 30 days as

$$f_0(h) = \frac{B_0(h + m)}{B_0(h)}$$

$$f_0(30) = \frac{B_0(120)}{B_0(30)} = \frac{0.9780}{0.9950} = 0.9829$$

---

[36] The concepts of a cash-and-carry strategy and the implied repo rate are applicable to any type of futures contract, but we cover them only with respect to T-bill futures.

[37] This formula is found by substituting $1 - r_0^d(h + m)[(h + m)/360]$ for $B_0(h + m)$ and $1 - r_0^d(h)(h/360)$ for $B_0(h)$ in the above equation for $r_0^{df}(h)$. This procedure expresses the spot prices in terms of their respective discount rates.

The discount rate implied by the futures price would be

$$r_0^{df}(h) = [1 - f_0(h)]\left(\frac{360}{m}\right)$$

$$r_0^{df}(30) = (1 - 0.9829)\left(\frac{360}{90}\right) = 0.0684$$

In other words, in the T-bill futures market, the rate would be stated as 6.84 percent, which would imply a futures price of 0.9829.[38] Alternatively, the implied futures discount rate could be obtained from the spot discount rates as

$$r_0^{df}(h) = \left\{ 1 - \left[\frac{1 - r_0^d(h + m)\left(\dfrac{h + m}{360}\right)}{1 - r_0^d(h)\left(\dfrac{h}{360}\right)} \right] \right\}\left(\frac{360}{m}\right)$$

$$r_0^{df}(30) = \left\{ 1 - \left[\frac{1 - 0.066\left(\dfrac{120}{360}\right)}{1 - 0.06\left(\dfrac{30}{360}\right)} \right] \right\}\left(\frac{360}{90}\right) = 0.0683$$

with a slight difference due to rounding.

To verify this result, one would buy the 120-day T-bill for 0.9780 and sell the futures at a price of 0.9829. Then, 30 days later, the T-bill would be a 90-day T-bill and would be delivered to settle the futures contract. The trader would receive the original futures price of 0.9829. The return per dollar invested would be

$$\frac{0.9829}{0.9780} = 1.0050$$

If, instead, the trader had purchased a 30-day T-bill at the price of 0.9950 and held it for 30 days, the return per dollar invested would be

$$\frac{1}{0.9950} = 1.0050$$

Thus, the purchase of the 120-day T-bill with its price in 30 days hedged by the sale of the futures contract is equivalent to purchasing a 30-day T-bill and holding it to maturity. Each transaction has the same return per dollar invested and is free of risk.

Suppose in the market, the futures price is 0.9850. The implied repo rate would be

$$r_0(h)* = \left[\frac{f_0(h)*}{B_0(h + m)} \right]^{365/h} - 1$$

$$= \left(\frac{0.9850}{0.9780}\right)^{365/30} - 1 = 0.0906$$

---

[38] We should also probably note that the IMM Index would be $100 - 6.84 = 93.16$. Thus, the futures price would be quoted in the market as 93.16.

Buying the 120-day T-bill for 0.9780 and selling a futures for 0.9850 generates a rate of return of $0.9850/0.9780 - 1 = 0.007157$. Annualizing this rate, $(1.007157)^{365/30} - 1 = 0.0906$. If financing could be obtained in the repo market for less than this annualized rate, the strategy would be attractive. If the trader could lend in the repo market at higher than this rate, he should buy the futures and sell short the T-bill to implicitly borrow at 9.06 percent and lend in the repo market at a higher rate.

Let us now recap the pricing of Treasury bill futures. We buy an (h + m)-day bond and sell a futures expiring on day h, which calls for delivery of an m-day T-bill. The futures price should be the price of the (h + m)-day T-bill compounded at the h-day risk-free rate. That rate is the rate of return on an h-day bill. The futures price can also be obtained as the ratio of the price of the (h + m)-day T-bill to the price of the h-day T-bill. Alternatively, we can express the futures price in terms of an implied discount rate, and we can derive the price in terms of the discount rates on the (h + m)-day T-bill and the h-day T-bill. Finally, remember that the actual futures price in the market relative to the price of the (h + m)-day T-bill implies a rate of return called the implied repo rate. The implied repo rate can be compared with the rate in the actual repo market to determine the attractiveness of an arbitrage transaction.

Exhibit 65-8 summarizes the important formulas involved in the pricing of T-bill futures. We then turn to the pricing of another short-term interest rate futures contract, the Eurodollar futures.

EXHIBIT 65-8   **Pricing Formulas for T-Bill Futures Contract**

Futures price = Underlying T-bill price compounded at risk-free rate

Futures price in terms of spot T-bills:

$$f_0(h) = \frac{B_0(h + m)}{B_0(h)}$$

Futures price as spot price compounded at risk-free rate:

$$f_0(h) = B_0(h + m)[1 + r_0(h)]^{h/365}$$

Discount rate implied by futures price:

$$r_0^{df}(h) = [1 - f_0(h)]\left(\frac{360}{m}\right) = \left\{1 - \left[\frac{1 - r_0^d(h + m)\left(\frac{h + m}{360}\right)}{1 - r_0^d(h)\left(\frac{h}{360}\right)}\right]\right\}\left(\frac{360}{m}\right)$$

Implied repo rate:

$$r_0(h)* = \left[\frac{f_0(h)*}{B_0(h + m)}\right]^{365/h} - 1$$

Practice Problem 3

A futures contract on a Treasury bill expires in 50 days. The T-bill matures in 140 days. The discount rates on T-bills are as follows:

50-day bill: 5.0 percent
140-day bill: 4.6 percent

A. Find the appropriate futures price by using the prices of the 50- and 140-day T-bills.

B. Find the futures price in terms of the underlying spot price compounded at the appropriate risk-free rate.

C. Convert the futures price to the implied discount rate on the futures.

D. Now assume that the futures contract is trading in the market at an implied discount rate 10 basis points lower than is appropriate, given the pricing model and the rule of no arbitrage. Demonstrate how an arbitrage transaction could be executed and show the outcome. Calculate the implied repo rate and discuss how it would be used to determine the profitability of the arbitrage.

▶ **Solution to A.** First, find the prices of the 50- and 140-day bonds:

$$B_0(50) = 1 - 0.05(50/360) = 0.9931$$
$$B_0(140) = 1 - 0.046(140/360) = 0.9821$$

The futures price is, therefore,

$$f_0(50) = \frac{0.9821}{0.9931} = 0.9889$$

▶ **Solution to B.** First, find the rate at which to compound the spot price of the 140-day T-bill. This rate is obtained from the 50-day T-bill:

$$[1 + r_0(h)]^{h/365} = \frac{1}{0.9931} = 1.0069$$

We actually do not need to solve for $r_0(h)$. The above says that based on the rate $r_0(h)$, every dollar invested should grow to a value of 1.0069. Thus, the futures price should be the spot price (the price of the 140-day T-bill) compounded by the factor 1.0069:

$$f_0(50) = 0.9821(1.0069) = 0.9889$$

Annualized, this rate would equal $(1.0069)^{365/50} - 1 = 0.0515$.

▶ **Solution to C.** Given the futures price of 0.9889, the implied discount rate is

$$r_0^{df}(50) = (1 - 0.9889)\left(\frac{360}{90}\right)$$
$$= 0.0444$$

> ▶ **Solution to D.** If the futures is trading for 10 basis points lower, it trades at a rate of 4.34 percent, so the futures price would be
>
> $$f_0(50) = 1 - 0.0434 \left(\frac{90}{360} \right)$$
> $$= 0.9892$$
>
> Do the following:
>
> ▶ Buy the 140-day bond at 0.9821
> ▶ Sell the futures at 0.9892
>
> This strategy provides a return per dollar invested of
>
> $$\frac{0.9892}{0.9821} = 1.0072$$
>
> which compares favorably with a return per dollar invested of 1.0069 if the futures is correctly priced.
>
> The implied repo rate is simply the annualization of this rate: $(1.0072)^{365/50} - 1 = 0.0538$. The cash-and-carry transaction would, therefore, earn 5.38 percent. Because the futures appears to be mispriced, we could likely obtain financing in the repo market at less than this rate.

OPTIONAL SEGMENT
ENDS

7.2.2 Pricing Eurodollar Futures

Based on the T-bill case, it is tempting to argue that the interest rate implied by the Eurodollar futures price would be the forward rate in the term structure of LIBOR. Unfortunately, that is not quite the case. In fact, the unusual construction of the Eurodollar futures contract relative to the Eurodollar spot market means that no risk-free combination of a Eurodollar time deposit and a Eurodollar futures contract can be constructed. Recall that the Eurodollar time deposit is an add-on instrument. Using $L_0(j)$ as the rate (LIBOR) on a j-day Eurodollar time deposit on day 0, if one deposits \$1, the deposit will grow to a value of $1 + L_0(j)(j/360)$ j days later. So, the present value of \$1 in j days is $1/[1 + L_0(j)(j/360)]$. The Eurodollar futures contract, however, is structured like the T-bill contract—as though the underlying were a discount instrument. So its price is stated in the form of $1 - L_0(j)(j/360)$. If we try the same arbitrage with Eurodollars that we did with T-bills, we cannot get the LIBOR that determines the spot price of a Eurodollar at expiration to offset the LIBOR that determines the futures price at expiration.

In other words, suppose that on day 0 we buy an (h + m)-day Eurodollar deposit that pays \$1 on day (h + m) and sell a futures at a price of $f_0(h)$. On day h, the futures expiration, the Eurodollar deposit has m days to go and is worth $1/[1 + L_h(m)(m/360)]$. The futures price at expiration is $f_h(h) = 1 - L_h(m)(m/360)$. The profit from the futures is $f_0(h) - [1 - L_h(m)(m/360)]$.

Adding this amount to the value of the m-day Eurodollar deposit we are holding gives a total position value of

$$\frac{1}{1 + L_h(m)\left(\dfrac{m}{360}\right)} + f_0(h) - [1 - L_h(m)]\left(\frac{m}{360}\right)$$

Although $f_0(h)$ is known when the transaction is initiated, $L_h(m)$ is not determined until the futures expiration. There is no way for the $L_h(m)$ terms to offset. This problem does not occur in the T-bill market because the spot price is a discount instrument and the futures contract is designed as a discount instrument.[39] It is, nonetheless, common for participants in the futures market to treat the Eurodollar rate as equivalent to the implied forward rate. Such an assumption would require the ability to conduct the risk-free arbitrage, which, as we have shown, is impossible. The differences are fairly small, but we shall not assume that the Eurodollar futures rate should equal the implied forward rate. In that case, it would take a more advanced model to solve the pricing problem. The essential points in pricing interest rate futures on short-term instruments can be understood by studying the T-bill futures market.

This mismatch in the design of spot and futures instruments in the Eurodollar market would appear to make the contract difficult to use as a hedging instrument. Note that in the above equation for the payoff of the portfolio combining a spot Eurodollar time deposit and a short Eurodollar futures contract, an increase (decrease) in LIBOR lowers (raises) the value of the spot Eurodollar deposit and raises (lowers) the payoff from the short Eurodollar futures. Thus, the Eurodollar futures contract can still serve as a hedging tool. The hedge will not be perfect but can still be quite effective. Indeed, the Eurodollar futures contract is a major hedging tool of dealers in over-the-counter derivatives.

We have now completed the treatment of futures contracts on short-term interest rate instruments. Now let us look at the pricing of Treasury bond futures.

7.2.3 Pricing Treasury Note and Bond Futures

Recall that in Section 6.2, we described the bond futures contract as one in which there are a number of deliverable bonds. When a given bond is delivered, the long pays the short the futures price times an adjustment term called the conversion factor. The conversion factor is the price of a $1 bond with coupon equal to that of the deliverable bond and yield equal to 6 percent, with calculations based on semiannual compounding. Bonds with a coupon greater (less) than 6 percent will have a conversion factor greater (less) than 1. Before we delve into the complexities added by this feature, however, let us start off by assuming a fairly generic type of contract: one in which the underlying is a single, specific bond.

---

[39] It is not clear why the Chicago Mercantile Exchange designed the Eurodollar contract as a discount instrument when the underlying Eurodollar deposit is an add-on instrument. The most likely reason is that the T-bill futures contract was already trading, was successful, and its design was well understood and accepted by traders. The CME most likely felt that this particular design was successful and should be continued with the Eurodollar contract. Ironically, the Eurodollar contract became exceptionally successful and the T-bill contract now has virtually no trading volume.

When examining bond forward contracts in Reading 64, we specified a time line and notation. We return to that specific time line and notation, which differs from those we used for examining short-term interest rate futures.

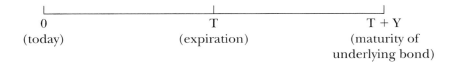

0	T	T + Y
(today)	(expiration)	(maturity of underlying bond)

Recall our notation from Reading 64:

$B_0^c(T + Y)$ = price at time 0 of coupon bond that matures at time T+Y. The bond has a maturity of Y at the futures expiration.

CI_i = coupon at time t_i, where the coupons occur at times t_1, t_2, . . ., t_n. Note that we care only about coupons prior to the futures expiration at T.

$f_0(T)$ = price at time 0 of futures expiring at time T.

$B_0(T)$ = price at time 0 of zero-coupon bond maturing at T.

We also need to know at time T the accumulated value of all coupons received over the period from 0 to T. We need the compound value from 0 to T of any coupons paid during the time the futures contract is alive. This value is denoted as FV(CI,0,T). We introduced this variable in Reading 64 and showed how to compute it, so you may wish to review that material. It is traditionally assumed that the interest rate at which these coupons are reinvested is known. We also assume that this interest rate applies to the period from 0 to T for money borrowed or lent. We denote this rate as

$r_0(T)$ = Interest rate at time 0 for period until time T

As described in the section on T-bill futures pricing, this is the rate that determines the price of a zero-coupon bond maturing at T.[40] Hence,

$$B_0(T) = \frac{1}{[1 + r_0(T)]^T}$$

The futures price at expiration is the price of the deliverable bond at expiration:

$$f_T(T) = B_T(T + Y)$$

Now we are ready to price this bond futures contract. On day 0, we buy the bond at the price $B_0^c(T + Y)$ and sell the futures at the price $f_0(T)$. Because the futures does not require any cash up front, its initial value is zero. The current value of the overall transaction is, therefore, just the value of the bond, $B_0^c(T + Y)$. This value represents the amount of money we must invest to engage in this transaction.

We hold this position until the futures expiration. During this time, we collect and reinvest the coupons. On day T, the futures expires. We deliver the bond and receive the futures price, $f_0(T)$. We also have the reinvested coupons, which have a value at T of FV(CI,0,T). These two amounts, $f_0(T)$ and FV(CI,0,T),

---

[40] Keep in mind, however, that this rate is not the discount rate that determines the price of the zero-coupon bond maturing at T. It is the rate of return, expressed as an annual rate. When working with T-bills, the symbol "T" represented Days/365, which is consistent with its use here with T-bonds.

are known when the transaction was initiated at time 0, so the transaction is risk-free. Therefore, the current value of the transaction, $B_0^c(T + Y)$, should be the discounted value of its value at T of $f_0(T) + FV(CI,0,T)$:

$$B_0^c(T + Y) = \frac{f_0(T) + FV(CI,0,T)}{[1 + r_0(T)]^T}$$

Note that we are simply discounting the known future value at T of the transaction at the risk-free rate of $r_0(T)$.[41]

We are, of course, more interested in the futures price, which is the only unknown in the above equation. Solving, we obtain

$$f_0(T) = B_0^c(T + Y)[1 + r_0(T)]^T - FV(CI,0,T) \qquad \textbf{(65-11)}$$

This equation is a variation of our basic cost-of-carry formula. The spot price, $B_0^c(T + Y)$, is compounded at the risk-free interest rate. We then subtract the compound future value of the reinvested coupons over the life of the contract. The coupon interest is like a negative cost of carry; it is a positive cash flow associated with holding the underlying bond.

Now let us work an example. Consider a $1 face value Treasury bond that pays interest at 7 percent semiannually. Thus, each coupon is $0.035. The bond has exactly five years remaining, so during that time it will pay 10 coupons, each six months apart. The yield on the bond is 8 percent. The price of the bond is found by calculating the present value of both the 10 coupons and the face value: The price is $0.9594.

Now consider a futures contract that expires in one year and three months: T = 1.25. The risk-free rate, $r_0(T)$, is 6.5 percent. The accumulated value of the coupons and the interest on them is

$$\$0.035(1.065)^{0.75} + \$0.035(1.065)^{0.25} = \$0.0722$$

The first coupon is paid in one-half a year and reinvests for three-quarters of a year. The second coupon is paid in one year and reinvests for one-quarter of a year.

Now the futures price is obtained as

$$f_0(T) = B_0^c(T + Y)[1 + r_0(T)]^T - FV(CI,0,T)$$
$$f_0(1.25) = \$0.9594(1.065)^{1.25} - \$0.0722 = \$0.9658$$

This is the price at which the futures should trade, given current market conditions. To verify this result, buy the five-year bond for $0.9594 and sell the futures for $0.9658. Hold the position for 15 months until the futures expiration. Collect and reinvest the coupons. When the futures expires, deliver the bond and receive the futures price of $0.9658. Then add the reinvested coupons of $0.0722 for a total of $0.9658 + $0.0722 = $1.0380. If we invest $0.9594 and end up with $1.0380 15 months later, the return is $1.0380/$0.9594 = 1.0819. For comparison purposes, we should determine the annual equivalent of this rate, which is found as $(1.0819)^{1/1.25} - 1 = 0.065$. This is the same 6.5 percent risk-free rate. If the futures contract trades at a higher price, the above transaction would result in a return greater than 6.5 percent. The amount available at expiration would

---

[41] We shall not take up the topic of the implied repo rate again, but note that if the futures is selling for $f_0(T)$, then $r_0(T)$ would be the implied repo rate.

be higher, clearly leading to a rate of return higher than 6.5 percent. If the futures trades at a lower price, the arbitrageur would sell short the bond and buy the futures, which would generate a cash inflow today. The amount paid back would be at less than the risk-free rate of 6.5 percent.[42]

Unfortunately, we now must complicate the matter a little by moving to the more realistic case with a delivery option. Bond futures contracts traditionally permit the short to choose which bond to deliver. This feature reduces the possibility of unusual price behavior of the deliverable bond caused by holders of short positions scrambling to buy a single deliverable bond at expiration. By allowing more than one bond to be deliverable, such problems are avoided. The contract is structured as though there is a standard hypothetical deliverable bond, which has a given coupon rate. The Chicago Board of Trade's contract uses a 6 percent rate. If the short delivers a bond with a higher (lower) coupon rate, the price received at delivery is adjusted upward (downward). The conversion factor is defined and calculated as the price of a $1 face value bond with a coupon and maturity equal to that of the deliverable bond and a yield of 6 percent. Each deliverable bond has its own conversion factor. The short designates which bond he will deliver, and that bond's conversion factor is multiplied by the final futures price to determine the amount the long will pay the short for the bond.

The availability of numerous deliverable bonds creates some confusion in pricing the futures contract, arising from the fact that the underlying cannot be uniquely identified, at least not on the surface. This confusion has given rise to the concept that one bond is always the best one to deliver. If a trader buys a given bond and sells the futures, he creates a risk-free hedge. If there are no arbitrage opportunities, the return from that hedge cannot exceed the risk-free rate. That return can, however, be *less* than the risk-free rate. How can this be? In all previous cases, if a return from a risk-free transaction is less than the risk-free rate, it should be a simple matter to reverse the transaction and capture an arbitrage profit. In this case, however, a reverse transaction would not work. If the arbitrageur sells short the bond and buys the futures, she must be assured that the short will deliver the bond from which the potential arbitrage profit was computed. But the short makes the delivery decision and in all likelihood would not deliver that particular bond.

Thus, the short can be long a bond and short futures and earn a return less than the risk-free rate. One bond, however, results in a return closest to the risk-free rate. Clearly that bond is the best bond to deliver. The terminology in the business is that this bond is the cheapest to deliver.

The cheapest-to-deliver bond is determined by selecting a given bond and computing the rate of return from buying that bond and selling the futures to hedge its delivery at expiration. This calculation is performed for all bonds. The one with the highest rate of return is the cheapest to deliver.[43] The cheapest-to-deliver bond can change, however, which can benefit the short and not the long. We ignore the details of determining the cheapest-to-deliver bond and assume that it has been identified. From here, we proceed to price the futures.

Let $CF(T)$ be the conversion factor for the bond we have identified as the cheapest to deliver. Now we go back to the arbitrage transaction described for the case where there is only one deliverable bond. Recall that we buy the bond, sell a futures, and reinvest the coupons on the bond. At expiration, we deliver the bond, receive the futures price $f_0(T)$, and have the reinvested coupons, which are worth $FV(CI,0,T)$. Now, in the case where the futures contract has

---

[42] Again, as in the section on T-bill futures, this analysis could be conducted in terms of the implied repo rate.

[43] As noted, this rate of return will not exceed the risk-free rate but will be the highest rate below the risk-free rate.

many deliverable bonds, we must recognize that when the bond is delivered, the long pays $f_0(T)$ times $CF(T)$. This adjustment does not add any risk to this risk-free transaction. Thus, the present value of the amount received at delivery, $f_0(T)CF(T) + FV(CI,0,T)$, should still equal the original price of the bond, which was the amount we invested to initiate the transaction:

$$B_0^c(T + Y) = \frac{f_0(T)CF(T) + FV(CI,0,T)}{[1 + r_0(T)]^T}$$

Solving for the futures price, we obtain

$$f_0(T) = \frac{B_0^c(T + Y)[1 + r_0(T)]^T - FV(CI,0,T)}{CF(T)}$$ **(65-12)**

Note that when we had only one deliverable bond, the formula did not have the $CF(T)$ term, but a better way to look at it is that for only one deliverable bond, the conversion factor is effectively 1, so Equation 65-12 would still apply.

Consider the same example we previously worked, but now we need a conversion factor. As noted above, the conversion factor is the price of a $1 bond with coupon and maturity equal to that of the deliverable bond on the expiration day and yield of 6 percent, with all calculations made assuming semiannual interest payments. As noted, we shall skip the specifics of this calculation here; it is simply a present value calculation. For this example, the 7 percent bond with maturity of three and three-quarter years on the delivery day would have a conversion factor of 1.0505. Thus, the futures price would be

$$f_0(T) = \frac{B_0^c(T + Y)[1 + r_0(T)]^T - FV(CI,0,T)}{CF(T)}$$

$$f_0(1.25) = \frac{0.9594(1.065)^{1.25} - 0.0722}{1.0505} = 0.9193$$

If the futures is priced higher than 0.9193, one can buy the bond and sell the futures to earn more than the risk-free rate. If the futures price is less than 0.9193, one can sell short the bond and buy the futures to end up borrowing at less than the risk-free rate. As noted previously, however, this transaction has a complication: If one goes short the bond and long the futures, this bond must remain the cheapest to deliver. Otherwise, the short will not deliver this particular bond and the arbitrage will not be successful.

Exhibit 65-9 reviews the important formulas for pricing Treasury bond futures contracts.

Practice Problem 4

Consider a three-year $1 par Treasury bond with a 7.5 percent annual yield and 8 percent semiannual coupon. Its price is $1.0132. A futures contract calling for delivery of this bond only expires in one year. The one-year risk-free rate is 7 percent.

A. Find the future value in one year of the coupons on this bond. Assume a reinvestment rate of 3.75 percent per six-month period.

B. Find the appropriate futures price.

C. Now suppose the bond is one of many deliverable bonds. The contract specification calls for the use of a conversion factor to determine the price paid for a given deliverable bond. Suppose the bond described here has a conversion factor of 1.0372. Now determine the appropriate futures price.

▶ **Solution to A.** One coupon of 0.04 will be invested for half a year at 3.75 percent (half of the rate of 7.5 percent). The other coupon is not reinvested but is still counted. Thus, $FV(CI,0,1) = 0.04(1.0375) + 0.04 = 0.0815$.

▶ **Solution to B.** $f_0(1) = 1.0132(1.07) - 0.0815 = 1.0026$

▶ **Solution to C.** $f_0(1) = \dfrac{1.0132(1.07) - 0.0815}{1.0372} = 0.9667$

EXHIBIT 65-9	**Pricing Formulas for Treasury Bond Futures Contract**

Futures price = Underlying T-bond price compounded at risk-free rate less Compound future value of reinvested coupons.

Futures price if underlying bond is the only deliverable bond:

$$f_0(T) = B_0^c(T + Y)[1 + r_0(T)]^T - FV(CI,0,T)$$

Futures price when there are multiple deliverable bonds:

$$f_0(T) = \frac{B_0^c(T + Y)[1 + r_0(T)]^T - FV(CI,0,T)}{CF(T)}$$

7.3 Pricing Stock Index Futures

Now let the underlying be either a portfolio of stocks or an individual stock.[44] The former are normally referred to as stock index futures, in which the portfolio is identical in composition to an underlying index of stocks. In this material, we focus on the pricing of stock index futures, but the principles are the same if the underlying is an individual stock.

In pricing stock index futures, we must account for the fact that the underlying stocks pay dividends.[45] Recall that in our previous discussions about the generic pricing of futures, we demonstrated that the futures price is lower as a result of the compound future value of any cash flows paid on the asset. Such cash flows consist of coupon interest payments if the underlying is a bond, or

---

[44] Futures on individual stocks have taken a long time to develop, primarily because of regulatory hurdles. They were introduced in the United States in late 2002 and, as of the publication date of this book, have achieved only modest trading volume. They currently trade in a few other countries such as the United Kingdom and Australia.

[45] Even if not all of the stocks pay dividends, at least some of the stocks almost surely pay dividends.

storage costs if the underlying incurs costs to store.[46] Dividends work exactly like coupon interest.

Consider the same time line we used before. Today is time 0, and the futures expires at time T. During the life of the futures, there are n dividends of $D_j, j = 1, 2, \ldots, n$. We assume these dividends are all known when the futures contract is initiated. Let

$FV(D,0,T)$ = the compound value over the period of 0 to T of all dividends collected and reinvested

We introduced this variable in Reading 64 and showed how to compute it, so you may wish to review that material. The other notation is the same we have previously used:

S_0 = current value of the stock index

$f_0(T)$ = futures price today of a contract that expires at T

r = risk-free interest rate over the period 0 to T

Now that we are no longer working with interest rate futures, we do not need the more flexible notation for interest rates on bonds of different maturities or interest rates at different time points. So we can use the simple notation of r as the risk-free interest rate, but we must keep in mind that it is the risk-free rate for the time period from 0 to T.

We undertake the following transaction: On day 0, we buy the stock portfolio that replicates the index. This transaction will require that we invest the amount S_0. We simultaneously sell the futures at the price $f_0(T)$.

On day T, the futures expires. We deliver the stock and receive the original futures price $f_0(T)$.[47] We also have the accumulated value of the reinvested dividends, $FV(D,0,T)$ for a total of $f_0(T) + FV(D,0,T)$. Because this amount is known at time 0, the transaction is risk free. Therefore, we should discount its value at the risk-free rate and set this equal to the initial value of the portfolio, S_0, as follows:

$$S_0 = \frac{f_0(T) + FV(D,0,T)}{(1 + r)^T}$$

Solving for the futures price gives

$$f_0(T) = S_0(1 + r)^T - FV(D,0,T) \qquad \textbf{(65-13)}$$

which is the cost-of-carry formula for stock index futures. Notice that it is virtually identical to that for bond futures. Ignoring the conversion factor necessitated by the delivery option, the only difference is that we use the compound future value of the dividends instead of the compound future value of the coupon interest.

Consider the following example. A stock index is at 1,452.45, and a futures contract on the index expires in three months. Thus, $T = 3/12 = 0.25$. The risk-free interest rate is 5.5 percent. The value of the dividends reinvested over the life of the futures is 7.26. The futures price should, therefore, be

$$f_0(T) = S_0(1 + r)^T - FV(D,0,T)$$
$$f_0(0.25) = 1,452.45(1.055)^{0.25} - 7.26$$
$$= 1,464.76$$

---

[46] We also allowed for the possibility of noncash costs, which we called the convenience yield, but there are no implicit costs or benefits associated with stock index futures.

[47] Virtually all stock index futures contracts call for cash settlement at expiration. See the explanation of the equivalence of delivery and cash settlement in Section 4 and Exhibit 65-2.

Thus, if the futures contract is selling for more than this price, an arbitrageur can buy the stocks and sell the futures. The arbitrageur would collect and reinvest the dividends and at expiration would receive a gain that would exceed the risk-free rate of 5.5 percent, a result of receiving more than 1,464.76 for the stocks. If the futures contract is selling for less than this price, the arbitrageur can sell short the stocks and buy the futures. After paying the dividends while holding the stocks,[48] the arbitrageur will end up buying back the stocks at a price that implies that he has borrowed money and paid it back at a rate less than the risk-free rate. The combined activities of all arbitrageurs will force the futures price to 1,464.76.

The stock index futures pricing formula has a number of variations. Suppose we define $FV(D,0,T)/(1 + r)^T$ as the present value of the dividends, $PV(D,0,T)$:

$$FV(D,0,T) = PV(D,0,T)(1 + r)^T$$

Substituting in the futures pricing formula above for $FV(D,0,T)$, we obtain

$$f_0(T) = [S_0 - PV(D,0,T)](1 + r)^T \qquad \textbf{(65-14)}$$

Notice here that the stock price is reduced by the present value of the dividends. This adjusted stock price is then compounded at the risk-free rate over the life of the futures.

In the problem we worked above, the present value of the dividends is found as

$$PV(D,0,T) = \frac{FV(D,0,T)}{(1 + r)^T}$$

$$PV(D,0,0.25) = \frac{7.26}{(1.055)^{0.25}} = 7.16$$

Then the futures price would be

$$f_0(T) = [S_0 - PV(D,0,T)](1 + r)^T$$
$$f_0(0.25) = (1{,}452.45 - 7.16)(1.055)^{0.25}$$
$$= 1{,}464.76$$

Another variation of the formula defines the yield as δ in the following manner:

$$\frac{1}{(1 + \delta)^T} = 1 - \frac{FV(D,0,T)}{S_0(1 + r)^T}$$

The exact solution for δ is somewhat complex, so we shall just leave it in the form above. Using this specification, we find that the futures pricing formula would be

$$f_0(T) = \left(\frac{S_0}{(1 + \delta)^T}\right)(1 + r)^T \qquad \textbf{(65-15)}$$

The stock price is, thus, discounted at the dividend yield, and this adjusted stock price is then compounded at the risk-free rate over the life of the futures.[49]

---

[48] Remember that a short seller must make restitution for any dividends paid while the position is short.

[49] Sometimes the futures price is written as $f_0(T) = S_0(1 + r - \delta)^T$ where the dividend yield is simply subtracted from the risk-free rate to give a net cost of carry. This formula is a rough approximation that we do not consider acceptable.

In the example above, the yield calculation is

$$\frac{1}{(1+\delta)^T} = 1 - \frac{FV(D,0,T)}{S_0(1+r)^T}$$

$$\frac{1}{(1+\delta)^T} = 1 - \frac{7.26}{1{,}452.45(1.055)^{0.25}} = 0.9951$$

Then $(1+\delta)^T$ is $1/0.9951 = 1.0049$ and the futures price is

$$f_0(T) = \left(\frac{S_0}{(1+\delta)^T}\right)(1+r)^T$$

$$f_0(0.25) = \left(\frac{1{,}452.45}{1.0049}\right)(1.055)^{0.25}$$

$$= 1{,}464.84$$

The difference between this and the answer we previously obtained is strictly caused by a rounding error.

Another variation of this formula is to express the yield as

$$\delta_* = \frac{PV(D,0,T)}{S_0} = \frac{FV(D,0,T)/(1+r)^T}{S_0}$$

This means that $FV(D,0,T) = S_0(1+r)^T\delta_*$. Substituting into our futures pricing formula for $FV(D,0,T)$, we obtain

$$f_0(T) = S_0(1 - \delta_*)(1+r)^T \qquad \textbf{(65-16)}$$

Here again, the stock price is reduced by the yield, and this "adjusted" stock price is compounded at the risk-free rate.

In the problem we worked above, the yield would be found as

$$\delta_* = \frac{PV(D,0,T)}{S_0}$$

$$\delta_* = \frac{7.16}{1{,}452.45} = 0.0049$$

Then the futures price would be

$$f_0(T) = S_0(1 - \delta_*)(1+r)^T$$

$$f_0(0.25) = 1{,}452.45(1 - 0.0049)(1.055)^{0.25}$$

$$= 1{,}464.81$$

Again, the difference between the two prices comes from rounding.

A common variation uses the assumption of continuous compounding. The continuously compounded risk-free rate is defined as $r^c = \ln(1+r)$. The continuously compounded dividend yield is $\delta^c = \ln(1+\delta)$. When working with discrete dividends, we obtained the relationship

$$\frac{1}{(1+\delta)^T} = 1 - \frac{FV(D,0,T)}{S_0(1+r)^T}$$

We calculated $(1 + \delta)^T$. To obtain δ^c, we take the natural log of this value and divide by T: $\delta^c = (1/T)\ln[(1 + \delta)^T]$. The formula for the futures price is

$$f_0(T) = S_0 e^{(r^c - \delta^c)T}$$

In the above formula, the opportunity cost, expressed as the interest rate, is reduced by the dividend yield. Thus, the formula compounds the spot price by the interest cost less the dividend benefits. An equivalent variation of the above formula is

$$f_0(T) = (S_0 e^{-\delta^c T}) e^{r^c T} \tag{65-17}$$

The expression in parentheses is the stock price discounted at the dividend yield rate. The result is an adjusted stock price with the present value of the dividends removed. This adjusted stock price is then compounded at the risk-free rate. So, as we have previously seen, the stock price less the present value of the dividends is compounded at the risk-free rate to obtain the futures price.

In the previous problem, $(1 + \delta)^T = 1.0049$. Then $\delta^c = (1/0.25)\ln(1.0049) = 0.0196$. The continuously compounded risk-free rate is $\ln(1.055) = 0.0535$. The futures price is, therefore, $f_0(0.25) = (1452.45 e^{-0.0196(0.25)}) e^{0.0535(0.25)} = 1464.81$; again the difference comes from rounding.

Exhibit 65-10 summarizes the formulas for pricing stock index futures contracts. Each of these formulas is consistent with the general formula for pricing futures. They are each based on the notion that a futures price is the spot price compounded at the risk-free rate, plus the compound future value of any other costs minus any cash flows and benefits. Alternatively, one can convert the

EXHIBIT 65-10   Pricing Formulas for Stock Index Futures Contract

Futures price = Stock index compounded at risk-free rate − Future value of dividends, or (Stock index − Present value of dividends) compounded at risk-free rate.

Futures price as stock index compounded at risk-free rate − Future value of dividends:

$$f_0(T) = S_0(1 + r)^T - FV(D,0,T)$$

Futures price as stock index − Present value of dividends compounded at risk-free rate:

$$f_0(T) = [S_0 - PV(D,0,T)](1 + r)^T$$

Futures price as stock index discounted at dividend yield, compounded at risk-free rate:

$$f_0(T) = \left(\frac{S_0}{(1 + \delta)^T}\right)(1 + r)^T \quad \text{or}$$

$$f_0(T) = S_0(1 - \delta^*)(1 + r)^T$$

Futures price in terms of continuously compounded rate and yield:

$$f_0(T) = S_0 e^{(r^c - \delta^c)T} \quad \text{or}$$

$$f_0(T) = (S_0 e^{-\delta^c T}) e^{r^c T}$$

compound future value of the costs net of benefits or cash flows of holding the asset to their current value and subtract this amount from the spot price before compounding the spot price at the interest rate. In this manner, the spot price adjusted for any costs or benefits is then compounded at the risk-free interest rate to give the futures price. These costs, benefits, and cash flows thus represent the linkage between spot and futures prices.

Practice Problem 5

A stock index is at 755.42. A futures contract on the index expires in 57 days. The risk-free interest rate is 6.25 percent. At expiration, the value of the dividends on the index is 3.94.

A. Find the appropriate futures price, using both the future value of the dividends and the present value of the dividends.

B. Find the appropriate futures price in terms of the two specifications of the dividend yield.

C. Using your answer in Part B, find the futures price under the assumption of continuous compounding of interest and dividends.

▶ **Solution to A.** $T = 57/365 = 0.1562$

$$f_0(0.1562) = 755.42(1.0625)^{0.1562} - 3.94 = 758.67$$

Alternatively, we can find the present value of the dividends:

$$PV(D,0,0.1562) = \frac{3.94}{(1.0625)^{0.1562}} = 3.90$$

Then we can find the futures price as $f_0(0.1562) = (755.42 - 3.90)(1.0625)^{0.1562} = 758.67$.

▶ **Solution to B.** Under one specification of the yield, we have

$$\frac{1}{(1+\delta)^T} = 1 - \frac{3.94}{755.42(1.0625)^{0.1562}} = 0.9948$$

We need the inverse of this amount, which is $1/0.9948 = 1.0052$. Then the futures price is

$$f_0(0.1562) = \left(\frac{755.42}{1.0052}\right)(1.0625)^{0.1562} = 758.66$$

Under the other specification of the dividend yield, we have

$$\delta^* = \frac{3.90}{755.42} = 0.0052$$

The futures price is $f_0(0.1562) = 755.42(1 - 0.0052)(1.0625)^{0.1562} = 758.64$, with the difference caused by rounding.

> ▶ **Solution to C.** The continuously compounded risk-free rate is $r^c = \ln(1.0625) = 0.0606$. The continuously compounded dividend yield is
>
> $$\frac{1}{0.1562}\ln(1.0052) = 0.0332$$
>
> The futures price would then be
>
> $$f_0(0.1562) = 755.42e^{(0.0606 - 0.0332)(0.1562)}$$
> $$= 758.66$$

7.4 Pricing Currency Futures

Given our assumptions about no marking to market, it will be a simple matter to learn how to price currency futures: We price them the same as currency forwards. Recall that in Reading 64 we described a currency as an asset paying a yield of r^f, which can be viewed as the foreign risk-free rate. Thus, in this sense, a currency futures can also be viewed like a stock index futures, whereby the dividend yield is analogous to the foreign interest rate.

Therefore, an arbitrageur can buy the currency for the spot exchange rate of S_0 and sell a futures expiring at T for $f_0(T)$, holding the position until expiration, collecting the foreign interest, and delivering the currency to receive the original futures price. An important twist, however, is that the arbitrageur must be careful to have the correct number of units of the currency on hand to deliver.

Consider a futures contract on one unit of the currency. If the arbitrageur purchases one unit of the currency up front, the accumulation of interest on the currency will result in having more than one unit at the futures expiration. To adjust for this problem, the arbitrageur should take $S_0/(1 + r^f)^T$ units of his own currency and buy $1/(1 + r^f)^T$ units of the foreign currency.[50] The arbitrageur holds this position and collects interest at the foreign rate. The accumulation of interest is accounted for by multiplying by the interest factor $(1 + r^f)^T$. At expiration, the number of units of the currency will have grown to $[1/(1 + r^f)^T][1 + r^f]^T = 1$. So, the arbitrageur would then have 1 unit of the currency. He delivers that unit and receives the futures price of $f_0(T)$.

To avoid an arbitrage opportunity, the present value of the payoff of $f_0(T)$ must equal the amount initially invested. To find the present value of the payoff, we must discount at the domestic risk-free rate, because that rate reflects the opportunity cost of the arbitrageur's investment of his own money. So, first we equate the present value of the future payoff, discounting at the domestic risk-free rate, to the amount initially invested:

$$\frac{f_0(T)}{(1 + r)^T} = \frac{S_0}{(1 + r^f)^T}$$

Then we solve for the futures price to obtain

$$f_0(T) = \left(\frac{S_0}{(1 + r^f)^T}\right)(1 + r)^T \tag{65-18}$$

---

[50] In other words, if S_0 buys 1 unit, then $S_0/(1 + r^f)^T$ buys $1/(1 + r^f)^T$ units.

This formula is the same one we used for currency forwards.

An alternative variation of this formula would apply when we use continuously compounded interest rates. The adjustment is very slight. In the formula above, dividing S_0 by $(1 + r^f)^T$ finds a present value by discounting at the foreign interest rate. Multiplying by $(1 + r)^T$ is finding a future value by compounding at the domestic interest rate. The continuously compounded analogs to those rates are $r^{fc} = \ln(1 + r^f)$ and $r^c = \ln(1 + r)$. Then the formula becomes

$$f_0(T) = (S_0 e^{-r^{fc}T}) e^{r^c T} \qquad \text{(65-19)}$$

We also saw this formula in Reading 64.

Consider a futures contract expiring in 55 days on the euro. Therefore, $T = 55/365 = 0.1507$. The spot exchange rate is \$0.8590. The foreign interest rate is 5.25 percent, and the domestic risk-free rate is 6.35 percent. The futures price should, therefore, be

$$f_0(T) = \left(\frac{S_0}{(1 + r^f)^T} \right) (1 + r)^T$$

$$f_0(0.1507) = \left(\frac{0.8590}{(1.0525)^{0.1507}} \right) (1.0635)^{0.1507} = 0.8603$$

If the futures is selling for more than this amount, the arbitrageur can buy the currency and sell the futures. He collects the foreign interest and converts the currency back at a higher rate than 0.8603, resulting in a risk-free return that exceeds the domestic risk-free rate. If the futures is selling for less than this amount, the arbitrageur can borrow the currency and buy the futures. The end result will be to receive money at the start and pay back money at a rate less than the domestic risk-free rate.

If the above problem were structured in terms of continuously compounded rates, the domestic rate would be $\ln(1.0635) = 0.0616$ and the foreign rate would be $\ln(1.0525) = 0.0512$. The futures price would then be

$$f_0(T) = (S_0 e^{-r^{fc}T}) e^{r^c T}$$

$$f_0(0.1507) = (0.85890 e^{-0.0512(0.1507)}) e^{0.0616(0.1507)} = 0.8603$$

which, of course, is the same price we calculated above.

Exhibit 65-11 summarizes the formulas for pricing currency futures.

EXHIBIT 65-11   **Pricing Formulas for Currency Futures Contract**

Futures price = (Spot exchange rate discounted by Foreign interest rate) compounded at Domestic interest rate:

Discrete interest: $f_0(T) = \left(\dfrac{S_0}{(1 + r^f)^T} \right) (1 + r)^T$

Continuous interest: $f_0(T) = (S_0 e^{-r^{fc}T}) e^{r^c T}$

Practice Problem 6

The spot exchange rate for the Swiss franc is $0.60. The U.S. interest rate is 6 percent, and the Swiss interest rate is 5 percent. A futures contract expires in 78 days.

A. Find the appropriate futures price.
B. Find the appropriate futures price under the assumption of continuous compounding.
C. Using Part A, execute an arbitrage resulting from a futures price of $0.62.

$T = 78/365 = 0.2137$

▶ **Solution to A.**

$$f_0(0.2137) = \frac{\$0.60}{(1.05)^{0.2137}}(1.06)^{0.2137} = \$0.6012$$

▶ **Solution to B.** The continuously compounded equivalent rates are

$$r^{fc} = \ln(1.05) = 0.0488$$
$$r^c = \ln(1.06) = 0.0583$$

The futures price is

$$f_0(0.2137) = (\$0.60e^{-0.0488(0.2137)})e^{0.0583(0.2137)}$$
$$= \$0.6012$$

▶ **Solution to C.** At $0.62, the futures price is too high, so we will need to sell the futures. First, however, we must determine how many units of the currency to buy. It should be

$$\frac{1}{(1.05)^{0.2137}} = 0.9896$$

So we buy this many units, which costs 0.9896($0.60) = $0.5938. We sell the futures at $0.62. We hold the position until expiration. During that time the accumulation of interest will make the 0.9896 units of the currency grow to 1.0000 unit. We convert the Swiss franc to dollars at the futures rate of $0.62. The return per dollar invested is

$$\frac{0.62}{0.5938} = 1.0441$$

This is a return of 1.0441 per dollar invested over 78 days. At the risk-free rate of 6 percent, the return over 78 days should be $(1.06)^{0.2137} = 1.0125$. Obviously, the arbitrage transaction is much better.

7.5 Futures Pricing: A Recap

We have now examined the pricing of short-term interest rate futures, intermediate- and long-term interest rate futures, stock index futures, and currency futures. Let us recall the intuition behind pricing a futures contract and see the commonality in each of those special cases. First recall that under the assumption of no marking to market, at expiration the short makes delivery and we assume that the long pays the full futures price at that point. An arbitrageur buys the asset and sells a futures contract, holds the asset for the life of the futures, and delivers it at expiration of the futures, at which time he is paid the futures price. In addition, while holding the asset, the arbitrageur accumulates costs and accrues cash flows, such as interest, dividends, and benefits such as a convenience yield. The value of the position at expiration will be the futures price net of these costs minus benefits and cash flows. The overall value of this transaction at expiration is known when the transaction is initiated; thus, the value at expiration is risk-free. The return from a risk-free transaction should equal the risk-free rate, which is the rate on a zero-coupon bond whose maturity is the futures expiration day. If the return is indeed this risk-free rate, then the futures price must equal the spot price compounded at the risk-free rate plus the compound value of these costs net of benefits and cash flows.

It should also be noted that although we have taken the more natural approach of buying the asset and selling the futures, we could just as easily have sold short the asset and bought the futures. Because short selling is usually a little harder to do as well as to understand, the approach we take is preferable from a pedagogical point of view. It is important, nonetheless, to remember that the ability to sell short the asset or the willingness of parties who own the asset to sell it to offset the buying of the futures is critical to establishing the results we have shown here. Otherwise, the futures pricing formulas would be inequalities—limited on one side but not restricted on the other.

We should remind ourselves that this general form of the futures pricing model also applied in Reading 64 in our discussion of forward contracts. Futures contracts differ from forward contracts in that the latter are subject to credit risk. Futures contracts are marked to market on a daily basis and guaranteed against losses from default by the futures clearinghouse, which has never defaulted. Although there are certain institutional features that distinguish futures from forwards, we consider those features separately from the material on pricing. Because the general economic and financial concepts are the same, for pricing purposes, we treat futures and forwards as the same.

THE ROLE OF FUTURES MARKETS AND EXCHANGES   8

We conclude this reading with a brief look at the role that futures markets and exchanges play in global financial systems and in society. Virtually all participants in the financial markets have heard of futures markets, but many do not understand the role that futures markets play. Some participants do not understand how futures markets function in global financial systems and often look at futures with suspicion, if not disdain.

Derivative markets provide price discovery and risk management, make the markets for the underlying assets more efficient, and permit trading at low transaction costs. These characteristics are also associated with futures markets. In fact, price discovery is often cited by others as the primary advantage of futures markets. Yet, all derivative markets provide these benefits. What characteristics do futures markets have that are not provided by comparable markets as forward markets?

First recall that a major distinction between futures and forwards is that futures are standardized instruments. By having an agreed-upon set of homogeneous contracts, futures markets can provide an orderly, liquid market in which traders can open and close positions without having to worry about holding these positions to expiration. Although not all futures contracts have a high degree of liquidity, an open position can nonetheless be closed on the exchange where the contract was initiated.[51] More importantly, however, futures contracts are guaranteed against credit losses. If a counterparty defaults, the clearinghouse pays and, as we have emphasized, no clearinghouse has ever defaulted. In this manner, a party can engage in a transaction to lock in a future price or rate without having to worry about the credit quality of the counterparty. Forward contracts are subject to default risk, but of course they offer the advantage of customization, the tailoring of a contract's terms to meet the needs of the parties involved.

With an open, standardized, and regulated market for futures contracts, their prices can be disseminated to other investors and the general public. Futures prices are closely watched by a vast number of market participants, many trying to discern an indication of the direction of future spot prices and some simply trying to determine what price they could lock in for future purchase or sale of the underlying asset. Although forward prices provide similar information, forward contracts are private transactions and their prices are not publicly reported. Futures markets thus provide transparency to the financial markets. They reveal the prices at which parties contract for future transactions.

Therefore, futures prices contribute an important element to the body of information on which investors make decisions. In addition, they provide opportunities to transact for future purchase or sale of an underlying asset without having to worry about the credit quality of the counterparty.

In Readings 64 and 65, we studied forward and futures contracts and showed that they have a lot in common. Both are commitments to buy or sell an asset at a future date at a price agreed on today. No money changes hands at the start of either transaction. We learned how to determine appropriate prices and values for these contracts. There are a variety of strategies and applications using forward and futures contracts. For now, however, we take a totally different approach and look at contracts that provide not the obligation but rather the right to buy or sell an asset at a later date at a price agreed on today. To obtain such a right, in contrast to agreeing to an obligation, one must pay money at the start. These instruments, called options, are the subject of Reading 66.

---

[51] Recall that there is no liquid market for previously opened forward contracts to be closed, but the holder of a forward contract can re-enter the market and establish a position opposite to the one previously established. If one holds a long forward contract to buy an asset in six months, one can then do a short forward contract to sell the asset in six months, and this transaction offsets the risk of changing market prices. The credit risk on both contracts remains. In some cases, the offsetting contract can be done with the same counterparty as in the original contract, permitting the two parties to arrange a single cash settlement to offset both contracts.

SUMMARY

► Futures contracts are standardized instruments that trade on a futures exchange, have a secondary market, and are guaranteed against default by means of a daily settling of gains and losses. Forward contracts are customized instruments that are not guaranteed against default and are created anywhere off of an exchange.

► Modern futures markets primarily originated in Chicago out of a need for grain farmers and buyers to be able to transact for delivery at future dates for grain that would, in the interim, be placed in storage.

► Futures transactions are standardized and conducted in a public market, are homogeneous, have a secondary market giving them an element of liquidity, and have a clearinghouse, which collects margins and settles gains and losses daily to provide a guarantee against default. Futures markets are also regulated at the federal government level.

► Margin in the securities markets is the deposit of money, the margin, and a loan for the remainder of the funds required to purchase a stock or bond. Margin in the futures markets is much smaller and does not involve a loan. Futures margin is more like a performance bond or down payment.

► Futures trading occurs on a futures exchange, which involves trading either in a physical location called a pit or via a computer terminal off of the floor of the futures exchange as part of an electronic trading system. In either case, a party to a futures contract goes long, committing to buy the underlying asset at an agreed-upon price, or short, committing to sell the underlying asset at an agreed-upon price.

► A futures trader who has established a position can re-enter the market and close out the position by doing the opposite transaction (sell if the original position was long or buy if the original position was short). The party has offset the position, no longer has a contract outstanding, and has no further obligation.

► Initial margin is the amount of money in a margin account on the day of a transaction or when a margin call is made. Maintenance margin is the amount of money in a margin account on any day other than when the initial margin applies. Minimum requirements exist for the initial and maintenance margins, with the initial margin requirement normally being less than 10 percent of the futures price and the maintenance margin requirement being smaller than the initial margin requirement. Variation margin is the amount of money that must be deposited into the account to bring the balance up to the required level. The settlement price is an average of the last few trades of the day and is used to determine the gains and losses marked to the parties' accounts.

► The futures clearinghouse engages in a practice called marking to market, also known as the daily settlement, in which gains and losses on a futures position are credited and charged to the trader's margin account on a daily basis. Thus, profits are available for withdrawal and losses must be paid quickly before they build up and pose a risk that the party will be unable to cover large losses.

► The margin balance at the end of the day is determined by taking the previous balance and accounting for any gains or losses from the day's activity, based on the settlement price, as well as any money added or withdrawn.

► Price limits are restrictions on the price of a futures trade and are based on a range relative to the previous day's settlement price. No trade can take place outside of the price limits. A limit move is when the price at which two parties would like to trade is at or beyond the price limit. Limit up is when the market price would be at or above the upper limit. Limit down is when the market price would be at or below the lower limit. Locked limit occurs when a trade cannot take place because the price would be above the limit up or below the limit down prices.

► A futures contract can be terminated by entering into an offsetting position very shortly before the end of the expiration day. If the position is still open when the contract expires, the trader must take delivery (if long) or make delivery (if short), unless the contract requires that an equivalent cash settlement be used in lieu of delivery. In addition, two participants can agree to alternative delivery terms, an arrangement called exchange for physicals.

► Delivery options are features associated with a futures contract that permit the short some flexibility in what to deliver, where to deliver it, and when in the expiration month to make delivery.

► Scalpers are futures traders who take positions for very short periods of time and attempt to profit by buying at the bid price and selling at the ask price. Day traders close out all positions by the end of the day. Position traders leave their positions open overnight and potentially longer.

► Treasury bill futures are contracts in which the underlying is $1,000,000 of a U.S. Treasury bill. Eurodollar futures are contracts in which the underlying is $1,000,000 of a Eurodollar time deposit. Treasury bond futures are contracts in which the underlying is $100,000 of a U.S. Treasury bond with a minimum 15-year maturity. Stock index futures are contracts in which the underlying is a well-known stock index, such as the S&P 500 or FTSE 100. Currency futures are contracts in which the underlying is a foreign currency.

► An expiring futures contract is equivalent to a spot transaction. Consequently, at expiration the futures price must converge to the spot price to avoid an arbitrage opportunity in which one can buy the asset and sell a futures or sell the asset and buy a futures to capture an immediate profit at no risk.

► The value of a futures contract just prior to marking to market is the accumulated price change since the last mark to market. The value of a futures contract just after marking to market is zero. These values reflect the claim a participant has as a result of her position in the contract.

► The price of a futures contract will equal the price of an otherwise equivalent forward contract one day prior to expiration, or if interest rates are known or constant, or if interest rates are uncorrelated with futures prices.

► A futures price is derived by constructing a combination of a long position in the asset and a short position in the futures. This strategy guarantees that the price received from the sale of the asset is known when the transaction is initiated. The futures price is then derived as the unknown value that eliminates the opportunity to earn an arbitrage profit off of the transaction.

► Futures prices are affected by the opportunity cost of funds tied up in the investment in the underlying asset, the costs of storing the underlying asset, any cash flows paid on the underlying asset, such as interest or dividends, and nonmonetary benefits of holding the underlying asset, referred to as the convenience yield.

► Backwardation describes a condition in which the futures price is lower than the spot price. Contango describes a condition in which the futures price is higher than the spot price.

► The futures price will not equal the expected spot price if the risk premium in the spot price is transferred from hedgers to futures traders. If the risk premium is transferred, then the futures price will be biased high or low relative to the expected future spot price. When the futures price is biased low (high), it is called normal backwardation (normal contango).

► T-bill futures prices are determined by going short a futures contract and going long a T-bill that will have the desired maturity at the futures expiration. At expiration, the T-bill is delivered or cash settled to a price locked in when the transaction was initiated through the sale of the futures. The correct futures price is the one that prohibits this combination from earning an arbitrage profit. Under the assumptions we make, the T-bill futures price is the same as the T-bill forward price.

► The implied repo rate is the rate of return implied by a transaction of buying a spot asset and selling a futures contract. If financing can be obtained in the repo market at less than the implied repo rate, the transaction should be undertaken. If financing can be supplied to the repo market at greater than the implied repo rate, the transaction should be reversed.

► Eurodollar futures cannot be priced as easily as T-bill futures, because the expiration price of a Eurodollar futures is based on a value computed as 1 minus a rate, whereas the value of the underlying Eurodollar time deposit is based on 1 divided by a rate. The difference is small but not zero. Hence, Eurodollar futures do not lend themselves to an exact pricing formula based on the notion of a cost of carry of the underlying.

► Treasury bond futures prices are determined by first identifying the cheapest bond to deliver, which is the bond that the short would deliver under current market conditions. Then one must construct a combination of a short futures contract and a long position in that bond. The bond is held, and the coupons are collected and reinvested. At expiration, the underlying bond is delivered and the futures price times the conversion factor for that bond is received. The correct futures price is the one that prevents this transaction from earning an arbitrage profit.

► Stock index futures prices are determined by constructing a combination of a long portfolio of stocks identical to the underlying index and a short futures contract. The stocks are held and the dividends are collected and reinvested. At expiration, the cash settlement results in the effective sale of the stock at the futures price. The correct futures price is the one that prevents this transaction from earning an arbitrage profit.

► Currency futures prices are determined by buying the underlying currency and selling a futures on the currency. The position is held, and the underlying currency pays interest at the foreign risk-free rate. At expiration, the currency is delivered and the futures price is received. The correct futures price is the one that prevents this transaction from earning an arbitrage profit.

► Futures markets serve our financial systems by making the markets for the underlying assets more efficient, by providing price discovery, by offering opportunities to trade at lower transaction costs, and by providing a means of managing risk. Futures markets also provide a homogeneous, standardized, and tradable instrument through which participants who might not have access to forward markets can make commitments to buy and sell assets at a future date at a locked-in price with no fear of credit risk. Because futures markets are so visible and widely reported on, they are also an excellent source of information, contributing greatly to the transparency of financial markets.

PROBLEMS FOR READING 65

1. Mary Craft is expecting large-capitalization stocks to rally close to the end of the year. She is pessimistic, however, about the performance of small-capitalization stocks. She decides to go long one December futures contract on the Dow Jones Industrial Average at a price of 9,020 and short one December futures contract on the S&P Midcap 400 Index at a price of 369.40. The multiplier for a futures contract on the Dow is $10, and the multiplier for a futures contract on the S&P Midcap 400 is $500. When Craft closes her position toward the end of the year, the Dow and S&P Midcap 400 futures prices are 9,086 and 370.20, respectively. How much is the net gain or loss to Craft?

2. **A.** The current price of gold is $300 per ounce. Consider the net cost of carry for gold to be zero. The risk-free interest rate is 6 percent. What should be the price of a gold futures contract that expires in 90 days?

   B. Using Part A above, illustrate how an arbitrage transaction could be executed if the futures contract is priced at $306 per ounce.

   C. Using Part A above, illustrate how an arbitrage transaction could be executed if the futures contract is priced at $303 per ounce.

3. Consider an asset priced at $90. A futures contract on the asset expires in 75 days. The risk-free interest rate is 7 percent. Answer the following questions, each of which is independent of the others, unless indicated otherwise.

   A. Find the appropriate futures price if the underlying asset has no storage costs, cash flows, or convenience yield.

   B. Find the appropriate futures price if the underlying asset's storage costs at the futures expiration equal $3.

   C. Find the appropriate futures price if the underlying asset has positive cash flows. The future value of these cash flows is $0.50 at the time of futures expiration.

   D. Find the appropriate futures price if the underlying asset's storage costs at the futures expiration equal $3.00 and the compound value at the time of the futures expiration of the positive cash flow from the underlying asset is $0.50.

   E. Using Part D above, illustrate how an arbitrage transaction could be executed if the futures contract is trading at $95.

   F. Using Part A above, determine the value of a long futures contract an instant before marking to market if the previous settlement price was $89.50.

   G. What happens to the value of the futures contract in Part F above as soon as it is marked to market?

4. A $1 face value bond pays an 8 percent semiannual coupon. The annual yield is 6 percent. The bond has 10 years remaining until maturity, and its price is $1.1488. Consider a futures contract calling for delivery of this bond only. The contract expires in 18 months. The risk-free rate is 5 percent.

   A. Compute the appropriate futures price.

   B. Assuming that the futures contract is appropriately priced, show the riskless strategy involving the bond and the futures contract that would earn the risk-free rate of return.

5. Consider a six-year $1 par Treasury bond. The bond pays a 6 percent semi-annual coupon, and the annual yield is 6 percent. The bond is priced at par. A futures contract expiring in 15 months calls for delivery of this bond only. The risk-free rate is 5 percent.

A. Find the future value in 15 months of the coupons on this bond.

B. Find the appropriate futures price.

C. Now suppose that the above bond is only one of many deliverable bonds. The contract specification calls for the use of a conversion factor to determine the price paid for a given deliverable bond. Suppose the bond described here has a conversion factor of 1.0567. Find the appropriate futures price.

6. A stock index is at 1,521.75. A futures contract on the index expires in 73 days. The risk-free interest rate is 6.10 percent. The value of the dividends reinvested over the life of the futures is 5.36.

A. Find the appropriate futures price.

B. Find the appropriate futures price in terms of the two specifications of the dividend yield.

C. Using your answer in Part B, find the futures price under the assumption of continuous compounding of interest and dividends.

7. A stock index is at 443.35. A futures contract on the index expires in 201 days. The price of the futures contract is 458.50. The risk-free interest rate is 6.50 percent. The value of the dividends reinvested over the life of the futures is 5.0.

A. Show that the futures contract above is mispriced by computing what the price of this futures contract should be.

B. Show how an arbitrageur could take advantage of the mispricing.

8. The spot exchange rate for the British pound is $1.4390. The U.S. interest rate is 6.3 percent, and the British interest rate is 5.8 percent. A futures contract on the exchange rate for the British pound expires in 100 days.

A. Find the appropriate futures price.

B. Find the appropriate futures price under the assumption of continuous compounding.

C. Suppose the actual futures price is $1.4650. Is the future contract mispriced? If yes, how could an arbitrageur take advantage of the mispricing? Use discrete compounding as in Part A.

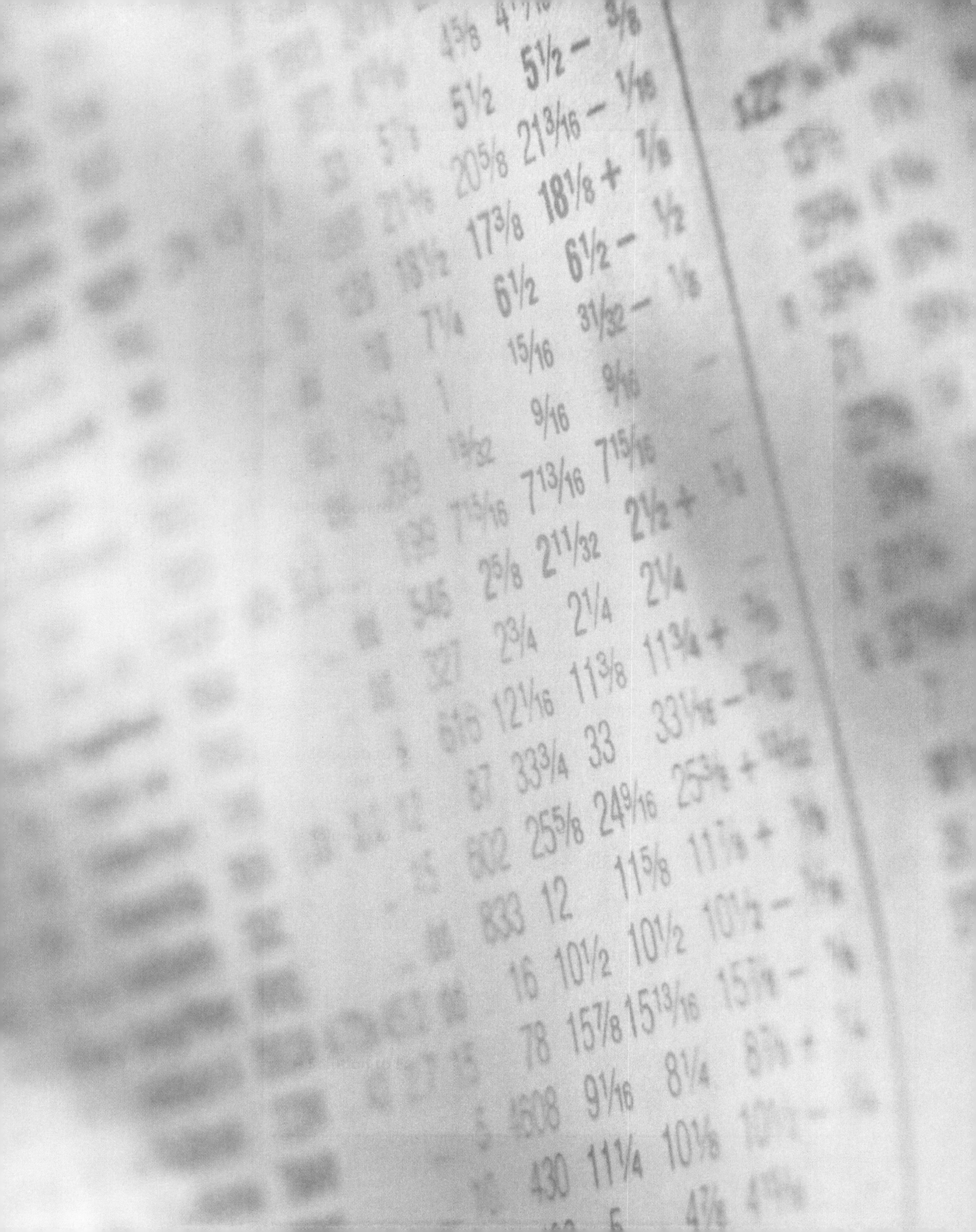

4⅝ 4⅞₁₆ — ⅝

5½ 5½ — ⅝

5½ 21³⁄₁₆ — ⅛

20⅝ 21³⁄₁₆ ⅞

17⅜ 18⅛ + ⅞

6½ 6½ — ½

6½ 3¹⁄₃₂ — ⅛

15/16

9/16 ⅝

7¹³⁄₁₆ 7¹⁵⁄₁₆

7¹⁵⁄₁₆ 7¹³⁄₁₆ 7¹⁵⁄₁₆

2⅝ 2¹¹⁄₃₂ 2½ +

23¾ 2¼ 2¼

12¹⁄₁₆ 11⅜ 11¾ +

33¾ 33 33⅛ —

25⅝ 24⁹⁄₁₆ 25⅝ +

12 11⅝ 11⅞ +

16 10½ 10½ 10⅛ —

78 15⅞ 15¹³⁄₁₆ 15⅞ —

9¹⁄₁₆ 8¼ 8⅛ +

430 11¼ 10⅛

STUDY SESSION 17
DERIVATIVE INVESTMENTS:
Options, Swaps, Interest Rate Derivatives, and Other Embedded Derivatives

This study session addresses options, swaps, interest rate derivatives, and embedded derivatives valuation and the prudent use of these instruments in a portfolio management context. Although the Black–Scholes–Merton model and the Black model are introduced, the practitioner-oriented emphasis is on the inputs, assumptions, and limitations of the models and their effect on valuation rather than on the calculation. Because derivatives are used largely to reduce risk or generate additional income, it is imperative to understand the relative cost/benefit of derivative strategies.

LEARNING OUTCOMES

Reading 66: Option Markets and Contracts
The candidate should be able to:

a. calculate and interpret the prices of a synthetic call option, synthetic put option, synthetic bond, and synthetic underlying stock, when provided with the formula for put–call parity, and explain why an investor would want to create such instruments;

b. calculate and interpret prices of interest rate options and options on assets using one- and two-period binomial models, when provided the formula;

c. explain the assumptions underlying the Black–Scholes–Merton model and their limitations;

d. explain how an option price, as represented by the Black–Scholes–Merton model, is affected by each of the input values (the option Greeks);

e. explain the delta of an option, and demonstrate how it is used in dynamic hedging;

f. explain the gamma effect on an option's price and delta and evaluate the effectiveness of delta hedging based on gamma's value;

g. discuss the effect of the underlying asset's cash flows on the price of an option;

h. demonstrate the methods for estimating the future volatility of the underlying asset (i.e., the historical volatility and the implied volatility methods);

i. illustrate how put–call parity for options on forwards (or futures) is established;

j. compare and contrast American options on forwards and futures to European options on forwards and futures, and identify the appropriate pricing model for European options.

Reading 67: Swap Markets and Contracts

The candidate should be able to:

a. distinguish between the pricing and valuation of swaps;

b. explain the equivalence of the following swaps to combinations of other instruments: interest rate swaps to a series of off-market forward rate agreements (FRAs) and a plain vanilla swap to a combination of an interest rate call and interest rate put;

c. calculate and interpret the fixed rate on a plain vanilla interest rate swap and the market value of the swap during its life, when provided with the formulas;

d. calculate and interpret the fixed rate, if applicable, and the foreign notional principal for a given domestic notional principal on a currency swap, and determine the market values of each of the different types of currency swaps during their lives, when provided with the formulas;

e. calculate and interpret the fixed rate, if applicable, on an equity swap and the market values of the different types of equity swaps during their lives; when provided with the formulas;

f. explain and interpret the characteristics of swaptions, including the difference between payer and receiver swaptions;

g. explain why swaptions exist, and illustrate how swaptions are used;

h. identify and calculate the possible payoffs and cash flows of an interest rate swaption, when provided with the formulas;

i. calculate and interpret the value of an interest rate swaption on the expiration day, when provided with the formulas;

j. explain how credit risk arises in a swap, which party bears the credit risk, at what point in a swap's life the credit risk is the greatest, and distinguish between current credit risk and potential credit risk;

k. define the swap spread and explain what it represents;

l. illustrate how swap credit risk is reduced by both netting and marking to market.

Reading 68: Interest Rate Derivative Instruments

The candidate should be able to:

a. characterize the change in the value of an interest rate swap for each counterparty when interest rates change;

b. demonstrate how both a cap and a floor are packages of 1) options on interest rates, and 2) options on fixed income instruments;

c. compute the payoff for a cap and a floor, and explain how a collar is created.

Reading 69: Swap Contracts, Convertible Securities, and Other Embedded Derivatives - Part II

The candidate should be able to:

a. compare and contrast structured notes to regular fixed-income securities;

b. describe the cash flow characteristics of dual-currency bonds, equity-index-linked notes, commodity-linked bull and bear bonds, and swap-linked notes.

$4\frac{5}{8}$ $4\frac{1}{16}$

$5\frac{1}{2}$ — $\frac{3}{8}$

$5\frac{1}{2}$ $5\frac{1}{2}$ —

$5\frac{1}{2}$ $21\frac{3}{16}$ — $\frac{1}{16}$

$20\frac{5}{8}$ $21\frac{3}{16}$ — $\frac{7}{8}$

$17\frac{3}{8}$ $18\frac{1}{8}$ +

$18\frac{1}{2}$ $6\frac{1}{2}$ — $\frac{1}{2}$

$6\frac{1}{2}$ $6\frac{1}{2}$ —

$7\frac{1}{4}$ $31\frac{1}{32}$ — $\frac{1}{8}$

$15\frac{1}{16}$

1 $9\frac{1}{16}$ $9\frac{1}{16}$

$1\frac{1}{32}$

$7\frac{13}{16}$ $7\frac{15}{16}$

$7\frac{5}{16}$ $7\frac{13}{16}$

$2\frac{5}{8}$ $2\frac{11}{32}$ $2\frac{1}{2}$ +

$2\frac{3}{4}$ $2\frac{1}{4}$ $2\frac{1}{4}$

$12\frac{1}{16}$ $11\frac{3}{8}$ $11\frac{3}{4}$ +

$6\frac{1}{8}$ $33\frac{3}{4}$ 33 $33\frac{1}{16}$ —

87 $25\frac{5}{8}$ $24\frac{9}{16}$ $25\frac{3}{8}$ +

602 12 $11\frac{5}{8}$ $11\frac{7}{8}$ +

833 $10\frac{1}{2}$ $10\frac{1}{2}$ $10\frac{1}{8}$ —

16 $15\frac{7}{8}$ $15\frac{13}{16}$ $15\frac{7}{8}$ +

78 $9\frac{1}{16}$ $8\frac{1}{4}$ $8\frac{1}{2}$ +

4508 $11\frac{1}{4}$ $10\frac{1}{8}$ $10\frac{1}{8}$

430 $4\frac{7}{8}$ $4\frac{7}{8}$

OPTION MARKETS AND CONTRACTS
by Don M. Chance

LEARNING OUTCOMES

The candidate should be able to:

a. calculate and interpret the prices of a synthetic call option, synthetic put option, synthetic bond, and synthetic underlying stock, when provided with the formula for put–call parity, and explain why an investor would want to create such instruments;

b. calculate and interpret prices of interest rate options and options on assets using one- and two-period binomial models, when provided the formula;

c. explain the assumptions underlying the Black–Scholes–Merton model and their limitations;

d. explain how an option price, as represented by the Black–Scholes–Merton model, is affected by each of the input values (the option Greeks);

e. explain the delta of an option, and demonstrate how it is used in dynamic hedging;

f. explain the gamma effect on an option's price and delta and evaluate the effectiveness of delta hedging based on gamma's value;

g. discuss the effect of the underlying asset's cash flows on the price of an option;

h. demonstrate the methods for estimating the future volatility of the underlying asset (i.e., the historical volatility and the implied volatility methods);

i. illustrate how put–call parity for options on forwards (or futures) is established;

j. compare and contrast American options on forwards and futures to European options on forwards and futures, and identify the appropriate pricing model for European options.

1

BEGINS

INTRODUCTION

In Reading 64 we examined forward contracts, and in Reading 65 we looked at futures contracts. We noted how similar forward and futures contracts are: Both are commitments to buy an underlying asset at a fixed price at a later date. Forward contracts, however, are privately created, over-the-counter customized instruments that carry credit risk. Futures contracts are publicly traded, exchange-listed standardized instruments that effectively have no credit risk. Now we turn to options. Like forwards and futures, they are derivative instruments that provide the opportunity to buy or sell an underlying asset with a specific expiration date. But in contrast, buying an option gives the *right*, not the obligation, to buy or sell an underlying asset. And whereas forward and futures contracts involve no exchange of cash up front, options require a cash payment from the option buyer to the option seller.

Yet options contain several features common to forward and futures contracts. For one, options can be created by any two parties with any set of terms they desire. In this sense, options can be privately created, over-the-counter, customized instruments that are subject to credit risk. In addition, however, there is a large market for publicly traded, exchange-listed, standardized options, for which credit risk is essentially eliminated by the clearinghouse.

Just as we examined the pricing of forwards and futures in the last two readings, we shall examine option pricing in this reading. We shall also see that options can be created out of forward contracts, and that forward contracts can be created out of options. With some simplifying assumptions, options can be created out of futures contracts and futures contracts can be created out of options.

Finally, we note that options also exist that have a futures or forward contract as the underlying. These instruments blend some of the features of both options and forwards/futures.

As background, we discuss the definitions and characteristics of options.

2

BASIC DEFINITIONS AND ILLUSTRATIONS OF OPTIONS CONTRACTS

An option is a financial derivative contract that provides a party the right to buy or sell an underlying at a fixed price by a certain time in the future. The party holding the right is the option buyer; the party granting the right is the option seller. There are two types of options, a **call** and a **put**. A call is an option granting the right to buy the underlying; a put is an option granting the right to sell the underlying. With the exception of some advanced types of options, a given option contract is either a call, granting the right to buy, or a put, granting the right to sell, but not both.[1] We emphasize that this right to buy or sell is held by the option buyer, also called the long or option holder, and granted by the option seller, also called the short or option **writer**.

To obtain this right, the option buyer pays the seller a sum of money, commonly referred to as the **option price**. On occasion, this option price is called the **option premium** or just the **premium**. This money is paid when the option contract is initiated.

2.1 Basic Characteristics of Options

The fixed price at which the option holder can buy or sell the underlying is called the **exercise price, strike price, striking price**, or **strike**. The use of this right to buy or sell the underlying is referred to as **exercise** or **exercising the option**. Like all derivative contracts, an option has an **expiration date**, giving rise to the notion of an option's **time to expiration**. When the expiration date arrives, an option that is not exercised simply expires.

What happens at exercise depends on the whether the option is a call or a put. If the buyer is exercising a call, she pays the exercise price and receives either the underlying or an equivalent cash settlement. On the opposite side of the transaction is the seller, who receives the exercise price from the buyer and delivers the underlying, or alternatively, pays an equivalent cash settlement. If the buyer is exercising a put, she delivers the stock and receives the exercise price or an equivalent cash settlement. The seller, therefore, receives the underlying and must pay the exercise price or the equivalent cash settlement.

As noted in the above paragraph, cash settlement is possible. In that case, the option holder exercising a call receives the difference between the market value of the underlying and the exercise price from the seller in cash. If the option holder exercises a put, she receives the difference between the exercise price and the market value of the underlying in cash.

There are two primary exercise styles associated with options. One type of option has **European-style exercise**, which means that the option can be exercised only on its expiration day. In some cases, expiration could occur during that day; in others, exercise can occur only when the option has expired. In either case, such an option is called a **European option**. The other style of exercise is **American-style exercise**. Such an option can be exercised on any day through the expiration day and is generally called an **American option**.[2]

Option contracts specify a designated number of units of the underlying. For exchange-listed, standardized options, the exchange establishes each term, with the exception of the price. The price is negotiated by the two parties. For an over-the-counter option, the two parties decide each of the terms through negotiation.

In an over-the-counter option—one created off of an exchange by any two parties who agree to trade—the buyer is subject to the possibility of the writer defaulting. When the buyer exercises, the writer must either deliver the stock or cash if a call, or pay for the stock or pay cash if a put. If the writer cannot do so for financial reasons, the option holder faces a credit loss. Because the option holder paid the price up front and is not required to do anything else, the seller does not face any credit risk. Thus, although credit risk is bilateral in forward contracts—the long assumes the risk of the short defaulting, and the short assumes the risk of the long

---

[1] Of course, a party could buy both a call and a put, thereby holding the right to buy *and* sell the underlying.

[2] It is worthwhile to be aware that these terms have nothing to do with Europe or America. Both types of options are found in Europe and America. The names are part of the folklore of options markets, and there is no definitive history to explain how they came into use.

defaulting—the credit risk in an option is unilateral. Only the buyer faces credit risk because only the seller can default. As we discuss later, in exchange-listed options, the clearinghouse guarantees payment to the buyer.

2.2 Some Examples of Options

Consider some call and put options on Sun Microsystems (SUNW). The date is 13 June and Sun is selling for $16.25. Exhibit 66-1 gives information on the closing prices of four options, ones expiring in July and October and ones with exercise prices of 15.00 and 17.50. The July options expire on 20 July and the October options expire on 18 October. In the parlance of the profession, these are referred to as the July 15 calls, July 17.50 calls, October 15 calls, and October 17.50 calls, with similar terminology for the puts. These particular options are American style.

Consider the July 15 call. This option permits the holder to buy SUNW at a price of $15 a share any time through 20 July. To obtain this option, one would pay a price of $2.35. Therefore, a writer received $2.35 on 13 June and must be ready to sell SUNW to the buyer for $15 during the period through 20 July. Currently, SUNW trades above $15 a share, but as we shall see in more detail later, the option holder has no reason to exercise the option right now.[3] To justify purchase of the call, the buyer must be anticipating that SUNW will increase in price before the option expires. The seller of the call must be anticipating that SUNW will not rise sufficiently in price before the option expires.

Note that the option buyer could purchase a call expiring in July but permitting the purchase of SUNW at a price of $17.50. This price is more than the $15.00 exercise price, but as a result, the option, which sells for $1.00, is considerably cheaper. The cheaper price comes from the fact that the July 17.50 call is less likely to be exercised, because the stock has a higher hurdle to clear. A buyer is not willing to pay as much and a seller is more willing to take less for an option that is less likely to be exercised.

Alternatively, the option buyer could choose to purchase an October call instead of a July call. For any exercise price, however, the October calls would be more expensive than the July calls because they allow a longer period for the stock to make the move that the buyer wants. October options are more likely to be exercised than July options; therefore, a buyer would be willing to pay more and the seller would demand more for the October calls.

EXHIBIT 66-1	Closing Prices of Selected Options on SUNW, 13 June			
Exercise Price	July Calls	October Calls	July Puts	October Puts
15.00	2.35	3.30	0.90	1.85
17.50	1.00	2.15	2.15	3.20

Note: Stock price is $16.25; July options expire on 20 July; October options expire on 18 October.

---

[3] The buyer paid $2.35 for the option. If he exercised it right now, he would pay $15.00 for the stock, which is worth only $16.25. Thus, he would have effectively paid $17.35 (the cost of the option of $2.35 plus the exercise price of $15) for a stock worth $16.25. Even if he had purchased the option previously at a much lower price, the current option price of $2.35 is the opportunity cost of exercising the option—that is, he can always sell the option for $2.35. Therefore, if he exercised the option, he would be throwing away the $2.35 he could receive if he sold it.

Suppose the buyer expects the stock price to go down. In that case, he might buy a put. Consider the October 17.50 put, which would cost the buyer $3.20. This option would allow the holder to sell SUNW at a price of $17.50 any time up through 18 October.[4] He has no reason to exercise the option right now, because it would mean he would be buying the option for $3.20 and selling a stock worth $16.25 for $17.50. In effect, the option holder would part with $19.45 (the cost of the option of $3.20 plus the value of the stock of $16.25) and obtain only $17.50.[5] The buyer of a put obviously must be anticipating that the stock will fall before the expiration day.

If he wanted a cheaper option than the October 17.50 put, he could buy the October 15 put, which would cost only $1.85 but would allow him to sell the stock for only $15.00 a share. The October 15 put is less likely to be exercised than the October 17.50, because the stock price must fall below a lower hurdle. Thus, the buyer is not willing to pay as much and the seller is willing to take less.

For either exercise price, purchase of a July put instead of an October put would be much cheaper but would allow less time for the stock to make the downward move necessary for the transaction to be worthwhile. The July put is cheaper than the October put; the buyer is not willing to pay as much and the seller is willing to take less because the option is less likely to be exercised.

In observing these option prices, we have obtained our first taste of some principles involved in pricing options.

Call options have a lower premium the higher the exercise price.
Put options have a lower premium the lower the exercise price.
Both call and put options are cheaper the shorter the time to expiration.[6]

These results should be intuitive, but later in this reading we show unequivocally why they must be true.

2.3 The Concept of Moneyness of an Option

An important concept in the study of options is the notion of an option's **moneyness**, which refers to the relationship between the price of the underlying and the exercise price. We use the terms **in-the-money, out-of-the-money,** and **at-the-money**. We explain the concept in Exhibit 66-2 with examples from the SUNW options. Note that **in-the-money options** are those in which exercising the option would produce a cash inflow that exceeds the cash outflow. Thus, calls are in-the-money when the value of the underlying exceeds the exercise price. Puts are in-the-money when the exercise price exceeds the value of the underlying. In our example, there are no at-the-money SUNW options, which would require that the stock value equal the exercise price; however, an at-the-money option can effectively be viewed as an **out-of-the-money option**, because its exercise would not bring in more money than is paid out.

As explained above, *one would not necessarily exercise an in-the-money option, but one would never exercise an out-of-the-money option.*

We now move on to explore how options markets are organized.

---

[4] Even if the option holder did not own the stock, he could use the option to sell the stock short.

[5] Again, even if the option were purchased in the past at a much lower price, the $3.20 current value of the option is an opportunity cost. Exercise of the option is equivalent to throwing away the opportunity cost.

[6] There is an exception to the rule that put options are cheaper the shorter the time to expiration. This statement is always true for American options but not always for European options. We explore this point later.

EXHIBIT 66-2	Moneyness of an Option		
In-the-Money		**Out-of-the-Money**	
Option	Justification	Option	Justification
July 15 call	16.25 > 15.00	July 17.50 call	16.25 < 17.50
October 15 call	16.25 > 15.00	October 17.50 call	16.25 < 17.50
July 17.50 put	17.50 > 16.25	July 15 put	15.00 < 16.25
October 17.50 put	17.50 > 16.25	October 15 put	15.00 < 16.25

Notes: Sun Microsystems options on 13 June; stock price is 16.25. See Exhibit 66-1 for more details. There are no options with an exercise price of 16.25, so no options are at-the-money.

3   THE STRUCTURE OF GLOBAL OPTIONS MARKETS

Although no one knows exactly how options first got started, contracts similar to options have been around for thousands of years. In fact, insurance is a form of an option. The insurance buyer pays the insurance writer a premium and receives a type of guarantee that covers losses. This transaction is similar to a put option, which provides coverage of a portion of losses on the underlying and is often used by holders of the underlying. The first true options markets were over-the-counter options markets in the United States in the 19th century.

3.1   Over-the-Counter Options Markets

In the United States, customized over-the-counter options markets were in existence in the early part of the 20th century and lasted well into the 1970s. An organization called the Put and Call Brokers and Dealers Association consisted of a group of firms that served as brokers and dealers. As brokers, they attempted to match buyers of options with sellers, thereby earning a commission. As dealers, they offered to take either side of the option transaction, usually laying off (hedging) the risk in another transaction. Most of these transactions were retail, meaning that the general public were their customers.

As we discuss in Section 3.2 below, the creation of the Chicago Board Options Exchange was a revolutionary event, but it effectively killed the Put and Call Brokers and Dealers Association. Subsequently, the increasing use of swaps facilitated a rebirth of the customized over-the-counter options market. Currency options, a natural extension to currency swaps, were in much demand. Later, interest rate options emerged as a natural outgrowth of interest rate swaps. Soon bond, equity, and **index options** were trading in a vibrant over-the-counter market. In contrast to the previous over-the-counter options market, however, the current one emerged as a largely wholesale market. Transactions are usually made with institutions and corporations and are rarely conducted directly with individuals. This market is much like the forward market described in Reading 64, with dealers offering to take either the long or short position in options and hedging that risk with transactions in other options or derivatives. There are no guarantees that the seller will perform; hence, the buyer faces credit risk. As such, option buyers must scrutinize sellers' credit risk and may require some risk reduction measures, such as collateral.

As previously noted, customized options have *all* of their terms—such as price, exercise price, time to expiration, identification of the underlying, settlement or delivery terms, size of the contract, and so on—determined by the two parties.

Like forward markets, over-the-counter options markets are essentially unregulated. In most countries, participating firms, such as banks and securities firms, are regulated by the appropriate authorities but there is usually no particular regulatory body for the over-the-counter options markets. In some countries, however, there are regulatory bodies for these markets.

Exhibit 66-3 on page 134 provides information on the leading dealers in over-the-counter currency and interest rate options as determined by *Risk* magazine in its annual surveys of banks and investment banks and also end users.

3.2 Exchange-Listed Options Markets

As briefly noted above, the Chicago Board Options Exchange was formed in 1973. Created as an extension of the Chicago Board of Trade, it became the first organization to offer a market for standardized options. In the United States, standardized options also trade on the Amex–Nasdaq, the Philadelphia Stock Exchange, and the Pacific Stock Exchange.[7] On a worldwide basis, standardized options are widely traded on such exchanges as LIFFE (the London International Financial Futures and Options Exchange) in London, Eurex in Frankfurt, and most other foreign exchanges. Exhibit 66-4 (page 135) shows the 20 largest options exchanges in the world. Note, perhaps surprisingly, that the leading options exchange is in Korea.

As described in Reading 64 on futures, the exchange fixes all terms of standardized instruments except the price. Thus, the exchange establishes the expiration dates and exercise prices as well as the minimum price quotation unit. The exchange also determines whether the option is European or American, whether the exercise is cash settlement or delivery of the underlying, and the contract size. In the United States, an option contract on an individual stock covers 100 shares of stock. Terminology such as "one option" is often used to refer to one option contract, which is really a set of options on 100 shares of stock. Index option sizes are stated in terms of a multiplier, indicating that the contract covers a hypothetical number of shares, as though the index were an individual stock. Similar specifications apply for options on other types of underlyings.

The exchange generally allows trading in exercise prices that surround the current stock price. As the stock price moves, options with exercise prices around the new stock price are usually added. The majority of trading occurs in options that are close to being at-the-money. Options that are far in-the-money or far out-of-the-money, called **deep-in-the-money** and **deep-out-of-the-money** options, are usually not very actively traded and are often not even listed for trading.

Most exchange-listed options have fairly short-term expirations, usually the current month, the next month, and perhaps one or two other months. Most of the trading takes place for the two shortest expirations. Some exchanges list options with expirations of several years, which have come to be called LEAPS, for **long-term equity anticipatory securities**. These options are fairly actively

---

[7] You may wonder why the New York Stock Exchange is not mentioned. Standardized options did trade on the NYSE at one time but were not successful, and the right to trade these options was sold to another exchange.

EXHIBIT 66-3	*Risk* Magazine Surveys of Banks, Investment Banks, and Corporate End Users to Determine the Top Three Dealers in Over-the-Counter Currency and Interest Rate Options

	Respondents	
Currencies	**Banks and Investment Banks**	**Corporate End Users**
Currency Options		
$/€	UBS Warburg	Citigroup
	Citigroup/Deutsche Bank	Royal Bank of Scotland
		Deutsche Bank
$/¥	UBS Warburg	Citigroup
	Credit Suisse First Boston	JP Morgan Chase
	JP Morgan Chase/Royal Bank of Scotland	UBS Warburg
$/£	Royal Bank of Scotland	Royal Bank of Scotland
	UBS Warburg	Citigroup
	Citigroup	Hong Kong Shanghai Banking Corp.
$/SF	UBS Warburg	UBS Warburg
	Credit Suisse First Boston	Credit Suisse First Boston
	Citigroup	Citigroup
Interest Rate Options		
$	JP Morgan Chase	JP Morgan Chase
	Deutsche Bank	Citigroup
	Bank of America	Deutsche Bank/Lehman Brothers
€	JP Morgan Chase	JP Morgan Chase
	Credit Suisse First Boston/ Morgan Stanley	Citigroup UBS Warburg
¥	JP Morgan Chase/Deutsche Bank	UBS Warburg
	Bank of America	Barclays Capital
		Citigroup
£	Barclays Capital	Royal Bank of Scotland
	Societe Generale Groupe	Citigroup
	Bank of America/Royal Bank of Scotland	Hong Kong Shanghai Banking Corp.
SF	UBS Warburg	UBS Warburg
	JP Morgan Chase	JP Morgan
	Credit Suisse First Boston	Goldman Sachs

Notes: $ = U.S. dollar, € = euro, ¥ = Japanese yen, £ = U.K. pound sterling, SF = Swiss franc

Source: Risk, September 2002, pp. 30–67 for Banks and Investment Banking dealer respondents, and June 2002, pp. 24–34 for Corporate End User respondents.

Results for Corporate End Users for Interest Rate Options are from *Risk,* July 2001, pp. 38–46. *Risk* omitted this category from its 2002 survey.

EXHIBIT 66-4	World's 20 Largest Options Exchanges
Exchange and Location	**Volume in 2001**
Korea Stock Exchange (Korea)	854,791,792
Chicago Board Options Exchange (United States)	306,667,851
MONEP (France)	285,667,686
Eurex (Germany and Switzerland)	239,016,516
American Stock Exchange (United States)	205,103,884
Pacific Stock Exchange (United States)	102,701,752
Philadelphia Stock Exchange (United States)	101,373,433
Chicago Mercantile Exchange (United States)	95,740,352
Amsterdam Exchange (Netherlands)	66,400,654
LIFFE (United Kingdom)	54,225,652
Chicago Board of Trade (United States)	50,345,068
OM Stockholm (Sweden)	39,327,619
South African Futures Exchange (South Africa)	24,307,477
MEFF Renta Variable (Spain)	23,628,446
New York Mercantile Exchange (United States)	17,985,109
Korea Futures Exchange (Korea)	11,468,991
Italian Derivatives Exchange (Italy)	11,045,804
Osaka Securities Exchange (Japan)	6,991,908
Bourse de Montreal (Canada)	5,372,930
Hong Kong Futures Exchange (China)	4,718,880

Note: Volume given is in number of contracts.

Source: Data supplied by *Futures Industry* magazine.

purchased, but most investors tend to buy and hold them and do not trade them as often as they do the shorter-term options.

The exchanges also determine on which companies they will list options for trading. Although specific requirements do exist, generally the exchange will list the options of any company for which it feels the options would be actively traded. The company has no voice in the matter. Options of a company can be listed on more than one exchange in a given country.

In Reading 65, we described the manner in which futures are traded. The procedure is very similar for exchange-listed options. Some exchanges have pit trading, whereby parties meet in the pit and arrange a transaction. Some exchanges use electronic trading, in which transactions are conducted through computers. In either case, the transactions are guaranteed by the clearinghouse. In the United States, the clearinghouse is an independent company called the **Options Clearing Corporation** or OCC. The OCC guarantees to the buyer that the clearinghouse will step in and fulfill the obligation if the seller reneges at exercise.

When the buyer purchases the option, the premium, which one might think would go to the seller, instead goes to the clearinghouse, which maintains it in a margin account. In addition, the seller must post some margin money, which is based on a formula that reflects whether the seller has a position that hedges the risk and whether the option is in- or out-of-the-money. If the price moves against the seller, the clearinghouse will force the seller to put up additional margin money. Although defaults are rare, the clearinghouse has always been successful in paying when the seller defaults. Thus, exchange-listed options are effectively free of credit risk.

Because of the standardization of option terms and participants' general acceptance of these terms, exchange-listed options can be bought and sold at any time prior to expiration. Thus, a party who buys or sells an option can re-enter the market before the option expires and offset the position with a sale or a purchase of the identical option. From the clearinghouse's perspective, the positions cancel.

As in futures markets, traders on the options exchange are generally either market makers or brokers. Some slight technical distinctions exist between different types of market makers in different options markets, but the differences are minor and do not concern us here. Like futures traders, option market makers attempt to profit by scalping (holding positions very short term) to earn the bid–ask spread and sometimes holding positions longer, perhaps closing them overnight or leaving them open for days or more.

When an option expires, the holder decides whether or not to exercise it. When the option is expiring, there are no further gains to waiting, so in-the-money options are always exercised, assuming they are in-the-money by more than the transaction cost of buying or selling the underlying or arranging a cash settlement when exercising. Using our example of the SUNW options, if at expiration the stock is at 16, the calls with an exercise price of 15 would be exercised. Most exchange-listed stock options call for actual delivery of the stock. Thus, the seller delivers the stock and the buyer pays the seller, through the clearinghouse, $15 per share. If the exchange specifies that the contract is cash settled, the seller simply pays the buyer $1. For puts requiring delivery, the buyer tenders the stock and receives the exercise price from the seller. If the option is out-of-the-money, it simply expires unexercised and is removed from the books. If the put is cash settled, the writer pays the buyer the equivalent cash amount.

Some nonstandardized exchange-traded options exist in the United States. In an attempt to compete with the over-the-counter options market, some exchanges permit some options to be individually customized and traded on the exchange, thereby benefiting from the advantages of the clearinghouse's credit guarantee. These options are primarily available only in large sizes and tend to be traded only by large institutional investors.

Like futures markets, exchange-listed options markets are typically regulated at the federal level. In the United States, federal regulation of options markets is the responsibility of the Securities and Exchange Commission; similar regulatory structures exist in other countries.

4 TYPES OF OPTIONS

Almost anything with a random outcome can have an option on it. Note that by using the word *anything*, we are implying that the underlying does not even need to be an asset. In this section, we shall discover the different types of options, identified by the nature of the underlying. Our focus in this book is on financial options, but it is important, nonetheless, to gain some awareness of other types of options.

4.1 Financial Options

Financial options are options in which the underlying is a financial asset, an interest rate, or a currency.

4.1.1 Stock Options

Options on individual stocks, also called **equity options**, are among the most popular. Exchange-listed options are available on most widely traded stocks and an option on any stock can potentially be created on the over-the-counter market. We have already given examples of stock options in an earlier section; we now move on to index options.

4.1.2 Index Options

Stock market indices are well known, not only in the investment community but also among many individuals who are not even directly investing in the market. Because a stock index is just an artificial portfolio of stocks, it is reasonable to expect that one could create an option on a stock index. Indeed, we have already covered forward and futures contracts on stock indices; options are no more difficult in structure.

For example, consider options on the S&P 500 Index, which trade on the Chicago Board Options Exchange and have a designated index contract multiplier of 250. On 13 June of a given year, the S&P 500 closed at 1241.60. A call option with an exercise price of $1,250 expiring on 20 July was selling for $28. The option is European style and settles in cash. The underlying, the S&P 500, is treated as though it were a share of stock worth $1,241.60, which can be bought, using the call option, for $1,250 on 20 July. At expiration, if the option is in-the-money, the buyer exercises it and the writer pays the buyer the $250 contract multiplier times the difference between the index value at expiration and $1,250.

In the United States, there are also options on the Dow Jones Industrial Average, the Nasdaq, and various other indices. There are nearly always options on the best-known stock indices in most countries.

Just as there are options on stocks, there are also options on bonds.

4.1.3 Bond Options

Options on bonds, usually called **bond options**, are primarily traded in the over-the-counter markets. Options exchanges have attempted to generate interest in options on bonds, but have not been very successful. Corporate bonds are not very actively traded; most are purchased and held to expiration. Government bonds, however, are very actively traded; nevertheless, options on them have not gained widespread acceptance on options exchanges. Options exchanges generate much of their trading volume from individual investors, who have far more interest in and understanding of stocks than bonds.

Thus, bond options are found almost exclusively in the over-the-counter market and are almost always options on government bonds. Consider, for example, a U.S. Treasury bond maturing in 27 years. The bond has a coupon of 5.50 percent, a yield of 5.75 percent, and is selling for $0.9659 per $1 par. An over-the-counter options dealer might sell a put or call option on the bond with an exercise price of $0.98 per $1.00 par. The option could be European or American. Its expiration day must be significantly before the maturity date of the bond. Otherwise, as the bond approaches maturity, its price will move toward par, thereby removing much of the uncertainty in its price. The option could be specified to settle with actual delivery of the bond or with a cash settlement. The parties would also specify that the contract covered a given notional principal, expressed in terms of a face value of the underlying bond.

Continuing our example, let us assume that the contract covers $5 million face value of bonds and is cash settled. Suppose the buyer exercises a call option when the bond price is at $0.995. Then the option is in-the-money by $0.995 − $0.98 = $0.015 per $1 par. The seller pays the buyer 0.015($5,000,000) = $75,000. If instead the contract called for delivery, the seller would deliver $5 million face value of bonds, which would be worth $5,000,000($0.995) = $4,975,000. The buyer would pay $5,000,000($0.98) = $4,900,000. Because the option is created in the over-the-counter market, the option buyer would assume the risk of the seller defaulting.

Even though bond options are not very widely traded, another type of related option is widely used, especially by corporations. This family of options is called **interest rate options**. These are quite different from the options we have previously discussed, because the underlying is not a particular financial instrument.

4.1.4 Interest Rate Options

In Reading 64, we devoted considerable effort to understanding the Eurodollar spot market and forward contracts on the Eurodollar rate or LIBOR, called FRAs. In this reading, we cover options on LIBOR. Although these are not the only interest rate options, their characteristics are sufficiently general to capture most of what we need to know about options on other interest rates. First recall that a Eurodollar is a dollar deposited outside of the United States. The primary Eurodollar rate is LIBOR, and it is considered the best measure of an interest rate paid in dollars on a nongovernmental borrower. These Eurodollars represent dollar-denominated time deposits issued by banks in London borrowing from other banks in London.

Before looking at the characteristics of interest rate options, let us set the perspective by recalling that FRAs are forward contracts that pay off based on the difference between the underlying rate and the fixed rate embedded in the contract when it is constructed. For example, consider a 3 × 9 FRA. This contract expires in three months. The underlying rate is six-month LIBOR. Hence, when the contract is constructed, the underlying Eurodollar instrument matures in nine months. *When the contract expires, the payoff is made immediately*, but the rate on which it is based, 180-day LIBOR, is set in the spot market, where it is assumed that interest will be paid 180 days later. Hence, the payoff on an FRA is discounted by the spot rate on 180-day LIBOR to give a present value for the payoff as of the expiration date.

Just as an FRA is a forward contract in which the underlying is an interest rate, an **interest rate option** is an option in which the underlying is an interest rate. Instead of an exercise price, it has an **exercise rate** (or **strike rate**), which is expressed on an order of magnitude of an interest rate. At expiration, the option payoff is based on the difference between the underlying rate in the market and the exercise rate. Whereas an FRA is a *commitment* to make one interest payment and receive another at a future date, an interest rate option is the *right* to make one interest payment and receive another. And just as there are call and put options, there is also an **interest rate call** and an **interest rate put**.

An interest rate call is an option in which the holder has the right to make a known interest payment and receive an unknown interest payment. The underlying is the unknown interest rate. If the unknown underlying rate turns out to be higher than the exercise rate at expiration, the option is in-the-money and is exercised; otherwise, the option simply expires. *An interest rate put is an option in which the holder has the right to make an unknown interest payment and receive a known interest payment.* If the unknown underlying rate turns out to be lower than the exercise rate at expiration, the option is in-the-money and is exercised; otherwise, the option simply expires. All interest rate option contracts have a specified size, which, as in FRAs, is called the notional principal. An interest rate option can be European or American style, but most tend to be European style. Interest rate options are settled in cash.

As with FRAs, these options are offered for purchase and sale by dealers, which are financial institutions, usually the same ones who offer FRAs. These dealers quote rates for options of various exercise prices and expirations. When a dealer takes an option position, it usually then offsets the risk with other transactions, often Eurodollar futures.

To use the same example we used in introducing FRAs, consider options expiring in 90 days on 180-day LIBOR. The option buyer specifies whatever exercise rate he desires. Let us say he chooses an exercise rate of 5.5 percent and a notional principal of $10 million.

Now let us move to the expiration day. Suppose that 180-day LIBOR is 6 percent. Then the call option is in-the-money. The payoff to the holder of the option is

$$(\$10{,}000{,}000)\,(0.06 - 0.055)\left(\frac{180}{360}\right) = \$25{,}000$$

This money is not paid at expiration, however; it is paid 180 days later. There is no reason why the payoff could not be made at expiration, as is done with an FRA. The delay of payment associated with interest rate options actually makes more sense, because these instruments are commonly used to hedge floating-rate loans in which the rate is set on a given day but the interest is paid later.

Note that the difference between the underlying rate and the exercise rate is multiplied by 180/360 to reflect the fact that the rate quoted is a 180-day rate but is stated as an annual rate. Also, the interest calculation is multiplied by the notional principal.

In general, the payoff of an interest rate call is

$$(\text{Notional Principal})\,\text{Max}\,(0, \text{Underlying rate at expiration}$$
$$- \text{Exercise rate})\left(\frac{\text{Days in underlying rate}}{360}\right) \qquad \textbf{(66-1)}$$

The expression Max(0,Underlying rate at expiration − Exercise rate) is similar to a form that we shall commonly see throughout this reading for all options. The payoff of a call option at expiration is based on the maximum of zero or the underlying minus the exercise rate. If the option expires out-of-the-money, then "Underlying rate at expiration − Exercise rate" is negative; consequently, zero is greater. Thus, the option expires with no value. If the option expires in-the-money, "Underlying rate at expiration − Exercise rate" is positive. Thus, the option expires worth this difference (multiplied by the notional principal and the Days/360 adjustment). The expression "Days in underlying rate," which we used in Reading 64, refers to the fact that the rate is specified as the rate on an instrument of a specific number of days to maturity, such as a 90-day or 180-day rate, thereby requiring that we multiply by 90/360 or 180/360 or some similar adjustment.

For an interest rate put option, the general formula is

$$(\text{Notional Principal})\,\text{Max}\,(0, \text{Exercise rate}$$
$$- \text{Underlying rate at expiration})\left(\frac{\text{Days in underlying rate}}{360}\right) \qquad \textbf{(66-2)}$$

For an exercise rate of 5.5 percent and an underlying rate at expiration of 6 percent, an interest rate put expires out-of-the-money. Only if the underlying rate is less than the exercise rate does the put option expire in-the-money.

As noted above, borrowers often use interest rate call options to hedge the risk of rising rates on floating-rate loans. Lenders often use interest rate put options to hedge the risk of falling rates on floating-rate loans. The form we have seen here, in which the option expires with a single payoff, is not the more commonly used variety of interest rate option. Floating-rate loans usually involve multiple interest payments. Each of those payments is set on a given date. To hedge the risk of interest rates increasing, the borrower would need options expiring on each rate reset date. Thus, the borrower would require a combination of interest rate call options. Likewise, a lender needing to hedge the risk of falling rates on a multiple-payment floating-rate loan would need a combination of interest rate put options.

A combination of interest rate calls is referred to as an **interest rate cap** or sometimes just a **cap**. A combination of interest rate puts is called an **interest rate floor** or sometimes just a **floor**.[8] Specifically, *an interest rate cap is a series of call options on an interest rate, with each option expiring at the date on which the floating loan rate will be reset, and with each option having the same exercise rate.*[9] Each option is independent of the others; thus, exercise of one option does not affect the right to exercise any of the others. Each component call option is called a **caplet**. *An interest rate floor is a series of put options on an interest rate, with each option expiring at the date on which the floating loan rate will be reset, and with each option having the same exercise rate.* Each component put option is called a **floorlet**. The price of an interest rate cap or floor is the sum of the prices of the options that make up the cap or floor.

A special combination of caps and floors is called an **interest rate collar**. *An interest rate collar is a combination of a long cap and a short floor or a short cap and a long floor.* Consider a borrower in a floating rate loan who wants to hedge the risk of rising interest rates but is concerned about the requirement that this hedge must have a cash outlay up front: the option premium. A collar, which adds a short floor to a long cap, is a way of reducing and even eliminating the up-front cost of the cap. The sale of the floor brings in cash that reduces the cost of the cap. It is possible to set the exercise rates such that the price received for the sale of the floor precisely offsets the price paid for the cap, thereby completely eliminating the up-front cost. This transaction is sometimes called a **zero-cost collar**. The term is a bit misleading, however, and brings to mind the importance of noting the true cost of a collar. Although the cap allows the borrower to be paid from the call options when rates are high, the sale of the floor requires the borrower to pay the counterparty when rates are low. Thus, the cost of protection against rising rates is the loss of the advantage of falling rates. Caps, floors, and collars are popular instruments in the interest rate markets.

Although interest rate options are primarily written on such rates as LIBOR, Euribor, and Euroyen, the underlying can be any interest rate.

---

[8] It is possible to construct caps and floors with options on any other type of underlying, but they are very often used when the underlying is an interest rate.

[9] Technically, each option need not have the same exercise rate, but they generally do.

4.1.5 Currency Options

As we noted in Reading 64, the currency forward market is quite large. The same is true for the currency options market. A **currency option** allows the holder to buy (if a call) or sell (if a put) an underlying currency at a fixed exercise rate, expressed as an exchange rate. Many companies, knowing that they will need to convert a currency X at a future date into a currency Y, will buy a call option on currency Y specified in terms of currency X. For example, say that a U.S. company will be needing €50 million for an expansion project in three months. Thus, it will be buying euros and is exposed to the risk of the euro rising against the dollar. Even though it has that concern, it would also like to benefit if the euro weakens against the dollar. Thus, it might buy a call option on the euro. Let us say it specifies an exercise rate of $0.90. So it pays cash up front for the right to buy €50 million at a rate of $0.90 per euro. If the option expires with the euro above $0.90, it can buy euros at $0.90 and avoid any additional cost over $0.90. If the option expires with the euro below $0.90, it does not exercise the option and buys euros at the market rate.

Note closely these two cases:

Euro expires above $0.90
Company buys €50 million at $0.90
Euro expires at or below $0.90
Company buys €50 million at the market rate

These outcomes can also be viewed in the following manner:

Dollar expires below €1.1111, that is, €1 > $0.90
Company sells $45 million (€50 million × $0.90) at €1.1111, equivalent to buying €50 million
Dollar expires above €1.1111, that is, €1 < $0.90
Company sells sufficient dollars to buy €50 million at the market rate

This transaction looks more like a put in which the underlying is the dollar and the exercise rate is expressed as €1.1111. Thus, the call on the euro can be viewed as a put on the dollar. Specifically, a call to buy €50 million at an exercise price of $0.90 is also a put to sell €50 million × $0.90 = $45 million at an exercise price of 1/$0.90, or €1.1111.

Most foreign currency options activity occurs on the customized over-the-counter markets. Some exchange-listed currency options trade on a few exchanges, but activity is fairly low.

4.2 Options on Futures

In Reading 64 we covered futures markets. One of the important innovations of futures markets is options on futures. These contracts originated in the United States as a result of a regulatory structure that separated exchange-listed options and futures markets. The former are regulated by the Securities and Exchange Commission, and the latter are regulated by the Commodity Futures Trading Commission (**CFTC**). SEC regulations forbid the trading of options side by side with their underlying instruments. Options on stocks trade on one exchange, and the underlying trades on another or on Nasdaq.

The futures exchanges got the idea that they could offer options in which the underlying is a futures contract; no such prohibitions for side-by-side trading existed under CFTC rules. As a result, the futures exchanges were able to add an attractive instrument to their product lines. The side-by-side trading of the option and its underlying futures made for excellent arbitrage linkages between these instruments. Moreover, some of the options on futures are designed to expire on the same day the underlying futures expires. Thus, the options on the futures are effectively options on the spot asset that underlies the futures.

A call option on a futures gives the holder the right to enter into a long futures contract at a fixed futures price. A put option on a futures gives the holder the right to enter into a short futures contract at a fixed futures price. The fixed futures price is, of course, the exercise price. Consider an option on the Eurodollar futures contract trading at the Chicago Mercantile Exchange. On 13 June of a particular year, an option expiring on 13 July was based on the July Eurodollar futures contract. That futures contract expires on 16 July, a few days after the option expires.[10] The call option with exercise price of 95.75 had a price of $4.60. The underlying futures price was 96.21. Recall that this price is the IMM index value, which means that the price is based on a discount rate of $100 - 96.21 = 3.79$. The contract size is $1 million.

The buyer of this call option on a futures would pay $0.046(\$1,000,000) = \$46,000$ and would obtain the right to buy the July futures contract at a price of 95.75. Thus, at that time, the option was in the money by $96.21 - 95.75 = 0.46$ per $100 face value. Suppose that when the option expires, the futures price is 96.00. Then the holder of the call would exercise it and obtain a long futures position at a price of 95.75. The price of the underlying futures is 96.00, so the margin account is immediately marked to market with a credit of 0.25 or $625.[11] The party on the short side of the contract is immediately set up with a short futures contract at the price of 95.75. That party will be charged the $625 gain that the long made. If the option is a put, exercise of it establishes a short position. The exchange assigns the put writer a long futures position.

4.3 Commodity Options

Options in which the asset underlying the option is a commodity, such as oil, gold, wheat, or soybeans, are also widely traded. There are exchange-traded as well as over-the-counter versions. Over-the-counter options on oil are widely used.

Our focus in this reading is on financial instruments so we will not spend any time on commodity options, but readers should be aware of the existence and use of these instruments by companies whose business involves the buying and selling of these commodities.

---

[10] Some options on futures expire a month or so before the futures expires. Others expire very close to, if not at, the futures expiration.

[11] If the contract is in-the-money by $96 - 95.75 = 0.25$ per $100 par, it is in-the-money by $0.25/100 = 0.0025$, or 0.25 percent of the face value. Because the face value is $1 million, the contract is in the money by $(0.0025)(90/360)(\$1,000,000) = \$625$. (Note the adjustment by 90/360) Another way to look at this calculation is that the futures price at 95.75 is $1 - (0.0425)(90/360) = \$0.989375$ per $1 par, or $989,375. At 96, the futures price is $1 - 0.04(90/360) = \$0.99$ per $1 par or $990,000. The difference is $625. So, exercising this option is like entering into a futures contract at a price of $989,375 and having the price immediately go to $990,000, a gain of $625. The call holder must deposit money to meet the Eurodollar futures margin, but the exercise of the option gives him $625. In other words, assuming he meets the minimum initial margin requirement, he is immediately credited with $625 more.

4.4 Other Types of Options

As derivative markets develop, options (and even some other types of derivatives) have begun to emerge on such underlyings as electricity, various sources of energy, and even weather. These instruments are almost exclusively customized over-the-counter instruments. Perhaps the most notable feature of these instruments is how the underlyings are often instruments that cannot actually be held. For example, electricity is not considered a storable asset because it is produced and almost immediately consumed, but it is nonetheless an asset and certainly has a volatile price. Consequently, it is ideally suited for options and other derivatives trading.

Consider weather. It is hardly an asset at all but simply a random factor that exerts an enormous influence on economic activity. The need to hedge against and speculate on the weather has created a market in which measures of weather activity, such as economic losses from storms or average temperature or rainfall, are structured into a derivative instrument. Option versions of these derivatives are growing in importance and use. For example, consider a company that generates considerable revenue from outdoor summer activities, provided that it does not rain. Obviously a certain amount of rain will occur, but the more rain, the greater the losses for the company. It could buy a call option on the amount of rainfall with the exercise price stated as a quantity of rainfall. If actual rainfall exceeds the exercise price, the company exercises the option and receives an amount of money related to the excess of the rainfall amount over the exercise price.

Another type of option, which is not at all new but is increasingly recognized in practice, is the real option. A real option is an option associated with the flexibility inherent in capital investment projects. For example, companies may invest in new projects that have the option to defer the full investment, expand or contract the project at a later date, or even terminate the project. In fact, most capital investment projects have numerous elements of flexibility that can be viewed as options. Of course, these options do not trade in markets the same way as financial and commodity options, and they must be evaluated much more carefully. They are, nonetheless, options and thus have the potential for generating enormous value.

Again, our emphasis is on financial options, but readers should be aware of the growing role of these other types of options in our economy. Investors who buy shares in companies that have real options are, in effect, buying real options. In addition, commodity and other types of options are sometimes found in investment portfolios in the form of "alternative investments" and can provide significant diversification benefits.

To this point, we have examined characteristics of options markets and contracts. Now we move forward to the all-important topic of how options are priced.

PRINCIPLES OF OPTION PRICING   5

In Readings 64 and 65, we discussed the pricing and valuation of forward and futures contracts. Recall that the value of a contract is what someone must pay to buy into it or what someone would receive to sell out of it. A forward or futures contract has zero value at the start of the contract, but the value turns positive or negative as prices or rates change. A contract that has positive value to one party and negative value to the counterparty can turn around and have negative value to the former and positive value to the latter as prices or rates change. The forward or futures price is the price that the parties agree will be paid on the future date to buy and sell the underlying.

With options, these concepts are different. An option has a positive value at the start. The buyer must pay money and the seller receives money to initiate the contract. Prior to expiration, the option always has positive value to the buyer and negative value to the seller. In a forward or futures contract, the two parties agree on the fixed price the buyer will pay the seller. This fixed price is set such that the buyer and seller do not exchange any money. The corresponding fixed price at which a call holder can buy the underlying or a put holder can sell the underlying is the exercise price. It, too, is negotiated between buyer and seller but still results in the buyer paying the seller money up front in the form of an option premium or price.[12]

Thus, what we called the forward or futures price corresponds more to the exercise price of an option. The option price *is* the option value: With a few exceptions that will be clearly noted, in this reading we do not distinguish between the option price and value.

In this section of the reading, we examine the principles of option pricing. These principles are characteristics of option prices that are governed by the rationality of investors. These principles alone do not allow us to calculate the option price. We do that in Section 6.

Before we begin, it is important to remind the reader that we assume all participants in the market behave in a rational manner such that they do not throw away money and that they take advantage of arbitrage opportunities. As such, we assume that markets are sufficiently competitive that no arbitrage opportunities exist.

Let us start by developing the notation, which is very similar to what we have used previously. Note that time 0 is today and time T is the expiration.

S_0, S_T = price of the underlying asset at time 0 (today) and time T (expiration)
X = exercise price
r = risk-free rate
T = time to expiration, equal to number of days to expiration divided by 365
c_0, c_T = price of European call today and at expiration
C_0, C_T = price of American call today and at expiration
p_0, p_T = price of European put today and at expiration
P_0, P_T = price of American put today and at expiration

On occasion, we will introduce some variations of the above as well as some new notation. For example, we start off with no cash flows on the underlying, but we shall discuss the effects of cash flows on the underlying in Section 5.7.

5.1 Payoff Values

The easiest time to determine an option's value is at expiration. At that point, there is no future. Only the present matters. An option's value at expiration is called its **payoff**. We introduced this material briefly in our basic descriptions of types of options; now we cover it in more depth.

At expiration, a call option is worth either zero or the difference between the underlying price and the exercise price, whichever is greater:

$$c_T = \text{Max}(0, S_T - X)$$
$$C_T = \text{Max}(0, S_T - X)$$

(66-3)

---

[12] For a call, there is no finite exercise price that drives the option price to zero. For a put, the unrealistic example of a zero exercise price would make the put price be zero.

Note that at expiration, a European option and an American option have the same payoff because they are equivalent instruments at that point.

The expression $Max(0, S_T - X)$ means to take the greater of zero or $S_T - X$. Suppose the underlying price exceeds the exercise price, $S_T > X$. In this case, the option is expiring in-the-money and the option is worth $S_T - X$. Suppose that at the instant of expiration, it is possible to buy the option for less than $S_T - X$. Then one could buy the option, immediately exercise it, and immediately sell the underlying. Doing so would cost c_T (or C_T) for the option and X to buy the underlying but would bring in S_T for the sale of the underlying. If c_T (or C_T) < $S_T - X$, this transaction would net an immediate risk-free profit. The collective actions of all investors doing this would force the option price up to $S_T - X$. The price could not go higher than $S_T - X$, because all that the option holder would end up with an instant later when the option expires is $S_T - X$. If $S_T < X$, meaning that the call is expiring out-of-the-money, the formula says the option should be worth zero. It cannot sell for less than zero because that would mean that the option seller would have to pay the option buyer. A buyer would not pay more than zero, because the option will expire an instant later with no value.

At expiration, a put option is worth either zero or the difference between the exercise price and the underlying price, whichever is greater.

$$p_T = Max(0, X - S_T)$$
$$P_T = Max(0, X - S_T)$$

(66-4)

Suppose $S_T < X$, meaning that the put is expiring in-the-money. At the instant of expiration, suppose the put is selling for less than $X - S_T$. Then an investor buys the put for p_T (or P_T) and the underlying for S_T and exercises the put, receiving X. If p_T (or P_T) < $X - S_T$, this transaction will net an immediate risk-free profit. The combined actions of participants doing this will force the put price up to $X - S_T$. It cannot go any higher, because the put buyer will end up an instant later with only $X - S_T$ and would not pay more than this. If $S_T > X$, meaning that the put is expiring out-of-the-money, it is worth zero. It cannot be worth less than zero because the option seller would have to pay the option buyer. It cannot be worth more than zero because the buyer would not pay for a position that, an instant later, will be worth nothing.

These important results are summarized along with an example in Exhibit 66-5. The payoff diagrams for the short positions are also shown and are obtained as the negative of the long positions. For the special case of $S_T = X$, meaning that both call and put are expiring at-the-money, we can effectively treat the option as out-of-the-money because it is worth zero at expiration.

The value $Max(0, S_T - X)$ for calls or $Max(0, X - S_T)$ for puts is also called the option's **intrinsic value** or **exercise value**. We shall use the former terminology. Intrinsic value is what the option is worth to exercise it based on current conditions. In this section, we have talked only about the option at expiration. Prior to expiration, an option will normally sell for more than its intrinsic value.[13] The difference between the market price of the option and its intrinsic value is called its **time value** or **speculative value**. We shall use the former terminology. The time value reflects the potential for the option's intrinsic value at expiration to be greater than its current intrinsic value. At expiration, of course, the time value is zero.

---

[13] We shall later see an exception to this statement for European puts, but for now take it as the truth.

EXHIBIT 66-5	Option Values at Expiration (Payoffs)		
		Example (X = 50)	
Option	**Value**	**$S_T = 52$**	**$S_T = 48$**
European call	$c_T = \text{Max}(0, S_T - X)$	$c_T = \text{Max}(0, 52 - 50) = 2$	$c_T = \text{Max}(0, 48 - 50) = 0$
American call	$C_T = \text{Max}(0, S_T - X)$	$C_T = \text{Max}(0, 52 - 50) = 2$	$C_T = \text{Max}(0, 48 - 50) = 0$
European put	$p_T = \text{Max}(0, X - S_T)$	$p_T = \text{Max}(0, 50 - 52) = 0$	$p_T = \text{Max}(0, 50 - 48) = 2$
American put	$P_T = \text{Max}(0, X - S_T)$	$P_T = \text{Max}(0, 50 - 52) = 0$	$P_T = \text{Max}(0, 50 - 48) = 2$

Notes: Results for the European and American calls correspond to Graph A. Results for Graph B are the negative of Graph A. Results for the European and American puts correspond to Graph C, and results for Graph D are the negative of Graph C.

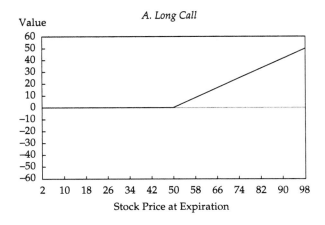

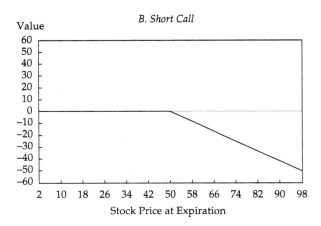

(Exhibit continued on next page ...)

EXHIBIT 66-5   (continued)

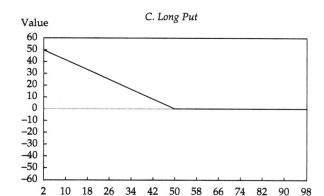

C. Long Put

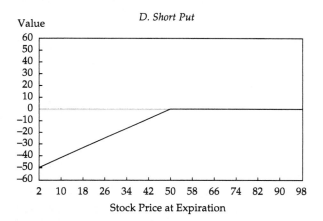

D. Short Put

Practice Problem 1

For Parts A through E, determine the payoffs of calls and puts under the conditions given.

A. The underlying is a stock index and is at 5,601.19 when the options expire. The multiplier is 500. The exercise price is

   i. 5,500

   ii. 6,000

B. The underlying is a bond and is at $1.035 per $1 par when the options expire. The contract is on $100,000 face value of bonds. The exercise price is

   i. $1.00

   ii. $1.05

C. The underlying is a 90-day interest rate and is at 9 percent when the options expire. The notional principal is $50 million. The exercise rate is

  i. 8 percent

  ii. 10.5 percent

D. The underlying is the Swiss franc and is at $0.775 when the options expire. The options are on SF500,000. The exercise price is

  i. $0.75

  ii. $0.81

E. The underlying is a futures contract and is at 110.5 when the options expire. The options are on a futures contract covering $1 million of the underlying. These prices are percentages of par. The exercise price is

  i. 110

  ii. 115

For Parts F and G, determine the payoffs of the strategies indicated and describe the payoff graph.

F. The underlying is a stock priced at $40. A call option with an exercise price of $40 is selling for $7. You buy the stock and sell the call. At expiration, the stock price is

  i. $52

  ii. $38

G. The underlying is a stock priced at $60. A put option with an exercise price of $60 is priced at $5. You buy the stock and buy the put. At expiration, the stock price is

  i. $68

  ii. $50

▶ **Solution to A.** **i.** Calls: $\text{Max}(0, 5601.19 - 5500) \times 500 = 50{,}595$
Puts: $\text{Max}(0, 5500 - 5601.19) \times 500 = 0$

    ii. Calls: $\text{Max}(0, 5601.19 - 6000) \times 500 = 0$
Puts: $\text{Max}(0, 6000 - 5601.19) \times 500 = 199{,}405$

▶ **Solution to B.** **i.** Calls: $\text{Max}(0, 1.035 - 1.00) \times \$100{,}000 = \$3{,}500$
Puts: $\text{Max}(0, 1.00 - 1.035) \times \$100{,}000 = \$0$

    ii. Calls: $\text{Max}(0, 1.035 - 1.05) \times \$100{,}000 = \$0$
Puts: $\text{Max}(0, 1.05 - 1.035) \times \$100{,}000 = \$1{,}500$

▶ **Solution to C.** **i.** Calls: $\text{Max}(0, 0.09 - 0.08) \times (90/360) \times$
$\$50{,}000{,}000 = \$125{,}000$
Puts: $\text{Max}(0, 0.08 - 0.09) \times (90/360) \times$
$\$50{,}000{,}000 = \$0$

    ii. Calls: $\text{Max}(0, 0.09 - 0.105) \times (90/360) \times$
$\$50{,}000{,}000 = \$0$
Puts: $\text{Max}(0, 0.105 - 0.09) \times (90/360) \times$
$\$50{,}000{,}000 = \$187{,}500$

▶ **Solution to D. i.** Calls: $\text{Max}(0, 0.775 - 0.75) \times \$500{,}000 = \$12{,}500$
Puts: $\text{Max}(0, 0.75 - 0.775) \times \$500{,}000 = \$0$

   ii. Calls: $\text{Max}(0, 0.775 - 0.81) \times \$500{,}000 = \$0$
Puts: $\text{Max}(0, 0.81 - 0.775) \times \$500{,}000 = \$17{,}500$

▶ **Solution to E. i.** Calls: $\text{Max}(0, 110.5 - 110) \times (1/100) \times \$1{,}000{,}000 = \$5{,}000$
Puts: $\text{Max}(0, 110 - 110.5) \times (1/100) \times \$1{,}000{,}000 = \$0$

   ii. Calls: $\text{Max}(0, 110.5 - 115) \times (1/100) \times \$1{,}000{,}000 = \$0$
Puts: $\text{Max}(0, 115 - 110.5) \times (1/100) \times \$1{,}000{,}000 = \$45{,}000$

▶ **Solution to F. i.** $52 - \text{Max}(0, 52 - 40) = 40$
   ii. $38 - \text{Max}(0, 38 - 40) = 38$

For any value of the stock price at expiration of 40 or above, the payoff is constant at 40. For stock price values below 40 at expiration, the payoff declines with the stock price. The graph would look similar to the short put in Panel D of Exhibit 66-5. This strategy is known as a covered call.

▶ **Solution to G. i.** $68 + \text{Max}(0, 60 - 68) = 68$
   ii. $50 + \text{Max}(0, 60 - 50) = 60$

For any value of the stock price at expiration of 60 or below, the payoff is constant at 60. For stock price values above 60 at expiration, the payoff increases with the stock price at expiration. The graph will look similar to the long call in Panel A of Exhibit 66-5. This strategy is known as a **protective put** and is covered later in this reading.

There is no question that everyone agrees on the option's intrinsic value; after all, it is based on the current stock price and exercise price. It is the time value that we have more difficulty estimating. So remembering that *Option price = Intrinsic value + Time value*, let us move forward and attempt to determine the value of an option today, prior to expiration.

5.2 Boundary Conditions

We start by examining some simple results that establish minimum and maximum values for options prior to expiration.

5.2.1 Minimum and Maximum Values

The first and perhaps most obvious result is one we have already alluded to: *The minimum value of any option is zero.* We state this formally as

$$c_0 \geq 0, C_0 \geq 0$$
$$p_0 \geq 0, P_0 \geq 0$$

(66-5)

No option can sell for less than zero, for in that case the writer would have to pay the buyer.

Now consider the maximum value of an option. It differs somewhat depending on whether the option is a call or a put and whether it is European or American. *The maximum value of a call is the current value of the underlying:*

$$c_0 \leq S_0, C_0 \leq S_0 \qquad \textbf{(66-6)}$$

A call is a means of buying the underlying. It would not make sense to pay more for the right to buy the underlying than the value of the underlying itself.

For a put, it makes a difference whether the put is European or American. One way to see the maximum value for puts is to consider the best possible outcome for the put holder. The best outcome is that the underlying goes to a value of zero. Then the put holder could sell a worthless asset for X. For an American put, the holder could sell it immediately and capture a value of X. For a European put, the holder would have to wait until expiration; consequently, we must discount X from the expiration day to the present. Thus, *the maximum value of a European put is the present value of the exercise price. The maximum value of an American put is the exercise price,*

$$P_0 \leq X/(1 + r)^T, P_0 \leq X \qquad \textbf{(66-7)}$$

where r is the risk-free interest rate and T is the time to expiration. These results for the maximums and minimums for calls and puts are summarized in Exhibit 66-6, which also includes a numerical example.

EXHIBIT 66-6	**Minimum and Maximum Values of Options**		
Option	Minimum Value	Maximum Value	Example ($S_0 = 52$, $X = 50$, $r = 5\%$, $T = 1/2$ year)
European call	$c_0 \geq 0$	$c_0 \leq S_0$	$0 \leq c_0 \leq 52$
American call	$C_0 \geq 0$	$C_0 \leq S_0$	$0 \leq C_0 \leq 52$
European put	$p_0 \geq 0$	$p_0 \leq X/(1 + r)^T$	$0 \leq p_0 \leq 48.80 \ [48.80 = 50/(1.05)^{0.5}]$
American put	$P_0 \geq 0$	$P_0 \leq X$	$0 \leq P_0 \leq 50$

5.2.2 *Lower Bounds*

The results we established in Section 5.2.1 do not put much in the way of restrictions on the option price. They tell us that the price is somewhere between zero and the maximum, which is either the underlying price, the exercise price, or the present value of the exercise price—a fairly wide range of possibilities. Fortunately, we can tighten the range up a little on the low side: We can establish a **lower bound** on the option price.

For American options, which are exercisable immediately, we can state that the lower bound of an American option price is its current intrinsic value:[14]

---

[14] Normally we have italicized sentences containing important results. This one, however, is a little different: We are stating it temporarily. We shall soon show that we can override one of these results with a lower bound that is higher and, therefore, is a better lower bound.

$$C_0 \geq \text{Max}(0, S_0 - X)$$
$$P_0 \geq \text{Max}(0, X - S_0)$$

(66-8)

The reason these results hold today is the same reason we have already shown for why they must hold at expiration. If the option is in-the-money and is selling for less than its intrinsic value, it can be bought and exercised to net an immediate risk-free profit.[15] The collective actions of market participants doing this will force the American option price up to at least the intrinsic value.

Unfortunately, we cannot make such a statement about European options—but we can show that the lower bound is either zero or the current underlying price minus the present value of the exercise price, whichever is greater. They cannot be exercised early; thus, there is no way for market participants to exercise an option selling for too little with respect to its intrinsic value. Fortunately, however, there is a way to establish a lower bound for European options. We can combine options with risk-free bonds and the underlying in such a way that a lower bound for the option price emerges.

First, we need the ability to buy and sell a risk-free bond with a face value equal to the exercise price and current value equal to the present value of the exercise price. This procedure is simple but perhaps not obvious. If the exercise price is X (say, 100), we buy a bond with a face value of X (100) maturing on the option expiration day. The current value of that bond is the present value of X, which is $X/(1 + r)^T$. So we buy the bond today for $X/(1 + r)^T$ and hold it until it matures on the option expiration day, at which time it will pay off X. We assume that we can buy or sell (issue) this type of bond. Note that this transaction involves borrowing or lending an amount of money equal to the present value of the exercise price with repayment of the full exercise price.

Exhibit 66-7 illustrates the construction of a special combination of instruments. We buy the European call and the risk-free bond and sell short the underlying asset. Recall that short selling involves borrowing the asset and selling it. At expiration, we shall buy back the asset. In order to illustrate the logic behind the lower bound for a European call in the simplest way, we assume that we can sell short without any restrictions.

In Exhibit 66-7 the two right-hand columns contain the value of each instrument when the option expires. The rightmost column is the case of the call

EXHIBIT 66-7   **A Lower Bound Combination for European Calls**

Transaction	Current Value	Value at Expiration	
		$S_T \leq X$	$S_T > X$
Buy call	c_0	0	$S_T - X$
Sell short underlying	$-S_0$	$-S_T$	$-S_T$
Buy bond	$X/(1 + r)^T$	X	X
Total	$c_0 - S_0 + X/(1 + r)^T$	$X - S_T \geq 0$	0

[15] Consider, for example, an in-the-money call selling for less than $S_0 - X$. One can buy the call for C_0, exercise it, paying X, and sell the underlying netting a gain of $S_0 - X - C_0$. This value is positive and represents an immediate risk-free gain. If the option is an in-the-money put selling for less than $X - S_0$, one can buy the put for P_0, buy the underlying for S_0, and exercise the put to receive X, thereby netting an immediate risk-free gain of $X - S_0 - P_0$.

expiring in-the-money, in which case it is worth $S_T - X$. In the other column, the out-of-the-money case, the call is worth zero. The underlying is worth $-S_T$ (the negative of its current value) in either case, reflecting the fact that we buy it back to cover the short position. The bond is worth X in both cases. The sum of all the positions is positive when the option expires out-of-the-money and zero when the option expires in-the-money. Therefore, in no case does this combination of instruments have a negative value. That means that we never have to pay out any money at expiration. We are guaranteed at least no loss at expiration and possibly something positive.

If there is a possibility of a positive outcome from the combination and if we know we shall never have to pay anything out from holding a combination of instruments, the cost of that combination must be positive—it must cost us something to enter into the position. We cannot take in money to enter into the position. In that case, we would be receiving money up front and never having to pay anything out. The cost of entering the position is shown in the second column, labeled the "Current Value." Because that value must be positive, we therefore require that $c_0 - S_0 + X/(1 + r)^T \geq 0$. Rearranging this equation, we obtain $c_0 \geq S_0 - X/(1 + r)^T$. Now we have a statement about the minimum value of the option, which can serve as a lower bound. This result is solid, because if the call is selling for less than $S_0 - X/(1 + r)^T$, an investor can buy the call, sell short the underlying, and buy the bond. Doing so would bring in money up front and, as we see in Exhibit 66-7, an investor would not have to pay out any money at expiration and might even get a little more money. Because other investors would do the same, the call price would be forced up until it is at least $S_0 - X/(1 + r)^T$.

But we can improve on this result. Suppose $S_0 - X/(1 + r)^T$ is negative. Then we are stating that the call price is greater than a negative number. But we already know that the call price cannot be negative. So we can now say that

$$c_0 \geq \text{Max}[0, S_0 - X/(1 + r)^T]$$

In other words, *the lower bound on a European call price is either zero or the underlying price minus the present value of the exercise price, whichever is greater.* Notice how this lower bound differs from the lower bound for the American call, $\text{Max}(0, S_0 - X)$. For the European call, we must wait to pay the exercise price and obtain the underlying. Therefore, the expression contains the current underlying value—the present value of its future value—as well as the present value of the exercise price. For the American call, we do not have to wait until expiration; therefore, the expression reflects the potential to immediately receive the underlying price minus the exercise price. We shall have more to say, however, about the relationship between these two values.

To illustrate the lower bound, let X = 50, r = 0.05, and T = 0.5. If the current underlying price is 45, then the lower bound for the European call is

$$\text{Max}[0, 45 - 50/(1.05)^{0.5}] = \text{Max}(0, 45 - 48.80) = \text{Max}(0, -3.80) = 0$$

All this calculation tells us is that the call must be worth no less than zero, which we already knew. If the current underlying price is 54, however, the lower bound for the European call is

$$\text{Max}(0, 54 - 48.80) = \text{Max}(0, 5.20) = 5.20$$

which tells us that the call must be worth no less than 5.20. With European puts, we can also see that the lower bound differs from the lower bound on American puts in this same use of the present value of the exercise price.

EXHIBIT 66-8	A Lower Bound Combination for European Puts		
		Value at Expiration	
Transaction	**Current Value**	$S_T < X$	$S_T \geq X$
Buy put	p_0	$X - S_T$	0
Buy underlying	S_0	S_T	S_T
Issue bond	$-X/(1 + r)^T$	$-X$	$-X$
Total	$p_0 + S_0 - X/(1 + r)^T$	0	$S_T - X \geq 0$

Exhibit 66-8 constructs a similar type of portfolio for European puts. Here, however, we buy the put and the underlying and borrow by issuing the zero-coupon bond. The payoff of each instrument is indicated in the two rightmost columns. Note that the total payoff is never less than zero. Consequently, the initial value of the combination must not be less than zero. Therefore, $p_0 + S_0 - X/(1 + r)^T \geq 0$. Isolating the put price gives us $p_0 \geq X/(1 + r)^T - S_0$. But suppose that $X/(1 + r)^T - S_0$ is negative. Then, the put price must be greater than a negative number. We know that the put price must be no less than zero. So we can now formally say that

$$p_0 \geq \text{Max}[0, X/(1 + r)^T - S_0]$$

In other words, *the lower bound of a European put is the greater of either zero or the present value of the exercise price minus the underlying price.* For the American put, recall that the expression was $\text{Max}(0, X - S_0)$. So for the European put, we adjust this value to the present value of the exercise price. The present value of the asset price is already adjusted to S_0.

Using the same example we did for calls, let $X = 50$, $r = 0.05$, and $T = 0.5$. If the current underlying price is 45, then the lower bound for the European put is

$$\text{Max}(0, 50/(1.05)^{0.5} - 45) = \text{Max}(0, 48.80 - 45) = \text{Max}(0, 3.80) = 3.80$$

If the current underlying price is 54, however, the lower bound is

$$\text{Max}(0, 48.80 - 54) = \text{Max}(0, -5.20) = 0$$

At this point let us reconsider what we have found. The lower bound for a European call is $\text{Max}[0, S_0 - X/(1 + r)^T]$. We also observed that an American call must be worth at least $\text{Max}(0, S_0 - X)$. But except at expiration, the European lower bound is greater than the minimum value of the American call.[16] We could not, however, expect an American call to be worth less than a European call. Thus the lower bound of the European call holds for American calls as well. Hence, we can conclude that

$$c_0 \geq \text{Max}[0, S_0 - X/(1 + r)^T]$$
$$C_0 \geq \text{Max}[0, S_0 - X/(1 + r)^T]$$

(66-9)

---

[16] We discuss this point more formally and in the context of whether it is ever worthwhile to exercise an American call early in Section 5.6.

For European puts, the lower bound is $\text{Max}[0, X/(1 + r)^T - S_0]$. For American puts, the minimum price is $\text{Max}(0, X - S_0)$. The European lower bound is lower than the minimum price of the American put, so the American put lower bound is not changed to the European lower bound, the way we did for calls. Hence,

$$p_0 \geq \text{Max}[0, X/(1 + r)^T - S_0]$$
$$P_0 \geq \text{Max}(0, X - S_0)$$

(66-10)

These results tell us the lowest possible price for European and American options.

Recall that we previously referred to an option price as having an intrinsic value and a time value. For American options, the intrinsic value is the value if exercised, $\text{Max}(0, S_0 - X)$ for calls and $\text{Max}(0, X - S_0)$ for puts. The remainder of the option price is the time value. For European options, the notion of a time value is somewhat murky, because it first requires recognition of an intrinsic value. Because a European option cannot be exercised until expiration, in a sense, all of the value of a European option is time value. The notion of an intrinsic value and its complement, a time value, is therefore inappropriate for European options, though the concepts are commonly applied to European options. Fortunately, understanding European options does not require that we separate intrinsic value from time value. We shall include them together as they make up the option price.

Practice Problem 2

Consider call and put options expiring in 42 days, in which the underlying is at 72 and the risk-free rate is 4.5 percent. The underlying makes no cash payments during the life of the options.

A. Find the lower bounds for European calls and puts with exercise prices of 70 and 75.

B. Find the lower bounds for American calls and puts with exercise prices of 70 and 75.

▶ **Solution to A.**
70 call: $\text{Max}[0, 72 - 70/(1.045)^{0.1151}] = \text{Max}(0, 2.35) = 2.35$
75 call: $\text{Max}[0, 72 - 75/(1.045)^{0.1151}] = \text{Max}(0, -2.62) = 0$
70 put: $\text{Max}[0, 70/(1.045)^{0.1151} - 72] = \text{Max}(0, -2.35) = 0$
75 put: $\text{Max}[0, 75/(1.045)^{0.1151} - 72] = \text{Max}(0, 2.62) = 2.62$

▶ **Solution to B.**
70 call: $\text{Max}[0, 72 - 70/(1.045)^{0.1151}] = \text{Max}(0, 2.35) = 2.35$
75 call: $\text{Max}[0, 72 - 75/(1.045)^{0.1151}] = \text{Max}(0, -2.62) = 0$
70 put: $\text{Max}(0, 70 - 72) = 0$
75 put: $\text{Max}(0, 75 - 72) = 3$

		Value at Expiration		
Transaction	Current Value	$S_T \leq X_1$	$X_1 < S_T < X_2$	$S_T \geq X_2$
Buy call ($X = X_1$)	$c_0(X_1)$	0	$S_T - X_1$	$S_T - X_1$
Sell call ($X = X_2$)	$-c_0(X_2)$	0	0	$-(S_T - X_2)$
Total	$c_0(X_1) - c_0(X_2)$	0	$S_T - X_1 > 0$	$X_2 - X_1 > 0$

EXHIBIT 66-9 — Portfolio Combination for European Calls Illustrating the Effect of Differences in Exercise Prices

5.3 The Effect of a Difference in Exercise Price

Now consider two options on the same underlying with the same expiration day but different exercise prices. Generally, the higher the exercise price, the lower the value of a call and the higher the price of a put. To see this, let the two exercise prices be X_1 and X_2, with X_1 being the smaller. Let $c_0(X_1)$ be the price of a European call with exercise price X_1 and $c_0(X_2)$ be the price of a European call with exercise price X_2. We refer to these as the X_1 call and the X_2 call. In Exhibit 66-9, we construct a combination in which we buy the X_1 call and sell the X_2 call.[17]

Note first that the three outcomes are all non-negative. This fact establishes that the current value of the combination, $c_0(X_1) - c_0(X_2)$ has to be non-negative. We have to pay out at least as much for the X_1 call as we take in for the X_2 call; otherwise, we would get money up front, have the possibility of a positive value at expiration, and never have to pay any money out. Thus, because $c_0(X_1) - c_0(X_2) \geq 0$, we restate this result as

$$c_0(X_1) \geq c_0(X_2)$$

This expression is equivalent to the statement that *a call option with a higher exercise price cannot have a higher value than one with a lower exercise price.* The option with the higher exercise price has a higher hurdle to get over; therefore, the buyer is not willing to pay as much for it. Even though we demonstrated this result with European calls, it is also true for American calls. Thus,[18]

$$C_0(X_1) \geq C_0(X_2)$$

In Exhibit 66-10 we construct a similar portfolio for puts, except that we buy the X_2 put (the one with the higher exercise price) and sell the X_1 put (the one with the lower exercise price).

Observe that the value of this combination is never negative at expiration; therefore, it must be non-negative today. Hence, $p_0(X_2) - p_0(X_1) \geq 0$. We restate this result as

$$p_0(X_2) \geq p_0(X_1)$$

---

[17] This transaction is also known as a bull spread.

[18] It is possible to use the results from this table to establish a limit on the difference between the prices of these two options, but we shall not do so here.

		Value at Expiration		
Transaction	Current Value	$S_T \leq X_1$	$X_1 < S_T < X_2$	$S_T \geq X_2$
Buy put ($X = X_2$)	$p_0(X_2)$	$X_2 - S_T$	$X_2 - S_T$	0
Sell put ($X = X_1$)	$-p_0(X_1)$	$-(X_1 - S_T)$	0	0
Total	$p_0(X_2) - p_0(X_1)$	$X_2 - X_1 > 0$	$X_2 - S_T > 0$	0

EXHIBIT 66-10 Portfolio Combination for European Puts Illustrating the Effect of Differences in Exercise Prices

Thus, *the value of a European put with a higher exercise price must be at least as great as the value of a European put with a lower exercise price.* These results also hold for American puts. Therefore,

$$P_0(X_2) \geq P_0(X_1)$$

Even though it is technically possible for calls and puts with different exercise prices to have the same price, *generally we can say that the higher the exercise price, the lower the price of a call and the higher the price of a put.* For example, refer back to Exhibit 66-1 and observe how the most expensive calls and least expensive puts have the lower exercise prices.

5.4 The Effect of a Difference in Time to Expiration

Option prices are also affected by the time to expiration of the option. Intuitively, one might expect that the longer the time to expiration, the more valuable the option. A longer-term option has more time for the underlying to make a favorable move. In addition, if the option is in-the-money by the end of a given period of time, it has a better chance of moving even further in-the-money over a longer period of time. If the additional time gives it a better chance of moving out-of-the-money or further out-of-the-money, the limitation of losses to the amount of the option premium means that the disadvantage of the longer time is no greater. In most cases, a longer time to expiration is beneficial for an option. We will see that longer-term American and European calls and longer-term American puts are worth no less than their shorter-term counterparts.

First let us consider each of the four types of options: European calls, American calls, European puts, and American puts. We shall introduce options otherwise identical except that one has a longer time to expiration than the other. The one expiring earlier has an expiration of T_1 and the one expiring later has an expiration of T_2. The prices of the options are $c_0(T_1)$ and $c_0(T_2)$ for the European calls, $C_0(T_1)$ and $C_0(T_2)$ for the American calls, $p_0(T_1)$ and $p_0(T_2)$ for the European puts, and $P_0(T_1)$ and $P_0(T_2)$ for the American puts.

When the shorter-term call expires, the European call is worth $\text{Max}(0, S_{T1} - X)$, but we have already shown that the longer-term European call is worth *at least* $\text{Max}(0, S_{T1} - X/(1+r)^{(T_2-T_1)})$, which is at least as great as this amount.[19] Thus, the longer-term European call is worth at least the value of the shorter-term European

---

[19] Technically, we showed this calculation using a time to expiration of T, but here the time to expiration is $T_2 - T_1$.

call. These results are not altered if the call is American. When the shorter-term American call expires, it is worth $\text{Max}(0, S_{T1} - X)$. The longer-term American call must be worth at least the value of the European call, so it is worth *at least* $\text{Max}[0, S - X/(1 + r)^{T_2 - T_1}]$. Thus, the longer-term call, European or American, is worth no less than the shorter-term call when the shorter-term call expires. Because this statement is always true, the longer-term call, European or American, is worth no less than the shorter-term call at any time prior to expiration. Thus,

$$c_0(T_2) \geq c_0(T_1)$$
$$C_0(T_2) \geq C_0(T_1)$$

(66-11)

Notice that these statements do not mean that the longer-term call is always worth more; it means that the longer-term call can be worth no less. With the exception of the rare case in which both calls are so far out-of-the-money or in-the-money that the additional time is of no value, the longer-term call will be worth more.

For European puts, we have a slight problem. For calls, the longer term gives additional time for a favorable move in the underlying to occur. For puts, this is also true, but there is one disadvantage to waiting the additional time. When a put is exercised, the holder receives money. The lost interest on the money is a disadvantage of the additional time. For calls, there is no lost interest. In fact, a call holder earns additional interest on the money by paying out the exercise price later. Therefore, it is not always true that additional time is beneficial to the holder of a European put. It is true, however, that the additional time is beneficial to the holder of an American put. An American put can always be exercised; there is no penalty for waiting. Thus, we have

$$p_0(T_2) \text{ can be either greater or less than } p_0(T_1)$$
$$P_0(T_2) \geq P_0(T_1)$$

(66-12)

So for European puts, either the longer-term or the shorter-term option can be worth more. The longer-term European put will tend to be worth more when volatility is greater and interest rates are lower.

Referring back to Exhibit 66-1, observe that the longer-term put and call options are more expensive than the shorter-term ones. As noted, we might observe an exception to this rule for European puts, but these are all American options.

5.5 Put–Call Parity

So far we have been working with puts and calls separately. To see how their prices must be consistent with each other and to explore common option strategies, let us combine puts and calls with each other or with a risk-free bond. We shall put together some combinations that produce equivalent results.

5.5.1 Fiduciary Calls and Protective Puts

First we consider an option strategy referred to as a **fiduciary call**. It consists of a European call and a risk-free bond, just like the ones we have been using, that matures on the option expiration day and has a face value equal to the exercise price of the call. The upper part of the table in Exhibit 66-11 shows the payoffs at expiration of the fiduciary call. We see that if the price of the underlying is below X at expiration, the call expires worthless and the bond is worth X. If the price of the underlying is above X at expiration, the call expires and is worth S_T (the underlying price) − X. So at expiration, the fiduciary call will end up worth X or

EXHIBIT 66-11	Portfolio Combinations for Equivalent Packages of Puts and Calls		

		Value at Expiration	
Transaction	Current Value	$S_T \leq X$	$S_T > X$
Fiduciary Call			
Buy call	c_0	0	$S_T - X$
Buy bond	$X/(1 + r)^T$	X	X
Total	$c_0 + X/(1 + r)^T$	X	S_T
Protective Put			
Buy put	p_0	$X - S_T$	0
Buy underlying asset	S_0	S_T	S_T
Total	$p_0 + S_0$	X	S_T

Value of Fiduciary Call and
Protective Put at Expiration

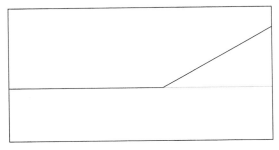

Stock Price at Expiration

S_T, whichever is greater. This type of combination is called a fiduciary call because it allows protection against downside losses and is thus faithful to the notion of preserving capital.

Now we construct a strategy known as a **protective put**, which consists of a European put and the underlying asset. If the price of the underlying is below X at expiration, the put expires and is worth $X - S_T$ and the underlying is worth S_T. If the price of the underlying is above X at expiration, the put expires with no value and the underlying is worth S_T. So at expiration, the protective put is worth X or S_T, whichever is greater. The lower part of the table in Exhibit 66-11 shows the payoffs at expiration of the protective put.

Thus, the fiduciary call and protective put end up with the same value. They are, therefore, identical combinations. To avoid arbitrage, their values today must be the same. The value of the fiduciary call is the cost of the call, c_0, and the cost of the bond, $X/(1 + r)^T$. The value of the protective put is the cost of the put, p_0, and the cost of the underlying, S_0. Thus,

$$c_0 + X/(1 + r)^T = p_0 + S_0 \qquad \text{(66-13)}$$

This equation is called **put–call parity** and is one of the most important results in options. It does not say that puts and calls are equivalent, but it does show an equivalence (parity) of a call/bond portfolio and a put/underlying portfolio.

Put–call parity can be written in a number of other ways. By rearranging the four terms to isolate one term, we can obtain some interesting and important results. For example,

$$c_0 = p_0 + S_0 - X/(1 + r)^T$$

means that a call is equivalent to a long position in the put, a long position in the asset, and a short position in the risk-free bond. The short bond position simply means to borrow by issuing the bond, rather than lend by buying the bond as we did in the fiduciary call portfolio. We can tell from the sign whether we should go long or short. Positive signs mean to go long; negative signs mean to go short.

5.5.2 Synthetics

Because the right-hand side of the above equation is equivalent to a call, we often refer to it as a **synthetic call**. To see that the synthetic call is equivalent to the actual call, look at Exhibit 66-12:

EXHIBIT 66-12	Call and Synthetic Call		

		Value at Expiration	
Transaction	Current Value	$S_T \leq X$	$S_T > X$
Call			
Buy call	c_0	0	$S_T - X$
Synthetic Call			
Buy put	p_0	$X - S_T$	0
Buy underlying asset	S_0	S_T	S_T
Issue bond	$-X/(1 + r)^T$	$-X$	$-X$
Total	$p_0 + S_0 - X/(1 + r)^T$	0	$S_T - X$

The call produces the value of the underlying minus the exercise price or zero, whichever is greater. The synthetic call does the same thing, but in a different way. When the call expires in-the-money, the synthetic call produces the underlying value minus the payoff on the bond, which is X. When the call expires out-of-the-money, the put covers the loss on the underlying and the exercise price on the put matches the amount of money needed to pay off the bond.

Similarly, we can isolate the put as follows:

$$p_0 = c_0 - S_0 + X/(1 + r)^T$$

which says that a put is equivalent to a long call, a short position in the underlying, and a long position in the bond. Because the left-hand side is a put, it follows that the right-hand side is a **synthetic put**. The equivalence of the put and synthetic put is shown in Exhibit 66-13.

As you can well imagine, there are numerous other combinations that can be constructed. Exhibit 66-14 shows a number of the more important combinations. There are two primary reasons that it is important to understand synthetic positions in option pricing. Synthetic positions enable us to price options, because they

| EXHIBIT 66-13 | Put and Synthetic Put | | | |

| Transaction | Current Value | Value at Expiration | |
		$S_T \leq X$	$S_T > X$
Put			
Buy put	p_0	$X - S_T$	0
Synthetic Put			
Buy call	c_0	0	$S_T - X$
Short underlying asset	$-S_0$	$-S_T$	$-S_T$
Buy bond	$X/(1+r)^T$	X	X
Total	$c_0 - S_0 + X/(1+r)^T$	$X - S_T$	0

produce the same results as options and have known prices. Synthetic positions also tell how to exploit mispricing of options relative to their underlying assets. Note that we can not only synthesize a call or a put, but we can also synthesize the underlying or the bond. As complex as it might seem to do this, it is really quite easy. First, we learn that *a fiduciary call is a call plus a risk-free bond maturing on the option expiration day with a face value equal to the exercise price of the option.* Then we learn that *a protective put is the underlying plus a put.* Then we learn the basic put–call parity equation: *A fiduciary call is equivalent to a protective put:*

$$c_0 + X/(1+r)^T = p_0 + S_0$$

Learn the put–call parity equation this way, because it is the easiest form to remember and has no minus signs.

| EXHIBIT 66-14 | Alternative Equivalent Combinations of Calls, Puts, the Underlying, and Risk-Free Bonds |

Strategy	Consisting of	Worth	Equates to	Strategy	Consisting of	Worth
Fiduciary call	Long call + Long bond	$c_0 + X/(1+r)^T$	=	Protective put	Long put + Long underlying	$p_0 + S_0$
Long call	Long call	c_0	=	Synthetic call	Long put + Long underlying + Short bond	$p_0 + S_0 - X/(1+r)^T$
Long put	Long put	p_0	=	Synthetic put	Long call + Short underlying + Long bond	$c_0 - S_0 + X/(1+r)^T$
Long underlying	Long underlying	S_0	=	Synthetic underlying	Long call + Long bond + Short put	$c_0 + X/(1+r)^T - p_0$
Long bond	Long bond	$X/(1+r)^T$	=	Synthetic bond	Long put + Long underlying + Short call	$p_0 + S_0 - c_0$

Next, we decide which instrument we want to synthesize. We use simple algebra to isolate that instrument, with a plus sign, on one side of the equation, moving all other instruments to the other side. We then see what instruments are on the other side, taking plus signs as long positions and minus signs as short positions. Finally, to check our results, we should construct a table like Exhibits 66-11 or 66-12, with the expiration payoffs of the instrument we wish to synthesize compared with the expiration payoffs of the equivalent combination of instruments. We then check to determine that the expiration payoffs are the same.

5.5.3 An Arbitrage Opportunity

In this section we examine the arbitrage strategies that will push prices to put–call parity. Suppose that in the market, prices do not conform to put–call parity. This is a situation in which price does not equal value. Recalling our basic equation, $c_0 + X/(1 + r)^T = p_0 + S_0$, we should insert values into the equation and see if the equality holds. If it does not, then obviously one side is greater than the other. We can view one side as overpriced and the other as underpriced, which suggests an arbitrage opportunity. To exploit this mispricing, we buy the underpriced combination and sell the overpriced combination.

Consider the following example involving call options with an exercise price of $100 expiring in half a year ($T = 0.5$). The risk-free rate is 10 percent. The call is priced at $7.50, and the put is priced at $4.25. The underlying price is $99.

The left-hand side of the basic put–call parity equation is $c_0 + X/(1 + r)^T = 7.50 + 100/(1.10)^{0.5} = 7.50 + 95.35 = 102.85$. The right-hand side is $p_0 + S_0 = 4.25 + 99 = 103.25$. So the right-hand side is greater than the left-hand side. This means that the protective put is overpriced. Equivalently, we could view this as the fiduciary call being underpriced. Either way will lead us to the correct strategy to exploit the mispricing.

We sell the overpriced combination, the protective put. This means that we sell the put and sell short the underlying. Doing so will generate a cash inflow of $103.25. We buy the fiduciary call, paying out $102.85. This series of transactions nets a cash inflow of $103.25 − $102.85 = $0.40. Now, let us see what happens at expiration.

> *The options expire with the underlying above 100:*
> The bond matures, paying $100.
> Use the $100 to exercise the call, receiving the underlying.
> Deliver the underlying to cover the short sale.
> The put expires with no value.
> Net effect: No money in or out.
> *The options expire with the underlying below 100:*
> The bond matures, paying $100.
> The put expires in-the-money; use the $100 to buy the underlying.
> Use the underlying to cover the short sale.
> The call expires with no value.
> Net effect: No money in our out.

So we receive $0.40 up front and do not have to pay anything out. The position is perfectly hedged and represents an arbitrage profit. The combined effects of other investors performing this transaction will result in the value of the protective put going down and/or the value of the fiduciary call going up until the two strategies are equivalent in value. Of course, it is possible that transaction costs might consume any profit, so small discrepancies will not be exploited.

It is important to note that regardless of which put–call parity equation we use, we will arrive at the same strategy. For example, in the above problem, the synthetic put (a long call, a short position in the underlying, and a long bond) is worth $7.50 − $99 + $95.35 = $3.85. The actual put is worth $4.25. Thus, we would conclude that we should sell the actual put and buy the synthetic put. To buy the synthetic put, we would buy the call, short the underlying, and buy the bond—precisely the strategy we used to exploit this price discrepancy.

In all of these examples based on put–call parity, we used only European options. Put–call parity using American options is considerably more complicated. The resulting parity equation is a complex combination of inequalities. Thus, we cannot say that a given combination exactly equals another; we can say only that one combination is more valuable than another. Exploitation of any such mispricing is somewhat more complicated, and we shall not explore it here.

Practice Problem 3

European put and call options with an exercise price of 45 expire in 115 days. The underlying is priced at 48 and makes no cash payments during the life of the options. The risk-free rate is 4.5 percent. The put is selling for 3.75, and the call is selling for 8.00.

A. Identify the mispricing by comparing the price of the actual call with the price of the synthetic call.

B. Based on your answer in Part A, demonstrate how an arbitrage transaction is executed.

▶ **Solution to A.** Using put–call parity, the following formula applies:

$$c_0 = p_0 + S_0 - X/(1 + r)^T$$

The time to expiration is $T = 115/365 = 0.3151$. Substituting values into the right-hand side:

$$c_0 = 3.75 + 48 - 45/(1.045)^{0.3151} = 7.37$$

Hence, the synthetic call is worth 7.37, but the actual call is selling for 8.00 and is, therefore, overpriced.

▶ **Solution to B.** Sell the call for 8.00 and buy the synthetic call for 7.37. To buy the synthetic call, buy the put for 3.75, buy the underlying for 48.00, and issue a zero-coupon bond paying 45.00 at expiration. The bond will bring in $45.00/(1.045)^{0.3151} = 44.38$ today. This transaction will bring in 8.00 − 7.37 = 0.63.

At expiration, the following payoffs will occur:

	$S_T < 45$	$S_T \geq 45$
Short call	0	$-(S_T - 45)$
Long put	$45 - S_T$	0
Underlying	S_T	S_T
Bond	-45	-45
Total	0	0

Thus there will be no cash in or out at expiration. The transaction will net a risk-free gain of $8.00 - 7.37 = 0.63$ up front.

5.6 American Options, Lower Bounds, and Early Exercise

As we have noted, American options can be exercised early and in this section we specify cases in which early exercise can have value. Because early exercise is never mandatory, the right to exercise early may be worth something but could never hurt the option holder. Consequently, the prices of American options must be no less than the prices of European options:

$$C_0 \geq c_0$$
$$P_0 \geq p_0$$

(66-14)

Recall that we already used this result in establishing the minimum price from the lower bounds and intrinsic value results in Section 5.2.2. Now, however, our concern is understanding the conditions under which early exercise of an American option might occur.

Suppose today, time 0, we are considering exercising early an in-the-money American call. If we exercise, we pay X and receive an asset worth S_0. But we already determined that a European call is worth at least $S_0 - X/(1 + r)^T$—that is, the underlying price minus the present value of the exercise price, which is more than $S_0 - X$. Because we just argued that the American call must be worth no less than the European call, it therefore must also be worth at least $S_0 - X/(1 + r)^T$. This means that the value we could obtain by selling it to someone else is more than the value we could obtain by exercising it. Thus, there is no reason to exercise the call early.

Some people fail to see the logic behind not exercising early. Exercising a call early simply gives the money to the call writer and throws away the right to decide at expiration if you want the underlying. It is like renewing a magazine subscription before the current subscription expires. Not only do you lose the interest on the money, you also lose the right to decide later if you want to renew. Without offering an early exercise incentive, the American call would have a price equal to the European call price. Thus, we must look at another case to see the value of the early exercise option.

If the underlying makes a cash payment, there may be reason to exercise early. If the underlying is a stock and pays a dividend, there may be sufficient reason to exercise just before the stock goes ex-dividend. By exercising, the option holder throws away the time value but captures the dividend. We shall skip the technical details of how this decision is made and conclude by stating that

▶ *When the underlying makes no cash payments, $C_0 = c_0$.*

▶ *When the underlying makes cash payments during the life of the option, early exercise can be worthwhile and C_0 can thus be higher than c_0.*

We emphasize the word *can*. It is possible that the dividend is not high enough to justify early exercise.

For puts, there is nearly always a possibility of early exercise. Consider the most obvious case, an investor holding an American put on a bankrupt company. The stock is worth zero. It cannot go any lower. Thus, the put holder would exercise immediately. As long as there is a possibility of bankruptcy, the American put will be worth more than the European put. But in fact, bankruptcy is not required for early exercise. The stock price must be very low, although we cannot say exactly how low without resorting to an analysis using option pricing models. Suffice it to say that *the American put is nearly always worth more than the European put: $P_0 > p_0$.*

5.7 The Effect of Cash Flows on the Underlying Asset

Both the lower bounds on puts and calls and the put–call parity relationship must be modified to account for cash flows on the underlying asset. In Readings 64 and 65, we discussed situations in which the underlying has cash flows. Stocks pay dividends, bonds pay interest, foreign currencies pay interest, and commodities have carrying costs. As we have done in the previous readings, we shall assume that these cash flows are either known or can be expressed as a percentage of the asset price. Moreover, as we did previously, we can remove the present value of those cash flows from the price of the underlying and use this adjusted underlying price in the results we have obtained above.

In the previous readings, we specified these cash flows in the form of the accumulated value at T of all cash flows incurred on the underlying over the life of the derivative contract. When the underlying is a stock, we specified these cash flows more precisely in the form of dividends, using the notation FV(D,0,T) as the future value, or alternatively PV(D,0,T) as the present value, of these dividends. When the underlying was a bond, we used the notation FV(CI,0,T) or PV(CI,0,T), where CI stands for "coupon interest." When the cash flows can be specified in terms of a yield or rate, we used the notation δ where $S_0/(1 + \delta)^T$ is the underlying price reduced by the present value of the cash flows.[20] Using continuous compounding, the rate can be specified as δ^c so that $S_0 e^{-\delta^c T}$ is the underlying price reduced by the present value of the dividends. For our purposes in this reading on options, let us just write this specification as PV(CF,0,T), which represents the present value of the cash flows on the underlying over the life of the options. Therefore, we can restate the lower bounds for European options as

$$c_0 \ge \text{Max}\,\{0,[S_0 - \text{PV(CF,0,T)}] - X/(1 + r)^T\}$$
$$p_0 \ge \text{Max}\,\{0,X/(1 + r)^T - [S_0 - \text{PV(CF,0,T)}]\}$$

---

[20] We actually used several specifications of the dividend yield in Reading 65, but we shall use just one here.

and put–call parity as

$$c_0 + X/(1 + r)^T = p_0 + [S_0 - PV(CF,0,T)]$$

which reflects the fact that, as we said, we simply reduce the underlying price by the present value of its cash flows over the life of the option.

5.8 The Effect of Interest Rates and Volatility

It is important to know that interest rates and volatility exert an influence on option prices. *When interest rates are higher, call option prices are higher and put option prices are lower.* This effect is not obvious and strains the intuition somewhat. When investors buy call options instead of the underlying, they are effectively buying an indirect leveraged position in the underlying. When interest rates are higher, buying the call instead of a direct leveraged position in the underlying is more attractive. Moreover, by using call options, investors save more money by not paying for the underlying until a later date. For put options, however, higher interest rates are disadvantageous. When interest rates are higher, investors lose more interest while waiting to sell the underlying when using puts. Thus, the opportunity cost of waiting is higher when interest rates are higher. Although these points may not seem completely clear, fortunately they are not critical. Except when the underlying is a bond or interest rate, interest rates do not have a very strong effect on option prices.

Volatility, however, has an extremely strong effect on option prices. *Higher volatility increases call and put option prices because it increases possible upside values and increases possible downside values of the underlying.* The upside effect helps calls and does not hurt puts. The downside effect does not hurt calls and helps puts. The reasons calls are not hurt on the downside and puts are not hurt on the upside is that when options are out-of-the-money, it does not matter if they end up more out-of-the-money. But when options are in-the-money, it does matter if they end up more in-the-money.

Volatility is a critical variable in pricing options. It is the only variable that affects option prices that is not directly observable either in the option contract or in the market. It must be estimated. We shall have more to say about volatility later in this reading.

5.9 Option Price Sensitivities

Later in this reading, we will study option price sensitivities in more detail. These sensitivity measures have Greek names:

- ▶ *Delta* is the sensitivity of the option price to a change in the price of the underlying.
- ▶ *Gamma* is a measure of how well the delta sensitivity measure will approximate the option price's response to a change in the price of the underlying.
- ▶ *Rho* is the sensitivity of the option price to the risk-free rate.
- ▶ *Theta* is the rate at which the time value decays as the option approaches expiration.
- ▶ *Vega* is the sensitivity of the option price to volatility.

6   DISCRETE-TIME OPTION PRICING: THE BINOMIAL MODEL

Until now, we have looked only at some basic principles of option pricing. Other than put–call parity, all we examined were rules and conditions, often suggesting limitations, on option prices. With put–call parity, we found that we could price a put or a call based on the prices of the combinations of instruments that make up the synthetic version of the instrument. If we wanted to determine a call price, we had to have a put; if we wanted to determine a put price, we had to have a call. What we need to be able to do is price a put or a call without the other instrument. In this section, we introduce a simple means of pricing an option. It may appear that we oversimplify the situation, but we shall remove the simplifying assumptions gradually, and eventually reach a more realistic scenario.

The approach we take here is called the **binomial model**. The word "binomial" refers to the fact that there are only two outcomes. In other words, we let the underlying price move to only one of two possible new prices. As noted, this framework oversimplifies things, but the model can eventually be extended to encompass all possible prices. In addition, we refer to the structure of this model as **discrete time**, which means that time moves in distinct increments. This is much like looking at a calendar and observing only the months, weeks, or days. Even at its smallest interval, we know that time moves forward at a rate faster than one day at a time. It moves in hours, minutes, seconds, and even fractions of seconds, and fractions of fractions of seconds. When we talk about time moving in the tiniest increments, we are talking about **continuous time**. We will see that the discrete time model can be extended to become a continuous time model. Although we present the continuous time model (Black–Scholes–Merton) in Section 7, we must point out that the binomial model has the advantage of allowing us to price American options. In addition, the binomial model is a simple model requiring a minimum of mathematics. Thus it is worthy of study in its own right.

6.1 The One-Period Binomial Model

We start off by having only one binomial period. This means that the underlying price starts off at a given level, then moves forward to a new price, at which time the option expires. Here we need to change our notation slightly from what we have been using previously. We let S be the current underlying price. One period later, it can move up to S^+ or down to S^-. Note that we are removing the time subscript, because it will not be necessary here. We let X be the exercise price of the option and r be the one period risk-free rate. The option is European style.

6.1.1 The Model

We start with a call option. If the underlying goes up to S^+, the call option will be worth c^+. If the underlying goes down to S^-, the option will be worth c^-. We know that if the option is expiring, its value will be the intrinsic value. Thus,

$$c^+ = \text{Max}(0, S^+ - X)$$
$$c^- = \text{Max}(0, S^- - X)$$

| EXHIBIT 66-15 | **One-Period Binomial Model** |

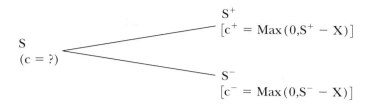

Exhibit 66-15 illustrates this scenario with a diagram commonly known as a **binomial tree**. Note how we indicate that the current option price, c, is unknown.

Now let us specify how the underlying moves. We identify a factor, u, as the up move on the underlying and d as the down move:

$$u = \frac{S^+}{S}$$

$$d = \frac{S^-}{S}$$

so that u and d represent 1 plus the rate of return if the underlying goes up and down, respectively. Thus, $S^+ = Su$ and $S^- = Sd$. To avoid an obvious arbitrage opportunity, we require that[21]

$$d < 1 + r < u$$

We are now ready to determine how to price the option. We assume that we have all information except for the current option price. In addition, we do not know in what direction the price of the underlying will move. We start by constructing an arbitrage portfolio consisting of one short call option. Let us now purchase an unspecified number of units of the underlying. Let that number be n. Although at the moment we do not know the value of n, we can figure it out quickly. We call this portfolio a hedge portfolio. In fact, n is sometimes called the **hedge ratio**. Its current value is H, where

$$H = nS - c$$

This specification reflects the fact that we own n units of the underlying worth S and we are short one call.[22] One period later, this portfolio value will go to either H^+ or H^-:

$$H^+ = nS^+ - c^+$$

$$H^- = nS^- - c^-$$

---

[21] This statement says that if the price of the underlying goes up, it must do so at a rate better than the risk-free rate. If it goes down, it must do so at a rate lower than the risk-free rate. If the underlying always does better than the risk-free rate, it would be possible to buy the underlying, financing it by borrowing at the risk-free rate, and be assured of earning a greater return from the underlying than the cost of borrowing. This would make it possible to generate an unlimited amount of money. If the underlying always does worse than the risk-free rate, one can buy the risk-free asset and finance it by shorting the underlying. This would also make it possible to earn an unlimited amount of money. Thus, the risky underlying asset cannot dominate or be dominated by the risk-free asset.

[22] Think of this specification as a plus sign indicating assets and a minus sign indicating liabilities.

Because we can choose the value of n, let us do so by setting H^+ equal to H^-. This specification means that regardless of which way the underlying moves, the portfolio value will be the same. Thus, the portfolio will be hedged. We do this by setting

$H^+ = H^-$, which means that

$nS^+ - c^+ = nS^- - c^-$

We then solve for n to obtain

$$n = \frac{c^+ - c^-}{S^+ - S^-} \qquad\qquad \textbf{(66-15)}$$

Because the values on the right-hand side are known, we can easily set n according to this formula. If we do so, the portfolio will be hedged. A hedged portfolio should grow in value at the risk-free rate.

$H^+ = H(1 + r)$, or

$H^- = H(1 + r)$

We know that $H^+ = nS^+ - c^+$, $H^- = nS^- - c^-$, and $H = nS - c$. We know the values of n, S^+, S^-, c^+, and c^-, as well as r. We can substitute and solve either of the above for c to obtain

$$c = \frac{\pi c^+ + (1 - \pi)c^-}{1 + r} \qquad\qquad \textbf{(66-16)}$$

where

$$\pi = \frac{1 + r - d}{u - d} \qquad\qquad \textbf{(66-17)}$$

We see that the call price today, c, is a weighted average of the next two possible call prices, c^+ and c^-. The weights are π and $1 - \pi$. This weighted average is then discounted one period at the risk-free rate.

It might appear that π and $1 - \pi$ are probabilities of the up and down movements, but they are not. In fact, the probabilities of the up and down movements are not required. It is important to note, however, that π and $1 - \pi$ are the probabilities that would exist if investors were risk neutral. Risk-neutral investors value assets by computing the expected future value and discounting that value at the risk-free rate. Because we are discounting at the risk-free rate, it should be apparent that π and $1 - \pi$ would indeed by the probabilities if the investor were **risk neutral**. In fact, we shall refer to them as **risk-neutral probabilities** and the process of valuing an option is often called **risk-neutral valuation**.[23]

------

[23] It may be helpful to contrast risk neutrality with risk aversion, which characterizes nearly all individuals. People who are risk neutral value an asset, such as an option or stock, by discounting the expected value at the risk-free rate. People who are risk averse discount the expected value at a higher rate, one that consists of the risk-free rate plus a risk premium. In the valuation of options, we are not making the assumption that people are risk neutral, but the fact that options can be valued by finding the expected value, using these special probabilities, and discounting at the risk-free rate creates the *appearance* that investors are assumed to be risk neutral. We emphasize the word "appearance," because no such assumption is being made. The terms "risk neutral probabilities" and "risk neutral valuation" are widely used in options valuation, although they give a misleading impression of the assumptions underlying the process.

6.1.2 One-Period Binomial Example

Suppose the underlying is a non-dividend-paying stock currently valued at $50. It can either go up by 25 percent or go down by 20 percent. Thus, u = 1.25 and d = 0.80.

$$S^+ = Su = 50(1.25) = 62.50$$
$$S^- = Sd = 50(0.80) = 40$$

Assume that the call option has an exercise price of 50 and the risk-free rate is 7 percent. Thus, the option values one period later will be

$$c^+ = Max(0,S^+ - X) = Max(0,62.50 - 50) = 12.50$$
$$c^- = Max(0,S^- - X) = Max(0,40 - 50) = 0$$

Exhibit 66-16 depicts the situation.

EXHIBIT 66-16   One-Period Binomial Example

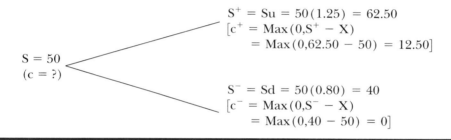

First we calculate π:

$$\pi = \frac{1 + r - d}{u - d} = \frac{1.07 - 0.80}{1.25 - 0.80} = 0.6$$

and, hence, $1 - \pi = 0.4$. Now, we can directly calculate the option price:

$$c = \frac{0.6(12.50) + 0.4(0)}{1.07} = 7.01$$

Thus, the option should sell for $7.01.

6.1.3 One-Period Binomial Arbitrage Opportunity

Suppose the option is selling for $8. If the option should be selling for $7.01 and it is selling for $8, it is overpriced—a clear case of price not equaling value. Investors would exploit this opportunity by selling the option and buying the underlying. The number of units of the underlying purchased for each option sold would be the value n:

$$n = \frac{c^+ - c^-}{S^+ - S^-} = \frac{12.50 - 0}{62.50 - 40} = 0.556$$

Thus, for every option sold, we would buy 0.556 units of the underlying. Suppose we sell 1,000 calls and buy 556 units of the underlying. Doing so would require an initial outlay of H = 556($50) − 1,000($8) = $19,800. One period later, the portfolio value will be either

$$H^+ = nS^+ - c^+ = 556(\$62.50) - 1,000(\$12.50) = \$22,250, \text{ or}$$
$$H^- = nS^- - c^- = 556(\$40) - 1,000(\$0) = \$22,240$$

These two values are not exactly the same, but the difference is due only to rounding the hedge ratio, n. We shall use the $22,250 value. If we invest $19,800 and end up with $22,250, the return is

$$\frac{\$22,250}{\$19,800} - 1 = 0.1237$$

that is, a risk-free return of more than 12 percent in contrast to the actual risk-free rate of 7 percent. Thus we could borrow $19,800 at 7 percent to finance the initial net cash outflow, capturing a risk-free profit of (0.1237 − 0.07) × $19,800 = $1,063 (to the nearest dollar) without any net investment of money. Other investors will recognize this opportunity and begin selling the option, which will drive down its price. When the option sells for $7.01, the initial outlay would be H = 556($50) − 1,000($7.01) = $20,790. The payoffs at expiration would still be $22,250. This transaction would generate a return of

$$\frac{\$22,250}{\$20,790} - 1 \approx 0.07$$

Thus, *when the option is trading at the price given by the model, a hedge portfolio would earn the risk-free rate*, which is appropriate because the portfolio would be risk free.

If the option sells for less than $7.01, investors would buy the option and sell short the underlying, which would generate cash up front. At expiration, the investor would have to pay back an amount less than 7 percent. All investors would perform this transaction, generating a demand for the option that would push its price back up to $7.01.

Practice Problem 4

Consider a one-period binomial model in which the underlying is at 65 and can go up 30 percent or down 22 percent. The risk-free rate is 8 percent.

A. Determine the price of a European call option with exercise prices of 70.

B. Assume that the call is selling for 9 in the market. Demonstrate how to execute an arbitrage transaction and calculate the rate of return. Use 10,000 call options.

▶ **Solution to A.** First find the underlying prices in the binomial tree. We have u = 1.30 and d = 1 − 0.22 = 0.78.

$$S^+ = Su = 65(1.30) = 84.50$$
$$S^- = Sd = 65(0.78) = 50.70$$

Then find the option values at expiration:

$$c^+ = \text{Max}(0, 84.50 - 70) = 14.50$$
$$c^- = \text{Max}(0, 50.70 - 70) = 0$$

The risk-neutral probability is

$$\pi = \frac{1.08 - 0.78}{1.30 - 0.78} = 0.5769$$

and $1 - \pi = 0.4231$. The call's price today is

$$c = \frac{0.5769(14.50) + 0.4231(0)}{1.08} = 7.75$$

▶ **Solution to B.** We need the value of n for calls:

$$n = \frac{c^+ - c^-}{S^+ - S^-} = \frac{14.50 - 0}{84.50 - 50.70} = 0.4290$$

The call is overpriced, so we should sell 10,000 call options and buy 4,290 units of the underlying.

Sell 10,000 calls at 9	+90,000
Buy 4,290 units of the underlying at 65	−278,850
Net cash flow	−188,850

So we invest 188,850. The value of this combination at expiration will be

If $S_T = 84.50$,

$$4,290(84.50) - 10,000(14.50) = 217,505$$

If $S_T = 50.70$,

$$4,290(50.70) - 10,000(0) = 217,503$$

These values differ by only a rounding error.
The rate of return is

$$\frac{217,505}{188,850} - 1 = 0.1517$$

Thus, we receive a risk-free return almost twice the risk-free rate. We could borrow the initial outlay of $188,850 at the risk-free rate and capture a risk-free profit without any net investment of money.

6.2 The Two-Period Binomial Model

In the example above, the movements in the underlying were depicted over one period, and there were only two outcomes. We can extend the model and obtain more-realistic results with more than two outcomes. Exhibit 66-17 shows how to do so with a two-period binomial tree.

EXHIBIT 66-17   **Two-Period Binomial Model**

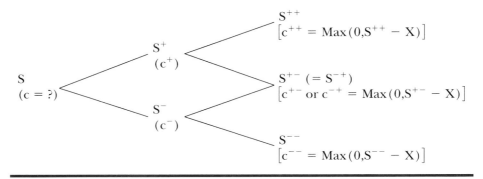

In the first period, we let the underlying price move from S to S^+ or S^- in the manner we did in the one-period model. That is, if u is the up factor and d is the down factor,

$$S^+ = Su$$
$$S^- = Sd$$

Then, with the underlying at S^+ after one period, it can either move up to S^{++} or down to S^{+-}. Thus,

$$S^{++} = S^+u$$
$$S^{+-} = S^+d$$

If the underlying is at S^- after one period, it can either move up to S^{-+} or down to S^{--}.

$$S^{-+} = S^-u$$
$$S^{--} = S^-d$$

We now have three unique final outcomes instead of two. Actually, we have four final outcomes, but S^{+-} is the same as S^{-+}. We can relate the three final outcomes to the starting price in the following manner:

$$S^{++} = S^+u = Suu = Su^2$$
$$S^{+-} \text{ (or } S^{-+}) = S^+d \text{ (or } S^-u) = Sud \text{ (or } Sdu)$$
$$S^{--} = S^-d = Sdd = Sd^2$$

Now we move forward to the end of the first period. Suppose we are at the point where the underlying price is S^+. Note that now we are back into the one-period model we previously derived. There is one period to go and two outcomes. The call price is c^+ and can go up to c^{++} or down to c^{+-}. Using what we know from the one-period model, the call price must be

$$c^+ = \frac{\pi c^{++} + (1 - \pi)c^{+-}}{1 + r}$$ **(66-18)**

where again we see that the call price is a weighted average of the next two possible call prices, then discounted back one period. If the underlying price is at S^-, the call price would be

$$c^- = \frac{\pi c^{-+} + (1 - \pi) c^{--}}{1 + r}$$

(66-19)

where in both cases the formula for π is still Equation 66-17:

$$\pi = \frac{1 + r - d}{u - d}$$

Now we step back to the starting point and find that the option price is still given as Equation 66-16:

$$c = \frac{\pi c^+ + (1 - \pi) c^-}{1 + r}$$

again, using the general form that the call price is a weighted average of the next two possible call prices, discounted back to the present. Other than requiring knowledge of the formula for π, the call price formula is simple and intuitive. It is an average, weighted by the risk-neutral probabilities, of the next two outcomes, then discounted to the present.[24]

Recall that the hedge ratio, n, was given as the difference in the next two call prices divided by the difference in the next two underlying prices. This will be true in all cases throughout the binomial tree. Hence, we have different hedge ratios at each time point:

$$n = \frac{c^+ - c^-}{S^+ - S^-}$$
$$n^+ = \frac{c^{++} - c^{+-}}{S^{++} - S^{+-}}$$
$$n^- = \frac{c^{-+} - c^{--}}{S^{-+} - S^{--}}$$

(66-20)

6.2.1 Two-Period Binomial Example

We can continue with the example presented in Section 6.1.2 in which the underlying goes up 25 percent or down 20 percent. Let us, however, alter the example a little. Suppose the underlying goes up 11.8 percent and down 10.56 percent, and we extend the number of periods to two. So, the up factor is 1.118 and the down factor is $1 - 0.1056 = 0.8944$. If the underlying goes up for two consecutive periods, it rises by a factor of $1.118(1.118) = 1.25$ (25 percent). If it goes down in both periods, it falls by a factor of $(0.8944)(0.8944) = 0.80$ (20 percent). This specification makes the highest and lowest prices unchanged. Let the risk-free rate be 3.44 percent per period. The π becomes $(1.0344 - 0.8944)/(1.118 - 0.8944) = 0.6261$. The underlying prices at expiration will be

---

[24] It is also possible to express the price today as a weighted average of the three final option prices discounted two periods, thereby skipping the intermediate step of finding c^+ and c^-; but little is gained by doing so and this approach is somewhat more technical.

| EXHIBIT 66-18 | Two-Period Binomial Example |

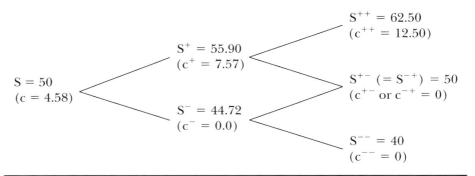

$$S^{++} = Su^2 = 50(1.118)(1.118) = 62.50$$
$$S^{+-} = Sud = 50(1.118)(0.8944) = 50$$
$$S^{--} = Sd^2 = 50(0.8944)(0.8944) = 40$$

When the options expire, they will be worth

$$c^{++} = Max(0,S^{++} - 50) = Max(0,62.50 - 50) = 12.50$$
$$c^{+-} = Max(0,S^{+-} - 50) = Max(0,50 - 50) = 0$$
$$c^{--} = Max(0,S^{--} - 50) = Max(0,40 - 50) = 0$$

The option values after one period are, therefore,

$$c^+ = \frac{\pi c^{++} + (1 - \pi)c^{+-}}{1 + r} = \frac{0.6261(12.50) + 0.3739(0)}{1.0344} = 7.57$$

$$c^- = \frac{\pi c^{-+} + (1 - \pi)c^{--}}{1 + r} = \frac{0.6261(0) + 0.3739(0)}{1.0344} = 0.0$$

So the option price today is

$$c = \frac{\pi c^+ + (1 - \pi)c^-}{1 + r} = \frac{0.6261(7.57) + 0.3739(0)}{1.0344} = 4.58$$

These results are summarized in Exhibit 66-18.

We shall not illustrate an arbitrage opportunity, because doing so requires a very long and detailed example that goes beyond our needs. Suffice it to say that if the option is mispriced, one can construct a hedged portfolio that will capture a return in excess of the risk-free rate.

| Practice Problem 5 |

Consider a two-period binomial model in which the underlying is at 30 and can go up 14 percent or down 11 percent each period. The risk-free rate is 3 percent per period.

A. Find the value of a European call option expiring in two periods with an exercise price of 30.

B. Find the number of units of the underlying that would be required at each point in the binomial tree to construct a risk-free hedge using 10,000 calls.

▶ **Solution to A.** First find the underlying prices in the binomial tree: We have u = 1.14 and d = 1 − 0.11 = 0.89.

$$S^+ = Su = 30(1.14) = 34.20$$
$$S^- = Sd = 30(0.89) = 26.70$$
$$S^{++} = Su^2 = 30(1.14)^2 = 38.99$$
$$S^{+-} = Sud = 30(1.14)(0.89) = 30.44$$
$$S^{--} = Sd^2 = 30(0.89)^2 = 23.76$$

Then find the option prices at expiration:

$$c^{++} = Max(0, 38.99 - 30) = 8.99$$
$$c^{+-} = Max(0, 30.44 - 30) = 0.44$$
$$c^{--} = Max(0, 23.76 - 30) = 0$$

We will need the value of π:

$$\pi = \frac{1.03 - 0.89}{1.14 - 0.89} = 0.56$$

and $1 - \pi = 0.44$. Then step back and find the option prices at time 1:

$$c^+ = \frac{0.56(8.99) + 0.44(0.44)}{1.03} = 5.08$$
$$c^- = \frac{0.56(0.44) + 0.44(0)}{1.03} = 0.24$$

The price today is

$$c = \frac{0.56(5.08) + 0.44(0.24)}{1.03} = 2.86$$

▶ **Solution to B.** The number of units of the underlying at each point in the tree is found by first computing the values of n.

$$n = \frac{5.08 - 0.24}{34.20 - 26.70} = 0.6453$$
$$n^+ = \frac{8.99 - 0.44}{38.99 - 30.44} = 1.00$$
$$n^- = \frac{0.44 - 0}{30.44 - 23.76} = 0.0659$$

The number of units of the underlying required for 10,000 calls would thus be 6,453 today, 10,000 at time 1 if the underlying is at 34.20, and 659 at time 1 if the underlying is at 26.70.

6.3 Binomial Put Option Pricing

In Section 6.2, the option was a call. It is a simple matter to make the option a put. We could step back through the entire example, changing all c's to p's and using the formulas for the payoff values of a put instead of a call. We should note, however, that if the same formula used for a call is used to calculate the hedge ratio, the minus sign should be ignored as it would suggest being long the stock (put) and short the put (stock) when the hedge portfolio should actually be long both instruments or short both instruments. The put moves opposite to the stock in the first place; hence, long or short positions in both instruments are appropriate.

Practice Problem 6

Repeating the data from Practice Problem 4, consider a one-period binomial model in which the underlying is at 65 and can go up 30 percent or down 22 percent. The risk-free rate is 8 percent. Determine the price of a European put option with exercise price of 70.

▶ **Solution.** First find the underlying prices in the binomial tree. We have u = 1.30 and d = 1 − 0.22 = 0.78.

$$S^+ = Su = 65(1.30) = 84.50$$
$$S^- = Sd = 65(0.78) = 50.70$$

Then find the option values at expiration:

$$p^+ = Max(0, 70 - 84.50) = 0$$
$$p^- = Max(0, 70 - 50.70) = 19.30$$

The risk-neutral probability is

$$\pi = \frac{1.08 - 0.78}{1.30 - 0.78} = 0.5769$$

and $1 - \pi = 0.4231$. The put price today is

$$p = \frac{0.5769(0) + 0.423(19.30)}{1.08} = 7.56$$

6.4 Binomial Interest Rate Option Pricing

In the examples above, the applications were appropriate for options on a stock, currency, or commodity.[25] Now we take a brief look at options on bonds and interest rates. A model for pricing these options must start with a model for the one-period interest rate and the prices of zero-coupon bonds.

We look at such a model in Exhibit 66-19. Note that this binomial tree is the first one we have seen with more than two time periods. At each point in the tree, we see a group of numbers. The first number is the one-period interest rate. The

---

[25] We have also been assuming that there are no cash flows on the underlying.

| EXHIBIT 66-19 | Binomial Interest Rate Tree |

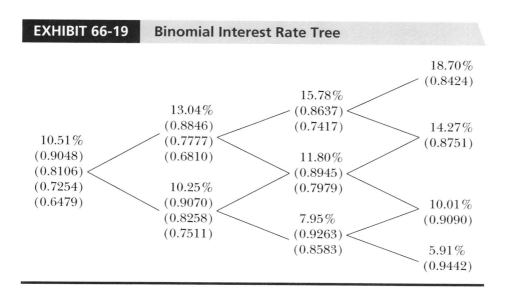

second set of numbers, which are in parentheses, represents the prices of $1 face value zero-coupon bonds of various maturities. At time 0, 0.9048 is the price of a one-period zero-coupon bond, 0.8106 is the price of a two-period zero-coupon bond, 0.7254 is the price of a three-period zero-coupon bond, and 0.6479 is the price of a four-period zero-coupon bond. The one-period bond price can be determined from the one-period rate—that is, 0.9048 = 1/1.1051, subject to some rounding off. The other prices cannot be determined solely from the one-period rate; we would have to see a tree of the two-, three-, and four-period rates. As we move forward in time, we lose one bond as the one-period bond matures.[26] Thus, at time 1, when the one-period rate is 13.04 percent, the two-period bond from the previous period, whose price was 0.8106, is now a one-period bond whose price is 1/1.1304 = 0.8846. Although we present these prices and rates here without derivation, they were determined using a model that prevents arbitrage opportunities in buying and selling bonds. We do not cover the actual derivation of the model here.

Now let us price a European option on a zero-coupon bond. First note that we need the option to expire before the bond matures, and it should have a reasonable exercise price. We shall work with the four-period zero-coupon bond. Exhibit 66-20 contains its price and the price of a two-period call option with an exercise price of $0.80 per $1 of par, as well as the one-period interest rate. The binomial interest rate tree in Exhibit 66-20 is based on the data in Exhibit 66-19. In parentheses in Exhibit 66-20 are the prices of the call option expiring at time 2.

First note that in binomial term structure models, the models are usually fit such that the risk-neutral probability, π, is 0.5. Thus we do not have to calculate π, as in the examples above. We must, however, do one thing quite differently. Whereas we have used a constant interest rate, we must now discount at a different interest rate, the one-period rate, given in Exhibit 66-19, depending on where we are in the tree.

---

[26] Technically we could show the bond we are losing as a bond with a price of $1.00, its face value, at its point of maturity.

EXHIBIT 66-20	Four-Period Zero-Coupon Bond and Two-Period Call Option with Exercise Price of 0.80

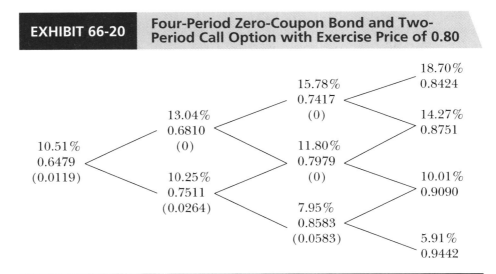

The payoff values at time 2 of the call with exercise price of 0.80 are

$$c^{++} = \text{Max}(0, 0.7417 - 0.80) = 0$$
$$c^{+-} = \text{Max}(0, 0.7979 - 0.80) = 0$$
$$c^{--} = \text{Max}(0, 0.8583 - 0.80) = 0.0583$$

These numbers appear in Exhibit 66-20 at time 2 along with the underlying bond prices and the one-period interest rates. Stepping back to time 1, we find the option prices as follows:

$$c^{+} = \frac{0.5(0) + 0.5(0)}{1.1304} = 0$$

$$c^{-} = \frac{0.5(0) + 0.5(0.0583)}{1.1025} = 0.0264$$

Note how we discount by the appropriate one-period rate, which is 10.25 percent for the bottom outcome at time 1 and 13.04 percent for the top outcome at time 1. Stepping back to time 0, the option price is, therefore,

$$c = \frac{0.5(0) + 0.5(0.0264)}{1.1051} = 0.0119$$

using the one-period rate of 10.51 percent. The call option is thus worth $0.0119 when the underlying zero-coupon bond paying $1 at time 4 is currently worth $0.6479.

Now let us price an option on a coupon bond. First, however, we must construct the tree of coupon bond prices. Exhibit 66-21 illustrates the price of a $1 face value, 11 percent coupon bond maturing at time 4 along with a call option expiring at time 2 with an exercise price of $0.95 per $1 of par.

We obtain the prices of the coupon bond from the prices of zero-coupon bonds. For example, at time 0, a four-period 11 percent coupon bond is equivalent to a combination of zero-coupon bonds with face value of 0.11 maturing at times 1, 2, and 3, and a zero-coupon bond with face value of 1.11 maturing at time 4. Thus,

EXHIBIT 66-21	Four-Period 11 Percent Coupon Bond and Two-Period Call Option with Exercise Price of 0.95

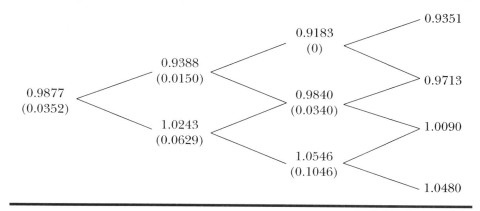

its price can be found by multiplying these face values by the prices of one-, two-, three-, and four-period zero-coupon bonds respectively, the prices of which are taken from Exhibit 66-19.

$$0.11(0.9048) + 0.11(0.8106) + 0.11(0.7254) + 1.11(0.6479) = 0.9877$$

At any other point in the tree, we use the same procedure, but of course fewer coupons remain.[27] Of course, pricing a coupon bond by decomposing it into a combination of zero-coupon bonds is basic fixed income material, which you have learned elsewhere in the CFA curriculum.

Now let us find the option prices. At time 2, the prices are

$$c^{++} = \text{Max}(0, 0.9183 - 0.95) = 0$$
$$c^{+-} = \text{Max}(0, 0.9840 - 0.95) = 0.0340$$
$$c^{--} = \text{Max}(0, 1.0546 - 0.95) = 0.1046$$

Stepping back to time 1, the prices are

$$c^{+} = \frac{0.5(0.0) + 0.5(0.0340)}{1.1304} = 0.0150$$

$$c^{-} = \frac{0.5(0.0340) + 0.5(0.1046)}{1.1025} = 0.0629$$

Stepping back to time 0, the option price is

$$c = \frac{0.5(0.0150) + 0.5(0.0629)}{1.1051} = 0.0352$$

Now let us look at options on interest rates. Recall that in Section 4.1.4, we illustrated how these options work. Their payoffs are based on the difference between the interest rate and an exercise rate. When the option expires, the payoff

---

[27] For example, consider the middle node at time 2. The coupon bond is now a two-period bond. The one- and two-period zero-coupon bond prices are 0.8945 and 0.7979, respectively (from Exhibit 66-19). Thus, the coupon bond price is 0.11(0.8945) + 1.11(0.7979) = 0.9840 as shown in Exhibit 66-21.

| EXHIBIT 66-22 | Two-Period Cap on One-Period Interest Rate with Exercise Rate of 10.5 Percent |

A. Pricing the Two-Period Caplet

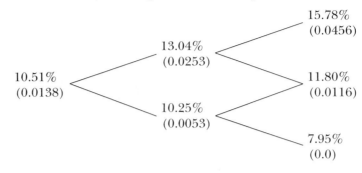

B. Pricing the One-Period Caplet

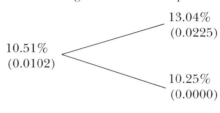

does not occur for one additional period. Thus, we have to discount the intrinsic value at expiration by the one-period interest rate. Recall that an interest rate cap is a set of interest rate call options expiring at various points in the life of a loan. The cap is generally set up to hedge the interest rate risk on a floating rate loan.

Exhibit 66-22 illustrates the pricing of a two-period cap with an exercise rate of 10.5 percent. This contract consists of two caplets: a one-period call option on the one-period interest rate with an exercise rate of 10.5 percent, and a two-period call option on the one-period interest rate with an exercise rate of 10.5 percent. We price the cap by pricing these two component options.

In Panel A, we price the two-period caplet. The values at time 2 are

$$c^{++} = \frac{\text{Max}(0, 0.1578 - 0.105)}{1.1578} = 0.0456$$

$$c^{+-} = \frac{\text{Max}(0, 0.1180 - 0.105)}{1.1180} = 0.0116$$

$$c^{--} = \frac{\text{Max}(0, 0.0795 - 0.105)}{1.0795} = 0.0$$

Note especially that we discount the payoff one period at the appropriate one-period rate, because the payoff does not occur until one period later. Stepping back to time 1:

$$c^{+} = \frac{0.5(0.0456) + 0.5(0.0116)}{1.1304} = 0.0253$$

$$c^{-} = \frac{0.5(0.0116) + 0.5(0.0)}{1.1025} = 0.0053$$

At time 0, the option price is

$$c = \frac{0.5(0.0253) + 0.5(0.0053)}{1.1051} = 0.0138$$

Panel B illustrates the same procedure for the one-period caplet. We shall omit the details because they follow precisely the pattern above. The one-period caplet price is 0.0102; thus the cap costs $0.0138 + 0.0102 = 0.0240$.

If the option is a floor, the procedure is precisely the same but the payoffs are based on the payoffs of a put instead of a call. Pricing a zero-cost collar, however, is considerably more complex. Remember that a zero-cost collar is a long cap and a short floor with the exercise rates set such that the premium on the cap equals the premium on the floor. We can arbitrarily choose the exercise rate on the cap or the floor, but the exercise rate on the other would have to be found by trial and error so that the premium offsets the premium on the other instrument.

Practice Problem 7

The diagram below is a two-period binomial tree containing the one-period interest rate and the prices of zero-coupon bonds. The first price is a one-period zero-coupon bond, the second is a two-period zero-coupon bond, and the third is a three-period zero-coupon bond. As we move forward, one bond matures and its price is removed. The maturity of each bond is then shorter by one period.

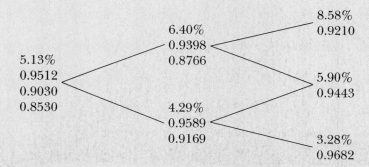

A. Find the price of a European put expiring in two periods with an exercise price of 1.01 on a three-period 6 percent coupon bond with $1.00 face value.

B. Find the price of a European put option expiring at time 2 with an exercise rate of 6 percent where the underlying is the one-period rate.

▶ **Solution to A.** First we have to find the price of the three-period $1.00 par, 6 percent coupon bond at expiration of the option (t = 2). We break the coupon bond up into zero-coupon bonds of one, two, and three periods to maturity. The face values of these zero-coupon bonds are 0.06, 0.06, and 1.06, respectively. The bond price at t = 2 is $1.06 discounted one period at the appropriate discount rate:

Bond prices at time 2:

$$
\begin{aligned}
&++\text{ outcome:} && 1.06(0.9210) = 0.9763 \\
&+-\text{ outcome:} && 1.06(0.9443) = 1.0010 \\
&--\text{ outcome:} && 1.06(0.9682) = 1.0263
\end{aligned}
$$

Now compute the put option values at expiration:

$$
\begin{aligned}
&++\text{ outcome:} && \text{Max}(0, 1.01 - 0.9763) = 0.0337 \\
&+-\text{ outcome:} && \text{Max}(0, 1.01 - 1.0010) = 0.0090 \\
&--\text{ outcome:} && \text{Max}(0, 1.01 - 1.0263) = 0.0000
\end{aligned}
$$

Now step back and compute the option values at time 1:

$$
+\text{ outcome:} \quad \frac{0.5(0.0337) + 0.5(0.0090)}{1.064} = 0.0201
$$

$$
-\text{ outcome:} \quad \frac{0.5(0.0090) + 0.5(0.0000)}{1.0429} = 0.0043
$$

Now step back and compute the option values at time 0:

$$
\frac{0.5(0.201) + 0.5(0.0043)}{1.0513} = 0.0116
$$

▶ **Solution to B.** First compute the put option values at expiration:

$$
p^{++} = \frac{\text{Max}(0, 0.06 - 0.0858)}{1.0858} = 0.0000
$$

$$
p^{+-} = \frac{\text{Max}(0, 0.06 - 0.0590)}{1.059} = 0.0009
$$

$$
p^{--} = \frac{\text{Max}(0, 0.06 - 0.0328)}{1.0328} = 0.0263
$$

Step back to time 2 and compute the option values:

$$
p^{+} = \frac{0.5(0.0000) + 0.5(0.0009)}{1.064} = 0.0004
$$

$$
p^{-} = \frac{0.5(0.0009) + 0.5(0.0263)}{1.0429} = 0.0130
$$

Now step back to time 0 and compute the option price as

$$
p = \frac{0.5(0.0004) + 0.5(0.0130)}{1.0513} = 0.0064
$$

6.5 American Options

The binomial model is also well suited for handling American-style options. At any point in the binomial tree, we can see whether the calculated value of the option is exceeded by its value if exercised early. If that is the case, we replace the calculated value with the exercise value.[28]

6.6 Extending the Binomial Model

In the examples in this reading, we divided an option's life into a given number of periods. Suppose we are pricing a one-year option. If we use only one binomial period, it will give us only two prices for the underlying, and we are unlikely to get a very good result. If we use two binomial periods, we will have three prices for the underlying at expiration. This result would probably be better but still not very good. But as we increase the number of periods, the result should become more accurate. In fact, in the limiting case, we are likely to get a very good result. By increasing the number of periods, we are moving from discrete time to continuous time.

Consider the following example of a one-period binomial model for a nine-month option. The asset is priced at 52.75. It can go up by 35.41 percent or down by 26.15 percent, so u = 1.3541 and d = 1 − 0.2615 = 0.7385. The risk-free rate is 4.88 percent. A call option has an exercise price of 50 and expires in nine months. Using a one-period binomial model would obtain an option price of 10.0259. Exhibit 66-23 shows the results we obtain if we divide the nine-month option life into an increasing number of periods of smaller and smaller length. The manner in which we fit the binomial tree is not arbitrary, however, because

EXHIBIT 66-23	Binomial Option Prices for Different Numbers of Time Periods
Number of Time Periods	**Option Price**
1	10.0259
2	8.4782
5	8.8305
10	8.6983
25	8.5862
50	8.6438
100	8.6160
500	8.6162
1000	8.6190

Notes: Call option with underlying price of 52.75, up factor of 1.3541, down factor of 0.7385, risk-free rate of 4.88 percent, and exercise price of 50. The variables u, d, and r are altered accordingly as the number of time periods increases.

---

[28] See Chapter 4 of *An Introduction to Derivatives and Risk Management*, 6th edition, Don M. Chance (South-Western College Publishing, 2004) for a treatment of this topic.

we have to alter the values of u, d, and the risk-free rate so that the underlying price move is reasonable for the life of the option. How we alter u and d is related to the volatility, a topic we cover in the next section. In fact, we need not concern ourselves with exactly how to alter any of these values. We need only to observe that our binomial option price appears to be converging to a value of around 8.62.

In the same way a sequence of rapidly taken still photographs converges to what appears to be a continuous sequence of a subject's movements, the binomial model converges to a continuous-time model, the subject of which is in our next section.

7 CONTINUOUS-TIME OPTION PRICING: THE BLACK–SCHOLES–MERTON MODEL

When we move to a continuous-time world, we price options using the famous Black–Scholes–Merton model. Named after its founders Fischer Black, Myron Scholes, and Robert Merton, this model resulted in the award of a Nobel Prize to Scholes and Merton in 1997.[29] (Fischer Black had died in 1995 and thus was not eligible for the prize.) The model can be derived either as the continuous limit of the binomial model, or through taking expectations, or through a variety of highly complex mathematical procedures. We are not concerned with the derivation here and instead simply present the model and its applications. First, however, let us briefly review its underlying assumptions.

7.1 Assumptions of the Model

7.1.1 The Underlying Price Follows a Geometric Lognormal Diffusion Process

This assumption is probably the most difficult to understand, but in simple terms, *the underlying price follows a lognormal probability distribution as it evolves through time.* A lognormal probability distribution is one in which the log return is normally distributed. For example, if a stock moves from 100 to 110, the return is 10 percent but the log return is $\ln(1.10) = 0.0953$ or 9.53 percent. Log returns are often called *continuously compounded returns.* If the log or continuously compounded return follows the familiar normal or bell-shaped distribution, the return is said to be lognormally distributed. The distribution of the return itself is skewed, reaching further out to the right and truncated on the left side, reflecting the limitation that an asset cannot be worth less than zero.

The lognormal distribution is a convenient and widely used assumption. It is almost surely not an exact measure in reality, but it suffices for our purposes.

7.1.2 The Risk-Free Rate Is Known and Constant

The Black–Scholes–Merton model does not allow interest rates to be random. Generally, we assume that *the risk-free rate is constant.* This assumption becomes a problem for pricing options on bonds and interest rates, and we will have to make some adjustments then.

---

[29] The model is more commonly called the Black–Scholes model, but we choose to give Merton the credit he is due that led to his co-receipt of the Nobel Prize.

7.1.3 The Volatility of the Underlying Asset Is Known and Constant

The volatility of the underlying asset, specified in the form of the standard deviation of the log return, is assumed to be known at all times and does not change over the life of the option. This assumption is the most critical, and we take it up again in a later section. In reality, the volatility is definitely not known and must be estimated or obtained from some other source. In addition, volatility is generally not constant. Obviously, the stock market is more volatile at some times than at others. Nonetheless, the assumption is critical for this model. Considerable research has been conducted with the assumption relaxed, but this topic is an advanced one and does not concern us here.

7.1.4 There Are No Taxes or Transaction Costs

We have made this assumption all along in pricing all types of derivatives. Taxes and transaction costs greatly complicate our models and keep us from seeing the essential financial principles involved in the models. It is possible to relax this assumption, but we shall not do so here.

7.1.5 There Are No Cash Flows on the Underlying

We have discussed this assumption at great length in pricing futures and forwards and earlier in this reading in studying the fundamentals of option pricing. The basic form of the Black–Scholes–Merton model makes this assumption, but it can easily be relaxed. We will show how to do this in Section 7.4.

7.1.6 The Options Are European

With only a few very advanced variations, the Black–Scholes–Merton model does not price American options. Users of the model must keep this in mind, or they may badly misprice these options. For pricing American options, the best approach is the binomial model with a large number of time periods.

7.2 The Black–Scholes–Merton Formula

Although the mathematics underlying the Black–Scholes–Merton formula are quite complex, the formula itself is not difficult, although it may appear so at first glance. The input variables are some of those we have already used: S_0 is the price of the underlying, X is the exercise price, r^c is the continuously compounded risk-free rate, and T is the time to expiration. The one other variable we need is the standard deviation of the log return on the asset. We denote this as σ and refer to it as the volatility. Then, the Black–Scholes–Merton formulas for the prices of call and put options are

$$
\begin{aligned}
c &= S_0 N(d_1) - X e^{-r^c T} N(d_2) \\
p &= X e^{-r^c T} [1 - N(d_2)] - S_0 [1 - N(d_1)]
\end{aligned}
\tag{66-21}
$$

where

$$
d_1 = \frac{\ln(S_0/X) + [r^c + (\sigma^2/2)]T}{\sigma\sqrt{T}}
\tag{66-22}
$$

$$
d_2 = d_1 - \sigma\sqrt{T}
$$

σ = the annualized standard deviation of the continuously compounded return on the stock

r^c = the continuously compounded risk-free rate of return

Of course, we have already seen the term "ln" and "e" in previous readings. We do, however, introduce two new and somewhat unusual looking terms, $N(d_1)$ and $N(d_2)$. These terms represent normal probabilities based on the values of d_1 and d_2. We compute the normal probabilities associated with values of d_1 and d_2 using the second equation above and insert these values into the formula as $N(d_1)$ and $N(d_2)$. Exhibit 66-24 presents a brief review of the normal probability distribution and explains how to obtain a probability value. Once we know how to look up a number in a normal probability table, we can then easily calculate d_1 and d_2, look them up in the table to obtain $N(d_1)$ and $N(d_2)$, and then insert the values of $N(d_1)$ and $N(d_2)$ into the above formula.

Consider the following example. The underlying price is 52.75 and has a volatility of 0.35. The continuously compounded risk-free rate is 4.88 percent. The option expires in nine months; therefore, $T = 9/12 = 0.75$. The exercise price is 50. First we calculate the values of d_1 and d_2:

$$d_1 = \frac{\ln(52.75/50) + (0.0488 + (0.35)^2/2)0.75}{0.35\sqrt{0.75}} = 0.4489$$

$$d_2 = 0.4489 - 0.35\sqrt{0.75} = 0.1458$$

To use the normal probability table in Appendix 66A, we must round off d_1 and d_2 to two digits to the right of the decimal. Thus we have $d_1 = 0.45$ and $d_2 = 0.15$. From the table, we obtain

$$N(0.45) = 0.6736$$
$$N(0.15) = 0.5596$$

Then we plug everything into the equation for c:

$$c = 52.75(0.6736) - 50e^{-0.0488(0.75)}(0.5596) = 8.5580$$

The value of a put with the same terms would be

$$p = 50e^{-0.0488(0.75)}(1 - 0.5596) - 52.75(1 - 0.6736) = 4.0110$$

At this point, we should note that the Black–Scholes–Merton model is extremely sensitive to rounding errors. In particular, the process of looking up values in the normal probability table is a major source of error. A number of other way exist to obtain $N(d_1)$ and $N(d_2)$, such as using Microsoft Excel's function "=normsdist()". Using a more precise method, such as Excel, the value of the call would be 8.619. Note that this is the value to which the binomial option price converged in the example we showed with 1,000 time periods in Exhibit 66-23. Indeed, the Black–Scholes–Merton model is said to be the continuous limit of the binomial model.

EXHIBIT 66-24   The Normal Probability Distribution

The normal probability distribution, or bell-shaped curve, gives the probability that a standard normal random variable will be less than or equal to a given value. The graph below shows the normal probability distribution; note that the curve is centered around zero. The values on the horizontal axis run from $-\infty$ to $+\infty$. If we were interested in a value of x of positive infinity, we would have $N(+\infty) = 1$. This expression means that the probability is 1.0 that we would obtain a value less than $+\infty$. If we were interested in a value of x of negative infinity, then $N(-\infty) = 0.0$. This expression means that there is zero probability of a value of x of less than negative infinity. Below, we are interested in the probability of a value less than x, where x is not infinite. We want $N(x)$, which is the area under the curve to the left of x.

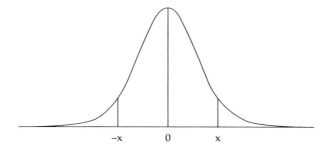

We obtain the values of $N(x)$ by looking them up in a table. Below is an excerpt from a table of values of x (the full table is given as Appendix 66A). Suppose $x = 1.12$. Then we find the row containing the value 1.1 and move over to the column containing 0.02. The sum of the row value and the column value is the value of x. The corresponding probability is seen as the value 0.8686. Thus, $N(1.12) = 0.8686$. This means that the probability of obtaining a value of less than 1.12 in a normal distribution is 0.8686.

x	0	0.01	0.02	0.03	0.04	0.05	0.06	0.07	0.08	0.09
0.60	0.7257	0.7291	0.7324	0.7357	0.7389	0.7422	0.7454	0.7486	0.7517	0.7549
0.70	0.7580	0.7611	0.7642	0.7673	0.7704	**0.7734**	0.7764	0.7794	0.7823	0.7852
0.80	0.7881	0.7910	0.7939	0.7967	0.7995	0.8023	0.8051	0.8078	0.8106	0.8133
0.90	0.8159	0.8186	0.8212	0.8238	0.8264	0.8289	0.8315	0.8340	0.8365	0.8389
1.00	0.8413	0.8438	0.8461	0.8485	0.8508	0.8531	0.8554	0.8577	0.8599	0.8621
1.10	0.8643	0.8665	**0.8686**	0.8708	0.8729	0.8749	0.8770	0.8790	0.8810	0.8830
1.20	0.8849	0.8869	0.8888	0.8907	0.8925	0.8944	0.8962	0.8980	0.8997	0.9015

Now, suppose the value of x is negative. Observe in the figure above that the area to the left of $-x$ is the same as the area to the right of $+x$. Therefore, if x is a negative number, $N(x)$ is found as $1 - N(-x)$. For example, let $x = -0.75$. We simply look up $N(-x) = N[-(-0.75)] = N(0.75) = 0.7734$. Then $N(-0.75) = 1 - 0.7734 = 0.2266$.

> **Practice Problem 8**
>
> Use the Black–Scholes–Merton model to calculate the prices of European call and put options on an asset priced at 68.5. The exercise price is 65, the continuously compounded risk-free rate is 4 percent, the options expire in 110 days, and the volatility is 0.38. There are no cash flows on the underlying.
>
> ▶ **Solutions.** The time to expiration will be T = 110/365 = 0.3014. Then d_1 and d_2 are
>
> $$d_1 = \frac{ln(68.5/65) + (0.04 + (0.38)^2/2)(0.3014)}{0.38\sqrt{0.3014}} = 0.4135$$
>
> $$d_2 = 0.4135 - 0.38\sqrt{0.3014} = 0.2049$$
>
> Looking up in the normal probability table, we have
>
> N(0.41) = 0.6591
> N(0.20) = 0.5793
>
> Plugging into the option price formula,
>
> $$c = 68.5(0.6591) - 65e^{-0.04(0.3014)}(0.5793) = 7.95$$
> $$p = 65e^{-0.04(0.3014)}(1 - 0.5793) - 68.5(1 - 0.6591) = 3.67$$

Let us now take a look at the various inputs required in the Black–Scholes–Merton model. We need to know where to obtain the inputs and how the option price varies with these inputs.

7.3 Inputs to the Black–Scholes–Merton Model

The Black–Scholes–Merton model has five inputs: the underlying price, the exercise price, the risk-free rate, the time to expiration, and the volatility.[30] As we have previously seen, call option prices should be higher the higher the underlying price, the longer the time to expiration, the higher the volatility, and the higher the risk-free rate. They should be lower the higher the exercise price. Put option prices should be higher the higher the exercise price and the higher the volatility. They should be lower the higher the underlying price and the higher the risk-free rate. As we saw, European put option prices can be either higher or lower the longer the time to expiration. American put option prices are always higher the longer the time to expiration, but the Black–Scholes–Merton model does not apply to American options.

These relationships are general to any European and American options and do not require the Black–Scholes–Merton model to understand them. Nonetheless, the Black–Scholes–Merton model provides an excellent opportunity to examine these relationships more closely. We can calculate and plot relation-

[30] Later we shall add one more input, cash flows on the underlying.

ships such as those mentioned, which are usually called the option Greeks, because they are often referred to with Greek names. Let us now look at each of the inputs and the various option Greeks.

7.3.1 The Underlying Price: Delta and Gamma

The price of the underlying is generally one of the easiest sources of input information. Suffice it to say that if an investor cannot obtain the price of the underlying, then she should not even be considering the option. The price should generally be obtained as a quote or trade price from a liquid, open market.

The relationship between the option price and the underlying price has a special name: It is called the **option delta**. In fact, the delta can be obtained approximately from the Black–Scholes–Merton formula as the value of $N(d_1)$ for calls and $N(d_1) - 1$ for puts. More formally, the delta is defined as

$$\text{Delta} = \frac{\text{Change in option price}}{\text{Change in underlying price}} \qquad \textbf{(66-23)}$$

The above definition for delta is exact; the use of $N(d_1)$ for calls and $N(d_1) - 1$ for puts is approximate. Later in this section, we shall see why $N(d_1)$ and $N(d_2)$ are approximations and when they are good or bad approximations.

Let us consider the example we previously worked, where S = 52.75, X = 50, r^c = 0.0488, T = 0.75, and σ = 0.35. Using a computer to obtain a more precise Black–Scholes–Merton answer, we get a call option price of 8.6186 and a put option price of 4.0717. $N(d_1)$, the call delta, is 0.6733, so the put delta is 0.6733 − 1 = −0.3267. Given that Delta = (Change in option price/Change in underlying price), we should expect that

Change in option price = Delta × Change in underlying price.

Therefore, for a $1 change in the price of the underlying, we should expect

Change in call option price = 0.6733(1) = 0.6733
Change in put option price = −0.3267(1) = −0.3267

This calculation would mean that

Approximate new call option price = 8.6186 + 0.6733 = 9.2919
Approximate new put option price = 4.0717 − 0.3267 = 3.7450

To test the accuracy of this approximation, we let the underlying price move up $1 to $53.75 and re-insert these values into the Black–Scholes–Merton model. We would then obtain

Actual new call option price = 9.3030
Actual new put option price = 3.7560

The delta approximation is fairly good, but not perfect.

Delta is important as a risk measure. *The delta defines the sensitivity of the option price to a change in the price of the underlying.* Traders, especially dealers in options, use delta to construct hedges to offset the risk they have assumed by buying and selling options. For example, recall from Reading 64 that FRA dealers offer to take either side of an FRA transaction. They then usually hedge the risk they have assumed by entering into other transactions. These same types of dealers offer to buy and sell options, hedging that risk with other transactions. For example, suppose we are a dealer offering to sell the call option we have been working with above. A customer buys 1,000 options for 8.619. We now are short 1,000 call options, which exposes us to considerable risk if the underlying goes up. So we must buy a certain number of units of the underlying to hedge this risk. We previously showed that the delta is 0.6733, so we would buy 673 units of the underlying at 52.75.[31] Assume for the moment that the delta tells us precisely the movement in the option for a movement in the underlying. Then suppose the underlying moves up $1:

Change in value of 673 long units of the underlying: $673(+\$1) = \$673$

Change in value of 1,000 short options: $1,000(+\$1)(0.6733) \approx \$673$

Because we are long the underlying and short the options, these values offset. At this point, however, the delta has changed. If we recalculate it, we would find it to be 0.6953. This would require that we have 695 units of the underlying, so we would need to buy an additional 22 units. We would borrow the money to do this. In some cases, we would need to sell off units of the underlying, in which case we would invest the money in the risk-free asset.

Let us consider how changes in the underlying price will change the delta. In fact, even if the underlying price does not change, the delta would still change as the option moves toward expiration. For a call, the delta will increase toward 1.0 as the underlying price moves up and will decrease toward 0.0 as the underlying price moves down. For a put, the delta will decrease toward -1.0 as the underlying price moves down and increase towards 0.0 as the underlying price moves up.[32] If the underlying price does not move, a call delta will move toward 1.0 if the call is in-the-money or 0.0 if the call is out-of-the-money as the call moves toward the expiration day. A put delta will move toward -1.0 if the put is in-the-money or 0.0 if the put is out-of-the-money as it moves toward expiration.

So the delta is constantly changing, which means that delta hedging is a dynamic process. In fact, delta hedging is often referred to as **dynamic hedging**. In theory, the delta is changing continuously and the hedge should be adjusted continuously, but continuous adjustment is not possible in reality. When the hedge is not adjusted continuously, we are admitting the possibility of much larger moves in the price of the underlying. Let us see what happens in that case.

Using our previous example, we allow an increase in the underlying price of $10 to $62.75. Then the call price should change by $0.6733(10) = 6.733$, and the put option price should change by $-0.3267(10) = -3.267$. Thus, the approximate prices would be

Approximate new call option price $= 8.619 + 6.733 = 15.3520$

Approximate new put option price $= 4.0717 - 3.267 = 0.8047$

The actual prices are obtained by recalculating the option values using the Black–Scholes–Merton model with an underlying price of 62.75. Using a computer for greater precision, we find that these prices are

---

[31] This transaction would require $673(\$52.75) = \$35,500$, less the $1,000(\$8.619) = \$8,619$ received from the sale of the option, for a total investment required of $26,881. We would probably borrow this money.

[32] Remember that the put delta is negative; hence, its movement is down toward -1.0 or up toward 0.0.

Actual new call option price = 16.3026

Actual new put option price = 1.7557

The approximations based on delta are not very accurate. In general, the larger the move in the underlying, the worse the approximation. This will make delta hedging less effective.

Exhibit 66-25 shows the relationship between the option price and the underlying price. Panel A depicts the relationship for calls and Panel B shows the corresponding relationship for puts. Notice the curvature in the relationship between the option price and the underlying price. Call option values definitely increase the greater the underlying value, and put option values definitely decrease. But the amount of change is not the same in each direction. $N(d_1)$ measures the slope of this line at a given point. As such, it measures only the slope for a very small change in the underlying. When the underlying changes by more than a very small amount, the curvature of the line comes into play and distorts the relationship between the option price and underlying price that is explained by the delta. The problem here is much like the relationship between a bond price and its yield. This first-order relationship between a bond price and its yield is called the duration; therefore, duration is similar to delta.

The curvature or second-order effect is known in the fixed income world as the convexity. In the options world, this effect is called **gamma**. Gamma is a numerical measure of how sensitive the delta is to a change in the underlying—in other words, how much the delta changes. When gamma is large, the delta

| EXHIBIT 66-25 | The Relationship between Option Price and Underlying Price X = 50, r^c = 0.0488, T = 0.75, σ = 0.35 |

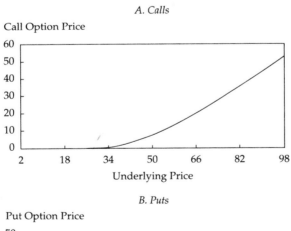

A. Calls

B. Puts

changes rapidly and cannot provide a good approximation of how much the option moves for each unit of movement in the underlying. We shall not concern ourselves with measuring and using gamma, but we should know a few things about the gamma and, therefore, about the behavior of the delta.

Gamma is larger when there is more uncertainty about whether the option will expire in- or out-of-the-money. This means that *gamma will tend to be large when the option is at-the-money and close to expiration.* In turn, this statement means that delta will be a poor approximation for the option's price sensitivity when it is at-the-money and close to the expiration day. Thus, a **delta hedge** will work poorly. When the gamma is large, we may need to use a gamma-based hedge, which would require that we add a position in another option to the delta-hedge position of the underlying and the option. We shall not take up this advanced topic here.

7.3.2 The Exercise Price

The exercise price is easy to obtain. It is specified in the option contract and does not change. Therefore, it is not worthwhile to speak about what happens when the exercise price changes, but we can talk about how the option price would differ if we choose an option with a different exercise price. As we have previously seen, the call option price will be lower the higher the exercise price and the put option price will be higher. This relationship is confirmed for our sample option in Exhibit 66-26.

EXHIBIT 66-26	**The Relationship between Option Price and Exercise Price** $S = 52.75$, $r^c = 0.0488$, $T = 0.75$, $\sigma = 0.35$

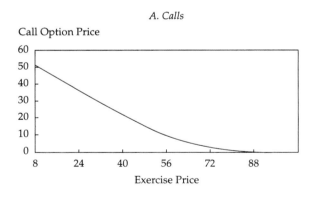

A. Calls

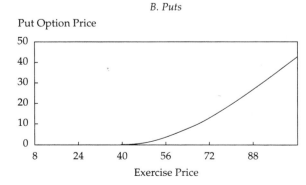

B. Puts

7.3.3 The Risk-Free Rate: Rho

The risk-free rate is the continuously compounded rate on the risk-free security whose maturity corresponds to the option's life. We have used the risk-free rate in previous readings; sometimes we have used the discrete version and sometimes the continuous version. As we have noted, the continuously compounded risk-free rate is the natural log of 1 plus the discrete risk-free rate.

For example, suppose the discrete risk-free rate quoted in annual terms is 5 percent. Then the continuous rate is

$$r^c = \ln(1 + r) = \ln(1.05) = 0.0488$$

Let us recall the difference in these two specifications. Suppose we want to find the present value of $1 in six months using both the discrete and continuous risk-free rates.

$$\text{Present value using discrete rate} = \frac{1}{(1 + r)^T} = \frac{1}{(1.05)^{0.5}} = 0.9759$$

$$\text{Present value using continuous rate} = e^{-r^cT} = e^{-0.0488(0.5)} = 0.9759$$

Obviously either specification will work. Because of how it uses the risk-free rate in the calculation of d_1, however, the Black–Scholes–Merton model requires the continuous risk-free rate.

The sensitivity of the option price to the risk-free rate is called the **rho**. We shall not concern ourselves with the calculation of rho. Technically, the Black–Scholes–Merton model assumes a constant risk-free rate, so it is meaningless to talk about the risk-free rate changing over the life of the option. We can, however, explore how the option price would differ if the current rate were different. Exhibit 66-27 on page 194 depicts this effect. Note how little change occurs in the option price over a very broad range of the risk-free rate. Indeed, *the price of a European option on an asset is not very sensitive to the risk-free rate.*[33]

7.3.4 Time to Expiration: Theta

Time to expiration is an easy input to determine. An option has a definite expiration date specified in the contract. We simply count the number of days until expiration and divide by 365, as we have done previously with forward and futures contracts.

Obviously, the time remaining in an option's life moves constantly towards zero. Even if the underlying price is constant, the option price will still change. We noted that American options have both an intrinsic value and a time value. For European options, all of the price can be viewed as time value. In either case, time value is a function of the option's moneyness, its time to expiration, and its volatility. The more uncertainty there is, the greater the time value. As expiration approaches, the option price moves toward the payoff value of the option at expiration, a process known as **time value decay**. The rate at which the time value decays is called the option's **theta**. We shall not concern ourselves with calculating the specific value of theta, but be aware that if the option price decreases as time moves forward, the theta will be negative. Exhibit 66-28 shows the time value decay for our sample option.

---

[33] When the underlying is an interest rate, however, there is a strong relationship between the option price and interest rates.

EXHIBIT 66-27	The Relationship between Option Price and Risk-Free Rate S = 52.75, X = 50, T = 0.75, σ = 0.35

A. Calls

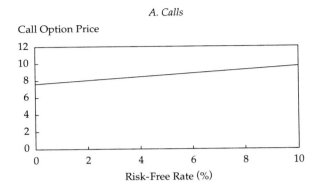

B. Puts

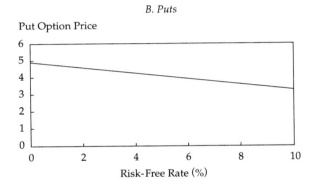

Note that both call and put values decrease as the time to expiration decreases. We previously noted that European put options do not necessarily do this. For some cases, European put options can increase in value as the time to expiration decreases, the case of a positive theta, but that is not so for our put.[34] *Most of the time, option prices are higher the longer the time to expiration. For European puts, however, some exceptions exist.*

7.3.5 Volatility: Vega

As we have previously noted, volatility is the standard deviation of the continuously compounded return on the stock. We have also noted that the volatility is an extremely important variable in the valuation of an option. It is the only variable that cannot be obtained easily and directly from another source. In addition, as we illustrate here, option prices are extremely sensitive to the volatility. We take up the subject of estimating volatility in Section 7.5.

---

[34] Positive put thetas tend to occur when the put is deep in-the-money, the volatility is low, the interest rate is high, and the time to expiration is low.

EXHIBIT 66-28	The Relationship between Option Price and Time to Expiration S = 52.75, X = 50, r^c = 0.0488, σ = 0.35. T Starts at 0.75 and Goes toward 0.0

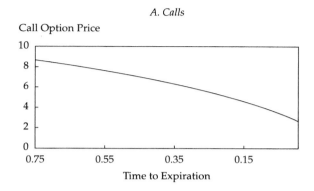

A. Calls

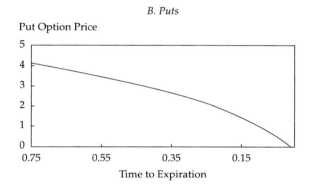

B. Puts

The relationship between option price and volatility is called the **vega**, which—albeit considered an option Greek—is not actually a Greek word.[35] We shall not concern ourselves with the actual calculation of the vega, but know that the vega is positive for both calls and puts, meaning that if the volatility increases, both call and put prices increase. Also, the vega is larger the closer the option is to being at-the-money.

In the problem we previously worked (S_0 = \$52.75, X = \$50, r^c = 0.0488, T = 0.75), at a volatility of 0.35, the option price was 8.619. Suppose we erroneously use a volatility of 0.40. Then the call price would be 9.446. An error in the volatility of this magnitude would not be difficult to make, especially for a variable that is not directly observable. Yet the result is a very large error in the option price.

Exhibit 66-29 displays the relationship between the option price and the volatility. Note that this relationship is nearly linear and that the option price varies over a very wide range, although this near-linearity is not the case for all options.

---

[35] So that all of these effects ("the Greeks") be named after Greek words, the term *kappa* is sometimes used to represent the relationship between an option price and its volatility. As it turns out, however, vega is used far more often than kappa and is probably easier to remember, given the "v" in vega and the "v" in volatility. Vega, however, is a star, not a letter, and its origin is Latin.

EXHIBIT 66-29	The Relationship between Option Price and Volatility S = 52.75, X = 50, r^c = 0.0488, T = 0.75

A. Calls

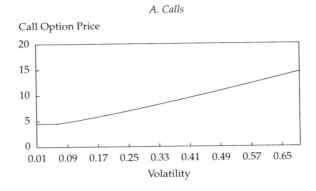

B. Puts

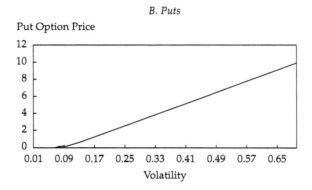

7.4 The Effect of Cash Flows on the Underlying

As we saw in Readings 64 and 65, cash flows on the underlying affect the prices of forward and futures contracts. It should follow that they would affect the prices of options. In studying the option boundary conditions and put–call parity earlier in this reading, we noted that we subtract the present value of the dividends from the underlying price and use this adjusted price to obtain the boundary conditions or to price the options using put–call parity. We do the same using the Black–Scholes–Merton model. Specifically, we introduced the expression PV(CF,0,T) for the present value of the cash flows on the underlying over the life of the option. So, we simply use $S_0 - PV(CF,0,T)$ in the Black–Scholes–Merton model instead of S_0.

Recall that in previous readings, we also used continuous compounding to express the cash flows. For stocks, we used a continuously compounded dividend yield; for currencies, we used a continuously compounded interest rate. In the case of stocks, we let δ^c represent the continuously compounded dividend rate. Then we substituted for $S_0 e^{-\delta^c T}$ for S_0 in the Black–Scholes–Merton formula. For a foreign currency, we let S_0 represent the exchange rate, which we discount using r^{fc}, the continuously compounded foreign risk-free rate. Let us work an example involving a foreign currency option.

Let the exchange rate of U.S. dollars for euros be $0.8475. The continuously compounded U.S. risk-free rate, which in this example is r^c, is 5.10 percent. The continuously compounded euro risk-free rate, r^{fc}, is 4.25 percent. A call option expires in 125 days (T = 125/365 = 0.3425) and has an exercise price of $0.90. The volatility of the continuously compounded exchange rate is 0.055.

The first thing we do is obtain the adjusted price of the underlying: $0.8475e^{-0.0425(0.3425)} = 0.8353$. We then use this value as S_0 in the formula for d_1 and d_2:

$$d_1 = \frac{ln(0.8353/0.90) + [0.051 + (0.055)^2/2](0.3425)}{0.055\sqrt{0.3425}} = -1.7590$$

$$d_2 = -1.7590 - 0.055\sqrt{0.3425} = -1.7912$$

Using the normal probability table, we find that

$$N(d_1) = N(-1.76) = 1 - 0.9608 = 0.0392$$
$$N(d_2) = N(-1.79) = 1 - 0.9633 = 0.0367$$

In discounting the exercise rate to evaluate the second term in the Black–Scholes–Merton expression, we use the domestic (here, U.S.) continuously compounded risk-free rate. The call option price would thus be

$$c = 0.8353(0.0392) - 0.90e^{-0.051(0.3425)}(0.0367) = 0.0003$$

Therefore, this call option on an asset worth $0.8475 would cost $0.0003.

Practice Problem 9

Use the Black–Scholes–Merton model adjusted for cash flows on the underlying to calculate the price of a call option in which the underlying is priced at 225, the exercise price is 200, the continuously compounded risk-free rate is 5.25 percent, the time to expiration is three years, and the volatility is 0.15. The effect of cash flows on the underlying is indicated below for two alternative approaches:

A. The present value of the cash flows over the life of the option is 19.72.

B. The continuously compounded dividend yield is 2.7 percent.

▶ **Solution to A.** Adjust the price of the underlying to $S_0 = 225 - 19.72 = 205.28$. Then insert into the Black–Scholes–Merton formula as follows:

$$d_1 = \frac{\ln(205.28/200) + [0.0525 + (0.15)^2/2]3.0}{0.15\sqrt{3.0}} = 0.8364$$

$$d_2 = 0.8364 - 0.15\sqrt{3.0} = 0.5766$$
$$N(0.84) = 0.7995$$
$$N(0.58) = 0.7190$$
$$c = 205.28(0.7995) - 200e^{-0.0525(3.0)}(0.7190) = 41.28$$

▶ **Solution to B.** Adjust the price of the underlying to $S_0 = 225e^{-0.027(3.0)} = 207.49$

$$d_1 = \frac{\ln(207.49/200) + [0.0525 + (0.15)^2/2]3.0}{0.15\sqrt{3.0}} = 0.8776$$

$$d_2 = 0.8776 - 0.15\sqrt{3.0} = 0.6178$$

$$N(0.88) = 0.8106$$

$$N(0.62) = 0.7324$$

$$c = 207.49(0.8106) - 200e^{-0.0525(3.0)}(0.7324) = 43.06$$

7.5 The Critical Role of Volatility

As we have previously stressed, volatility is an extremely important variable in the pricing of options. In fact, with the possible exception of the cash flows on the underlying, it is the only variable that cannot be directly observed and easily obtained. It is, after all, the volatility over the life of the option; therefore, it is not past or current volatility but rather the future volatility. Differences in opinion on option prices nearly always result from differences of opinion about volatility. But how does one obtain a number for the future volatility?

7.5.1 Historical Volatility

The most logical starting place to look for an estimate of future volatility is past volatility. When the underlying is a publicly traded asset, we usually can collect some data over a recent past period and estimate the standard deviation of the continuously compounded return.

Exhibit 66-30 illustrates this process for a sample of 12 monthly prices of a particular stock. We convert these prices to returns, convert the returns to continuously compounded returns, find the variance of the series of continuously compounded returns, and then convert the variance to the standard deviation. In this example, the data are monthly returns, so we must annualize the variance by multiplying it by 12. Then we take the square root to obtain the historical estimate of the annual standard deviation or volatility.

The historical estimate of the volatility is based only on what happened in the past. To get the best estimate, we must use a lot of prices, but that means going back farther in time. The farther back we go, the less current the data become, and the less reliable our estimate of the volatility. We now look at a way of obtaining a more current estimate of the volatility, but one that raises questions as well as answers them.

7.5.2 Implied Volatility

In a market in which options are traded actively, we can reasonably assume that the market price of the option is an accurate reflection of its true value. Thus, by setting the Black–Scholes–Merton price equal to the market price, we can work backwards to infer the volatility. This procedure enables us to determine the volatility that option traders are using to price the option. This volatility is called the **implied volatility**.

Unfortunately, determining implied volatility is not a simple task. We cannot simply solve the Black–Scholes–Merton equation for the volatility. It is a complicated function with the volatility appearing several times, in some cases as σ^2.

EXHIBIT 66-30	Estimating Historical Volatility			
Month	Price	Return	Log Return	(Log Return − Average)^2
0	100			
1	102	0.020000	0.019803	0.000123
2	99	−0.029412	−0.029853	0.001486
3	97	−0.020202	−0.020409	0.000847
4	89	−0.082474	−0.086075	0.008982
5	103	0.157303	0.146093	0.018878
6	104	0.009709	0.009662	0.000001
7	102	−0.019231	−0.019418	0.000790
8	99	−0.029412	−0.029853	0.001486
9	104	0.050505	0.049271	0.001646
10	102	−0.019231	−0.019418	0.000790
11	105	0.029412	0.028988	0.000412
12	111	0.057143	0.055570	0.002197
		Sum	0.104360	0.037639
		Average	0.008697	

The variance is estimated as follows:

$$\sigma^2 = \frac{\sum_{i=1}^{N}(R_i^c - \overline{R}^c)^2}{N-1}$$

where R_i^c is the continuously compounded return for observation i (shown above in the fourth column and calculated as $\ln(1 + R_i)$, where i goes from 1 to 12) and R_i is the ith return, $\overline{R}^c$ is the average return over the entire sample, and N is the number of observations in the sample (here, N = 12). Then

$$\sigma^2 = \frac{0.037639}{11} = 0.003422$$

Because this sample consists of monthly returns, to obtain the annual variance, we must multiply this number by 12 (or 52 for weekly, or 250—the approximate number of trading days in a year—for daily). Thus

$$\sigma^2 = 12(0.003422) = 0.041064$$

The annual standard deviation or volatility is, therefore,

$$\sigma = \sqrt{0.041064} = 0.2026$$

So the historical volatility estimate is 20.26 percent.

There are some mathematical techniques that speed up the estimation of the implied volatility. Here, however, we shall look at only the most basic method: trial and error.

Recall the option we have been working with. The underlying price is 52.75, the exercise price is 50, the risk-free rate is 4.88 percent, and the time to expiration is 0.75. In our previous examples, the volatility was 0.35. Using these values in the Black–Scholes–Merton model, we obtained a call option price of 8.619. Suppose we observe the option selling in the market for 9.25. What volatility would produce this price?

We have already calculated a price of 8.619 at a volatility of 0.35. Because the call price varies directly with the volatility, we know that it would take a volatility greater than 0.35 to produce a price higher than 8.619. We do not know how much higher, so we should just take a guess. Let us try a volatility of 0.40. Using the Black–Scholes–Merton formula with a volatility of 0.40, we obtain a price of 9.446. This is too high, so we try a lower volatility. We keep doing this in the following manner:

Volatility	Black–Scholes–Merton Price
0.35	8.619
0.40	9.446
0.39	9.280
0.38	9.114

So now we know that the correct volatility lies between 0.38 and 0.39, closer to 0.39. In solving for the implied volatility, we must decide either how close to the option price we want to be or how many significant digits we want in the implied volatility. If we choose four significant digits in the implied volatility, a value of 0.3882 would produce the option price of 9.2500. Alternatively, if we decide that we want to be within 0.01 of the option price, we would find that the implied volatility is in the range of 38.76 to 38.88 percent.

Thus, if the option is selling for about 9.25, we say that the market is pricing it at a volatility of 0.3882. This number represents the market's best estimate of the true volatility of the underlying asset; it can be viewed as a more current source of volatility information than the past volatility. Unfortunately, a circularity exists in the argument. If one uses the Black–Scholes–Merton model to determine if an option is over- or underpriced, the procedure for extracting the implied volatility assumes that the market correctly prices the option. The only way to use the implied volatility in identifying mispriced options is to interpret the implied volatility as either too high or too low, which would require an estimate of true volatility. Nonetheless, the implied volatility is a source of valuable information on the uncertainty in the underlying, and option traders use it routinely.

All of this material on continuous-time option pricing has been focused on options in which the underlying is an asset. As we described earlier in this reading, there are also options on futures. Let us take a look at the pricing of options on futures, which will pave the way for a continuous-time pricing model for options on interest rates, another case in which the underlying is not an asset.

PRICING OPTIONS ON FORWARD AND FUTURES CONTRACTS AND AN APPLICATION TO INTEREST RATE OPTION PRICING

8

Earlier in this reading, we discussed how options on futures contracts are active, exchange-traded options in which the underlying is a futures contract. In addition, there are over-the-counter options in which the underlying is a forward contract. In our treatment of these instruments, we assume constant interest rates. As we learned in Readings 64 and 65, this assumption means that futures and forward contracts will have the same prices. European options on futures and forward contracts will, therefore, have the same prices. American options on forwards will differ in price from American options on futures, and we discuss this later.

First we take a quick look at the basic rules that we previously developed for options on underlying assets. If the underlying asset is a futures contract, the payoff values of the options at expiration are

$$c_T = \text{Max}[0, f_T(T) - X]$$
$$p_T = \text{Max}[0, X - f_T(T)]$$

(66-24)

where $f_T(T)$ is the price of a futures contract at T in which the contract expires at T. Thus, $f_T(T)$ is the futures price at expiration. These formulas are, of course, the same as for options when the underlying is an asset, with the futures price substituted for the asset price. When the option and the futures expire simultaneously, the futures price at expiration, $f_T(T)$, converges to the asset price, S_T, making the above payoffs precisely the same as those of the option on the underlying asset.

The minimum and maximum values for options on forwards or futures are the same as those we obtained for options on assets, substituting the futures price for the asset price. Specifically,

$$0 \le c_0 \le f_0(T)$$
$$0 \le C_0 \le f_0(T)$$
$$0 \le p_0 \le X/(1 + r)^T$$
$$0 \le P_0 \le X$$

(66-25)

We also established lower bounds for European options and intrinsic values for American options and used these results to establish the minimum prices of these options. For options on futures, the lower bounds are

$$c_0 \ge \text{Max}\{0, [f_0(T) - X]/(1 + r)^T\}$$
$$p_0 \ge \text{Max}\{0, [X - f_0(T)]/(1 + r)^T\}$$

(66-26)

where $f_0(T)$ is the price at time 0 of a futures contract expiring at T. Therefore, the price of a European call or put on the futures is either zero or the difference between the futures price and exercise price, as formulated above, discounted to the present. For American options on futures, early exercise is possible. Thus, we express their lowest prices as the intrinsic values:

$$C_0 \ge \text{Max}[0, f_0(T) - X]$$
$$P_0 \ge \text{Max}[0, X - f_0(T)]$$

(66-27)

Because these values are greater than the lower bounds, we maintain these values as the minimum prices of American calls.[36]

As we have previously pointed out, with the assumption of constant interest rates, futures prices and forward prices are the same. We can treat European options on futures the same way as options on forwards. American options on futures will differ from American options on forwards. Now we explore how put–call parity works for options on forwards.

8.1 Put–Call Parity for Options on Forwards

In an earlier section, we examined put–call parity. Now we take a look at the parity between puts and calls on forward contracts and their underlying forward contracts. First recall the notation: $F(0,T)$ is the price established at time 0 for a forward contract expiring at time T. Let c_0 and p_0 be the prices today of calls and puts on the forward contract. We shall assume that the puts and calls expire when the forward contract expires. The exercise price of the options is X. The payoff of the call is $Max(0, S_T - X)$, and the payoff of the put is $Max(0, X - S_T)$.[37] We construct a combination consisting of a long call and a long position in a zero-coupon bond with face value of $X - F(0,T)$. We construct another combination consisting of a long position in a put and a long position in a forward contract. Exhibit 66-31 shows the results.

As the exhibit demonstrates, both combinations produce a payoff of either $X - F(0,T)$ or $S_T - F(0,T)$, whichever is greater. The call and bond combination is thus equivalent to the put and forward contract combination. Hence, to prevent an arbitrage opportunity, the initial values of these combinations must be the same. The initial value of the call and bond combination is $c_0 + [X - F(0,T)]/(1 + r)^T$. The forward contract has zero initial value, so the initial value of the put and forward contract combination is only the initial value of the put, p_0. Therefore,

EXHIBIT 66-31	Portfolio Combinations for Equivalent Packages of Puts, Calls, and Forward Contracts (Put–Call Parity for Forward Contracts)		
		Value at Expiration	
Transaction	Current Value	$S_T \leq X$	$S_T > X$
Call and Bond			
Buy call	c_0	0	$S_T - X$
Buy bond	$[X - F(0,T)]/(1 + r)^T$	$X - F(0,T)$	$X - F(0,T)$
Total	$c_0 + [X - F(0,T)]/(1 + r)^T$	$X - F(0,T)$	$S_T - F(0,T)$
Put and Forward			
Buy put	p_0	$X - S_T$	0
Buy forward contract	0	$S_T - F(0,T)$	$S_T - F(0,T)$
Total	p_0	$X - F(0,T)$	$S_T - F(0,T)$

[36] In other words, we cannot use the European lower bound as the lowest price of an American call or put, as we could with calls when the underlying was an asset instead of a futures.

[37] Recall that the option payoffs are given by the underlying price at expiration, because the forward contract expires when the option expires. Therefore, the forward price at expiration is the underlying price at expiration.

$$c_0 + [X - F(0,T)]/(1 + r)^T = p_0 \qquad \text{(66-28)}$$

This equation is **put–call parity for options on forward contracts**.

Note that we seem to have implied that the bond is a long position, but that might not be the case. The bond should have a face value of $X - F(0,T)$. We learned in Reading 64 that $F(0,T)$ is determined in the market as the underlying price compounded at the risk-free rate.[38] Because there are a variety of options with different exercise prices, any one of which could be chosen, it is clearly possible for X to exceed or be less than $F(0,T)$. If $X > F(0,T)$, we are long the bond, because the payoff of $X - F(0,T)$ is greater than zero, meaning that we get back money from the bond. If $X < F(0,T)$, we issue the bond, because the payoff of $X - F(0,T)$ is less than zero, meaning that we must pay back money. Note the special case when $X = F(0,T)$. The bond is effectively out of the picture. Then $c_0 = p_0$.

Now recall from Reading 64 that with discrete interest compounding and no storage costs, the forward price is the spot price compounded at the risk-free rate. So,

$$F(0,T) = S_0(1 + r)^T$$

If we substitute this result for $F(0,T)$ in the put–call parity equation for options on forwards, we obtain

$$p_0 + S_0 = c_0 + X/(1 + r)^T$$

which is the put–call parity equation for options on the underlying that we learned earlier in this reading. Indeed, put–call parity for options on forwards and put–call parity for options on the underlying asset are the same. The only difference is that in the former, the forward contract and the bond replace the underlying. Given the equivalence of options on the forward contract and options on the underlying, we can refer to put–call parity for options on forwards as **put–call–forward parity**. The equation

$$c_0 + [X - F(0,T)]/(1 + r)^T = p_0$$

expresses the relationship between the forward price and the prices of the options on the underlying asset, or alternatively between the forward price and the prices of options on the forward contract. We can also rearrange the equation to isolate the forward price and obtain

$$F(0,T) = (c_0 - p_0)(1 + r)^T + X$$

which shows how the forward price is related to the put and call prices and to the exercise price.

Now observe in Exhibit 66-32 how a synthetic forward contract can be created out of options.

In the top half of the exhibit is a forward contract. Its payoff at expiration is $S_T - F(0,T)$. In the bottom half of the exhibit is a **synthetic forward contract**, which consists of a long call, a short put, and a long risk-free bond with a face value equal to the exercise price minus the forward price. Note that this bond can actually be short if the exercise price of these options is lower than the forward price. The forward contract and synthetic forward contract have the same payoffs,

---

[38] We are, of course, assuming no cash flows or costs on the underlying asset.

EXHIBIT 66-32	Forward Contract and Synthetic Forward Contract			

		Value at Expiration	
Transaction	**Current Value**	$S_T \leq X$	$S_T > X$
Forward Contract			
Long forward contract	0	$S_T - F(0,T)$	$S_T - F(0,T)$
Synthetic Forward Contract			
Buy call	c_0	0	$S_T - X$
Sell put	$-p_0$	$-(X - S_T)$	0
Buy (or sell) bond	$[X - F(0,T)]/(1+r)^T$	$X - F(0,T)$	$X - F(0,T)$
Total	$c_0 - p_0 + [X - F(0,T)]/(1+r)^T$	$S_T - F(0,T)$	$S_T - F(0,T)$

so their initial values must be equal. The initial value of the forward contract is zero, so the initial value of the synthetic forward contract must be zero. Thus,

$$c_0 - p_0 + [X - F(0,T)]/(1+r)^T = 0$$

Solving for $F(0,T)$, we obtain the equation for the forward price in terms of the call, put, and bond that was given previously. So a synthetic forward contract is a combination consisting of a long call, a short put, and a zero-coupon bond with face value of $X - F(0,T)$.

Consider the following example: The options and a forward contract expire in 50 days, so $T = 50/365 = 0.1370$. The risk-free rate is 6 percent, and the exercise price is 95. The call price is 5.50, the put price is 10.50, and the forward price is 90.72. Substituting in the above equation, we obtain

$$5.50 - 10.50 + \frac{95 - 90.72}{(1.06)^{0.1370}} = -0.7540$$

which is supposed to be zero. The left-hand side replicates a forward contract. Thus, the synthetic forward is underpriced. We buy it and sell the actual forward contract. So if we buy the call, sell the put, and buy the bond with face value $95 - 90.72 = 4.28$, we bring in 0.7540. At expiration, the payoffs are as follows.

The options and forward expire with the underlying above 95:
   The bond matures and pays off $95 - 90.72 = 4.28$.
   Exercise the call, paying 95 and obtaining the underlying.
   Deliver the underlying and receive 90.72 from the forward contract.
   The put expires with no value.
   Net effect: No money in or out.

The options and forward expire with the underlying at or below 95:
   The bond matures and pays off $95 - 90.72 = 4.28$.
   Buy the underlying for 95 with the short put.
   Deliver the underlying and receive 90.72 from the forward contract.
   The call expires with no value.
   Net effect: No money in or out.

So we take in 0.7540 up front and never have to pay anything out. The pressure of other investors doing this will cause the call price to increase and the put price to decrease until the above equation equals zero or is at least equal to the transaction costs that would be incurred to exploit any discrepancy from zero.

Similarly, an option can be created from a forward contract. If a long forward contract is equivalent to a long call, short put, and zero-coupon bond with face value of $X - F(0,T)$, then a long call is a long forward, long put, and a zero-coupon bond with face value of $F(0,T) - X$. A long put is a long call, short forward, and a bond with face value of $X - F(0,T)$. These results are obtained just by rearranging what we learned here about forwards and options.

These results hold strictly for European options; some additional considerations exist for American options, but we do not cover them here.

Practice Problem 10

Determine if a forward contract is correctly priced by using put–call–forward parity. The option exercise price is 90, the risk-free rate is 5 percent, the options and the forward contract expire in two years, the call price is 15.25, the put price is 3.00, and the forward price is 101.43.

▶ **Solution.** First note that the time to expiration is $T = 2.0$. There are many ways to express put–call–forward parity. We use the following specification:

$$p_0 = c_0 + [X - F(0,T)]/(1 + r)^T$$

The right-hand side is the synthetic put and consists of a long call, a short forward contract, and a bond with face value of $X - F(0,T)$. Substituting the values into the right-hand side, we obtain

$$p_0 = 15.25 + (90 - 101.43)/(1.05)^{2.0} = 4.88$$

Because the actual put is selling for 3.00, it is underpriced. So we should buy the put and sell the synthetic put. To sell the synthetic put we should sell the call, buy the forward contract, and hold a bond with face value $F(0,T) - X$. Doing so will generate the following cash flow up front:

Buy put:	-3.00
Sell call:	$+15.25$
Buy bond:	$-(101.43 - 90)/(1.05)^{2.0} = -10.37$
Total:	$+1.88$

Thus the transaction brings in 1.88 up front. The payoffs at expiration are

	$S_T < 90$	$S_T \geq 90$
Long put	$90 - S_T$	0
Short call	0	$-(S_T - 90)$
Long bond	$101.43 - 90$	$101.43 - 90$
Long forward	$S_T - 101.43$	$S_T - 101.43$
Total	0	0

Therefore, no money flows in or out at expiration.

8.2 Early Exercise of American Options on Forward and Futures Contracts

As we noted earlier, the holder of an American put option may want to exercise it early. For American call options on underlying assets that make no cash payments, however, there is no justification for exercising the option early. If the underlying asset makes a cash payment, such as a dividend on a stock or interest on a bond, it may be justifiable to exercise the call option early.

For American options on futures, it may be worthwhile to exercise both calls and puts early. Even though early exercise is never justified for American calls on underlying assets that make no cash payments, early exercise can be justified for American call options on futures. Deep-in-the money American call options on futures behave almost identically to the underlying, but the investor has money tied up in the call. If the holder exercises the call and establishes a futures position, he earns interest on the futures margin account. A similar argument holds for deep-in-the-money American put options on futures. The determination of the timing of early exercise is a specialist topic so we do not explore it here.

If the option is on a forward contract instead of a futures contract, however, these arguments are overshadowed by the fact that a forward contract does not pay off until expiration, in contrast to the mark-to-market procedure of futures contracts. Thus, if one exercised either a call or a put on a forward contract early, doing so would only establish a long or short position in a forward contract. This position would not pay any cash until expiration. No justification exists for exercising early if one cannot generate any cash from the exercise. Therefore, an American call on a forward contract is the same as a European call on a forward contract, but American calls on futures are different from European calls on futures and carry higher prices.

8.3 The Black Model

The usual model for pricing European options on futures is called the Black model, named after Fischer Black of Black–Scholes–Merton fame. The formula is

$$c = e^{-r^c T}[f_0(T)N(d_1) - XN(d_2)]$$
$$p = e^{-r^c T}(X[1 - N(d_2)] - f_0(T)[1 - N(d_1)])$$

where

$$d_1 = \frac{\ln(f_0(T)/X) + (\sigma^2/2)T}{\sigma\sqrt{T}}$$
$$d_2 = d_1 - \sigma\sqrt{T}$$
$$f_0(T) = \text{the futures price}$$

and the other terms are those we have previously used. The volatility, σ, is the volatility of the continuously compounded change in the futures price.[39]

---

[39] If we were using the model to price options on forward contracts, we would insert $F(0,T)$, the forward price, instead of the futures price. Doing so would produce some confusion because we have never subscripted the forward price, arguing that it does not change. Therefore, although we could use the formula to price options on forwards at time 0, how could we use the formula to price options on forwards at a later time, say time t, prior to expiration? In that case, we would have to use the price of a newly constructed forward contract that expires at T, $F(t,T)$. Of course, with constant interest rates, these forward prices, $F(0,T)$ and $F(t,T)$, would be identical to the analogous futures price, $f_0(T)$ and $f_t(T)$. So, for ease of exposition we use the futures price.

Although the Black model may appear to give a somewhat different formula, it can be obtained directly from the Black–Scholes–Merton formula. Recall that the futures price in terms of the underlying spot price would be $f_0(T) = S_0 e^{r^c T}$. If we substitute the right-hand-side for $f_0(T)$ in the Black formula for d_1, we obtain the Black–Scholes–Merton formula for d_1.[40] Then if we substitute the right-hand side of the above for $f_0(T)$ in the Black formula for c_0 and p_0, we obtain the Black–Scholes–Merton formula for c_0 and p_0. These substitutions should make sense: The prices of options on futures equal the prices of options on the asset when the options and futures expire simultaneously.

The procedure should be straightforward if you have mastered substituting the asset price and other inputs into the Black–Scholes–Merton formula. Also, note that as with the Black–Scholes–Merton formula, the formula applies only to European options. As we noted in the previous section, early exercise of American options on futures is often justified, so we cannot get away with using this formula for American options on futures. We can, however, use the formula for American options on forwards, because they are never exercised early.

Practice Problem 11

The price of a forward contract is 139.19. A European option on the forward contract expires in 215 days. The exercise price is 125. The continuously compounded risk-free rate is 4.25 percent. The volatility is 0.15.

A. Use the Black model to determine the price of the call option.

B. Determine the price of the underlying from the above information and use the Black–Scholes–Merton model to show that the price of an option on the underlying is the same as the price of the option on the forward.

The time to expiration is $T = 215/365 = 0.5890$.

▶ **Solution to A.** First find d_1 and d_2, then $N(d_1)$ and $N(d_2)$, and then the call price:

$$d_1 = \frac{ln(139.19/125) + [(0.15)^2/2]\,0.5890}{0.15\sqrt{0.5890}} = 0.9916$$

$$d_2 = 0.9916 - 0.15\sqrt{0.5890} = 0.8765$$

$$N(0.99) = 0.8389$$

$$N(0.88) = 0.8106$$

$$c = e^{-0.0425(0.5890)}[139.19(0.8389) - 125(0.8106)] = 15.06$$

▶ **Solution to B.** We learned in Reading 64 that if there are no cash flows on the underlying and the interest is compounded continuously, the forward price is given by the formula $F(0, T) = S_0 e^{r^c T}$. We can thus find the spot price as

$$S_0 = F(0,T)e^{-r^c T} = 139.19 e^{-0.0425(0.5890)} = 135.75$$

---

[40] This action requires us to recognize that $ln(S_0 e^{r^c T}/X) = ln(S_0/X) + r^c T$.

Then we simply use the Black–Scholes–Merton formula:

$$d_1 = \frac{ln(135.75/125) + (0.0425 + (0.15)^2/2)(0.5890)}{0.15\sqrt{0.5890}} = 0.9916$$

$$d_2 = 0.9916 - 0.15\sqrt{0.5890} = 0.8765$$

These are the same values as in Part A, so $N(d_1)$ and $N(d_2)$ will be the same. Plugging into the formula for the call price gives

$$c = 135.75(0.8389) - 125e^{-0.0425(0.5890)}(0.8106) = 15.06$$

This price is the same as in Part A.

8.4 Application of the Black Model to Interest Rate Options

Earlier in this reading, we described options on interest rates. These derivative instruments parallel the FRAs that we covered in Reading 64, in that they are derivatives in which the underlying is not a bond but rather an interest rate. Pricing options on interest rates is a challenging task. We showed how this is done using binomial trees. It would be nice if the Black–Scholes–Merton model could be easily used to price interest rate options, but the process is not so straightforward. Pricing options on interest rates requires a sophisticated model that prohibits arbitrage among interest-rate related instruments and their derivatives. The Black–Scholes–Merton model is not sufficiently general to use in this manner. Nonetheless, practitioners often employ the Black model to price interest rate options. Somewhat remarkably, perhaps, it is known to give satisfactory results. Therefore, we provide a quick overview of this practice here.

Suppose we wish to price a one-year interest rate cap, consisting of three caplets. One caplet expires in 90 days, one 180 days, and one in 270 days.[41] The exercise rate is 9 percent. To use the Black model, we use the forward rate as though it were $f_0(T)$. Therefore, we also require its volatility and the risk-free rate for the period to the option's expiration.[42] Recalling that there are three caplets and we have to price each one individually, let us first focus on the caplet expiring in 90 days. We first specify that $T = 90/365 = 0.2466$. Then we need the forward rate today for the period day 90 to day 180. Let this rate be 9.25 percent. We shall assume its volatility is 0.03. We then need the continuously compounded risk-free rate for 90 days, which we assume to be 9.60 percent. So now we have the following input variables:

---

[41] A one-year cap will have three individual caplets. The first expires in 90 days and pays off in 180 days, the second expires in 180 days and pays off in 270 days, and the third expires in 270 days and pays off in 360 days. The tendency to think that a one-year cap using quarterly periods should have four caplets is incorrect because there is no caplet expiring right now and paying off in 90 days. It would make no sense to create an option that expires immediately. Also, in a one-year loan, the rate is set at the start and reset only three times; hence, only three caplets are required.

[42] It is important to note here that the Black model requires that all inputs be in continuous compounding format. Therefore, the forward rate and risk-free rate would need to be the continuously compounded analogs to the discrete rates. Because the underlying is usually LIBOR, which is a discrete rate quoted on the basis of a 360-day year, some adjustments must be made to convert to a continuous rate quoted on the basis of a 365-day year. We will not address these adjustments here.

$$T = 0.2466$$
$$f_0(T) = 0.0925$$
$$\sigma = 0.03$$
$$X = 0.09$$
$$r^c = 0.096$$

Inserting these inputs into the Black model produces

$$d_1 = \frac{ln(0.0925/0.09) + [(0.03)^2/2](0.2466)}{0.03\sqrt{0.2466}} = 1.8466$$

$$d_2 = 1.8466 - 0.03\sqrt{0.2466} = 1.8317$$

$$N(1.85) = 0.9678$$

$$N(1.83) = 0.9664$$

$$c_0 = e^{-0.096(0.2466)}[0.0925(0.9678) - 0.09(0.9664)] = 0.00248594$$

(Because of the order of magnitude of the inputs, we carry the answer out to eight decimal places.) But this answer is not quite what we need. The formula gives the answer under the assumption that the option payoff occurs at the option expiration. As we know, interest rate options pay off later than their expirations. This option expires in 90 days and pays off 90 days after that. Therefore, we need to discount this result back from day 180 to day 90 using the forward rate of 9.25 percent.[43] We thus have

$$0.00248594e^{-0.0925(0.2466)} = 0.00242988$$

Another adjustment is necessary. Because the underlying price and exercise price are entered as rates, the resulting answer is a rate. Moreover, the underlying rate and exercise rate are expressed as annual rates, so the answer is an annual rate. Interest rate option prices are always quoted as periodic rates (which are prices for $1 notional principal). We would adjust this rate by multiplying by 90/360.[44] The price would thus be

$$0.00242988(90/360) = 0.00060747$$

Finally, we should note that this price is valid for a $1 notional principal option. If the notional principal were $1 million, the option price would be

$$\$1,000,000(0.00060747) = \$607.47$$

We have just priced the first caplet of this cap. To price the second caplet, we need the forward rate for the period 180 days to 270 days, we would use $180/365 = 0.4932$ as the time to expiration, and we need the risk-free rate for 180 days. To price the third caplet, we need the forward rate for the period 270 days to 360 days, we would use $270/365 = 0.7397$ as the time to expiration, and we need the risk-free rate for 270 days. The price of the cap would be the sum of the prices of the three component caplets. If we were pricing a floor, we would price the component floorlets using the Black model for puts.

---

[43] Be very careful in this discounting procedure. The exponent in the exponential should have a time factor of the number of days between the option expiration and its payoff. Because there are 90 days between days 90 and 180, we use $90/365 = 0.2466$. This value is not quite the same as the time until the option expiration, which today is 90 but which will count down to zero.

[44] It is customary in the interest rate options market to use 360 in the denominator to make this adjustment, even though we have used 365 in other places.

Although the Black model is frequently used to price interest rate options, binomial models, as we illustrated earlier, are somewhat more widely used in this area. These models are more attuned to deriving prices that prohibit arbitrage opportunities using any of the diverse instruments whose prices are given by the term structure. When you use the Black model to price interest rate options, there is some risk, perhaps minor, of having a counterparty be able to do arbitrage against you. Yet somehow the Black model is used often, and professionals seem to agree that it works remarkably well.

Practice Problem 12

Use the Black model to price an interest rate put that expires in 280 days. The forward rate is currently 6.8 percent, the 280-day continuously compounded risk-free rate is 6.25 percent, the exercise rate is 7 percent, and the volatility is 0.02. The option is based on a 180-day underlying rate, and the notional principal is $10 million.

► **Solution.** The time to expiration is $T = 280/365 = 0.7671$. Calculate the value of d_1, d_2, and $N(d_1)$, $N(d_2)$, and p_0 using the Black model:

$$d_1 = \frac{ln(0.068/0.07) + [(0.02)^2/2]0.7671}{0.02\sqrt{0.7671}} = -1.6461$$

$d_2 = -1.6461 - 0.02\sqrt{0.7671} = -1.6636$

$N(-1.65) = 1 - N(1.65) = 1 - 0.9505 = 0.0495$

$N(-1.66) = 1 - N(1.66) = 1 - 0.9515 = 0.0485$

$p_0 = e^{-0.0625(0.7671)}[0.07(1 - 0.0485) - 0.068(1 - 0.0495)]$

$\quad = 0.00187873$

This formula assumes the option payoff is made at expiration. For an interest rate option, that assumption is false. This is a 180-day rate, so the payoff is made 180 days later. Therefore, we discount the payoff over 180 days using the forward rate:

$e^{-0.068(180/365)}(0.00187873) = 0.00181677$

Interest rate option prices must reflect the fact that the rate used in the formula is quoted as an annual rate. So, we must multiply by 180/360 because the transaction is based on a 180-day rate:

$0.00181677(180/360) = 0.00090839$

Then we multiply by the notional principal:

$\$10,000,000(0.00090839) = \$9,084$

THE ROLE OF OPTIONS MARKETS   9

As we did with futures markets, we conclude the reading by looking at the important role options markets play in the financial system. Derivative markets provide price discovery and risk management, make the markets for the underlying assets more efficient, and permit trading at low transaction costs. These features are also associated with options markets. Yet, options offer further advantages that some other derivatives do not offer.

For example, forward and futures contracts have bidirectional payoffs. They have the potential for a substantial gain in one direction and a substantial loss in the other direction. The advantage of taking such a position lies in the fact that one need pay no cash up front. In contrast, options offer the feature that, if one is willing to pay cash up front, one can limit the loss in a given direction. In other words, options have unidirectional payoffs. This feature can be attractive to the holder of an option. To the writer, options offer the opportunity to be paid cash up front for a willingness to assume the risk of the unidirectional payoff. An option writer can assume the risk of potentially a large loss unmatched by the potential for a large gain. In fact, the potential gain is small. But for this risk, the option writer receives money up front.

Options also offer excellent devices for managing the risk of various exposures. An obvious one is the protective put, which we saw earlier and which can protect a position against loss by paying off when the value of the underlying is down.

Recall that futures contracts offer price discovery, the revelation of the prices at which investors will contract today for transactions to take place later. Options, on the other hand, provide volatility discovery. Through the implied volatility, investors can determine the market's assessment of how volatile it believes the underlying asset is. This valuable information can be difficult to obtain from any other source.

Futures offer advantages over forwards, in that futures are standardized, tend to be actively traded in a secondary market, and are protected by the exchange's clearinghouse against credit risk. Although some options, such as interest rate options, are available only in over-the-counter forms, many options exist in both over-the-counter and exchange-listed forms. Hence, one can often customize an option if necessary or trade it on an exchange.

In Reading 64, we covered forward contracts; in Reading 65, we covered futures contracts; and in this reading we covered option contracts. We have one more major class of derivative instruments, swaps, which we now turn to in Reading 67.

SUMMARY

▶ Options are rights to buy or sell an underlying at a fixed price, the exercise price, for a period of time. The right to buy is a call; the right to sell is a put. Options have a definite expiration date. Using the option to buy or sell is the action of exercising it. The buyer or holder of an option pays a price to the seller or writer for the right to buy (a call) or sell (a put) the underlying instrument. The **writer of an option** has the corresponding potential obligation to sell or buy the underlying.

▶ European options can be exercised only at expiration; American options can be exercised at any time prior to expiration. Moneyness refers to the characteristic that an option has positive intrinsic value. The payoff is the value of the option at expiration. An option's intrinsic value is the value that can be captured if the option is exercised. Time value is the component of an option's price that reflects the uncertainty of what will happen in the future to the price of the underlying.

▶ Options can be traded as standardized instruments on an options exchange, where they are protected from default on the part of the writer, or as customized instruments on the over-the-counter market, where they are subject to the possibility of the writer defaulting. Because the buyer pays a price at the start and does not have to do anything else, the buyer cannot default.

▶ The underlying instruments for options are individual stocks, stock indices, bonds, interest rates, currencies, futures, commodities, and even such random factors as the weather. In addition, a class of options called real options is associated with the flexibility in capital investment projects.

▶ Like FRAs, which are forward contracts in which the underlying is an interest rate, interest rate options are options in which the underlying is an interest rate. However, FRAs are commitments to make one interest payment and receive another, whereas interest rate options are rights to make one interest payment and receive another.

▶ Option payoffs, which are the values of options when they expire, are determined by the greater of zero or the difference between underlying price and exercise price, if a call, or the greater of zero or the difference between exercise price and underlying price, if a put. For interest rate options, the exercise price is a specified rate and the underlying price is a variable interest rate.

▶ Interest rate options exist in the form of caps, which are call options on interest rates, and floors, which are put options on interest rates. Caps consist of a series of call options, called caplets, on an underlying rate, with each option expiring at a different time. Floors consist of a series of put options, called floorlets, on an underlying rate, with each option expiring at a different time.

▶ The minimum value of European and American calls and puts is zero. The maximum value of European and American calls is the underlying price. The maximum value of a European put is the present value of the exercise price. The maximum value of an American put is the exercise price.

▶ The lower bound of a European call is established by constructing a portfolio consisting of a long call and risk-free bond and a short position in the underlying asset. This combination produces a non-negative value at expiration, so its current value must be non-negative. For this situation to occur, the call price has to be worth at least the underlying price minus the present value of the exercise price. The lower bound of a European put is established by constructing a portfolio consisting of a long put, a long position in the underlying, and the issuance of a zero-coupon bond. This combination produces a non-negative value at expiration so its current value must be non-negative. For this to occur, the put price has to be at least as much as the present value of the exercise price minus the underlying price. For both calls and puts, if this lower bound is negative, we invoke the rule that an option price can be no lower than zero.

▶ The lowest price of a European call is referred to as the lower bound. The lowest price of an American call is also the lower bound of a European call. The lowest price of a European put is also referred to as the lower bound. The lowest price of an American put, however, is its intrinsic value.

▶ Buying a call with a given exercise price and selling an otherwise identical call with a higher exercise price creates a combination that always pays off with a non-negative value. Therefore, its current value must be non-negative. For this to occur, the call with the lower exercise price must be worth at least as much as the other call. A similar argument holds for puts, except that one would buy the put with the higher exercise price. This line of reasoning shows that the put with the higher exercise price must be worth at least as much as the one with the lower exercise price.

▶ A longer-term European or American call must be worth at least as much as a corresponding shorter-term European or American call. A longer-term American put must be worth at least as much as a shorter-term American put. A longer-term European put, however, can be worth more or less than a shorter-term European put.

▶ A fiduciary call, consisting of a European call and a zero-coupon bond, produces the same payoff as a protective put, consisting of the underlying and a European put. Therefore, their current values must be the same. For this equivalence to occur, the call price plus bond price must equal the underlying price plus put price. This relationship is called put–call parity and can be used to identify combinations of instruments that synthesize another instrument by rearranging the equation to isolate the instrument you are trying to create. Long positions are indicated by positive signs, and short positions are indicated by negative signs. One can create a synthetic call, a synthetic put, a synthetic underlying, and a synthetic bond, as well as synthetic short positions in these instruments for the purpose of exploiting mispricing in these instruments.

▶ Put–call parity violations exist when one side of the equation does not equal the other. An arbitrageur buys the lower-priced side and sells the higher-priced side, thereby earning the difference in price, and the positions offset at expiration. The combined actions of many arbitrageurs performing this set of transactions would increase the demand and price for the under-priced instruments and decrease the demand and price for the overpriced instruments, until the put–call parity relationship is upheld.

▶ American option prices must always be no less than those of otherwise equivalent European options. American call options, however, are never exercised early unless there is a cash flow on the underlying, so they can sell for the same as their European counterparts in the absence of such a cash flow. American put options nearly always have a possibility of early exercise, so they ordinarily sell for more than their European counterparts.

▶ Cash flows on the underlying affect an option's boundary conditions and put–call parity by lowering the underlying price by the present value of the cash flows over the life of the option.

$$\pi = \frac{1 + r - d}{v - d}$$

$$C = \frac{\pi c^+ + (1 - \pi) c^-}{1 + r}$$

hedge ratio:
$$n = \frac{c^+ - c^-}{S^+ - S^-}$$

▶ A higher interest rate increases a call option's price and decreases a put option's price.

▶ In a one-period binomial model, the underlying asset can move up to one of two prices. A portfolio consisting of a long position in the underlying and a short position in a call option can be made risk-free and, therefore, must return the risk-free rate. Under this condition, the option price can be obtained by inferring it from a formula that uses the other input values. The option price is a weighted average of the two option prices at expiration, discounted back one period at the risk-free rate.

▶ If an option is trading for a price higher than that given in the binomial model, one can sell the option and buy a specific number of units of the underlying, as given by the model. This combination is risk free but will earn a return higher than the risk-free rate. If the option is trading for a price lower than the price given in the binomial model, a short position in a specific number of units of the underlying and a long position in the option will create a risk-free loan that costs less than the risk-free rate.

▶ In a two-period binomial model, the underlying can move to one of two prices in each of two periods; thus three underlying prices are possible at the option expiration. To price an option, start at the expiration and work backward, following the procedure in the one-period model in which an option price at any given point in time is a weighted average of the next two possible prices discounted at the risk-free rate.

▶ To calculate the price of an option on a zero-coupon bond or a coupon bond, one must first construct a binomial tree of the price of the bond over the life of the option. To calculate the price of an option on an interest rate, one should use a binomial tree of interest rates. Then the option price is found by starting at the option expiration, determining the payoff and successively working backwards by computing the option price as the weighted average of the next two option prices discounted back one period. For the case of options on bonds or interest rates, a different discount rate is used at different parts of the tree.

▶ For an option of a given expiration, a greater pricing accuracy is obtained by dividing the option's life into a greater number of time periods in a binomial tree. As more time periods are added, the discrete-time binomial price converges to a stable value as though the option is being modeled in a continuous-time world.

▶ The assumptions under which the Black–Scholes–Merton model is derived state that the underlying asset follows a geometric lognormal diffusion process, the risk-free rate is known and constant, the volatility of the underlying asset is known and constant, there are no taxes or transaction costs, there are no cash flows on the underlying, and the options are European.

Delta: $\dfrac{\Delta \text{ option } \$}{\Delta \text{ underlying } \$}$

▶ To calculate the value of an option using the Black–Scholes–Merton model, enter the underlying price, exercise price, risk-free rate, volatility, and time to expiration into a formula. The formula will require you to look up two normal probabilities, obtained from either a table or preferably a computer routine.

▶ The change in the option price for a change in the price of the underlying is called the delta. The change in the option price for a change in the risk-free rate is called the rho. The change in the option price for a change in the time to expiration is called the theta. The change in the option price for a change in the volatility is called the vega.

► The delta is defined as the change in the option price divided by the change in the underlying price. The option price change can be approximated by the delta times the change in the underlying price. To construct a delta-hedged position, a short (long) position in each call is matched with a long (short) position in delta units of the underlying. Changes in the underlying price will generate offsetting changes in the value of the option position, provided the changes in the underlying price are small and occur over a short time period. A delta-hedged position should be adjusted as the delta changes and time passes.

► If changes in the price of the underlying are large or the delta hedge is not adjusted over a longer time period, the hedge may not be effective. This effect is due to the instability of the delta and is called the gamma effect. If the gamma effect is large, option price changes will not be very close to the changes as approximated by the delta times the underlying price change.

► Cash flows on the underlying are accommodated in option pricing models by reducing the price of the underlying by the present value of the cash flows over the life of the option.

► Volatility can be estimated by calculating the standard deviation of the continuously compounded returns from a sample of recent data for the underlying. This is called the historical volatility. An alternative measure, called the implied volatility, can be obtained by setting the Black–Scholes–Merton model price equal to the market price and inferring the volatility. The implied volatility is a measure of the volatility the market is using to price the option.

► The payoffs of a call on a forward contract and an appropriately chosen zero-coupon bond are equivalent to the payoffs of a put on the forward contract and the forward contract. Thus, their current values must be the same. For this equality to occur, the call price plus the bond price must equal the put price. The appropriate zero-coupon bond is one with a face value equal to the exercise price minus the forward price. This relationship is called put–call–forward (or futures) parity.

► There is no justification for exercising American options on forward contracts early, so they are equivalent to European options on forwards. American options on futures, both calls and puts, can sometimes be exercised early, so they are different from European options on futures and carry a higher price.

► The Black model can be used to price European options on forwards or futures by entering the forward price, exercise price, risk-free rate, time to expiration, and volatility into a formula that will also require the determination of two normal probabilities.

► The Black model can be used to price European options on interest rates by entering the **forward interest rate** into the model for the forward or futures price and the exercise rate for the exercise price.

► Options are useful in financial markets because they provide a way to limit losses to the premium paid while permitting potentially large gains. They can be used for hedging purposes, especially in the case of puts, which can be used to limit the loss on a long position in an asset. Options also provide information on the volatility of the underlying asset. Options can be standardized and exchange-traded or customized in the over-the-counter market.

APPENDIX 66A   Cumulative Probabilities for a Standard Normal Distribution
$P(X \leq x) = N(x)$ for $x \geq 0$ or $1 - N(-x)$ for $x < 0$

x	0	0.01	0.02	0.03	0.04	0.05	0.06	0.07	0.08	0.09
0.00	0.5000	0.5040	0.5080	0.5120	0.5160	0.5199	0.5239	0.5279	0.5319	0.5359
0.10	0.5398	0.5438	0.5478	0.5517	0.5557	0.5596	0.5636	0.5675	0.5714	0.5753
0.20	0.5793	0.5832	0.5871	0.5910	0.5948	0.5987	0.6026	0.6064	0.6103	0.6141
0.30	0.6179	0.6217	0.6255	0.6293	0.6331	0.6368	0.6406	0.6443	0.6480	0.6517
0.40	0.6554	0.6591	0.6628	0.6664	0.6700	0.6736	0.6772	0.6808	0.6844	0.6879
0.50	0.6915	0.6950	0.6985	0.7019	0.7054	0.7088	0.7123	0.7157	0.7190	0.7224
0.60	0.7257	0.7291	0.7324	0.7357	0.7389	0.7422	0.7454	0.7486	0.7517	0.7549
0.70	0.7580	0.7611	0.7642	0.7673	0.7704	0.7734	0.7764	0.7794	0.7823	0.7852
0.80	0.7881	0.7910	0.7939	0.7967	0.7995	0.8023	0.8051	0.8078	0.8106	0.8133
0.90	0.8159	0.8186	0.8212	0.8238	0.8264	0.8289	0.8315	0.8340	0.8365	0.8389
1.00	0.8413	0.8438	0.8461	0.8485	0.8508	0.8531	0.8554	0.8577	0.8599	0.8621
1.10	0.8643	0.8665	0.8686	0.8708	0.8729	0.8749	0.8770	0.8790	0.8810	0.8830
1.20	0.8849	0.8869	0.8888	0.8907	0.8925	0.8944	0.8962	0.8980	0.8997	0.9015
1.30	0.9032	0.9049	0.9066	0.9082	0.9099	0.9115	0.9131	0.9147	0.9162	0.9177
1.40	0.9192	0.9207	0.9222	0.9236	0.9251	0.9265	0.9279	0.9292	0.9306	0.9319
1.50	0.9332	0.9345	0.9357	0.9370	0.9382	0.9394	0.9406	0.9418	0.9429	0.9441
1.60	0.9452	0.9463	0.9474	0.9484	0.9495	0.9505	0.9515	0.9525	0.9535	0.9545
1.70	0.9554	0.9564	0.9573	0.9582	0.9591	0.9599	0.9608	0.9616	0.9625	0.9633
1.80	0.9641	0.9649	0.9656	0.9664	0.9671	0.9678	0.9686	0.9693	0.9699	0.9706
1.90	0.9713	0.9719	0.9726	0.9732	0.9738	0.9744	0.9750	0.9756	0.9761	0.9767
2.00	0.9772	0.9778	0.9783	0.9788	0.9793	0.9798	0.9803	0.9808	0.9812	0.9817
2.10	0.9821	0.9826	0.9830	0.9834	0.9838	0.9842	0.9846	0.9850	0.9854	0.9857
2.20	0.9861	0.9864	0.9868	0.9871	0.9875	0.9878	0.9881	0.9884	0.9887	0.9890
2.30	0.9893	0.9896	0.9898	0.9901	0.9904	0.9906	0.9909	0.9911	0.9913	0.9916
2.40	0.9918	0.9920	0.9922	0.9925	0.9927	0.9929	0.9931	0.9932	0.9934	0.9936
2.50	0.9938	0.9940	0.9941	0.9943	0.9945	0.9946	0.9948	0.9949	0.9951	0.9952
2.60	0.9953	0.9955	0.9956	0.9957	0.9959	0.9960	0.9961	0.9962	0.9963	0.9964
2.70	0.9965	0.9966	0.9967	0.9968	0.9969	0.9970	0.9971	0.9972	0.9973	0.9974
2.80	0.9974	0.9975	0.9976	0.9977	0.9977	0.9978	0.9979	0.9979	0.9980	0.9981
2.90	0.9981	0.9982	0.9982	0.9983	0.9984	0.9984	0.9985	0.9985	0.9986	0.9986
3.00	0.9987	0.9987	0.9987	0.9988	0.9988	0.9989	0.9989	0.9989	0.9990	0.9990

PROBLEMS FOR READING 66

1. Consider the following information on put and call options on a stock:

Call price, $c_0 = \$4.50$

Put price, $p_0 = \$6.80$

Exercise price, $X = \$70$

Days to option expiration $= 139$

Current stock price, $S_0 = \$67.32$

Risk-free rate, $r = 5$ percent

A. Use put–call parity to calculate prices of the following:

   i. Synthetic call option

   ii. Synthetic put option

   iii. Synthetic bond

   iv. Synthetic underlying stock

B. For each of the synthetic instruments in Part A, identify any mispricing by comparing the actual price with the synthetic price.

C. Based on the mispricing in Part B, illustrate an arbitrage transaction using a synthetic call.

D. Based on the mispricing in Part B, illustrate an arbitrage transaction using a synthetic put.

2. A stock currently trades at a price of $100. The stock price can go up 10 percent or down 15 percent. The risk-free rate is 6.5 percent.

A. Use a one-period binomial model to calculate the price of a call option with an exercise price of $90.

B. Suppose the call price is currently $17.50. Show how to execute an arbitrage transaction that will earn more than the risk-free rate. Use 100 call options.

C. Suppose the call price is currently $14. Show how to execute an arbitrage transaction that replicates a loan that will earn less than the risk-free rate. Use 100 call options.

3. Suppose a stock currently trades at a price of $150. The stock price can go up 33 percent or down 15 percent. The risk-free rate is 4.5 percent.

A. Use a one-period binomial model to calculate the price of a put option with exercise price of $150.

B. Suppose the put price is currently $14. Show how to execute an arbitrage transaction that will earn more than the risk-free rate. Use 10,000 put options.

C. Suppose the put price is currently $11. Show how to execute an arbitrage transaction that will earn more than the risk-free rate. Use 10,000 put options.

4. Consider a two-period binomial model in which a stock currently trades at a price of $65. The stock price can go up 20 percent or down 17 percent each period. The risk-free rate is 5 percent.

A. Calculate the price of a call option expiring in two periods with an exercise price of $60.

B. Based on your answer in Part A, calculate the number of units of the underlying stock that would be needed at each point in the binomial tree to construct a risk-free hedge. Use 10,000 calls.

    C. Calculate the price of a call option expiring in two periods with an exercise price of $70.

    D. Based on your answer in Part C, calculate the number of units of the underlying stock that would be needed at each point in the binomial tree to construct a risk-free hedge. Use 10,000 calls.

5. Consider a two-period binomial model in which a stock currently trades at a price of $65. The stock price can go up 20 percent or down 17 percent each period. The risk-free rate is 5 percent.

    A. Calculate the price of a put option expiring in two periods with exercise price of $60.

    B. Based on your answer in Part A, calculate the number of units of the underlying stock that would be needed at each point in the binomial tree in order to construct a risk-free hedge. Use 10,000 puts.

    C. Calculate the price of a put option expiring in two periods with an exercise price of $70.

    D. Based on your answer in Part C, calculate the number of units of the underlying stock that would be needed at each point in the binomial tree in order to construct a risk-free hedge. Use 10,000 puts.

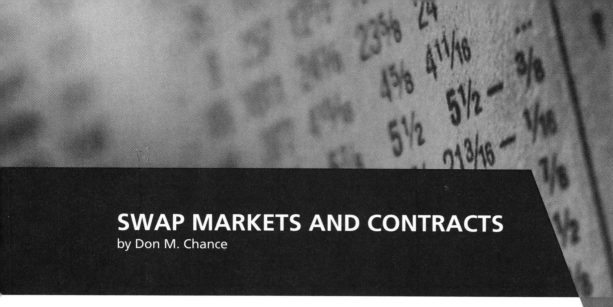

SWAP MARKETS AND CONTRACTS
by Don M. Chance

LEARNING OUTCOMES

The candidate should be able to:

a. distinguish between the pricing and valuation of swaps;

b. explain the equivalence of the following swaps to combinations of other instruments: interest rate swaps to a series of off-market forward rate agreements (FRAs) and a plain vanilla swap to a combination of an interest rate call and interest rate put;

c. calculate and interpret the fixed rate on a plain vanilla interest rate swap and the market value of the swap during its life, when provided with the formulas;

d. calculate and interpret the fixed rate, if applicable, and the foreign notional principal for a given domestic notional principal on a currency swap, and determine the market values of each of the different types of currency swaps during their lives, when provided with the formulas;

e. calculate and interpret the fixed rate, if applicable, on an equity swap and the market values of the different types of equity swaps during their lives; when provided with the formulas;

f. explain and interpret the characteristics of swaptions, including the difference between payer and receiver swaptions;

g. explain why swaptions exist, and illustrate how swaptions are used;

h. identify and calculate the possible payoffs and cash flows of an interest rate swaption, when provided with the formulas;

i. calculate and interpret the value of an interest rate swaption on the expiration day, when provided with the formulas;

j. explain how credit risk arises in a swap, which party bears the credit risk, at what point in a swap's life the credit risk is the greatest, and distinguish between current credit risk and potential credit risk;

k. define the swap spread and explain what it represents;

l. illustrate how swap credit risk is reduced by both netting and marking to market.

Analysis of Derivatives for the CFA® Program, by Don M. Chance, Copyright © 2003 by Association for Investment Management and Research. Reprinted with permission.

1

INTRODUCTION

This reading completes the survey of the main types of derivative instruments. Preceding readings covered forward contracts, futures contracts, and options. This reading covers swaps. Although swaps were the last of the main types of derivatives to be invented, they are clearly not the least important. In fact, judging by the size of the swap market, they are probably the most important. The Bank for International Settlements estimated the notional principal of the global over-the-counter derivatives market as of 30 June 2001 at $100 trillion. Of that amount, interest rate and currency swaps account for about $61 trillion, with interest rate swaps representing about $57 trillion of that total.[1] Indeed, interest rate swaps have had overwhelming success as a derivative product. They are widely used by corporations, financial institutions, and governments.

Recall first that *a swap is an agreement between two parties to exchange a series of future cash flows*. For most types of swaps, one party makes payments that are determined by a random outcome, such as an interest rate, a currency rate, an equity return, or a commodity price. These payments are commonly referred to as variable or *floating*. The other party either makes variable or floating payments determined by some other random factor or makes fixed payments. At least one type of swap involves both parties making fixed payments, but the values of those payments vary due to random factors.

In forwards, futures, and options, the terminology of *long* and *short* has been used to describe buyers and sellers. These terms are not used as often in swaps. The preferred terminology usually designates a party as being the floating- (or variable-) rate payer or the fixed-rate payer. Nonetheless, in swaps in which one party receives a floating rate and the other receives a fixed rate, the former is usually said to be long and the latter is said to be short. This usage is in keeping with the fact that parties who go long in other instruments pay a known amount and receive a claim on an unknown amount. In some swaps, however, both sides are floating or variable, and this terminology breaks down.

1.1 Characteristics of Swap Contracts

Although technically a swap can have a single payment, most swaps involve multiple payments. Thus, we refer to a swap as a *series* of payments. In fact, we have already covered a swap with one payment, which is just a forward contract. Hence, a swap is basically a series of forward contracts. We will elaborate further in Section 4.1.2, but with this idea in mind, we can see that a swap is like an agreement to buy something over a period of time. We might be paying a variable price or a price that has already been fixed: we might be paying an uncertain price, or we might already know the price we shall pay.

---

[1] Equity and commodity swaps account for less than the notional principal of currency swaps.

When a swap is initiated, neither party pays any amount to the other. Therefore, a swap has zero value at the start of the contract. Although it is not absolutely necessary for this condition to be true, swaps are typically done in this fashion. Neither party pays anything up front. There is, however, a technical exception to this point in regard to currency swaps. Each party pays the notional principal to the other, but the amounts exchanged are equivalent, though denominated in two different currencies.

Each date on which the parties make payments is called a **settlement date**, sometimes called a payment date, and the time between settlement dates is called the **settlement period**. On a given settlement date when payments are due, one party makes a payment to the other, which in turn makes a payment to the first party. With the exception of currency swaps and a few variations associated with other types of swaps, both sets of payments are made in the same currency. Consequently, the parties typically agree to exchange only the net amount owed from one party to the other, a practice called **netting**. In currency swaps and a few other special cases, the payments are not made in the same currency; hence, the parties usually make separate payments without netting. Note the implication that swaps are generally settled in cash. It is quite rare for swaps to call for actual physical delivery of an underlying asset.

A swap always has a **termination date**, the date of the final payment. We can think of this date as its expiration date, as we do with other derivatives. The original time to maturity is sometimes called the *tenor* of a swap.

The swap market is almost exclusively an over-the-counter market, so swaps contracts are customized to the parties' specific needs. Several of the leading futures exchanges have created futures contracts on swaps. These contracts allow participants to hedge and speculate on the rates that will prevail in the swap market at future dates. Of course, these contracts are not swaps themselves but, as derivatives of swaps, they can in some ways serve as substitutes for swaps. These futures contracts have been moderately successful, but their volume is insignificant compared with the over-the-counter market for swaps.

As we have discussed in previous readings, over-the-counter instruments are subject to default risk. Default is possible whenever a payment is due. When a series of payments is made, there is default risk potential throughout the life of the contract, depending on the financial condition of the two parties. But default can be somewhat complicated in swaps. Suppose, for example, that on a settlement date, Party A owes Party B a payment of $50,000 and Party B owes Party A a payment of $12,000. Agreeing to net, Party A owes Party B $38,000 for that particular payment. Party A may be illiquid, or perhaps even bankrupt, and unable to make the payment. But it may be the case that the market value of the swap, which reflects the present value of the remaining payments, could be positive from the perspective of Party A and negative from the perspective of Party B. In that case, Party B owes Party A more for the remaining payments. We will learn how to determine the market value of a swap in Section 4.2 of this reading.

The handling of default in swaps can be complicated, depending on the contract specifications and the applicable laws under which the contract was written. In most cases, the above situation would be resolved by having A be in default but possessing an asset, the swap, that can be used to help settle its other liabilities. We shall discuss the default risk of swaps in more detail in Section 7.

1.2 Termination of a Swap

As we noted earlier, a swap has a termination or expiration date. Sometimes, however, a party could want to terminate a swap before its formal expiration. This scenario is much like a party selling a bond before it matures or selling an exchange-traded option or futures contract before its expiration. With swaps, early termination can take place in several ways.

As we mentioned briefly and will cover in more detail later, a swap has a market value that can be calculated during its life. If a party holds a swap with a market value of $125,000, for example, it can settle the swap with the counterparty by having the counterparty pay it $125,000 in cash. This payment terminates the transaction for both parties. From the opposite perspective, a party holding a swap with a negative market value can terminate the swap by paying the market value to the counterparty. Terminating a swap in this manner is possible only if the counterparties specify in advance that such a transaction can be made, or if they reach an agreement to do so without having specified in advance. In other words, this feature is not automatically available and must be agreed to by both parties.

Many swaps are terminated early by entering into a separate and offsetting swap. For example, suppose a corporation is engaged in a swap to make fixed payments of 5 percent and receive floating payments based on LIBOR, with the payments made each 15 January and 15 July. Three years remain on the swap. That corporation can offset the swap by entering into an entirely new swap in which it makes payments based on LIBOR and receives a fixed rate with the payments made each 15 January and 15 July for three years. The swap fixed rate is determined by market conditions at the time the swap is initiated. Thus, the fixed rate on the new swap is not likely to match the fixed rate on the old swap, but the effect of this transaction is simply to have the floating payments offset; the fixed payments will net out to a known amount. Hence, the risk associated with the floating rate is eliminated. The default risk, however, is not eliminated because both swaps remain in effect.

Another way to terminate a swap early is sell the swap to another counterparty. Suppose a corporation holds a swap worth $75,000. If it can obtain the counterparty's permission, it can find another party to take over its payments. In effect, it sells the swap for $75,000 to that party. This procedure, however, is not commonly used.

A final way to terminate a swap early is by using a swaption. This instrument is an option to enter into a swap at terms that are established in advance. Thus, a party could use a swaption to enter into an offsetting swap, as described above. We shall cover swaptions in more detail in Section 6.

2   THE STRUCTURE OF GLOBAL SWAP MARKETS

The global swaps market is much like the global forward and over-the-counter options markets, which we covered in some detail in Readings 64 and 66. It is made up of dealers, which are banks and investment banking firms. These dealers make markets in swaps, quoting bid and ask prices and rates, thereby offering to take either side of a swap transaction. Upon taking a position in a swap, the dealer generally offsets the risk by making transactions in other markets. The counterparties to swaps are either end users or other dealers. The end users are often corporations with risk management problems that can be solved by engaging in a swap—a corporation or other end user is usually exposed to or needs an exposure to some type of risk that arises from interest rates, exchange rates, stock prices, or commodity prices. The end user contacts a dealer that makes a market in swaps. The two engage in a transaction, at which point the dealer assumes some risk from the end user. The dealer then usually lays off the risk by engaging in a transaction with another party. That transaction could be something as simple as a futures contract, or it could be an over-the-counter transaction with another dealer.

Risk magazine conducts annual surveys of participants in various derivative products. Exhibit 67-1 presents the results of those surveys for currency and

EXHIBIT 67-1	*Risk* Magazine Surveys of Banks, Investment Banks, and Corporate End Users to Determine the Top Three Dealers in Currency and Interest Rate Swaps	

	Respondents	
Currencies	**Banks and Investment Banks**	**Corporate End Users**
Currency Swaps		
$/€	UBS Warburg	Citigroup
	JP Morgan Chase	Royal Bank of Scotland
	Deutsche Bank	Bank of America
$/¥	JP Morgan Chase	Citigroup
	UBS Warburg	Bank of America
	Credit Suisse First Boston/ Deutsche Bank	JP Morgan Chase
$/£	Royal Bank of Scotland	Royal Bank of Scotland
	JP Morgan Chase	Citigroup
	Goldman Sachs	Deutsche Bank
$/SF	UBS Warburg	UBS Warburg
	Goldman Sachs	Citigroup
	Credit Suisse First Boston	Credit Suisse First Boston
Interest Rate Swaps (2–10 years)		
$	JP Morgan Chase	JP Morgan Chase
	Bank of America	Bank of America
	Morgan Stanley	Royal Bank of Scotland
€	JP Morgan Chase	Royal Bank of Scotland
	Deutsche Bank	Deutsche Bank
	Morgan Stanley	Citigroup
¥	JP Morgan Chase	Royal Bank of Scotland
	Deutsche Bank	Barclays Capital
	Bank of America	Citigroup/JP Morgan Chase
£	Royal Bank of Scotland	Royal Bank of Scotland
	Barclays Capital	Barclays Capital
	UBS Warburg	Deutsche Bank
SF	UBS Warburg	UBS Warburg
	Credit Suisse First Boston	Credit Suisse First Boston
	Zürcher Kantonalbank	Zürcher Kantonalbank

Note: $ = U.S. dollar, € = euro, ¥ = Japanese yen, £ = U.K. pound sterling, SF = Swiss franc

Source: Risk, September 2002, pp. 30–67 for banks and investment banking dealer respondents, and June 2002, pp. 24–34 for corporate end user respondents. Ratings for swaps with maturities less than 2 years and greater than 10 years are also provided in the September 2002 issue of *Risk.*

interest rate swaps. One survey provides opinions of banks and investment banks that are swaps dealers. In the other survey, the respondents are end users. The results give a good idea of the major players in this market. It is interesting to note the disagreement between how dealers view themselves and how end users view them. Also, note that the rankings change, sometimes drastically, from year to year.

3   TYPES OF SWAPS

We alluded to the fact that the underlying asset in a swap can be a currency, interest rate, stock, or commodity. We now take a look at these types of swaps in more detail.

3.1 Currency Swaps

In a currency swap, each party makes interest payments to the other in different currencies.[2] Consider this example. The U.S. retailer Target Corporation (NYSE: TGT) does not have an established presence in Europe. Let us say that it has decided to begin opening a few stores in Germany and needs €9 million to fund construction and initial operations. TGT would like to issue a fixed-rate euro-denominated bond with face value of €9 million, but the company is not very well known in Europe. European investment bankers have given it a quote for such a bond. Deutsche Bank, AG (NYSE: DB), however, tells TGT that it should issue the bond in dollars and use a swap to convert it into euros.

Suppose TGT issues a five-year US$10 million bond at a rate of 6 percent. It then enters into a swap with DB in which DB will make payments to TGT in U.S. dollars at a fixed rate of 5.5 percent and TGT will make payments to DB in euros at a fixed rate of 4.9 percent each 15 March and 15 September for five years. The payments are based on a notional principal of 10 million in dollars and 9 million in euros. We assume the swap starts on 15 September of the current year. The swap specifies that the two parties exchange the notional principal at the start of the swap and at the end. Because the payments are made in different currencies, netting is not practical, so each party makes its respective payments.[3]

Thus, the swap is composed of the following transactions:
15 September:

▶ DB pays TGT €9 million
▶ TGT pays DB $10 million

---

[2] It is important at this point to clear up some terminology confusion. Foreign currency is often called *foreign exchange* or sometimes *FX*. There is another transaction called an *FX swap*, which sounds as if it might be referring to a currency swap. In fact, an FX swap is just a long position in a forward contract on a foreign currency and a short position in a forward contract on the same currency with a different expiration. Why this transaction is called a swap is not clear, but this transaction existed before currency swaps were created. In futures markets, the analogous transaction is called a *spread*, reflecting as it does the risk associated with the spread between the prices of futures contracts with different expirations.

[3] In this example, we shall assume 180 days between payment dates. In practice, exact day counts are usually used, leading to different fixed payment amounts in one six-month period from those of another. In the example here, we are only illustrating the idea behind swap cash flows, so it is convenient to keep the fixed payments the same. Later in the reading, we shall illustrate situations in which the exact day count is used, leading to fixed payments that vary slightly.

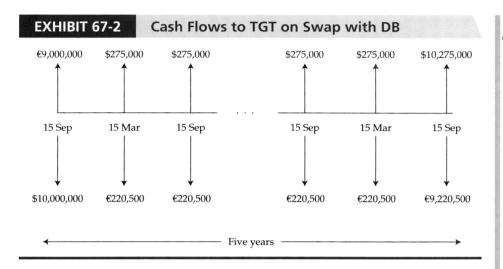

EXHIBIT 67-2   Cash Flows to TGT on Swap with DB

€9,000,000 $275,000 $275,000 $275,000 $275,000 $10,275,000

15 Sep   15 Mar   15 Sep   . . . 15 Sep   15 Mar   15 Sep

$10,000,000 €220,500   €220,500   €220,500   €220,500   €9,220,500

◄———————————————— Five years ————————————————►

Each 15 March and 15 September for five years:

▶ DB pays TGT 0.055(180/360)$10 million = $275,000
▶ TGT pays DB 0.049(180/360) €9 million = €220,500

15 September five years after initiation:

▶ DB pays TGT $10 million
▶ TGT pays DB €9 million

Note that we have simplified the interest calculations a little. In this example, we calculated semiannual interest using the fraction 180/360. Some parties might choose to use the exact day count in the six-month period divided by 365 days. LIBOR and Euribor transactions, the predominant rates used in interest rate swaps, nearly always use 360 days, as mentioned in previous readings. Exhibit 67-2 shows the stream of cash flows from TGT's perspective.

Note that the Target–Deutsche Bank transaction looks just like TGT is issuing a bond with face value of €9 million and that bond is purchased by DB. TGT converts the €9 million to $10 million and buys a dollar-denominated bond issued by DB. Note that TGT, having issued a bond denominated in euros, accordingly makes interest payments to DB in euros. DB, appropriately, makes interest payments in dollars to TGT. At the end, they each pay off the face values of the bonds they have issued. We emphasize that the Target–Deutsche Bank transaction *looks like* what we have just described. In fact, neither TGT nor DB actually issues or purchases a bond. They exchange only a series of cash flows that replicated the issuance and purchase of these bonds.

Exhibit 67-3 illustrates how such a combined transaction would work. TGT issues a bond in dollars (Exhibit 67-3, Panel A). It takes the dollars and passes them through to DB, which gives TGT the €9 million it needs. On the interest payment dates, the swap generates $275,000 of the $300,000 in interest TGT needs to pay its bondholders (Panel B). In turn, TGT makes interest payments in euros. Still, small dollar interest payments are necessary because TGT cannot issue a dollar bond at the swap rate. At the end of the transaction, TGT receives $10 million back from DB and passes it through to its bondholders (Panel C). TGT pays DB €9 million, thus effectively paying off a euro-denominated bond.

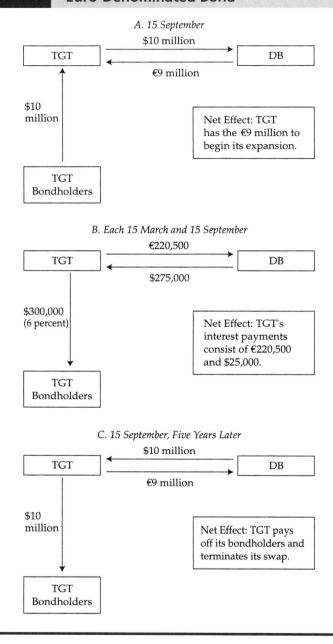

EXHIBIT 67-3   Issuing a Dollar-Denominated Bond and Using a Currency Swap to Convert a Euro-Denominated Bond

A. 15 September

TGT → $10 million → DB

TGT ← €9 million ← DB

$10 million ↑ TGT Bondholders

Net Effect: TGT has the €9 million to begin its expansion.

B. Each 15 March and 15 September

TGT → €220,500 → DB

TGT ← $275,000 ← DB

$300,000 (6 percent) ↓ TGT Bondholders

Net Effect: TGT's interest payments consist of €220,500 and $25,000.

C. 15 September, Five Years Later

TGT ← $10 million ← DB

TGT → €9 million → DB

$10 million ↓ TGT Bondholders

Net Effect: TGT pays off its bondholders and terminates its swap.

TGT has effectively issued a dollar-denominated bond and converted it to a euro-denominated bond. In all likelihood, it can save on interest expense by funding its need for euros in this way, because TGT is better known in the United States than in Europe. Its swap dealer, DB, knows TGT well and also obviously has a strong presence in Europe. Thus, DB can pass on its advantage in euro bond markets to TGT. In addition, had TGT issued a euro-denominated bond, it would have assumed no credit risk. By entering into the swap, TGT assumes a remote possibility of DB defaulting. Thus, TGT saves a little money by assuming some credit risk.

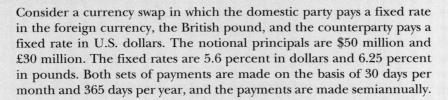

Consider a currency swap in which the domestic party pays a fixed rate in the foreign currency, the British pound, and the counterparty pays a fixed rate in U.S. dollars. The notional principals are $50 million and £30 million. The fixed rates are 5.6 percent in dollars and 6.25 percent in pounds. Both sets of payments are made on the basis of 30 days per month and 365 days per year, and the payments are made semiannually.

A. Determine the initial exchange of cash that occurs at the start of the swap.

B. Determine the semiannual payments.

C. Determine the final exchange of cash that occurs at the end of the swap.

D. Give an example of a situation in which this swap might be appropriate.

▶ **Solution to A.** At the start of the swap:
  Domestic party pays counterparty $50 million
  Counterparty pays domestic party £30 million

▶ **Solution to B.** Semiannually:
  Domestic party pays counterparty £30,000,000(0.0625)(180/365)
  = £924,658
  Counterparty pays domestic party $50,000,000(0.056)(180/365)
  = $1,380,822

▶ **Solution to C.** At the end of the swap:
  Domestic party pays counterparty £30,000,000
  Counterparty pays domestic party $50,000,000

▶ **Solution to D.** This swap would be appropriate for a U.S. company that issues a dollar-denominated bond but would prefer to borrow in British pounds.

Returning to the Target swap, recall that Target effectively converted a fixed-rate loan in dollars to a fixed-rate loan in euros. Suppose instead that TGT preferred to borrow in euros at a floating rate. It then would have specified that the swap required it to make payments to DB at a floating rate. Had TGT preferred to issue the dollar-denominated bond at a floating rate, it would have specified that DB pay it dollars at a floating rate.

Although TGT and DB exchanged notional principal, some scenarios exist in which the notional principals are not exchanged. For example, suppose many years later, TGT is generating €10 million in cash semi annually and converting it back to dollars on 15 January and 15 July. It might then wish to lock in the conversion rate by entering into a currency swap that would require it to pay a dealer €10 million and receive a fixed amount of dollars. If the euro fixed rate were 5 percent, a notional principal of €400 million would generate a payment of 0.05(180/360)€400 million = €10 million. If the exchange rate is, for example, $0.85, the equivalent dollar notional principal would be $340 million. If the dollar fixed rate is 6 percent, TGT would receive 0.06(180/360)$340 million =

$10.2 million.[4] These payments would occur twice a year for the life of the swap. TGT might then lock in the conversion rate by entering into a currency swap with notional principal amounts that would allow it to receive a fixed amount of dollars on 15 January and 15 July. There would be not reason to specify an exchange of notional principal. As we previously described, there are four types of currency swaps. Using the original Target–Deutsche Bank swap as an example, the semi-annual payments would be

A. TGT pays euros at a fixed rate; DB pays dollars at a fixed rate.

B. TGT pays euros at a fixed rate; DB pays dollars at a floating rate.

C. TGT pays euros at a floating rate; DB pays dollars at a floating rate.

D. TGT pays euros at a floating rate; DB pays dollars at a fixed rate.

Or, reversing the flow, TGT could be the payer of dollars and DB could be the payer of euros:

E. TGT pays dollars at a fixed rate; DB pays euros at a fixed rate.

F. TGT pays dollars at a fixed rate; DB pays euros at a floating rate.

G. TGT pays dollars at a floating rate; DB pays euros at a floating rate.

H. TGT pays dollars at a floating rate; DB pays euros at a fixed rate.

Suppose we combine Swap A with Swap H. With TGT paying euros at a fixed rate and DB paying euros at a fixed rate, the euro payments wash out and the net effect is

I. TGT pays dollars at a floating rate; DB pays dollars at a fixed rate.

Suppose we combine Swap B with Swap E. Similarly, the euro payments again wash out, and the net effect is

J. TGT pays dollars at a fixed rate; DB pays dollars at a floating rate.

Suppose we combine Swap C with Swap F. Likewise, the euro floating payments wash out, and the net effect is

K. TGT pays dollars at a fixed rate; DB pays dollars at a floating rate.

Lastly, suppose we combine Swap D with Swap G. Again, the euro floating payments wash out, and the net effect is

L. TGT pays dollars at a floating rate; DB pays dollars at a fixed rate.

Of course, the net results of I and L are equivalent, and the net results of J and K are equivalent. What we have shown here, however, is that combinations of currency swaps eliminate the currency flows and leave us with transactions in only one currency. A swap in which both sets of interest payments are made in the same currency is an interest rate swap.

---

[4] It might appear that TGT has somehow converted cash flows worth €10million($0.085) = $8.5 million into cash flows worth $10.2 million. Recall, however, that the €10 million cash flows are generated yearly and $0.85 is the *current* exchange rate. We cannot apply the current exchange rate to a series of cash flows over various future dates. We would apply the respective forward exchange rates, not the spot rate, to the series of future euro cash flows.

3.2 Interest Rate Swaps

As we discovered in the above paragraph, an interest rate swap can be created as a combination of currency swaps. Of course, no one would create an interest rate swap that way; doing so would require two transactions when only one would suffice. Interest rate swaps evolved into their own market. In fact, the interest rate swap market is much bigger than the currency swap market, as we have seen in the notional principal statistics.

As previously noted, one way to look at an interest rate swap is that it is a currency swap in which both currencies are the same. Consider a swap to pay Currency A fixed and Currency B floating. Currency A could be dollars, and B could be euros. But what if A and B are both dollars, or A and B are both euros? The first case is a dollar-denominated plain vanilla swap; the second is a euro-denominated plain vanilla swap. *A* **plain vanilla swap** *is simply an interest rate swap in which one party pays a fixed rate and the other pays a floating rate, with both sets of payments in the same currency.* In fact, the plain vanilla swap is probably the most common derivative transaction in the global financial system.

Note that because we are paying in the same currency, there is no need to exchange notional principals at the beginning and at the end of an interest rate swap. In addition, the interest payments can be, and nearly always are, netted. If one party owes $X and the other owes $Y, the party owing the greater amount pays the net difference, which greatly reduces the credit risk (as we discuss in more detail in Section 7). Finally, we note that there is no reason to have both sides pay a fixed rate. The two streams of payments would be identical in that case. So in an interest rate swap, either one side always pays fixed and the other side pays floating, or both sides paying floating, but never do both sides pay fixed.[5]

Thus, in a plain vanilla interest rate swap, one party makes interest payments at a fixed rate and the other makes interest payments at a floating rate. Both sets of payments are on the same notional principal and occur on regularly scheduled dates. For each payment, the interest rate is multiplied by a fraction representing the number of days in the settlement period over the number of days in a year. In some cases, the settlement period is computed assuming 30 days in each month; in others, an exact day count is used. Some cases assume a 360-day year; others use 365 days.

Let us now illustrate an interest rate swap. Suppose that on 15 December, General Electric Company (NYSE: GE) borrows money for one year from a bank such as Bank of America (NYSE: BAC). The loan is for $25 million and specifies that GE will make interest payments on a quarterly basis on the 15th of March, June, September, and December for one year at the rate of LIBOR plus 25 basis points. At the end of the year, it will pay back the principal. On the 15th of December, March, June, and September, LIBOR is observed and sets the rate for that quarter. The interest is then paid at the end of the quarter.[6]

GE believes that it is getting a good rate, but fearing a rise in interest rates, it would prefer a fixed-rate loan. It can easily convert the floating-rate loan to a fixed-rate loan by engaging in a swap. Suppose it approaches JP Morgan Chase (NYSE: JPM), a large dealer bank, and requests a quote on a swap to pay a fixed rate and receive LIBOR, with payments on the dates of its loan payments. The bank prices the swap (a procedure we cover in Section 4) and quotes a fixed rate

---

[5] The case of both sides paying floating is called a basis swap, which we shall cover in Section 5.

[6] Again, we assume 90 days in each interest payment period for this example. The exact payment dates are not particularly important for illustrative purposes.

| EXHIBIT 67-4 | Cash Flows to GE on Swap with JPM |

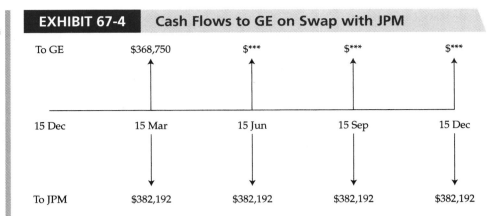

*** Computed as $25,000,000(L)90/360, where L is LIBOR on the previous settlement date.

of 6.2 percent.[7] The fixed payments will be made based on a day count of 90/365, and the floating payments will be made based on 90/360. Current LIBOR is 5.9 percent. Therefore, the first fixed payment, which GE makes to JPM, is $25,000,000(0.062)(90/365) = $382,192. This is also the amount of each remaining fixed payment.

The first floating payment, which JPM makes to GE, is $25,000,000(0.059) (90/360) = $368,750. Of course, the remaining floating payments will not be known until later. Exhibit 67-4 shows the pattern of cash flows on the swap from GE's perspective.

Practice Problem 2

Determine the upcoming payments in a plain vanilla interest rate swap in which the notional principal is €70 million. The end user makes semiannual fixed payments at the rate of 7 percent, and the dealer makes semiannual floating payments at Euribor, which was 6.25 percent on the last settlement period. The floating payments are made on the basis of 180 days in the settlement period and 360 days in a year. The fixed payments are made on the basis of 180 days in the settlement period and 365 days in a year. Payments are netted, so determine which party pays which and what amount.

▶ **Solution.** The fixed payments are €70,000,000(0.07)(180/365) = €2,416,438.
The upcoming floating payment is €70,000,000(0.0625)(180/360) = €2,187,500.
The net payment is that the party paying fixed will pay the party paying floating

$$€2,416,438 - €2,187,500 = €228,938.$$

---

[7] Typically the rate is quoted as a spread over the rate on a U.S. Treasury security with a comparable maturity. Suppose the yield on a two-year Treasury note is 6 percent. Then the swap would be quoted as 20 basis points over the two-year Treasury rate. By quoting the rate in the this manner, GE knows what it is paying over the Treasury rate, a differential called the swap spread, which is a type of credit risk premium we discuss in Section 7. In addition, a quote in this form protects the bank from the rate changing drastically either during the phone conversation or shortly thereafter. Thus, the quote can stay in effect for a reasonable period of time while GE checks out quotes from other dealers.

Note in Exhibit 67-4 that we did not show the notional principal, because it was not exchanged. We could implicitly show that GE received $25 million from JPM and paid $25 million to JPM at the start of the swap. We could also show that the same thing happens at the end. If we look at it that way, it appears as if GE has issued a $25 million fixed-rate bond, which was purchased by JPM, which in turn issued a $25 million floating-rate bond, which was in turn purchased by GE. We say that *it appears* as if this is what happened: In fact, neither party actually issued a bond, but they have generated the cash flows that would occur if GE had issued such a fixed-rate bond, JPM had issued such a **floating-rate bond**, and each purchased the bond of the other. In other words, we could include the principals on both sides to make each set of cash flows look like a bond, yet the overall cash flows would be the same as on the swap.

So let us say that GE enters into this swap. Exhibit 67-5 shows the net effect of the swap and the loan. GE pays LIBOR plus 25 basis points to Bank of America on its loan, pays 6.2 percent to JPM, and receives LIBOR from JPM. The net effect is that GE pays $6.2 + 0.25 = 6.45$ percent fixed.

Now, JPM is engaged in a swap to pay LIBOR and receive 6.2 percent. It is exposed to the risk of LIBOR increasing. It would, therefore, probably engage in some other type of transaction to offset this risk. One transaction commonly used in this situation is to sell Eurodollar futures. As discussed in Reading 65, Eurodollar futures prices move $25 in value for each basis point move in LIBOR. JPM will determine how sensitive its position is to a move in LIBOR and sell an appropriate number of futures to offset the risk. Note that Bank of America is exposed to LIBOR as well, but in the banking industry, floating-rate loans are often made because the funding that the bank obtained to make the loan was probably already at LIBOR or a comparable floating rate.

It is possible but unlikely that GE could get a fixed-rate loan at a better rate. The swap involves some credit risk: the possibility, however small, that JPM will default. In return for assuming that risk, GE in all likelihood would get a better rate than it would if it borrowed at a fixed rate. JPM is effectively a wholesaler of risk, using its powerful position as one of the world's leading banks to facilitate the buying and selling of risk for companies such as GE. Dealers profit from the spread between the rates they quote to pay and the rates they quote to receive. The swaps market is, however, extremely competitive and the spreads have been squeezed very tight, which makes it very challenging for dealers to make a profit. Of course, this competition is good for end users, because it gives them more attractive rates.

EXHIBIT 67-5	GE's Conversion of a Floating-Rate Loan to a Fixed-Rate Loan Using an Interest Rate Swap with JPM

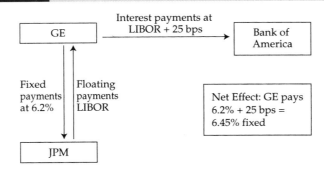

3.3 Equity Swaps

By now, it should be apparent that a swap requires at least one variable rate or price underlying it. So far, that rate has been an interest rate.[8] In an equity swap, the rate is the return on a stock or stock index. This characteristic gives the equity swap two features that distinguish it from interest rate and currency swaps.

First, the party making the fixed-rate payment could also have to make a variable payment based on the equity return. Suppose the end user pays the equity payment and receives the fixed payment, i.e., it pays the dealer the return on the S&P 500 Index, and the dealer pays the end user a fixed rate. If the S&P 500 increases, the return is positive and the end user pays that return to the dealer. If the S&P 500 goes down, however, its return is obviously negative. In that case, the end user would pay the dealer the *negative return on the S&P 500*, which means that it would receive that return from the dealer. For example, if the S&P 500 falls by 1 percent, the dealer would pay the end user 1 percent, in addition to the fixed payment the dealer makes in any case. So the dealer, or in general the party receiving the equity return, could end up making *both* a fixed-rate payment and an equity payment.

The second distinguishing feature of an equity swap is that the payment is not known until the end of the settlement period, at which time the return on the stock is known. In an interest rate or currency swap, the floating interest rate is set at the beginning of the period.[9] Therefore, one always knows the amount of the upcoming floating interest payment.[10]

Another important feature of some equity swaps is that the rate of return is often structured to include both dividends and capital gains. In interest rate and currency swaps, capital gains are not paid.[11] Finally, we note that in some equity swaps, the notional principal is indexed to change with the level of the stock, although we will not explore such swaps in this reading.[12]

Equity swaps are commonly used by asset managers. Let us consider a situation in which an asset manager might use such a swap. Suppose that the Vanguard Asset Allocation Fund (Nasdaq: VAAPX) is authorized to use swaps. On the last day of December, it would like to sell $100 million in U.S. large-cap equities and invest the proceeds at a fixed rate. It believes that a swap allowing it to pay the total return on the S&P 500, while receiving a fixed rate, would achieve this objective. It would like to hold this position for one year, with payments to be made on the last day of March, June, September, and December. It enters into such a swap with Morgan Stanley (NYSE: MWD).

Specifically, the swap covers a notional principal of $100 million and calls for VAAPX to pay MWD the return on the S&P 500 Total Return Index and for MWD to pay VAAPX a fixed rate on the last day of March, June, September, and December for one year. MWD prices the swap at a fixed rate of 6.5 percent. The fixed payments will be made using an actual day count/365 days convention. There are 90 days between 31 December and 31 March, 91 days between

---

[8] Currency swaps also have the element that the exchange rate is variable.

[9] Technically, there are interest rate swaps in which the floating rate is set at the end of the period, at which time the payment is made. We shall briefly mention these swaps in Section 5.

[10] In a currency swap, however, one does not know the exchange rate until the settlement date.

[11] In some kinds of interest rate swaps, the total return on a bond, which includes dividends and capital gains, is paid. This instrument is called a **total return swap** and is a common variety of a credit derivative.

[12] Some interest rate swaps also have a notional principal that changes, which we shall briefly discuss in Section 5.

EXHIBIT 67-6	Cash Flows to VAAPX on Equity Swap with MWD

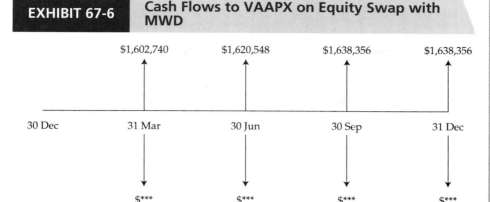

*** Computed as $100,000,000R, where R is the return on the S&P 500 Total Return Index from the previous settlement date.

31 March and 30 June, 92 days between 30 June and 30 September, and 92 days between 30 September and 31 December. Thus, the fixed payments will be

31 March: $100,000,000(0.065)(90/365) = $1,602,740

30 June: $100,000,000(0.065)(91/365) = $1,620,548

30 September: $100,000,000(0.065)(92/365) = $1,638,356

31 December: $100,000,000(0.065)(92/365) = $1,638,356

Exhibit 67-6 shows the cash flow stream to VAAPX.

Suppose that on the day the swap is initiated, 31 December, the S&P 500 Total Return Index is at 3,517.76. Now suppose that on 31 March, the index is at 3,579.12. The return on the index is

$$\frac{3,579.12}{3,517.76} - 1 = 0.0174$$

Thus, the return is 1.74 percent. The equity payment that VAAPX would make to MWD would be $100,000,000(0.0174) = $1,740,000.

Of course, this amount would not be known until 31 March, and only the difference between this amount and the fixed payment would be paid. Then on 31 March, the index value of 3,579.12 would be the base for the following period. Suppose that on 30 June, the index declines to 3,452.78. Then the return for the second quarter would be

$$\frac{3,452.78}{3,579.12} - 1 = -0.0353$$

Therefore, the loss is 3.53 percent, requiring a payment of $100,000,000(0.0353) = $3,530,000.

Because this amount represents a loss on the S&P 500, MWD would make a payment to VAAPX. In addition, MWD would also owe VAAPX the fixed payment of $1,620,548. It is as though VAAPX sold out of its position in stock, thereby avoiding the loss of about $3.5 million, and moved into a fixed-income position, thereby picking up a gain of about $1.6 million.

Practice Problem 3

A mutual fund has arranged an equity swap with a dealer. The swap's notional principal is $100 million, and payments will be made semi-annually. The mutual fund agrees to pay the dealer the return on a small-cap stock index, and the dealer agrees to pay the mutual fund based on one of the two specifications given below. The small-cap index starts off at 1,805.20; six months later, it is at 1,796.15.

A. The dealer pays a fixed rate of 6.75 percent to the mutual fund, with payments made on the basis of 182 days in the period and 365 days in a year. Determine the first payment for both parties and, under the assumption of netting, determine the net payment and which party makes it.

B. The dealer pays the return on a large-cap index. The index starts off at 1155.14 and six months later is at 1148.91. Determine the first payment for both parties and, under the assumption of netting, determine the net payment and which party makes it.

▶ **Solution to A.** The fixed payment is $100,000,000(0.0675)182/365 = $3,365,753. The equity payment is

$$\left(\frac{1796.15}{1805.20} - 1\right)\$100,000,000 = -\$501,329$$

Because the fund pays the equity return and the equity return is negative, the dealer must pay the equity return. The dealer also pays the fixed return, so the dealer makes both payments, which add up to $3,365,753 + $501,329 = $3,867,082. The net payment is $3,867,082, paid by the dealer to the mutual fund.

▶ **Solution to B.** The large-cap equity payment is

$$\left(\frac{1148.91}{1155.14} - 1\right)\$100,000,000 = -\$539,329$$

The fund owes −$501,329, so the dealer owes the fund $501,329. The dealer owes −$539,329, so the fund owes the dealer $539,329. Therefore, the fund pays the dealer the net amount of $539,329 − $501,329 = $38,000.

Exhibit 67-7 illustrates what VAAPX has accomplished. It is important to note that the conversion of its equity assets into fixed income is not perfect. VAAPX does not hold a portfolio precisely equal to the S&P 500 Total Return Index. To the extent that VAAPX's portfolio generates a return that deviates from the index, some mismatching can occur, which can be a problem. As an alternative, VAAPX can request that MWD give it a swap based on the precise portfolio that VAAPX wishes to sell off. In that case, however, MWD would assess a charge by lowering the fixed rate it pays or raising the rate VAAPX pays to it.[13]

---

[13] Note, however, that VAAPX is converting not its entire portfolio but simply a $100 million portion of it.

EXHIBIT 67-7	VAAPX's Conversion of an Equity Position into a Fixed-Income Position

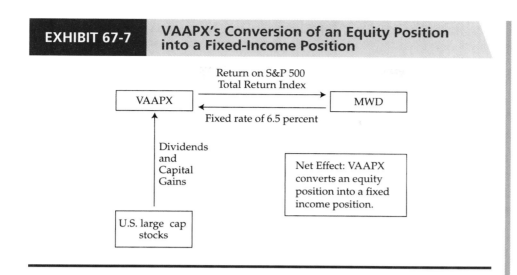

In our previous VAAPX example, the fund wanted to move some money out of a large-cap equity position and invest the proceeds at a fixed rate. Suppose instead that they do not want to move the proceeds into a fixed-rate investment. VAAPX could structure a swap to pay it a floating rate or the return on some other equity index. For example, an asset allocation from U.S. large-cap stocks to U.S. small-cap stocks could be accomplished by having MWD pay the return on the S&P 500 Small Cap 600 Index.

Suppose VAAPX wanted to move out of a position in U.S. stocks and into a position in U.K. large-cap stocks. It could structure the swap to have MWD pay it the return on the FTSE (Financial Times Stock Exchange) 100 Index. Note, however, that this index is based on the prices of U.K. stocks as quoted in pounds sterling. If VAAPX wanted the exposure in pounds—that is, it wanted the currency risk as well as the risk of the U.K. stock market—the payments from MWD to VAAPX would be made in pounds. VAAPX could, however, ask for the payments in dollars. In that case, MWD would hedge the currency risk and make payments in dollars.

Although our focus is on currency, interest rate, and equity products, we shall take a very brief look at some other types of swaps.

3.4 Commodity and Other Types of Swaps

Just as currencies, interest rates, and equities can be used to structure swaps, so too can commodities and just about anything that has a random outcome and to which a corporation, financial institution, or even an individual is exposed. Commodity swaps are very commonly used. For example, airlines enter into swaps to hedge their future purchases of jet fuel. They agree to make fixed payments to a swap dealer on regularly scheduled dates and receive payments determined by the price of jet fuel. Gold mining companies use swaps to hedge future deliveries of gold. Other parties dealing in such commodities as natural gas and precious metals often use swaps to lock in prices for future purchases and sales. In addition, swaps can be based on non-storable commodities, like electricity and the weather. In the case of the weather, payments are made based on a measure of a particular weather factor, such as amounts of rain, snowfall, or weather-related damage.

We have now introduced and described the basic structure of swaps. We have made many references to the pricing and valuation of swaps, and we now move on to explore how this is done.

PRICING AND VALUATION OF SWAPS

In Reading 64, we took our first look at the concepts of pricing and valuation when we examined forward contracts on assets and FRAs, which are essentially forward contracts on interest rates. Recall that a forward contract requires no cash payment at the start and commits one party to buy and another to sell an asset at a later date. An FRA commits one party to make a single fixed-rate interest payment and the other to make a single floating-rate interest payment. A swap extends that concept by committing one party to making a series of floating payments. The other party commits to making a series of fixed or floating payments. For swaps containing any fixed terms, such as a fixed rate, pricing the swap means to determine those terms at the start of the swap. Some swaps do not contain any fixed terms; we explore examples of both types of swaps.

All swaps have a market value. Valuation of a swap means to determine the market value of the swap based on current market conditions. The fixed terms, such as the fixed rate, are established at the start to give the swap an initial market value of zero. As we have already discussed, a zero market value means that neither party pays anything to the other at the start. Later during the life of the swap, as market conditions change, the market value will change, moving from zero from both parties' perspective to a positive value for one party and a negative value for the other. When a swap has zero value, it is neither an asset nor a liability to either party. When the swap has positive value to one party, it is an asset to that party; from the perspective of the other party, it thus has negative value and is a liability.

We begin the process of pricing and valuing swaps by learning how swaps are comparable to other instruments. If we know that one financial instrument is equivalent to another, we can price one instrument if we know or can determine the price of the other instrument.

4.1 Equivalence of Swaps and Other Instruments

In this section, we look at how swaps are similar to other instruments. Because our focus is on currency, interest rate, and equity swaps, we do not discuss commodity swaps here.

4.1.1 Swaps and Assets

We have already alluded to the similarity between swaps and assets. For example, a currency swap is identical to issuing a fixed- or floating-rate bond in one currency, converting the proceeds to the other currency, and using the proceeds to purchase a fixed- or floating-rate bond denominated in the other currency. An interest rate swap is identical to issuing a fixed- or floating-rate bond and using the proceeds to purchase a floating- or fixed-rate bond. The notional principal is equivalent to the face value on these hypothetical bonds.

Equity swaps appear to be equivalent to issuing one type of security and using the proceeds to purchase another, where at least one of the types of securities is a stock or stock index. For example, a pay-fixed, receive-equity swap looks like issuing a fixed-rate bond and using the proceeds to buy a stock or index portfolio. As it turns out, however, these two transactions are not exactly the same, although they are close. The stock position in the transaction is not the same as a buy-and-hold position; some adjustments are required on the settlement dates to replicate the cash flows of a swap. We shall take a look at this process of replicating an equity swap in Section 4.2.3. For now, simply recognize that an equity swap is like issuing bonds and buying stock, but not buying and holding stock.

The equivalence of a swap to transactions we are already familiar with, such as owning assets, is important because it allows us to price and value the swap using simple instruments, such as the underlying currency, interest rate, or stock. We do not require other derivatives to replicate the cash flows of a swap. Nonetheless, other derivatives can be used to replicate the cash flows of a swap, and it is worth seeing why this is true.

4.1.2 Swaps and Forward Contracts

Recall that a forward contract, whether on an interest rate, a currency, or an equity, is an agreement for one party to make a fixed payment to the other, while the latter party makes a variable payment to the former. A swap extends this notion by combining a series of forward contracts into a single transaction. There are, however, some subtle differences between swaps and forward contracts. For example, swaps are a series of equal fixed payments, whereas the component contracts of a series of forward contracts would almost always be priced at different fixed rates.[14] In this context we often refer to a swap as a series of off-market forward contracts, reflecting the fact that the implicit forward contracts that make up the swap are all priced at the swap fixed rate and not at the rate at which they would normally be priced in the market. In addition, in interest rate swaps, the next payment that each party makes is known. That would obviously not be the case for a single forward contract. Other subtleties distinguish currency swaps from a series of currency forwards and equity swaps from a series of equity forwards, but in general, it is acceptable to view a swap as a series of forward contracts.

4.1.3 Swaps and Futures Contracts

It is a fairly common practice to equate swaps to futures contracts. This practice is partially correct, but only to the extent that futures contracts can be equated to forward contracts. We saw in Reading 65 that futures contracts are equivalent to forward contracts only when future interest rates are known. Obviously this condition can never truly be met, and because swaps are often used to manage uncertain interest rates, the equivalence of futures with swaps is not always appropriate. Moreover, swaps are highly customized contracts, whereas futures are standardized with respect to expiration and the underlying instrument. Although it is common to equate a swap with a series of futures contracts, this equality holds true only in very limited cases.[15]

4.1.4 Swaps and Options

Finally, we note that swaps can be equated to combinations of options. Buying a call and selling a put would force the transacting party to make a net payment if the underlying is below the exercise rate at expiration, and would result in receipt of a payment if the underlying is above the exercise rate at expiration.

---

[14] For example, a series of FRAs would have different fixed rates unless the term structure is flat.

[15] It is possible only in extremely rare circumstances for futures expirations to line up with swap settlement dates and thereby provide perfect equivalence. That does not mean, however, that futures cannot be used to hedge in a delta-hedging sense, as described in Reading 66. A futures price has a given sensitivity to the underlying, and futures are often highly liquid. A dealer, having entered into a swap, can determine the swap's sensitivity to the underlying and execute the appropriate number of futures transactions to balance the volatility of the swap to that of the futures. Indeed, this method is standard for hedging plain vanilla swaps using the Eurodollar futures contract.

This payment will be equivalent to a swap payment if the exercise rate is set at the fixed rate on the swap. Therefore, a swap is equivalent to a combination of options with expirations at the swap payment dates. The connection between swaps and options is relatively straightforward for interest rate instruments, but less so for currency and equity instruments. Nonetheless, we can generally consider swaps as equivalent to combinations of options.

In this section, we have learned that swaps can be shown to be equivalent to combinations of assets, combinations of forward contracts, combinations of futures contracts, and combinations of options. Thus, to price and value swaps we can choose any of these approaches. We choose the simplest: swaps and assets.

4.2 Pricing and Valuation

As in previous readings, our goal is to determine the market value of the derivative transaction of interest, in this case, swaps. At the start of a swap, the market value is set to zero. The process of pricing the swap involves finding the terms that force that market value to zero. To determine the market value of a swap, we replicate the swap using other instruments that produce the same cash flows. Knowing the values of these other instruments, we are able to value the swap. This value can be thought of as what the swap is worth if we were to sell it to someone else. In addition, we can think of the value as what we might assign to it on our balance sheet. The swap can have a positive value, making it an asset, or a negative value, making it a liability.

As we noted in Section 4.1, swaps are equivalent to a variety of instruments, but we prefer to use the simplest instruments to replicate the swap. The simplest instruments are the underlying assets: bonds, stocks, and currencies. Therefore, we shall use these underlying instruments to replicate the swap.

To understand the pricing of currency, interest rate, and equity swaps, we shall have to first take a brief digression to examine an instrument that plays an important role in their pricing. We shall see that the floating-rate security will have a value of 1.0, its par, at the start and on any coupon reset date. Recall that we have made numerous references to floating rates and floating payments. Accordingly, we must first obtain a solid understanding of floating-rate notes.

As we did in Reading 64, let us first set up a time line that indicates where we are and where the interest payments on the floating-rate note will occur:

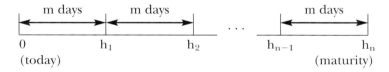

We start at time 0. The interest payments will occur on days h_1, h_2, . . . , h_{n-1}, and h_n, so there are n interest payments in all. Day h_n is the maturity date of the floating-rate note. The time interval between payments is m days. The underlying rate is an m-day interest rate.

For simplicity, we will use LIBOR as the underlying rate and denote it with the symbol we have previously used, $L_i(m)$, which stands for the m-day LIBOR on day i. If i = 1, we are referring to day h_1, which might, for example, be 180 days after day 0. Thus, $h_1 = 180$. $L_0(180)$ is the 180-day LIBOR on day 0. Then h_2 would likely be 360 and $L_0(2m) = L_0(360)$, the 360-day LIBOR on day 0. We denote $B_0(h_j)$ as the present value factor on a zero-coupon instrument paying $1 at its maturity date. As an example, to discount payments 180 and 360 days later, we multiply the payment amount by the following respective factors:

$$B_0(180) = \frac{1}{1 + L_0(180) \times (180/360)}$$

$$B_0(360) = \frac{1}{1 + L_0(360) \times (360/360)}$$

We can think of these discount factors as the values of spot LIBOR deposits that pay \$1 at maturity, 180 and 360 days later.

On day 0, the floating rate is set for the first period and the interest to be paid at that rate is paid on day h_1. Then on day h_1, the rate is set for the second period and the interest is paid on day h_2. This process continues so that on day h_{n-1} the rate is set for the last period, and the final interest payment and the principal are paid on day h_n. Let the principal be 1.0.

Suppose today is day h_{n-1} and LIBOR on that day is $L_{n-1}(m)$. Remember that this rate is the m-day LIBOR in the market at that time. Therefore, looking ahead to day h_n, we anticipate receiving 1.0, the final principal payment, plus $L_{n-1}(m) \times (m/360)$. What is the value of this amount on day h_{n-1}? We would discount it by the appropriate m-day LIBOR in the following manner:

Value at h_{n-1} = (Payment at h_n)(One-period discount factor)

$$= [1.0 + L_{n-1}(m) \times (m/360)]\left[\frac{1}{1.0 + L_{n-1}(m) \times (m/360)}\right] = 1.0$$

The value is 1.0, its par value. Now step back to day h_{n-2}, at which time the rate is $L_{n-2}(m)$. Looking ahead to day h_{n-1} we shall receive an interest payment of $L_{n-2}(m) \times (m/360)$. We do not receive the principal on day h_{n-1}, but it is appropriate to discount the market value on day h_{n-1}, which we just determined is 1.0.[16] Thus, the value of the floating-rate security will be

Value at h_{n-2} = (Payment at h_{n-1})(One-period discount factor)

$$= [1.0 + L_{n-2}(m) \times (m/360)]\left[\frac{1}{1.0 + L_{n-2}(m) \times (m/360)}\right] = 1.0$$

We continue this procedure, stepping back until we reach time 0. The floating-rate security will have a value of 1.0, its par, at the start and on any coupon reset date.[17] We shall use this result to help us price and value swaps.

In previous material in this reading, we have covered currency swaps first. We did so because we showed that an interest rate swap is just a currency swap in which both currencies are the same. A currency swap is thus the more general instrument of the two. For the purposes of this section, however, it will be easier to price and value a currency swap if we first price and value an interest rate swap.

---

[16] All we are doing here is discounting the upcoming cash flow and the market value of the security on the next payment date. This procedure is not unique to floating-rate securities; it is standard valuation procedure for any type of security. What is special and different for floating-rate securities is that the market value goes back to par on each payment date.

[17] Floating-rate securities are designed to allow the coupon to catch up with market interest rates on a regularly scheduled basis. The price can deviate from par during the period between reset dates. In addition, if there is any credit risk and that risk changes during the life of the security, its price can deviate from par at any time, including at the coupon reset date. We are assuming no credit risk here.

4.2.1 Interest Rate Swaps

Pricing an interest rate swap means finding the fixed rate that equates the present value of the fixed payments to the present value of the floating payments, a process that sets the market value of the swap to zero at the start. Using the time line illustrated earlier, the swap cash flows will occur on days $h_1, h_2, \ldots, h_{n-1}$, and h_n, so there are n cash flows in the swap. Day h_n is the expiration date of the swap. The time interval between payments is m days. We can thus think of the swap as being on an m-day interest rate, which will be LIBOR in our examples.

As previously mentioned, the payments in an interest rate swap are a series of fixed and floating interest payments. They do not include an initial and final exchange of notional principals. As we already observed, such payments would be only an exchange of the same money. But if we introduce the notional principal payments as though they were actually made, we have not done any harm. The cash flows on the swap are still the same. The advantage of introducing the notional principal payments is that we can now treat the fixed and floating sides of the swap as though they were fixed- and floating-rate bonds.

So we introduce a hypothetical final notional principal payment of $1 on a swap starting at day 0 and ending on day h_n, in which the underlying is an m-day rate. The fixed swap interest payment *rate*, FS(0,n,m), gives the fixed payment *amount* corresponding to the $1 notional principal. Thus, the present value of a series of fixed interest payments at the swap rate FS(0,n,m) plus a final principal payment of 1.0 is

$$\sum_{j=1}^{n} FS(0, n, m) B_0(h_j) + \$1 \times B_0(h_n), \text{ or}$$

$$FS(0, n, m) \sum_{j=1}^{n} B_0(h_j) + B_0(h_n)$$

Here the summation simply represents the sum of the present value factors for each payment. The expression $B_0(h_n)$ is the present value factor for the final hypothetical notional principal payment of 1.0.

Now we must find the present value of the floating payments, and here we use what we learned about floating-rate notes. Remember that a floating-rate note with $1 face will have a value of $1 at the start and at any coupon reset date. If the swap's floating payments include a final principal payment, we can treat them like a floating-rate note. Hence, we know their value is $1.

Now all we have to do is equate the present value of the fixed payments to the present value of the floating payments

$$FS(0, n, m) \sum_{j=1}^{n} B_0(h_j) + B_0(h_n) = 1.0$$

and solve for the fixed rate FS(0,n,m) that will result in equality of these two streams of payments. The solution is as follows:

$$FS(0, n, m) = \frac{1.0 - B_0(h_n)}{\sum_{j=1}^{n} B_0(h_j)}$$

(67-1)

The swap fixed payment is 1.0 minus the last present value factor divided by the sum of the present value factors for each payment. Thus, we have priced the swap.

One can use several other ways to find the fixed payment on a swap, but this method is unquestionably the simplest. In fact, this formulation shows that the fixed rate on a swap is simply the coupon rate on a par bond whose payments coincide with those on the swap.[18]

Let us now work a problem. Consider a one-year swap with quarterly payments on days 90, 180, 270, and 360. The underlying is 90-day LIBOR. The annualized LIBOR spot rates today are

$$L_0(90) \quad = 0.0345$$

$$L_0(180) = 0.0358$$

$$L_0(270) = 0.0370$$

$$L_0(360) = 0.0375$$

The present value factors are obtained as follows:

$$B_0(90) \quad = \frac{1}{1 + 0.0345(90/360)} = 0.9914$$

$$B_0(180) = \frac{1}{1 + 0.0358(180/360)} = 0.9824$$

$$B_0(270) = \frac{1}{1 + 0.0370(270/360)} = 0.9730$$

$$B_0(360) = \frac{1}{1 + 0.0375(360/360)} = 0.9639$$

The fixed payment is found as

$$FS(0, n, m) = FS(0,4,90) = \frac{1 - 0.9639}{0.9914 + 0.9824 + 0.9730 + 0.9639} = 0.0092$$

Therefore, the quarterly fixed payment will be 0.0092 for each $1 notional principal. Of course, this rate is quarterly; it is customary to quote it as an annual rate. We would thus see the rate quoted as $0.0092 \times (360/90) = 0.0368$, or 3.68 percent. We would also have to adjust our payment by multiplying by the actual notional principal. For example, if the actual notional principal were $30 million, the payment would be $(0.0092)\$30$ million $= \$276,000$.

In determining the fixed rate on the swap, we have essentially found the fixed payment that sets the present value of the floating payments plus a hypothetical notional principal of 1.0 equal to the present value of the fixed payments plus a hypothetical notional principal of 1.0. We have thus made the market value of the swap equal to zero at the start of the transaction. This equality makes sense, because neither party pays any money to the other.

Now suppose we have entered into the swap. Let us move forward into the life of the swap, at which time interest rates have changed, and determine its market value. Rather than present mathematical equations for determining its value, we shall work through this example informally. We shall see that the procedure is simple and intuitive. Suppose we have now moved 60 days into the life of the swap. At day 60, we face a new term structure of LIBORs. Because the

---

[18] Technically, bond interest payments are usually found by dividing the annual rate by 2 if the payments are semiannual, whereas swap payments do, on occasion, use day counts such as 181/365 to determine semiannual payments. When we refer to a par bond, we are assuming the payments are structured exactly like those on the swap.

upcoming payments occur in 30, 120, 210, and 300 days, we want the term structure for 30, 120, 210, and 300 days, which is given as follows:

$$L_{60}(30) = 0.0425$$

$$L_{60}(120) = 0.0432$$

$$L_{60}(210) = 0.0437$$

$$L_{60}(300) = 0.0444$$

The new set of discount factors is

$$B_{60}(30) = \frac{1}{1 + 0.0425(30/360)} = 0.9965$$

$$B_{60}(120) = \frac{1}{1 + 0.0432(120/360)} = 0.9858$$

$$B_{60}(210) = \frac{1}{1 + 0.0437(210/360)} = 0.9751$$

$$B_{60}(300) = \frac{1}{1 + 0.0444(300/360)} = 0.9643$$

We must value the swap from the perspective of one of the parties. Let us look at it as though we were the party paying fixed and receiving floating. Finding the present value of the remaining fixed payments of 0.0092 is straightforward. This present value, including the hypothetical notional principal, is 0.0092(0.9965 + 0.9858 + 0.9751 + 0.9643) + 1.0(0.9643) = 1.0004.

Now we must find the present value of the floating payments. Recall that on day 0, the 90-day LIBOR was 3.45 percent. Thus, the first floating payment will be 0.0345(90/360) = 0.0086. We know that we should discount this payment back 30 days, but what about the remaining floating payments? Remember that we know that the market value of the remaining payments on day 90, including the hypothetical final notional principal, is 1.0. So, we can discount 1.00 + 0.0086 = 1.0086 back 30 days to obtain 1.0086(0.9965) = 1.0051.

The present value of the remaining floating payments, plus the hypothetical notional principal, is 1.0051, and the present value of the remaining fixed payments, plus the hypothetical notional principal, is 1.0004. Therefore, the value of the swap is 1.0051 − 1.0004 = 0.0047 per $1 notional principal. If, for example, the actual swap were for a notional principal of $30 million, the market value would be $30 million(0.0047) = $141,000.

Practice Problem 4

Consider a one-year interest rate swap with semiannual payments.

A. Determine the fixed rate on the swap and express it in annualized terms. The term structure of LIBOR spot rates is given as follows:

Days	Rate
180	7.2%
360	8.0%

B. Ninety days later, the term structure is as follows:

Days	Rate
90	7.1%
270	7.4%

Determine the market value of the swap from the perspective of the party paying the floating rate and receiving the fixed rate. Assume a notional principal of $15 million.

▶ **Solution to A.** First calculate the present value factors for 180 and 360 days:

$$B_0(180) = \frac{1}{1 + 0.072(180/360)} = 0.9653$$

$$B_0(360) = \frac{1}{1 + 0.08(360/360)} = 0.9259$$

The fixed rate is $\frac{1 - 0.9259}{0.9653 + 0.9259} = 0.0392$. The fixed payment would, therefore, be 0.0392 per $1 notional principal. The annualized rate would be 0.0392(360/180) = 0.0784.

▶ **Solution to B.** Calculate the new present value factors for 90 and 270 days:

$$B_{90}(90) = \frac{1}{1 + 0.071(90/360)} = 0.9826$$

$$B_{90}(270) = \frac{1}{1 + 0.0074(270/360)} = 0.9474$$

The present value of the remaining fixed payments plus hypothetical $1 notional principal is 0.0392(0.9826 + 0.9474) + 1.0(0.9474) = 1.0231.

The 180-day rate at the start was 7.2 percent, so the first floating payment would be 0.072(180/360) = 0.036. The present value of the floating payments plus hypothetical $1 notional principal will be 1.036(0.9826) = 1.0180. The market value of a pay-floating, receive-fixed swap is, therefore, 1.0231 − 1.0180 = 0.0051. For a notional principal of $15 million, the market value is $15,000,000(0.0051) = $76,500.

Note that we valued the swap from the perspective of the party paying the fixed rate. From the counterparty's perspective, the value of the swap would be the negative of the value to the fixed-rate payer.

Although an interest rate swap is like a series of FRAs, or a long position in an interest rate cap and a short position in an interest rate floor with the exercise rate set at the fixed rate on a swap, pricing and valuing an interest rate swap as either of these instruments is more difficult than what we have done here. To price the swap as a series of FRAs, we would need to calculate the forward rates, which is not difficult but would add another step. If we priced a swap as a combination of caps and floors, we would need to price these options. As we saw in Reading 66, interest rate option pricing can be somewhat complex. In addition, we would have to find the exercise rate on the cap and floor that equated their values, which would require trial and error. What we have seen here is the trick that if we add the notional principal to both sides of an interest rate swap, we do not change the swap payments, but we make the cash flows on each side of the swap equivalent to those of a bond. Then we can price the swap as though it were a pair of bonds, one long and the other short. One side is like a floating-rate bond, which we know is priced at par value at the time of issuance as well as on any reset date. The other side is like a fixed-rate bond. Because the value of the fixed-rate bond must equal that of the floating-rate bond at the start, we know that the coupon on a par value bond is the fixed rate on the swap.

Having discussed the pricing and valuation of interest rate swaps, we can now move on to currency swaps, taking advantage of what we know about pricing interest rate swaps. As we have already noted, an interest rate swap is just like a currency swap in which both currencies are the same.

4.2.2 Currency Swaps

Recall the four types of currency swaps: (1) pay one currency fixed, receive the other fixed, (2) pay one currency fixed, receive the other floating, (3) pay one currency floating, receive the other fixed, and (4) pay one currency floating, receive the other floating. In determining the fixed rate on a swap, we must keep in mind one major point: The fixed rate is the rate that makes the present value of the payments made equal the present value of the payments received. In the fourth type of currency swap mentioned here, both sides pay floating so there is no need to find a fixed rate. But all currency swaps have two notional principals, one in each currency. We can arbitrarily set the notional principal in the domestic currency at one unit. We then must determine the equivalent notional principal in the other currency. This task is straightforward: We simply convert the one unit of domestic currency to the equivalent amount of foreign currency, dividing 1.0 by the exchange rate.

Consider the first type of currency swap, in which we pay the foreign currency at a fixed rate and receive the domestic currency at a fixed rate. What are the two fixed rates? We will see that they are the fixed rates on plain vanilla interest rate swaps in the respective countries.

Because we know that the value of a floating-rate security with $1 face value is $1, we know that the fixed rate on a plain vanilla interest rate swap is the rate on a $1 par bond in the domestic currency. That rate results in the present value of the interest payments and the hypothetical notional principal being equal to 1.0 unit of the domestic currency. Moreover, for a currency swap, the notional principal is typically paid, so we do not even have to call it hypothetical. We know that the fixed rate on the domestic leg of an interest rate swap is the appropriate domestic fixed rate for a currency swap in which the domestic notional principal is 1.0 unit of the domestic currency.

What about the fixed rate for the foreign payments on the currency swap? To answer that question, let us assume the point of view of a resident of the foreign country. Given the term structure in the foreign country, we might be interested in first pricing plain vanilla interest rate swaps in that country. So, we know that the fixed rate on interest rate swaps in that country would make the present value of the interest and principal payments equal 1.0 unit of that currency.

Now let us return to our domestic setting. We know that the fixed rate on interest rate swaps in the foreign currency makes the present value of the foreign interest and principal payments equal to 1.0 unit of the foreign currency. We multiply by the spot rate, S_0, to obtain the value of those payments in our domestic currency: 1.0 times S_0 equals S_0, which is now in terms of the domestic currency. This amount does not equal the present value of the domestic payments, but if we set the notional principal on the foreign side of the swap equal to $1/S_0$, then the present value of the foreign payments will be $S_0(1/S_0) = 1.0$ unit of our domestic currency, which is what we want.

Let us now summarize this argument:

► The fixed rate on plain vanilla swaps in our country makes the present value of the domestic interest and principal payments equal 1.0 unit of the domestic currency.

► The fixed rate on plain vanilla swaps in the foreign country makes the present value of the foreign interest and principal payments equal 1.0 unit of the foreign currency.

► A notional principal of $1/S_0$ units of foreign currency makes the present value of the foreign interest and principal payments equal $1/S_0$ units of the foreign currency.

► Conversion of $1/S_0$ units of foreign currency at the current exchange rate of S_0 gives 1.0 unit of domestic currency.

► Therefore, the present value of the domestic payments equals the present value of the foreign payments.

► The fixed rates on a currency swap are, therefore, the fixed rates on plain vanilla interest rate swaps in the respective countries.

Of course, if the domestic notional principal is any amount other than 1.0, we multiply the domestic notional principal by $1/S_0$ to obtain the foreign notional principal. Then the actual swap payments are calculated by multiplying by the overall respective notional principals.

The second and third types of currency swaps each involve one side paying fixed and the other paying floating. The rate on the fixed side of each of these swaps is, again, just the fixed rate on an interest rate swap in the given country. The payments on the floating side automatically have the same present value as the payments on the fixed side. We again use 1.0 unit of domestic currency and $1/S_0$ units of foreign currency as the notional principal.

For the last type of currency swap, in which both sides pay floating, we do not need to price the swap because both sides pay a floating rate. Again, the notional principals are 1.0 unit of domestic currency and $1/S_0$ units of foreign currency.

In the example we used in pricing interest rate swaps, we were given a term structure for a one-year swap with quarterly payments. We found that the fixed payment was 0.0092, implying an annual rate of 3.68 percent. Let us now work through a currency swap in which the domestic currency is the dollar and the foreign currency is the Swiss franc. The current exchange rate is $0.80. We shall use the same term structure used previously for the domestic term structure: $L_0(90) = 0.0345$, $L_0(180) = 0.0358$, $L_0(270) = 0.0370$, and $L_0(360) = 0.0375$. The Swiss term structure, denoted with a superscript SF, is

$$L_0^{SF}(90) = 0.0520$$

$$L_0^{SF}(180) = 0.0540$$

$$L_0^{SF}(270) = 0.0555$$

$$L_0^{SF}(360) = 0.0570$$

The present value factors are

$$B_0^{SF}(90) = \frac{1}{1 + 0.0520(90/360)} = 0.9872$$

$$B_0^{SF}(180) = \frac{1}{1 + 0.0540(180/360)} = 0.9737$$

$$B_0^{SF}(270) = \frac{1}{1 + 0.0555(270/360)} = 0.9600$$

$$B_0^{SF}(360) = \frac{1}{1 + 0.0570(360/360)} = 0.9461$$

The fixed payment is easily found as

$$FS^{SF}(0, n, m) = FS^{SF}(0,4,90) = \frac{1 - 0.9461}{0.9872 + 0.9737 + 0.9600 + 0.9461} = 0.0139$$

The quarterly fixed payment is thus SF0.0139 for each SF1.00 of notional principal. This translates into an annual rate of $0.0139(360/90) = 0.0556$ or 5.56 percent, so in Switzerland we would quote the fixed rate on a plain vanilla interest rate swap in Swiss francs as 5.56 percent.

Our currency swap involving dollars for Swiss francs would have a fixed rate of 3.68 percent in dollars and 5.56 percent in Swiss francs. The notional principal would be $1.0 and 1/$0.80 = SF1.25. Summarizing, we have the following terms for the four swaps:

Swap 1: Pay dollars fixed at 3.68 percent, receive SF fixed at 5.56 percent.
Swap 2: Pay dollars fixed at 3.68 percent, receive SF floating.
Swap 3: Pay dollars floating, receive SF fixed at 5.56 percent.
Swap 4: Pay dollars floating, receive SF floating.

In each case, the notional principal is $1 and SF1.25, or more generally, SF1.25 for every dollar of notional principal.

As we did with interest rate swaps, we move 60 days forward in time. We have a new U.S. term structure, given in the interest rate swap problem, and a new Swiss franc term structure, which is given below:

$$L_{60}^{SF}(30) = 0.0600$$

$$L_{60}^{SF}(120) = 0.0615$$

$$L_{60}^{SF}(210) = 0.0635$$

$$L_{60}^{SF}(300) = 0.0653$$

The new set of discount factors is

$$B_{60}^{SF}(30) = \frac{1}{1 + 0.0600(30/360)} = 0.9950$$

$$B_{60}^{SF}(120) = \frac{1}{1 + 0.0615(120/360)} = 0.9799$$

$$B_{60}^{SF}(210) = \frac{1}{1 + 0.0635(210/360)} = 0.9643$$

$$B_{60}^{SF}(300) = \frac{1}{1 + 0.0653(300/360)} = 0.9484$$

The new exchange rate is \$0.82. Now let us value each swap in turn, taking advantage of what we already know about the values of the U.S. dollar interest rate swaps calculated in the previous section. Recall we found that

Present value of dollar fixed payments = 1.0004
Present value of dollar floating payments = 1.0051

Let us find the comparable numbers for the Swiss franc payments. In other words, we position ourselves as a Swiss resident or institution and obtain the values of the fixed and floating streams of Swiss franc payments per SF1 notional principal. The present value of the remaining Swiss fixed payments is

0.0139(0.9950 + 0.9799 + 0.9643 + 0.9484) + 1.0(0.9484) = 1.0024

Recall that in finding the present value of the floating payments, we simply recognize that on the next payment date, we shall receive a floating payment of 0.052(90/360) = 0.013, and the market value of the remaining payments will be 1.0.[19] Thus, we can discount 1.0130 back 30 days to obtain 1.0130(0.9950) = 1.0079.

These two figures are based on SF1 notional principal. We convert them to the actual notional principal in Swiss francs by multiplying by SF1.25. Thus,

Present value of SF fixed payments = 1.0024(1.25) = SF1.2530
Present value of SF floating payments = 1.0079(1.25) = SF1.2599

Now we need to convert these figures to dollars by multiplying by the current exchange rate of \$0.82. Thus,

Present value of SF fixed payments in dollars = 1.2530(\$0.82) = \$1.0275
Present value of SF floating payments in dollars = 1.2599(\$0.82) = \$1.0331

Now we can value the four currency swaps:

Value of swap to receive SF fixed, pay \$ fixed
$$= +\$1.0275 - \$1.0004 = +\$0.0271$$
Value of swap to receive SF floating, pay \$ fixed
$$= +\$1.0331 - \$1.0004 = +\$0.0327$$

---

[19] The first floating payment was set when the swap was initiated at the 90-day rate of 5.2 percent times 90/360.

Value of swap to receive SF fixed, pay $ floating
$$= +\$1.0275 - \$1.0051 = +\$0.0224$$
Value of swap to receive SF floating, pay $ floating
$$= +\$1.0331 - \$1.0051 = +\$0.0280$$

Note that all of these numbers are positive. Therefore, our swaps are showing gains as a result of the combination of interest rate changes in the two countries as well as the exchange rate change. To the counterparty, the swaps are worth these same numerical amounts, but the signs are negative.

Practice Problem 5

Consider a one-year currency swap with semiannual payments. The two currencies are the U.S. dollar and the euro. The current exchange rate is $0.75.

A. The term structure of interest rates for LIBOR and Euribor are

Days	LIBOR	Euribor
180	7.2%	6.0%
360	8.0%	6.6%

Determine the fixed rate in euros and express it in annualized terms. Note that the LIBOR rates are the same as in Practice Problem 4, in which we found that the fixed payment in dollars was 0.0392.

B. Ninety days later, the term structure is as follows:

Days	LIBOR	Euribor
90	7.1%	5.5%
270	7.4%	6.0%

The new exchange rate is $0.70. Determine the market values of swaps to pay dollars and receive euros. Consider all four swaps that are covered in the reading. Assume a notional principal of $20 million and the appropriate amount for euros. Note that the LIBOR rates are the same as in Practice Problem 4, in which we found that the present value of the fixed payments (floating payments) plus the hypothetical $1 notional principal was $1.0231 ($1.0180).

▶ **Solution to A.** The fixed payment in dollars is the same as in Practice Problem 4: 0.0392. To determine the fixed rate in euros, we first compute the discount factors:

$$B_0^{\€}(180) = \frac{1}{1 + 0.06(180/360)} = 0.9709$$

$$B_0^{\unicode{x20AC}}(360) = \frac{1}{1 + 0.066(360/360)} = 0.9381$$

The fixed rate in euros is, therefore, $\dfrac{1 - 0.9381}{0.9709 + 0.9381} = 0.0324$.

On an annual basis, this rate would be $0.0324(360/180) = 0.0648$.

▶ **Solution to B.** Recalculate the euro discount factors:

$$B_{90}^{\unicode{x20AC}}(90) = \frac{1}{1 + 0.055(90/360)} = 0.9864$$

$$B_{90}^{\unicode{x20AC}}(270) = \frac{1}{1 + 0.060(270/360)} = 0.9569$$

The present value of the fixed payments plus hypothetical €1 notional principal is €0.0324(0.9864 + 0.9569) + €1.0(0.9569) = €1.0199.

The 180-day rate at the start of the swap was 6 percent, so the first floating payment would be $0.06(180/360) = 0.03$. The present value of the floating payments plus hypothetical notional principal of €1 is €1.03(0.9864) = €1.0160.

The euro notional principal, established at the start of the swap, is $1/\$0.75 = €1.3333$. Converting the euro payments to dollars at the new exchange rate and multiplying by the euro notional principal, we obtain the following values for the four swaps (where we use the present values of U.S. dollar fixed and floating payments as found in Practice Problem 4, repeated in the statement of Part B above).

- ▶ Pay \$ fixed, receive € fixed = $-\$1.0231 + €1.3333(\$0.70)1.0199$
  $= -\$0.0712$
- ▶ Pay \$ fixed, receive € floating = $-\$1.0231 + €1.3333(\$0.70)1.0160$
  $= -\$0.0749$
- ▶ Pay \$ floating, receive € fixed = $-\$1.0180 + €1.3333(\$0.70)1.0199$
  $= -\$0.0661$
- ▶ Pay \$ floating, receive € floating = $-\$1.0180 + €1.3333(\$0.70)1.0160$
  $= -\$0.0698$

Now we turn to equity swaps. It is tempting to believe that we will not use any more information regarding the term structure in pricing and valuing equity swaps. In fact, for equity swaps in which one side pays either a fixed or floating rate, the results we have obtained for interest rate swaps will be very useful.

4.2.3 Equity Swaps

In this section, we explore how to price and value three types of equity swaps: (1) a swap to pay a fixed rate and receive the return on the equity, (2) a swap to pay a floating rate and receive the return on the equity, and (3) a swap to pay the return on one equity and receive the return on another.

To price or value an equity swap, we must determine a combination of stock and bonds that replicates the cash flows on the swap. As we saw with interest rate and currency swaps, such a replication is not difficult to create. We issue a bond and buy a bond, with one being a fixed-rate bond and the other being a floating-rate bond. If we are dealing with a currency swap, we require that one of the bonds be denominated in one currency and the other be denominated in the other currency. With an equity swap, it would appear that a replicating strategy would involve issuing a bond and buying the stock or vice versa, but this is not exactly how to replicate an equity swap. Remember that in an equity swap, we receive cash payments representing the return on the stock, and that is somewhat different from payments based on the price.

Pricing a Swap to Pay a Fixed Rate and Receive the Return on the Equity   By example, we will demonstrate how to price an n-payment m-day rate swap to pay a fixed rate and receive the return on equity. Suppose the notional principal is $1, the swap involves annual settlements and lasts for two years (n = 2), and the returns on the stock for each of the two years are 10 percent for the first year and 15 percent for the second year. The equity payment on the swap would be $0.10 the first year and $0.15 the second. If, however, we purchased the stock instead of doing the equity swap, we would have to sell the stock at the end of the first year or we would not generate any cash. Suppose at the end of the first year, the stock is at $1.10. We sell the stock, withdraw $0.10, and reinvest $1.00 in the stock. At the end of the second year the stock would be at $1.15. We then sell the stock, taking cash of $0.15. But we have $1.00 left over. To get rid of, or offset, this cash flow, suppose that when we purchased the stock we borrowed the present value of $1.00 for two years. Then two years later, we would pay back $1.00 on that loan. This procedure would offset the $1.00 in cash we have from the stock. The fixed payments on the swap can be easily replicated. If the fixed payment is denoted as FS(0,n,m), we simply borrow the present value of FS(0,n,m) for one year and also borrow the present value of FS(0,n,m) for two years. When we pay those loans back, we will have replicated the fixed payments on the swap.

For the more general case of n payments, we do the following to replicate the swap whose fixed payments are FS(0,n,m):

1. Invest $1.00 in the stock.
2. Borrow the present value of $1.00 to be paid back at the swap expiration, day h_n. This is the amount $B_0(h_n)$.
3. Take out a series of loans requiring that we pay back FS(0,n,m) at time h_1, and also at time h_2, and at all remaining times through time h_n.

Note that this transaction is like issuing debt and buying stock. The amount of money required to do this is

$$\$1 - B_0(h_n) - FS(0, n, m) \sum_{j=1}^{n} B_0(h_j)$$

Because no money changes hands at the start, the initial value of the swap is zero. We set the expression above to zero and solve for the fixed payment FS(0,n,m) to obtain

$$FS(0, n, m) = \frac{1.0 - B_0(h_n)}{\sum_{j=1}^{n} B_0(h_j)}$$

This is precisely the formula (Equation 67-1) for the fixed rate on an interest rate swap or a currency swap.

Pricing a Swap to Pay a Floating Rate and Receive the Return on the Equity If, instead, the swap involves the payment of a floating rate for the equity return, no further effort is needed because there is no fixed rate for which we must solve. We know from our understanding of interest rate swaps that the present value of the floating payments equals the present value of the fixed payments, which equals the notional principal of 1.0. The market value of the swap is zero at the start, as it should be.

Pricing a Swap to Pay the Return on One Equity and Receive the Return on Another Equity Let $S_0(1)$ and $S_1(1)$ be the level of Stock Index 1 at times 0 and 1, and let $S_0(2)$ and $S_1(2)$ be the level of Stock Index 2 at times 0 and 1. Assume we pay the return on Index 2 and receive the return on Index 1. We need to replicate the cash flows on this swap by investing in these two stocks using some type of strategy. Suppose we sell short $1.00 of Index 2, taking the proceeds and investing in $1.00 of Index 1. Then at time 1, we liquidate the position in Index 1, as described above, withdrawing the cash and reinvesting the $1.00 back into Index 1. We cover the short position in Index 2, taking the proceeds and re-shorting Index 2. We continue in this manner throughout the life of the swap. This strategy replicates the cash flows on the swap. Thus, going long one stock and short the other replicates this swap. Of course, there is no fixed rate and thus no need to price the swap. The market value at the start is zero as it should be.

Now let us look at how to determine the market values of each of these swaps during their lives. In other words, after the swap has been initiated, we move forward in time. We must take into account where we are in the life of the swap and how interest rates and the equity price have changed.

Valuing a Swap to Pay the Fixed Rate and Receive the Return on the Equity
Let us use the same U.S. term structure we have already been using for interest rate and currency swaps. Our equity swap is for one year and will involve fixed quarterly payments. Recall that the fixed payment on the interest rate swap is 0.0092, corresponding to an annual rate of 3.68 percent. This will be the rate on the swap to pay fixed and receive the equity payment.

Now let us move 60 days into the life of the swap, at which time we have a new term structure as given in the interest rate swap example. We started off with a stock price of S_0, and now the stock price is S_{60}. The stock payment we will receive at the first settlement in 30 days is $S_{90}/S_0 - 1$. Let us write this amount as

$$\left(\frac{1}{S_0}\right)S_{90} - 1$$

Sixty days into the life of the swap, we could replicate this payment by purchasing $1/S_0$ shares of stock, currently at S_{60}. Doing so will cost $(1/S_0)S_{60}$. Then at the first settlement, we shall have stock worth $(1/S_0)S_{90}$. We sell that stock, withdrawing cash of $(1/S_0)S_{90} - 1$. We then take the $1 left over and roll it into the stock again, which will replicate the return the following period, as described above. This procedure will leave $1 left over at the end. Thus, sixty days into the swap, to replicate the remaining cash flows, we do the following:

1. Invest $(1/S_0)S_{60}$ in the stock.
2. Borrow the present value of $1.00 to be paid back at the swap expiration, time h_n. This is the amount $B_{60}(h_n)$.
3. Take out a series of loans requiring that we pay back $FS(0,n,m)$ at time h_1, and also at time h_2, and at all remaining times through time h_n.

For the general case of day t, the market value of the swap is

$$\left(\frac{S_t}{S_0}\right) - B_t(h_n) - FS(0,n,m) \sum_{j=1}^{n} B_t(h_j) \qquad \textbf{(67-2)}$$

The first term reflects the investment in the stock necessary to replicate the equity return. The second term is the loan for the present value of $1.00 due at the expiration date of the swap. The third term is the series of loans of the amount FS(0,n,m) due at the various swap settlement dates. Note that all discounting is done using the new term structure. Of course, the overall market value figure would then be multiplied by the notional principal.

Let us calculate these results for our pay-fixed, receive-equity swap 60 days into its life. Suppose the stock index was at 1405.72 when the swap was initiated. Now it is at 1436.59. We use the same term structure at 60 days that we used for the interest rate swap example. The market value of the swap is

$$\left(\frac{1436.59}{1405.72}\right) - 0.9643 - (0.0092)(0.9965 + 0.9858 + 0.9751 + 0.9643)$$
$$= 0.0216$$

Thus, 60 days into its life, the market value of this fixed-for-equity swap is positive at $0.0216 per $1 notional principal.

Valuing a Swap to Pay a Floating Rate and Receive the Return on the Equity
We can value this swap in two ways. The first will require that we discount the next floating rate and the par value, as we did with interest rate swaps. We can do this because we recognize that a floating-rate security is worth its par value on the payment date. As long as we add the notional principal, we can assume the floating payments are those of a floating-rate bond. The notional principal offsets the $1 left over at the end from holding the stock and withdrawing all of the profits on each settlement date. The calculation of the market value of this swap is simple. We just determine the value of $1 invested in the stock since the last settlement period, minus the present value of the floating leg. With the upcoming floating payment being 0.0086, the market value of the swap is, therefore,

$$\left(\frac{1436.59}{1405.72}\right) - (1.0086)(0.9965) = 0.0169$$

Another, and probably easier, way to arrive at this answer is to recognize that

▶ a swap to pay fixed and receive the equity return is worth 0.0216, and
▶ a swap to pay floating and receive fixed is worth −0.0047.[20]

If we did both of these swaps, the fixed payments would offset and would leave the equivalent of the equity swap. The value would then be 0.0216 − 0.0047 = 0.0169.

Valuing a Swap to Pay One Equity Return and Receive Another   Now we need to value the swap to pay the return on Index 2 and receive the return on Index 1, 60 days into the swap's life. Let the following be the values of the indices on days 0 and 60.

---

[20] In Section 4.2.1, we found the value of a swap to pay fixed and receive floating to be 0.0047. Therefore, a swap to pay floating and receive fixed is worth −0.0047.

	Day 0	Day 60
Index 1	1405.72	1436.59
Index 2	5255.18	5285.73

As we previously described, this swap can be replicated by going long Index 1 and short Index 2. The market value calculation is simple: We find the value of $1 invested in Index 1 since the last settlement day minus the value of $1 invested in Index 2 since the last settlement day. Thus, the market value of the position is

$$\left(\frac{1436.59}{1405.72}\right) - \left(\frac{5285.73}{5255.18}\right) = 0.0161$$

Of course, all of these results are per $1 notional principal, so we would have to multiply by the actual notional principal to get the overall market value of this equity-for-equity swap.

Practice Problem 6

Consider an equity swap that calls for semiannual payments for one year. The party will receive the return on the Dow Jones Industrial Average (DJIA), which starts off at 10033.27. The current LIBOR term structure is

Days	Rate
180	7.2%
360	8.0%

A. In Practice Problem 4, we determined that the fixed rate for a one-year interest rate swap given the above term structure was 0.0392. Given this term structure data, what is the fixed rate in an equity swap calling for the party to pay a fixed rate and receive the return on the DJIA?

B. Find the market value of the swap 90 days later if the new term structure is

Days	Rate
90	7.1%
270	7.4%

The notional principal of the swap is $60 million. The DJIA is at 9955.14. Again, these are the same rates as in Practice Problem 4, for which we computed $B_{90}(90) = 0.9826$ and $B_{90}(270) = 0.9474$.

   C. Recompute the market value under the assumption that the counterparty pays a floating rate instead of a fixed rate.

   D. Recompute the market value under the assumption that the counterparty pays the return on the Dow Jones Transportation Index, which started off at 2835.17 and 90 days later is 2842.44.

▶ **Solution to A.** Because this term structure is the same as in Practice Problem 4, the fixed rate is the same at 0.0392. The fact that the party here receives an equity return rather than a floating interest rate does not affect the magnitude of the fixed payment.

▶ **Solution to B.** Using the 180- and 360-day discount factors at 90 days from Practice Problem 4, the market value of the swap to pay a fixed rate and receive the equity return is

$$\left(\frac{9955.14}{10033.27}\right) - 0.9474 - 0.0392(0.9826 + 0.9474) = -0.0309$$

Multiplying by the notional principal of $60 million, we obtain a market value of $60,000,000(-0.0309) = -\$1,854,000$.

▶ **Solution to C.** Because the first floating payment would be at the rate of 7.2 percent and is, therefore, 0.036, the market value of the swap to pay a floating rate and receive the equity return is

$$\left(\frac{9955.14}{10033.27}\right) - 1.036(0.9826) = -0.0258$$

Adjusting for the notional principal, the market value is $60,000,000(-0.0258) = -\$1,548,000$.

▶ **Solution to D.** The market value of the swap to pay the return on the Dow Jones Transportation Average and receive the return on the DJIA is

$$\left(\frac{9955.14}{10033.27}\right) - \left(\frac{2842.44}{2835.17}\right) = -0.0104$$

Adjusting for the notional principal, the market value is $60,000,000(-0.0104) = -\$624,000$.

4.3 Some Concluding Comments on Swap Valuation

Let us review some important results on swap valuation and pricing. Because the market value of the swap when initiated is zero, pricing the swap means to find the terms of the swap that will make its market value be zero. If the swap pays a fixed rate, we must find the fixed rate that makes the present value of the fixed payments equal the present value of the floating payments. If both sides of the swap involve floating payments, there are no terms to determine. For currency swaps, we also have to determine the notional principal in one currency that is equivalent to a given notional principal in another currency.

    The market value of a swap starts off at zero but changes to either a positive or negative value as the swap evolves through its life and market conditions change. To determine the market value of a swap, we must determine the present value of the remaining stream of payments, netting one against the other.

The market value of a swap gives a number that represents what the swap is worth to each party. If the market value is positive, the swap is like an asset. The amount due to one party is worth more than the amount that party owes. If it is negative, the swap is like a liability. The amount that party owes is worth more than the amount owed to it. The market value of a swap is also sometimes known as the **replacement value**. This notion views the swap as an instrument whose value can potentially be lost through default. If a party is holding a positive value swap and the other party defaults, that value is lost and would require that amount of money to replace it. We discuss this point further in Section 7.

VARIATIONS OF SWAPS   5

So far we have covered the most common types of swaps: fixed-for-floating interest rate swaps, various combinations of fixed and floating currency swaps, and equity swaps involving fixed payments, floating payments, or the returns on another equity. We must also mention some other types of swaps.

We briefly referred to the **basis swap**, in which both sides pay a floating rate. A typical basis swap involves one party paying LIBOR and the other paying the T-bill rate. As we learned in Reading 65, the term *basis* refers to the spread between two prices, usually the spot and futures prices. Here it is simply the spread between two rates, LIBOR and the T-bill rate. Because LIBOR is always more than the T-bill rate, the two parties negotiate a fixed spread such that the party paying LIBOR actually pays LIBOR minus the spread.[21] LIBOR is the borrowing rate of high-quality London banks, and the T-bill rate is the default-free borrowing rate of the U.S. government. The difference between LIBOR and the T-bill rate is thus a reflection of investors' perception of the general level of credit risk in the market. Basis swaps are usually employed for speculative purposes by end users who believe the spread between LIBOR and the T-bill rate will change.[22] A basis swap of this type is, therefore, usually a position taken in anticipation of a change in the relative level of credit risk in the market. As noted, both sides are floating, and typically both sides use 360-day years in their calculations.[23]

Another type of swap we sometimes encounter is not all that different from a plain vanilla or basis swap. In a **constant maturity swap**, one party pays a fixed rate, or a short-term floating rate such as LIBOR, and the other party pays a floating rate that is the rate on a security known as a **constant maturity treasury (CMT)** security. The transaction is also sometimes known as a CMT swap. This underlying instrument is a hypothetical U.S. Treasury note, meaning that its maturity is in the 2- to 10-year range, with a constant maturity. Obviously the reference to a particular CMT cannot be referring to a single note, because the maturity of any security decreases continuously. As mentioned, the note is hypothetical. For example, for a two-year CMT security, when there is an actual two-year note, that note is the CMT security. Otherwise, the yield on a CMT security

---

[21] Alternatively, the counterparty could pay the T-bill rate plus the spread.

[22] The spread between LIBOR and the T-bill rate is called the TED spread. It is considered an indicator of the relative state of credit risk in the markets. LIBOR represents the rate on a private borrower (London banks); the T-bill rate is the U.S. government borrowing rate. When the global economy weakens, the TED spread tends to widen because rates based on the credit risk of private borrowers will increase while the U.S. government remains a risk-free borrower.

[23] Of course, a basis swap need not be based on LIBOR and the T-bill rate, so other conventions can be used.

is interpolated from the yields of securities with surrounding maturities. The distinguishing characteristic of a constant maturity swap is that the maturity of the underlying security exceeds the length of the settlement period. For example, a CMT swap might call for payments every six months, with the rate based on the one-year CMT security. In contrast, a standard swap settling every six months would nearly always be based on a six-month security. Otherwise, however, a constant maturity swap possesses the general characteristics of a plain vanilla swap.

One interesting variant of an interest rate swap is an **overnight index swap (OIS)**. This instrument commits one party to paying a fixed rate as usual. The floating rate, however, is the cumulative value of a single unit of currency invested at an overnight rate during the settlement period. The overnight rate changes daily. This instrument is used widely in Europe but not in the United States.

Amortizing and **accreting swaps** are those in which the notional principal changes according to a formula related to the underlying. The more common of the two is the amortizing swap, sometimes called an **index amortizing swap**. In this type of interest rate swap, the notional principal is indexed to the level of interest rates. The notional principal declines with the level of interest rates according to a predefined schedule. This feature makes the swap similar to certain asset-backed securities, such as mortgage-backed securities, which prepay some of their principal as rates fall. An index amortizing swap is often used to hedge this type of security.

Diff swaps combine elements of interest rate, currency, and equity swaps. In a typical diff swap, one party pays the floating interest rate of one country and the other pays the floating interest rate of another country. Both sets of payments, however, are made in a single currency. So one set of payments is based on the interest rate of one country, but the payment is made in the currency of another country. This swap is a pure play on the interest rate differential between two countries and is basically a currency swap with the currency risk hedged. Alternatively, in equity diff swaps, the return on a foreign stock index is paid in the domestic currency.

An **arrears swap** is a special type of interest rate swap in which the floating payment is set at the end of the period and the interest is paid at that same time. This procedure stands in contrast to the typical interest rate swap, in which the payment is set on one settlement date and the interest is paid on the next settlement date.

In a **capped swap**, the floating payments have a limit as to how high they can be. Similarly, a **floored swap** has a limit on how low the floating payments can be.

There is no limit to the number of variations that can be found in swaps, and it is not worthwhile to examine them beyond the basic, most frequently used types. We must, however, cover an important variation of a swap that combines elements of both swaps and options.

6 SWAPTIONS

A **swaption** *is an option to enter into a swap*. Although swaptions can be designed in a variety of ways, we shall focus exclusively on the most widely used swaption, the plain vanilla interest rate swaption. This is a swaption to pay the fixed rate and receive the floating rate or the other way around. It allows the holder to establish a fixed rate on the underlying swap in advance and have the option of entering into the swap with that fixed rate or allowing the swaption to expire and entering into the swap at the fixed rate that prevails in the market.

6.1 Basic Characteristics of Swaptions

The two types of swaptions are a **payer swaption** and a **receiver swaption**. A payer swaption allows the holder to enter into a swap as the fixed-rate payer and floating-rate receiver. A receiver swaption allows the holder to enter into a swap as the fixed-rate receiver and floating-rate payer. Therefore, these terms refer to the fixed rate and are comparable to the terms *call* and *put* used for other types of options. Although it is not apparent at this point, a payer swaption is a put and a receiver swaption is a call.

Swaptions have specific expiration dates. Like ordinary options, swaptions can be European style (exercisable only at expiration) or American style (exercisable at any time prior to expiration). A swaption is based on a specific underlying swap. For example, consider a European payer swaption that expires in two years and allows the holder to enter into a three-year swap with semiannual payments every 15 January and 15 July. The payments will be made at the rate of 6.25 percent and will be computed using the 30/360 adjustment. The underlying swap is based on LIBOR, and the notional principal is $10 million. Of course, a swaption has a price or premium, which is an amount paid by the buyer to the seller up front.

Note that this swaption expires in two years and the underlying swap expires three years after that. This arrangement is called a 2 × 5 swaption, a terminology we used in explaining FRAs. The underlying can be viewed as a five-year swap at the time the swaption is initiated and will be a three-year swap when the swaption expires.

Finally, there are a number of ways to settle a swaption at expiration. Recall that ordinary options can allow for either physical delivery or cash settlement. We will explore the comparable concepts for swaptions in Section 6.3.

6.2 Uses of Swaptions

Swaptions have a variety of purposes. Now, however, we take a brief glance at why swaptions exist.

Swaptions are used by parties who anticipate the need for a swap at a later date but would like to establish the fixed rate today, while providing the flexibility to not engage in the swap later or engage in the swap at a more favorable rate in the market. These parties are often corporations that expect to need a swap later and would like to hedge against unfavorable interest rate moves while preserving the flexibility to gain from favorable moves.

Swaptions are used by parties entering into a swap to give them the flexibility to terminate the swap. In Section 1.2, we discussed why a party engaged in a swap might wish to terminate it before expiration. Suppose the party in a swap is paying fixed and receiving floating. If it owned a receiver swaption, it could exercise the swaption, thereby entering into a swap to receive a fixed rate and pay a floating rate. It would then have offset the floating parts of the swap, effectively removing any randomness from the position.[24] But the only way the party could do so would require having previously purchased a swaption. Similarly, parties engaged in a receive-fixed, pay-floating swap can effectively offset it by exercising a payer swaption.

Swaptions are used by parties to speculate on interest rates. As with any interest rate sensitive instrument, swaptions can be used to speculate. Their prices move with interest rates and, like all options, they contain significant leverage. Thus, they are appropriate instruments for interest rate speculators.

[24] Note, however, that both swaps are still in effect even though the floating sides offset. Because both swaps remain in effect, there is credit risk on the two transactions.

6.3 Swaption Payoffs

When a swaption is exercised, it effectively creates a stream of equivalent payments, commonly referred to in the financial world as an annuity. This stream is a series of interest payments equal to the difference between the exercise rate and the market rate on the underlying swap when the swaption is exercised.

Consider a European payer swaption that expires in two years and is exercisable into a one-year swap with quarterly payments, using 90/360 as the day-count adjustment. The exercise rate is 3.60 percent. The notional principal is $20 million. Now, suppose we are at the swaption expiration and the term structure is the one we obtained when pricing the interest rate swap earlier in this reading. We repeat that information here:

Maturity	Rate	Discount Factor
90 days	3.45%	0.9914
180 days	3.58%	0.9824
270 days	3.70%	0.9730
360 days	3.75%	0.9639

Under these conditions, we found that the swap fixed payment is 0.0092, equating to an annual fixed rate of 3.68 percent.

The holder of the swaption has the right to enter into a swap to pay 3.60 percent, whereas in the market such a swap would require payment at a rate of 3.68 percent. Therefore, here at expiration this swaption does appear to offer an advantage over the market rate. Let us consider the three possible ways to exercise this swaption.

The holder can exercise the swaption, thereby entering into a swap to pay 3.60 percent. The quarterly payment at the rate of 3.60 percent would be $20,000,000(0.0360)(90/360) = $180,000. The swaption holder would then be engaged in a swap to pay $180,000 quarterly and receive LIBOR. The first floating payment would be at 3.45 percent[25] and would be $20,000,000(0.0345)(90/360) = $172,500. The remaining floating payments would, of course, be determined later. The payment stream is illustrated in Exhibit 67-8, Panel A.

Alternatively, the holder can exercise the swaption, thereby entering into a swap to pay 3.60 percent, and then enter into a swap in the market to receive fixed and pay floating. The fixed rate the holder would receive is 3.68 percent, the market-determined fixed rate at the time the swaption expires. The quarterly fixed payment at 3.68 percent would be $20,000,000(0.0368)(90/360) = $184,000. Technically, the LIBOR payments are still made, but the same amount is paid and received. Hence, they effectively offset. Panel B illustrates this payment stream. This arrangement would be common if the counterparty to the second swap is not the same as the counterparty to the swaption.

The holder can arrange to receive a net payment stream of $184,000 − $180,000 = $4,000. Panel C illustrates this payment stream. In this case, the counterparty to the second swap is probably the same as the counterparty to the swap created by exercising the swaption, who would be the counterparty to the swaption. Because the floating payments are eliminated, the amount of cash passing between the parties is reduced, which mitigates the credit risk.

---

[25] The first floating payment is at 3.45 percent because this is the 90-day rate in effect at the time the swap is initiated.

EXHIBIT 67-8	**Cash Flows from Swaptions**

A. Exercise of Payer Swaption, Entering into a Pay-Fixed, Receive-Floating Swap

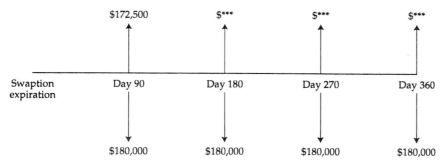

***Computed as $20,000,000(L)90/360$, where L is LIBOR on the previous settlement date.

B. Exercise of Payer Swaption, Entering into a Pay-Fixed, Receive-Floating Swap and Entering into a Receive-Fixed, Pay-Floating Swap at the Market Rate

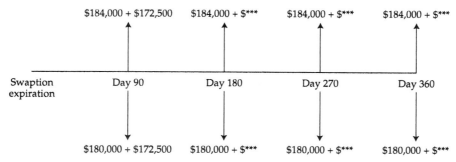

***Computed as $20,000,000(L)90/360$, where L is LIBOR on the previous settlement date.

C. Exercise of Swaption with Offsetting Swap Netted

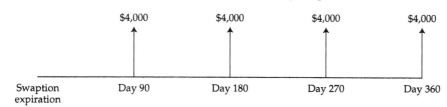

D. Cash Settlement

The holder can receive an up-front cash payment. We can easily determine the amount. It is simply the present value of the payment stream shown in Panel C, which we can obtain using the discount factors shown above:

$$\$4,000(0.9914 + 0.9824 + 0.9730 + 0.9639) = \$15,643$$

This pure cash settlement is illustrated in Panel D.

Other than transaction costs and the credit risk associated with the newly created swaps, each of these means of exercising a swaption has the same value. Of course, the two parties would have to agree up front which of these means to use at expiration. Cash settlement is the most common.

Therefore, the payoff of a payer swaption in which the exercise rate is x and the market rate on the underlying swap is FS(0,n,m) is

$$\text{Max}[0, \text{FS}(0, n, m) - x] \sum_{j=1}^{n} B_0(h_j) \qquad \textbf{(67-3)}$$

Similarly, the payoff of a receiver swaption would be

$$\text{Max}[0, x - \text{FS}(0, n, m)] \sum_{j=1}^{n} B_0(h_j) \qquad \textbf{(67-4)}$$

Of course, these figures would be multiplied by the actual notional principal. So we see that a swaption effectively creates an annuity. The present value factors are not relevant in determining whether the swaption will be exercised. Exercise is determined solely on the relationship between the swap rate at expiration and the exercise rate. The present value factors are used to convert the stream of net payments obtained upon exercise of the swap into a current value. Now, let us take a brief look at how a swaption is priced.

6.4 Pricing and Valuation of Swaptions

We shall show here, perhaps somewhat surprisingly, that an interest rate swaption is like an option on a coupon bond. Restating our result given about, the payoff of a payer swaption is

$$\text{Max}[0, \text{FS}(0, n, m) - x] \sum_{j=1}^{n} B_0(h_j)$$

This expression finds the present value of the difference between the fixed rate on the swap and the exercise rate on the swaption if that difference is positive. Otherwise, the payoff is zero. Recall from Section 4.2.1 (Equation 67-1) that the fixed rate on an interest rate swap is

$$\text{FS}(0, n, m) = \frac{1.0 - B_0(h_n)}{\displaystyle\sum_{j=1}^{n} B_0(h_j)}$$

Substituting the fixed rate into the payoff equation, we obtain

$$\text{Max}\left[0, \frac{1.0 - B_0(h_n)}{\displaystyle\sum_{j=1}^{n} B_0(h_j)} - x\right] \sum_{j=1}^{n} B_0(h_j)$$

which can be rewritten as

$$\text{Max}\left\{0,\ 1.0 - \left[x\sum_{j=1}^{n} B_0(h_j) + B_0(h_N) \right]\right\}$$

Note the term in brackets,

$$x\sum_{j=1}^{n} B_0(h_j) + B_0(h_N)$$

which is the same as the market value at the swaption expiration of a coupon bond of $1.00 par value, in which the coupon is x. Thus, the swaption payoff is effectively $\text{Max}(0, 1.0 - \text{Market value of coupon bond})$. This amount is the payoff of a put option on a coupon bond with coupon of x, a face value of 1.0, and a maturity of the swap expiration date. The exercise price is the par value of 1.0, and the exercise rate of the swaption is the coupon rate on the bond. Hence, we can value the swaption as though it were simply a put on a bond. In a similar manner, the payoff of a receiver swaption can be shown to be that of a call option on this coupon bond.

Now you can see why, as we stated earlier, a payer swaption is a put option and a receiver swaption is a call option. More specifically, a payer swaption is a put option on a bond and a receiver swaption is a call option on a bond.

Practice Problem 7

Calculate the market value of a receiver swaption at the expiration if the exercise rate is 4 percent and the term structure is given below:

Days	Rate
180	7.2%
360	8.0%

These are the same rates as in Practice Problem 4. The swaption is on a swap that will make payments in 180 and 360 days, and the notional principal is $25 million. Also, show that this payoff is equivalent to that of a call option on a bond.

▶ **Solution.** Based on a fixed rate of 0.0392 from Practice Problem 4, the market value is $\text{Max}(0, 0.04 - 0.0392)(0.9653 + 0.9259) = 0.0015$.

Based on a notional principal of $25 million, this is a market value of $25,000,000(0.0015) = \$37,500$.

This payoff is equivalent to that of a call option on a bond with an exercise price of 1.0, its par value. At this point in time, the expiration of the option, the bond on which this call is based would have a market value of $0.04(0.9653 + 0.9259) + 1.0(0.9259) = 1.0015$.

Therefore, the payoff of a call on this bond is $\text{Max}(0, 1.0015 - 1.0) = 0.0015$—the same as that of the swaption.

With that result in mind, we could value the swaption using any of a number of approaches to valuing bond options. We shall not take up the pricing of swaptions here, as it is a somewhat advanced topic and the issues are somewhat complicated. It is not a straightforward matter to apply the Black–Scholes–Merton or Black models to pricing bond options. We discussed the valuation of options on bonds in Reading 66, noting that the binomial model is probably the best way to do so.

6.5 Forward Swaps

We have seen in this book that options represent rights and forward contracts represent commitments. Just as there are options to enter swaps, there are also forward contracts to enter into swaps, called **forward swaps**. They are not as widely used as swaptions but do offer the advantage, as is always the case with forwards, that one does not have to pay any cash up front as with an option premium. Forward swaps are priced by pricing the swap off of the forward term structure instead of the spot term structure.

7   CREDIT RISK AND SWAPS

In this reading, we have mentioned on a few occasions that swaps are subject to credit risk. Indeed, as we have emphasized throughout the book, *all* over-the-counter derivatives are subject to credit risk. In this section, we examine some of the issues involved in the credit risk of swaps.

Recall that a swap has zero market value at the start. It starts off as neither an asset nor a liability. Once the swap is engaged and market conditions change, the market value becomes positive for one party and negative for the other. The party holding the positive value swap effectively owns an asset, which represents a claim against the counterparty. This claim is a netting of the amount owed by the counterparty and the amount that the party owes, with the former exceeding the latter. The party holding the positive-value swap thus assumes credit risk. The counterparty could declare bankruptcy, leaving the party holding the positive-value swap with a claim that is subject to the legal process of bankruptcy. In most swap arrangements, netting is legally recognized, so the claim has a value based on the net amount. Of course, as we described in the reading, currency swaps are generally not netted so the credit risk is greater on currency swaps.

The party to which the swap has a negative value is not subject to credit risk. It owes more than is owed to it, so the other party faces the risk.

During the life of the swap, however, the market value to a given party can change from positive to negative or vice versa. Hence, the party not facing credit risk at a given moment is not entirely free of risk, because the swap value could turn positive for it later.

The timing of credit risk is in the form of immediate or **current credit risk** and deferred or **potential credit risk**. The former arises when a payment is immediately due and cannot be made by one party. The latter reflects the ever-present possibility that, although a counterparty may currently be able to make payments, it may be unable to make future payments.

Let us work through an example illustrating these points. Consider two parties A and B who are engaged in a swap. At a given payment date, the payment of Party A to Party B is $100,000 and the payment of Party B to Party A is $35,000. As is customarily the case, Party A must pay $65,000 to Party B. Once the payment is made, we shall assume that the market value of the swap is $1,250,000, which is an asset to A and a liability to B.

Suppose Party A is unable to pay and declares bankruptcy. Then Party B does not make any payment to Party A. Party A is bankrupt, but the swap is an asset to A. Given the $65,000 owed by A to B, the claim of A against B is $1,250,000 − $65,000 = $1,185,000. We emphasize in this example that A is the bankrupt party, but the swap is an asset to A, representing its claim against B. If B were holding the positive market value of the swap, it would have a claim of $1,250,000 + $65,000 = $1,315,000 on A as A enters into the bankruptcy process.

Let us change the example a little by having A not be bankrupt on the payment date. It makes its payment of $65,000 to B and moves forward. But a few months later, before the next payment, A declares bankruptcy. Its payment is not immediately due, but it has essentially stated that it will not make its next payment or any payments thereafter. To determine the financial implications of the event, the two parties must compute the market value of the swap. Suppose the value is now $1,100,000 and is positive to A. Then A, the bankrupt party, holds a claim against B of $1,100,000. The fact that A is bankrupt does not mean that it cannot have a claim against someone else, just as a bankrupt corporation can be owed money for inventory it has sold but on which it has not yet collected payment.

Of course, A could be bankrupt and B's claim against A could be the greater. In fact, with A bankrupt, there is a very good possibility that this scenario would be the case. Then, of course, B would simply be another of A's many creditors.

Exactly what happens to resolve these claims in each of these situations is a complex legal issue and is beyond the scope of our level of treatment. In addition, the bankruptcy laws vary somewhat around the world, so the potential exists for different treatments of the same situation. Most countries do recognize the legality of netting, however, so it would be rare that a party would be able to claim the full amount owed it without netting out the amount it owes.

The credit risk in a swap varies during its life. An interest rate or equity swap has no final principal payments. The credit risk in either of these swap types is greater during the middle of its life. This occurs because near the end of the life of the swap, not many payments remain, so there is not much money at risk. And at the beginning of the life of the swap, the credit risk is usually low because the parties would probably not engage in the swap if a great deal of credit risk already were present at the start. Therefore, the greatest potential for credit losses is during the middle of the life of the swap. For currency swaps, in which the notional principals are typically exchanged at the end of the life of the swap, the credit risk is concentrated between the middle and the end of its life.

The parties that engage in swaps are generally of good credit quality, but the fear of default is still a significant concern. Yet, perhaps surprisingly, the rates that all parties pay on swaps are the same, regardless of either party's credit quality. As we have illustrated here, a plain vanilla swap, in which one party pays a floating rate and the other pays a fixed rate, has the fixed rate determined by the term structure for that underlying rate. Therefore, if a party wanted to engage in a swap to pay LIBOR and receive a fixed rate, it would get the fixed rate based on the LIBOR term structure, regardless of its credit quality or that of the counterparty, provided that the two parties agreed to do the transaction. Implicit in the fixed rate, however, is the spread between LIBOR and the default-free rate. As we described earlier in the reading, swap rates are quoted with respect to a spread over the equivalent default-free rate. Thus, a one-year swap rate of 3.68 percent as in our example might be quoted as 50 basis points over the rate on a one-year U.S. Treasury note, implying that the one-year U.S. Treasury note rate was 3.18 percent. This differential is called the **swap spread**.

It is important to note that the swap spread is not a measure of the credit risk on a given swap but rather a reflection of the general level of credit risk in the global economy. The LIBOR term structure reflects the borrowing rate for London banks, which are generally highly rated but not default free. Whenever a recession approaches or credit concerns arise, this spread widens and fixed-rate payers on swaps end up paying more. Of course, floating-rate payers end up paying more as well, but the additional cost to them is less obvious up front because the floating rates change over the life of the swap.

So all parties pay the same rate, but clearly some parties are better credit risks than others. In addition, virtually no parties are default free, and many are of lower credit quality than the typical London bank on which LIBOR is based. How do parties manage the credit risk in swaps? There are a number of methods, which we shall discuss in more detail in Reading 9. For right now, however, we cover one such method that we have seen before with respect to forward contracts and that is routinely used in the futures market: marking to market.

Reconsider the interest rate swap we covered earlier in the reading in which the payments are made quarterly in the amount of 0.0092 per \$1 notional principal. The swap lasts for one year, so there are four payments. Suppose the parties agree to mark the contract to market halfway through its life—that is, in six months, immediately after the payment is made. Suppose we are at that point and the term structure is as follows:

$$L_{180}(90) = 0.0390$$
$$L_{180}(180) = 0.0402$$

Note that we are at day 180, and the upcoming payments occur in 90 and 180 days. We thus need to calculate $B_{180}(270)$ and $B_{180}(360)$. These present value factors are

$$B_{180}(270) = \frac{1}{1 + 0.039(90/360)} = 0.9903$$

$$B_{180}(360) = \frac{1}{1 = 0.0402(180/360)} = 0.9803$$

Now we can compute the market value of the swap. The present value of the remaining fixed payments, plus the hypothetical notional principal, is $0.0092(0.9903 + 0.9803) + 1.0(0.9803) = 0.9984$.

Because the 90-day floating rate is 3.90 percent, the next floating payment will be $0.0390(90/360) = 0.00975$. Of course, we do not know the last floating payment, but it does not matter because the present value of the remaining floating payments, plus hypothetical notional principal, is automatically 1.0 because we are on the coupon reset date. Therefore, the market value of the swap to the party receiving floating and paying fixed is the present value of the floating payments, 1.0, minus the present value of the fixed payments, 0.9984, or $1.0 - 0.9984 = 0.0016$.

If the two parties marked this swap to market, the party paying floating and receiving fixed would pay the other party a lump sum cash payment of \$0.0016 per \$1 notional principal. The two parties would then reprice the swap. The new payment would be

$$FS(0, n, m) = FS(0,2,90) = \frac{1 - 0.9803}{0.9903 + 0.9803} = 0.01$$

Thus, the fixed payment would be 0.01 for the rest of the swap.

Practice Problem 8

Consider a two-year swap to pay a fixed rate and receive a floating rate with semiannual payments. The fixed rate is 0.0462. Now, 360 days later, the term structure is

Days	Rate
180	10.1%
360	10.4%

The next floating payment will be 0.045. The swap calls for marking to market after 180 days, and, therefore, will now be marked to market. Determine the market value, identify which party pays which, and calculate the new fixed rate.

▶ **Solution.** First find the discount factors:

$$B_{360}(540) = \frac{1}{1 + 0.101(180/360)} = 0.9519$$

$$B_{360}(720) = \frac{1}{1 + 0.104(360/360)} = 0.9058$$

The market value of the fixed payments plus $1 hypothetical notional principal is $0.0462(0.9519 + 0.9058) + 1.0(0.9058) = 0.9916$.

The market value of the floating payments plus $1 hypothetical notional principal is $1.045(0.9519) = 0.9947$.

Therefore, the market value to the party paying fixed and receiving floating is $0.9947 - 0.9916 = 0.0031$.

This amount would be paid by the party paying floating and receiving fixed. The new fixed rate would then be

$$\frac{1 - 0.9058}{0.9519 + 0.9058} = 0.0507$$

This rate would be quoted as an annual rate of $5.07\%(360/180) = 10.14\%$.

As in the futures market, marking a swap contract to market results in the two parties terminating the contract and automatically engaging in a new swap. In essence, the arrangement commits the two parties to terminating the swap and re-establishing it on a predetermined schedule. This process reduces the credit risk by requiring one party to pay the other any amount due at a time prior to the expiration date of the swap. The effect is to reduce the extent to which the swap can go deeply underwater to one of the parties, who may be facing financial problems.

8   THE ROLE OF SWAP MARKETS

In each of the preceding three readings, we have discussed the role played by the markets represented by the various derivative instruments. The swap market is extremely large, consisting of dealers and end users engaging in customized transactions that involve a series of payments. As we showed in this reading, swaps can be equivalent to various other derivative instruments. Moreover, we used transactions in assets to replicate swaps. Hence, an obvious question is why swaps exist when the same results can be obtained using other instruments.

First let us ignore the obvious counter-question of why other instruments exist when swaps serve the same purpose. In the race to see which derivative instrument is more popular, swaps have clearly won. We can only surmise the reason why.

The tremendous popularity of swaps results largely from the popularity of interest rate swaps. For several reasons, these instruments have been embraced by corporations as tools for managing interest rate risk. One is that interest rate swaps, certainly the plain vanilla type, are simple instruments, rarely requiring technology, computational skills, or financial know-how beyond what exists in most corporate treasury offices. In short, they are easy to understand. In addition, interest rate swaps can easily be viewed as a pair of loans. Borrowing and lending money is second nature to corporations. Corporations view engaging in swaps as nothing more than an extension of their regular practice of borrowing and lending money. Many corporations are restricted in their use of options and futures, but they can usually justify swaps as nothing more than variations of loans. Also, swaps are so easily tailored to alter the interest rate patterns on most corporate loans that they seem to go hand in hand with the typical fixed- and floating-rate loans that corporations take out. Many corporations borrow money and combine the loan with a swap right from the start. Finally, we should note that some dealer firms have exploited the attractions of swaps by aggressive selling. In some cases, corporations entered into ill-advised and occasionally complex, exotic swaps. We do not suggest that most dealers have engaged in unethical actions (although some certainly have) but rather that, as in all sales-oriented activities, customers do not always get impartial advice from sales personnel. In some cases, corporations have used swaps to step over the line from good risk management into speculation on risks they know nothing about. In short, at least part of the success of swaps has probably not been for the right reasons.

But using swaps for the wrong reason does not sufficiently explain the success of these instruments. If it were the primary motivation for their use, swaps would die out as a risk management tool. Instead, swaps have grown in popularity. Swaps provide a mechanism for managing the risks associated with a series of payments. Although forward contracts and other instruments can manage that risk, a swap is more of a portfolio approach to managing risk—a package of risk management tools all rolled up into one. Given that risk often exists in a series, swaps are ideal instruments for managing it. Other instruments may be able to do the job, but they must be carefully constructed with a certain amount of financial ingenuity.

SUMMARY

▶ Swaps are over-the-counter contracts in which two parties agree to pay a series of cash flows to each other. At least one series is floating or variable and related to an interest rate, exchange rate, equity price, or commodity price; the other can be fixed or floating. Swaps have zero value at the start and have payments made on scheduled payment or settlement dates and a final termination or expiration date. When swap payments are made in the same currency, the payments are usually netted. Swaps are subject to default on the part of either party.

▶ Swaps can be terminated by having one party pay the market value of the swap to the other party, by entering into a swap in which the variable payments offset, by selling the swap to another party, or by exercising a swaption to enter into an offsetting swap.

▶ In a currency swap, each party makes payments to the other in different currencies. A currency swap can have one party pay a fixed rate in one currency and the other pay a fixed rate in the other currency; have both pay a floating rate in their respective currencies; have the first party pay a fixed rate in one currency and the second party pay a floating rate in the other currency; or have the first party pay a floating rate in one currency and the second pay a fixed rate in the other currency. In currency swaps, the notional principal is usually exchanged at the beginning and at the end of the life of the swap, although this exchange is not mandatory.

▶ The payments on a currency swap are calculated by multiplying the notional principal by the fixed or floating interest rate times a day-count adjustment. This procedure is done in each currency, and the respective parties make their separate payments to each other. The payments are not netted.

▶ In a plain vanilla interest rate swap, one party makes payments at a fixed rate and the other makes payments at a floating rate, with no exchange of notional principal. A typical plain vanilla swap involves one party paying a fixed rate and the other paying a floating rate such as LIBOR. Swaps are often done by a party borrowing floating at a rate tied to LIBOR; that party then uses a pay-fixed, receive-floating swap to offset the risk of its exposure to LIBOR and effectively convert its loan to a fixed-rate loan.

▶ The payments on an interest rate swap are calculated by multiplying the notional principal by the fixed or floating interest rate times a day-count adjustment. The respective amounts are netted so that the party owing the greater amount makes a net payment to the other.

▶ The three types of equity swaps involve one party paying a fixed rate, a floating rate, or the return on another equity, while the other party pays an equity return. Therefore, an equity swap is a swap in which at least one party pays the return on a stock or stock index.

▶ The equity payment (or payments, if both sides of the swap are related to an equity return) on an equity swap is calculated by multiplying the return on the stock over the settlement period by the notional principal. If there is a fixed or floating payment, it is calculated in the same manner as in an interest rate swap. With payments in a single currency, the two sets of payments are netted.

► Swap pricing means to determine the fixed rate and any relevant terms, such as the foreign notional principal on a currency swap, at the start of the swap. Valuation means to determine the market value of the swap, which is the present value of one stream of payments less the present value of the other stream of payments. The market value of a swap is zero at the start but will change to positive for one party and negative for the other during the life of the swap, as market conditions change and time passes.

► Swaps can be viewed as combinations of assets. Currency swaps are like issuing a bond denominated in one currency and using the proceeds to buy a bond denominated in another currency. Interest rate swaps are like issuing a fixed-rate bond and using the proceeds to buy a floating-rate bond or vice versa. Equity swaps are like issuing a bond and using the proceeds to buy stock or vice versa. Equity swaps with both sides paying an equity return are like selling short one stock and using the proceeds to buy another stock. The stock position is not, however, a buy-and-hold position and requires some rebalancing.

► An interest rate swap is like a series of off-market FRAs, meaning that the rate on each FRA is set at the swap rate, not at the rate it would be set at if priced as an FRA with zero market value at the start. In addition, the first payment on a swap is just an exchange of known amounts of cash. Currency swaps and equity swaps are similar to forward contracts, but the connection is not as straightforward as in interest rate swaps.

► Interest rate swaps are like being long (short) interest rate calls and short (long) interest rate puts. Currency swaps and equity swaps are also similar to combinations of options, but the connection is not as straightforward.

► The fixed rate on an interest rate swap equates the present value of the fixed payments plus a hypothetical notional principal to the present value of the floating payments plus a hypothetical notional principal. The notional principals offset but permit these swaps to be treated like bonds. The fixed rate is then equivalent to the fixed rate on a par bond with the same payments as on the swap. The market value of the swap during its life is found by determining the difference in the market values of the floating- and fixed-rate bonds later during their lives under the new term structure.

► The fixed rate on a currency swap are the same as the fixed rates on plain vanilla interest rate swaps in the given countries. The foreign notional principal for a domestic notional principal of one unit is the inverse of the exchange rate. In other words, it is the foreign currency equivalent of the domestic notional principal. Because a currency swap is like issuing a bond in one currency and using the proceeds to buy a bond in another currency, the market value of a currency swap during its life is found by determining the difference in the market values of the two bonds during their lives using the new term structures in the two countries. The foreign bond value must be converted to its domestic equivalent by using the new exchange rate.

► The fixed rate on an equity swap is the same as the fixed rate on a plain vanilla interest rate swap. The market value of an equity swap involving fixed or floating payments during its life is found as the present value of the equity payments less the present value of the fixed or floating payments necessary to replicate the equity swap payment. The market value of an equity swap in which both sides make equity payments is the market value of a long position in one equity and a short position in the other, assuming the positions are liquidated at each settlement date and gains and losses are paid out.

▶ A swaption is an option to enter into a swap. The two types of interest rate swaptions are payer swaptions, which allow the holder to enter into a swap to pay the fixed rate and receive the floating rate, and receiver swaptions, which allow the holder to enter into a swap to receive the fixed rate and pay the floating rate. Swaptions are based on a specific underlying swap and have an exercise rate and an expiration date. At expiration, they can be exercised to enter into the underlying swap. Swaptions require an up-front premium.

▶ Swaptions exist to allow users the flexibility to enter into swaps at later dates but establish the terms in advance. If market conditions are not favorable to exercising a swaption, the holder can allow the swaption to expire and obtain more favorable terms by entering into a swap at the market rate. Swaptions are used by parties who anticipate a need to enter into a swap at a later date, who anticipate the need to terminate an already-existing swap, or who wish to speculate on interest rates.

▶ The payoffs of an interest rate swaption are like those of an option on a coupon-bearing bond. The option has an exercise price of par value, and the coupon rate is the exercise rate on the swaption. A payer swaption is like a put on the bond, and a receiver swaption is like a call on the bond.

▶ At expiration, an interest rate payer swaption is worth the maximum of zero or the present value of the difference between the market swap rate and the exercise rate, valued as an annuity extending over the remaining life of the underlying swap. To value a receiver swaption at expiration, we take the difference between the exercise rate and the market swap rate, adjusted for its present value over the life of the underlying swap. These figures must be multiplied by the notional principal.

▶ The market value of a swaption at expiration can be received in one of four ways: by exercising the swaption to enter into the underlying swap, by exercising the swaption and entering into an offsetting swap that keeps both swaps in force, by exercising the swaption and entering into an offsetting swap that eliminates both swaps and pays a series of payments equal to the net difference in the fixed rates on the two swaps, or by exercising the swaption and receiving a lump sum cash payment.

▶ A forward swap is a forward contract to enter into a swap. It commits both parties to entering into a swap at a later date at a fixed rate agreed on today. In contrast to a swaption, which is the right to enter into a swap, a forward swap is a binding commitment to enter into a swap.

▶ Credit risk arises in a swap due to the possibility that a party will not be able to make its payments. Current credit risk is the risk of a party being unable to make the upcoming payment. Potential credit risk is the risk of a party being unable to make future payments. Credit risk is faced only by the party that is owed the greater amount.

▶ The credit risk in an interest rate or equity swap is greatest during the middle of the swap's life. The risk is small at the beginning of the swap because the parties would not engage in the swap if the credit risk were significant at the start. The risk is low at the end of the life of the swap because of the small number of remaining payments. For currency swaps, the payment of notional principal shifts the credit risk more toward the end of the life of the swap. In addition, because the payments are typically not netted, the credit risk on currency swaps is greater than on interest rate swaps.

▶ The swap spread is the difference between the fixed rate on a swap and the yield on a default-free security of the same maturity as the swap. The spread indicates the average credit risk in the global economy but not the credit risk in a given swap.

► Netting reduces the credit risk in a swap by reducing the amount of money passing from any one party to another. The amount owed by a party is deducted from the amount due to a party, and only the net is paid. Marking a swap to market is a process in which the parties agree to periodically calculate the market value of the swap and have the party owing the greater amount pay the market value to the other party. The fixed rate is then reset on the swap until it is marked to market again or terminates. This procedure forces the party to which the swap is losing money to pay the other party before getting too deeply in debt.

► Swaps play an important role in the financial system by providing a simple means of managing a series of risks. Their popularity has arisen largely from corporate use in managing interest rate exposure.

PROBLEMS FOR READING 67

1. Consider a two-year interest rate swap with semiannual payments. Assume a notional principal of $25 million.

   A. Calculate the annualized fixed rate on the swap. The current term structure of LIBOR interest rates is as follows:

      $L_0(180) = 0.0585$
      $L_0(360) = 0.0605$
      $L_0(540) = 0.0624$
      $L_0(720) = 0.0665$

   B. Calculate the market value of the swap 120 days later 1) from the point of view of the party paying the floating rate and receiving the fixed rate and 2) from the point of view of the party paying the fixed rate and receiving the floating rate. The term structure 120 days later is as follows:

      $L_{120}(60) = 0.0613$
      $L_{120}(240) = 0.0629$
      $L_{120}(420) = 0.0653$
      $L_{120}(600) = 0.0697$

2. Consider a one-year interest rate swap with quarterly payments. Assume a notional principal of $15 million.

   A. Calculate the annualized fixed rate on the swap. The current term structure of LIBOR interest rates is as follows:

      $L_0(90) = 0.0656$
      $L_0(180) = 0.0640$
      $L_0(270) = 0.0621$
      $L_0(360) = 0.0599$

   B. Calculate the market value of the swap 30 days later 1) from the point of view of the party paying the floating rate and receiving the fixed rate and 2) from the point of view of the party paying the fixed rate and receiving the floating rate. The term structure 30 days later is as follows:

      $L_{30}(60) = 0.0384$
      $L_{30}(150) = 0.0379$
      $L_{30}(240) = 0.0382$
      $L_{30}(330) = 0.0406$

3. Consider a two-year currency swap with semiannual payments. The domestic currency is the U.S. dollar, and the foreign currency is the U.K. pound. The current exchange rate is $1.41 per pound.

   A. Calculate the annualized fixed rates for dollars and pounds. The current U.S. term structure is the same as in Problem 8, Part A:

      $L_0(180) = 0.0585$
      $L_0(360) = 0.0605$
      $L_0(540) = 0.0624$
      $L_0(720) = 0.0665$

The U.K. term structure is

$$L_0^£(180) = 0.0493$$
$$L_0^£(360) = 0.0505$$
$$L_0^£(540) = 0.0519$$
$$L_0^£(720) = 0.0551$$

B. Now move forward 120 days. The new exchange rate is $1.35 per pound, and the new U.S. term structure is the same as in Problem 8, Part B:

$$L_{120}(60) = 0.0613$$
$$L_{120}(240) = 0.0629$$
$$L_{120}(420) = 0.0653$$
$$L_{120}(600) = 0.0697$$

The new U.K. term structure is

$$L_{120}^£(60) = 0.0517$$
$$L_{120}^£(240) = 0.0532$$
$$L_{120}^£(420) = 0.0568$$
$$L_{120}^£(600) = 0.0583$$

Assume that the notional principal is $1 or the corresponding amount in British pounds. Calculate the market values of the following swaps:

  i. Pay £ fixed and receive $ fixed.

  ii. Pay £ floating and receive $ fixed.

  iii. Pay £ floating and receive $ floating.

  iv. Pay £ fixed and receive $ floating.

4. Consider a one-year currency swap with quarterly payments. The domestic currency is the U.S. dollar, and the foreign currency is the euro. The current exchange rate is $0.86 per euro.

  A. Calculate the annualized fixed rates for dollars and euros. The current U.S. term structure is the same as in Problem 9, Part A:

$$L_0(90) = 0.0656$$
$$L_0(180) = 0.0640$$
$$L_0(270) = 0.0621$$
$$L_0(360) = 0.0599$$

The Euribor term structure is

$$L_0(90) = 0.0682$$
$$L_0(180) = 0.0673$$
$$L_0(270) = 0.0661$$
$$L_0(360) = 0.0668$$

  B. Now move forward 30 days. The new exchange rate is $0.82 per euro, and the new U.S. term structure is the same as in Problem 9, Part B:

$$L_{30}(60) = 0.0384$$
$$L_{30}(150) = 0.0379$$
$$L_{30}(240) = 0.0382$$
$$L_{30}(330) = 0.0406$$

The new Euribor term structure is

$$L_{30}^{€}(60) = 0.0583$$
$$L_{30}^{€}(150) = 0.0605$$
$$L_{30}^{€}(240) = 0.0613$$
$$L_{30}^{€}(330) = 0.0651$$

Assume that the notional principal is \$1 or the corresponding amount in euros. Calculate the market values of the following swaps:

   i. Pay € fixed and receive \$ fixed.

   ii. Pay € floating and receive \$ fixed.

   iii. Pay € floating and receive \$ floating.

   iv. Pay € fixed and receive \$ floating.

5. Consider a one-year currency swap with semiannual payments. The two currencies are the U.K. pound and the euro. The current exchange rate is £0.61 per euro.

   A. Calculate the annualized fixed rates for pounds and euros. The current U.K. term structure is

$$L_0^{€}(180) = 0.0623$$
$$L_0^{€}(360) = 0.0665$$

   The Euribor term structure is

$$L_0^{€}(180) = 0.0563$$
$$L_0^{€}(360) = 0.0580$$

   B. Now move forward 60 days. The new exchange rate is £0.57 per euro, and the new British term structure is

$$L_{60}^{£}(120) = 0.0585$$
$$L_{60}^{£}(300) = 0.0605$$

   The new Euribor term structure is

$$L_{60}^{£}(120) = 0.0493$$
$$L_{60}^{£}(300) = 0.0505$$

   Assume that the notional principal is £1 or the corresponding amount in euros. Calculate the market values in pounds of the following swaps:

   i. Pay £ fixed and receive € fixed.

   ii. Pay £ floating and receive € fixed.

   iii. Pay £ floating and receive € floating.

   iv. Pay £ fixed and receive € floating.

6. An asset manager wishes to enter into a two-year equity swap in which he will receive the rate of return on the S&P 500 Index in exchange for paying a fixed interest rate. The S&P 500 stock index is at 1150.89 at the beginning of the swap. The swap calls for semiannual payments.

   A. Calculate the annualized fixed rate on the swap. The current term structure of interest rates is as follows:

$$L_0(180) = 0.0458$$
$$L_0(360) = 0.0528$$
$$L_0(540) = 0.0624$$
$$L_0(720) = 0.0665$$

B. Calculate the market value of the swap 160 days later if the new term structure is

$$L_{160}(20) = 0.0544$$
$$L_{160}(200) = 0.0629$$
$$L_{160}(380) = 0.0679$$
$$L_{160}(560) = 0.0697$$

The S&P 500 is at 1204.10. The notional principal of the swap is $100 million.

7. Assume an asset manager enters into a one-year equity swap in which he will receive the return on the Nasdaq 100 Index in return for paying a floating interest rate. The swap calls for quarterly payments. The Nasdaq 100 is at 1561.27 at the beginning of the swap. Ninety days later, the rate $L_{90}(90)$ is 0.0432. Calculate the market value of the swap 100 days from the beginning of the swap if the Nasdaq 100 is at 1595.72 and the term structure is

$$L_{100}(80) = 0.0427$$
$$L_{100}(170) = 0.0481$$
$$L_{100}(260) = 0.0544$$

The notional principal of the swap is $50 million.

8. Consider an equity swap in which the asset manager receives the return on the Russell 2000 Index in return for paying the return on the DJIA. At the inception of the equity swap, the Russell 2000 is at 478.19 and the DJIA is at 9867.33. Calculate the market value of the swap a few months later when the Russell 2000 is at 524.29 and the DJIA is at 10016. The notional principal of the swap is $15 million.

9. Consider a European receiver swaption that expires in one year and is on a two-year swap that will make semiannual payments. The swaption has an exercise rate of 7 percent. The notional principal is $50 million. At expiration, the term structure of interest rates is as follows:

$$L_0(180) = 0.0420$$
$$L_0(360) = 0.0474$$
$$L_0(540) = 0.0544$$
$$L_0(720) = 0.0661$$

A. List the four possible ways this swaption could be exercised, and indicate the relevant cash flows in each case.

B. Show that the payoff on the swaption is equivalent to that of a call option on a bond with exercise price of $1 (the par value of the bond).

10. Consider a European payer swaption that expires in one year and is on a two-year swap that will make semiannual payments. The swaption has an exercise rate of 5 percent. The notional principal is $10 million. At expiration, the term structure of interest rates is as follows:

$$L_0(180) = 0.0583$$
$$L_0(360) = 0.0605$$
$$L_0(540) = 0.0614$$
$$L_0(720) = 0.0651$$

A. List the four possible ways this swaption could be exercised, and indicate the relevant cash flows in each case.

B. Show that the payoff on the swaption is equivalent to that of a put option on a bond with exercise price of $1 (the par value of the bond).

11. Consider a European receiver swaption that expires in two years and is on a one-year swap that will make quarterly payments. The swaption has an exercise rate of 6.5 percent. The notional principal is $100 million. At expiration, the term structure of interest rates is as follows:

$$L_0(90) = 0.0373$$
$$L_0(180) = 0.0429$$
$$L_0(270) = 0.0477$$
$$L_0(360) = 0.0538$$

A. Calculate the market value of the swaption at expiration.

B. Show that the payoff is equivalent to that of a call option on a bond with exercise price of $1 (the par value of the bond).

12. A two-year swap with semiannual payments pays a floating rate and receives a fixed rate. The term structure at the beginning of the swap is

$$L_0(180) = 0.0583$$
$$L_0(360) = 0.0616$$
$$L_0(540) = 0.0680$$
$$L_0(720) = 0.0705$$

In order to mitigate the credit risk of the parties engaged in the swap, the swap will be marked to market in 180 days. Suppose it is now 180 days later and the swap is being marked to market. The new term structure is

$$L_{180}(180) = 0.0429$$
$$L_{180}(360) = 0.0538$$
$$L_{180}(540) = 0.0618$$

A. Calculate the market value of the swap per $1 notional principal and indicate which party pays which.

B. Calculate the new fixed rate on the swap at which the swap would proceed after marking to market.

13. A one-year swap with quarterly payments pays a fixed rate and receives a floating rate. The term structure at the beginning of the swap is

$$L_0(90) = 0.0252$$
$$L_0(180) = 0.0305$$
$$L_0(270) = 0.0373$$
$$L_0(360) = 0.0406$$

In order to mitigate the credit risk of the parties engaged in the swap, the swap will be marked to market in 90 days. Suppose it is now 90 days later and the swap is being marked to market. The new term structure is

$$L_{90}(90) = 0.0539$$
$$L_{90}(180) = 0.0608$$
$$L_{90}(270) = 0.0653$$

A. Calculate the market value of the swap per $1 notional principal and indicate which party pays which.

B. Calculate the new fixed rate on the swap at which the swap would proceed after marking to market.

4⅝ 4⁷/₁₆ — ⁹/₁₆

5½ 5½ — ⁹/₁₆

5½ 21³/₁₆ — 1/₁₆

20⅝ 21³/₁₆

17⅜ 18⅛ + ⅞

6½ 6½ — ½

7¼ 6½ 3¹/₃₂ — ⅛

15/₁₆

9/₁₆ 9/₁₆

⁷/₃₂

7⁵/₁₆ 7¹³/₁₆ 7¹⁵/₁₆

2⅝ 2¹¹/₃₂ 2½ +

2¾ 2¼ 2¼

12¹/₁₆ 11⅜ 11¾ +

87 33¾ 33 33⅛ —

802 25⅝ 24⁹/₁₆ 25⅜ +

833 12 11⅝ 11⅝ +

16 10½ 10½ 10½ —

78 15⅞ 15¹³/₁₆ 15⅞ —

608 9¹/₁₆ 8¼ 8¾

430 11¼ 10⅝ 10⅛ —

INTEREST RATE DERIVATIVE INSTRUMENTS

by Frank J. Fabozzi

READING
68

LEARNING OUTCOMES

The candidate should be able to:

a. characterize the change in the value of an interest rate swap for each counter-party when interest rates change;

b. demonstrate how both a cap and a floor are packages of (1) options on interest rates, and (2) options on fixed income instruments;

c. compute the payoff for a cap and a floor, and explain how a collar is created.

INTRODUCTION 1

In this reading we turn our attention to financial contracts that are popularly referred to as **interest rate derivative instruments** because they derive their value from some cash market instrument or reference interest rate. These instruments include futures, forwards, options, swaps, caps, and floors. In this reading we will discuss the basic features of these instruments and in the next we will see how they are valued.

Why would a portfolio manager be motivated to use interest rate derivatives rather than the corresponding cash market instruments? There are three principal reasons for doing this when there is a well-developed interest rate derivatives market for a particular cash market instrument. First, typically it costs less to execute a transaction or a strategy in the interest rate derivatives market in order to alter the interest rate risk exposure of a portfolio than to make the adjustment in the corresponding cash market. Second, portfolio adjustments typically can be accomplished faster in the interest rate derivatives market than in the corresponding cash market. Finally, interest rate derivative may be able to absorb a greater dollar transaction amount without an adverse effect on the price of the derivative instrument compared to the price effect on the cash market instrument; that is, the interest rate derivative may be more liquid than the cash market. To summarize: There are three potential advantages that motivate the use of interest rate derivatives: cost, speed, and liquidity.

2 INTEREST RATE FUTURES

A **futures contract** is an agreement that requires a party to the agreement either to buy or sell something at a designated future date at a predetermined price. Futures contracts are products created by exchanges. Futures contracts based on a financial instrument or a financial index are known as **financial futures**. Financial futures can be classified as (1) stock index futures, (2) interest rate futures, and (3) currency futures. Our focus in this reading is on interest rate futures.

A. Mechanics of Futures Trading

A futures contract is an agreement between a buyer (seller) and an established exchange or its clearinghouse in which the buyer (seller) agrees to take (make) delivery of something (the **underlying**) at a specified price at the end of a designated period of time. The price at which the parties agree to transact in the future is called the **futures price**. The designated date at which the parties must transact is called the **settlement date** or **delivery date**.

1. Liquidating a Position

Most financial futures contracts have settlement dates in the months of March, June, September, and December. This means that at a predetermined time in the contract settlement month the contract stops trading, and a price is determined by the exchange for settlement of the contract. The contract with the closest settlement date is called the **nearby futures contract**. The next futures contract is the one that settles just after the nearby futures contract. The contract farthest away in time from settlement is called the **most distant futures contract**.

A party to a futures contract has two choices on liquidation of the position. First, the position can be liquidated prior to the settlement date. For this purpose, the party must take an offsetting position in the same contract. For the buyer of a futures contract, this means selling the same number of the identical futures contracts; for the seller of a futures contract, this means buying the same number of identical futures contracts.

The alternative is to wait until the settlement date. At that time the party purchasing a futures contract accepts delivery of the underlying at the agreed-upon price; the party that sells a futures contract liquidates the position by delivering the underlying at the agreed-upon price. For some interest rate futures contracts, settlement is made in cash only. Such contracts are referred to as **cash settlement contracts**.

2. The Role of the Clearinghouse

Associated with every futures exchange is a clearinghouse, which performs several functions. One of these functions is to guarantee that the two parties to the transaction will perform.

When an investor takes a position in the futures market, the clearinghouse takes the opposite position and agrees to satisfy the terms set forth in the contract. Because of the clearinghouse, the investor need not worry about the financial strength and integrity of the party taking the opposite side of the contract. After initial execution of an order, the relationship between the two parties ends. The clearinghouse interposes itself as the buyer for every sale and the seller for every purchase. Thus investors are free to liquidate their positions without involving the other party in the original contract, and without worrying that the other party may default. This is the reason that we define a futures contract as an agreement between a party and a clearinghouse associated with an exchange. Besides its guarantee function, the clearinghouse makes it simple for parties to a futures contract to unwind their positions prior to the settlement date.

3. Margin Requirements

When a position is first taken in a futures contract, the investor must deposit a minimum dollar amount per contract as specified by the exchange. This amount is called **initial margin** and is required as deposit for the contract. The initial margin may be in the form of an interest-bearing security such as a Treasury bill. As the price of the futures contract fluctuates, the value of the margin account changes. Marking to market means effectively replacing the initiation price with a current settlement price. The contract thus has a new settlement price. At the end of each trading day, the exchange determines the current settlement price for the futures contract. This price is used to mark to market the investor's position, so that any gain or loss from the position is reflected in the margin account.[1]

Maintenance margin is the minimum level (specified by the exchange) to which the margin account may fall to as a result of an unfavorable price movement before the investor is required to deposit additional margin. The additional margin deposited is called **variation margin**, and it is an amount necessary to bring the account back to its initial margin level. This amount is determined from the process of marking the position to market. Unlike initial margin, variation margin must be in cash, not interest-bearing instruments. Any excess margin in the account may be withdrawn by the investor. If a party to a futures contract who is required to deposit variation margin fails to do so within 24 hours, the futures position is closed out.

Although there are initial and maintenance margin requirements for buying securities on margin, the concept of margin differs for securities and futures. When securities are acquired on margin, the difference between the price of the security and the initial margin is borrowed from the broker. The security purchased serves as collateral for the loan, and the investor pays interest. For futures contracts, the initial margin, in effect, serves as "good faith" money, an indication that the investor will satisfy the obligation of the contract.

B. Forward Contracts

A **forward contract**, just like a futures contract, is an agreement for the future delivery of something at a specified price at the end of a designated period of time. Futures contracts are standardized agreements as to the delivery date (or month) and quality of the deliverable, and are traded on organized exchanges.

---

[1] For a further discussion of margin requirements and illustrations of how the margin account changes as the futures price changes, see Don M. Chance, *Analysis of Derivatives for the CFA Program* (Charlottesville, VA: Association for Investment Management and Research, 2003), pp.86–91.

A forward contract differs in that it is usually non-standardized (that is, the terms of each contract are negotiated individually between buyer and seller), there is no clearinghouse, and secondary markets are often non-existent or extremely thin. Unlike a futures contract, which is an exchange-traded product, a forward contract is an over-the-counter instrument.

Futures contracts are marked to market at the end of each trading day. Consequently, futures contracts are subject to interim cash flows as additional margin may be required in the case of adverse price movements, or as cash is withdrawn in the case of favorable price movements. A forward contract *may* or *may not be marked to market*, depending on the wishes of the two parties. For a forward contract that is *not* marked to market, there are no interim cash flow effects because no additional margin is required.

Finally, the parties in a forward contract are exposed to credit risk because either party may default on its obligation. This risk is called **counterparty risk**. This risk is minimal in the case of futures contracts because the clearinghouse associated with the exchange guarantees the other side of the transaction. In the case of a forward contract, both parties face counterparty risk. Thus, there exists **bilateral counterparty risk**.

Other than these differences, most of what we say about futures contracts applies equally to forward contracts.

C. Risk and Return Characteristics of Futures Contracts

When an investor takes a position in the market by buying a futures contract, the investor is said to be in a **long position** or to be **long futures**. The buyer of the futures contract is also referred to as the "long." If, instead, the investor's opening position is the sale of a futures contract, the investor is said to be in a **short position** or to be **short futures**. The seller of the futures contract is also referred to as the "short." The buyer of a futures contract will realize a profit if the futures price increases; the seller of a futures contract will realize a profit if the futures price decreases.

When a position is taken in a futures contract, the party need not put up the entire amount of the investment. Instead, only initial margin must be put up. Consequently, an investor can effectively create a leveraged position by using futures. At first, the leverage available in the futures market may suggest that the market benefits only those who want to speculate on price movements. This is not true. As we shall see in Level III, futures markets can be used to control interest rate risk. Without the effective leverage possible in futures transactions, the cost of reducing price risk using futures would be too high for many market participants.

D. Exchange-Traded Interest Rate Futures Contracts

Interest rate futures contracts can be classified by the maturity of their underlying security. Short-term interest rate futures contracts have an underlying security that matures in less than one year. Examples of these are futures contracts in which the underlying is a 3-month Treasury bill and a 3-month Eurodollar **certificate of deposit**. The maturity of the underlying security of long-term futures contracts exceeds one year. Examples of these are futures contracts in which the underlying is a Treasury coupon security, a 10-year agency note, and a municipal bond index. Our focus will be on futures contracts in which the underlying is a Treasury coupon security (a Treasury bond or a Treasury note). These contracts are the most widely used by managers of bond portfolios and we begin with the specifications of the Treasury bond futures contract. We will also discuss the agency note futures contracts.

There are futures contracts on non-U.S. government securities traded throughout the world. Many of them are modeled after the U.S. Treasury futures contracts and consequently, the concepts discussed below apply directly to those futures contracts.

1. Treasury Bond Futures

The Treasury bond futures contract is traded on the Chicago Board of Trade (CBOT). The underlying instrument for a Treasury bond futures contract is $100,000 par value of a hypothetical 20-year coupon bond. The coupon rate on the hypothetical bond is called the **notional coupon**.

The futures price is quoted in terms of par being 100. Quotes are in 32nds of 1%. Thus a quote for a Treasury bond futures contract of 97-16 means 97 and $^{16}\!/_{32}$ or 97.50. So, if a buyer and seller agree on a futures price of 97-16, this means that the buyer agrees to accept delivery of the hypothetical underlying Treasury bond and pay 97.50% of par value and the seller agrees to accept 97.50% of par value. Since the par value is $100,000, the futures price that the buyer and seller agree to for this hypothetical Treasury bond is $97,500.

The minimum price fluctuation for the Treasury bond futures contract is $\frac{1}{32}$ of 1%, which is referred to as "a 32nd." The dollar value of a 32nd for $100,000 par value (the par value for the underlying Treasury bond) is $31.25. Thus, the minimum price fluctuation is $31.25 for this contract.

We have been referring to the underlying as a hypothetical Treasury bond. The seller of a Treasury bond futures contract who decides to make delivery rather than liquidate the position by buying back the contract prior to the settlement date must deliver some Treasury bond issue. But what Treasury bond issue? The CBOT allows the seller to deliver one of several Treasury bonds that the CBOT designates as acceptable for delivery. The specific issues that the seller may deliver are published by the CBOT for all contracts by settlement date. The CBOT makes its determination of the Treasury bond issues that are acceptable for delivery from all outstanding Treasury bond issues that have at least 15 years to maturity from the date of delivery.

Exhibit 68-1 shows the Treasury bond issues that the seller could have selected to deliver to the buyer of the CBOT Treasury bond futures contract as of May 29, 2002. Should the U.S. Department of the Treasury issue any Treasury bonds that meet the CBOT criteria for eligible delivery, those issues would be added to the list. Notice that for the Treasury bond futures contract settling (i.e., maturing) in March 2005, notice that there are 25 eligible issues. For contracts settling after March 2005, there are fewer than 25 eligible issues due to the shorter maturity of each previous eligible issue that results in a maturity of less than 15 years.

Although the underlying Treasury bond for this contract is a hypothetical issue and therefore cannot itself be delivered into the futures contract, the contract is not a cash settlement contract. The only way to close out a Treasury bond futures contract is to either initiate an offsetting futures position, or to deliver a Treasury bond issue satisfying the above-mentioned criteria into the futures contract.

a. Conversion Factors   The delivery process for the Treasury bond futures contract makes the contract interesting. At the settlement date, the seller of a futures contract (the short) is now required to deliver to the buyer (the long) $100,000 par value of a 6% 20-year Treasury bond. Since no such bond exists, the seller

OPTIONAL SEGMENT

EXHIBIT 68-1 U.S. Treasury Bond Issues Acceptable for Delivery and Conversion Factors

Eligible for Delivery as of May 29, 2002.

Issue		Conversion Factors									
		Mar. 2005	Jun. 2005	Sep. 2005	Dec. 2005	Mar. 2006	Jun. 2006	Sep. 2006	Dec. 2006	Mar. 2007	Jun. 2007
5¼	11/15/28	0.9062	0.9065	0.9071	0.9075	0.9081	0.9084	0.9090	0.9095	0.9101	0.9105
5¼	02/15/29	0.9056	0.9062	0.9065	0.9071	0.9075	0.9081	0.9084	0.9090	0.9095	0.9101
5⅜	02/15/31	0.9185	0.9189	0.9191	0.9196	0.9198	0.9203	0.9206	0.9210	0.9213	0.9218
5	08/15/28	0.9376	0.9381	0.9383	0.9387	0.9389	0.9394	0.9396	0.9400	0.9403	0.9407
6	02/15/26	0.9999	1.0000	0.9999	1.0000	0.9999	1.0000	0.9999	1.0000	0.9999	1.0000
6⅛	11/15/27	1.0153	1.0151	1.0152	1.0150	1.0150	1.0148	1.0148	1.0146	1.0146	1.0144
6⅛	08/15/29	1.0158	1.0158	1.0156	1.0156	1.0154	1.0155	1.0153	1.0153	1.0151	1.0152
6¼	08/15/23	1.0274	1.0273	1.0270	1.0269	1.0265	1.0264	1.0261	1.0260	1.0256	1.0255
6¼	05/15/30	1.0322	1.0319	1.0319	1.0316	1.0316	1.0313	1.0313	1.0310	1.0310	1.0307
6⅜	08/15/27	1.0456	1.0455	1.0451	1.0450	1.0446	1.0444	1.0441	1.0439	1.0435	1.0433
6	11/15/26	1.0600	1.0595	1.0593	1.0588	1.0585	1.0580	1.0578	1.0573	1.0570	1.0565
6⅝	02/15/27	1.0752	1.0749	1.0744	1.0741	1.0735	1.0732	1.0726	1.0722	1.0716	1.0713
6¾	08/15/26	1.0893	1.0889	1.0882	1.0878	1.0871	1.0867	1.0860	1.0855	1.0848	1.0843
6⅞	08/15/25	1.1017	1.1011	1.1003	1.0998	1.0990	1.0984	1.0976	1.0970	1.0961	1.0955
7⅛	02/15/23	1.1217	1.1209	1.1197	1.1189	1.1177	1.1168	1.1156	1.1147	1.1135	1.1125
7¼	08/15/22	1.1331	1.1321	1.1308	1.1298	1.1285	1.1274	1.1261	1.1250	1.1236	1.1225
7	11/15/24	1.1711	1.1697	1.1687	1.1673	1.1663	1.1649	1.1637	1.1623	1.1612	1.1597
7⅝	11/15/22	1.1746	1.1730	1.1717	1.1701	1.1687	1.1671	1.1657	1.1640	1.1625	1.1607
7⅝	02/15/25	1.1864	1.1853	1.1839	1.1828	1.1813	1.1801	1.1786	1.1774	1.1759	1.1746
7⅞	02/15/21	1.1892	1.1875	1.1855	1.1838	—	—	—	—	—	—
8	11/15/21	1.2077	1.2056	1.2039	1.2018	1.2000	1.1979	1.1960	—	—	—
8⅛	05/15/21	1.2166	1.2144	1.2125	1.2102	1.2083	—	—	—	—	—
8⅛	08/15/21	1.2185	1.2166	1.2144	1.2125	1.2102	1.2083	—	—	—	—
8¾	05/15/20	1.2695	—	—	—	—	—	—	—	—	—
8¾	08/15/20	1.2721	1.2695	—	—	—	—	—	—	—	—
No. of Eligible issues		25	24	23	23	22	21	20	19	19	19

Source: Chicago Board of Trade

must choose from one of the acceptable deliverable Treasury bonds that the CBOT has specified. Suppose the seller is entitled to deliver $100,000 of a 5% 20-year Treasury bond to settle the futures contract. The value of this bond is less than the value of a 6% 20-year bond. If the seller delivers the 5% 20-year bond, this would be unfair to the buyer of the futures contract who contracted to receive $100,000 of a 6% 20-year Treasury bond. Alternatively, suppose the seller delivers $100,000 of a 7% 20-year Treasury bond. The value of a 7% 20-year Treasury bond is greater than that of a 6% 20-year bond, so this would be a disadvantage to the seller.

How can this problem be resolved? To make delivery equitable to both parties, the CBOT has introduced **conversion factors** for adjusting the price of each Treasury issue that can be delivered to satisfy the Treasury bond futures contract. The conversion factor is determined by the CBOT before a contract with a specific settlement date begins trading.[2] The adjusted price is found by multiplying the conversion factor by the futures price. The adjusted price is called the **converted price**.

Exhibit 68-1 shows conversion factors as of May 29, 2002. The conversion factors are shown by contract settlement date. Note that the conversion factor depends not only on the issue delivered but also on the settlement date of the contract. For example, look at the first issue in Exhibit 68-1, the 5¼% coupon bond maturing 11/15/28. For the Treasury bond futures contract settling (i.e., maturing) in March 2005, the conversion factor is 0.9062. For the December 2005 contract, the conversion factor is 0.9075.

The price that the buyer must pay the seller when a Treasury bond is delivered is called the **invoice price**. The invoice price is the futures settlement price plus accrued interest. However, as just noted, the seller can deliver one of several acceptable Treasury issues and to make delivery fair to both parties, the invoice price must be adjusted based on the actual Treasury issue delivered. It is the conversion factors that are used to adjust the invoice price. The invoice price is:

invoice price = contract size × futures settlement price × conversion factor
+ accrued interest

Suppose the Treasury March 2006 futures contract settles at 105-16 and that the issue delivered is the 8% of 11/15/21. The futures contract settlement price of 105-16 means 105.5% of par value or 1.055 times par value. As indicated in Exhibit 68-1, the conversion factor for this issue for the March 2006 contract is 1.2000. Since the contract size is $100,000, the invoice price the buyer pays the seller is:

$100,000 × 1.055 × 1.2000 + accrued interest = $126,600
+ accrued interest

b. Cheapest-to-Deliver Issue   As can be seen in Exhibit 68-1, there can be more than one issue that is permitted to be delivered to satisfy a futures contract. In fact, for the March 2005 contract, there are 25 deliverable or eligible bond issues. It is the short that has the option of selecting which one of the deliverable bond issues if he decides to deliver.[3] The decision of which one of the bond

PRACTICE QUESTION 1

Suppose that the June 200X Treasury bond futures contract settles at 97-24 and the issue delivered has a conversion factor of 1.17. Assume that the accrued interest for the issue delivered is $3,800 per $100,000 par value. What is the invoice price the buyer pays the seller?

---

[2] The conversion factor is based on the price that a deliverable bond would sell for at the beginning of the delivery month if it were to yield 6%.

[3] Remember that the short can always unwind his position by buying the same futures contract before the settlement date.

issues a short will elect to deliver is *not* made arbitrarily. There is an economic analysis that a short will undertake in order to determine the best bond issue to deliver. In fact, as we will see, all of the elements that go into the economic analysis will be the same for all participants in the market who are either electing to deliver or who are anticipating delivery of one of the eligible bond issues. In this section, how the best bond issue to deliver is determined will be explained.

The economic analysis is not complicated. The basic principle is as follows. Suppose that an investor enters into the following two transactions *simultaneously*:

1. buys one of the deliverable bond issues today with borrowed money and

2. sells a futures contract

The two positions (i.e., the long position in the deliverable bond issue purchased and the short position in the futures contract) will be held to the delivery date. At the delivery date, the bond issue purchased will be used to satisfy the short's obligation to deliver an eligible bond issue. The simultaneous transactions above and the delivery of the acceptable bond issue purchased to satisfy the short position in the futures contract is called a ***cash and carry trade***. We will discuss this in more detail in the next reading where the importance of selecting the best bond issue to deliver for the pricing of a futures contract is explained.

Let's look at the economics of this cash and carry trade. The investor (who by virtue of the fact that he sold a futures contract is the short), has synthetically created a short-term investment vehicle. The reason is that the investor has purchased a bond issue (one of the deliverable bond issues) and at the delivery date delivers that bond issue and receives the futures price. So, the investor knows the cost of buying the bond issue and knows how much will be received from the investment. The amount received is the coupon interest until the delivery date, any reinvestment income from reinvesting coupon payments, and the futures price at the delivery date. (Remember that the futures price at the delivery date for a given deliverable bond issue will be its converted price.) Thus, the investor can calculate the rate of return that will be earned on the investment. In the futures market, this rate of return is called the **implied repo rate**.

An implied repo rate can be calculated for *every* deliverable bond issue. For example, suppose that there are N deliverable bond issues that can be delivered to satisfy a bond futures contract. Market participants who want to know either the best issue to deliver or what issue is likely to be delivered will calculate an implied repo rate for all N eligible bond issues. Which would be the best issue to deliver by a short? Since the implied repo rate is the rate of return on an investment, the best bond issue is the one that has the *highest* implied repo rate (i.e., the highest rate of return). The bond issue with the highest implied repo rate is called the **cheapest-to-deliver issue**.

Now that we understand the economic principle for determining the best bond issue to deliver (i.e., the cheapest-to-deliver issue), let's look more closely at how one calculates the implied repo rate for each deliverable bond issue. This rate is computed using the following information for a given deliverable bond issue:

1. the price plus accrued interest at which the Treasury issue could be purchased

2. the converted price plus the accrued interest that will be received upon delivery of that Treasury bond issue to satisfy the short futures position

3. the coupon payments that will be received between today and the date the issue is delivered to satisfy the futures contract.

4. the reinvestment income that will be realized on the coupon payments between the time the interim coupon payment is received and the date that the issue is delivered to satisfy the Treasury bond futures contract.

The first three elements are known. The last element will depend on the reinvestment rate that can be earned. While the reinvestment rate is unknown, typically this is a small part of the rate of return and not much is lost by assuming that the implied repo rate can be predicted with certainty.

The general formula for the implied repo rate is as follows:

$$\text{implied repo rate} = \frac{\text{dollar return}}{\text{cost of the investment}} \times \frac{360}{\text{days}_1}$$

where days_1 is equal to the number of days until settlement of the futures contract. Below we will explain the other components in the formula for the implied repo rate.

Let's begin with the dollar return. The **dollar return** for an issue is the difference between the **proceeds received** and the **cost of the investment**. The proceeds received are equal to the proceeds received at the settlement date of the futures contract and any interim coupon payment plus interest from reinvesting the interim coupon payment. The proceeds received at the settlement date include the converted price (i.e., futures settlement price multiplied by the conversion factor for the issue) and the accrued interest received from delivery of the issue. That is,

$$\text{proceeds received} = \text{converted price} + \text{accrued interest received} \\ + \text{interim coupon payment} + \text{interest from reinvesting} \\ \text{the interim coupon payment}$$

As noted earlier, all of the elements are known except the interest from reinvesting the interim coupon payment. This amount is estimated by assuming that the coupon payment can be reinvested at the term repo rate. At Level III we describe the repo market and the term repo rate. The **term repo rate** is not only a borrowing rate for an investor who wants to borrow in the repo market but also the rate at which an investor can invest proceeds on a short-term basis. For how long is the reinvestment of the interim coupon payment? It is the number of days from when the interim coupon payment is received and the actual delivery date to satisfy the futures contract. The reinvestment income is then computed as follows:

$$\text{interest from reinvesting the interim coupon payment} = \text{interim coupon} \\ \times \text{term repo rate} \times (\text{days}_2/360)$$

where

$$\text{days}_2 = \text{number of days between when the interim coupon payment is} \\ \text{received and the actual delivery date of the futures contract}$$

The reason for dividing days_2 by 360 is that the ratio represents the number of days the interim coupon is reinvested as a percentage of the number of days in a year as measured in the money market.

The cost of the investment is the amount paid to purchase the issue. This cost is equal to the purchase price plus accrued interest paid. That is,

$$\text{cost of the investment} = \text{purchase price} + \text{accrued interest paid}$$

Thus, the dollar return for the numerator of the formula for the implied repo rate is equal to

dollar return = proceeds received - cost of the investment

The dollar return is then divided by the cost of the investment.[4]

So, now we know how to compute the numerator and the denominator in the formula for the implied repo rate. The second ratio in the formula for the implied repo rate simply involves annualizing the return using a convention in the money market for the number of days. (Recall that in the money market the convention is to use a 360 day year.) Since the investment resulting from the cash and carry trade is a synthetic money market instrument, 360 days are used.

Let's compute the implied repo rate for a hypothetical issue that may be delivered to satisfy a hypothetical Treasury bond futures contract. Assume the following for the deliverable issue and the futures contract:

Futures contract

    futures price = 96

    days to futures delivery date ($days_1$) = 82 days

Deliverable issue

    price of issue = 107

    accrued interest paid = 3.8904

    coupon rate = 10%

    days remaining before interim coupon paid = 40 days

    interim coupon = $5

    number of days between when the interim coupon payment is received
       and the actual delivery date of the futures contract ($days_2$) = 42

    conversion factor = 1.1111

    accrued interest received at futures settlement date = 1.1507

Other information:

    42-day term repo rate = 3.8%

Let's begin with the proceeds received. We need to compute the converted price and the interest from reinvesting the interim coupon payment. The converted price is:

$$converted\ price = futures\ price \times conversion\ factor$$
$$= 96 \times 1.1111 = 106.6656$$

The interest from reinvesting the interim coupon payment depends on the term repo rate. The term repo rate is assumed to be 3.8%. Therefore,

$$interest\ from\ reinvesting\ the\ interim\ coupon\ payment = \$5 \times 0.038 \times \left(\frac{42}{360}\right)$$
$$= 0.0222$$

---

[4] Actually, the cost of the investment should be adjusted because the amount that the investor ties up in the investment is reduced if there is an interim coupon payment. We will ignore this adjustment here.

To summarize:

converted price	=	106.6656
accrued interest received at futures settlement date	=	1.1507
interim coupon payment	=	5.0000
interest from reinvesting the interim coupon payment	=	0.0222
proceeds received	=	112.8385

The cost of the investment is the purchase price for the issue plus the accrued interest paid, as shown below:

$$\text{cost of the investment} = 107 + 3.8904 = 110.8904$$

The implied repo rate is then:

$$\text{implied repo rate} = \frac{112.8385 - 110.8904}{110.8904} \times \frac{360}{82} = 0.0771 = 7.71\%$$

Once the implied repo rate is calculated for each deliverable issue, the cheapest-to-deliver issue will be the one that has the highest implied repo rate (i.e., the issue that gives the maximum return in a cash-and-carry trade). As explained in the next chapter, this issue plays a key role in the pricing of a Treasury bond futures contract.

While an eligible bond issue may be the cheapest to deliver today, changes in factors may cause some other eligible bond issue to be the cheapest to deliver at a future date. A sensitivity analysis can be performed to determine how a change in yield affects the cheapest to deliver.

PRACTICE QUESTION 2

Calculate the implied repo rate for a hypothetical issue that is deliverable for a Treasury bond futures contract assuming the following for the deliverable issue and the futures contract:

Futures contract
Futures price = 97
days to futures delivery date (days$_1$) = 62 days

Deliverable issue
price of issue = 95
accrued interest paid = 3.0110
coupon rate = 7%
days remaining before interim coupon made = 25 day
interim coupon = $3.50
number of days between when the interim coupon payment is received and the actual delivery date of the futures contract (day$_2$) = 37 days
conversion factor = 0.9710
accrued interest received at futures settlement date = 0.7096

Other information:
37-day repo rate = 4.7%

c. Other Delivery Options   In addition to the choice of which acceptable Treasury issue to deliver—sometimes referred to as the **quality option** or **swap option**—the short has at least two more options granted under CBOT delivery guidelines. The short is permitted to decide when in the delivery month delivery actually will take place. This is called the **timing option**. The other option is the right of the short to give notice of intent to deliver up to 8:00 p.m. Chicago time after the closing of the exchange (3:15 p.m. Chicago time) on the date when the futures settlement price has been fixed. This option is referred to as the **wild card option**. The quality option, the timing option, and the wild card option (in sum referred to as the **delivery options**), mean that the long position can never be sure which Treasury bond will be delivered or when it will be delivered. These three delivery options are summarized in Exhibit 68-2.

d. Delivery Procedure   For a short who wants to deliver, the delivery procedure involves three days. The first day is the **position day**. On this day, the short notifies the CBOT that it intends to deliver. The short has until 8:00 p.m. central standard time to do so. The second day is the **notice day**. On this day, the short specifies which particular issue will be delivered. The short has until 2:00 p.m. central standard time to make this declaration. (On the last possible notice day in the delivery month, the short has until 3:00 p.m.) The CBOT then selects the long to whom delivery will be made. This is the long position that has been outstanding for the greatest period of time. The long is then notified by 4:00 p.m. that delivery will be made. The third day is the **delivery day**. By 10:00 a.m. on this day the short must have in its account the Treasury issue that it specified on the notice day and by 1:00 p.m. must deliver that bond to the long that was assigned by the CBOT to accept delivery. The long pays the short the invoice price upon receipt of the bond.

2. Treasury Note Futures

The three Treasury note futures contracts are 10-year, 5-year, and 2-year note contracts. All three contracts are modeled after the Treasury bond futures contract and are traded on the CBOT.

   The underlying instrument for the 10-year Treasury note futures contract is $100,000 par value of a hypothetical 10-year, 6% Treasury note. Several acceptable Treasury issues may be delivered by the short. An issue is acceptable if the maturity is not less than 6.5 years and not greater than 10 years from the first day of the delivery month. Delivery options are granted to the short position.

EXHIBIT 68-2	Delivery Options Granted to the Short (Seller) of a CBOT Treasury Bond Futures Contract
Delivery option	**Description**
Quality or swap option	Choice of which acceptable Treasury issue to deliver
Timing option	Choice of when in delivery month to deliver
Wild card option	Choice to deliver after the closing price of the futures contract is determined

For the 5-year Treasury note futures contract, the underlying is $100,000 par value of a 6% notional coupon U.S. Treasury note that satisfies the following conditions: (1) an original maturity of not more than 5 years and 3 months, (2) a remaining maturity no greater than 5 years and 3 months, and (3) a remaining maturity not less than 4 years and 2 months.

The underlying for the 2-year Treasury note futures contract is $200,000 par value of a 6% notional coupon U.S. Treasury note with a remaining maturity of not more than 2 years and not less than 1 year and 9 months. Moreover, the original maturity of the note delivered to satisfy the 2-year futures cannot be more than 5 years and 3 months.

3. Agency Note Futures Contract

In 2000, the CBOT and the Chicago Mercantile Exchange (CME) began trading in futures contracts in which the underlying is a Fannie Mae or Freddie Mac agency debenture security. (Agency debentures are explained at Level I.) The underlying for the CBOT 10-year agency note futures contract is a Fannie Mae benchmark note or Freddie Mac reference note having a par value of $100,000 and a notional coupon of 6%. The 10-year agency note futures contract of the CME is similar to that of the CBOT, but has a notional coupon of 6.5% instead of 6%.

As with the Treasury futures contract, more than one issue is deliverable for both the CBOT and CME agency note futures contract. The contract delivery months are March, June, September, and December. As with the Treasury futures contract a conversion factor applies to each eligible issue for each contract settlement date. Because many issues are deliverable, one issue is the cheapest-to-deliver issue. This issue is found in exactly the same way as with the Treasury futures contract.

INTEREST RATE OPTIONS

An **option** is a contract in which the writer of the option grants the buyer of the option the right, but not the obligation, to purchase from or sell to the writer something at a specified price within a specified period of time (or at a specified date). The **writer**, also referred to as the **seller**, grants this right to the buyer in exchange for a certain sum of money, called the **option price** or **option premium**. The price at which the underlying for the contract may be bought or sold is called the **exercise price** or **strike price**. The date after which an option is void is called the **expiration date**. Our focus is on options where the "something" underlying the option is an interest rate instrument or an interest rate.

When an option grants the buyer the right to purchase the designated instrument from the writer (seller), it is referred to as a **call option**, or **call**. When the option buyer has the right to sell the designated instrument to the writer, the option is called a **put option**, or **put**.

An option is also categorized according to when the option buyer may exercise the option. There are options that may be exercised at any time up to and including the expiration date. Such an option is referred to as an **American option**. There are options that may be exercised only at the expiration date. An option with this feature is called a **European option**. An option that can be exercised prior to maturity but only on designated dates is called a **modified American, Bermuda**, or **Atlantic option**.

A. Risk and Return Characteristics of Options

The maximum amount that an option buyer can lose is the option price. The maximum profit that the option writer can realize is the option price at the time of sale. The option buyer has substantial upside return potential, while the option writer has substantial downside risk.

It is assumed in this reading that the reader has an understanding of the basic positions that can be created with options. These positions include:

1. long call position (buying a call option)
2. short call position (selling a call option)
3. long put position (buying a put option)
4. short put position (selling a put option)

Exhibit 68-3 shows the payoff profile for these four option positions *assuming that each option position is held to the expiration date and not exercised early.*

B. Differences Between Options and Futures Contracts

Unlike a futures contract, one party to an option contract is not obligated to transact. Specifically, the option buyer has the right, but not the obligation, to transact. The option writer does have the obligation to perform. In the case of a futures contract, both buyer and seller are obligated to perform. Of course, a futures buyer does not pay the seller to accept the obligation, while an option buyer pays the option seller an option price.

Consequently, the risk/reward characteristics of the two contracts are also different. In the case of a futures contract, the buyer of the contract realizes a dollar-for-dollar gain when the price of the futures contract increases and suffers a dollar-for-dollar loss when the price of the futures contract drops. The opposite occurs for the seller of a futures contract. Options do not provide this symmetric risk/reward relationship. The most that the buyer of an option can lose is the

EXHIBIT 68-3	Payoff of Basic Option Positions if Held to Expiration Date

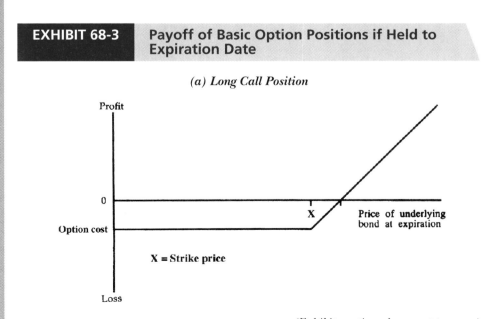

(a) Long Call Position

(Exhibit continued on next page ...)

EXHIBIT 68-3 (continued)

(b) Short Call Position

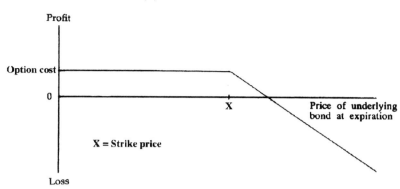

(c) Long Put Position

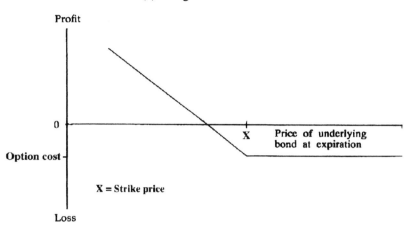

(d) Short Put Position

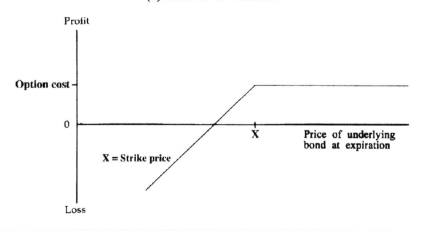

option price. While the buyer of an option retains all the potential benefits, the gain is always reduced by the amount of the option price. The maximum profit that the writer may realize is the option price; this is compensation for accepting substantial downside risk.

Both parties to a futures contract are required to post margin. There are no margin requirements for the buyer of an option once the option price has been paid in full. Because the option price is the maximum amount that the investor can lose, no matter how adverse the price movement of the underlying, there is no need for margin. Because the writer of an option has agreed to accept all of the risk (and none of the reward) of the position in the underlying, the writer is generally required to put up the option price received as margin. In addition, as price changes occur that adversely affect the writer's position, the writer is required to deposit additional margin (with some exceptions) as the position is marked to market.

C. Exchange-Traded Versus OTC Options

Options, like other financial instruments, may be traded either on an organized exchange or in the over-the-counter (OTC) market. An exchange that wants to create an options contract must obtain approval from regulators. Exchange-traded options have three advantages. First, the strike price and expiration date of the contract are standardized.[5] Second, as in the case of futures contracts, the direct link between buyer and seller is severed after the order is executed because of the interchangeability of exchange-traded options. The clearinghouse performs the same guarantor function in the options market that it does in the futures market. Finally, transaction costs are lower for exchange-traded options than for OTC options.

The higher cost of an OTC option reflects the cost of customizing the option for the many situations where an institutional investor needs to have a tailor-made option because the standardized exchange-traded option does not satisfy its investment objectives. Investment banking firms and commercial banks act as principals as well as brokers in the OTC options market. While an OTC option is less liquid than an exchange-traded option, this is typically not of concern to an institutional investor—most institutional investors use OTC options as part of an asset/liability strategy and intend to hold them to expiration.

Exchange-traded interest rate options can be written on a fixed income security or an interest rate futures contract. The former options are called *options on physicals*. For reasons to be explained later, options on interest rate futures are more popular than options on physicals. However, portfolio managers have made increasingly greater use of OTC options.

1. Exchange-Traded Futures Options

There are futures options on all the interest rate futures contracts mentioned earlier in this reading. An option on a futures contract, commonly referred to as a **futures option**, gives the buyer the right to buy from or sell to the writer a designated futures contract at the strike price at any time during the life of the option. If the futures option is a call option, the buyer has the right to purchase

---

[5] Exchanges have developed put and call options issued by their clearinghouse that are customized with respect to expiration date, exercise style, and strike price. These options are called *flexible exchange options* and are nicknamed "Flex" options.

one designated futures contract at the strike price. That is, the buyer has the right to acquire a long futures position in the underlying futures contract. If the buyer exercises the call option, the writer acquires a corresponding short position in the same futures contract.

A put option on a futures contract grants the buyer the right to sell one designated futures contract to the writer at the strike price. That is, the option buyer has the right to acquire a short position in the designated futures contract. If the put option is exercised, the writer acquires a corresponding long position in the designated futures contract.

As the parties to the futures option will realize a position in a futures contract when the option is exercised, the question is: what will the futures price be? What futures price will the long be required to pay for the futures contract, and at what futures price will the short be required to sell the futures contract?

Upon exercise, the futures price for the futures contract will be set equal to the strike price. The position of the two parties is then immediately marked-to-market in terms of the then-current futures price. Thus, the futures position of the two parties will be at the prevailing futures price. At the same time, the option buyer will receive from the option seller the economic benefit from exercising. In the case of a call futures option, the option writer must pay the difference between the current futures price and the strike price to the buyer of the option. In the case of a put futures option, the option writer must pay the option buyer the difference between the strike price and the current futures price.

For example, suppose an investor buys a call option on some futures contract in which the strike price is 85. Assume also that the futures price is 95 and that the buyer exercises the call option. Upon exercise, the call buyer is given a long position in the futures contract at 85 and the call writer is assigned the corresponding short position in the futures contract at 85. The futures positions of the buyer and the writer are immediately marked-to-market by the exchange. Because the prevailing futures price is 95 and the strike price is 85, the long futures position (the position of the call buyer) realizes a gain of 10, while the short futures position (the position of the call writer) realizes a loss of 10. The call writer pays the exchange 10 and the call buyer receives from the exchange 10. The call buyer, who now has a long futures position at 95, can either liquidate the futures position at 95 or maintain a long futures position. If the former course of action is taken, the call buyer sells his futures contract at the prevailing futures price of 95. There is no gain or loss from liquidating the position. Overall, the call buyer realizes a gain of 10 (less the option purchase price). The call buyer who elects to hold the long futures position will face the same risk and reward of holding such a position, but still realizes a gain of 10 from the exercise of the call option.

Suppose instead that the futures option with a strike price of 85 is a put rather than a call, and the current futures price is 60 rather than 95. Then, if the buyer of this put option exercises it, the buyer would have a short position in the futures contract at 85; the option writer would have a long position in the futures contract at 85. The exchange then marks the position to market at the then-current futures price of 60, resulting in a gain to the put buyer of 25 and a loss to the put writer of the same amount. The put buyer now has a short futures position at 60 and can either liquidate the short futures position by buying a futures contract at the prevailing futures price of 60 or maintain the short futures position. In either case the put buyer realizes a gain of 25 (less the option purchase price) from exercising the put option.

There are no margin requirements for the buyer of a futures option once the option price has been paid in full. Because the option price is the maximum amount that the buyer can lose regardless of how adverse the price movement of the underlying instrument, there is no need for margin. Because the writer (seller) of a futures option has agreed to accept all of the risk (and none of the reward) of the position in the underlying instrument, the writer (seller) is required to deposit not only the margin required on the interest rate futures contract position but also (with certain exceptions) the option price that is received from writing the option.

The price of a futures option is quoted in 64ths of 1% of par value. For example, a price of 24 means $^{24}\!/\!_{64}$ of 1% of par value. Since the par value of a Treasury bond futures contract is $100,000, an option price of 24 means: $[(^{24}\!/\!_{64})/100] \times \$100,000 = \$375$. In general, the price of a futures option quoted at Q is equal to:

$$\text{Option price} = \left[\frac{Q/64}{100}\right] \times \$100,000$$

There are three reasons that futures options have largely supplanted options on fixed income securities as the options vehicle of choice for institutional investors who want to use exchange-traded options. First, unlike options on fixed income securities, options on Treasury coupon futures do not require payments for accrued interest to be made. Consequently, when a futures option is exercised, the call buyer and the put writer need not compensate the other party for accrued interest. Second, futures options are believed to be "cleaner" instruments because of the reduced likelihood of delivery squeezes. Market participants who must deliver an instrument are concerned that at the time of delivery the instrument to be delivered will be in short supply, resulting in a higher price to acquire the instrument. As the deliverable supply of futures contracts is infinite for futures options currently traded, there is no concern about a delivery squeeze. Finally, in order to price any option, it is imperative to know at all times the price of the underlying instrument. In the bond market, current prices are not as easily available as price information on the futures contract. The reason is that as bonds trade in the OTC market there is no single reporting system with recent price information. Thus, an investor who wanted to purchase an option on a Treasury bond would have to call several dealer firms to obtain a price. In contrast, futures contracts are traded on an exchange and, as a result, price information is reported.

2. Over-the-Counter Options

Institutional investors who want to purchase an option on a specific Treasury security or a Ginnie Mae passthrough security can do so on an over-the-counter basis. There are government and mortgage-backed securities dealers who make a

PRACTICE QUESTION 3

a. Suppose an investor purchases a call option on a Treasury bond futures contract with a strike price of 98. Also assume that at the expiration date the price of the Treasury bond futures contract is 103. Will the investor exercise the call option and, if so, what will the investor and the writer of the call option receive?

b. Suppose an investor purchases a put option on a Treasury bond futures contract with a strike price of 105. Also assume that at the expiration date the price of the Treasury bond futures contract is 96. Will the investor exercise the put option and, if so, what will the investor and the writer of the put option receive?

market in options on specific securities. OTC options, also called **dealer options**, usually are purchased by institutional investors who want to hedge the risk associated with a specific security. For example, a thrift may be interested in hedging its position in a specific mortgage passthrough security. Typically, the maturity of the option coincides with the time period over which the buyer of the option wants to hedge, so the buyer is not concerned with the option's liquidity.

In the absence of a clearinghouse the parties to any over-the-counter contract are exposed to counterparty risk.[6] In the case of forward contracts where both parties are obligated to perform, both parties face counterparty risk. In contrast, in the case of an option, once the option buyer pays the option price, it has satisfied its obligation. It is only the seller that must perform if the option is exercised. Thus, the option buyer is exposed to counterparty risk—the risk that the option seller will fail to perform.

OTC options can be customized in any manner sought by an institutional investor. Basically, if a dealer can reasonably hedge the risk associated with the opposite side of the option sought, it will create the option desired by a customer. OTC options are not limited to European or American type. Dealers also create modified American (Bermuda or Atlantic) type options.

ENDS

INTEREST RATE SWAPS   4

In an interest rate swap, two parties agree to exchange periodic interest payments. The dollar amount of the interest payments exchanged is based on some predetermined dollar principal, which is called the **notional principal** or **notional amount**. The dollar amount each counterparty pays to the other is the agreed-upon periodic interest rate times the notional principal. The only dollars that are exchanged between the parties are the interest payments, not the notional principal. In the most common type of swap, one party agrees to pay the other party fixed interest payments at designated dates for the life of the contract. This party is referred to as the **fixed-rate payer**. The fixed rate that the fixed-rate payer must make is called the **swap rate**. The other party, who agrees to make interest rate payments that float with some reference rate, is referred to as the **fixed-rate receiver**.

The reference rates that have been used for the floating rate in an interest rate swap are those on various money market instruments: Treasury bills, the London interbank offered rate, commercial paper, bankers acceptances, certificates of deposit, the **federal funds rate**, and the prime rate. The most common is the **London interbank offered rate (LIBOR)**. LIBOR is the rate at which prime banks offer to pay on Eurodollar deposits available to other prime banks for a given maturity. Basically, it is viewed as the global cost of bank borrowing. There is not just one rate but a rate for different maturities. For example, there is a 1-month LIBOR, 3-month LIBOR, 6-month LIBOR, etc.

To illustrate an interest rate swap, suppose that for the next five years party X agrees to pay party Y 6% per year (the swap rate), while party Y agrees to pay party X 6-month LIBOR (the reference rate). Party X is the fixed-rate payer, while party Y is the fixed-rate receiver. Assume that the notional principal is $50

---

[6] There are well-established institutional arrangements for mitigating counterparty risk in not only OTC options but also the other OTC derivatives described in this reading (swaps, caps, and floors). These arrangement include limiting exposure to a specific counterparty, marking to market positions, collateralizing trades, and netting arrangement. For a discussion of these arrangements, see Chance, *Analysis of Derivatives for the CFA Program*, pp. 595–598.

PRACTICE QUESTION 4

Suppose that party G and party H enter into a 4-year interest rate swap. The notional amount for the swap is $100 million and the reference rate is 3-month LIBOR. Suppose that the payments are made quarterly by both the fixed-rate payer and the fixed-rate receiver. Also assume that the swap rate is 4.4%.

a. What are the payments that must be made by the fixed-rate payer every quarter?

b. Suppose for the first floating-rate payment 3-month LIBOR is 7.2%. What is the amount of the first floating-rate payment that must be made by the fixed-rate receiver?

million, and that payments are exchanged every six months for the next five years. This means that every six months, party X (the fixed-rate payer) will pay party Y $1.5 million (6% times $50 million divided by 2). The amount that party Y (the fixed-rate receiver) will pay party X will be 6-month LIBOR times $50 million divided by 2. If 6-month LIBOR is 5% at the beginning of the 6-month period, party Y will pay party X $1.25 million (5% times $50 million divided by 2). Mechanically, the floating-rate is determined at the beginning of a period and paid in arrears—that is, it is paid at the end of the period. The two payments are actually netted out so that $0.25 million will be paid from party X to party Y. Note that we divide by two because one-half year's interest is being paid. This is illustrated in panel a of Exhibit 68-4.

The convention that has evolved for quoting a swap rate is that a dealer sets the floating rate equal to the reference rate and then quotes the fixed rate that will apply. The fixed rate is the swap rate and reflects a "spread" above the Treasury yield curve with the same term to maturity as the swap. This spread is called the **swap spread**.

A. Entering Into a Swap and Counterparty Risk

Interest rate swaps are OTC instruments. This means that they are not traded on an exchange. An institutional investor wishing to enter into a swap transaction can do so through either a securities firm or a commercial bank that transacts in swaps.[7] These entities can do one of the following. First, they can arrange or broker a swap between two parties that want to enter into an interest rate swap. In this case, the securities firm or commercial bank is acting in a brokerage capacity. The broker is not a party to the swap.

The second way in which a securities firm or commercial bank can get an institutional investor into a swap position is by taking the other side of the swap. This means that the securities firm or the commercial bank is a dealer rather than a broker in the transaction. Acting as a dealer, the securities firm or the commercial bank must hedge its swap position in the same way that it hedges its position in other securities that it holds. Also it means that the dealer (which we refer to as a **swap dealer**) is the counterparty to the transaction. If an institu-

---

[7] Don't get confused here about the role of commercial banks. A bank can use a swap in its asset/liability management. Or, a bank can transact (buy and sell) swaps to clients to generate fee income. It is in the latter sense that we are discussing the role of a commercial bank in the swap market here.

EXHIBIT 68-4	Summary of How the Value of a Swap to Each Counterparty Changes When Interest Rates Change

a. Initial position

Swap rate	= 6%		Settlement	= semiannual
Reference rate	= 6-month LIBOR		Term of swap	= 5 years
Notional amount	= $50 million		Payment by fixed-rate payer	= $1.5 million

Every six months

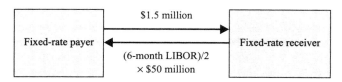

b. Interest rates increase such that swap rate is 7% for new swaps

Fixed-rate payer pays initial swap rate of 6% to obtain 6-month LIBOR
   Advantage to fixed-rate payer: pays only 6% not 7% to obtain 6-month LIBOR

Fixed-rate receiver pays 6-month LIBOR
   Disadvantage to fixed-rate receiver: receives only 6% in exchange for 6-month LIBOR, not 7%

Results of a rise in interest rates:

Party	Value of swap
Fixed-rate payer	Increases
Fixed-rate receiver	Decreases

c. Interest rates decrease such that swap rate is 5% for new swaps

Fixed-rate payer pays initial swap rate of 6% to obtain 6-month LIBOR
   Disadvantage to fixed-rate payer: must pay 6% not 5% to obtain 6-month LIBOR

Fixed-rate receiver pays 6-month LIBOR
   Advantage to fixed-rate receiver: receives 6% in exchange for 6-month LIBOR, not 5%

Results of a decrease in interest rates:

Party	Value of swap
Fixed-rate payer	Decreases
Fixed-rate receiver	Increases

tional investor entered into a swap with a swap dealer, the institutional investor will look to the swap dealer to satisfy the obligations of the swap; similarly, that same swap dealer looks to the institutional investor to fulfill its obligations as set forth in the swap.

The risk that the two parties take on when they enter into a swap is that the other party will fail to fulfill its obligations as set forth in the swap agreement. That is, each party faces default risk and therefore there is bilateral counterparty risk.

B. Risk/Return Characteristics of an Interest Rate Swap

The value of an interest rate swap will fluctuate with market interest rates. As interest rates rise, the fixed-rate payer is receiving a higher 6-month LIBOR (in our illustration). He would need to pay more for a new swap. Let's consider our hypothetical swap. Suppose that interest rates change immediately after parties X and Y enter into the swap. Panel a in Exhibit 68-4 shows the transaction. First, consider what would happen if the market demanded that in any 5-year swap the fixed-rate payer must pay 7% in order to receive 6-month LIBOR. If party X (the fixed-rate payer) wants to sell its position to party A, then party A will benefit by having to pay only 6% (the original swap rate agreed upon) rather than 7% (the current swap rate) to receive 6-month LIBOR. Party X will want compensation for this benefit. Consequently, the value of party X's position has increased. Thus, if interest rates increase, the fixed-rate payer will realize a profit and the fixed-rate receiver will realize a loss. Panel b in Exhibit 68-4 summarizes the results of a rise in interest rates.

Next, consider what would happen if interest rates decline to, say, 5%. Now a 5-year swap would require a new fixed-rate payer to pay 5% rather than 6% to receive 6-month LIBOR. If party X wants to sell its position to party B, the latter would demand compensation to take over the position. In other words, if interest rates decline, the fixed-rate payer will realize a loss, while the fixed-rate receiver will realize a profit. Panel c in Exhibit 68-4 summarizes the results of a decline in interest rates

While we know in what direction the change in the value of a swap will be for the counterparties when interest rates change, the question is how much will the value of the swap change. We show how to compute the change in the value of a swap in the next reading.

C. Interpreting a Swap Position

There are two ways that a swap position can be interpreted: (1) a package of forward (futures) contracts and (2) a package of cash flows from buying and selling cash market instruments.

1. Package of Forward (Futures) Contracts

Contrast the position of the counterparties in an interest rate swap summarized above to the position of the long and short interest rate futures (forward) contract. The long futures position gains if interest rates decline and loses if interest rates rise—this is similar to the risk/return profile for a floating-rate payer. The risk/return profile for a fixed-rate payer is similar to that of the short futures position: a gain if interest rates increase and a loss if interest rates decrease. By taking a closer look at the interest rate swap we can understand why the risk/return relationships are similar.

Consider party X's position in our previous swap illustration. Party X has agreed to pay 6% and receive 6-month LIBOR. More specifically, assuming a $50 million notional principal, X has agreed to buy a commodity called "6-month LIBOR" for $1.5 million. This is effectively a 6-month forward contract where X agrees to pay $1.5 million in exchange for delivery of 6-month LIBOR. If interest rates increase to 7%, the price of that commodity (6-month LIBOR) is higher, resulting in a gain for the fixed-rate payer, who is effectively long a 6-month forward contract on 6-month LIBOR. The floating-rate payer is effectively short a 6-month forward contract on 6-month LIBOR. There is therefore an implicit forward contract corresponding to each exchange date.

Now we can see why there is a similarity between the risk/return relationship for an interest rate swap and a forward contract. If interest rates increase to, say, 7%, the price of that commodity (6-month LIBOR) increases to $1.75 million (7% times $50 million divided by 2). The long forward position (the fixed-rate payer) gains, and the short forward position (the floating-rate payer) loses. If interest rates decline to, say, 5%, the price of our commodity decreases to $1.25 million (5% times $50 million divided by 2). The short forward position (the floating-rate payer) gains, and the long forward position (the fixed-rate payer) loses.

Consequently, interest rate swaps can be viewed as a package of more basic interest rate derivatives, such as forwards.[8] The pricing of an interest rate swap will then depend on the price of a package of forward contracts with the same settlement dates in which the underlying for the forward contract is the same reference rate. We will make use of this principle in the next reading when we explain how to value swaps.

While an interest rate swap may be nothing more than a package of forward contracts, it is not a redundant contract for several reasons. First, maturities for forward or futures contracts do not extend out as far as those of an interest rate swap; an interest rate swap with a term of 15 years or longer can be obtained. Second, an interest rate swap is a more transactionally efficient instrument. By this we mean that in one transaction an entity can effectively establish a payoff equivalent to a package of forward contracts. The forward contracts would each have to be negotiated separately. Third, the interest rate swap market has grown in liquidity since its introduction in 1981; interest rate swaps now provide more liquidity than forward contracts, particularly long-dated (i.e., long-term) forward contracts.

2. Package of Cash Market Instruments

To understand why a swap can also be interpreted as a package of cash market instruments, consider an investor who enters into the transaction below:

▶ buy $50 million par of a 5-year floating-rate bond that pays 6-month LIBOR every six months

▶ finance the purchase by borrowing $50 million for five years on terms requiring a 6% annual interest rate payable every six months

As a result of this transaction, the investor

▶ receives a floating rate every six months for the next five years

▶ pays a fixed rate every six months for the next five years

---

[8] More specifically, an interest rate swap is equivalent to a package of **forward rate agreements**. A forward rate agreement (FRA) is the over-the-counter equivalent of the exchange-traded futures contracts on short-term rates. Typically, the short-term rate is LIBOR. The elements of an FRA are the contract rate, reference rate, settlement rate, notional amount, and settlement date.

EXHIBIT 68-5	Cash Flow for the Purchase of a 5-Year Floating-Rate Bond Financed by Borrowing on a Fixed-Rate Basis

Transaction:
- Purchase for $50 million a 5-year floating-rate bond: floating rate = LIBOR, semiannual payments
- Borrow $50 million for five years: fixed rate = 6%, semiannual payments

Six Month Period	Cash Flow (In Millions of Dollars) From:		
	Floating-Rate Bond*	Borrowing at 5%	Net = Same as swap
0	−$50	+$50.0	$0
1	$+(LIBOR_1/2) \times 50$	−1.5	$+(LIBOR_1/2) \times 50 - 1.5$
2	$+(LIBOR_2/2) \times 50$	−1.5	$+(LIBOR_2/2) \times 50 - 1.5$
3	$+(LIBOR_3/2) \times 50$	−1.5	$+(LIBOR_3/2) \times 50 - 1.5$
4	$+(LIBOR_4/2) \times 50$	−1.5	$+(LIBOR_4/2) \times 50 - 1.5$
5	$+(LIBOR_5/2) \times 50$	−1.5	$+(LIBOR_5/2) \times 50 - 1.5$
6	$+(LIBOR_6/2) \times 50$	−1.5	$+(LIBOR_6/2) \times 50 - 1.5$
7	$+(LIBOR_7/2) \times 50$	−1.5	$+(LIBOR_7/2) \times 50 - 1.5$
8	$+(LIBOR_8/2) \times 50$	−1.5	$+(LIBOR_8/2) \times 50 - 1.5$
9	$+(LIBOR_9/2) \times 50$	−1.5	$+(LIBOR_9/2) \times 50 - 1.5$
10	$+(LIBOR_{10}/2) \times 50 + 50$	−51.5	$+(LIBOR_{10}/2) \times 50 - 1.5$

* The subscript for LIBOR indicates the 6-month LIBOR as per the terms of the floating-rate bond at time t.

The cash flows for this transaction are set forth in Exhibit 68-5. The second column of the exhibit shows the cash flow from purchasing the 5-year floating-rate bond. There is a $50 million cash outlay and then ten cash inflows. The amount of the cash inflows is uncertain because they depend on future LIBOR. The next column shows the cash flow from borrowing $50 million on a fixed-rate basis. The last column shows the net cash flow from the entire transaction. As the last column indicates, there is no initial cash flow (no cash inflow or cash outlay). In all ten 6-month periods, the net position results in a cash inflow of LIBOR and a cash outlay of $1.5 million. This net position, however, is identical to the position of a fixed-rate payer/floating-rate receiver.

It can be seen from the net cash flow in Exhibit 68-5 that a fixed-rate payer has a cash market position that is equivalent to a long position in a floating-rate bond and a short position in a fixed-rate bond—the short position being the equivalent of borrowing by issuing a fixed-rate bond.

What about the position of a floating-rate payer? It can be easily demonstrated that the position of a floating-rate payer is equivalent to purchasing a fixed-rate bond and financing that purchase at a floating rate, where the floating rate is the reference rate for the swap. That is, the position of a floating-rate payer is equivalent to a long position in a fixed-rate bond and a short position in a floating-rate bond.

D. Describing the Counterparties to a Swap Agreement

The terminology used to describe the position of a party in the swap markets combines cash market jargon and futures market jargon, given that a swap position can be interpreted as a position in a package of cash market instruments or a package of futures/forward positions. As we have said, the counterparty to an interest rate swap is either a fixed-rate payer or floating-rate payer.

Exhibit 68-6 lists how the counterparties to an interest rate swap agreement are described.[9] To understand why the fixed-rate payer is viewed as "short the bond market," and the floating-rate payer is viewed as "long the bond market," consider what happens when interest rates change. Those who borrow on a fixed-rate basis will benefit if interest rates rise because they have locked in a lower interest rate. But those who have a short bond position will also benefit if interest rates rise. Thus, a fixed-rate payer can be said to be short the bond market. A floating-rate payer benefits if interest rates fall. A long position in a bond also benefits if interest rates fall, so terminology describing a floating-rate payer as long the bond market is not surprising. From our discussion of the interpretation of a swap as a package of cash market instruments, describing a swap in terms of the sensitivities of long and short cash positions follows naturally.[10]

INTEREST RATE CAPS AND FLOORS   5

There are agreements between two parties whereby one party for an upfront premium agrees to compensate the other at specific time periods if the reference rate is different from a predetermined level. If one party agrees to pay the other when the reference rate exceeds a predetermined level, the agreement is referred to as an **interest rate cap** or **ceiling**. The agreement is referred to as an

EXHIBIT 68-6	Describing the Parties to a Swap Agreement
Fixed-rate payer	**Fixed-rate receiver**
• pays fixed rate in the swap	• pays floating rate in the swap
• receives floating in the swap	• receives fixed in the swap
• is short the bond market	• is long the bond market
• has bought a swap	• has sold a swap
• is long a swap	• is short a swap
• has established the price sensitivities of a longer-term fixed-rate liability and a floating-rate asset	• has established the price sensitivities of a longer-term fixed-rate asset and a floating-rate liability

---

[9] Robert F. Kopprasch, John Macfarlane, Daniel R. Ross, and Janet Showers, "The Interest Rate Swap Market: Yield Mathematics, Terminology, and Conventions," Chapter 58 in Frank J. Fabozzi and Irving M. Pollack (eds.), *The Handbook of Fixed Income Securities* (Homewood, IL: Dow Jones-Irwin, 1987).

[10] It is common for market participants to refer to one leg of a swap as the "funding leg" and the other as the "asset leg." This jargon is the result of the interpretation of a swap as a leveraged position in the asset. The payment of the floating-rate is referred to as the "funding leg" and the fixed-rate side is referred to as the "asset side."

interest rate floor if one party agrees to pay the other when the reference rate falls below a predetermined level. The predetermined level is called the **strike rate**. The strike rate for a cap is called the **cap rate**; the strike rate for a floor is called the **floor rate**.

The terms of a cap and floor agreement include:

1. the reference rate

2. the strike rate (cap rate or floor rate) that sets the ceiling or floor

3. the length of the agreement

4. the frequency of settlement

5. the notional principal

For example, suppose that C buys an interest rate cap from D with the following terms:

1. the reference rate is 3-month LIBOR.

2. the strike rate is 6%.

3. the agreement is for four years.

4. settlement is every three months.

5. the notional principal is $20 million.

Under this agreement, every three months for the next four years, D will pay C whenever 3-month LIBOR exceeds 6% at a settlement date. The payment will equal the dollar value of the difference between 3-month LIBOR and 6% times the notional principal divided by 4. For example, if three months from now 3-month LIBOR on a settlement date is 8%, then D will pay C 2% (8% minus 6%) times $20 million divided by 4, or $100,000. If 3-month LIBOR is 6% or less, D does not have to pay anything to C.

In the case of an interest rate floor, assume the same terms as the interest rate cap we just illustrated. In this case, if 3-month LIBOR is 8%, C receives nothing from D, but if 3-month LIBOR is less than 6%, D compensates C for the difference. For example, if 3-month LIBOR is 5%, D will pay C $50,000 (6% minus 5% times $20 million divided by 4).[11]

A. Risk/Return Characteristics

In an interest rate agreement, the buyer pays an upfront fee which represents the maximum amount that the buyer can lose and the maximum amount that the seller (writer) can gain. The only party that is required to perform is the seller of the interest rate agreement. The buyer of an interest rate cap benefits if the reference rate rises above the strike rate because the seller must compensate the buyer. The buyer of an interest rate floor benefits if the reference rate falls below the strike rate, because the seller must compensate the buyer.

The seller of an interest rate cap or floor does not face counterparty risk once the buyer pays the fee. In contrast, the buyer faces counterparty risk. Thus, as with options, there is unilateral counterparty risk.

---

[11] Interest rate caps and floors can be combined to create an *interest rate collar*. This is done by buying an interest rate cap and selling an interest rate floor. The purchase of the cap sets a maximum rate; the sale of the floor sets a minimum rate. The range between the maximum and minimum rate is called the collar.

PRACTICE QUESTION 5

Suppose that a 4-year cap has a cap rate of 7% and a notional amount of $100 million. The frequency of settlement is quarterly and the reference rate is 3-month LIBOR. Assume that 3-month LIBOR for the next four quarters is as shown below. What is the payoff for each quarter?

Period	3-month LIBOR
1	6.7%
2	7.0%
3	7.4%
4	7.6%

B. Interpretation of a Cap and Floor Position

In an interest rate cap and floor, the buyer pays an upfront fee, which represents the maximum amount that the buyer can lose and the maximum amount that the seller of the agreement can gain. The only party that is required to perform is the seller of the interest rate agreement. The buyer of an interest rate cap benefits if the reference rate rises above the strike rate because the seller must compensate the buyer. The buyer of an interest rate floor benefits if the reference rate falls below the strike rate because the seller must compensate the buyer.

How can we better understand interest rate caps and interest rate floors? In essence these contracts are equivalent to a *package of interest rate options* at different time periods. As with a swap, a complex contract can be seen to be a package of basic contracts—options in the case of caps and floors. Each of the interest rate options comprising a cap are called **caplets**; similarly, each of the interest rate options comprising a floor are called **floorlets**.

The question is what type of package of options is a cap and a floor. Note the following very carefully! It depends on whether the underlying is a rate or a fixed-income instrument. If the underlying is considered a fixed-income instrument, its value changes inversely with interest rates. Therefore:

► for a call option on a fixed-income instrument:

1. interest rates increase → fixed-income instrument's price decreases → call option value decreases

and

2. interest rates decrease → fixed-income instrument's price increases → call option value increases

► for a put option on a fixed-income instrument

1. interest rates increase → fixed-income instrument's price decreases → put option value increases

and

2. interest rates decrease → fixed-income instrument's price increases → put option value decreases

To summarize the situation for call and put options on a fixed-income instrument:

Value of:	When interest rates increase	decrease
long call	decrease	increase
short call	increase	decrease
long put	increase	decrease
short put	decrease	increase

For a cap and floor, the situation is as follows

Value of:	When interest rates increase	decrease
short cap	decrease	increase
long cap	increase	decrease
short floor	increase	decrease
long floor	decrease	increase

Therefore, buying a cap (long cap) is equivalent to buying a package of puts on a fixed-income instrument and buying a floor (long floor) is equivalent to buying a package of calls on a fixed-income instrument.

Caps and floors can also be seen as packages of options on interest rates. In the over-the-counter market one can purchase an option on an interest rate. These options work as follows in terms of their payoff. There is a strike rate. For a call option on an interest rate, there is a payoff if the reference rate is greater than the strike rate. This means that when interest rates increase, the call option's value increases and when interest rates decrease, the call option's value decreases. As can be seen from the payoff for a cap and a floor summarized above, this is the payoff of a long cap. Consequently, a cap is equivalent to a package of call options on an interest rate. For a put option on an interest rate, there is a payoff when the reference rate is less than the strike rate. When interest rates increase, the value of the put option on an interest rate decreases, as does the value of a long floor position (see the summary above); when interest rates decrease, the value of the put on an interest rate increases, as does the value of a long floor position (again, see the summary above). Thus, a floor is equivalent to a package of put options on an interest rate.

When market participants talk about the equivalency of caps and floors in terms of put and call options, they must specify the underlying. For example, a long cap is equivalent to a package of call options on interest rates or a package of put options on a fixed-income instrument.

C. Creation of an Interest Rate Collar

Interest rate caps and floors can be combined by borrowers to create an **interest rate collar**. This is done by buying an interest rate cap and selling an interest rate floor. The purchase of the cap sets a maximum interest rate that a borrower would have to pay if the reference rate rises. The sale of a floor sets the minimum interest rate that a borrower can benefit from if the reference rate declines. Therefore, there is a range for the interest rate that the borrower must pay if the reference rate changes. The net premium that a borrower who wants to create a collar must pay is the difference between the premium paid to purchase the cap and the premium received to sell the floor.

For example, consider the following collar created by a borrower: a cap purchased with a strike rate of 7% and a floor sold with a strike rate of 4%. If the reference rate exceeds 7%, the borrower receives a payment; if the reference rate is less than 4%, the borrower makes a payment. Thus, the borrower's cost will have a range from 4% to 7%. Note, however, that the borrower's effective interest cost is adjusted by the net premium that the borrower must pay.

SUMMARY

▶ A futures contract is an agreement between a buyer (seller) and an established exchange or its clearinghouse in which the buyer (seller) agrees to take (make) delivery of something at a specified price at the end of a designated period of time.

▶ A forward contract is an agreement for the future delivery of something at a specified price at a designated time, but differs from a futures contract in that it is usually non-standardized and traded in the over-the-counter market.

▶ An investor who takes a long futures position realizes a gain when the futures price increases; an investor who takes a short futures position realizes a gain when the futures price decreases.

▶ The parties to a futures contract are required to satisfy margin requirements.

▶ Parties to over-the-counter interest rate contracts are exposed to counter-party risk which is the risk that the counterparty will not satisfy its contractual obligations.

▶ For the Treasury bond futures contract the underlying instrument is $100,000 par value of a hypothetical 20-year 6% coupon Treasury bond.

▶ Conversion factors are used to adjust the invoice price of a Treasury bond futures contract to make delivery equitable to both parties.

▶ The short in a Treasury bond futures contract has several delivery options: quality option (or swap option), timing option, and wildcard option.

▶ For all the issues that may be delivered to satisfy a Treasury futures contract, a rate of return can be computed in a cash and carry trade; the rate of return is called the implied repo rate.

▶ For all the issues that may be delivered to satisfy a Treasury futures contract, the cheapest-to-deliver issue is the one with the highest implied repo rate.

▶ By varying the yield on Treasury bonds, it can be determined which issue will become the new cheapest-to-deliver issue.

▶ There are futures contracts in which the underlying is a Fannie Mae and Freddie Mac debenture.

▶ An option is a contract in which the writer of the option grants the buyer of the option the right, but not the obligation, to purchase from or sell to the writer something at a specified price within a specified period of time (or at a specified date).

▶ The option buyer pays the option writer (seller) a fee, called the option price (or premium).

▶ A call option allows the option buyer to purchase the underlying from the option writer at the strike price; a put option allows the option buyer to sell the underlying to the option writer at the strike price.

▶ Interest rate options include options on fixed income securities and options on interest rate futures contracts; the latter, called futures options, are the preferred exchange-traded vehicle for implementing investment strategies.

▶ Because of the difficulties of hedging particular fixed income securities, some institutional investors have found over-the-counter options more useful.

▶ An interest rate swap is an agreement specifying that the parties exchange interest payments at designated times, with a generic or vanilla swap calling for one party to make fixed-rate payments and the other to make floating-rate payments based on a notional principal.

▶ The swap rate is the interest rate paid by the fixed-rate payer.

▶ The swap spread is the spread paid by the fixed-rate payer over the on-the-run Treasury rate with the same maturity as the swap agreement.

▶ The convention in quoting swaps is to quote the payments made by the floating-rate payer flat (that is, without a spread) and the fixed-rate payer payments as a spread to the on-the-run Treasury with the same maturity as the swap (the swap spread)

▶ A swap position can be interpreted as either a package of forward/futures contracts or a package of cash flows from buying and selling cash market instruments.

▶ An interest rate cap specifies that one party receive a payment if the reference rate is above the cap rate; an interest rate floor specifies that one party receive a payment if a reference rate is below the floor rate.

▶ The terms of a cap and floor set forth the reference rate, the strike rate, the length of the agreement, the frequency of reset, and the notional amount.

▶ In an interest rate cap and floor, the buyer pays an upfront fee, which represents the maximum amount that the buyer can lose and the maximum amount that the seller of the agreement can gain.

▶ Buying a cap is equivalent to buying a package of puts on a fixed income security and buying a floor is equivalent to buying a package of calls on a fixed income security.

▶ If an option is viewed as one in which the underlying is an interest rate, then buying a cap is equivalent to buying a package of calls on interest rates and buying a floor is equivalent to buying a package of puts on interest rates.

▶ An interest collar is created by buying an interest rate cap and selling an interest rate floor.

▶ Forward contracts and swaps expose the parties to bilateral counterparty risk while buyers of OTC options, caps, and floors face unilateral counterparty risk.

PROBLEMS FOR READING 68

1. In an interest rate swap what is meant by the swap rate and the swap spread?

2. Suppose that Ted Munson, a portfolio manager, enters into a 3-year interest rate swap with a commercial bank that is a swap dealer. The notional amount for the swap is $40 million and the reference rate is 3-month LIBOR. Suppose that the payments are made quarterly. The swap rate that Mr. Munson agrees to pay is 5.6%.

    a. Who is the fixed-rate payer and who is the fixed-rate receiver in this swap?

    b. What are the payments that must be made by the fixed-rate payer every quarter?

    c. Suppose for the first floating-rate payment 3-month LIBOR is 3.6%. What is the amount of the first floating-rate payment that must be made by the fixed-rate receiver?

3. Give two interpretations of an interest rate swap and explain why an interest rate swap can be interpreted in each way.

4. Suppose that interest rates decrease subsequent to the inception of an interest rate swap.

    a. What is the effect on the value of the swap from the perspective of the fixed-rate payer?

    b. What is the effect on the value of the swap from the perspective of the fixed-rate receiver?

5. Why is the fixed-rate payer in an interest rate swap said to be "short the bond market"?

6. Suppose that a 1-year cap has a cap rate of 8% and a notional amount of $10 million. The frequency of settlement is quarterly and the reference rate is 3-month LIBOR. Assume that 3-month LIBOR for the next four quarters is as shown below. What is the payoff for each quarter?

Period	3-month LIBOR
1	8.7%
2	8.0%
3	7.8%
4	8.2%

7. Suppose that a 1-year floor has a floor rate of 4% and a notional amount of $20 million. The frequency of settlement is quarterly and the reference rate is 3-month LIBOR. Assume that 3-month LIBOR for the next four quarters is as shown below. What is the payoff for each quarter?

Period	3-month LIBOR
1	4.7%
2	4.4%
3	3.8%
4	3.4%

8. What counterparty risk is the seller of an interest rate floor exposed to?

9. a. What is an interest rate cap or floor equivalent to?

  b. What is a caplet and a floorlet?

SWAP CONTRACTS, CONVERTIBLE SECURITIES, AND OTHER EMBEDDED DERIVATIVES - PART II

by Frank K. Reilly and Keith C. Brown

LEARNING OUTCOMES

The candidate should be able to:

a. compare and contrast structured notes to regular fixed-income securities;

....

b. describe the cash flow characteristics of dual-currency bonds, equity-index-linked notes, commodity-linked bull and bear bonds, and swap-linked notes.

The first part of this reading is assigned as Reading 46 in Volume 4.

OTHER EMBEDDED DERIVATIVES   5

For many years, the nature of borrowing and lending in securitized capital markets remained quite stable, with companies typically issuing bonds at par value and paying either a fixed or floating rate of interest in the same currency in which the money was borrowed. With few exceptions, the choice of maturity or coupon structure was driven by the economic situation faced by the borrower, rather than the investor. Over the past decade, however, this scenario has greatly changed with the development of the structured note market. Generally speaking, structured notes are debt issues that have their principal or coupon payments linked to some other underlying variable. Examples include bonds whose coupons are tied to the appreciation of an equity index, such as the S&P 500, or a **zero coupon bond** with a principal amount tied to the appreciation of an oil price index.

Crabbe and Argilagos (1994) and Das (2001) have pointed out several common features that distinguish structured notes from regular fixed-income securities, two of which are important for our discussion. First, structured notes are designed for and targeted to a specific investor with a very particular need. That is, these are not generic instruments but products tailored to address an investor's special constraints, which often are themselves created by tax, regulatory, or institutional policy restrictions. Second, after structuring the financing to meet the investor's needs, the issuer typically will hedge that unique exposure with swaps or exchange-traded derivatives. Inasmuch as the structured note most likely required an embedded derivative to create the desired payoff structure for the investor, this unwinding of the derivative position by the issuer generates an additional source of profit opportunity for the bond underwriter.

The growth of this market has been quite rapid. From its ostensible origin in the mid-1980s, by 2003 about $100 billion of these notes were issued annually. Equally impressive is the wide variety of economic risks that have been embedded and the maze of new acronyms that has accompanied these innovations (e.g., FLAG, **LYON**, SPEL, STEER, PERCS, and ICON). We will take a detailed look at four such structures representative of the major exposures an investor might desire: currency, equity, commodity, and interest rates.

Dual Currency Bonds

A dual currency bond is a debt instrument that has coupons denominated in a different currency than its principal amount. They have been popular funding instruments, particularly in the Euromarkets, for more than a decade and have been designed to include virtually all the world's major currencies. These bonds can be viewed as a combination of two simpler financial instruments: (1) a single-currency fixed-coupon bond, and (2) a forward contract to exchange the bond's principal into a predetermined amount of a foreign currency. They often are sold to investors who are willing to take a view over the longer term in the foreign exchange markets. By having the currency forward attached to the bond, fixed-income portfolio managers who might otherwise be restricted from trading in FX have the potential to enhance their performance if their beliefs about future market conditions prove correct.

To demonstrate a structure typical of these products, consider a five-year bond paying an annual coupon of 9 percent in U.S. dollars and redemption amount of JPY 110,000. The initial price of the bond is USD 1,020, relative to a par value of USD 1,000. Assuming further that a regular five-year, dollar-denominated bond of comparable risk yielding 9 percent could have been issued at par, this means that the forward contract portion of the dual currency instrument is off market because it carries a present value of USD 20. Exhibit 69-16 shows the cash flows for this structure from the investor's point of view. It also demonstrates how it can be assembled from its more basic component parts.

Notice that the embedded forward contract allows the bondholder to exchange the USD 1,000 for JPY 110,000, generating an implied *nominal* exchange rate of JPY 110/USD (or, equivalently, USD 0.0091/JPY). However,

EXHIBIT 69-16   Cash Flows for a Dual Currency Bond from the Investor's Perspective

Transaction	Year 0	1	2	3	4	5
1. Long 9% USD bond	−USD 1,000	+USD 90	+USD 90	+USD 90	+USD 90	+USD 1,090
2. Long yen forward (pay USD, receive JPY)	−USD 20	—	—	—	—	+JPY 110,000 and −USD 1,000
3. Long dual currency bond (Transaction 1 + Transaction 2)	−USD 1,020	−USD 90	+USD 90	+USD 90	+USD 90	+JPY 110,000 and +USD 90

given that the investor has to pay an additional USD 20 today for this future transaction, this is not the *effective* exchange rate that the investor faces. Indeed, the fact that the investor is willing to pay the additional USD 20 suggests that JPY 110/USD is a favorable price to purchase yen forward. The effective exchange rate built into this transaction can be established by dividing JPY 110,000 by the sum of USD 1,000 and the future value (in Year 5) of USD 20. Calculating this latter amount as 30.77 [$= 20 \times (1.09)^5$], the effective exchange rate becomes JPY 106.72/USD [$= 110,000 \div (1,000 + 30.77)$].

There are at least two reasons why this dual currency bond might trade at a premium over a single-currency 9 percent coupon bond of comparable creditworthiness. First, it is possible that the five-year forward exchange rate between yen and dollars is JPY 106.72/USD, meaning that at USD 1,020, the bond is priced properly. The more likely possibility, though, is that the five-year forward rate actually is JPY 110/USD and that investors are paying up for a desirable FX exposure that they cannot acquire in any other way. If this is true, the issuer—who is effectively short the regular dollar bond and short in the yen forward—can unwind its derivative position at a profit, thereby reducing its funding cost below 9 percent. That is, the issuer's commitment to sell JPY 110,000 to the investor in Year 5 can be offset by a long position in a separate yen forward (which, once again, is usually done with the bond's underwriter as the counterparty) at the market forward exchange rate of JPY 110/JSD. Thus, the issuer's net borrowing cost can be calculated by solving for the yield as follows:

$$1,020 = \sum_{t=1}^{5} \frac{90}{(1 + y)^t} + \frac{1,000}{(1 + y)^5}$$

or $y = 8.49$ percent. This 51-basis-point differential from the plain vanilla borrowing rate of 9 percent represents the issuer's compensation for creating an investment vehicle that is tailored to the needs of the investor.

Equity-Index Linked Notes

In July of 2002, Bank of America Corporation raised capital by issuing a class of unsecured senior debt securities called S&P 500 Return Linked Notes. These particular instruments are an example of a wider class of structured notes known as **variable principal redemption (VPR)** securities because the amount of the bond's principal that is refunded to the investor at maturity is not fixed but instead depends on the returns to an equity index. These particular VPR bonds mature on July 2, 2007, and—as their name implies—have their redemption amount tied to movements in the S&P 500 index between the origination and maturity dates. Other VPR notes that have traded in the market in recent years have tied the principal redemption to a wide variety of global stock indexes, including the Dow Jones Industrial Average, the Russell 1000, the FT-SE 100, and the Nikkei 225.

Bank of America designed this VPR note so that it would pay no coupons prior to maturity. Further, at maturity the bondholder receives the original issue price (stated here as 100 percent of minimum face value) plus a "supplemental redemption amount," the value of which depends on the level at which the S&P 500 index settles relative to a predetermined initial level. Given that this supplemental amount cannot be less than zero, the total payout to the investor at maturity can be written:

$$100 + \max\left[0, \left\{100 \times \left(\frac{\text{Final SPX Value} - \text{Initial SPX Value}}{\text{Initial SPX Value}}\right) \times 1.22\right\}\right]$$

where the initial S&P 500 (i.e., SPX) index value was specified as 973.53. The factor 1.22 indicates that the investor actually receives 122% of the return to the SPX over the five-year period, provided that return is positive.

From the preceding description, recognize that the VPR structure combines a five-year, zero-coupon bond with a SPX index call option, both of which were issued by Bank of America. Thus, the structured note investor essentially owns a "portfolio" that is (1) long in a bond and (2) long in an index call option position. This particular security might have been designed for those investors who wanted to participate in the equity market but, for regulatory or taxation reasons, were not permitted to do so directly. For example, the manager of a fixed-income mutual fund might be able to enhance her return performance by purchasing this bond and then hoping for an appreciating stock market. Notice that the use of the call option in this design makes it fairly easy for Bank of America to market to its institutional customers in that it is a no-lose proposition; the worst-case scenario for the investor is that she simply gets her money back without interest in five years. (Of course, the customer does carry the bank's credit risk for this period.) Thus, unlike the dual currency bond where the investor could either gain or lose from changing exchange rates, at origination this VPR issue had no downside exposure to stock price declines.

The call option embedded in this structure is actually a partial position. To see this, we can rewrite the option portion of the note's redemption value as:

$$\max\left[0, \left\{100 \times 1.22 \times \left(\frac{\text{Final SPX} - 973.53}{973.53}\right)\right\}\right]$$
$$= \max\left[0, \left\{\left(\frac{122}{973.53}\right)(\text{Final SPX} - 973.53)\right\}\right]$$

or

$$(0.1253)\{\max[0, (\text{Final SPX} - 973.53)]\}$$

Thus, given that a regular index option would have a terminal payoff of max [0, Final SPX − X], where X is the exercise price, the derivative in the VPR represents 12.53 percent of this amount. The terminal payoffs to the VPR embedded option are shown in Exhibit 69-17, along with those to a regular index call option for several potential July 2007 levels of the S&P 500 index. Notice that although both the VPR and regular options become in the money at the same point (i.e., 973.53), only the latter produces a dollar-for-dollar payoff with increasing values of the index beyond this level. The payoff to the call feature in the structured note still rises for any S&P 500 level above 973.53, but gains only $0.1253 for every one point gained by the index.

Exhibit 69-18 provides a different way to visualize the VPR investment structure. In particular, notice that for the initial (i.e., July 2002) payment of $100, the investor has purchased the equivalent of a five-year zero-coupon bond maturing in July 2007 plus a partial call option on the index on the S&P 500 index. Thus, the $100 initial payment can be split into the value of the zero-coupon bond—which is simply $100 discounted to the present at Bank of America's five-year bond yield—and the remainder, which must be the value of the embedded SPX call option at the origination date. This way of viewing the instrument also makes valuing the VPR at any point in its life a more transparent process. That is, it must always be the case that the value of the entire structure is just the value of the bond portion plus the value of the option component; any price synergy for the packaging will be a market-driven phenomenon.

EXHIBIT 69-17	Terminal Payoffs to VPR Embedded Call Option and Regular Index Call Option (X = 973.53)	
Final SPX Value	**Regular Index Call**	**VPR Call**
875	0.00	0.00
900	0.00	0.00
925	0.00	0.00
950	0.00	0.00
975	1.47	0.18
1000	26.47	3.32
1025	51.47	6.45
1050	76.47	9.58
1075	101.47	12.72
1100	126.47	15.85
1125	151.47	18.98
1150	176.47	22.12
1175	201.47	25.25
1200	226.47	28.38
1225	251.47	31.51
1250	276.47	34.65
1275	301.47	37.78
1300	326.47	40.91
1325	351.47	44.05
1350	376.47	47.18
1375	401.47	50.31
1400	426.47	53.45

To see how this might work, consider that on January 3, 2005, the closing level for the S&P 500 was 1,202.08. Further, the semiannually compounded yield of a zero-coupon (i.e., "stripped") Treasury bond on this date was 3.17 percent, while a Bank of America bond maturing at about the same time as the VPR issue carried a yield of 3.65 percent. (This 48-basis-point credit spread was appropriate for Bank of America's credit rating of Aa2 and AA by Moody's and Standard & Poor's, respectively.) Given the remaining time to maturity (i.e., two years and six months, or five half-years), the bond portion of the VPR issue should be worth:

$$\text{VPR Bond Value} = \frac{100}{\left(1 + \dfrac{.0365}{2}\right)^5} = \$91.354.$$

The value of a regular call option on a stock index can be calculated with the dividend yield-adjusted version of the Black-Scholes model. To perform this computation, three additional inputs are needed. First, the S&P 500 dividend yield on January 3, 2005, was 1.80 percent. Second, the continuously compounded

EXHIBIT 69-18   **Illustrating the VPR Transaction**

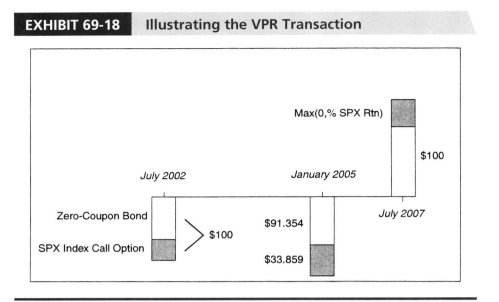

equivalent of the quoted risk-free rate is 3.15 percent.[1] Finally, the volatility of SPX index returns over the time to VPR issue's maturity is assumed to be 15.54 percent, a level approximated from the prevailing implied volatilities for traded index options on that date.

The value of an index call option with an exercise price of 973.53 can now be generated by the **Black-Scholes formula** using the following inputs: $S = 1,202.08$, $X = 973.53$, $T = 2.50$, $RFR = 0.0315$, $D = 0.018$, and $\sigma = 0.1554$. Under these conditions we have:

$$d_1 = [ln(1202.08e^{-(.018)2.50}/973.53) + (.0315 + 0.5(.1554)^2)(2.50)]$$
$$\div (.1554[2.50]^{1/2}) = 1.1185$$

and

$$d_2 = 1.1185 - .1554[2.50]^{1/2} = 0.8728$$

so that $N(d_1) = 0.8682$ and $N(d_2) = 0.8086$. Thus the index call's Black-Scholes value is:

$$C_0 = (1202.08)(e^{-(.018)2.50})(0.8682) - (973.53)(e^{-(.0315)2.50})(0.8086) = 270.221$$

The value of the embedded VPR call is then established by multiplying 270.221 by 0.1253, which leaves a value of $33.859. Therefore, as shown in Exhibit 69-18, on this particular date the VPR issue was valued at $125.213 (= 91.354 + 33.859). Finally, notice that since the January 3, 2005, index value (i.e., 1,202.08) was already substantially greater than the initial (i.e., exercise) level, the VPR call feature is deep in the money and the value of the embedded option can be further broken down into $28.637 [= (.1253)(1202.08 − 973.53)] of intrinsic value and $5.222 (= 33.859 − 28.637) of **time premium**.

---

[1] This value can be established by solving for r in the following equation:
$$e^r = (1 + (.0317/2))^2$$
or
$$r = ln[(1 + (.0317/2))^2] = 0.0315$$

Commodity-Linked Bull and Bear Bonds

Besides linking their payoffs to currency or equity indexes, fixed-income securities can be designed to give an investor exposure to commodity price movements as well. The commodities involved in these structures are seldom exchanged but instead represented in the form of "cash settlement only" derivatives. Thus, virtually no theoretical limit exists to the number of different underlying assets that can be embedded into a bond issue. However, recall that innovation in the structured note market is dictated by investor demands, which to date have tended to concentrate on either oil or precious metals. As in the previous examples, the primary attractions to the investor of gaining the desired exposure through the purchase of structured notes are their convenience and their ability to avoid restrictions on taking commodity positions directly.

A particularly interesting form of the commodity-linked bond is the so-called bull-and-bear note. This structure gets its name from a bond that is issued in two portions: a bull tranche, whose principal redemption amount increases directly with the price of the designated commodity; and a bear tranche, whose principal refunding declines with increasing commodity prices. One of the first issues of this kind occurred in October 1986 when the Kingdom of Denmark raised $120 million in two separate $60 million tranches, each having a different payoff structure depending on the movement of an index of gold prices.[2] Both of these gold-linked note tranches had a seven-year maturity, paid an annual coupon of 3 percent, and were issued at a price of 100.125 percent of par value. The principal redemptions for each $1,000 of face value for the two tranches were:

Bull Redemption: $1,000 × [1.158 × (Index at Redemption ÷ Initial Index)]

and

Bear Redemption: $1,000 × {2.78 − [1.158 × (Index at Redemption ÷ Initial Index)]}

Finally, for both tranches, maximum and minimum redemption levels of $2,280 and $500, respectively, were set.

Exhibit 69-19 shows the redemption amount that the Kingdom of Denmark is obligated to pay on each tranche for a series of gold index levels relative to the initial level, which was set at 426.50. The final column of this display shows what the average redemption value is when the two tranches are considered together. Notice that this average amount does not vary—that is, *the issuer has no net exposure to gold price movements.* Unlike the dual currency bond example considered earlier, which required the issuer to adopt an additional derivative position to offset the instrument's inherent FX exposure, the virtue of this two-tranche approach is that the commodity exposure is neutralized internally. That is, the Kingdom of Denmark is effectively both long and short gold in equal amounts across the bear and bull segments, respectively. An immediate consequence of this is that they have a fixed funding cost for the full $120 million issue, calculated by solving:

$$1,001.25 = \sum_{t=1}^{7} \frac{30}{(1 + y)^t} + \frac{1,390}{(1 + y)^7}$$

or $y = 7.42$ percent. At the time this deal was launched, a regular seven-year, par-value debt issue would have required a yield of about 8 percent, a fact that

---

[2] Additional details of this bull-and-bear structure are explained in Walmsley (1998), who also provides descriptions of an exhaustive set of such deals. It is recommended reading for anyone wishing to learn more about the development of these innovative products.

EXHIBIT 69-19	Redemption Values for the Bull-and-Bear Gold-Linked Note (in U.S. Dollars)		
Terminal Gold Index	Bull Tranche	Bear Tranche	Average
100	500	2,280	1,390
150	500	2,280	1,390
200	543	2,237	1,390
250	679	2,101	1,390
300	815	1,965	1,390
350	950	1,830	1,390
400	1,086	1,694	1,390
450	1,222	1,558	1,390
500	1,358	1,422	1,390
550	1,493	1,287	1,390
600	1,629	1,151	1,390
650	1,765	1,015	1,390
700	1,901	879	1,390
750	2,036	744	1,390
800	2,172	608	1,390
850	2,280	500	1,390
900	2,280	500	1,390

underscores the Kingdom of Denmark's incentive to create this structure in the first place.

The attraction for the investors, of course, is the ability to purchase a fixed-income security that also allows for participation in gold price movements. In exchange for accepting a lower-than-market coupon, buyers of the bull (bear) tranche will receive a redemption value that exceeds their purchase price if the gold index increases (declines). Exhibit 69-20, which shows the redemption values for the two tranches in a graphical form, suggests that the commodity derivatives embedded in this transaction are not simple forward or option positions. Rather, the minimum and maximum principal payoffs effectively convert the gold exposure into a call option money spread—a bull spread for the bull tranche, a bear for the bear. The investors, who undoubtedly will be different people for the two positions, pay for this spread position through a reduction in their average yield to maturity relative to the regular bond.

Swap-Linked Notes

As we have seen, interest rate swaps are efficient mechanisms for transforming the cash flows of existing debt issues. They also are quite useful in the new-issue market when the desired rate exposures of the borrower and lender do not coincide naturally. Imagine, for example, that Company LMN wishes to raise $50 million by issuing a fixed-rate note with semiannual coupon payments over a three-year period. Having launched a similar issue in the capital markets recently, however, LMN finds that little appetite exists for another one of its fixed-rate notes. On the other hand, a large institutional investor is willing to

EXHIBIT 69-20	Redemption Values for the Bull-And-Bear Gold-Linked Note

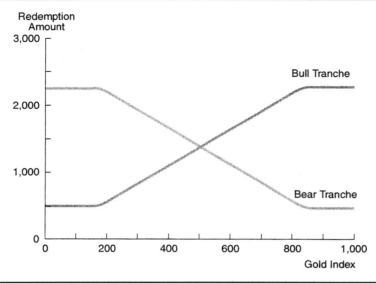

accept LMN's credit risk on a privately placed loan, providing that the deal can be structured to its satisfaction. In particular, the fund manager for this investment company thinks that interest rates are going to decline substantially over the next few years and wants to design the loan contract to take advantage of that possibility. Accordingly, she wants the semiannual coupon on the note to move inversely with the level of some variable interest rate index, such as LIBOR. This sort of arrangement is known as a *reverse floating-rate* contract; the coupon rate changes as the general level of interest rates moves but in the opposite direction.

Suppose the specific structure that LMN and the investor agree on resets the coupon on a semiannual basis at a level equal to 12 percent minus LIBOR. Thus, if six-month LIBOR on a particular settlement date is 7.5 percent, the coupon payment will be 4.5 percent ($\times$ .5 $\times$ $50,000,000). Conversely, a LIBOR of only 3.75 percent would generate a coupon of 8.25 percent. In this way, the investor gains the desired benefit from falling rates and does so in a convenient form that entails less credit risk than if it had transformed a regular bond issue with a derivative on its own. In addition, the reverse floater will actually benefit more from a rate decline than would a fixed-rate note of identical maturity. Specifically, while the price of a fixed-rate bond paying constant coupons will appreciate when yields fall, the reverse floater will increase the investor's periodic cash flow as well.

Unfortunately, although this design satisfies the investor's requirements, it does not do the same for the issuer. This discrepancy can be easily remedied, though, by combining Company LMN's debt position with a swap in which it receives the fixed rate and pays LIBOR. This is illustrated in Exhibit 69-21, assuming a three-year fixed swap rate of 6.5 percent against six-month LIBOR. One helpful way to see how a swap must be written to fix the coupon on this reverse rate structure is to notice that paying a coupon of 12 percent minus LIBOR is equivalent to paying a coupon of 12 percent and receiving one of LIBOR. Thus, to neutralize LMN's floating-rate exposure, it must pay out LIBOR on the swap.

Exhibit 69-21 also shows that the net synthetic fixed-rate funding cost to Company LMN is 5.5 percent (assuming the swap fixed rate has been converted to an actual/360 basis). This will only be true, however, whenever LIBOR does not exceed 12 percent. If LIBOR is greater than 12 percent, the benefit from paying

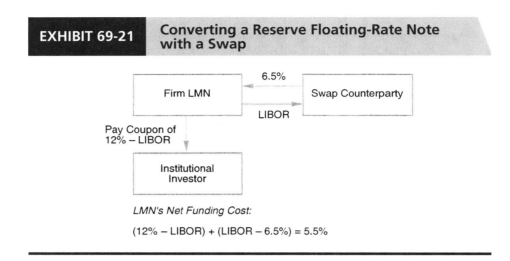

EXHIBIT 69-21   Converting a Reserve Floating-Rate Note with a Swap

LMN's Net Funding Cost:

(12% − LIBOR) + (LIBOR − 6.5%) = 5.5%

lower coupons to the investor will stop—the coupon rate can never go negative—but LMN will continue having to make the higher net settlement payment on the swap, which raises the effective borrowing cost above 5.5 percent. Consequently, because there is an implicit cap on LIBOR built into the reverse floating-rate loan, Company LMN will need to offset this by purchasing an actual cap agreement with an exercise rate of 12 percent and a notional principal of $50 million. This option will not be expensive because it is quite far out of the money but it will not be free, which means the net funding cost will be somewhat greater than 5.5 percent.

Earlier in the reading, we saw that an interest rate swap can be interpreted as a pair of capital market transactions. In this particular case, a "receive 6.5 percent fixed, pay LIBOR" swap can be viewed as a portfolio long in a fixed-rate note paying 6.5 percent and short in a LIBOR-based floating-rate note. Recalling that "+" represents a long position and "−" represents a short position, the synthetic fixed-rate issue from Company LMN's perspective can be written as follows:

$$
\begin{aligned}
-(\text{Synthetic Fixed Rate Bond at } 5.5\%) = {} & -(\text{Reverse Floater at } 12\% - \text{LIBOR}) \\
& + (\text{Receive } 6.5\%, \text{Pay LIBOR Swap}) \\
& + (\text{Cap at } 12\% \text{ Exercise Rate}) \\
= {} & -(\text{Reverse Floater at } 12\% - \text{LIBOR}) \\
& - (\text{FRN at LIBOR}) + (\text{Fixed Rate} \\
& \quad \text{Bond at } 6.5\%) \\
& + (\text{Cap at } 12\% \text{ Exercise Rate})
\end{aligned}
$$

As in the previous examples, this sort of structured solution would only make sense to the issuer if it could ultimately obtain funding cost that was lower than a direct fixed-rate loan. The biggest reason for this is that while a direct fixed-rate loan would carry no credit risk for Company LMN, the structured loan would because of the swap and cap positions. Thus, the swap-based borrowing is never as good as a direct approach and, therefore, requires a lower cost to entice the issuer.

As a final extension of this concept, consider what would have happened if the institutional investor decided to take an even more aggressive view of falling interest rates and requested that the coupon reset the formula to 18.4 percent minus (2 × LIBOR). Such a design is called a *leveraged* reverse floating-rate note, with the leverage coming from the fact that the coupon increases twice as fast as the decline in yields. Exhibit 69-22 indicates that to convert this to a fixed-rate issue, Company LMN would have to enter into two $50 million receive-fixed swaps (or, more practically, one contract with a notional principal of $100 million). As before, to fix its funding cost completely, it also would have to purchase two

EXHIBIT 69-22	Converting a Leveraged Reserve Floater with Two Swaps

Firm LMN

2 x 6.5% →

2 x LIBOR ←

Swap Counterparty

Pay Coupon of
18.4% – (2 x LIBOR) ↓

Institutional
Investor

LMN's Net Funding Cost:

[18.4% – (2 x LIBOR)] + ([2 x LIBOR) – (2 x 6.5%)] = 5.4%

$50 million cap agreements with a cap rate of 9.2 percent (= 18.4 percent ÷ 2). This converted position, which would have a net funding cost of 5.4 percent before factoring in the cost of the caps, can be represented as

$$
\begin{aligned}
-(\text{Synthetic Fixed-Rate Bond at } 5.4\%) &= -(\text{Reverse Floater at } 18.4\% \\
&\quad - 2 \times \text{LIBOR}) \\
&\quad + (2 \text{ Receive } 6.5\%, \text{Pay LIBOR Swaps}) \\
&\quad + (2 \text{ Caps at } 9.2\% \text{ Exercise Rate}) \\
&= -(\text{Reverse Floater at } 18.4\% \\
&\quad - 2 \times \text{LIBOR}) \\
&\quad - (2 \text{ FRNs at LIBOR}) + (2 \text{ Fixed-Rate} \\
&\quad \text{Bonds at } 6.5\%) \\
&\quad + (2 \text{ Caps at } 9.2\% \text{ Exercise Rate})
\end{aligned}
$$

As Brown and Smith (1995) explain, although the net coupon on this swapped leveraged structure is lower than on the swapped unleveraged reverse floater, the cost of the required options will be more than twice as expensive since two contracts must be purchased at a lower cap rate.

VALUING FLEXIBILITY: AN INTRODUCTION TO REAL OPTIONS

6

OPTIONAL SEGMENT
BEGINS

Recently, energy companies have begun to open gas-fired power plants that generate electricity at an expense 50 percent to 70 percent greater than those of other, more cost-effective plants. Coy (1999) notes that these new, "inefficient" plants are intended to operate only when the price of electricity is high enough to justify the cost. The energy firms hope to make a profit on the new plants because power prices have become increasingly volatile and the new plants—although they cost more to run—are much less costly to fire up and shut down on short notice than traditional plants. Although these "peaking" plants are also cheaper to build, their main attraction lies in their *flexibility:* they allow energy companies to supply more electricity when prices are high and to cease production almost immediately when electricity prices have dropped.

How should investors value companies that possess this sort of operational flexibility? Conventional net present value calculations ignore the benefits of flexibility and may therefore undervalue projects that allow companies to react rapidly to changing circumstances. For example, the fact that these new power plants are expected to run only part of the year is easily incorporated into a standard value calculation. However, predicting the future cash flows based on factors like expected running time, expected electricity prices, or expected production costs will fail to capture the most valuable feature of these plants: namely, that they will only be generating electricity when the price of a megawatt-hour of electricity exceeds the cost of producing it. This is in contrast to conventional plants that produce electricity more cheaply overall but are sometimes forced to sell below-cost power because shutting down and then restarting the facility would be prohibitively expensive.

As we have seen earlier, options give their holders the right, but not the obligation, to trade an asset at a predetermined exercise price by a prespecified future date. So far, the derivative contracts we have discussed are exchanged in financial markets and the asset underlying the derivative contract is often another financial instrument (such as a share of common stock, a government bond, or a futures contract). However, options are also embedded in real assets owned by firms; these are known as **real options**. A pharmaceutical company, for instance, owns valuable options in the form of its collection of drug patents. The firm has the right, but not the obligation, to develop marketable drugs based on its patents and will do so if the value of those drugs (in terms of discounted present value) exceeds the cost of development and regulatory approval. In the language of derivative contracting, these costs can be considered as the strike price for the development option. For the energy example, the peaking plant in effect gives the firm the right but not the obligation to buy Y megawatt-hours of electricity at an exercise price X, where Y is the total capacity of the plant and X is the generating cost per megawatt-hour.

Although real options have existed ever since humans first walked the earth—for instance, storing food and other necessities gave people a valuable option, allowing them to consume more (or less) than the amount produced in a given time period—a number of recent changes have made understanding them more important than ever. These factors include (1) the *pace of technological innovation*, which has made a company's long-term planning more difficult to assess for managers and investors alike; (2) *deregulation and privatization*, which have created new incentives for firms to analyze and use real options in order to gain a competitive advantage; and (3) *advances in derivatives pricing theory* and *decreases in the computing costs*, making it easier to interpret and value real options, which are often quite complex in practice.

Company Valuation with Real Options

To highlight the advantages of the real options derivative-based approach over traditional company valuation methods, we present the case of the fictional GoldFlex Corporation.[3] One of GoldFlex's assets is a lease on a gold mine, which expires in exactly one year from now (i.e, Year 1). GoldFlex geologists estimate that the mine—which is currently idle—holds 100,000 Troy ounces of gold and that extraction costs are $260/ounce. The current (i.e, Year 0) spot price of an ounce of gold is $264.40, while the Year 1 forward contract price equals $268.40. For simplicity, we will assume that all the gold is extracted at the end of the year. To be able to mine gold in a year, the company must spend $1,000,000 today to restore the mining facilities to working order. Suppose further that the spot price of gold in one year will be either $290 or $240 and that the one-year risk-free rate is 5 percent. How should an investor establish the value of GoldFlex's mining lease?

---

[3] This example follows a greatly simplified approach based on the valuation method first introduced by Brennan and Schwartz (1985).

To see the issues, first recognize that GoldFlex could sell all of its gold at the current forward price. Since the resulting sales proceeds a year from now would then be known, assuming that extraction costs and the quantity of gold are known with certainty, the appropriate discount rate is the one-year T-bill (i.e., risk-free) yield. Thus, the value of the mine calculated using a traditional net present value approach would be

$$NPV = \{[(268.40 - 260) \times 100,000] \div 1.05\} - 1,000,000 = -\$200,000$$

Of course, this calculation suggests that the lease has no value because opening the mine would be a money-losing project. However, the traditional approach ignores the value of flexibility: if gold prices decline in the future, management can shut down production and leave the gold in the ground. Once we consider the possibility of shutting down, the cash flows from the mine can be viewed in a different and more realistic manner.

The main premise behind the derivatives-based approach to valuing a real asset with embedded timing options (such as the mine) is that it is possible for an investor to assemble a portfolio of financial securities that will have the same pattern of future cash flows with the same level of risk. Specifically, such an investor could value the potential future cash flows by creating a hypothetical portfolio consisting of risk-free, one-year T-bills and gold forward contracts that would exactly mimic the mining operation. This *replicating portfolio* will have the same possible cash flows as the gold mine, so its value in an **efficient capital market** should also be the same. For example, we can use the two-state framework to view the valuation question as follows:

TODAY (YEAR 0)		IN ONE YEAR (YEAR 1)	
	Gold Price		Cash Flow
	$290		$3,000,000
Spend $1 Million to Reopen Mine?			[= (290 − 260) × 100,000]
	$240		$0 (No Production)

How many forward contracts are necessary to build a security position that duplicates these cash flows? Notice that the other asset involved in this process is risk free, so all the variation in the cash flows of the replicating portfolio must come from the payoff to the forward contract. With the assumed Year 1 gold price forecasts, a long position in a one-year gold forward contract will leave the investor with either a profit of $21.60 (= 290 − 268.40) or a loss of −$28.40 (= 240 − 268.40) per ounce. The difference between these two payoffs equals $50 [= $21.6 − (−$28.4)], while the difference between the two possible cash flows from the mine is $3,000,000. Therefore, the number of forward contracts necessary to form a replicating portfolio (where each contract stipulates the delivery of one ounce of gold) *is*

$$(3,000,000) \div (50) = 60,000$$

To find the amount of the T-bill investment needed in the replicating portfolio, notice that if the price of gold drops to $240 in one year, the holder of 60,000 forward contracts will lose $1,704,000 (= 28.4 × 60,000), while the cash flow from the mine would be zero. The payoff from the risk-free investment must make up for the difference, so the amount that must be invested in one-year T-bills to form a "synthetic mine" is

$$1,704,000 \div 1.05 = \$1,622,857$$

Exhibit 69-23 summarizes the process of creating this replicating portfolio.

Given that this portfolio of securities has, by design, the same future cash flows as the mine with the same level of volatility, in an efficient capital market the replicating portfolio and the mine should have the same present value. This can be expressed as

(Value of Gold Forward Position) + (Value of T-bill Position)
= (Value of Mine Lease)

Since the present value of an "at-market" forward contract is zero, the replicating portfolio (and therefore the lease on the mine) is worth \$1,622,857, which

---

EXHIBIT 69-23	Creating a "Real Options" Replicating Portfolio

Step 1: Design a portfolio containing F forward contracts and T invested in a risk-free security that has the same future payoffs as the mine:

"Up" State (Gold Price = \$290): $[F \times (290 - 268.4)]$
                                     $+ [(1.05) \times (T)] = \$3,000,000$
"Down" State (Gold Price = \$240): $[F \times (240 - 268.4)]$
                                     $+ [(1.05) \times (T)] = \$0$

Step 2: Solve for F and T simultaneously:
a. Rewrite the "down" state cash flow equation:

$$T = F \times [(-28.4) \div (-1.05)] = F \times [(28.4) \div (1.05)]$$

b. Insert the "down" state T value into the "up" state cash flow equation:

$$[F \times (21.6)] + [(1.05) \times F \times [(28.4) \div (1.05)]] = 50 \times F = 3,000,000$$

c. Solve for F:

$$F = (3,000,000) \div 50 = 60,000$$

d. Solve for T from 2(a):

$$T = (60,000) \times [(28.4) \div (1.05)] = \$1,622,857$$

(*Note:* This is the "real options" value of the mine lease cash flows, before netting out the initial reopening expense.)

Step 3: Confirm the equality of replicating portfolio and mine future cash flows:

"Up" State: $[(60,000) \times (21.6)] + (1.05)(1,622,857) = \$3,000,000$
"Down" State: $[(60,000) \times (-28.4)] + (1.05)(1,622,857) = 0$

is greater than the $1,000,000 required to restore the facilities. Investors using traditional discounted cash flow analysis will consider the lease worthless and ignore an important asset when valuing GoldFlex. Also, recognize that increased volatility in future gold prices will have no effect on the traditional valuation estimate, while it would increase the value of the lease when using the real options methodology since greater uncertainty generally leads to higher option values.

Of course, in practice, real options are much more complex than this example. For instance, gold production typically takes place steadily during the year, so the analysis may require either a continuous-time (e.g., Black-Scholes) option valuation model or an expansion of the prior binomial tree approach to include a large number of subintervals. Note also that extraction costs and the exact amount of the gold deposits are rarely known with certainty. The problem of having uncertain extraction costs can be solved by realizing that the lease on the mine in effect becomes an *exchange option*, a problem that was first considered by Margrabe (1978). In this context, the leaseholder effectively has an option to exchange the gold in the mine for the extraction costs (e.g., the cost of the required equipment, material and manpower).[4]

THE INTERNET

Investments Online

Otherwise straightforward financial instruments (e.g., bonds) can become quite complex when they have swap agreements attached or when they contain embedded options, such as convertible and call features or warrants. Several Web sites can help students and investors learn more about these advanced applications of derivatives:

www.isda.org The Web site of the **International Swaps and Derivatives Association**, which is the leading trade organization representing over-the-counter derivative market makers. Among other things, ISDA is committed to advancing the understanding and treatment of derivatives and risk management from public policy and regulatory capital perspectives. Their Web site contains a wealth of information about the nature and use of swap contracts.

www.numa.com This is the Web site of Numa Financial Systems. It provides access to a substantial amount of educational and strategic information concerning derivative securities. Of particular note is the availability of financial calculators for computing the value of options, multiple options, warrants, and convertible bonds.

www.goldmansachs.com A page on the Goldman Sachs Web site that features research papers on quantitative strategies by Goldman analysts, many of which involve derivative applications.

www.calamos.com Calamos Investments specializes in research, investment, and management of convertible securities. It offers a variety of mutual funds, as well. News, analysis, and market updates are available here.

www.dir.co.jp/InfoManage/datarsc.html The site of the Daiwa Convertible Bond Index (DCBI) includes data and information on how the index is constructed.

www.optionscentral.com The Options Clearing Corporation is the issuer and guarantor of all exchange-traded options contracts in the United States. Its home page allows users to download free software. It features a strategies for options trading and has a number of resource links to exchanges that trade options.

www.amex.com A link on the Web site of the American Stock Exchange contains details of several structured products, such as the VPR equity-index-linked notes.

---

[4] We would like to thank Professor Andras Marosi for his contributions to this section.

SUMMARY

▶ The genius of modern financial markets is that they continuously provide new products and strategies to meet the constantly changing needs of anyone willing to pay the required price. In this chapter, we explore several ways in which derivatives can aid in that development process. In particular, we see that innovation sometimes takes the form of creating a new set of instruments, such as interest rate swaps, while at other times it involves packaging existing securities in a creative way. Structured notes, which combine bonds with a derivative position based on a different sort of underlying asset, are a good example of this latter approach. It is important to keep in mind that the ultimate purpose of this **financial engineering** is to help borrowers and lenders manage one of four types of potential exposures: interest rate, currency, equity, or commodity price risk.

▶ We began our discussion with an examination of the market for OTC interest rate agreements. Although forward rate agreements are the most basic product in this category, interest rate swaps are the most popular. Swap contracts can be interpreted in three unique ways: as a series of FRAs, as a portfolio of bond positions, or as a zero-cost collar, which consists of a pair of cap and floor agreements. We then extended the plain vanilla swap concept to include contracts designed to handle other exposures, such as currency and equity swaps. Since all of these agreements are traded off of the organized exchanges, they are extremely flexible in the terms available— the primary appeal to investors and issuers.

▶ We conclude with an analysis of several ways in which derivatives can be embedded into other securities to create customized payoff distributions. Because these hybrid structures often are designed to the specific needs of a particular investor, the investor must "pay up" for the customization. Warrants, which are call options on common stock issued directly by the company itself, can be attached to a debt issue to offer investors the upside potential of equity with the safety of a bond. Further, bonds and preferred stock issues can be set up to allow for conversion into common stock at the investor's option. In both cases, the issuing firm will likely end up with a lower front-end funding cost because of the options it has implicitly sold. Finally, a class of instruments known as structured notes carries this concept even further by embedding into bonds derivatives that often are based on exposures that may not appear on the issuer's balance sheet. These instruments epitomize how much value derivatives can add when they are used properly, and are indicative of the ways in which investors are likely to see them appear in the market for years to come. Finally, we discuss how the derivative features embedded in physical assets (i.e., real options) can be used by investors to value companies.

PORTFOLIO MANAGEMENT

STUDY SESSION

Study Session 18 Capital Market Theory and the Portfolio Management Process

TOPIC LEVEL LEARNING OUTCOME

The candidate should be able to estimate the return and determine the risk of various securities, and apply the basic principles of the portfolio management process to specific scenarios.

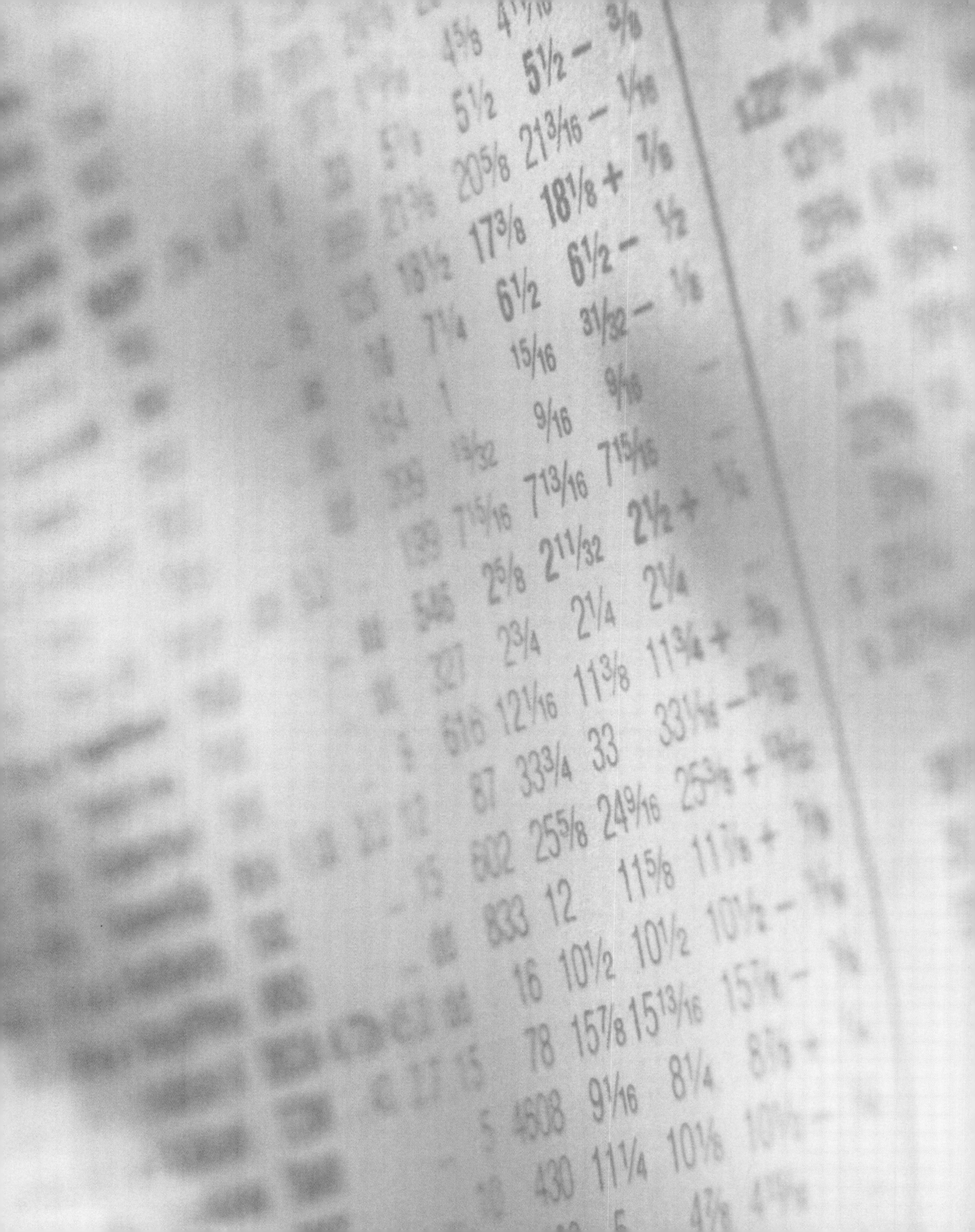

STUDY SESSION 18
CAPITAL MARKET THEORY AND THE PORTFOLIO MANAGEMENT PROCESS

READING ASSIGNMENTS

The first reading in this study session reintroduces the capital asset pricing model—a foundation of knowledge for this study session and one of the most important concepts in modern financial economics, providing a relationship between the expected risk and expected return of an asset. The second reading introduces a simplified approach to managing portfolio risk, differentiating between systematic and security-specific risk. The third reading illustrates a generalized version of some of the concepts introduced in the first two readings, using a multifactor approach to evaluate risk and return expectations. The fourth and fifth readings link the portfolio process to valuation.

LEARNING OUTCOMES

Reading 70: The Capital Asset Pricing Model
The candidate should be able to:

a. discuss the assumptions of the capital market theory, explain how the presence of a risk-free asset changes the portfolio possibilities relative to the Markowitz efficient frontier, and describe the market portfolio and the role it plays in the formation of the capital market line (CML);

b. discuss the security market line (SML) and how it differs from the CML, calculate the beta of a risky asset, and calculate and interpret, based on the SML, the expected return for an asset; determine whether the asset is undervalued, overvalued, or properly valued; and outline the appropriate trading strategy;

c. evaluate the effect on the SML of relaxing each of its main underlying assumptions.

Reading 71: Index Models

The candidate should be able to:

a. discuss how the Index Model can help simplify the Capital Asset Pricing Model framework and procedure developed in the prior reading;

b. distinguish between systematic and unsystematic risk, and discuss why the expected risk is a function of the number and characteristics of assets in the investment portfolio;

c. explain the problems when estimating individual asset betas and portfolio betas over time, and discuss systematic ways to help predict betas.

Reading 72: Arbitrage Pricing Theory and Multifactor Models of Risk and Return

The candidate should be able to:

a. compare and contrast the assumptions of the arbitrage pricing theory (APT) to the assumptions of the CAPM and the Index Model;

b. explain how the risk factors in a multifactor model are chosen, and describe the macroeconomic and microeconomic factors that have been used.

Reading 73: The Theory of Active Portfolio Management

The candidate should be able to:

a. explain how the theory of active portfolio management can be reconciled with the notion that markets are at equilibrium;

b. discuss the steps and the approach of the Treynor-Black model for security selection;

c. describe how the composition of the active portfolio changes when short positions are prohibited and when there are imperfect forecasts of alpha values.

Note:
Candidates are not responsible, within Reading 73, for deriving or memorizing the formulas introduced in sections 4–6.

Reading 74: The Portfolio Management Process and the Investment Policy Statement

The candidate should be able to:

a. explain the importance of the portfolio perspective;

b. describe the steps of the portfolio management process and the components of those steps;

c. define investment objectives and constraints and explain and distinguish among the types of investment objectives and constraints;

d. discuss the role of the investment policy statement in the portfolio management process and explain the elements of an investment policy statement;

e. explain how capital market expectations and the investment policy statement help influence the strategic asset allocation decision and discuss how the investment time horizon may influence investors' ability to take risk, and help modify investors' strategic asset allocation;

f. contrast the types of investment time horizons, determine the time horizon for a particular investor, and evaluate the effects of this time horizon on portfolio choice;

g. justify ethical conduct as a requirement for managing investment portfolios.

THE CAPITAL ASSET PRICING MODEL
by Zvi Bodie, Alex Kane, and Alan J. Marcus

LEARNING OUTCOMES

The candidate should be able to:

a. discuss the assumptions of the capital market theory, explain how the presence of a risk-free asset changes the portfolio possibilities relative to the Markowitz efficient frontier, and describe the market portfolio and the role it plays in the formation of the capital market line (CML);

b. discuss the security market line (SML) and how it differs from the CML, calculate the beta of a risky asset, and calculate and interpret, based on the SML, the expected return for an asset; determine whether the asset is undervalued, overvalued, or properly valued; and outline the appropriate trading strategy;

c. evaluate the effect on the SML of relaxing each of its main underlying assumptions.

THE CAPITAL ASSET PRICING MODEL

1

The capital asset pricing model is a set of predictions concerning equilibrium expected returns on risky assets. Harry Markowitz laid down the foundation of modern portfolio management in 1952. The CAPM was developed 12 years later in articles by William Sharpe,[1] John Lintner,[2] and Jan Mossin.[3] The time for this gestation indicates that the leap from Markowitz's portfolio selection model to the CAPM is not trivial.

We will approach the CAPM by posing the question "what if," where the "if" part refers to a simplified world. Positing an admittedly unrealistic world allows a

---

[1] William Sharpe, "Capital Asset Prices: A Theory of Market Equilibrium," *Journal of Finance,* September 1964.

[2] John Lintner, "The Valuation of Risk Assets and the Selection of Risky Investments in Stock Portfolios and Capital Budgets," *Review of Economics and Statistics,* February 1965.

[3] Jan Mossin, "Equilibrium in a Capital Asset Market," *Econometrica,* October 1966.

relatively easy leap to the "then" part. Once we accomplish this, we can add complexity to the hypothesized environment one step at a time and see how the conclusions must be amended. This process allows us to derive a reasonably realistic and comprehensible model.

We summarize the simplifying assumptions that lead to the basic version of the CAPM in the following list. The thrust of these assumptions is that we try to ensure that individuals are as alike as possible, with the notable exceptions of initial wealth and risk aversion. We will see that conformity of investor behavior vastly simplifies our analysis.

1. There are many investors, each with an endowment (wealth) that is small compared to the total endowment of all investors. Investors are price-takers, in that they act as though security prices are unaffected by their own trades. This is the usual perfect competition assumption of microeconomics.

2. All investors plan for one identical holding period. This behavior is myopic (shortsighted) in that it ignores everything that might happen after the end of the single-period horizon. Myopic behavior is, in general, suboptimal.

3. Investments are limited to a universe of publicly traded financial assets, such as stocks and bonds, and to risk-free borrowing or lending arrangements. This assumption rules out investment in nontraded assets such as education (human capital), private enterprises, and governmentally funded assets such as town halls and international airports. It is assumed also that investors may borrow or lend any amount at a fixed, risk-free rate.

4. Investors pay no taxes on returns and no transaction costs (commissions and service charges) on trades in securities. In reality, of course, we know that investors are in different tax brackets and that this may govern the type of assets in which they invest. For example, tax implications may differ depending on whether the income is from interest, dividends, or capital gains. Furthermore, actual trading is costly, and commissions and fees depend on the size of the trade and the good standing of the individual investor.

5. All investors are rational mean-variance optimizers, meaning that they all use the Markowitz portfolio selection model.

6. All investors analyze securities in the same way and share the same economic view of the world. The result is identical estimates of the probability distribution of future cash flows from investing in the available securities; that is, for any set of security prices, they all derive the same **input list** to feed into the Markowitz model. Given a set of security prices and the risk-free interest rate, all investors use the same expected returns and covariance matrix of security returns to generate the **efficient frontier** and the unique **optimal risky portfolio**. This assumption is often referred to as **homogeneous expectations** or beliefs.

These assumptions represent the "if" of our "what if" analysis. Obviously, they ignore many real-world complexities. With these assumptions, however, we can gain some powerful insights into the nature of equilibrium in security markets.

We can summarize the equilibrium that will prevail in this hypothetical world of securities and investors briefly. The rest of the reading explains and elaborates on these implications.

1. All investors will choose to hold a portfolio of risky assets in proportions that duplicate representation of the assets in the **market portfolio** (*M*), which includes all traded assets. For simplicity, we generally refer to all risky

assets as *stocks*. The proportion of each stock in the market portfolio equals the market value of the stock (price per share multiplied by the number of shares outstanding) divided by the total market value of all stocks.

2. Not only will the market portfolio be on the efficient frontier, but it also will be the tangency portfolio to the optimal **capital allocation line (CAL)** derived by each and every investor. As a result, the *capital market line* (**CML**), the line from the risk-free rate through the market portfolio, *M*, is also the best attainable capital allocation line. All investors hold *M* as their optimal risky portfolio, differing only in the amount invested in it versus in the risk-free asset.

3. The risk premium on the market portfolio will be proportional to its risk and the degree of risk aversion of the representative investor. Mathematically,

$$E(r_M) - r_f = \overline{A}\sigma_M^2 \times .01$$

where σ_M^2 is the variance of the market portfolio and $\overline{A}$ is the average degree of risk aversion across investors.[4] Note that because *M* is the optimal portfolio, which is efficiently diversified across all stocks, σ_M^2 is the systematic risk of this universe.

4. The risk premium on *individual* assets will be proportional to the risk premium on the market portfolio, *M*, and the *beta coefficient* of the security relative to the market portfolio. Beta measures the extent to which returns on the stock and the market move together. Formally, beta is defined as

$$\beta_i = \frac{Cov(r_i, r_M)}{\sigma_M^2}$$

and the risk premium on individual securities is

$$E(r_i) - r_f = \frac{Cov(r_i, r_M)}{\sigma_M^2}[E(r_M) - r_f] = \beta_i[E(r_M) - r_f]$$

We will elaborate on these results and their implications shortly.

Why Do All Investors Hold the Market Portfolio?

What is the market portfolio? When we sum over, or aggregate, the portfolios of all individual investors, lending and borrowing will cancel out (since each lender has a corresponding borrower), and the value of the aggregate risky portfolio will equal the entire wealth of the economy. This is the market portfolio, *M*. The proportion of each stock in this portfolio equals the market value of the stock (price per share times number of shares outstanding) divided by the sum of the market values of all stocks.[5] The CAPM implies that as individuals attempt to optimize their personal portfolios, they each arrive at the same portfolio, with weights on each asset equal to those of the market portfolio.

Given the assumptions of the previous section, it is easy to see that all investors will desire to hold identical risky portfolios. If all investors use identical Markowitz

---

[4] The scale factor .01 arises because we measure returns as percentages rather than decimals.

[5] As noted previously, we use the term "stock" for convenience; the market portfolio properly includes all assets in the economy.

analysis (Assumption 5) applied to the same universe of securities (Assumption 3) for the same time horizon (Assumption 2) and use the same input list (Assumption 6), they all must arrive at the same determination of the optimal risky portfolio, the portfolio on the efficient frontier identified by the tangency line from T-bills to that frontier, as in Figure 70-1. This implies that if the weight of GM stock, for example, in each common risky portfolio is 1%, then GM also will comprise 1% of the market portfolio. The same principle applies to the proportion of any stock in each investor's risky portfolio. As a result, the optimal risky portfolio of all investors is simply a share of the market portfolio in Figure 70-1.

Now suppose that the optimal portfolio of our investors does not include the stock of some company, such as Delta Airlines. When all investors avoid Delta stock, the demand is zero, and Delta's price takes a free fall. As Delta stock gets progressively cheaper, it becomes ever more attractive and other stocks look relatively less attractive. Ultimately, Delta reaches a price where it is attractive enough to include in the optimal stock portfolio.

Such a price adjustment process guarantees that all stocks will be included in the optimal portfolio. It shows that *all* assets have to be included in the market portfolio. The only issue is the price at which investors will be willing to include a stock in their optimal risky portfolio.

This may seem a roundabout way to derive a simple result: If all investors hold an identical risky portfolio, this portfolio has to be *M*, the market portfolio. Our intention, however, is to demonstrate a connection between this result and its underpinnings, the equilibrating process that is fundamental to security market operation.

The Passive Strategy Is Efficient

We define the CML (capital market line) as the CAL (capital allocation line) that is constructed from a money market account (or T-bills) and the market portfolio. Perhaps now you can fully appreciate why the CML is an interesting CAL. In the simple world of the CAPM, *M* is the optimal tangency portfolio on the efficient frontier, as shown in Figure 70-1.

FIGURE 70-1   The Efficient Frontier and the Capital Market Line

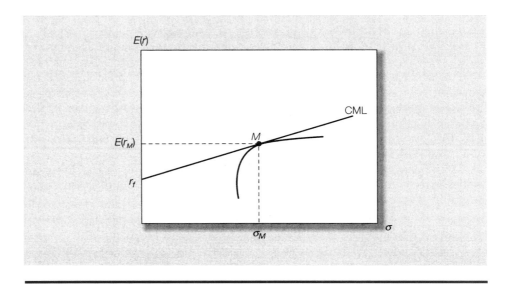

diversified portfolio will be so very highly correlated with the market that a stock's beta relative to the market will still be a useful risk measure.

In fact, several authors have shown that modified versions of the CAPM will hold true even if we consider differences among individuals leading them to hold different portfolios. For example, Brennan[8] examined the impact of differences in investors' personal tax rates on market equilibrium, and Mayers[9] looked at the impact of nontraded assets such as human capital (earning power). Both found that although the market portfolio is no longer each investor's optimal risky portfolio, the expected return–beta relationship should still hold in a somewhat modified form.

If the expected return-beta relationship holds for any individual asset, it must hold for any combination of assets. Suppose that some portfolio P has weight w_k for stock k, where k takes on values $1, \ldots, n$. Writing out the CAPM equation 70-8 for each stock, and multiplying each equation by the weight of the stock in the portfolio, we obtain these equations, one for each stock:

$$
\begin{aligned}
w_1 E(r_1) &= w_1 r_f + w_1 \beta_1 [E(r_M) - r_f] \\
+ w_2 E(r_2) &= w_2 r_f + w_2 \beta_2 [E(r_M) - r_f] \\
+ \cdots &= \cdots \\
+ w_n E(r_n) &= w_n r_f + w_n \beta_n [E(r_M) - r_f] \\
\hline
E(r_P) &= r_f + \beta_P [E(r_M) - r_f]
\end{aligned}
$$

Summing each column shows that the CAPM holds for the overall portfolio because $E(r_P) = \sum_k w_k E(r_k)$ is the expected return on the portfolio, and $\beta_P = \sum_k w_k \beta_k$ is the portfolio beta. Incidentally, this result has to be true for the market portfolio itself,

$$
E(r_M) = r_f + \beta_M [E(r_M) - r_f]
$$

Indeed, this is a tautology because $\beta_M = 1$, as we can verify by noting that

$$
\beta_M = \frac{\text{Cov}(r_M, r_M)}{\sigma_M^2} = \frac{\sigma_M^2}{\sigma_M^2}
$$

This also establishes 1 as the weighted-average value of beta across all assets. If the market beta is 1, and the market is a portfolio of all assets in the economy, the weighted-average beta of all assets must be 1. Hence betas greater than 1 are considered aggressive in that investment in high-beta stocks entails above-average sensitivity to market swings. Betas below 1 can be described as defensive.

A word of caution: We are all accustomed to hearing that well-managed firms will provide high rates of return. We agree this is true if one measures the *firm's* return on investments in plant and equipment. The CAPM, however, predicts returns on investments in the *securities* of the firm.

Let us say that everyone knows a firm is well run. Its stock price will therefore be bid up, and consequently returns to stockholders who buy at those high prices will not be excessive. Security prices, in other words, already reflect public information about a firm's prospects; therefore only the risk of the company (as measured by beta in the context of the CAPM) should affect expected returns. In a

[8] Michael J. Brennan, "Taxes, Market Valuation, and Corporate Finance Policy," *National Tax Journal*, December 1973.

[9] David Mayers, "Nonmarketable Assets and Capital Market Equilibrium under Uncertainty," in *Studies in the Theory of Capital Markets*, ed. M. C. Jensen (New York: Praeger, 1972).

rational market investors receive high expected returns only if they are willing to bear risk.

Of course, investors do not directly observe or determine expected returns on securities. Rather, they observe security prices and bid those prices up or down. Expected rates of return are determined by the prices investors must pay compared to the cash flows those investments might garner. The connection between security expected returns and the market-price equilibrium process is described in more detail in the Appendix to this reading.

CONCEPT CHECK 3

Suppose that the risk premium on the market portfolio is estimated at 8% with a standard deviation of 22%. What is the risk premium on a portfolio invested 25% in GM and 75% in Ford, if they have betas of 1.10 and 1.25, respectively?

The Security Market Line

We can view the expected return–beta relationship as a reward–risk equation. The beta of a security is the appropriate measure of its risk because beta is proportional to the risk that the security contributes to the optimal risky portfolio.

Risk-averse investors measure the risk of the optimal risky portfolio by its variance. In this world we would expect the reward, or the risk premium on individual assets, to depend on the *contribution* of the individual asset to the risk of the portfolio. The beta of a stock measures the stock's contribution to the variance of the market portfolio. Hence we expect, for any asset or portfolio, the required risk premium to be a function of beta. The CAPM confirms this intuition, stating further that the security's risk premium is directly proportional to both the beta and the risk premium of the market portfolio; that is, the risk premium equals $\beta[E(r_M) - r_f]$.

The expected return–beta relationship can be portrayed graphically as the **security market line (SML)** in Figure 70-2. Because the market beta is 1, the slope is the risk premium of the market portfolio. At the point on the horizontal axis where $\beta = 1$ (which is the market portfolio's beta) we can read off the vertical axis the expected return on the market portfolio.

It is useful to compare the security market line to the capital market line. The CML graphs the risk premiums of *efficient* portfolios (i.e., portfolios composed of the market and the risk-free asset) as a function of portfolio standard deviation. This is appropriate because standard deviation is a valid measure of risk for efficiently diversified portfolios that are candidates for an investor's overall portfolio. The SML, in contrast, graphs *individual asset* risk premiums as a function of asset risk. The relevant measure of risk for individual assets held as parts of well-diversified portfolios is not the asset's standard deviation or variance; it is, instead, the contribution of the asset to the portfolio variance, which we measure by the asset's beta. The SML is valid for both efficient portfolios and individual assets.

The security market line provides a benchmark for the evaluation of investment performance. Given the risk of an investment, as measured by its beta, the SML provides the required rate of return necessary to compensate investors for both risk as well as the time value of money.

FIGURE 70-2   The Security Market Line

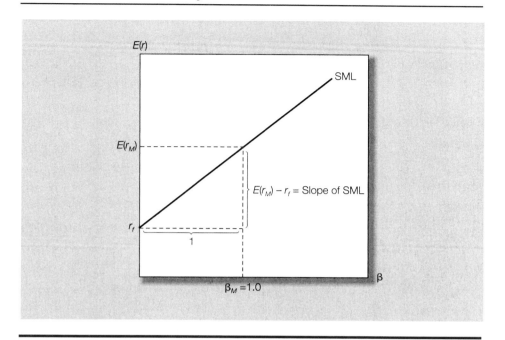

Because the security market line is the graphic representation of the expected return-beta relationship, "fairly priced" assets plot exactly on the SML; that is, their expected returns are commensurate with their risk. Given the assumptions we made at the start of this section, all securities must lie on the SML in market equilibrium. Nevertheless, we see here how the CAPM may be of use in the money-management industry. Suppose that the SML relation is used as a benchmark to assess the fair expected return on a risky asset. Then security analysis is performed to calculate the return actually expected. (Notice that we depart here from the simple CAPM world in that some investors now apply their own unique analysis to derive an "input list" that may differ from their competitors'.) If a stock is perceived to be a good buy, or underpriced, it will provide an expected return in excess of the fair return stipulated by the SML. Underpriced stocks therefore plot above the SML: Given their betas, their expected returns are greater than dictated by the CAPM. Overpriced stocks plot below the SML.

The difference between the fair and actually expected rates of return on a stock is called the stock's **alpha**, denoted α. For example, if the market return is expected to be 14%, a stock has a beta of 1.2, and the T-bill rate is 6%, the SML would predict an expected return on the stock of $6 + 1.2(14 - 6) = 15.6\%$. If one believed the stock would provide an expected return of 17%, the implied alpha would be 1.4% (see Figure 70-3).

One might say that security analysis (which we treat in Part 5) is about uncovering securities with nonzero alphas. This analysis suggests that the starting point of portfolio management can be a passive market-index portfolio. The portfolio manager will then increase the weights of securities with positive alphas and decrease the weights of securities with negative alphas.

The CAPM is also useful in capital budgeting decisions. For a firm considering a new project, the CAPM can provide the *required rate of return* that the project

FIGURE 70-3   The SML and a Positive-Alpha Stock

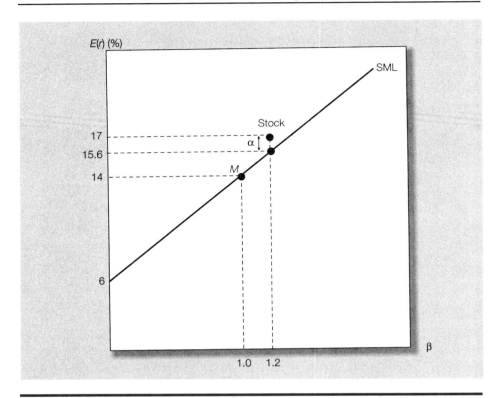

needs to yield, based on its beta, to be acceptable to investors. Managers can use the CAPM to obtain this cutoff internal rate of return (IRR), or "hurdle rate" for the project.

The box on page 346 describes how the CAPM can be used in capital budgeting. It also discusses some empirical anomalies concerning the model. The article asks whether the CAPM is useful for capital budgeting in light of these shortcomings; it concludes that even given the anomalies cited, the model still can be useful to managers who wish to increase the fundamental value of their firms.

E-INVESTMENTS: BETA AND SECURITY RETURNS

Fidelity provides data on the risk and return of its funds at www.fidelity.com. Find the annual return and beta of one of Fidelity's equity funds over the last year (look under *Snapshot*). Use the CAPM to estimate the required rate of return and calculate the alpha of the fund over the most recent annual period. You can find recent performance of several market indexes at finance.yahoo.com. Yahoo! also contains current Treasury rates (click on *Bonds—Rates*). What market risk premium seems reasonable to you? How have the Fidelity funds done for their investors?

Example 70-1

Using the CAPM

Yet another use of the CAPM is in utility rate-making cases.[10] In this case the issue is the rate of return that a regulated utility should be allowed to earn on its investment in plant and equipment. Suppose that the equity-holders have invested $100 million in the firm and that the beta of the equity is .6. If the T-bill rate is 6% and the market risk premium is 8%, then the fair profits to the firm would be assessed as 6 + .6(8) = 10.8% of the $100 million investment, or $10.8 million. The firm would be allowed to set prices at a level expected to generate these profits.

CONCEPT CHECK 4

Stock XYZ has an expected return of 12% and risk of $\beta = 1$. Stock ABC has expected return of 13% and $\beta = 1.5$. The market's expected return is 11%, and $r_f = 5\%$.

a. According to the CAPM, which stock is a better buy?

b. What is the alpha of each stock? Plot the SML and each stock's risk-return point on one graph. Show the alphas graphically.

The risk-free rate is 8% and the expected return on the market portfolio is 16%. A firm considers a project that is expected to have a beta of 1.3.

a. What is the required rate of return on the project?

b. If the expected IRR of the project is 19%, should it be accepted?

EXTENSIONS OF THE CAPM   **2**

The assumptions that allowed Sharpe to derive the simple version of the CAPM are admittedly unrealistic. Financial economists have been at work ever since the CAPM was devised to extend the model to more realistic scenarios.

There are two classes of extensions to the simple version of the CAPM. The first attempts to relax the assumptions that we outlined at the outset of the reading. The second acknowledges the fact that investors worry about sources of risk other than the uncertain value of their securities, such as unexpected changes in relative prices of consumer goods. This idea involves the introduction of additional risk factors besides security returns.

---

[10] This application is fast disappearing, as many states are in the process of deregulating their public utilities and allowing a far greater degree of free market pricing. Nevertheless, a considerable amount of rate setting still takes place.

The CAPM with Restricted Borrowing:
The Zero-Beta Model

The CAPM is predicated on the assumption that all investors share an identical input list that they feed into the Markowitz algorithm. Thus all investors agree on the location of the efficient (minimum-variance) frontier, where each portfolio has the lowest variance among all feasible portfolios at a target expected rate of return. When all investors can borrow and lend at the safe rate, r_f, all agree on the optimal tangency portfolio and choose to hold a share of the market portfolio.

However, when borrowing is restricted, as it is for many financial institutions, or when the borrowing rate is higher than the lending rate because borrowers pay a default premium, the market portfolio is no longer the common optimal portfolio for all investors.

When investors no longer can borrow at a common risk-free rate, they may choose risky portfolios from the entire set of efficient frontier portfolios according to how much risk they choose to bear. The market is no longer the common optimal portfolio. In fact, with investors choosing different portfolios, it is no longer obvious whether the market portfolio, which is the aggregate of all investors' portfolios, will even be on the efficient frontier. If the market portfolio is no longer mean-variance efficient, then the expected return–beta relationship of the CAPM will no longer characterize market equilibrium.

An equilibrium expected return-beta relationship in the case of restrictions on risk-free investments has been developed by Fischer Black.[11] Black's model is fairly difficult and requires a good deal of facility with mathematics. Therefore, we will satisfy ourselves with a sketch of Black's argument and spend more time with its implications.

Black's model of the CAPM in the absence of a risk-free asset rests on the three following properties of mean-variance efficient portfolios:

1. Any portfolio constructed by combining efficient portfolios is itself on the efficient frontier.

2. Every portfolio on the efficient frontier has a "companion" portfolio on the bottom half (the inefficient part) of the **minimum-variance frontier** with which it is uncorrelated. Because the portfolios are uncorrelated, the companion portfolio is referred to as the **zero-beta portfolio** of the efficient portfolio.

   The expected return of an efficient portfolio's zero-beta companion portfolio can be derived by the following graphical procedure. From any efficient portfolio such as P in Figure 70-4 draw a tangency line to the vertical axis. The intercept will be the expected return on portfolio P's zero-beta companion portfolio, denoted Z(P). The horizontal line from the intercept to the minimum-variance frontier identifies the standard deviation of the zero-beta portfolio. Notice in Figure 70-4 that different efficient portfolios such as P and Q have different zero-beta companions.

   These tangency lines are helpful constructs only. They do *not* signify that one can invest in portfolios with expected return-standard deviation pairs along the line. That would be possible only by mixing a risk-free asset with the tangency portfolio. In this case, however, we assume that risk-free assets are not available to investors.

---

[11] Fischer Black, "Capital Market Equilibrium with Restricted Borrowing," *Journal of Business*, July 1972.

FIGURE 70-4   Efficient Portfolios and Their Zero-Beta Companions

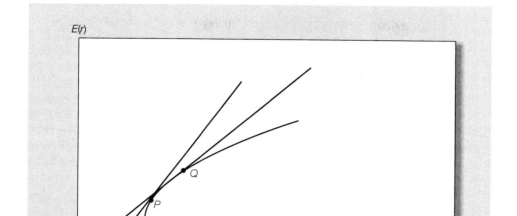

3. The expected return of any asset can be expressed as an exact, linear function of the expected return on any two frontier portfolios. Consider, for example, the minimum-variance frontier portfolios P and Q. Black showed that the expected return on any asset i can be expressed as

$$E(r_i) = E(r_Q) + [E(r_P) - E(r_Q)]\frac{\mathrm{Cov}(r_i, r_P) - \mathrm{Cov}(r_P, r_Q)}{\sigma_P^2 - \mathrm{Cov}(r_P, r_Q)} \quad \text{(70-9)}$$

Note that Property 3 has nothing to do with market equilibrium. It is a purely mathematical property relating frontier portfolios and individual securities.

With these three properties, the Black model can be applied to any of several variations: no risk-free asset at all, risk-free lending but no risk-free borrowing, and borrowing at a rate higher than r_f. We show here how the model works for the case with risk-free lending but no borrowing.

Imagine an economy with only two investors, one relatively risk averse and one risk tolerant. The risk-averse investor will choose a portfolio on the CAL supported by portfolio T in Figure 70-5, that is, he will mix portfolio T with lending at the risk-free rate. T is the tangency portfolio on the efficient frontier from the risk-free lending rate, r_f. The risk-tolerant investor is willing to accept more risk to earn a higher-risk premium; she will choose portfolio S. This portfolio lies along the efficient frontier with higher risk and return than portfolio T. The aggregate risky portfolio (i.e., the market portfolio, M) will be a combination of T and S, with weights determined by the relative wealth and degrees of risk aversion of the two investors. Since T and S are each on the efficient frontier, so is M (from Property 1).

FIGURE 70-5   Capital Market Equilibrium with No Borrowing

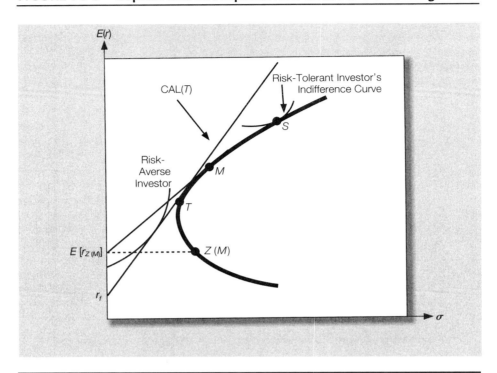

TALES FROM THE FAR SIDE

Financial markets' evaluation of risk determines the way firms invest. What if the markets are wrong?

Investors are rarely praised for their good sense. But for the past two decades a growing number of firms have based their decisions on a model which assumes that people are perfectly rational. If they are irrational, are businesses making the wrong choices?

The model, known as the "capital-asset pricing model," or CAPM, has come to dominate modern finance. Almost any manager who wants to defend a project—be it a brand, a factory or a corporate merger—must justify his decision partly based on the CAPM. The reason is that the model tells a firm how to calculate the return that its investors demand. If shareholders are to benefit, the returns from any project must clear this "hurdle rate."

Although the CAPM is complicated, it can be reduced to five simple ideas:

▶ Investors can eliminate some risks—such as the risk that workers will strike, or that a firm's boss will quit—by diversifying across many regions and sectors.

▶ Some risks, such as that of a global recession, cannot be eliminated through diversification. So even a basket of all of the stocks in a stock market will still be risky.

▶ People must be rewarded for investing in such a risky basket by earning returns above those that they can get on safer assets, such as Treasury bills.

▶ The rewards on a specific investment depend only on the extent to which it affects the market basket's risk.

(continued)

TALES FROM THE FAR SIDE *(continued)*

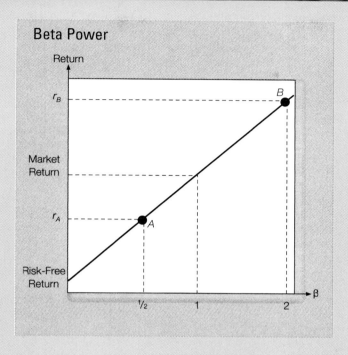

Beta Power

▶ Conveniently, that contribution to the market basket's risk can be captured by a single measure—dubbed "beta"—which expresses the relationship between the investments risk and the market's.

Beta is what makes the CAPM so powerful. Although an investment may face many risks, diversified investors should care only about those that are related to the market basket. Beta not only tells managers how to measure those risks, but it also allows them to translate them directly into a hurdle rate. If the future profits from a project will not exceed that rate, it is not worth shareholders' money.

The diagram shows how the CAPM works. Safe investments, such as Treasury bills, have a beta of zero. Riskier investments should earn a premium over the risk-free rate which increases with beta. Those whose risks roughly match the market's have a beta of one, by definition, and should earn the market return.

So suppose that a firm is considering two projects, A and B. Project A has a beta of 1/2: when the market rises or falls by 10%, its returns tend to rise or fall by 5%. So its risk premium is only half that of the market. Project B's risk premium is twice that of the market, so it must earn a higher return to justify the expenditure.

Never Knowingly Underpriced

But there is one small problem with the CAPM: Financial economists have found that beta is not much use for explaining rates of return on firms' shares. Worse, there appears to be another measure which explains these returns quite well.

That measure is the ratio of a firm's book value (the value of its assets at the time they entered the balance sheet) to its market value. Several studies have found that, on average, companies that have high book-to-market ratios tend to earn excess returns over long periods, even after adjusting for the risks that are associated with beta.

(continued)

TALES FROM THE FAR SIDE *(continued)*

The discovery of this **book-to-market effect** has sparked a fierce debate among financial economists. All of them agree that some risks ought to carry greater rewards. But they are now deeply divided over how risk should be measured. Some argue that since investors are rational, the book-to-market effect must be capturing an extra risk factor. They conclude, therefore, that managers should incorporate the book-to-market effect into their hurdle rates. They have labeled this alternative hurdle rate the "new estimator of expected return," or NEER.

Other financial economists, however, dispute this approach. Since there is no obvious extra risk associated with a high book-to-market ratio, they say, investors must be mistaken. Put simply, they are **underpricing** high book-to-market stocks, causing them to earn abnormally high returns. If managers of such firms try to exceed those inflated hurdle rates, they will forgo many profitable investments. With economists now at odds, what is a conscientious manager to do?

In a new paper,* Jeremy Stein, an economist at the Massachusetts Institute of Technology's business school, offers a paradoxical answer. If investors are rational, then beta cannot be the only measure of risk, so managers should stop using it. Conversely, if investors are irrational, then beta is still the right measure in many cases. Mr. Stein argues that if beta captures an asset's fundamental risk—that is, its contribution to the market basket's risk—then it will often make sense for managers to pay attention to it, even if investors are somehow failing to.

Often, but not always. At the heart of Mr. Stein's argument lies a crucial distinction—that between (a) boosting a firm's long-term value and (b) trying to raise its share price. If investors are rational, these are the same thing: any decision that raises long-term value will instantly increase the share price as well. But if investors are making predictable mistakes, a manager must choose.

For instance, if he wants to increase today's share price—perhaps because he wants to sell his shares, or to fend off a takeover attempt—he must usually stick with the NEER approach, accommodating investors' misperceptions. But if he is interested in long-term value, he should usually continue to use beta. Showing a flair for marketing, Mr. Stein labels this far-sighted alternative to NEER the "fundamental asset risk"—or FAR—approach.

Mr. Stein's conclusions will no doubt irritate many company bosses, who are fond of denouncing their investors' myopia. They have resented the way in which CAPM—with its assumption of investor infallibility—has come to play an important role in boardroom decision-making. But it now appears that if they are right, and their investors are wrong, then those same far-sighted managers ought to be the CAPM's biggest fans.

---

* Jeremy Stein, "Rational Capital Budgeting in an Irrational World," *The Journal of Business,* October 1996.
Source: "Tales from the FAR Side," *The Economist,* November 16, 1996, p. 8.

From Property 2, *M* has a companion zero-beta portfolio on the minimum-variance frontier, $Z(M)$, shown in Figure 70-5. Moreover, by Property 3 we can express the return on any security in terms of M and $Z(M)$ as in equation 70-9. But, since by construction $\text{Cov}[r_M, r_{Z(M)}] = 0$, the expression simplifies to

$$E(r_i) = E[r_{Z(M)}] + E[r_M - r_{Z(M)}]\frac{\text{Cov}(r_i, r_M)}{\sigma_M^2} \tag{70-10}$$

where *P* from equation 70-9 has been replaced by *M* and *Q* has been replaced by $Z(M)$. Equation 70-10 may be interpreted as a variant of the simple CAPM, in which r_f has been replaced with $E[r_{Z(M)}]$.

There is a more realistic scenario, where investors lend at the risk-free rate and borrow at a higher rate. The same arguments that we have just employed can also be used to establish the zero-beta CAPM in this situation.

CONCEPT CHECK 5

Suppose that the zero-beta portfolio exhibits returns that are, on average, greater than the rate on T-bills. Is this fact relevant to the question of the validity of the CAPM?

Lifetime Consumption and the CAPM

One of the restrictive assumptions for the simple version of the CAPM is that investors are myopic—they plan for one common holding period. Investors actually may be concerned with a lifetime consumption plan and a desire to leave a bequest to children. Consumption plans that are feasible for them depend on current wealth and future rates of return on the investment portfolio. These investors will want to rebalance their portfolios as often as required by changes in wealth.

However, Eugene Fama[12] showed that, even if we extend our analysis to a multiperiod setting, the single-period CAPM still may be appropriate. The key assumptions that Fama used to replace myopic **planning horizons** are that investor preferences are unchanging over time and the risk-free interest rate and probability distribution of security returns do not change unpredictably over time. Of course, this latter assumption is also unrealistic. A variant of the CAPM allows for such unpredictability.

THE CAPM AND LIQUIDITY   3

Liquidity refers to the cost and ease with which an asset can be converted into cash, that is, sold. Traders have long recognized the importance of liquidity, and some evidence suggests that illiquidity can reduce market prices substantially. For example, one study[13] finds that market discounts on closely held (and therefore nontraded) firms can exceed 30%. The nearby box focuses on the relationship between liquidity and stock returns.

A rigorous treatment of the value of liquidity was first developed by Amihud and Mendelson.[14] Several studies show that liquidity plays an important role in explaining rates of return on financial assets.[15] Chordia, Roll, and Subrahmanyam[16] find commonality across stocks in the variable cost of liquidity:

---

[12] Eugene F. Fama, "Multiperiod Consumption-Investment Decisions," *American Economic Review* 60 (1970).

[13] Shannon P. Pratt, *Valuing a Business: The Analysis of Closely Held Companies*, 2nd ed. (Homewood, IL.: Dow Jones–Irwin, 1989).

[14] Yakov Amihud and Haim Mendelson, "Asset Pricing and the Bid–Ask Spread," *Journal of Financial Economics* 17 (1986), pp. 223–49.

[15] For example, Venkat Eleswarapu, "Cost of Transacting and Expected Returns in the NASDAQ Market," *Journal of Finance* 2, no. 5 (1993), pp. 2113–27.

[16] Tarun Chordia, Richard Roll, and Avanidhar Subrahmanyam, "Commonality and Liquidity," *Journal of Financial Economics*, April 2000.

STOCK INVESTORS PAY HIGH PRICE FOR LIQUIDITY

Given a choice between liquid and illiquid stocks, most investors, to the extent they think of it at all, opt for issues they know are easy to get in and out of.

But for long-term investors who don't trade often—which includes most individuals—that may be unnecessarily expensive. Recent studies of the performance of listed stocks show that, on average, less-liquid issues generate substantially higher returns—as much as several percentage points a year at the extremes. . . .

Illiquidity Payoff

Among the academic studies that have attempted to quantify this illiquidity payoff is a recent work by two finance professors, Yakov Amihud of New York University and Tel Aviv University, and Haim Mendelson of the University of Rochester. Their study looks at New York Stock Exchange issues over the 1961–1980 period and defines liquidity in terms of bid–asked spreads as a percentage of overall share price.

Market makers use spreads in quoting stocks to define the difference between the price they'll bid to take stock off an investor's hands and the price they'll offer to sell stock to any willing buyer. The bid price is always somewhat lower because of the risk to the broker of tying up precious capital to hold stock in inventory until it can be resold.

If a stock is relatively illiquid, which means there's not a ready flow of orders from customers clamoring to buy it, there's more of a chance the broker will lose money on the trade. To hedge this risk, market makers demand an even bigger discount to service potential sellers, and the spread will widen further.

The study by Profs. Amihud and Mendelson shows that liquidity spreads— measured as a percentage discount from the stock's total price—ranged from less than 0.1%, for widely held International Business Machines Corp., to as much as 4% to 5%. The widest-spread group was dominated by smaller, low-priced stocks.

The study found that, overall, the least-liquid stocks averaged an 8.5 percent-a-year higher return than the most-liquid stocks over the 20-year period. On average, a one percentage point increase in the spread was associated with a 2.5% higher annual return for New York Stock Exchange stocks. The relationship held after results were adjusted for size and other risk factors.

An extension of the study of **Big Board** stocks done at *The Wall Street Journal*'s request produced similar findings. It shows that for the 1980–85 period, a one percentage-point-wider spread was associated with an extra average annual gain of 2.4%. Meanwhile, the least-liquid stocks out-performed the most-liquid stocks by almost six percentage points a year.

Cost of Trading

Since the cost of the spread is incurred each time the stock is traded, illiquid stocks can quickly become prohibitively expensive for investors who trade frequently. On the other hand, long-term investors needn't worry so much about spreads, since they can amortize them over a longer period.

In terms of investment strategy, this suggests "that the small investor should tailor the types of stocks he or she buys to his expected holding period," Prof. Mendelson says. If the investor expects to sell within three months, he says, it's better to pay up for the liquidity and get the lowest spread. If the investor plans to hold the stock for a year or more, it makes sense to aim at stocks with spreads of 3% or more to capture the extra return.

Source: Barbara Donnelly, *The Wall Street Journal,* April 28, 1987, p. 37. Reprinted by permission of *The Wall Street Journal.* © 1987 Dow Jones & Company, Inc. All Rights Reserved Worldwide.

quoted spreads, quoted depth, and effective spreads covary with the market and industrywide liquidity. Hence, liquidity risk is systematic and therefore difficult to diversify. We believe that liquidity will become an important part of standard valuation, and therefore present here a simplified version of their model.

Recall Assumption 4 of the CAPM, that all trading is costless. In reality, no security is perfectly liquid, in that all trades involve some transaction cost. Investors prefer more liquid assets with lower transaction costs, so it should not surprise us to find that all else equal, relatively illiquid assets trade at lower prices or, equivalently, that the expected return on illiquid assets must be higher. Therefore, an **illiquidity premium** must be impounded into the price of each asset.

We start with the simplest case, in which we ignore systematic risk. Imagine a world with a large number of uncorrelated securities. Because the securities are uncorrelated, well-diversified portfolios of these securities will have standard deviations near zero and the market portfolio will be virtually as safe as the risk-free asset. In this case, the market risk premium will be zero. Therefore, despite the fact that the beta of each security is 1.0, the expected rate of return on all securities will equal the risk-free rate, which we will take to be the T-bill rate.

Assume that investors know in advance for how long they intend to hold their portfolios, and suppose that there are n types of investors, grouped by investment horizon. Type 1 investors intend to liquidate their portfolios in one period, Type 2 investors in two periods, and so on, until the longest-horizon investors (Type n) intend to hold their portfolios for n periods.

We assume that there are only two classes of securities: liquid and illiquid. The liquidation cost of a class L (more liquid) stock to an investor with a horizon of h years (a Type h investor) will reduce the per-period rate of return by $c_L/h\%$. For example, if the combination of commissions and the **bid–asked spread** on a security resulted in a liquidation cost of 10%, then the per-period rate of return for an investor who holds stock for 5 years would be reduced by approximately 2% per year, whereas the return on a 10-year investment would fall by only 1% per year.[17] Class I (illiquid) assets have higher liquidation costs that reduce the per-period return by $c_I/h\%$, where c_I is greater than c_L. Therefore, if you intend to hold a class L security for h periods, your expected rate of return *net* of transaction costs is $E(r_L) - c_L/h$. There is no liquidation cost on T-bills.

The following table presents the expected return investors would realize from the risk-free asset and class L and class I stock portfolios *assuming* that the simple CAPM is correct and all securities have an expected return of r.

Asset:	Risk-Free	Class L	Class I
Gross rate of return:	r	r	r
One-period liquidation cost:	0	c_L	c_I

[17] This simple structure of liquidation costs allows us to derive a correspondingly simple solution for the effect of liquidity on expected returns. Amihud and Mendelson used a more general formulation, but then needed to rely on complex and more difficult-to-interpret mathematical programming. All that matters for the qualitative results below, however, is that illiquidity costs be less onerous to longer-term investors.

Investor Type		Net Rate of Return	
1	r	$r - c_L$	$r - c_I$
2	r	$r - c_L/2$	$r - c_I/2$
$\vdots$	$\vdots$	$\vdots$	$\vdots$
n	r	$r - c_L/n$	$r - c_I/n$

These net rates of return would be inconsistent with a market in equilibrium, because with equal gross rates of return all investors would prefer to invest in zero-transaction-cost T-bills. As a result, both class L and class I stock prices must fall, causing their expected returns to rise until investors are willing to hold these shares.

Suppose, therefore, that each gross return is higher by some fraction of liquidation cost. Specifically, assume that the gross expected return on class L stocks is $r + xc_L$ and that of class I stocks is $r + yc_I$. The *net* rate of return on class L stocks to an investor with a horizon of h will be $(r + xc_L) - c_L/h = r + c_L(x - 1/h)$. In general, the rates of return to investors will be:

Asset:	Risk-Free	Class L	Class I
Gross rate of return:	r	$r + xc_L$	$r + yc_I$
One-period liquidation cost:	0	c_L	c_I

Investor Type		Net Rate of Return	
1	r	$r + c_L(x - 1)$	$r + c_I(y - 1)$
2	r	$r + c_L(x - 1/2)$	$r + c_I(y - 1/2)$
$\vdots$	$\vdots$	$\vdots$	$\vdots$
n	r	$r + c_L(x - 1/n)$	$r + c_I(y - 1/n)$

Notice that the liquidation cost has a greater impact on per-period returns for shorter-term investors. This is because the cost is amortized over fewer periods. As the horizon becomes very large, the per-period impact of the transaction cost approaches zero and the net rate of return approaches the gross rate.

Figure 70-6 graphs the net rate of return on the three asset classes for investors of differing horizons. The more illiquid stock has the lowest net rate of return for very short investment horizons because of its large liquidation costs. However, in equilibrium, the stock must be priced at a level that offers a rate of return high enough to induce some investors to hold it, implying that its gross rate of return must be higher than that of the more liquid stock. Therefore, for long enough investment horizons, the net return on class I stocks will exceed that on class L stocks.

Both stock classes underperform T-bills for very short investment horizons, because the transactions costs then have the largest per-period impact. Ultimately, however, because the *gross* rate of return of stocks exceeds r, for a sufficiently long investment horizon, the more liquid stocks in class L will dominate

FIGURE 70-6   Net Returns As a Function of Investment Horizon

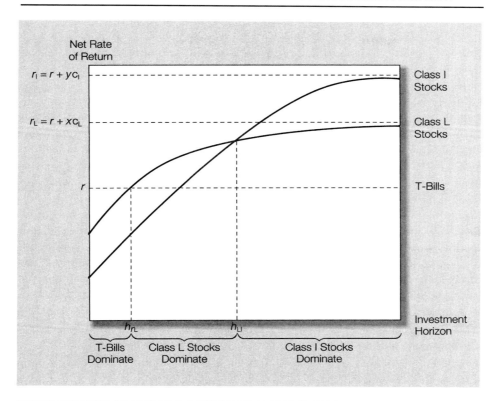

bills. The threshold horizon can be read from Figure 70-6 as h_{TL}. Anyone with a horizon that exceeds h_{TL} will prefer class L stocks to T-bills. Those with horizons below h_{TL} will choose bills. For even longer horizons, because c_I exceeds c_L, the net rate of return on relatively illiquid class I stocks will exceed that on class L stocks. Therefore, investors with horizons greater than h_{LI} will specialize in the most illiquid stocks with the highest gross rate of return. These investors are harmed least by the effect of trading costs.

Now we can determine equilibrium illiquidity premiums. For the marginal investor with horizon h_{LI}, the *net* return from class I and L stocks is the same. Therefore,

$$r + c_L(x - 1/h_{LI}) = r + c_I(y - 1/h_{LI})$$

We can use this equation to solve for the relationship between x and y as follows:

$$y = \frac{1}{h_{LI}} + \frac{c_L}{c_I}\left(x - \frac{1}{h_{LI}}\right)$$

The expected gross return on illiquid stocks is then

$$r_I = r + c_I y = r + \frac{c_I}{h_{LI}} + c_L\left(x - \frac{1}{h_{LI}}\right) = r + c_L x + \frac{1}{h_{LI}}(c_I - c_L) \qquad \textbf{(70-11)}$$

Recalling that the expected gross return on class L stocks is $r_L = r + c_L x$, we conclude that the illiquidity premium of class I versus class L stocks is

$$r_I - r_L = \frac{1}{h_{LI}}(c_I - c_L) \qquad \textbf{(70-12)}$$

Similarly, we can derive the liquidity premium of class L stocks over T-bills. Here, the marginal investor who is indifferent between bills and class L stocks will have investment horizon h_{rL} and a net rate of return just equal to r. Therefore, $r + c_L(x - 1/h_{rL}) = r$, implying that $x = 1/h_{rL}$, and the liquidity premium of class L stocks must be $xc_L = c_L/h_{rL}$. Therefore,

$$r_L - r = \frac{1}{h_{rL}}c_L \qquad \textbf{(70-13)}$$

There are two lessons to be learned from this analysis. First, as predicted, equilibrium expected rates of return are bid up to compensate for transaction costs, as demonstrated by equations 70-12 and 70-13. Second, the illiquidity premium is *not* a linear function of transaction costs. In fact, the incremental illiquidity premium steadily declines as transaction costs increase. To see that this is so, suppose that c_L is 1% and $c_I - c_L$ is also 1%. Therefore, the transaction cost increases by 1% as you move out of bills into the more liquid stock class, and by another 1% as you move into the illiquid stock class. Equation 70-13 shows that the illiquidity premium of class L stocks over no-transaction-cost bills is then $1/h_{rL}$, and equation 70-12 shows that the illiquidity premium of class I over class L stocks is $1/h_{LI}$. But h_{LI} exceeds h_{rL} (see Figure 70-5), so we conclude that the incremental effect of illiquidity declines as we move into ever more illiquid assets.

The reason for this last result is simple. Recall that investors will self-select into different asset classes, with longer-term investors holding assets with the highest gross return but that are the most illiquid. For these investors, the effect of illiquidity is less costly because trading costs can be amortized over a longer horizon. Therefore, as these costs increase, the investment horizon associated with the holders of these assets also increases, which mitigates the impact on the required gross rate of return.

CONCEPT CHECK 6

Consider a very illiquid asset class of stocks, class V, with $c_V > c_I$. Use a graph like Figure 70-6 to convince yourself that there is an investment horizon, h_{IV}, for which an investor would be indifferent between stocks in illiquidity classes I and V. Analogously to equation 70-12, in equilibrium, the differential in gross returns must be

$$r_V - r_I = \frac{1}{h_{IV}}(c_V - c_I)$$

Our analysis so far has focused on the case of uncorrelated assets, allowing us to ignore issues of systematic risk. This special case turns out to be easy to generalize. If we were to allow for correlation among assets due to common systematic risk factors, we would find that the illiquidity premium is simply additive to the risk premium of the usual CAPM.[18] Therefore, we can generalize the CAPM expected return–beta relationship to include a liquidity effect as follows:

$$E(r_i) - r_f = \beta_i[E(r_M) - r_f] + f(c_i)$$

where $f(c_i)$ is a function of trading costs that measures the effect of the illiquidity premium given the trading costs of security i. We have seen that $f(c_i)$ is increasing in c_i but at a decreasing rate. The usual CAPM equation is modified because each investor's optimal portfolio is now affected by liquidation cost as well as risk–return considerations.

The model can be generalized in other ways as well. For example, even if investors do not know their investment horizon for certain, as long as investors do not perceive a connection between unexpected needs to liquidate investments and security returns, the implications of the model are essentially unchanged, with expected horizons replacing actual horizons in equations 70-12 and 70-13.

Amihud and Mendelson provided a considerable amount of empirical evidence that liquidity has a substantial impact on gross stock returns. For a preview of the quantitative significance of the illiquidity effect, examine Figure 70-7,

FIGURE 70-7   The Relationship Between Illiquidity and Average Returns

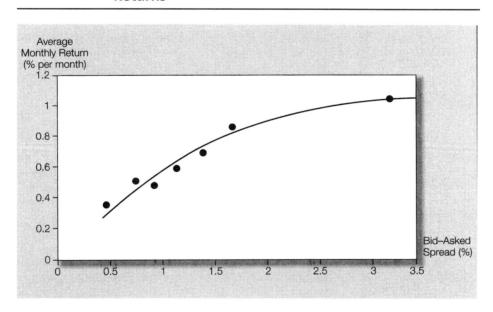

Source: Derived from Yakov Amihud and Haim Mendelson, "Asset Pricing and the Bid–Ask Spread," *Journal of Financial Economics* 17 (1986), pp. 223–49.

---

[18] The only assumption necessary to obtain this result is that for each level of beta, there are many securities within that risk class, with a variety of transaction costs. (This is essentially the same assumption used by Modigliani and Miller in their famous capital structure irrelevance proposition.) Thus our earlier analysis could be applied within each risk class, resulting in an illiquidity premium that simply adds on to the systematic risk premium.

which is derived from their study. It shows that average monthly returns over the 1961–1980 period rose from .35% for the group of stocks with the lowest bid–asked spread (the most liquid stocks) to 1.024% for the highest-spread stocks. This is an annualized differential of about 8%, nearly equal to the historical average risk premium on the S&P 500 index! Moreover, as their model predicts, the effect of the spread on average monthly returns is nonlinear, with a curve that flattens out as spreads increase.

SUMMARY

▶ The CAPM assumes that investors are single-period planners who agree on a common input list from security analysis and seek mean-variance optimal portfolios.

▶ The CAPM assumes that security markets are ideal in the sense that:

A. They are large, and investors are price-takers.

B. There are no taxes or transaction costs.

C. All risky assets are publicly traded.

D. Investors can borrow and lend any amount at a fixed risk-free rate.

▶ With these assumptions, all investors hold identical risky portfolios. The CAPM holds that in equilibrium the market portfolio is the unique mean-variance efficient tangency portfolio. Thus a passive strategy is efficient.

▶ The CAPM market portfolio is a value-weighted portfolio. Each security is held in a proportion equal to its market value divided by the total market value of all securities.

▶ If the market portfolio is efficient and the average investor neither borrows nor lends, then the risk premium on the market portfolio is proportional to its variance, σ_M^2, and to the average coefficient of risk aversion across investors, A:

$$E(r_M) - r_f = .01 \times \overline{A}\sigma_M^2$$

▶ The CAPM implies that the risk premium on any individual asset or portfolio is the product of the risk premium on the market portfolio and the beta coefficient:

$$E(r_i) - r_f = \beta_i[E(r_M) - r_f]$$

where the beta coefficient is the covariance of the asset with the market portfolio as a fraction of the variance of the market portfolio

$$\beta_i = \frac{Cov(r_i, r_M)}{\sigma_M^2}$$

▶ When risk-free investments are restricted but all other CAPM assumptions hold, then the simple version of the CAPM is replaced by its zero-beta version. Accordingly, the risk-free rate in the expected return-beta relationship is replaced by the zero-beta portfolio's expected rate of return:

$$E(r_i) = E[r_{Z(M)}] + \beta_i E[r_M - r_{Z(M)}]$$

▶ The simple version of the CAPM assumes that investors are myopic. When investors are assumed to be concerned with lifetime consumption and bequest plans, but investors' tastes and security return distributions are stable over time, the market portfolio remains efficient and the simple version of the expected return-beta relationship holds.

▶ Liquidity costs can be incorporated into the CAPM relationship. When there is a large number of assets with any combination of beta and liquidity cost c_i, the expected return is bid up to reflect this undesired property according to

$$E(r_i) - r_f = \beta_i[E(r_M) - r_f] + f(c_i)$$

WEBSITES

finance.yahoo.com (Enter the ticker symbol, then link to the *Profile* report.)

moneycentral.msn.com/investor/home.asp (Enter the ticker symbol, then link to the *Company Report* from the *Research* menu on the left.)

www.wallpost.com (*see Profiles*)

www.411stocks.com

www.thomsoninvest.net (enter ticker symbol)

The sites listed above contain estimates of beta coefficients for individual securities and mutual funds.

www.efficientfrontier.com

This site contains practical information related to modern portfolio theory and portfolio allocation.

www.moneychimp.com/articles/valuation/capm.htm

Try the CAPM calculator at Moneychimp.com.

APPENDIX 70

Demand for Stocks and Equilibrium Prices

In this section, we will make more explicit the links between the quest for efficiently diversified portfolios, which drives investor demand for securities, and the process by which equilibrium expected rates of return are established. To understand how market equilibrium is formed we need to connect the determination of optimal portfolios with security analysis and the actual buy/sell transactions of investors. We will show how the quest for **efficient diversification** leads to a demand schedule for shares. In turn, the supply and demand for shares determine equilibrium prices and expected rates of return.

Imagine a simple world with only two corporations: Bottom Up Inc. (BU) and Top Down Inc. (TD). Stock prices and market values are shown in Table 70-1. Investors can also invest in a money market fund (MMF) which yields a risk-free interest rate of 5%.

Sigma Fund is a new actively managed mutual fund that has raised $220 million to invest in the stock market. The security analysis staff of Sigma believes that neither BU nor TD will grow in the future and therefore, that each firm will pay level annual dividends for the foreseeable future. This is a useful simplifying assumption because, if a stock is expected to pay a stream of level dividends, the income derived from each share is a perpetuity. Therefore, the present value of each share—often called the *intrinsic value* of the share—equals the dividend divided by the appropriate discount rate. A summary of the report of the security analysts appears in Table 70-2.

The expected returns in Table 70-2 are based on the assumption that next year's dividends will conform to Sigma's forecasts, and share prices will be equal to intrinsic values at year-end. The standard deviations and the correlation coefficient between the two stocks were estimated by Sigma's security analysts from past returns and assumed to remain at these levels for the coming year.

Using these data and assumptions Sigma easily generates the efficient frontier shown in Figure 70-1 and computes the optimal portfolio proportions corresponding to the tangency portfolio. These proportions, combined with the total investment budget, yield the fund's buy orders. With a budget of $220 million, Sigma wants a position in BU of $220,000,000 × .8070 = $177,540,000, or $177,540,000/39 = 4,552,308 shares, and a position in TD of $220,000,000 × .1930 = $42,460,000, which corresponds to 1,088,718 shares.

TABLE 70-1 Share Prices and Market Values of Bottom Up (BU) and Top Down (TD)

	BU	TD
Price per share ($)	39.00	39.00
Shares outstanding	5,000,000	4,000,000
Market value ($ millions)	195	156

TABLE 70-2 Capital Market Expectations of Portfolio Manager		
	BU	**TD**
Expected annual dividend ($/share)	6.40	3.80
Discount rate = Required return* (%)	16	10
Expected end-of-year price† ($/share)	40	38
Current price	39	39
Expected return (%): Capital gain	2.56	−2.56
Dividend yield	16.41	9.74
Total expected return for the year	18.97	7.18
Standard deviation of rate of return	40%	20%
Correlation coefficient between rates of return on BU and TD	.20	

* Based on assessment of risk.
† Obtained by discounting the dividend perpetuity at the required rate of return.

Sigma's Demand for Shares

The expected rates of return that Sigma used to derive its demand for shares of BU and TD were computed from the forecast of year-end stock prices and the current prices. If, say, a share of BU could be purchased at a lower price, Sigma's forecast of the rate of return on BU would be higher. Conversely, if BU shares

FIGURE 70-1   Sigma's Efficient Frontier and Optimal Portfolio

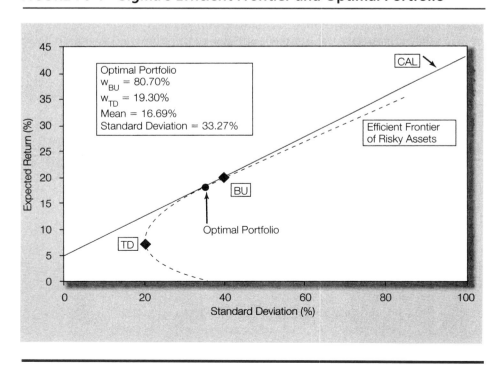

TABLE 70-3 Calculation of Sigma's Demand for BU Shares					
Current Price ($)	Capital Gain (%)	Dividend Yield (%)	Expected Return (%)	BU Optimal Proportion	Desired BU Shares
45.0	−11.11	14.22	3.11	−.4113	−2,010,582
42.5	−5.88	15.06	9.18	.3192	1,652,482
40.0	0	16.00	16.00	.7011	3,856,053
37.5	6.67	17.07	23.73	.9358	5,490,247
35.0	14.29	18.29	32.57	1.0947	6,881,225

were selling at a higher price, expected returns would be lower. A new expected return would result in a different optimal portfolio and a different demand for shares.

We can think of Sigma's demand schedule for a stock as the number of shares Sigma would want to hold at different share prices. In our simplified world, producing the demand for BU shares is not difficult. First, we revise Table 70-2 to recompute the expected return on BU at different current prices given the forecast year-end price. Then, for each price and associated expected return, we construct the optimal portfolio and find the implied position in BU. A few samples of these calculations are shown in Table 70-3. The first four columns in Table 70-3 show the expected returns on BU shares given their current price. The optimal proportion (column 5) is calculated using these expected returns. Finally, Sigma's investment budget, the optimal proportion in BU and the current price of a BU share determine the desired number of shares. Note that we compute the demand for BU shares *given* the price and expected return for TD. This means that the entire demand schedule must be revised whenever the price and expected return on TD is changed.

Sigma's demand curve for BU stock is given by the Desired Shares column in Table 70-3 and is plotted in Figure 70-2. Notice that the demand curve for the stock slopes downward. When BU's stock price falls, Sigma will desire more shares for two reasons: (1) an income effect—at a lower price Sigma can purchase more shares with the same budget, and (2) a **substitution effect**—the increased expected return at the lower price will make BU shares more attractive relative to TD shares. Notice that one can desire a negative number of shares, that is, a short position. If the stock price is high enough, its expected return will be so low that the desire to sell will overwhelm diversification motives and investors will want to take a short position. Figure 70-2 shows that when the price exceeds $44, Sigma wants a short position in BU.

The demand curve for BU shares assumes that the price and therefore expected return of TD remain constant. A similar demand curve can be constructed for TD shares given a price for BU shares. As before, we would generate the demand for TD shares by revising Table 70-2 for various current prices of TD, leaving the price of BU unchanged. We use the revised expected returns to calculate the optimal portfolio for each possible price of TD, ultimately obtaining the demand curve shown in Figure 70-3 on page 364.

FIGURE 70-2   Supply and Demand for BU Shares

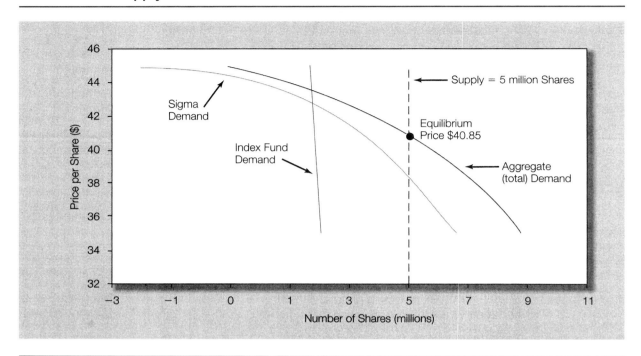

Index Funds' Demands for Stock

We have seen that index funds play an important role in portfolio selection, so let's see how an index fund would derive its demand for shares. Suppose that $130 million of investor funds in our hypothesized economy are given to an index fund—named Index—to manage. What will it do?

Index is looking for a portfolio that will mimic the market. Suppose current prices and market values are as in Table 70-1. Then the required proportions to mimic the market portfolio are:

$$w_{BU} = 195/(195 + 156) = .5556(55.56\%); w_{TD} = 1 - .5556 = .4444(44.44\%)$$

With $130 million to invest, Index will place $.5556 \times \$130$ million $= \$72.22$ million in BU shares. Table 70-4 shows a few other points on Index's demand curve for BU shares. The second column of the table shows the proportion of BU in total stock market value at each assumed price. In our two-stock example, this is BU's value as a fraction of the combined value of BU and TD. The third column is Index's desired dollar investment in BU and the last column shows shares demanded. The bold row corresponds to the case we analyzed in Table 70-1, for which BU is selling at $39.

Index's demand curve for BU shares is plotted in Figure 70-2 next to Sigma's demand, and in Figure 70-3 for TD shares. Index's demand is smaller than Sigma's because its budget is smaller. Moreover, the demand curve of the index fund is very steep, or "inelastic," that is, demand hardly responds to price changes. This is because an index fund's demand for shares does not respond to

TABLE 70-4	Calculation of Index Demand for BU Shares		
Current Price	BU Market-Value Proportion	Dollar Investment* ($ million)	Shares Desired
$45.00	.5906	76.772	1,706,037
42.50	.5767	74.966	1,763,908
40.00	.5618	73.034	1,825,843
39.00	**.5556**	**72.222**	**1,851,852**
37.50	.5459	70.961	1,892,285
35.00	.5287	68.731	1,963,746

* Dollar investment = BU proportion × $130 million.

expected returns. Index funds seek only to replicate market proportions. As the stock price goes up, so does its proportion in the market. This leads the index fund to invest more in the stock. Nevertheless, because each share costs more, the fund will desire fewer shares.

Equilibrium Prices and the Capital Asset Pricing Model

Market prices are determined by supply and demand. At any one time, the supply of shares of a stock is fixed, so supply is vertical at 5,000,000 shares of BU in Figure 70-2 and 4,000,000 shares of TD in Figure 70-3. Market demand is obtained by "horizontal aggregation," that is, for each price we add up the **quantity demanded** by all investors. You can examine the horizontal aggregation of the demand curves of Sigma and Index in Figures 70-2 and 70-3. The equilibrium prices are at the intersection of supply and demand.

However, the prices shown in Figures 70-2 and 70-3 will likely not persist for more than an instant. The reason is that the equilibrium price of BU ($40.85) was generated by demand curves derived by assuming that the price of TD was $39. Similarly, the equilibrium price of TD ($38.41) is an equilibrium price only when BU is at $39, which also is not the case. A full equilibrium would require that the demand curves derived for each stock be consistent with the actual prices of all other stocks. Thus, our model is only a beginning. But it does illustrate the important link between security analysis and the process by which portfolio demands, market prices, and expected returns are jointly determined. The CAPM treats the problem of finding a set of mutually consistent equilibrium prices and expected rates of return across all stocks. The model here illustrates the process that underlies the adjustment of market expected returns to demand pressures.

One might wonder why we originally posited that Sigma expects BU's share price to increase only by year-end when we have just argued that the adjustment to the new equilibrium price ought to be instantaneous. The reason is that when Sigma observes a market price of $39, it must assume that this *is* an equilibrium price based on investor beliefs *at the time*. Sigma believes that the market will catch up to its (presumably) superior estimate of intrinsic value of the firm by year-end, when its better assessment about the firm becomes widely adopted. In

FIGURE 70-3   Supply and Demand for TD Shares

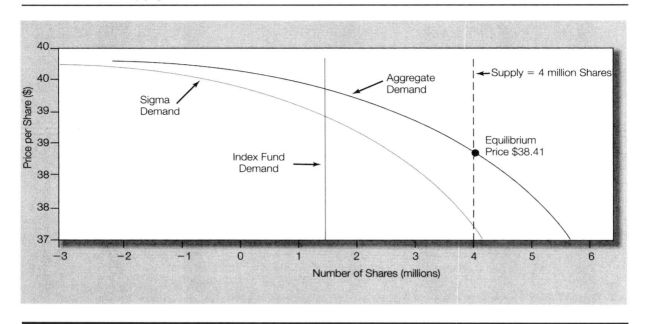

our simple example, Sigma is the only active manager, so its demand for "low-priced" BU stock would move the price immediately. But more realistically, since Sigma would be a small player compared to the entire stock market, the stock price would barely move in response to Sigma's demand, and the price would remain around $39 until Sigma's assessment was adopted by the average investor.

INDEX MODELS
by Zvi Bodie, Alex Kane, and Alan J. Marcus

LEARNING OUTCOMES

The candidate should be able to:

a. discuss how the Index Model can help simplify the Capital Asset Pricing Model framework and procedure developed in the prior reading;

b. distinguish between systematic and unsystematic risk, and discuss why the expected risk is a function of the number and characteristics of assets in the investment portfolio;

c. explain the problems when estimating individual asset betas and portfolio betas over time, and discuss systematic ways to help predict betas.

A SINGLE-INDEX SECURITY MARKET   1

Systematic Risk versus Firm-Specific Risk

The success of a portfolio selection rule depends on the quality of the input list, that is, the estimates of expected security returns and the covariance matrix. In the long run, efficient portfolios will beat portfolios with less reliable input lists and consequently inferior reward-to-risk trade-offs.

Suppose your security analysts can thoroughly analyze 50 stocks. This means that your input list will include the following:

$$
\begin{aligned}
n &= 50 \text{ estimates of expected returns} \\
n &= 50 \text{ estimates of variances} \\
(n^2 - n)/2 &= \underline{1{,}225} \text{ estimates of covariances} \\
& \ \ 1{,}325 \text{ estimates}
\end{aligned}
$$

This is a formidable task, particularly in light of the fact that a 50-security portfolio is relatively small. Doubling n to 100 will nearly quadruple the number of estimates to 5,150. If $n = 3,000$, roughly the number of NYSE stocks, we need more than 4.5 *million* estimates.

Another difficulty in applying the Markowitz model to portfolio optimization is that errors in the assessment or estimation of correlation coefficients can lead to nonsensical results. This can happen because some sets of correlation coefficients are mutually inconsistent, as the following example demonstrates:[1]

Asset	Standard Deviation (%)	Correlation Matrix		
		A	B	C
A	20	1.00	0.90	0.90
B	20	0.90	1.00	0.00
C	20	0.90	0.00	1.00

Suppose that you construct a portfolio with weights: -1.00; 1.00; 1.00, for assets A; B; C, respectively, and calculate the portfolio variance. You will find that the portfolio variance appears to be negative (-200). This of course is not possible because portfolio variances cannot be negative: we conclude that the inputs in the estimated correlation matrix must be mutually inconsistent. Of course, *true* correlation coefficients are always consistent.[2] But we do not know these true correlations and can only estimate them with some imprecision. Unfortunately, it is difficult to determine whether a correlation matrix is inconsistent, providing another motivation to seek a model that is easier to implement.

Covariances between security returns tend to be positive because the same economic forces affect the fortunes of many firms. Some examples of common economic factors are business cycles, interest rates, technological changes, and cost of labor and raw materials. All these (interrelated) factors affect almost all firms. Thus unexpected changes in these variables cause, simultaneously, unexpected changes in the rates of return on the entire stock market.

Suppose that we summarize all relevant economic factors by one macroeconomic indicator and assume that it moves the security market as a whole. We further assume that, beyond this common effect, all remaining uncertainty in stock returns is firm specific; that is, there is no other source of correlation between securities. Firm-specific events would include new inventions, deaths of key employees, and other factors that affect the fortune of the individual firm without affecting the broad economy in a measurable way.

We can summarize the distinction between macroeconomic and firm-specific factors by writing the holding-period return on security i as

$$r_i = E(r_i) + m_i + e_i \qquad \text{(71-1)}$$

where $E(r_i)$ is the expected return on the security as of the beginning of the holding period, m_i is the impact of unanticipated macro events on the security's return during the period, and e_i is the impact of unanticipated firm-specific events. Both m_i and e_i have zero expected values because each represents the impact of unanticipated events, which by definition must average out to zero.

We can gain further insight by recognizing that different firms have different sensitivities to macroeconomic events. Thus if we denote the unanticipated

[1] We are grateful to Andrew Kaplin and Ravi Jagannathan, Kellogg Graduate School of Management, Northwestern University, for this example.

[2] The mathematical term for a correlation matrix that cannot generate negative portfolio variance is "positive definite."

components of the macro factor by F, and denote the responsiveness of security i to macroevents by beta, β_i, then the macro component of security i is $m_i = \beta_i F$, and then Equation 71-1 becomes[3]

$$r_i = E(r_i) + \beta_i F + e_i \qquad \textbf{(71-2)}$$

Equation 71-2 is known as a **single-factor model** for stock returns. It is easy to imagine that a more realistic decomposition of security returns would require more than one factor in Equation 71-2. We treat this issue later in the reading. For now, let us examine the simple case with only one macro factor.

Of course, a factor model is of little use without specifying a way to measure the factor that is posited to affect security returns. One reasonable approach is to assert that the rate of return on a broad index of securities such as the S&P 500 is a valid proxy for the common macro factor. This approach leads to an equation similar to the factor model, which is called a **single-index model** because it uses the market index to proxy for the common or systematic factor.

According to the **index model**, we can separate the actual or realized rate of return on a security into macro (systematic) and micro (firm-specific) components in a manner similar to that in Equation 71-2. We write the rate of return on each security as a sum of three components:

	Symbol
1. The stock's expected return if the market is neutral, that is, if the market's excess return, $r_M - r_f$, is zero	α_j
2. The component of return due to movements in the overall market; β_j is the security's responsiveness to market movements	$\beta_j(r_M - r_f)$
3. The unexpected component due to unexpected events that are relevant only to this security (firm specific)	e_j

The holding-period excess return on the stock can be stated as

$$r_i - r_f = \alpha_i + \beta_i (r_M - r_f) + e_i$$

Let us denote excess returns over the risk-free rate by capital R and rewrite this equation as

$$R_i = \alpha_i + \beta_i R_M + e_i \qquad \textbf{(71-3)}$$

We write the index model in terms of excess returns over r_f rather than in terms of total returns because the level of the stock market return represents the state of the macro economy only to the extent that it exceeds or falls short of the rate of return on risk-free T-bills. For example, in 2003, when T-bills were yielding only 1% or 2%, a return of 8% or 9% on the stock market would be considered good news. In contrast, in the early 1980s, when bills were yielding over 10%, that same 8% or 9% would signal disappointing macroeconomic news.[4]

---

[3] You may wonder why we choose the notation β for the responsiveness coefficient because β already has been defined in Reading 70 in the context of the CAPM. The choice is deliberate, however. Our reasoning will be obvious shortly.

[4] Practitioners often use a "modified" index model that is similar to Equation 71-3 but that uses total rather than excess returns. This practice is most common when daily data are used. In this case the rate of return on bills is on the order of only about .01% per day, so total and excess returns are almost indistinguishable.

Equation 71-3 says that each security has two sources of risk: *market or systematic risk*, attributable to its sensitivity to macroeconomic factors as reflected in R_M, and *firm-specific risk,* as reflected in *e*. If we denote the variance of the excess return on the market, R_M, as σ_M^2, then we can break the variance of the rate of return on each stock into two components:

	Symbol
1. The variance attributable to the uncertainty of the common macroeconomic factor	$\beta_i^2\,\sigma_M^2$
2. The variance attributable to firm-specific uncertainty	$\sigma^2(e_i)$

The covariance between R_M and e_i is zero because e_i is defined as firm specific, that is, independent of movements in the market. Hence the variance of the rate of return on security *i* equals the sum of the variances due to the common and the firm-specific components:

$$\sigma_i^2 = \beta_i^2\sigma_M^2 + \sigma^2(e_i)$$

What about the covariance between the rates of return on two stocks? This may be written:

$$\text{Cov}(R_i, R_j) = \text{Cov}(\alpha_i + \beta_i\,R_M + e_i,\, \alpha_j + \beta_j\,R_M + e_j)$$

But since α_i and α_j are constants, their covariance with any variable is zero. Further, the firm-specific terms $(e_i,\,e_j)$ are assumed uncorrelated with the market and with each other. Therefore, the only source of covariance in the returns between the two stocks derives from their common dependence on the common factor, R_M. In other words, the covariance between stocks is due to the fact that the returns on each depend in part on economywide conditions. Thus,

$$\text{Cov}(R_i, R_j) = \text{Cov}(\beta_iR_M, \beta_jR_M) = \beta_i\beta_j\sigma_M^2 \qquad \textbf{(71-4)}$$

These calculations show that if we have

n estimates of the expected excess returns, $E(R_i)$
n estimates of the sensitivity coefficients, β_i
n estimates of the firm-specific variances, $\sigma^2(e_i)$
1 estimate for the variance of the (common) macroeconomic factor, σ_M^2,

then these $(3n + 1)$ estimates will enable us to prepare the input list for this single-index security universe. Thus for a 50-security portfolio we will need 151 estimates rather than 1,325; for the entire New York Stock Exchange, about 3,000 securities, we will need 9,001 estimates rather than approximately 4.5 million!

It is easy to see why the index model is such a useful abstraction. For large universes of securities, the number of estimates required for the Markowitz procedure using the index model is only a small fraction of what otherwise would be needed.

Another advantage is less obvious but equally important. The index model abstraction is crucial for specialization of effort in security analysis. If a covariance term had to be calculated directly for each security pair, then security analysts could not specialize by industry. For example, if one group were to specialize in the computer industry and another in the auto industry, who would have the common background to estimate the covariance *between* IBM and GM? Neither group would have the deep understanding of other industries necessary to make an informed judgment of co-movements among industries. In contrast, the index model suggests a simple way to compute covariances. Covariances among securities are due to the influence of the single common factor, represented by the market index return, and can be easily estimated using Equation 71-4.

The simplification derived from the index model assumption is, however, not without cost. The "cost" of the model lies in the restrictions it places on the structure of asset return uncertainty. The classification of uncertainty into a simple dichotomy—macro versus micro risk—oversimplifies sources of real-world uncertainty and misses some important sources of dependence in stock returns. For example, this dichotomy rules out industry events, events that may affect many firms within an industry without substantially affecting the broad macroeconomy.

Statistical analysis shows that relative to a single index, the firm-specific components of some firms are correlated. Examples are the nonmarket components of stocks in a single industry, such as computer stocks or auto stocks. At the same time, statistical significance does not always correspond to economic significance. Economically speaking, the question that is more relevant to the assumption of a single-index model is whether portfolios constructed using covariances that are estimated on the basis of the single-factor or single-index assumption are significantly different from, and less efficient than, portfolios constructed using covariances that are estimated directly for each pair of stocks.

CONCEPT CHECK 1

Suppose that the index model for the excess returns of stocks A and B is estimated with the following results:

$$R_A = 1.0\% + .9R_M + e_A$$
$$R_B = -2.0\% + 1.1R_M + e_B$$
$$\sigma_M = 20\%$$
$$\sigma(e_A) = 30\%$$
$$\sigma(e_B) = 10\%$$

Find the standard deviation of each stock and the covariance between them.

Estimating the Index Model

Equation 71-3 also suggests how we might go about actually measuring market and firm-specific risk. Suppose that we observe the excess return on the market index and a specific asset over a number of holding periods. We use as an example monthly excess returns on the S&P 500 index and GM stock for a 1-year period. We can summarize the results for a sample period in a **scatter diagram**, as illustrated in Figure 71-1.

The horizontal axis in Figure 71-1 measures the excess return (over the risk-free rate) on the market index, whereas the vertical axis measures the excess return on the asset in question (GM stock in our example). A pair of excess returns (one for the market index, one for GM stock) constitutes one point on this scatter diagram. The points are numbered 1 through 12, representing excess returns for the S&P 500 and GM for each month from January through December. The single-index model states that the relationship between the excess returns on GM and the S&P 500 is given by

$$R_{GMt} = \alpha_{GM} + \beta_{GM}R_{Mt} + e_{GMt}$$

Note the resemblance of this relationship to a **regression equation**.

In a single-variable regression equation, the dependent variable plots around a straight line with an intercept α and a slope β. The deviations from the line, e, are assumed to be mutually uncorrelated as well as uncorrelated with the independent variable. Because these assumptions are identical to those of the index model we can look at the index model as a regression model. The sensitivity of GM to the market, measured by β_{GM}, is the slope of the regression line. The intercept of the regression line is α_{GM}, representing the average firm-specific excess return when the market's excess return is zero. Deviations of particular observations from the regression line in any period are denoted e_{GMt} and called **residuals**. Each of these residuals is the difference between the actual stock return and the return that would be predicted from the regression equation describing the usual relationship between the stock and the market; therefore, residuals measure the impact of firm-specific events during the particular month. The parameters of interest, α, β, and $Var(e)$, can be estimated using standard regression techniques.

Estimating the regression equation of the single-index model gives us the **security characteristic line** (SCL), which is plotted in Figure 71-1. (The regression results and raw data appear in Table 71-1.) The SCL is a plot of the typical excess return on a security as a function of the excess return on the market.

This sample of holding-period returns is, of course, too small to yield reliable statistics. We use it only for demonstration. For this sample period we find that the beta coefficient of GM stock, as estimated by the slope of the regression line, is 1.1357, and that the intercept for this SCL is −2.59% per month.

FIGURE 71-1 Security Characteristic Line (SCL) for GM

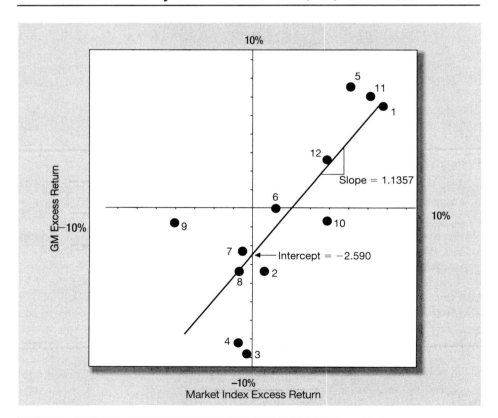

TABLE 71-1 Characteristic Line for GM Stock

Month	GM Return	Market Return	Monthly T-Bill Rate	Excess GM Return	Excess Market Return
January	6.06	7.89	0.65	5.41	7.24
February	−2.86	1.51	0.58	−3.44	0.93
March	−8.18	0.23	0.62	−8.79	−0.38
April	−7.36	−0.29	0.72	−8.08	−1.01
May	7.76	5.58	0.66	7.10	4.92
June	0.52	1.73	0.55	−0.03	1.18
July	−1.74	−0.21	0.62	−2.36	−0.83
August	−3.00	−0.36	0.55	−3.55	−0.91
September	−0.56	−3.58	0.60	−1.16	−4.18
October	−0.37	4.62	0.65	−1.02	3.97
November	6.93	6.85	0.61	6.32	6.25
December	3.08	4.55	0.65	2.43	3.90
Mean	0.02	2.38	0.62	−0.60	1.75
Standard deviation	4.97	3.33	0.05	4.97	3.32

Regression results $r_{GM} - r_f = \alpha + \beta(r_M - r_f)$

	α	β
Estimated coefficient	−2.590	1.1357
Standard error of estimate	(1.547)	(0.309)

Variance of residuals = 12.601

Standard deviation of residuals = 3.550

$R^2 = .575$

For each month, t, our estimate of the residual, e_t, which is the deviation of GM's excess return from the prediction of the SCL, equals

Deviation = Actual − Predicted return
$$e_{GMt} = R_{GMt} - (\beta_{GM}R_{Mt} + \alpha_{GM})$$

These residuals are estimates of the monthly unexpected *firm-specific* component of the rate of return on GM stock. Hence we can estimate the firm-specific variance by[5]

$$\sigma^2(e_{GM}) = \frac{1}{10}\sum_{t=1}^{12}e_t^2 = 12.60$$

[5] Because the mean of e_t is zero, e_t^2 is the squared deviation from its mean. The average value of e_t^2 is therefore the estimate of the variance of the firm-specific component. We divide the sum of squared residuals by the degrees of freedom of the regression, $n - 2 = 12 - 2 = 10$, to obtain an unbiased estimate of $\sigma^2(e)$.

The <u>stand</u>ard deviation of the firm-specific component of GM's return, $\sigma(e_{GM})$, is $\sqrt{12.60} = 3.55\%$ per month, equal to the standard deviation of the regression residual.

The Index Model and Diversification

The index model, first suggested by Sharpe,[6] also offers insight into portfolio diversification. Suppose that we choose an equally weighted portfolio of n securities. The excess rate of return on each security is given by

$$R_i = \alpha_i + \beta_i R_M + e_i$$

Similarly, we can write the excess return on the portfolio of stocks as

$$R_P = \alpha_P + \beta_P R_M + e_P \qquad \textbf{(71-5)}$$

We now show that, as the number of stocks included in this portfolio increases, the part of the portfolio risk attributable to nonmarket factors becomes ever smaller. This part of the risk is diversified away. In contrast, the market risk remains, regardless of the number of firms combined into the portfolio.

To understand these results, note that the excess rate of return on this equally weighted portfolio, for which each portfolio weight $w_i = 1/n$, is

$$R_P = \sum_{i=1}^{n} w_i R_i = \frac{1}{n}\sum_{i=1}^{n} R_i = \frac{1}{n}\sum_{i=1}^{n} (\alpha_i + \beta_i R_M + e_i)$$

$$= \frac{1}{n}\sum_{i=1}^{n} \alpha_i + \left(\frac{1}{n}\sum_{i=1}^{n} \beta_i\right) R_M + \frac{1}{n}\sum_{i=1}^{n} e_i \qquad \textbf{(71-6)}$$

Comparing Equations 71-5 and 71-6, we see that the portfolio has a sensitivity to the market given by

$$\beta_P = \frac{1}{n}\sum_{i=1}^{n} \beta_i$$

which is the average of the individual β_is. It has a nonmarket return component of a constant (intercept)

$$\alpha_P = \frac{1}{n}\sum_{i=1}^{n} \alpha_i$$

which is the average of the individual alphas, plus the zero mean variable

$$e_P = \frac{1}{n}\sum_{i=1}^{n} e_i$$

which is the average of the firm-specific components. Hence the portfolio's variance is

$$\sigma_P^2 = \beta_P^2 \sigma_M^2 + \sigma^2(e_P) \qquad \textbf{(71-7)}$$

---

[6] William F. Sharpe, "A Simplified Model of Portfolio Analysis," *Management Science*, January 1963.

The systematic risk component of the portfolio variance, which we defined as the component that depends on marketwide movements, is $\beta_P^2 \, \sigma_M^2$ and depends on the sensitivity coefficients of the individual securities. This part of the risk depends on portfolio beta and σ_M^2 and will persist regardless of the extent of portfolio diversification. No matter how many stocks are held, their common exposure to the market will be reflected in portfolio systematic risk.[7]

In contrast, the nonsystematic component of the portfolio variance is $\sigma^2(e_P)$ and is attributable to firm-specific components, e_i. Because these e_is are independent, and all have zero expected value, the law of averages can be applied to conclude that as more and more stocks are added to the portfolio, the firm-specific components tend to cancel out, resulting in ever-smaller nonmarket risk. Such risk is thus termed *diversifiable*. To see this more rigorously, examine the formula for the variance of the equally weighted "portfolio" of firm-specific components. Because the e_is are uncorrelated,

$$\sigma^2(e_P) = \sum_{i=1}^{n}\left(\frac{1}{n}\right)^2 \sigma^2(e_i) = \frac{1}{n}\overline{\sigma}^2(e)$$

where $\overline{\sigma}^2(e)$ is the average of the firm-specific variances. Because this average is independent of n, when n gets large, $\sigma^2(e_P)$ becomes negligible.

To summarize, as diversification increases, the total variance of a portfolio approaches the systematic variance, defined as the variance of the market factor multiplied by the square of the portfolio sensitivity coefficient, β_P^2. This is shown in Figure 71-2.

FIGURE 71-2   The Variance of a Portfolio with Risk Coefficient β_P in the Single-Factor Economy

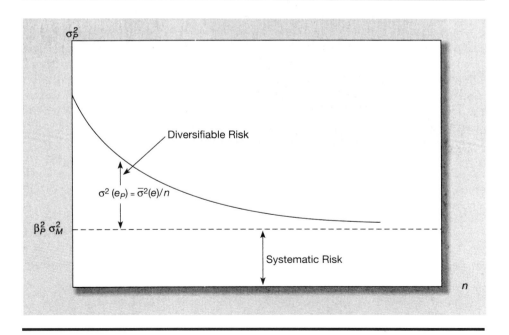

[7] Of course, one can construct a portfolio with zero systematic risk by mixing negative β and positive β assets. The point of our discussion is that the vast majority of securities have a positive β, implying that well-diversified portfolios with small holdings in large numbers of assets will indeed have positive systematic risk.

Figure 71-2 shows that as more and more securities are combined into a portfolio, the portfolio variance decreases because of the diversification of firm-specific risk. However, the power of diversification is limited. Even for very large n, part of the risk remains because of the exposure of virtually all assets to the common, or market, factor. Therefore, this systematic risk is said to be nondiversifiable.

This analysis is borne out by empirical evidence. These empirical results are similar to the theoretical graph presented in Figure 71-2.

CONCEPT CHECK 2

Reconsider the two stocks in Concept Check 1. Suppose we form an equally weighted portfolio of A and B. What will be the nonsystematic standard deviation of that portfolio?

---

2   THE CAPM AND THE INDEX MODEL

Actual Returns versus Expected Returns

The CAPM is an elegant model. The question is whether it has real-world value—whether its implications are borne out by experience. There is a range of empirical evidence on this point, but for now we focus briefly on a more basic issue: Is the CAPM testable even in principle?

For starters, one central prediction of the CAPM is that the market portfolio is a mean-variance efficient portfolio. Consider that the CAPM treats all traded risky assets. To test the efficiency of the CAPM market portfolio, we would need to construct a value-weighted portfolio of a huge size and test its efficiency. So far, this task has not been feasible. An even more difficult problem, however, is that the CAPM implies relationships among *expected* returns, whereas all we can observe are actual or realized holding-period returns, and these need not equal prior expectations. Even supposing we could construct a portfolio to represent the CAPM market portfolio satisfactorily, how would we test its mean-variance efficiency? We would have to show that the **reward-to-variability ratio** of the market portfolio is higher than that of any other portfolio. However, this reward-to-variability ratio is set in terms of expectations, and we have no way to observe these expectations directly.

The problem of measuring expectations haunts us as well when we try to establish the validity of the second central set of CAPM predictions, the expected return–beta relationship. This relationship is also defined in terms of expected returns $E(r_i)$ and $E(r_M)$:

$$E(r_i) = r_f + \beta_i[E(r_M) - r_f] \tag{71-8}$$

The upshot is that, as elegant and insightful as the CAPM is, we must make additional assumptions to make it implementable and testable.

The Index Model and Realized Returns

We have said that the CAPM is a statement about ex ante or expected returns, whereas in practice all anyone can observe directly are ex post or realized returns. To make the leap from expected to realized returns, we can employ the index model, which we will use in excess return form as

$$R_i = \alpha_i + \beta_i R_M + e_i \tag{71-9}$$

We saw in Section 1 how to apply standard regression analysis to estimate Equation 71-9 using observable realized returns over some sample period. Let us now see how this framework for statistically decomposing actual stock returns meshes with the CAPM.

We start by deriving the covariance between the returns on stock i and the market index. By definition, the firm-specific or nonsystematic component is independent of the marketwide or systematic component, that is, $Cov(R_M, e_i) = 0$. From this relationship, it follows that the covariance of the excess rate of return on security i with that of the market index is

$$\begin{aligned} Cov(R_i, R_M) &= Cov(\beta_i R_M + e_i, R_M) \\ &= \beta_i Cov(R_M, R_M) + Cov(e_i, R_M) \\ &= \beta_i \sigma_M^2 \end{aligned}$$

Note that we can drop α_i from the covariance terms because α_i is a constant and thus has zero covariance with all variables.

Because $Cov(R_i, R_M) = \beta_i \sigma_M^2$, the sensitivity coefficient, β_i, in equation 71-9, which is the slope of the regression line representing the index model, equals

$$\beta_i = \frac{Cov(R_i, R_M)}{\sigma_M^2}.$$

The index model beta coefficient turns out to be the same beta as that of the CAPM expected return–beta relationship, except that we replace the (theoretical) market portfolio of the CAPM with the well-specified and observable market index.

CONCEPT CHECK 3

The data below describe a three-stock financial market that satisfies the single-index model.

Stock	Capitalization	Beta	Mean Excess Return	Standard Deviation
A	$3,000	1.0	10%	40%
B	$1,940	0.2	2	30
C	$1,360	1.7	17	50

The single factor in this economy is perfectly correlated with the value-weighted index of the stock market. The standard deviation of the market index portfolio is 25%.

a. What is the mean excess return of the index portfolio?

b. What is the covariance between stock B and the index?

c. Break down the variance of stock B into its systematic and firm-specific components.

The Index Model and the Expected Return–Beta Relationship

Recall that the CAPM expected return–beta relationship is, for any asset i and the (theoretical) market portfolio,

$$E(r_i) - r_f = \beta_i[E(r_M) - r_f]$$

where $\beta_i = \text{Cov}(R_i, R_M)/\sigma_M^2$. This is a statement about the mean of expected excess returns of assets relative to the mean excess return of the (theoretical) market portfolio.

If the index M in Equation 71-9 represents the true market portfolio, we can take the expectation of each side of the equation to show that the index model specification is

$$E(r_i) - r_f = \alpha_i + \beta_i[E(r_M) - r_f]$$

A comparison of the index model relationship to the CAPM expected return–beta relationship (Equation 71-8) shows that the CAPM predicts that α_i should be zero for all assets. The alpha of a stock is its expected return in excess of (or below) the fair expected return as predicted by the CAPM. If the stock is fairly priced, its alpha must be zero.

We emphasize again that this is a statement about *expected* returns on a security. After the fact, of course, some securities will do better or worse than expected and will have returns higher or lower than predicted by the CAPM; that is, they will exhibit positive or negative alphas over a sample period. But this superior or inferior performance could not have been forecast in advance.

Therefore, if we estimate the index model for several firms, using Equation 71-9 as a regression equation, we should find that the ex post or realized alphas (the regression intercepts) for the firms in our sample center around zero. If the initial expectation for alpha were zero, as many firms would be expected to have a positive as a negative alpha for some sample period. The CAPM states that the *expected* value of alpha is zero for all securities, whereas the index model representation of the CAPM holds that the *realized* value of alpha should average out to zero for a sample of historical observed returns. Just as important, the sample alphas should be unpredictable, that is, independent from one sample period to the next.

Some interesting evidence on this property was first compiled by Michael Jensen,[8] who examined the alphas realized by mutual funds over the period 1945 to 1964. Figure 71-3 shows the frequency distribution of these alphas, which do indeed seem to be distributed around zero. More recent studies come to the same conclusion.

There is yet another applicable variation on the intuition of the index model, the **market model**. Formally, the market model states that the return "surprise" of any security is proportional to the return surprise of the market, plus a firm-specific surprise:

$$r_i - E(r_i) = \beta_i[r_M - E(r_M)] + e_i$$

This equation divides returns into firm-specific and systematic components somewhat differently from the index model. If the CAPM is valid, however, you

---

[8] Michael C. Jensen, "The Performance of Mutual Funds in the Period 1945–1964," *Journal of Finance* 23 (May 1968).

FIGURE 71-3   Frequency Distribution of Alphas

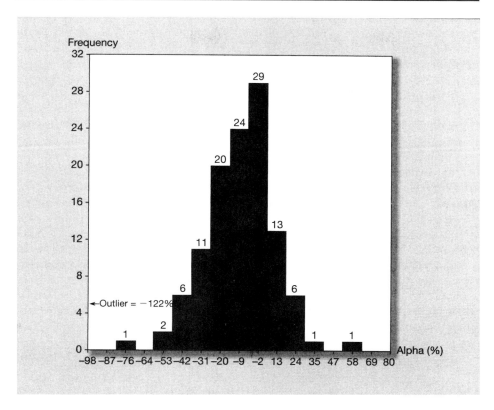

Source: Michael C. Jensen, "The Performance of Mutual Funds in the Period 1945–1964," *Journal of Finance* 23 (May 1968).

can confirm that, substituting for $E(r_i)$ from Equation 71-8, the market model equation becomes identical to the index model. For this reason the terms "index model" and "market model" often are used interchangeably.

CONCEPT CHECK 4

Can you sort out the nuances of the following maze of models?

a. CAPM
b. Single-factor model
c. Single-index model
d. Market model

THE INDUSTRY VERSION OF THE INDEX MODEL   3

Not surprisingly, the index model has attracted the attention of practitioners. To the extent that it is approximately valid, it provides a convenient benchmark for security analysis.

A modern practitioner using the CAPM, who has neither special information about a security nor insight that is unavailable to the general public, will conclude that the security is "properly" priced. By properly priced, the analyst means that the expected return on the security is commensurate with its risk, and therefore plots on the security market line. For instance, if one has no **private information** about GM's stock, then one should expect

$$E(r_{GM}) = r_f + \beta_{GM}[E(r_M) - r_f]$$

A portfolio manager who has a forecast for the market index, $E(r_M)$, and observes the risk-free T-bill rate, r_f, can use the model to determine the benchmark expected return for any stock. The beta coefficient, the market risk, σ_M^2, and the firm-specific risk, $\sigma^2(e)$, can be estimated from historical SCLs, that is, from regressions of security excess returns on market index excess returns.

There are many sources for such regression results. One widely used source is Research Computer Services Department of Merrill Lynch, which publishes a monthly *Security Risk Evaluation* book, commonly called the "beta book". The websites listed at the end of the chapter also provide security betas.

Security Risk Evaluation uses the S&P 500 as the proxy for the market portfolio. It relies on the 60 most recent monthly obeservations to calculate regression parameters. Merrill Lynch and most services[9] use total returns, rather than excess returns (deviations from T-bill rates), in the regressions. In this way they estimate a variant of our index model, which is

$$r = a + br_M + e* \qquad \text{(71-10)}$$

instead of

$$r - r_f = \alpha + \beta(r_M - r_f) + e \qquad \text{(71-11)}$$

To see the effect of this departure, we can rewrite Equation 71-11 as

$$r = r_f + \alpha + \beta r_M - \beta r_f + e = \alpha + r_f(1 - \beta) + \beta r_M + e \qquad \text{(71-12)}$$

Comparing Equations 71-10 and 71-12, you can see that if r_f is constant over the sample period, both equations have the same independent variable, r_M, and residual, e. Therefore, the slope coefficient will be the same in the two regressions.[10]

However, the intercept that Merrill Lynch calls alpha is really an estimate of $\alpha + r_f(1 - \beta)$. The apparent justification for this procedure is that, on a monthly basis, $r_f(1 - \beta)$ is small and is apt to be swamped by the volatility of actual stock returns. But it is worth noting that for $\beta \neq 1$, the regression intercept in Equation 71-10 will not equal the index model alpha as it does when excess returns are used as in Equation 71-11.

Another way the Merrill Lynch procedure departs from the index model is in its use of percentage changes in price instead of total rates of return. This means that the index model variant of Merrill Lynch ignores the dividend component of stock returns.

Table 71-2 illustrates a page from the beta book which includes estimates for GM. The third column, Close Price, shows the stock price at the end of the sam-

[9] Value Line is another common source of security betas. Value Line uses weekly rather than monthly data and uses the New York Stock Exchange index instead of the S&P 500 as the market proxy.

[10] Actually, r_f does vary over time and so should not be grouped casually with the constant term in the regression. However, variations in r_f are tiny compared with the swings in the market return. The actual volatility in the T-bill rate has only a small impact on the estimated value of β.

TABLE 71-2 Market Sensitivity Statistics

Ticker Symbol	Security Name	June 1994 Close Price	Beta	Alpha	R-SQR	RESID STD DEV-N	Standard Error Beta	Standard Error Alpha	Adjusted Beta	Number of Observations
GBND	General Binding Corp	18.375	0.52	−0.06	0.02	10.52	0.37	1.38	0.68	60
GBDC	General Bldrs Corp	0.930	0.58	−1.03	0.00	17.38	0.62	2.28	0.72	60
GNCMA	General Communication Inc Class A	3.750	1.54	0.82	0.12	14.42	0.51	1.89	1.36	60
GCCC	General Computer Corp	8.375	0.93	1.67	0.06	12.43	0.44	1.63	0.95	60
GDC	General Datacomm Inds Inc	16.125	2.25	2.31	0.16	18.32	0.65	2.40	1.83	60
GD	General Dynamics Corp	40.875	0.54	0.63	0.03	9.02	0.32	1.18	0.69	60
GE	General Elec Co	46.625	1.21	0.39	0.61	3.53	0.13	0.46	1.14	60
JOB	General Employment Enterpris	4.063	0.91	1.20	0.01	20.50	0.73	2.69	0.94	60
GMCC	General Magnaplate Corp	4.500	0.97	0.00	0.04	14.18	0.50	1.86	0.98	60
GMW	General Microwave Corp	8.000	0.95	0.16	0.12	8.83	0.31	1.16	0.97	60
GIS	General MLS Inc	54.625	1.01	0.42	0.37	4.82	0.17	0.63	1.01	60
GM	General MTRS Corp	50.250	0.80	0.14	0.11	7.78	0.28	1.02	0.87	60 ←
GPU	General Pub Utils Cp	26.250	0.52	0.20	0.20	3.69	0.13	0.48	0.68	60
GRN	General RE Corp	108.875	1.07	0.42	0.31	5.75	0.20	0.75	1.05	60
GSX	General SIGNAL Corp	33.000	0.86	−0.01	0.22	5.85	0.21	0.77	0.91	60

Source: Modified from *Security Risk Evaluation*, 1994, Research Computer Services Department of Merrill Lynch, Pierce, Fenner and Smith, Inc., pp. 9–17. Based on S&P 500 index, using straight regression.

ple period. The next two columns show the beta and alpha coefficients. Remember that Merrill Lynch's alpha is actually an estimate of $\alpha + r_f(1 - \beta)$.

The next column, R-SQR, shows the square of the correlation between r_i and r_M. The R-square statistic, R^2, which is sometimes called the *coefficient of determination*, gives the fraction of the variance of the dependent variable (the return on the stock) that is explained by movements in the independent variable (the return on the S&P 500 index). Recall from Section 1 that the part of the total variance of the rate of return on an asset, σ^2, that is explained by market returns is the systematic variance, $\beta^2 \sigma_M^2$. Hence the R-square is systematic variance over total variance, which tells us what fraction of a firm's volatility is attributable to market movements:

$$R^2 = \frac{\beta^2 \sigma_M^2}{\sigma^2}$$

The firm-specific variance, $\sigma^2(e)$, is the part of the asset variance that is unexplained by the market index. Therefore, because

$$\sigma^2 = \beta^2 \sigma_M^2 + \sigma^2(e)$$

the coefficient of determination also may be expressed as

$$R^2 = 1 - \frac{\sigma^2(e)}{\sigma^2}$$ (71-13)

Accordingly, the column following *R-SQR* reports the standard deviation of the nonsystematic component, $\sigma(e)$, calling it RESID STD DEV-*N*, in reference to the fact that the *e* is estimated from the regression residuals. This variable is an estimate of firm-specific risk.

The following two columns appear under the heading of Standard Error. These are statistics that allow us to test the precision and significance of the regression coefficients. The standard error of an estimate is the standard deviation of the possible estimation error of the coefficient. A rule of thumb is that if an estimated coefficient is less than twice its standard error, we cannot reject the hypothesis that the true coefficient is zero. The ratio of the coefficient to its standard error is the *t*-statistic. A *t*-statistic greater than 2 is the traditional cutoff for statistical significance. The two columns of the standard error of the estimated beta and alpha allow us a quick check on the statistical significance of these estimates.

The next-to-last column is called Adjusted Beta. The motivation for adjusting beta estimates is that, on average, the beta coefficients of stocks seem to move toward 1 over time. One explanation for this phenomenon is intuitive. A business enterprise usually is established to produce a specific product or service, and a new firm may be more unconventional than an older one in many ways, from technology to management style. As it grows, however, a firm often diversifies, first expanding to similar products and later to more diverse operations. As the firm becomes more conventional, it starts to resemble the rest of the economy even more. Thus its beta coefficient will tend to change in the direction of 1.

Another explanation for this phenomenon is statistical. We know that the average beta over all securities is 1. Thus, before estimating the beta of a security, our best forecast of the beta would be that it is 1. When we estimate this beta coefficient over a particular sample period, we sustain some unknown sampling error of the estimated beta. The greater the difference between our beta estimate and 1, the greater is the chance that we incurred a large estimation error and that beta in a subsequent sample period will be closer to 1.

E-INVESTMENTS: BETA ESTIMATES

Go to one of the sites listed in the Related Websites section. Find the betas of 10 stocks from different industries. What sorts of factors might explain the differences among these betas? Do the firms in industries that are more sensitive to the business cycle appear to have higher betas? Find betas of four firms in the same industry. Are the beta estimates for firms within an industry more similar than beta estimates across industries?

The sample estimate of the beta coefficient is the best guess for that sample period. Given that beta has a tendency to evolve toward 1, however, a forecast of the future beta coefficient should adjust the sample estimate in that direction.

Merrill Lynch adjusts beta estimates in a simple way.[11] It takes the sample estimate of beta and averages it with 1, using weights of two-thirds and one-third:

Adjusted beta = 2/3 sample beta + 1/3(1)

---

[11] A more sophisticated method is described in Oldrich A. Vasicek, "A Note on Using Cross-Sectional Information in Bayesian Estimation of Security Betas," *Journal of Finance* 28 (1973), pp. 1233–39.

Example 71-1

Adjusted Beta

For the 60 months used in Table 71-2, GM's beta was estimated at .80. Therefore, its adjusted beta is $2/3 \times .80 + 1/3 = .87$, taking it a third of the way toward 1.

In the absence of special information concerning GM, if our forecast for the market index is 14% and T-bills pay 6%, we learn from the Merrill Lynch beta book that the CAPM forecast for the rate of return on GM stock is

$$E(r_{GM}) = r_f + \text{adjusted beta} \times [E(r_M) - r_f]$$
$$= 6 + .87 \,(14 - 6) = 12.96\%$$

The sample period regression alpha is .14%. Because GM's beta is less than 1, we know that this means that the index model alpha estimate is somewhat smaller. As in Equation 71-12, we have to subtract $(1 - \beta) r_f$ from the regression alpha to obtain the index model alpha. Even so, the standard error of the alpha estimate is 1.02. The estimate of alpha is far less than twice its standard error. Consequently, we cannot reject the hypothesis that the true alpha is zero.

CONCEPT CHECK 5

What was GM's CAPM alpha per month during the period covered by the Merrill Lynch regression if during this period the average monthly rate of return on T-bills was .6%?

Always remember that these alpha estimates are ex post (after the fact) measures. They do not mean that anyone could have forecast these alpha values ex ante (before the fact). In fact, the name of the game in security analysis is to forecast alpha values ahead of time. A well-constructed portfolio that includes long positions in future positive-alpha stocks and short positions in future negative-alpha stocks will outperform the market index. The key term here is "well constructed," meaning that the portfolio has to balance concentration on high-alpha stocks with the need for risk-reducing diversification. The beta and residual variance estimates from the index model regression make it possible to achieve this goal.

Note that GM's RESID STD DEV-N is 7.78% per month and its R^2 is .11. This tells us that $\sigma_{GM}^2(e) = 7.78^2 = 60.53$ and, because $R^2 = 1 - \sigma^2(e)/\sigma^2$, we can solve for the estimate of GM's total standard deviation by rearranging Equation 71-13 as follows:

$$\sigma_{GM} = \left[\frac{\sigma_{GM}^2(e)}{1 - R^2} \right]^{1/2} = \left(\frac{60.53}{.89} \right)^{1/2} = 8.25\% \text{ per month}$$

This is GM's monthly standard deviation for the sample period. Therefore, the annualized standard deviation for that period was $8.25\sqrt{12} = 28.58\%$.

Finally, the last column shows the number of observations, which is 60 months, unless the stock is newly listed and fewer observations are available.

Predicting Betas

We saw in the previous section that betas estimated from past data may not be the best estimates of future betas: Betas seem to drift toward 1 over time. This suggests that we might want a forecasting model for beta.

One simple approach would be to collect data on beta in different periods and then estimate a regression equation:

$$\text{Current beta} = a + b\,(\text{Past beta}) \tag{71-14}$$

Given estimates of a and b, we would then forecast future betas using the rule

$$\text{Forecast beta} = a + b\,(\text{Current beta})$$

There is no reason, however, to limit ourselves to such simple forecasting rules. Why not also investigate the predictive power of other financial variables in forecasting beta? For example, if we believe that firm size and debt ratios are two determinants of beta, we might specify an expanded version of Equation 71-14 and estimate

$$\text{Current beta} = a + b_1(\text{Past beta}) + b_2(\text{Firm size}) + b_3(\text{Debt ratio})$$

Now we would use estimates of a and b_1 through b_3 to forecast future betas.

Such an approach was followed by Rosenberg and Guy[12] who found the following variables to help predict betas:

1. Variance of earnings.
2. Variance of cash flow.
3. Growth in earnings per share.
4. Market capitalization (firm size).
5. Dividend yield.
6. Debt-to-asset ratio.

Rosenberg and Guy also found that even after controlling for a firm's financial characteristics, industry group helps to predict beta. For example, they found that the beta values of gold mining companies are on average .827 lower than would be predicted based on financial characteristics alone. This should not be surprising; the $-.827$ "adjustment factor" for the gold industry reflects the fact that gold values are inversely related to market returns.

Table 71-3 presents beta estimates and adjustment factors for a subset of firms in the Rosenberg and Guy study.

TABLE 71-3 Industry Betas and Adjustment Factors

Industry	Beta	Adjustment Factor
Agriculture	0.99	−.140
Drugs and medicine	1.14	−.099

(Table continued on next page …)

---

[12] Barr Rosenberg and J. Guy, "Prediction of Beta from Investment Fundamentals, Parts 1 and 2," *Financial Analysts Journal*, May–June and July–August 1976.

TABLE 71-3 Industry Betas and Adjustment Factors (continued)		
Industry	**Beta**	**Adjustment Factor**
Telephone	0.75	−.288
Energy utilities	0.60	−.237
Gold	0.36	−.827
Construction	1.27	.062
Air transport	1.80	.348
Trucking	1.31	.098
Consumer durables	1.44	.132

CONCEPT CHECK 6

Compare the first five and last four industries in Table 71-3. What characteristic seems to determine whether the adjustment factor is positive or negative?

INDEX MODELS AND TRACKING PORTFOLIOS   4

Suppose a portfolio manager believes she has identified an underpriced portfolio. Her security analysis team estimates the index model equation for this portfolio (using the S&P 500 index) in excess return form and obtains the following estimates:

$$R_P = .04 + 1.4R_{\text{S\&P500}} + e_P \qquad \text{(71-15)}$$

Therefore, P has an alpha value of 4% (which measures the extent of mispricing) and a beta of 1.4. The manager is confident in the quality of her security analysis but is wary about the performance of the broad market in the near term. If she buys the portfolio, and the market as a whole turns down, she still could lose money on her investment (which has a large positive beta) even if her team is correct that the portfolio is underpriced on a relative basis. She would like a position that takes advantage of her team's analysis but is independent of the performance of the overall market.

To this end, a **tracking portfolio** (T) can be constructed. A tracking portfolio for portfolio P is a portfolio designed to match the systematic component of P's return. The idea is for the portfolio to "track" the market-sensitive component of P's return. This means the tracking portfolio must have the same beta on the index portfolio as P and as little **nonsystematic risk** as possible.

A tracking portfolio for P will have a levered position in the S&P 500 to achieve a beta of 1.4. Therefore, T includes positions of 1.4 in the S&P 500 and − 0.4 in T-bills. Because T is constructed from the index and bills, it has an alpha value of zero.

Now consider buying portfolio P but at the same time offsetting systematic risk by assuming a short position in the tracking portfolio. The short position in T cancels out the systematic exposure of the long position in P: the overall combined position is thus *market neutral*. Therefore, even if the market does poorly, the combined position should not be affected. But the alpha on portfolio P will remain intact. The combined portfolio, C, provides a return per dollar of

$$R_C = R_P - R_T = (.04 + 1.4R_{S\&P500} + e_P) - 1.4R_{S\&P500} = .04 + e_P \qquad \textbf{(71-16)}$$

While this portfolio is still risky (due to the residual risk, e_P), the systematic risk has been eliminated, and if P is reasonably well-diversified, the remaining non-systematic risk will be small. Thus the objective is achieved: the manager can take advantage of the 4% alpha without inadvertently taking on market exposure.

EXCEL APPLICATION

Estimating Beta Coefficients

The spreadsheet Betas, which you will find on the Online Learning Center (www.mhhe.com/bkm), contains 60 months' returns for 10 individual stocks. Returns are calculated over the 5 years ending in December 2000. The spreadsheet also contains returns for S&P 500 Index and the observed risk-free rates as measured by the 1-year Treasury bill. With this data, monthly excess returns for the individual securities and the market as measured by the S&P 500 Index can be used with the regression module in Excel. The spreadsheet also contains returns on an equally weighted portfolio of the individual securities. The regression module is available under Tools Data Analysis. The dependent variable is the security excess return. The independent variable is the market excess return.

A sample of the output from the regression is shown below. The estimated beta coefficient for American Express is 1.21, and 48% of the variance in returns for American Express can be explained by the returns on the S&P 500 Index.

	A	B	C	D	E	F
1	SUMMARY OUTPUT	AXP				
2						
3	*Regression Statistics*					
4	Multiple R	0.69288601				
5	R Square	0.48009103				
6	Adjusted R Square	0.47112708				
7	Standard Error	0.05887426				
8	Observations	60				
9						
10	ANOVA					
11		*df*	*SS*	*MS*	*F*	*Significance F*
12	Regression	1	0.185641557	0.1856416	53.55799	8.55186E-10
13	Residual	58	0.201038358	0.0034662		
14	Total	59	0.386679915			
15						
16		*Coefficients*	*Standard*	*t Stat*	*P-value*	*Lower 95%*
17			*Error*			
18	Intercept	0.01181687	0.00776211	1.522379	0.133348	−0.003720666
19	X Variable 1	1.20877413	0.165170705	7.3183324	8.55E-10	0.878149288

This "long-short strategy" is characteristic of the activity of many *hedge funds.* Hedge fund managers identify an underpriced security and then try to attain a "pure play" on the perceived underpricing. They hedge out all extraneous risk, focusing the bet only on the perceived "alpha." Tracking funds are the vehicle used to hedge the exposures to which they do *not* want exposure. Hedge fund managers use index regressions such as those discussed here, as well as more-sophisticated variations, to create the tracking portfolios at the heart of their hedging strategies.

SUMMARY

▶ A single-factor model of the economy classifies sources of uncertainty as systematic (macroeconomic) factors or firm-specific (microeconomic) factors. The index model assumes that the macro factor can be represented by a broad index of stock returns.

▶ The single-index model drastically reduces the necessary inputs in the Markowitz portfolio selection procedure. It also aids in specialization of labor in security analysis.

▶ According to the index model specification, the systematic risk of a portfolio or asset equals $\beta^2\sigma_M^2$ and the covariance between two assets equals $\beta_i\beta_j\sigma_M^2$.

▶ The index model is estimated by applying regression analysis to excess rates of return. The slope of the regression curve is the beta of an asset, whereas the intercept is the asset's alpha during the sample period. The regression line is also called the *security characteristic line*. The regression beta is equivalent to the CAPM beta, except that the regression uses actual returns and the CAPM is specified in terms of expected returns. The CAPM predicts that the average value of alphas measured by the index model regression will be zero.

▶ Practitioners routinely estimate the index model using total rather than excess rates of return. This makes their estimate of alpha equal to $\alpha + r_f(1 - \beta)$.

▶ Betas show a tendency to evolve toward 1 over time. Beta forecasting rules attempt to predict this drift. Moreover, other financial variables can be used to help forecast betas.

WEBSITES

All the following sites provide estimated beta coefficients based on the single-index model:

www.dailystocks.com

finance.yahoo.com (Enter ticker symbol of company, then link to *Profile* report.)

moneycentral.msn.com

www.bloomberg.com

wallpost.com

www.quicken.com (Enter ticker symbol, then see the *Fundamentals* report for beta and growth rates of the company.)

45/8 47/8
51/2 51/2 −
51/2 213/16 −
205/8 213/16 7/8
173/8 181/8 +
61/2 61/2 −
71/4 31/32 −
15/16
9/16 9/8
715/16 713/16 715/16
25/8 211/32 21/2 +
23/4 21/4 21/4
121/16 113/8 113/4 +
87 333/4 33 331/4 −
602 255/8 249/16 253/8 +
833 12 115/8 117/8 +
16 101/2 101/2 101/8 −
78 157/8 1513/16 157/8 −
508 91/16 81/4 81/8 +
430 111/4 101/8 101/8

ARBITRAGE PRICING THEORY AND MULTIFACTOR MODELS OF RISK AND RETURN

by Zvi Bodie, Alex Kane, and Alan J. Marcus

LEARNING OUTCOMES

The candidate should be able to:

a. compare and contrast the assumptions of the arbitrage pricing theory (APT) to the assumptions of the CAPM and the Index Model;

b. explain how the risk factors in a multifactor model are chosen, and describe the macroeconomic and microeconomic factors that have been used.

MULTIFACTOR MODELS: AN OVERVIEW   1

The index model introduced in Reading 71 gave us a way of decomposing stock variability into market or systematic risk, due largely to macroeconomic events, versus firm-specific or idiosyncratic effects that can be diversified in large portfolios. In the index model, the return on the market portfolio summarized the broad impact of macro factors. Sometimes, however, rather than using a market proxy, it is more useful to focus directly on the ultimate sources of risk. This can be useful in risk assessment, for example, when measuring one's exposures to particular sources of uncertainty. Factor models are tools that allow us to describe and quantify the different factors that affect the rate of return on a security during any time period.

Factor Models of Security Returns

To illustrate, we will start by examining a single-factor model like the one introduced in Reading 71. As noted there, uncertainty in asset returns has two sources: a common or macroeconomic factor, and firm-specific events. The common factor is constructed to have zero expected value, since we use it to measure *new* information concerning the macroeconomy which, by definition, has zero expected value.

If we call F the deviation of the common factor from its expected value, β_i the sensitivity of firm i to that factor, and e_i the firm-specific disturbance, the factor model states that the actual return on firm i will equal its initially expected return plus a (zero expected value) random amount attributable to unanticipated economywide events, plus another (zero expected value) random amount attributable to firm-specific events.

Formally, the **single-factor model** is described by equation 72-1:

$$r_i = E(r_i) + \beta_i F + e_i \qquad\qquad \textbf{(72-1)}$$

where $E(r_i)$ is the expected return on stock i. Notice that if the macro factor has a value of 0 in any particular period (i.e., no macro surprises), the return on the security will equal its previously expected value, $E(r_i)$, plus the effect of firm-specific events only. All the nonsystematic components of returns, the e_is, are uncorrelated among themselves and uncorrelated with the factor F.

Example 72-1

Factor Models

To make the factor model more concrete, consider an example. Suppose that the macro factor, F, is taken to be news about the state of the business cycle, measured by the unexpected percentage change in gross domestic product (GDP), and that the consensus is that GDP will increase by 4% this year. Suppose also that a stock's β value is 1.2. If GDP increases by only 3%, then the value of F would be -1%, representing a 1% disappointment in actual growth versus expected growth. Given the stock's beta value, this disappointment would translate into a return on the stock that is 1.2% lower than previously expected. This macro surprise, together with the firm-specific disturbance, e_i, determine the total departure of the stock's return from its originally expected value.

CONCEPT CHECK 1

Suppose you currently expect the stock in Example 72-1 to earn a 10% rate of return. Then some macroeconomic news suggests that GDP growth will come in at 5% instead of 4%. How will you revise your estimate of the stock's expected rate of return?

The factor model's decomposition of returns into systematic and firm-specific components is compelling, but confining systematic risk to a single factor is not. Indeed, when we motivated the index model in Reading 71, we noted that the systematic or macro factor summarized by the market return arises from a number of sources, for example, uncertainty about the business cycle, interest rates, inflation, and so on. The market return reflects both macro factors as well as the average sensitivity of firms to those factors. When we estimate a single-index regression, therefore, we implicitly impose an (incorrect) assumption that each stock has the same relative sensitivity to each risk factor. If stocks actually differ in their betas relative to the various macroeconomic factors, then lumping all systematic sources of risk into one variable such as the return on the market index will ignore the nuances that better explain individual-stock returns.

It stands to reason that a more explicit representation of systematic risk, allowing for the possibility that different stocks exhibit different sensitivities to its various components, would constitute a useful refinement of the single-factor model. It is easy to see that models that allow for several factors—**multifactor models**—can provide better descriptions of security returns.

Apart from their use in building models of equilibrium security pricing, multifactor models are useful in risk management applications. These models give us a simple way to measure our exposure to various macroeconomic risks, and construct portfolios to hedge those risks.

Let's start with a two-factor model. Suppose the two most important macroeconomic sources of risk are uncertainties surrounding the state of the business cycle, news of which we will again measure by unanticipated growth in GDP and changes in interest rates. We will call any unexpected decline in interest rates, which ought to be good news for stocks, IR. The return on any stock will respond both to sources of macro risk as well as to its own firm-specific influences. We therefore can write a two-factor model describing the rate of return on stock i in some time period as follows:

$$r_i = E(r_i) + \beta_{iGDP}GDP + \beta_{iIR}IR + e_i$$ (72-2)

The two macro factors on the right-hand side of the equation comprise the systematic factors in the economy. As in the single-factor model, both of these macro factors have zero expectation: they represent changes in these variables that have not already been anticipated. The coefficients of each factor in equation 72-2 measure the sensitivity of share returns to that factor. For this reason the coefficients are sometimes called **factor sensitivities**, **factor loadings**, or, equivalently, **factor betas**. Also as before, e_i reflects firm-specific influences.

To illustrate the advantages of multifactor models in understanding the sources of macro risk, consider two firms, one a regulated electric-power utility in a mostly residential area, the other an airline. Because residential demand for electricity is not very sensitive to the business cycle, the utility is likely to have a low beta on GDP. But the utility's stock price may have a relatively high sensitivity to interest rates. Since the cash flow generated by the utility is relatively stable, its present value behaves much like that of a bond, varying inversely with interest rates. Conversely, the performance of the airline is very sensitive to economic activity but is less sensitive to interest rates. It will have a high GDP beta and a lower interest rate beta. Suppose that on a particular day, there is a piece of news suggesting that the economy will expand. GDP is expected to increase, but so are interest rates. Is the "macro news" on this day good or bad? For the utility, this is bad news: its dominant sensitivity is to rates. But for the airline, which responds more to GDP, this is good news. Clearly a one-factor or single-index model cannot capture such differential responses to varying sources of macroeconomic uncertainty.

Example 72-2

Risk Assessment Using Multifactor Models

Suppose we estimate the two-factor model in equation 72-2 for Northeast Airlines and find the following result:

$$r = .10 + 1.8(GDP) + .7(IR) + e$$

> This tells us that based on currently available information, the expected rate of return for Northeast is 10%, but that for every percentage point increase in GDP beyond current expectations, the return on Northeast shares increases on average by 1.8%, while for every unanticipated percentage point that interest rates decrease, Northeast's shares rise on average by .7%.
>
> The factor betas can provide a framework for a hedging strategy. The idea for an investor who wishes to hedge a source of risk is to establish an opposite factor exposure to offset that particular source of risk. Often, futures contracts can be used to hedge particular factor exposures.

A Multifactor Security Market Line

As it stands, the multifactor model is no more than a *description* of the factors that affect security returns. There is no "theory" in the equation. The obvious question left unanswered by a factor model like equation 72-2 is where $E(r)$ comes from, in other words, what determines a security's expected rate of return. This is where we need a theoretical model of equilibrium security returns.

In the previous two readings we developed one example of such a model: the Security Market Line of the Capital Asset Pricing Model. The CAPM asserts that securities will be priced to give investors an expected return comprised of two components: the risk-free rate, which is compensation for the time value of money, and a risk premium, determined by multiplying a benchmark risk premium (i.e., the risk premium offered by the market portfolio) times the relative measure of risk, beta:

$$E(r) = r_f + \beta[E(r_M) - r_f]$$ (72-3)

If we denote the risk premium of the market portfolio by RP_M, then a useful way to rewrite equation 72-3 is as follows:

$$E(r) = r_f + \beta\mathrm{RP}_M$$ (72-4)

We pointed out in Reading 71 that you can think of beta as measuring the exposure of a stock or portfolio to marketwide or macroeconomic risk factors. Therefore, one interpretation of the SML is that investors are rewarded with a higher expected return for their exposure to macro risk, based on both the sensitivity to that risk (beta) as well as the compensation for bearing each unit of that source of risk (i.e., the risk premium, RP_M), but are *not* rewarded for exposure to firm-specific uncertainty (the residual term e_i in equation 72-1).

How might this single-factor view of the world generalize once we recognize the presence of multiple sources of systematic risk? We will work out the details of the argument in the next section, but before getting lost in the trees, we will start with the lay of the forest, motivating intuitively the results that are to come. Perhaps not surprisingly, a multifactor index model gives rise to a multifactor security market line in which the risk premium is determined by the exposure to *each* systematic risk factor, and by a risk premium associated with each of those factors.

For example, in a two-factor economy in which risk exposures can be measured by equation 72-2, we would conclude that the expected rate of return on a security would be the sum of:

1. The risk-free rate of return.

2. The sensitivity to GDP risk (i.e., the GDP beta) times the risk premium for GDP risk.

3. The sensitivity to interest rate risk (i.e., the interest rate beta) times the risk premium for interest rate risk.

This assertion is expressed as follows in equation 72-5. In that equation, for example, β_{GDP} denotes the sensitivity of the security return to unexpected changes in GDP growth, and RP_{GDP} is the risk premium associated with "one unit" of GDP exposure, i.e., the exposure corresponding to a GDP beta of 1.0. Here then is a two-factor security market line.

$$E(r) = r_f + \beta_{GDP}RP_{GDP} + \beta_{IR}RP_{IR} \qquad \textbf{(72-5)}$$

If you look back at equation 72-4, you will see that equation 72-5 is a generalization of the simple security market line. In the usual SML, the benchmark risk premium is given by the market portfolio, $RP_M = E(r_M) - r_f$, but once we generalize to multiple risk sources, each with its own risk premium, we see that the insights are highly similar.

We still need to specify how to estimate the risk premium for each factor. Analogously to the simple CAPM, the risk premium associated with each factor can be thought of as the risk premium of a portfolio that has a beta of 1.0 on that particular factor and a beta of zero on all other factors. In other words, it is the risk premium one might expect to earn by taking a "pure play" on that factor. We will return to this below, but for now, let's just take the factor risk premia as given and see how a multifactor SML might be used.

Example 72-3

A Multifactor SML

Think about our regression estimates for Northeast Airlines in Example 72-2. Northeast has a GDP beta of 1.8 and an interest rate beta of .7. Suppose the risk premium for one unit of exposure to GDP risk is 6%, while the risk premium for one unit of exposure to interest rate risk is 3%. Then the overall risk premium on the Northeast portfolio should equal the sum of the risk premiums required as compensation for each source of systematic risk.

The risk premium attributable to GDP risk should be the stock's exposure to that risk multiplied by the risk premium of the first factor portfolio, 6%. Therefore, the portion of the firm's risk premium that is compensation for its exposure to the first factor is 1.8 × 6% = 10.8%. Similarly, the risk premium attributable to interest rate risk is .7 × 3% = 2.1%. The total risk premium should be 10.8 + 2.1 = 12.9%. Therefore, if the risk-free rate is 4%, the total return on the portfolio should be

4.0%	Risk-free rate
+ 10.8	+ Risk premium for exposure to GDP risk
+ 2.1	+ Risk premium for exposure to interest rate risk
16.9%	Total expected return

More concisely,

$$E(r) = 4\% + 1.8 \times 6\% + .7 \times 3\% = 16.9\%$$

The multifactor model clearly gives us a much richer way to think about risk exposures and compensation for those exposures than the single-index model or CAPM. Let us now fill in some of the gaps in the argument and more carefully explore the link between multifactor models of security returns and multifactor security market lines.

CONCEPT CHECK 2

Suppose the risk premia in Example 72-3 were $RP_{GDP} = 4\%$ and $RP_{IR} = 2\%$. What would be the new value for the equilibrium expected rate of return on Northeast Airlines?

---

2   ARBITRAGE PRICING THEORY

Stephen Ross developed the **arbitrage pricing theory** (APT) in 1976.[1] Like the CAPM, the APT predicts a Security Market Line linking expected returns to risk, but the path it takes to its SML is quite different. Ross's APT relies on three key propositions: (i) security returns can be described by a factor model; (ii) there are sufficient securities to diversify away idiosyncratic risk; and (iii) well-functioning security markets do not allow for the persistence of arbitrage opportunities. We begin with a simple version of Ross's model, which assumes that only one systematic factor affects security returns. However, the usual discussion of the APT is concerned with the multifactor case, so we treat this more general case as well.

Arbitrage, Risk Arbitrage, and Equilibrium

An **arbitrage** opportunity arises when an investor can earn riskless profits without making a net investment. A trivial example of an arbitrage opportunity would arise if shares of a stock sold for different prices on two different exchanges. For example, suppose IBM sold for $60 on the NYSE but only $58 on Nasdaq. Then you could buy the shares on Nasdaq and simultaneously sell them on the NYSE, clearing a riskless profit of $2 per share without tying up any of your own capital. The **Law of One Price** states that if two assets are equivalent in all economically relevant respects, then they should have the same market price. The Law of One Price is enforced by arbitrageurs: if they observe a violation of the law, they will engage in *arbitrage activity*—simultaneously buying the asset where it is cheap and selling where it is expensive. In the process, they will bid up the price where it is low and force it down where it is high until the arbitrage opportunity is eliminated.

The idea that market prices will move to rule out arbitrage opportunities is perhaps the most fundamental concept in capital market theory. Violation of this restriction would indicate the grossest form of market irrationality.

The critical property of a risk-free arbitrage portfolio is that any investor, regardless of risk aversion or wealth, will want to take an infinite position in it. Because those large positions will quickly force prices up or down until the opportunity vanishes, security prices should satisfy a "no-arbitrage condition," that is, a condition that rules out the existence of arbitrage opportunities.

---

[1] Stephen A. Ross, "Return, Risk and Arbitrage," in I. Friend and J. Bicksler, eds., *Risk and Return in Finance* (Cambridge, MA: Ballinger, 1976).

There is an important difference between arbitrage and risk–return dominance arguments in support of equilibrium price relationships. A dominance argument holds that when an equilibrium price relationship is violated, many investors will make limited portfolio changes, depending on their degree of risk aversion. Aggregation of these limited portfolio changes is required to create a large volume of buying and selling, which in turn restores equilibrium prices. By contrast, when arbitrage opportunities exist each investor wants to take as large a position as possible; hence it will not take many investors to bring about the price pressures necessary to restore equilibrium. Therefore, implications for prices derived from no-arbitrage arguments are stronger than implications derived from a risk–return dominance argument.

The CAPM is an example of a dominance argument, implying that all investors hold mean-variance efficient portfolios. If a security is mispriced, then investors will tilt their portfolios toward the underpriced and away from the overpriced securities. Pressure on equilibrium prices results from many investors shifting their portfolios, each by a relatively small dollar amount. The assumption that a large number of investors are mean-variance sensitive is critical. In contrast, the implication of a no-arbitrage condition is that a few investors who identify an arbitrage opportunity will mobilize large dollar amounts and quickly restore equilibrium.

Practitioners often use the terms "arbitrage" and "arbitrageurs" more loosely than our strict definition. "Arbitrageur" often refers to a professional searching for mispriced securities in specific areas such as merger-target stocks, rather than to one who seeks strict (risk-free) arbitrage opportunities. Such activity is sometimes called **risk arbitrage** to distinguish it from pure arbitrage.

To leap ahead, we will discuss "derivative" securities such as futures and options, whose market values are determined by prices of other securities. For example, the value of a call option on a stock is determined by the price of the stock. For such securities, strict arbitrage is a practical possibility, and the condition of no-arbitrage leads to exact pricing. In the case of stocks and other "primitive" securities whose values are not determined strictly by another asset or bundle of assets, no-arbitrage conditions must be obtained by appealing to diversification arguments.

Well-Diversified Portfolios

Now we look at the risk of a portfolio of stocks. We first show that if a portfolio is well diversified, its firm-specific or nonfactor risk becomes negligible, so that only factor (or systematic) risk remains. If we construct an n-stock portfolio with weights w_i, $\Sigma w_i = 1$, then the rate of return on this portfolio is as follows:

$$r_P = E(r_P) + \beta_P F + e_P \qquad \textbf{(72-6)}$$

where

$$\beta_P = \Sigma w_i \beta_i$$

is the weighted average of the β_i of the n securities. The portfolio nonsystematic component (which is uncorrelated with F) is $e_P = \Sigma w_i e_i$ which similarly is a weighted average of the e_i of the n securities.

We can divide the variance of this portfolio into systematic and nonsystematic sources, as we saw in Reading 71. The portfolio variance is

$$\sigma_P^2 = \beta_P^2 \sigma_F^2 + \sigma^2(e_P)$$

where σ_F^2 is the variance of the factor F and $\sigma^2(e_P)$ is the nonsystematic risk of the portfolio, which is given by

$$\sigma^2(e_P) = \text{Variance}(\Sigma w_i e_i) = \Sigma w_i^2 \sigma^2(e_i)$$

Note that in deriving the nonsystematic variance of the portfolio, we depend on the facts that the firm-specific e_is are uncorrelated and hence that the variance of the "portfolio" of nonsystematic e_is is the weighted sum of the individual nonsystematic variances with the square of the investment proportions as weights.

If the portfolio were equally weighted, $w_i = 1/n$, then the nonsystematic variance would be

$$\sigma^2(e_P) = \text{Variance}(\Sigma w_i e_i) = \Sigma\left(\frac{1}{n}\right)^2 \sigma^2(e_i) = \frac{1}{n}\Sigma\frac{\sigma^2(e_i)}{n} = \frac{1}{n}\overline{\sigma}^2(e_i)$$

where the last term is the average value across securities of nonsystematic variance. In words, the nonsystematic variance of the portfolio equals the average nonsystematic variance divided by n. Therefore, when the portfolio gets large in the sense that n is large, its nonsystematic variance approaches zero. This is the effect of diversification.

We conclude that for the equally weighted portfolio, the nonsystematic variance approaches zero as n becomes ever larger. This property is true of portfolios other than the equally weighted one. *Any* portfolio for which each w_i becomes consistently smaller as n gets large (more precisely, for which each w_i^2 approaches zero as n increases) will satisfy the condition that the portfolio nonsystematic risk will approach zero. In fact, this property motivates us to define a **well-diversified portfolio** as one that is diversified over a large enough number of securities with each weight, w_i, small enough that for practical purposes the nonsystematic variance, $\sigma^2(e_P)$, is negligible.

CONCEPT CHECK 3

a. A portfolio is invested in a very large number of shares (n is large). However, one-half of the portfolio is invested in stock 1, and the rest of the portfolio is equally divided among the other $n - 1$ shares. Is this portfolio well diversified?

b. Another portfolio also is invested in **n shares, where** n is very large. Instead of equally weighting with portfolio weights of 1/n in each stock, the weights in half the securities are 1.5/n while the weights in the other shares are .5/n. Is this portfolio well diversified?

Because the expected value of e_P for any well-diversified portfolio is zero, and its variance also is effectively zero, we can conclude that any realized value of e_P will be virtually zero. Rewriting equation 72-1, we conclude that for a well-diversified portfolio, for all practical purposes

$$r_P = E(r_P) + \beta_P F$$

Large (mostly institutional) investors can hold portfolios of hundreds and even thousands of securities; thus the concept of well-diversified portfolios clearly is operational in contemporary financial markets.

Betas and Expected Returns

Because nonfactor risk can be diversified away, only factor risk should command a risk premium in market equilibrium. Nonsystematic risk across firms cancels out in well-diversified portfolios; one would not expect investors to be rewarded for bearing risk that can be eliminated through diversification. Instead, only the systematic risk of a portfolio of securities should be related to its expected returns.

The solid line in Figure 72-1A plots the return of a well-diversified Portfolio A with $\beta_A = 1$ for various realizations of the systematic factor. The expected return of Portfolio A is 10%; this is where the solid line crosses the vertical axis. At this point the systematic factor is zero, implying no macro surprises. If the macro factor is positive, the portfolio's return exceeds its expected value; if it is negative, the portfolio's return falls short of its mean. The return on the portfolio is therefore

$$E(r_A) + \beta_A F = 10\% + 1.0 \times F$$

FIGURE 72-1   Returns as a Function of the Systematic Factor. Panel A, Well-Diversified Portfolio A. Panel B, Single Stock (S).

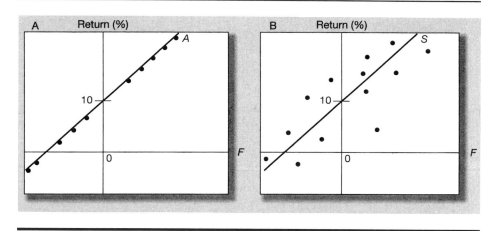

FIGURE 72-2   Returns as a Function of the Systematic Factor: An Arbitrage Oportunity

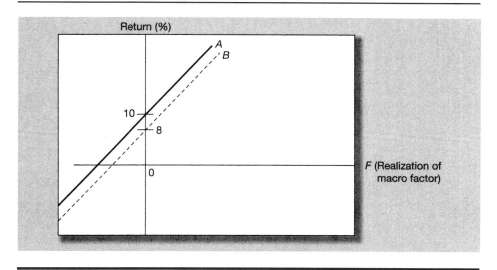

Compare Figure 72-1A with Figure 72-1B, which is a similar graph for a single stock (*S*) with $\beta_s = 1$. The undiversified stock is subject to nonsystematic risk, which is seen in a scatter of points around the line. The well-diversified portfolio's return, in contrast, is determined completely by the systematic factor.

Now consider Figure 72-2, where the dashed line plots the return on another well-diversified portfolio, Portfolio *B*, with an expected return of 8% and β_B also equal to 1.0. Could Portfolios *A* and *B* coexist with the return pattern depicted? Clearly not: No matter what the systematic factor turns out to be, Portfolio *A* outperforms Portfolio *B*, leading to an arbitrage opportunity.

If you sell short $1 million of *B* and buy $1 million of *A*, a zero net investment strategy, your riskless payoff would be $20,000, as follows:

$$
\begin{array}{ll}
(.10 + 1.0 \times F) \times \$1\text{ million} & \text{from long position in } A \\
- (.08 + 1.0 \times F) \times \$1\text{ million} & \text{from short position in } B \\
\hline
.02 \times \$1\text{ million} = \$20,000 & \text{net proceeds}
\end{array}
$$

Your profit is risk-free because the factor risk cancels out across the long and short positions. Moreover, the strategy requires zero net investment. You should pursue it on an infinitely large scale until the return discrepancy between the two portfolios disappears. Well-diversified portfolios with equal betas must have equal expected returns in market equilibrium, or arbitrage opportunities exist.

What about portfolios with different betas? We show now that their risk premiums must be proportional to beta. To see why, consider Figure 72-3. Suppose that the risk-free rate is 4% and that a well-diversified portfolio, *C*, with a beta of .5, has an expected return of 6%. Portfolio *C* plots below the line from the risk-free asset to Portfolio *A*. Consider, therefore, a new portfolio, *D*, composed of half of Portfolio *A* and half of the risk-free asset. Portfolio *D*'s beta will be $(.5 \times 0 + .5 \times 1.0) = .5$, and its expected return will be $(.5 \times 4 + .5 \times 10) = 7\%$. Now Portfolio *D* has an equal beta but a greater expected return than Portfolio *C*. From our analysis in the previous paragraph we know that this constitutes an arbitrage opportunity.

We conclude that, to preclude arbitrage opportunities, the expected return on all well-diversified portfolios must lie on the straight line from the risk-free asset in Figure 72-3. The equation of this line will dictate the expected return on all well-diversified portfolios.

FIGURE 72-3   An arbitrage opportunity

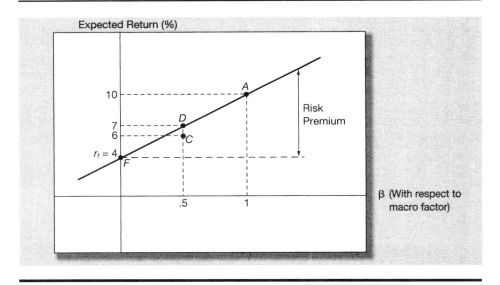

Notice in Figure 72-3 that risk premiums are indeed proportional to portfolio betas. The risk premium is depicted by the vertical arrow, which measures the distance between the risk-free rate and the expected return on the portfolio. The risk premium is zero for $\beta = 0$ and rises in direct proportion to β.

The One-Factor Security Market Line

Now consider the market index portfolio, M, as a well-diversified portfolio, and let us measure the systematic factor as the unexpected return on that portfolio. Because the index portfolio must be on the line in Figure 72-4 and the beta of the index portfolio is 1, we can determine the equation describing that line. As Figure 72-4 shows, the intercept is r_f and the slope is $E(r_M) - r_f$ [rise $= E(r_M) - r_f$; run $= 1$], implying that the equation of the line is

$$E(r_P) = r_f + \left[E(r_M) - r_f\right]\beta_P \tag{72-7}$$

Hence, Figures 72-3 and 72-4 imply an SML relation equivalent to that of the CAPM.

Example 72-4

Arbitrage and the Security Market Line

Suppose the market index is a well-diversified portfolio with expected return 10% and that deviations of its return from expectation (i.e., $r_M -$ 10%) can serve as the systematic factor. The T-bill rate is 4%. Then the SML (equation 72-7) implies that the expected rate of return on well-diversified Portfolio E with a beta of $\frac{2}{3}$ should be 4% $+$ $\frac{2}{3}$ (10 $-$ 4) $=$ 8%. What if its expected return actually is 9%? Then there will be an arbitrage opportunity.

Buy $1 of the stock and sell $1 of a portfolio that is invested $\frac{1}{3}$ in T-bills and $\frac{2}{3}$ in the market. This portfolio by construction has the same beta as Portfolio E. The return on this portfolio is $\frac{1}{3} r_f + r_M = \frac{1}{3} \times 4\%$ $+ \frac{2}{3} r_M$. The net return on the combined position is:

$1 $\times$ [.09 + $\frac{2}{3}$ (r_M − .10)]	Invest $1 in portfolio E with expected return 9% and beta of $\frac{2}{3}$ on surprise in market return.
− $1 ($\frac{1}{3}$ $\times$ .04 + $\frac{2}{3}$ r_M)	Sell portfolio invested $\frac{1}{3}$ in T-bills and $\frac{2}{3}$ in the market index.
$1 $\times$ .01	Total

The profit per dollar invested is risk-free and precisely equal to the deviation of expected return from the SML.

CONCEPT CHECK 4

Continue to use the data in Example 72-4. Now consider Portfolio G which is well diversified with a beta of 1/3 and expected return of 5%. Does an arbitrage opportunity exist? If so, what is the arbitrage strategy? Show that the strategy results in risk-free profits with zero net investment.

We have used the no-arbitrage condition to obtain an expected return–beta relationship identical to that of the CAPM, without the restrictive assumptions of the CAPM. As noted, this derivation depends on three assumptions: a factor model describing security returns, a sufficient number of securities to form well-diversified portfolios, and the absence of arbitrage opportunities. This last restriction gives rise to the name of the approach: Arbitrage Pricing Theory. Our demonstration suggests that despite its restrictive assumptions, the main conclusion of the CAPM, namely, the SML expected return–beta relationship, should be at least approximately valid.

It is worth noting that in contrast to the CAPM, the APT does not require that the benchmark portfolio in the SML relationship be the true market portfolio. Any well-diversified portfolio lying on the SML of Figure 72-4 may serve as the benchmark portfolio. For example, one might define the **benchmark portfolio** as the well-diversified portfolio most highly correlated with whatever systematic factor is thought to affect stock returns. Accordingly, the APT has more flexibility than does the CAPM because problems associated with an unobservable market portfolio are not a concern.

In addition, the APT provides further justification for use of the index model in the practical implementation of the SML relationship. Even if the index portfolio is not a precise proxy for the true market portfolio, which is a cause of considerable concern in the context of the CAPM, we now know that if the index portfolio is sufficiently well diversified, the SML relationship should still hold true according to the APT.

FIGURE 72-4   The security market line

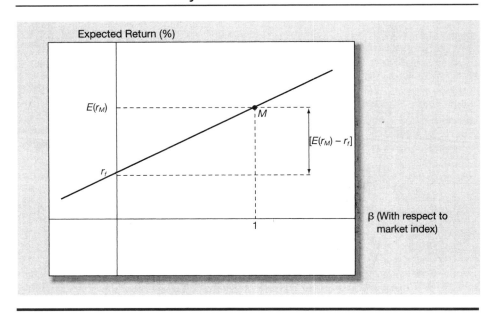

So far we have demonstrated the APT relationship for well-diversified portfolios only. The CAPM expected return–beta relationship applies to single assets, as well as to portfolios. In the next section we generalize the APT result one step further.

INDIVIDUAL ASSETS AND THE APT **3**

We have demonstrated that if arbitrage opportunities are to be ruled out, each well-diversified portfolio's expected excess return must be proportional to its beta. The question is whether this relationship tells us anything about the expected returns on the component stocks. The answer is that if this relationship is to be satisfied by all well-diversified portfolios, it must be satisfied by *almost* all individual securities, although a full proof of this proposition is somewhat difficult. We can illustrate the argument less formally.

Suppose that the expected return–beta relationship is violated for all single assets. Now create a pair of well-diversified portfolios from these assets. What are the chances that in spite of the fact that for any pair of assets the relationship does *not* hold, the relationship *will* hold for both well-diversified portfolios? The chances are small, but it is possible that the relationships among the single securities are violated in offsetting ways so that somehow it holds for the pair of well-diversified portfolios.

Now construct yet a third well-diversified portfolio. What are the chances that the violations of the relationships for single securities are such that the third portfolio also will fulfill the no-arbitrage expected return–beta relationship? Obviously, the chances are smaller still, but the relationship is possible. Continue with a fourth well-diversified portfolio, and so on. If the no-arbitrage expected return–beta relationship has to hold for infinitely many different, well-diversified portfolios, it must be virtually certain that the relationship holds for all but a small number of individual securities.

We use the term *virtually certain* advisedly because we must distinguish this conclusion from the statement that all securities surely fulfill this relationship. The reason we cannot make the latter statement has to do with a property of well-diversified portfolios.

Recall that to qualify as well diversified, a portfolio must have very small positions in all securities. If, for example, only one security violates the expected return–beta relationship, then the effect of this violation on a well-diversified portfolio will be too small to be of importance for any practical purpose, and meaningful arbitrage opportunities will not arise. But if many securities violate the expected return–beta relationship, the relationship will no longer hold for well-diversified portfolios, and arbitrage opportunities will be available. Consequently, we conclude that imposing the no-arbitrage condition on a single-factor security market implies maintenance of the expected return–beta relationship for all well-diversified portfolios and for all but possibly a *small* number of individual securities.

The APT and the CAPM

The APT serves many of the same functions as the CAPM. It gives us a benchmark for rates of return that can be used in capital budgeting, security evaluation, or investment performance evaluation. Moreover, the APT highlights the crucial distinction between nondiversifiable risk (factor risk) that requires a reward in the form of a risk premium and diversifiable risk that does not.

The APT is an extremely appealing model. It depends on the assumption that a rational equilibrium in capital markets precludes arbitrage opportunities. A violation of the APT's pricing relationships will cause extremely strong pressure to restore them even if only a limited number of investors become aware of the disequilibrium. Furthermore, the APT yields an expected return–beta relationship using a well-diversified portfolio that practically can be constructed from a large number of securities.

In contrast, the CAPM is derived assuming an inherently unobservable "market" portfolio. The CAPM argument rests on mean-variance efficiency; that is, if any security violates the expected return–beta relationship, then many investors (each relatively small) will tilt their portfolios so that their combined overall pressure on prices will restore an equilibrium that satisfies the relationship.

In spite of these apparent advantages, the APT does not fully dominate the CAPM. The CAPM provides an unequivocal statement on the expected return–beta relationship for all securities, whereas the APT implies that this relationship holds for all but perhaps a small number of securities. Because it focuses on the no-arbitrage condition, without the further assumptions of the market or index model, the APT cannot rule out a violation of the expected return–beta relationship for any particular asset. For this, we need the CAPM assumptions and its dominance arguments.

4   A MULTIFACTOR APT

We have assumed so far that there is only one systematic factor affecting stock returns. This simplifying assumption is in fact too simplistic. We've noted that it is easy to think of several factors driven by the business cycle that might affect stock returns: interest rate fluctuations, inflation rates, oil prices, and so on. Presumably, exposure to any of these factors will affect a stock's risk and hence its expected return. We can derive a multifactor version of the APT to accommodate these multiple sources of risk.

Suppose that we generalize the factor model expressed in equation 72-1 to a two-factor model:

$$r_i = E(r_i) + \beta_{i1}F_1 + \beta_{i2}F_2 + e_i \qquad \textbf{(72-8)}$$

In Example 72-2, Factor 1 was the departure of GDP growth from expectations, and Factor 2 was the unanticipated decline in interest rates. Each factor has zero expected value because each measures the *surprise* in the systematic variable rather than the level of the variable. Similarly, the firm-specific component of unexpected return, e_i, also has zero expected value. Extending such a two-factor model to any number of factors is straightforward.

Establishing a multifactor APT is similar to the one-factor case. But first we must introduce the concept of a **factor portfolio,** which is a well-diversified portfolio constructed to have a beta of 1 on one of the factors and a beta of 0 on any other factor. We can think of a factor portfolio as a *tracking portfolio.* That is, the returns on such a portfolio track the evolution of particular sources of macroeconomic risk, but are uncorrelated with other sources of risk. It is possible to form such factor portfolios because we have a large number of securities to choose from, and a relatively small number of factors. Factor portfolios will serve as the benchmark portfolios for a multifactor security market line.

To generalize the argument in Example 72-5, note that the factor exposures of any portfolio, P, are given by its betas, β_{P1} and β_{P2}. A competing portfolio, Q, can be formed by investing in factor portfolios with the following weights: β_{P1} in

Example 72-5

Multifactor SML

Suppose that the two factor portfolios, Portfolios 1 and 2, have expected returns $E(r_1) = 10\%$ and $E(r_2) = 12\%$. Suppose further that the risk-free rate is 4%. The risk premium on the first factor portfolio is $10\% - 4\% = 6\%$, whereas that on the second factor portfolio is $12\% - 4\% = 8\%$.

Now consider a well-diversified portfolio, Portfolio A, with beta on the first factor, $\beta_{A1} = .5$, and beta on the second factor, $\beta_{A2} = .75$. The multifactor APT states that the overall risk premium on this portfolio must equal the sum of the risk premiums required as compensation for each source of systematic risk. The risk premium attributable to risk factor 1 should be the portfolio's exposure to factor 1, β_{A1}, multiplied by the risk premium earned on the first factor portfolio, $E(r_1) - r_f$. Therefore, the portion of Portfolio A's risk premium that is compensation for its exposure to the first factor is $\beta_{A1}[E(r_1) - r_f] = .5(10\% - 4\%) = 3\%$, whereas the risk premium attributable to risk factor 2 is $\beta_{A2}[E(r_2) - r_f] = .75(12\% - 4\%) = 6\%$. The total risk premium on the portfolio should be $3 + 6 = 9\%$ and the total return on the portfolio should be $4\% + 9\% = 13\%$.

the first factor portfolio, β_{P2} in the second factor portfolio, and $1 - \beta_{P1} - \beta_{P2}$ in T-bills. By construction, portfolio Q will have betas equal to those of Portfolio P and expected return of

$$E(r_Q) = \beta_{P1}E(r_1) + \beta_{P2}E(r_2) + (1 - \beta_{P1} - \beta_{P2})r_f$$
$$= r_f + \beta_{P1}[E(r_1) - r_f] + \beta_{P2}[E(r_2) - r_f] \qquad \textbf{(72-9)}$$

Using the numbers in Example 72-5:

$$E(r_Q) = 4 + .5 \times (10 - 4) + .75 \times (12 - 4) = 13\%$$

Because Portfolio Q has precisely the same exposures as Portfolio A to the two sources of risk, their expected returns also ought to be equal. So Portfolio A also ought to have an expected return of 13%. If it does not, then there will be an arbitrage opportunity.

Example 72-6

Mispricing and Arbitrage

Suppose that the expected return on Portfolio A were 12% rather than 13%. This return would give rise to an arbitrage opportunity. Form a portfolio from the factor portfolios with the same betas as Portfolio A. This requires weights of .5 on the first factor portfolio, .75 on the second factor portfolio, and $-.25$ on the risk-free asset. This portfolio has exactly the same factor betas as Portfolio A: It has a beta of .5 on the first factor because of its .5 weight on the first factor portfolio, and a beta of .75 on the second factor. (The weight of $-.25$ on risk-free T-bills does not affect the sensitivity to either factor.)

Now invest $1 in Portfolio Q and sell (short) $1 in Portfolio A. Your net investment is zero, but your expected dollar profit is positive and equal to

$$\$1 \times E(r_Q) - \$1 \times E(r_A) = \$1 \times .13 - \$1 \times .12 = \$.01$$

Moreover, your net position is riskless. Your exposure to each risk factor cancels out because you are long $1 in Portfolio Q and short $1 in Portfolio A, and both of these well-diversified portfolios have exactly the same factor betas. Thus, if Portfolio A's expected return differs from that of Portfolio Q's, you can earn positive risk-free profits on a zero net investment position. This is an arbitrage opportunity.

CONCEPT CHECK 5

Using the factor portfolios of Example 72.5, find the equilibrium rate of return on a portfolio with $\beta_1 = .2$ and $\beta_2 = 1.4$.

We conclude that any well-diversified portfolio with betas β_{P1} and β_{P2} must have the return given in equation 72-9 if arbitrage opportunities are to be precluded. If you compare equations 72-3 and 72-9, you will see that equation 72-9 is simply a generalization of the one-factor SML.

Finally, the extension of the multifactor SML of equation 72-9 to individual assets is precisely the same as for the one-factor APT. Equation 72-9 cannot be satisfied by every well-diversified portfolio unless it is satisfied by virtually every security taken individually. Equation 72-9 thus represents the multifactor SML for an economy with multiple sources of risk.

We pointed out earlier that one application of the CAPM is to provide "fair" rates of return for regulated utilities. The multifactor APT can be used to the same ends. The nearby box summarizes a study in which the APT was applied to find the cost of capital for regulated electric companies.

5   WHERE SHOULD WE LOOK FOR FACTORS?

One shortcoming of the multifactor APT is that it gives no guidance concerning the determination of the relevant risk factors or their risk premiums. Two principles guide us when we specify a reasonable list of factors. First, we want to limit ourselves to systematic factors with considerable ability to explain security returns. If our model calls for hundreds of explanatory variables, it does little to simplify our description of security returns. Second, we wish to choose factors that seem likely to be important risk factors, i.e., factors that concern investors sufficiently that they will demand meaningful risk premiums to bear exposure to those sources of risk.

One example of the multifactor approach is the work of Chen, Roll, and Ross[2] who chose the following set of factors based on the ability of these factors

---

[2] N. Chen, R. Roll, and S. Ross, "Economic Forces and the Stock Market," *Journal of Business* 59 (1986), pp. 383–403.

to paint a broad picture of the macroeconomy. Their set is obviously but one of many possible sets that might be considered.

IP   = % change in industrial production
EI   = % change in expected inflation
UI   = % change in **unanticipated inflation**
CG = excess return of long-term corporate bonds over long-term government bonds
GB = excess return of long-term government bonds over T-bills

This list gives rise to the following five-factor model of security returns during holding period t as a function of the change in the set of macroeconomic indicators:

$$r_{it} = \alpha_i + \beta_{iIP}IP_t + \beta_{iEI}EI_t + \beta_{iUI}UI_t + \beta_{iCG}CG_t + \beta_{iGB}GB_t + e_{it} \quad \textbf{(72-10)}$$

Equation 72-10 is a multidimensional security characteristic line (SCL), with five factors. As before, to estimate the betas of a given stock we can use regression analysis. Here, however, because there is more than one factor, we estimate a *multiple* regression of the returns of the stock in each period on the five macroeconomic factors. The residual variance of the regression estimates the firm-specific risk. We discuss the results of this model in the next reading, which focuses on empirical evidence on security pricing.

An alternative approach to specifying macroeconomic factors as candidates for relevant sources of systematic risk uses firm characteristics that seem on empirical grounds to proxy for exposure to systematic risk. In other words, the factors are chosen as variables that on past evidence seem to predict high average returns and therefore may be capturing risk premiums. One example of this approach is the so-called Fama and French three-factor model,[3]

$$r_{it} = \alpha_i + \beta_{iM}R_{Mt} + \beta_{iSMB}SMB_t + \beta_{iHML}HML_t + e_{it} \quad \textbf{(72-11)}$$

where

SMB   = Small Minus Big, i.e., the return of a portfolio of small stocks in excess of the return on a portfolio of large stocks
HML   = High Minus Low, i.e., the return of a portfolio of stocks with a high book-to-market ratio in excess of the return on a portfolio of stocks with a low book-to-market ratio

Note that in this model the market index does play a role and is expected to capture systematic risk originating from macroeconomic factors.

These two firm-characteristic variables are chosen because of long-standing observations that corporate capitalization (firm size) and book-to-market ratio seem to be predictive of average stock returns. Fama and French justify this model on empirical grounds: while SMB and HML are not themselves obvious candidates for relevant risk factors, the hope is that these variables proxy for yet-unknown more-fundamental variables. For example, Fama and French point out that firms with high ratios of book to market value are more likely to be in financial distress and that small stocks may be more sensitive to changes in business conditions. Thus, these variables may capture sensitivity to risk factors in the macroeconomy.

---

[3] Eugene F. Fama and Kenneth R. French, "Multifactor Explanations of Asset Pricing Anomalies," *Journal of Finance* 51 (1996), pp. 55–84.

USING THE APT TO FIND COST OF CAPITAL

Elton, Gruber, and Mei* use the APT to derive the cost of capital for electric utilities. They assume that the relevant risk factors are unanticipated developments in the term structure of interest rates, the level of interest rates, inflation rates, the business cycle (measured by GDP), foreign exchange rates, and a summary measure they devise to measure other macro factors.

Their first step is to estimate the risk premium associated with exposure to each risk source. They accomplish this in a two-step strategy:

1. *Estimate "factor loadings" (i.e., betas) of a large sample of firms.* Regress returns of 100 randomly selected stocks against the systematic risk factors. They use a time-series regression for each stock (e.g., 60 months of data), therefore estimating 100 regressions, one for each stock.

2. *Estimate the reward earned per unit of exposure to each risk factor.* For each month, regress the return of each stock against the five betas estimated. The coefficient on each beta is the extra average return earned as beta increases, i.e., it is an estimate of the risk premium for that risk factor from that month's data. These estimates are of course subject to sampling error. Therefore, average the risk premium estimates across the 12 months in each year. The *average* response of return to risk is less subject to sampling error.

The risk premia found for 1990 are in the second column of the table at the top of the next column.

Notice that some risk premia are negative. The interpretation of this result is that risk premium should be positive for risk factors you don't want exposure to, but *negative* for factors you *do* want exposure to. For example, you should desire securities that have higher returns when inflation increases and be willing to accept lower expected returns on such securities; this shows up as a negative risk premium.

Therefore, the expected return on any security should be related to its factor betas as follows:

$$r_f + .425\beta_{\text{term struc}} - .051\beta_{\text{int rate}} - .049\beta_{\text{ex rate}} + .041\beta_{\text{bus cycle}} - .069\beta_{\text{inflation}} + .530\beta_{\text{other}}$$

Finally, to obtain the cost of capital for a particular firm, the authors estimate the firm's betas against each source of risk, multiply each factor beta by the "cost of factor risk" from the table below, sum over all risk sources to obtain the total risk premium, and add the risk-free rate.

For example, the beta estimates for Niagra Mohawk appear in the last column of the table below. Therefore its cost of capital is

$$
\begin{aligned}
\text{Cost of capital} &= r_f + .425 \times 1.0615 - .051(-2.4167) \\
&\quad - .049(1.3235) + .041(.1292) \\
&\quad - .069(-.5220) + .530(.3046) \\
&= r_f + .72
\end{aligned}
$$

In other words, the monthly cost of capital for Niagra Mohawk is .72% above the monthly risk-free rate. Its annualized risk premium is therefore .72% × 12 = 8.64%.

Factor	Factor Risk Premium	Factor Betas for Niagra Mohawk
Term structure	.425	1.0615
Interest rates	−.051	−2.4167
Exchange rates	−.049	1.3235
Business cycle	.041	.1292
Inflation	−.069	−.5220
Other Macro Factors	.530	.3046

* Edwin J. Elton, Martin J. Gruber, and Jianping Mei, "Cost of Capital Using Arbitrage Pricing Theory: A Case Study of Nine New York Utilities," *Financial Markets, Institutions, and Instruments* 3 (August 1994), pp. 46–68.

The problem with empirical approaches such as the Fama-French model, which use proxies for extramarket sources of risk, is that none of the factors in the proposed models can be clearly identified as hedging a significant source of uncertainty. Black[4] points out that when researchers scan and rescan the database of security returns in search of explanatory factors (an activity often called data-snooping), they may eventually uncover past "patterns" that are due purely to chance. Black observes that return premiums to factors such as firm size have largely vanished since first discovered. However, Fama and French point out that size and book-to-market ratios have predicted average returns in various time periods and in markets all over the world, thus mitigating potential effects of data-snooping.

A MULTIFACTOR CAPM   6

The CAPM presupposes that the only relevant source of risk arises from variations in security returns, and therefore a representative (market) portfolio can capture this entire risk. As a result, individual-stock risk can be defined by the contribution to overall portfolio risk; hence, the risk premium on an individual stock is solely determined by its beta on the market portfolio. But is this narrow view of risk warranted?

Consider a relatively young investor whose future wealth is determined in large part by labor income. The stream of future labor income is also risky and may be intimately tied to the fortunes of the company for which the investor works. Such an investor might choose an investment portfolio that will help to diversify labor-income risk. For that purpose, stocks with lower-than-average correlation with future labor income would be favored, that is, such stocks will receive higher weights in the individual portfolio than their weights in the market portfolio. Put another way, using this broader notion of risk, these investors no longer consider the market portfolio as efficient and the rationale for the CAPM expected return–beta relationship no longer applies.

In principle, the CAPM may still hold if the hedging demands of various investors are equally distributed across different types of securities so that deviations of portfolio weights from those of the market portfolio are offsetting. But if hedging demands are common to many investors, the prices of securities with desirable hedging characteristics will be bid up and the expected return reduced, which will invalidate the CAPM expected return–beta relationship. For example, suppose the prices of energy stocks were driven up by investors who buy such stocks to hedge uncertainty about energy expenditures. At those higher stock prices, expected rates of return will be lower than dictated by the expected return–beta relationship of the CAPM. The simple SML relationship needs to be generalized to account for the effects of extramarket **hedging demands** on equilibrium rates of return.

Merton[5] has shown that these hedging demands will result in an expanded or multifactor version of the CAPM that recognizes the multidimensional nature of risk. His model is called the **multifactor CAPM** or, alternatively, the Intertemporal CAPM (ICAPM for short). The focal point of Merton's model is not dollar returns per se, but the consumption and investment made possible by the investor's wealth. Each source of risk to consumption or investment opportunities may in principle command its own risk premium.

---

[4] Fischer Black, "Beta and Return," *Journal of Portfolio Management* 20 (1993), pp. 8–18.

[5] Robert C. Merton, "An Intertemporal Capital Asset Pricing Model," *Econometrica* 41 (1973), pp. 867–87.

In the case of energy price risk, for example, Merton's model would imply that the expected return–beta relationship of the single-factor CAPM would be generalized to the following two-factor relationship:

$$E(r_i) = r_f + \beta_{iM} [E(r_M) - r_f] + \beta_{ie} [E(r_e) - r_f]$$

where β_{iM} is the beta of security i with respect to the market portfolio, and β_{ie} is the beta with respect to energy price risk. Similarly, $E(r_e) - r_f$ is the risk premium associated with exposure to energy price uncertainty. The rate of return of the portfolio that best hedges energy price uncertainty is r_e. This equation, therefore, is a two-factor CAPM. More generally, we will have a beta and a risk premium for every significant source of risk that consumers try to hedge.

Notice that this expanded version of the CAPM provides a prediction for security returns identical to that of the multifactor APT. Therefore, there is no contradiction between these two theories of the risk premium. The CAPM approach does offer one notable advantage, however. In contrast to the APT, which is silent on the relevant systematic factors, the CAPM provides guidance as to where to look for those factors. The important factors will be those sources of risk that large groups of investors try to offset by establishing extramarket hedge portfolios. By specifying the likely sources of risk against which dominant groups of investors attempt to hedge, we identify the dimensions along which the CAPM needs to be generalized.

When a source of risk has an effect on expected returns, we say that this risk "is priced." While the single-factor CAPM predicts that only market risk will be priced, the ICAPM predicts that other sources of risk also may be priced. Merton suggested a list of possible common sources of uncertainty that might affect expected security returns. Among these are uncertainties in labor income, prices of important **consumption goods** (e.g., energy prices), or changes in future investment opportunities (e.g., changes in the riskiness of various asset classes). However, it is difficult to predict whether there exists sufficient demand for hedging these sources of uncertainty to affect security returns.

CONCEPT CHECK 6

Consider the following regression results for Stock X.

$$r_X = 2\% + 1.2 \text{ (percentage change in oil prices)}$$

a. If I live in Louisiana, where the local economy is heavily dependent on oil industry profits, does Stock X represent a useful asset to hedge my overall economic well-being?

b. What if I live in Massachusetts, where most individuals and firms are energy *consumers*?

c. If energy consumers are far more numerous than energy producers, will high oil-beta stocks have higher or lower expected rates of return in market equilibrium than low oil-beta stocks?

SUMMARY

► Multifactor models seek to improve the explanatory power of single-factor models by explicitly accounting for the various systematic components of security risk. These models use indicators intended to capture a wide range of macroeconomic risk factors.

► Once we allow for multiple risk factors, we conclude that the security market line also ought to be multidimensional, with exposure to each risk factor contributing to the total risk premium of the security.

► A (risk-free) arbitrage opportunity arises when two or more security prices enable investors to construct a zero net investment portfolio that will yield a sure profit. The presence of arbitrage opportunities will generate a large volume of trades that puts pressure on security prices. This pressure will continue until prices reach levels that preclude such arbitrage.

► When securities are priced so that there are no risk-free arbitrage opportunities, we say that they satisfy the no-arbitrage condition. Price relationships that satisfy the no-arbitrage condition are important because we expect them to hold in real-world markets.

► Portfolios are called "well-diversified" if they include a large number of securities and the investment proportion in each is sufficiently small. The proportion of a security in a well-diversified portfolio is small enough so that for all practical purposes a reasonable change in that security's rate of return will have a negligible effect on the portfolio's rate of return.

► In a single-factor security market, all well-diversified portfolios have to satisfy the expected return–beta relationship of the CAPM to satisfy the no-arbitrage condition. If all well-diversified portfolios satisfy the expected return–beta relationship, then all but a small number of securities also must satisfy this relationship.

► The APT does not require the restrictive assumptions of the CAPM and its (unobservable) market portfolio. The price of this generality is that the APT does not guarantee this relationship for all securities at all times.

► A multifactor APT generalizes the single-factor model to accommodate several sources of systematic risk. The multidimensional security market line predicts that exposure to each risk factor contributes to the security's total risk premium by an amount equal to the factor beta times the risk premium of the factor portfolio that tracks that source of risk.

► A multifactor extension of the single-factor CAPM, the ICAPM, is a model of the **risk–return trade-off** that predicts the same multidimensional security market line as the APT. The ICAPM suggests that priced risk factors will be those sources of risk that lead to significant hedging demand by a substantial fraction of investors.

WEBSITES

www.onelook.com/?w=arbitrage+pricing+theory
APT is defined here.
www.aimr.com/pdf/apgapt.pdf
This site serves as a practitioner's guide to APT.
www.bus.ed.ac.uk/cfm/cfmr021.htm
This site offers an application of CAPM and APT to the Italian stock market.
www.datalife.com/mall/pages/glossary/GLOSS_R.HTM
Visit this site for a discussion of several risks that generate return volatility.

THE THEORY OF ACTIVE PORTFOLIO MANAGEMENT

by Zvi Bodie, Alex Kane, and Alan J. Marcus

LEARNING OUTCOMES

The candidate should be able to:

a. explain how the theory of active portfolio management can be reconciled with the notion that markets are at equilibrium;

b. discuss the steps and the approach of the Treynor-Black model for security selection;

c. describe how the composition of the active portfolio changes when short positions are prohibited and when there are imperfect forecasts of alpha values.

THE LURE OF ACTIVE MANAGEMENT   1

How can a theory of active portfolio management be reconciled with the notion that markets are in equilibrium?

Market efficiency prevails when many investors are willing to depart from maximum diversification, or a passive strategy, by adding mispriced securities to their portfolios in the hope of realizing abnormal returns. The competition for such returns ensures that prices will be near their "fair" values. Most managers will not beat the passive strategy on a risk-adjusted basis. However, in the competition for rewards to investing, exceptional managers might beat the average forecasts built into market prices.

There is both economic logic and some empirical evidence to indicate that exceptional portfolio managers can beat the average forecast. Let us discuss economic logic first. We must assume that if no analyst can beat the passive strategy, investors will be smart enough to divert their funds from strategies entailing expensive analysis to less expensive passive strategies. In that case funds under active management will dry up, and prices will no longer reflect sophisticated forecasts. The consequent profit opportunities will lure back active managers who once again will become successful.[1] Of course, the critical assumption is that investors allocate management funds wisely. Direct evidence on that has yet to be produced.

Note:
Candidates are not responsible, within Reading 73, for deriving or memorizing the formulas introduced in sections 4–6.

---

[1] This point is worked out fully in Danford J. Grossman and Joseph E. Stiglitz, "On the Impossibility of Informationally Efficient Markets," *American Economic Review* 70 (June 1980)

As for empirical evidence, consider the following: (1) Some portfolio managers have produced streaks of abnormal returns that are hard to label as lucky outcomes; (2) the "noise" in realized rates is enough to prevent us from rejecting outright the hypothesis that some money managers have beaten the passive strategy by a statistically small, yet economically significant, margin; and (3) some anomalies in realized returns have been sufficiently persistent to suggest that portfolio managers who identified them in a timely fashion could have beaten the passive strategy over prolonged periods.

These conclusions persuade us that there is a role for a theory of active portfolio management. Active management has an inevitable lure even if investors agree that security markets are nearly efficient.

Suppose that capital markets are perfectly efficient, that an easily accessible market-index portfolio is available, and that this portfolio is for all practical purposes the efficient risky portfolio. Clearly, in this case security selection would be a futile endeavor. You would be better off with a passive strategy of allocating funds to a money market fund (the safe asset) and the market-index portfolio. Under these simplifying assumptions the optimal investment strategy seems to require no effort or know-how.

Such a conclusion, however, is too hasty. Recall that the proper allocation of investment funds to the risk-free and risky portfolios requires some analysis because y, the fraction to be invested in the risky market portfolio, M, is given by

$$y = \frac{E(r_M) - r_f}{.01 A \sigma_M^2} \qquad\qquad \textbf{(73-1)}$$

where $E(r_M) - r_f$ is the risk premium on M, σ_M^2 its variance, and A is the investor's coefficient of risk aversion. Any rational allocation therefore requires an estimate of σ_M and $E(r_M)$. Even a passive investor needs to do some forecasting, in other words.

Forecasting $E(r_M)$ and s_M is further complicated by the existence of security classes that are affected by different environmental factors. Long-term bond returns, for example, are driven largely by changes in the term structure of interest rates, whereas equity returns depend on changes in the broader economic environment, including macroeconomic factors beyond interest rates. Once our investor determines relevant forecasts for separate sorts of investments, she might as well use an optimization program to determine the proper mix for the portfolio. It is easy to see how the investor may be lured away from a purely passive strategy, and we have not even considered temptations such as international stock and bond portfolios or sector portfolios.

In fact, even the definition of a "purely passive strategy" is problematic, because simple strategies involving only the market-index portfolio and risk-free assets now seem to call for **market analysis**. For our purposes we define purely passive strategies as those that use only index funds and weight those funds by fixed proportions that do not vary in response to perceived market conditions. For example, a portfolio strategy that always places 60% in a stock market–index fund, 30% in a bond-index fund, and 10% in a money market fund is a purely passive strategy.

More important, the lure into active management may be extremely strong because the potential profit from active strategies is enormous. At the same time, competition among the multitude of active managers creates the force driving market prices to near efficiency levels. Although enormous profits may be increasingly difficult to earn, decent profits to the better analysts should be the rule rather than the exception. For prices to remain efficient to some degree, some analysts must be able to eke out a reasonable profit. Absence of profits would decimate the active investment management industry, eventually allowing prices to stray from informationally efficient levels. The theory of managing active portfolios is the concern of this reading.

OBJECTIVES OF ACTIVE PORTFOLIOS 　　　2

What does an investor expect from a professional portfolio manager, and how does this expectation affect the operation of the manager? If the client were risk neutral, that is, indifferent to risk, the answer would be straightforward. The investor would expect the portfolio manager to construct a portfolio with the highest possible expected rate of return. The portfolio manager follows this dictum and is judged by the realized average rate of return.

When the client is risk averse, the answer is more difficult. Without a normative theory of portfolio management, the manager would have to consult each client before making any portfolio decision in order to ascertain that reward (average return) is commensurate with risk. Massive and constant input would be needed from the client-investors, and the economic value of professional management would be questionable.

Fortunately, the theory of mean-variance efficient portfolio management allows us to separate the "product decision," which is how to construct a mean-variance efficient risky portfolio, and the "consumption decision," or the investor's allocation of funds between the efficient risky portfolio and the safe asset. We have seen that construction of the optimal risky portfolio is purely a technical problem, resulting in a single optimal risky portfolio appropriate for all investors. Investors will differ only in how they apportion investment to that risky portfolio and the safe asset.

Another feature of the mean-variance theory that affects portfolio management decisions is the criterion for choosing the optimal risky portfolio. The optimal risky portfolio for any investor is the one that maximizes the reward-to-variability ratio, or the expected excess rate of return (over the risk-free rate) divided by the standard deviation. A manager who uses this Markowitz methodology to construct the optimal risky portfolio will satisfy all clients regardless of risk aversion. Clients, for their part, can evaluate managers using statistical methods to draw inferences from realized rates of return about prospective, or ex ante, reward-to-variability ratios.

William Sharpe's assessment of mutual fund performance[2] is the seminal work in the area of portfolio performance evaluation. The reward-to-variability ratio has come to be known as **Sharpe's measure**:

$$S = \frac{E(r_P) - r_f}{\sigma_P}$$

It is now a common criterion for tracking performance of professionally managed portfolios.

Briefly, mean-variance portfolio theory implies that the objective of professional portfolio managers is to maximize the (ex ante) Sharpe measure, which entails maximizing the slope of the CAL (capital allocation line). A "good" manager is one whose CAL is steeper than the CAL representing the passive strategy

---

[2] William F. Sharpe, "Mutual Fund Performance," *Journal of Business, Supplement on Security Prices* 39 (January 1966).

of holding a market-index portfolio. Clients can observe rates of return and compute the realized **Sharpe measure** (the ex post CAL) to evaluate the relative performance of their manager.

Ideally, clients would like to invest their funds with the most able manager, one who consistently obtains the highest Sharpe measure and presumably has real forecasting ability. This is true for all clients regardless of their degree of risk aversion. At the same time, each client must decide what fraction of investment funds to allocate to this manager, placing the remainder in a safe fund. If the manager's Sharpe measure is constant over time (and can be estimated by clients), the investor can compute the optimal fraction to be invested with the manager from equation 73-1, based on the portfolio long-term average return and variance. The remainder will be invested in a money market fund.

The manager's ex ante Sharpe measure from updated forecasts will be constantly varying. Clients would have liked to increase their allocation to the risky portfolio when the forecasts are optimistic, and vice versa. However, it would be impractical to constantly communicate updated forecasts to clients and for them to constantly revise their allocation between the risky portfolios and risk-free asset.

Allowing managers to shift funds between their optimal risky portfolio and a safe asset according to their forecasts alleviates the problem. Indeed, many stock funds allow the managers reasonable flexibility to do just that.

3   MARKET TIMING

Consider the results of the following two different investment strategies:

1. An investor who put $1,000 in 30-day commercial paper on January 1, 1927, and rolled over all proceeds into 30-day paper (or into 30-day T-bills after they were introduced) would have ended on December 31, 1978, fifty-two years later, with $3,600.

2. An investor who put $1,000 in the NYSE index on January 1, 1927, and reinvested all dividends in that portfolio would have ended on December 31, 1978, with $67,500.

Suppose we defined perfect **market timing** as the ability to tell (with certainty) at the beginning of each month whether the NYSE portfolio will outperform the 30-day paper portfolio. Accordingly, at the beginning of each month, the **market timer** shifts all funds into either cash equivalents (30-day paper) or equities (the NYSE portfolio), whichever is predicted to do better. Beginning with $1,000 on the same date, how would the perfect timer have ended up 52 years later?

This is how Nobel Laureate Robert Merton began a seminar with finance professors 25 years ago. As he collected responses, the boldest guess was a few million dollars. The correct answer: $5.36 *billion*.[3]

CONCEPT CHECK 1

What was the monthly and annual compounded rate of return for the three strategies over the period 1926 to 1978?

---

[3] This demonstration has been extended to recent data with similar results.

These numbers highlight the power of compounding. This effect is particularly important because more and more of the funds under management represent retirement savings. The horizons of such investments may not be as long as 52 years but are measured in decades, making compounding a significant factor.

Another result that may seem surprising at first is the huge difference between the end-of-period value of the all-safe asset strategy ($3,600) and that of the all-equity strategy ($67,500). Why would anyone invest in safe assets given this historical record? If you have internalized the lessons of previous readings, you know the reason: risk. The average rates of return and the standard deviations on the all-bills and all-equity strategies for this period are:

	Arithmetic Mean	Standard Deviation
Bills	2.55	2.10
Equities	10.70	22.14

The significantly higher standard deviation of the rate of return on the equity portfolio is commensurate with its significantly higher average return.

Can we also view the rate-of-return premium on the perfect-timing fund as a risk premium? The answer must be "no," because the perfect timer never does worse than either bills or the market. The extra return is not compensation for the possibility of poor returns but is instead attributable to superior analysis. It is the value of superior information that is reflected in the tremendous end-of-period value of the portfolio.

The monthly rate-of-return statistics for the all-equity portfolio and the timing portfolio are:

Per Month	All Equities (%)	Perfect Timer No Charge (%)	Perfect Timer Fair Charge (%)
Average rate of return	0.85	2.58	0.55
Average excess return over return on safe asset	0.64	2.37	0.34
Standard deviation	5.89	3.82	3.55
Highest return	38.55	38.55	30.14
Lowest return	−29.12	0.06	−7.06
Coefficient of skewness	0.42	4.28	2.84

Ignore for the moment the fourth column ("Perfect Timer—Fair Charge"). The results of rows 1 and 2 are self-explanatory. The third row, standard deviation, requires some discussion. The standard deviation of the monthly rate of return earned by the perfect market timer was 3.82%, far greater than the volatility of T-bill returns over the same period. Does this imply that (perfect) timing is a riskier strategy than investing in bills? No. For this analysis standard deviation is a misleading measure of risk.

To see why, consider how you might choose between two hypothetical strategies: The first offers a sure rate of return of 5%; the second strategy offers an uncertain return that is given by 5% *plus* a random number that is zero with probability .5 and 5% with probability .5. The characteristics of each strategy are:

	Strategy 1 (%)	Strategy 2 (%)
Expected return	5	7.5
Standard deviation	0	2.5
Highest return	5	10.0
Lowest return	5	5.0

Clearly, Strategy 2 dominates Strategy 1 because its rate of return is *at least* equal to that of Strategy 1 and sometimes greater. No matter how risk averse you are, you will always prefer Strategy 2, despite its significant standard deviation. Compared to Strategy 1, Strategy 2 provides only "good surprises," so the standard deviation in this case cannot be a measure of risk.

These two strategies are analogous to the case of the perfect timer compared with an all-equity or all-bills strategy. In every period the perfect timer obtains at least as good a return, in some cases a better one. Therefore the timer's standard deviation is a misleading measure of risk compared to an all-equity or all-bills strategy.

Returning to the empirical results, you can see that the highest rate of return is identical for the all-equity and the timing strategies, whereas the lowest rate of return is positive for the perfect timer and disastrous for all the all-equity portfolio. Another reflection of this is seen in the coefficient of skewness, which measures the asymmetry of the distribution of returns. Because the equity portfolio is almost (but not exactly) normally distributed, its coefficient of skewness is very low at .42. In contrast, the perfect timing strategy effectively eliminates the negative tail of the distribution of portfolio returns (the part below the risk-free rate). Its returns are "skewed to the right," and its coefficient of skewness is therefore quite large, 4.28.

Now for the fourth column, "Perfect Timer—Fair Charge," which is perhaps the most interesting. Most assuredly, the perfect timer will charge clients for such a valuable service. (The perfect timer may have otherworldly predictive powers, but saintly benevolence is unlikely.)

Subtracting a fair fee (discussed later) from the monthly rate of return of the timer's portfolio gives us an average rate of return lower than that of the passive, all-equity strategy. However, because the fee is *constructed* to be fair, the two portfolios (the all-equity strategy and the market-timing-with-fee strategy) must be equally attractive after risk adjustment. In this case, again, the standard deviation of the market timing strategy (with fee) is of no help in adjusting for risk because the coefficient of skewness remains high, 2.84. In other words, **mean-variance analysis** is inadequate for valuing market timing. We need an alternative approach.

Valuing Market Timing as an Option

The key to analyzing the pattern of returns to the perfect market timer is to recognize that perfect foresight is equivalent to holding a call option on the equity portfolio. The perfect timer invests 100% in either the safe asset or the equity portfolio, whichever will yield the higher return. This is shown in Figure 73-1. The rate of return is bounded from below by r_f.

FIGURE 73-1   Rate of Return of a Perfect Market Timer

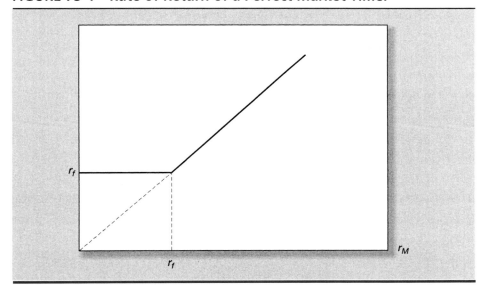

To see the value of information as an option, suppose that the market index currently is at S_0 and that a call option on the index has an exercise price of $X = S_0(1 + r_f)$. If the market outperforms bills over the coming period, S_T will exceed X, whereas it will be less than X otherwise. Now look at the payoff to a portfolio consisting of this option and S_0 dollars invested in bills:

	$S_T < X$	$S_T \geq X$
Bills	$S_0(1 + r_f)$	$S_0(1 + r_f)$
Option	0	$S_T - X$
Total	$S_0(1 + r_f)$	S_T

The portfolio pays the risk-free return when the market is bearish (i.e., the market return is less than the risk-free rate), and it pays the market return when the market is bullish and beats bills. Such a portfolio is a perfect market timer. Consequently, we can measure the value of perfect ability as the value of the call option, because a call enables the investor to earn the market return only when it exceeds r_f. This insight lets Merton[4] value timing ability using the theory of option of valuation, and calculate the fair charge for it.

The Value of Imperfect Forecasting

Unfortunately, managers are not perfect forecasters. It seems pretty obvious that if managers are right most of the time, they are doing very well. However, when we say "most of the time," we cannot mean merely the percentage of the time a manager is right. The weather forecaster in Tucson, Arizona, who *always* predicts no rain, may be right 90% of the time. But a high success rate for a "stopped-clock" strategy clearly is not evidence of forecasting ability.

Similarly, the appropriate measure of market forecasting ability is not the overall proportion of correct forecasts. If the market is up two days out of three and a forecaster always predicts market advance, the two-thirds success rate is not

[4] Robert C. Merton, "On Market Timing and Investment Performance: An Equilibrium Theory of Value for Market Forecasts," *Journal of Business,* July 1981.

a measure of forecasting ability. We need to examine the proportion of bull markets ($r_M > r_f$) correctly forecast *and* the proportion of bear markets ($r_M < r_f$) correctly forecast.

If we call P_1 the proportion of the correct forecasts of bull markets and P_2 the proportion for bear markets, then $P_1 + P_2 - 1$ is the correct measure of timing ability. For example, a forecaster who always guesses correctly will have $P_1 = P_2 = 1$, and will show ability of 1 (100%). An analyst who always bets on a bear market will mispredict all bull markets ($P_1 = 0$), will correctly "predict" all bear markets ($P_2 = 1$), and will end up with timing ability of $P_1 + P_2 - 1 = 0$. If C denotes the (call option) value of a perfect market timer, then $(P_1 + P_2 - 1)C$ measures the value of imperfect forecasting ability.

CONCEPT CHECK 2

What is the market timing score of someone who flips a fair coin to predict the market?

---

4   SECURITY SELECTION: THE TREYNOR-BLACK MODEL

Overview of the Treynor-Black Model

Security analysis is the other form of active portfolio management besides timing the overall market. Suppose that you are an analyst studying individual securities. It is quite likely that you will turn up several securities that appear to be mispriced. They offer positive anticipated alphas to the investor. But how do you exploit your analysis? Concentrating a portfolio on these securities entails a cost, namely, the firm-specific risk that you could shed by more fully diversifying. As an active manager you must strike a balance between aggressive exploitation of perceived security mispricing and diversification motives that dictate that a few stocks should not dominate the portfolio.

Treynor and Black[5] developed an optimizing model for portfolio managers who use security analysis. It represents a portfolio management theory that assumes security markets are *nearly* efficient. The essence of the model is this:

1. Security analysts in an active investment management organization can analyze in depth only a limited number of stocks out of the entire universe of securities. The securities not analyzed are assumed to be fairly priced.
2. For the purpose of efficient diversification, the market index portfolio is the baseline portfolio, which the model treats as the passive portfolio.
3. The macro forecasting unit of the investment management firm provides forecasts of the expected rate of return and variance of the passive (market-index) portfolio.
4. The objective of security analysis is to form an active portfolio of a necessarily limited number of securities. Perceived mispricing of the analyzed securities is what guides the composition of this active portfolio.

---

[5] Jack Treynor and Fischer Black, "How to Use Security Analysis to Improve Portfolio Selection," *Journal of Business,* January 1973.

5. Analysts follow several steps to make up the active portfolio and evaluate its expected performance:

   a. Estimate the beta of each analyzed security and its residual risk. From the beta and macro forecast, $E(r_M) - r_f$, determine the *required* rate of return of the security.

   b. Given the degree of mispricing of each security, determine its expected return and expected *abnormal* return (alpha).

   c. The cost of less-than-full diversification comes from the nonsystematic risk of the mispriced stock, the variance of the stock's residual, $\sigma^2(e)$, which offsets the benefit (alpha) of specializing in an underpriced security.

   d. Use the estimates for the values of alpha, beta, and $\sigma^2(e)$ to determine the optimal weight of each security in the active portfolio.

   e. Compute the alpha, beta, and $\sigma^2(e)$ of the active portfolio from the weights of the securities in the portfolio.

6. The macroeconomic forecasts for the passive index portfolio and the composite forecasts for the active portfolio are used to determine the optimal risky portfolio, which will be a combination of the passive and active portfolios.

Treynor and Black's model did not take the industry by storm. This is unfortunate for several reasons:

1. Just as even imperfect market timing ability has enormous value, security analysis of the sort Treynor and Black proposed has similar potential value.[6] Even with far from perfect security analysis, proper active management can add value.

2. The Treynor-Black model is conceptually easy to implement. Moreover, it is useful even when some of its simplifying assumptions are relaxed.

3. The model lends itself to use in decentralized organizations. This property is essential to efficiency in complex organizations.

Portfolio Construction

Assuming that all securities are fairly priced, and using the index model as a guideline for the rate of return on fairly priced securities, the rate of return on the *i*th security is given by

$$r_i = r_f + \beta_i(r_M - r_f) + e_i \qquad \textbf{(73-2)}$$

where e_i is the zero mean, firm-specific disturbance.

Absent security analysis, Treynor and Black (TB) took equation 73-2 to represent the rate of return on all securities and assumed that the market portfolio, *M*, is the efficient portfolio. For simplicity, they also assumed that the nonsystematic components of returns, e_i, are independent across securities. As for market timing, TB assumed that the forecast for the **passive portfolio** already has been made, so that the expected return on the market index, r_M, as well as its variance, σ_M^2, has been assessed.

---

[6] Alex Kane, Alan Marcus, and Robert Trippi, "The Valuation of Security Analysis," *Journal of Portfolio Management*, Spring 1999.

Now a portfolio manager unleashes a team of security analysts to investigate a subset of the universe of available securities. The objective is to form an active portfolio of positions in the analyzed securities to be mixed with the index portfolio. For each security, k, that is researched, we write the rate of return as

$$r_k = r_f + \beta_k(r_M - r_f) + e_k + \alpha_k \tag{73-3}$$

where α_k represents the extra expected return (called the *abnormal return*) attributable to any perceived mispricing of the security. Thus, for each security analyzed the research team estimates the parameters α_k, β_k, and $\sigma^2(e_k)$. If all the α_k turn out to be zero, there would be no reason to depart from the passive strategy and the index portfolio M would remain the manager's choice. However, this is a remote possibility. In general, there will be a significant number of nonzero alpha values, some positive and some negative.

One way to get an overview of the TB methodology is to examine what we should do with the active portfolio once we determine it. Suppose that the **active portfolio** (A) has been constructed somehow and has the parameters α_A, β_A, and $\sigma^2(e_A)$. Its total variance is the sum of its systematic variance, $\beta_A^2 \sigma_M^2$, plus the nonsystematic variance, $\sigma^2(e_A)$. Its covariance with the market index portfolio, M, is

$$\text{Cov}(r_A, r_M) = \beta_A \sigma_M^2$$

Figure 73-2 shows the optimization process with the active and passive portfolios. The dashed efficient frontier represents the universe of all securities assuming that they are all fairly priced, that is, that all alphas are zero. By definition, the market index, M, is on this efficient frontier and is tangent to the (dashed) capital market line (CML). In practice, the analysts do not need to know this frontier. They need only to observe the market-index portfolio and construct a portfolio resulting in a capital allocation line that lies above the

FIGURE 73-2   The Optimization Process with Active and Passive Portfolios

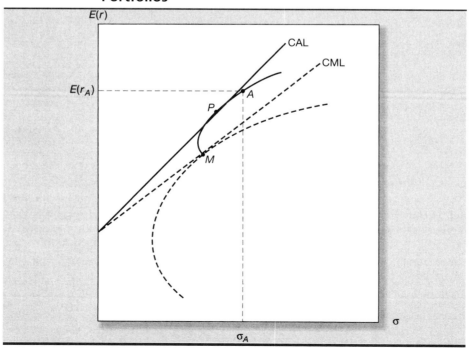

CML. Given their perceived superior analysis, they will view the market-index portfolio as inefficient: The active portfolio, A, constructed from mispriced securities, must lie, by design, above the CML.

To locate the active portfolio A in Figure 73-2, we need its expected return and standard deviation. The standard deviation is

$$\sigma_A = \left[\beta_A^2 \sigma_M^2 + \sigma^2(e_A)\right]^{1/2}$$

Because of the positive alpha value that is forecast for A, it may plot above the (dashed) CML with expected return

$$E(r_A) = \alpha_A + r_f + \beta_A[E(r_M) - r_f]$$

The optimal combination of the active portfolio, A, with the passive portfolio, M, is a simple application of the construction of optimal risky portfolios from two component assets. Because the active portfolio is not perfectly correlated with the market-index portfolio, we need to account for their mutual correlation in the determination of the optimal allocation between the two portfolios. This is evident from the solid efficient frontier that passes through M and A in Figure 73-2. It supports the optimal capital allocation line (CAL) and identifies the optimal risky portfolio, P, which combines portfolios A and M and is the tangency point of the CAL to the efficient frontier. The active portfolio A in this example is not the ultimate efficient portfolio, because we need to mix A with the passive market portfolio to achieve optimal diversification.

Let us now outline the algebraic approach to this optimization problem. If we invest a proportion, w, in the active portfolio and $1 - w$ in the market index, the portfolio return will be

$$r_p(w) = wr_A + (1 - w)r_M$$

To find the weight, w, which provides the best (i.e., the steepest) CAL, we use equation 73-4, which describes the optimal risky portfolio composed of two risky assets (in this case, A and M) when there is a risk-free asset:

$$w_A = \frac{\left[E(r_A) - r_f\right]\sigma_M^2 - \left[E(r_M) - r_f\right]\text{Cov}(r_A, r_M)}{\left[E(r_A) - r_f\right]\sigma_M^2 + \left[E(r_M) - r_f\right]\sigma_A^2 - \left[E(r_A) - r_f + E(r_M) - r_f\right]\text{Cov}(r_A, r_M)}$$

(73-4)

Now recall that

$$E(r_A) - r_f = \alpha_A + \beta_A R_M \qquad \text{where } R_M = E(r_M) - r_f$$

$$\text{Cov}(R_A, R_M) = \beta_A \sigma_M^2 \qquad \text{where } R_A = E(r_A) - r_f$$

$$\sigma_A^2 = \beta_A^2 \sigma_M^2 + \sigma^2(e_A)$$

$$[E(r_A) - r_f] + [E(r_M) - r_f] = (\alpha_A + \beta R_M) + R_M = \alpha_A + R_M(1 + \beta_A)$$

Substituting these expressions into equation 73-4, dividing both numerator and denominator by σ_M^2, and collecting terms yields the expression for the optimal weight in portfolio A, w^*,

$$w^* = \frac{\alpha_A}{\alpha_A(1 - \beta_A) + R_M \dfrac{\sigma^2(e_A)}{\sigma_M^2}}$$

(73-5)

Let's begin with the simple case where $\beta_A = 1$ and substitute into equation 73-5. Then the optimal weight, w_0, is

$$w_0 = \frac{\dfrac{\alpha_A}{R_M}}{\dfrac{\sigma^2(e_A)}{\sigma_M^2}} = \frac{\alpha_A/\sigma^2(e_A)}{R_M/\sigma_M^2} \qquad \textbf{(73-6)}$$

Here is some intuition for this result. If the systematic risk of the active portfolio is average, that is, $\beta_A = 1$, then the optimal weight is the "relative advantage" of portfolio A as measured by the ratio: alpha/[market excess return], divided by the "disadvantage" of A, that is, the ratio: [nonsystematic risk of A]/[market risk]. Some algebra applied to equation 73-5 reveals the relationship between w_0 and w^*:

$$w^* = \frac{w_0}{1 + (1 - \beta_A) w_0} \qquad \textbf{(73-7)}$$

w^* increases when β_A increases because the greater the systematic risk, β_A, of the active portfolio, A, the smaller is the benefit from diversifying it with the index, M, and the more beneficial it is to take advantage of the mispriced securities. However, we expect the beta of the active portfolio to be in the neighborhood of 1.0 and the optimal weight, w^*, to be close to w_0.

What is the reward-to-variability ratio of the optimal risky portfolio once we find the best mix, w^*, of the active and passive index portfolios? It turns out that if we compute the square of Sharpe's measure of the risky portfolio, we can separate the contributions of the index and active portfolios as follows:

$$S_P^2 = S_M^2 + \frac{\alpha_A^2}{\sigma^2(e_A)} = \left[\frac{R_M}{\sigma_M} \right]^2 + \left[\frac{\alpha_A}{\sigma(e_A)} \right]^2 \qquad \textbf{(73-8)}$$

This decomposition of the Sharpe measure of the optimal risky portfolio, which by the way is valid *only* for the optimal portfolio, tells us how to construct the active portfolio. Equation 73-8 shows that the highest Sharpe measure for the risky portfolio will be attained when we construct an active portfolio that maximizes the value of $\alpha_A/\sigma(e_A)$. The ratio of alpha to residual standard deviation of the active portfolio will be maximized when we choose a weight for the kth analyzed security as follows:

$$w_k = \frac{\alpha_k/\sigma^2(e_k)}{\displaystyle\sum_{i=1}^{n} \alpha_i/\sigma^2(e_i)} \qquad \textbf{(73-9)}$$

This makes sense: The weight of a security in the active portfolio depends on the ratio of the degree of mispricing, α_k, to the nonsystematic risk, $\sigma^2(e_k)$, of the security. The denominator, the sum of the ratio across securities, is a scale factor to guarantee that portfolio weights sum to one.

Note from equation 73-8 that the square of Sharpe's measure of the optimal risky portfolio is increased over the square of the Sharpe measure of the passive (market-index) portfolio by the amount

$$\left[\frac{\alpha_A}{\sigma(e_A)} \right]^2$$

The ratio of the degree of mispricing, α_A, to the nonsystematic standard deviation, $\sigma(e_A)$, is therefore a natural performance measure of the active component of the risky portfolio. Sometimes this is called the **information ratio**.

We can calculate the contribution of a single security in the active portfolio to the portfolio's overall performance. When the active portfolio contains n analyzed securities, the total improvement in the squared Sharpe measure equals the sum of the squared information ratios of the analyzed securities,

$$\left[\frac{\alpha_A}{\sigma(e_A)}\right]^2 = \sum_{i=1}^{n}\left[\frac{\alpha_i}{\sigma(e_i)}\right]^2 \qquad \textbf{(73-10)}$$

The information ratio for each security; $\alpha_i/\sigma(e_i)$, is a measure of the contribution of that security to the performance of the active portfolio.

The best way to illustrate the Treynor-Black process is through an example that can be easily worked out in a spreadsheet. Suppose that the macroforecasting unit of Drex Portfolio Inc. (DPF) issues a forecast for a 15% market return. The forecast's standard error is 20%. The risk-free rate is 7%. The macro data can be summarized as follows:

$$R_M = E(r_M) - r_f = 8\%; \sigma_M = 20\%$$

At the same time the security analysis division submits to the portfolio manager the following forecast of annual returns for the three securities that it covers:

Stock	α	β	$\sigma(e)$	$\alpha/\sigma(e)$
1	7%	1.6	45%	.1556
2	-5	1.0	32	-.1563
3	3	0.5	26	.1154

E-INVESTMENTS: CALCULATING THE INFORMATION RATIO

Go to www.the401k.com. Click through *Reference*, then *Focus on 401(k) Newsletter*, where you can choose the Second Quarter 2001 newsletter. This choice allows you to review the calculation of the information ratio. How can the portfolio manager take extra risk to "beat" the market indexes? What does the information ratio measure?

Note that the alpha estimates appear reasonably moderate. The estimates of the residual standard deviations are correlated with the betas, just as they are in reality. The magnitudes also reflect typical values for NYSE stocks. Equations 73-10, 73-8, and the analyst input table allow a quick calculation of the DPF portfolio's Sharpe measure.

$$S_P = \left[(8/20)^2 + .1556^2 + .1563^2 + .1154^2\right]^{1/2} = \sqrt{.2220} = .4711$$

Compare the result with the Sharpe ratio for the market-index portfolio, which is only $8/20 = .40$. We now proceed to compute the composition and performance of the active portfolio.

First, let us construct the optimal active portfolio implied by the security analyst input list. To do so we compute the **appraisal ratios** as follows (remember to use decimal representations of returns in the formulas):

Stock	$\alpha/\sigma^2(e)$	$\dfrac{\alpha_k}{\sigma^2(e_k)} / \displaystyle\sum_{i=1}^{3} \dfrac{\alpha_i}{\sigma^2(e_i)}$
1	$.07/.45^2 =\ \ .3457$	$.3457/.3012 =\ \ \ 1.1477$
2	$-.05/.32^2 = -.4883$	$-.4883/.3012 = -1.6212$
3	$.03/.26^2 =\ \ .4438$	$.4438/.3012 =\ \ \ 1.4735$
Total	$.3012$	1.0000

The last column presents the optimal positions of each of the three securities in the active portfolio. Obviously, Stock 2, with a negative alpha, has a negative weight. The magnitudes of the individual positions in the active portfolio (e.g., 114.77% in Stock 1) seem quite extreme. However, this should not concern us because the active portfolio will later be mixed with the well-diversified market-index portfolio, resulting in much more moderate positions, as we shall see shortly.

The forecasts for the stocks, together with the proposed composition of the active portfolio, lead to the following parameter estimates for the active portfolio:

$$\alpha_A = 1.1477 \times .07 + (-1.6212) \times (-.05) + 1.4735 \times .03$$
$$= .2056 = 20.56\%$$
$$\beta_A = 1.1477 \times 1.6 + (-1.6212) \times 1.0 + 1.4735 \times .5 = .9519$$
$$\sigma(e_A) = \left[1.1477^2 \times .45^2 + (-1.6212)^2 \times .32^2 + 1.4735^2 \times .26^2\right]^{1/2}$$
$$= .8262 = 82.62\%$$
$$\sigma^2(e_A) = .8262^2 = .6826$$

Note that the negative weight (short position) on the negative alpha stock results in a positive contribution to the alpha of the active portfolio. Note also that because of the assumption that the stock residuals are uncorrelated, the active portfolio's residual variance is simply the weighted sum of the individual stock residual variances, with the squared portfolio proportions as weights.

The parameters of the active portfolio are now used to determine its proportion in the overall risky portfolio:

$$w_0 = \frac{\alpha_A/\sigma^2(e_A)}{R_M/\sigma_M^2} = \frac{.2056/.6826}{.08/.04} = .1506$$

$$w^* = \frac{w_0}{1 + (1-\beta_A)w_0} = \frac{.1506}{1 + (1 - .9519) \times .1506} = .1495$$

Although the active portfolio's alpha is impressive (20.56%), its proportion in the overall risky portfolio, before adjustment for beta, is only 15.06%, because of its large nonsystematic standard deviation (82.62%). Such is the importance of diversification. As it happens, the beta of the active portfolio is almost 1.0, and hence the adjustment for beta (from w_0 to w^*) is small, from 15.06% to 14.95%. The direction of the change makes sense. If the beta of the active portfolio is low (less than 1.0), there is more potential gain from diversification, hence a smaller position in the active portfolio is called for. If the beta of the active portfolio were significantly greater than 1.0, a larger correction in the opposite direction would be called for.

The proportions of the individual stocks in the active portfolio, together with the proportion of the active portfolio in the overall risky portfolio, determine the proportions of each individual stock in the overall risky portfolio.

Stock	Final Position
1	$.1495 \times 1.1477 = \quad .1716$
2	$.1495 \times (-1.6212) = -.2424$
3	$.1495 \times 1.4735 = \quad .2202$
Active portfolio	$.1495$
Market portfolio	$.8505$
	1.0000

The parameters of the active portfolio and market-index portfolio are now used to forecast the performance of the optimal, overall risky portfolio. When optimized, a property of the risky portfolio is that its squared Sharpe measure exceeds that of the passive portfolio by the square of the active portfolio's information ratio:

$$S_P^2 = \left[\frac{R_M}{\sigma_M}\right]^2 + \left[\frac{\alpha_A}{\sigma(e_A)}\right]^2$$
$$= .16 + .0619 = .2219$$

and hence the Sharpe measure of the DPF portfolio is $\sqrt{.2219} = .4711$, compared with .40 for the passive portfolio.

Another measure of the gain from increasing the Sharpe measure is the M^2 statistic. M^2 is calculated by comparing the expected return of a portfolio on the capital allocation line supported by portfolio P, CAL(P), with a standard deviation equal to that of the market index, to the expected return on the market index. In other words, we mix portfolio P with the risk-free asset to obtain a new portfolio P^* that has the same standard deviation as the market portfolio. Since both portfolios have equal risk, we can compare their expected returns. The M^2 statistic is the difference in expected returns. Portfolio P^* can be obtained by investing a fraction σ_M/σ_P in P and a fraction $(1 - \sigma_M/\sigma_P)$ in the risk-free asset. The risk premium on CAL(P^*) with total risk σ_M is given by

$$R_{P^*} = E(r_{P^*}) - r_f = S_P \sigma_M = .4711 \times .20 = .0942, \text{ or } 9.42\% \qquad \textbf{(73-11)}$$

and

$$M^2 = [R_{P^*} - R_M] = 9.42 - 8 = 1.42\% \qquad \textbf{(73-12)}$$

At first blush, an incremental expected return of 1.42% seems paltry compared with the alpha values submitted by the analyst. This seemingly modest improvement is the result of diversification motives: To mitigate the large risk of individual stocks (verify that the standard deviation of stock 1 is 55%)

and maximize the portfolio Sharpe measure (which compares excess return to total volatility), we must diversify the active portfolio by mixing it with *M*. Note also that this improvement has been achieved with only three stocks, and with forecasts and portfolio rebalancing only once a year. Increasing the number of stocks and the frequency of forecasts can improve the results dramatically.

For example, suppose the analyst covers three more stocks that turn out to have alphas and risk levels identical to the first three. Use equation 73-10 to show that the squared appraisal ratio of the active portfolio will double. By using equation 73-8, it is easy to show that the new Sharpe measure will rise to .5327. Equation 73-12 then implies that M^2 rises to 2.65%, almost double the previous value. Increasing the frequency of forecasts and portfolio rebalancing will deploy the power of compounding to improve annual performance even more.

CONCEPT CHECK 3

a. When short positions are prohibited, the manager simply discards stocks with negative alphas. Using the preceding example, what would be the composition of the active portfolio if short sales were disallowed? Find the cost of the short-sale restriction in terms of the decline in performance (M^2) of the new overall risky portfolio.

b. What is the contribution of security selection to portfolio performance if the macro forecast is adjusted upward, for example, to $R_M = 12\%$, and short sales are again allowed?

5 MULTIFACTOR MODELS AND ACTIVE PORTFOLIO MANAGEMENT

Portfolio managers use various multifactor models of security returns. So far our analytical framework for active portfolio management seems to rest on the validity of the index model, that is, on a single-factor security model. Using a multifactor model will not affect the construction of the active portfolio because the entire TB analysis focuses on the residuals of the index model. If we were to replace the one-factor model with a multifactor model, we would continue to form the active portfolio by calculating each security's alpha relative to its fair return (given its betas on *all* factors), and again we would combine the active portfolio with the portfolio that would be formed in the absence of security analysis. The multifactor framework, however, does raise several new issues.

You saw in Reading 71 how the index model simplifies the construction of the input list necessary for portfolio optimization programs. If

$$r_i - r_f = \alpha_i + \beta_i (r_M - r_f) + e_i$$

adequately describes the security market, then the variance of any asset is the sum of systematic and nonsystematic risk: $\sigma^2(r_i) = \beta_i^2 \sigma_M^2 + \sigma^2(e_i)$, and the covariance between any two assets is $\beta_i\beta_j\sigma_M^2$.

How do we generalize this rule to use in a multifactor model? To simplify, let us consider a two-factor world, and let us call the two factor portfolios M and H. Then we generalize the index model to

$$r_i - r_f = \beta_{iM}(r_M - r_f) + \beta_{iH}(r_H - r_f) + \alpha_i + e_i$$
$$= R_\beta + \alpha_i + e_i$$

(73-13)

β_{iM} and β_{iH} are the betas of the security relative to portfolios M and H. Given the rates of return on the factor portfolios, r_M and r_H, the fair excess rate of return over r_f on a security is denoted R_β and its expected abnormal return is α_i.

How can we use equation 73-13 to form optimal portfolios? As before, investors wish to maximize the Sharpe measures of their portfolios. The factor structure of equation 73-13 can be used to generate the inputs for the Markowitz portfolio selection algorithm. The variance and covariance estimates are now more complex, however:

$$\sigma^2(r_i) = \beta_{iM}^2 \sigma_M^2 + \beta_{iH}^2 \sigma_H^2 + 2\beta_{iM}\beta_{iH} \operatorname{Cov}(r_M, r_H) + \sigma^2(e_i)$$
$$\operatorname{Cov}(r_i, r_j) = \beta_{iM}\beta_{jM}\sigma_M^2 + \beta_{iH}\beta_{jH}\sigma_H^2 + (\beta_{iM}\beta_{jH} + \beta_{jM}\beta_{iH})\operatorname{Cov}(r_M, r_H)$$

Nevertheless, the informational economy of the factor model still is valuable, because we can estimate a covariance matrix for an n-security portfolio from

n estimates of β_{iM}
n estimates of β_{iH}
n estimates of $\sigma^2(e_i)$
1 estimate of σ_M^2
1 estimate of σ_H^2

rather than $n(n+1)/2$ separate variance and covariance estimates. Thus the factor structure continues to simplify portfolio construction data requirements.

The factor structure also suggests an efficient method to allocate research effort. Analysts can specialize in forecasting means and variances of different factor portfolios. Having established factor betas, they can form a covariance matrix to be used together with expected security returns generated by the CAPM or APT to construct an optimal passive risky portfolio. If active analysis of individual stocks also is attempted, the procedure of constructing the optimal active portfolio and its optimal combination with the passive portfolio is identical to that followed in the single-factor case.

In the case of the multifactor market even passive investors (meaning those who accept market prices as "fair") need to do a considerable amount of work. They need forecasts of the expected return and volatility of each factor return, *and* they need to determine the appropriate weights on each factor portfolio to maximize their **expected utility**. Such a process is straightforward in principle, but it quickly becomes computationally demanding.

IMPERFECT FORECASTS OF ALPHA VALUES AND THE USE OF THE TREYNOR-BLACK MODEL IN INDUSTRY

6

Suppose an analyst is assigned to a security and provides you with a forecast of $\alpha = 20\%$. It looks like a great opportunity! Using this forecast in the Treynor-Black algorithm, we'll end up tilting our portfolio heavily toward this security.

Should we go out on a limb? Before doing so, any reasonable manager would ask: "How good is the analyst?" Unless the answer is a resounding "good," a reasonable manager would discount the forecast. We can quantify this notion.

Suppose we have a record of an analyst's past forecast of alpha, α^f. Relying on the index model and obtaining reliable estimates of the stock beta, we can estimate the true alphas (after the fact) from the average realized excess returns on the security, $\overline{R}$, and the index, $\overline{R}_M$, that is,

$$\alpha = \overline{R} - \beta \overline{R}_M$$

To measure the forecasting accuracy of the analyst, we can estimate a regression of the forecasts on the realized alpha:

$$\alpha^f = a_0 + a_1\alpha + \varepsilon$$

The coefficients a_0 and a_1 reflect potential bias in the forecasts, which we will ignore for simplicity; that is, we will suppose $a_0 = 0$ and $a_1 = 1$. Because the forecast errors are uncorrelated with the true alpha, the variance of the forecast is

$$\sigma_{\alpha^f}^2 = \sigma_\alpha^2 + \sigma_\varepsilon^2$$

The quality of the forecasts can be measured by the squared correlation coefficient between the forecasts and realization, equivalently, the ratio of explained variance to total variance

$$\rho^2 = \frac{\sigma_\alpha^2}{\sigma_\alpha^2 + \sigma_\varepsilon^2}$$

This equation shows us how to "discount" analysts' forecasts to reflect their precision. Knowing the quality of past forecasts, ρ^2, we "shrink" any new forecast, α^f, to $\rho^2\alpha^f$, to minimize forecast error. This procedure is quite intuitive: If the analyst is perfect, that is, $\rho^2 = 1$, we take the forecast at face value. If analysts' forecasts have proven to be useless, with $\rho^2 = 0$, we ignore the forecast. The quality of the forecast gives us the precise shrinkage factor to use.

Suppose the analysts' forecasts of the alpha of the three stocks in our previous example are all of equal quality, $\rho^2 = .2$. Shrinking the forecasts of alpha by a factor of .2 and repeating the optimization process, we end up with a much smaller weight on the active portfolio (.03 instead of .15), a much smaller Sharpe measure (.4031 instead of .4711), and a much smaller M^2 (.06% instead of 1.42%).

The reduction in portfolio expected performance does not reflect an inferior procedure. Rather, accepting alpha forecasts without acknowledging and adjusting for their imprecision would be naïve. We must adjust our expectations to the quality of the forecasts.

In reality, we can expect the situation to be much worse. A forecast quality of .2, that is, a correlation coefficient between alpha forecasts and realizations of $\sqrt{.2} = .45$, is most likely unrealistic in nearly efficient markets. Moreover, we don't even know this quality, and its estimation introduces yet another potential error into the optimization process. Finally, the other parameters we use in the TB model—market expected return and variance, security betas and residual variances—are also estimated with errors. Thus, under realistic circumstances, we would be fortunate to obtain even the meager results we have just uncovered.

So, should we ditch the TB model? Before we do, let's make one more calculation. The "meager" Sharpe measure of .4031 squares to .1625, larger than the market's squared Sharpe measure of .16 by .0025. Suppose we cover 300 securities instead of three, that is, 100 sets identical to the one we analyzed. From equations 73-8 and 73-10 we know that the increment to the squared Sharpe measure will rise to $100 \times .0025 = .25$. The squared Sharpe measure of the risky portfolio will rise to $.16 + .25 = .41$, a Sharpe measure of .64, and an M^2 of 4.8%! Moreover, some of the estimation errors of the other parameters that plague us when we use three securities will offset one another and be diversified away with many more securities covered.[7]

What we see here is a demonstration of the value of security analysis we mentioned at the outset. In the final analysis, the value of the active management depends on forecast quality. The vast demand for active management suggests that this quality is not negligible. The optimal way to exploit analysts' forecasts is with the TB model.

---

[7] Empirical work along these lines can be found in: Alex Kane, Tae-Hwan Kim, and Halbert White, "The Power of Portfolio Optimization," UCSD Working Paper, July 2000.

SUMMARY

▶ A truly passive portfolio strategy entails holding the market-index portfolio and a money market fund. Determining the optimal allocation to the market portfolio requires an estimate of its expected return and variance, which in turn suggests delegating some analysis to professionals.

▶ Active portfolio managers attempt to construct a risky portfolio that maximizes the reward-to-variability (Sharpe) ratio.

▶ The value of perfect market timing ability is considerable. The rate of return to a perfect market timer will be uncertain. However, its risk characteristics are not measurable by standard measures of portfolio risk, because perfect timing dominates a passive strategy, providing "good" surprises only.

▶ Perfect timing ability is equivalent to the possession of a call option on the market portfolio, whose value can be determined using option valuation techniques such as the Black-Scholes formula.

▶ With imperfect timing, the value of a timer who attempts to forecast whether stocks will outperform bills is determined by the conditional probabilities of the true outcome given the forecasts: $P_1 + P_2 - 1$. Thus if the value of perfect timing is given by the option value, C, then imperfect timing has the value $(P_1 + P_2 - 1)C$.

▶ The Treynor-Black security selection model envisions that a macroeconomic forecast for market performance is available and that security analysts estimate abnormal expected rates of return, α, for various securities. Alpha is the expected rate of return on a security beyond that explained by its beta and the security market line.

▶ In the Treynor-Black model the weight of each analyzed security is proportional to the ratio of its alpha to its nonsystematic risk, $\sigma^2(e)$.

▶ Once the active portfolio is constructed, its alpha value, nonsystematic risk, and beta can be determined from the properties of the component securities. The optimal risky portfolio, P, is then constructed by holding a position in the active portfolio according to the ratio of α_A to $\sigma^2(e_A)$, divided by the analogous ratio for the market-index portfolio. Finally, this position is adjusted using the beta of the active portfolio.

▶ When the overall risky portfolio is constructed using the optimal proportions of the active portfolio and passive portfolio, its performance, as measured by the square of Sharpe's measure, is improved (over that of the passive, market-index, portfolio) by the amount $[\alpha_A/\sigma(e_A)]^2$.

▶ The contribution of each security to the overall improvement in the performance of the active portfolio is determined by its degree of mispricing and nonsystematic risk. The contribution of each security to portfolio performance equals $[\alpha_i/\sigma(e_i)]^2$, so that for the optimal risky portfolio,

$$S_P^2 = \left[\frac{E(r_M) - r_f}{\sigma_M} \right]^2 + \sum_{i=1}^{n} \left[\frac{\alpha_i}{\sigma(e_i)} \right]^2$$

▶ Applying the Treynor-Black model to a multifactor framework is straightforward. The forecast of the market-index mean and standard deviation must be replaced with forecasts for an optimized passive portfolio based on a multifactor model. The proportions of the factor portfolios are calculated using the familiar efficient frontier algorithm. The active portfolio is constructed on the basis of residuals from the multifactor model.

► Implementing the model with imperfect forecasts requires estimation of bias and precision of raw forecasts. The adjusted forecast is obtained by applying the estimated co-efficients to the raw forecasts.

WEBSITES

www.investorsoftware.net/InvestorPrimer/InvestmentPerformance.html

www.nysscpa.org/cpajournal/2001/0600/features/f064401.htm

Learn more about the Sharpe measure at these sites.

www.sniper.at

www.stockmarkettiming.com

The sites above give valuable market timing information.

www.financewise.com/public/edit/riskm/ewrm/ewrm-port-x.htm

www.financewise.com/public/edit/riskm/ewrm/ewrm-portfolio.htm

www.business.com/directory/financial_services/commercial_finance/
treasury/insurance_and_risk_management/sources_and_managing_risk/
portfolio_diversification

Visit these sites for further information on the Treynor-Black Model.

www.russell.com/AU/Institutional_Investors/Russell_Library/Investment_
Articles_and_Updates/Information_Ratios_Explained.asp

www.the401k.com/news/quarter11997/information_ratio.html

Visit these sites to gain a better understanding of the information ratio.

THE PORTFOLIO MANAGEMENT PROCESS AND THE INVESTMENT POLICY STATEMENT

by John L. Maginn, Donald L. Tuttle, Dennis W. McLeavey, and Jerald E. Pinto

LEARNING OUTCOMES

The candidate should be able to:

a. explain the importance of the portfolio perspective;

b. describe the steps of the portfolio management process and the components of those steps;

c. define investment objectives and constraints and explain and distinguish among the types of investment objectives and contraints;

d. discuss the role of the investment policy statement in the portfolio management process and explain the elements of an investment policy statement;

e. explain how capital market expectations and the investment policy statement help influence the strategic asset allocation decision and discuss how the investment time horizon may influence investors' ability to take risk, and help modify investors' strategic asset allocation;

f. contrast the types of investment time horizons, determine the time horizon for a particular investor, and evaluate the effects of this time horizon on portfolio choice;

g. justify ethical conduct as a requirement for managing investment portfolios.

INTRODUCTION   1

In setting out to master the concepts and tools of portfolio management, we first need a coherent description of the portfolio management process. The **portfolio management process** is an integrated set of steps undertaken in a consistent manner to create and maintain an appropriate portfolio (combination of assets) to meet clients' stated goals. The process we present in this reading is a distillation of the shared elements of current practice.

Because it serves as the foundation for the process, we also introduce the investment policy statement through a discussion of its main components. An **investment policy statement** (IPS) is a written document that clearly sets out a client's return objectives and risk tolerance over that client's relevant time horizon, along with applicable constraints such as liquidity needs, tax considerations, regulatory requirements, and unique circumstances.

The portfolio management process moves from planning, through execution, and then to feedback. In the planning step, investment objectives and policies are formulated, capital market expectations are formed, and strategic asset allocations are established. In the execution step, the portfolio manager constructs the portfolio. In the feedback step, the manager monitors and evaluates the portfolio compared with the plan. Any changes suggested by the feedback must be examined carefully to ensure that they represent long-run considerations.

The investment policy statement provides the foundation of the portfolio management process. In creating an IPS, the manager writes down the client's special characteristics and needs. The IPS must clearly communicate the client's objectives and constraints. The IPS thereby becomes a plan that can be executed by any advisor or portfolio manager the client might subsequently hire. A properly developed IPS disciplines the portfolio management process and helps ensure against ad hoc revisions in strategy.

When combined with capital market expectations, the IPS forms the basis for a strategic asset allocation. **Capital market expectations** concern the risk and return characteristics of **capital market instruments** such as stocks and bonds. The **strategic asset allocation** establishes acceptable exposures to IPS-permissible asset classes to achieve the client's long-run objectives and constraints.

The portfolio perspective underlies the portfolio management process and IPS. The next sections illustrate this perspective.

2   INVESTMENT MANAGEMENT

Investment management is the service of professionally investing money. As a profession, investment management has its roots in the activities of European investment bankers in managing the fortunes created by the Industrial Revolution. By the beginning of the 21st century, investment management had become an important part of the financial services sector of all developed economies. By the end of 2003, the United States alone had approximately 15,000 money managers (registered investment advisors) responsible for investing more than $23 trillion, according to Standard & Poor's *Directory of Registered Investment Advisors* (2004). No worldwide count of investment advisors is available, but looking at another familiar professionally managed investment, the number of mutual funds stood at about 54,000 at year-end 2003; of these funds only 15 percent were U.S. based.[1]

The economics of investment management are relatively simple. An investment manager's revenue is fee driven; primarily, fees are based on a percentage of the average amount of assets under management and the type of investment program run for the client, as spelled out in detail in the investment management contract or other governing document. Consequently, an investment management firm's size is judged by the amount of assets under management, which is thus directly related to manager's revenue, another measure of size. Traditionally, the value of an investment management business (or a first estimate of value) is determined as a multiple of its annual fee income.

To understand an investment management firm or product beyond its size, we need to know not only its investment disciplines but also the type or types of investor it primarily serves. Broadly speaking, investors can be described as institutional or individual. Institutional investors are entities such as pension funds, foundations and endowments, insurance companies, and banks that ultimately serve as financial intermediaries between individuals and financial markets. The investment policy decisions of institutional investors are typically made by investment committees or trustees, with at least some members having a professional background in finance. The committee members or trustees frequently also bear a fiduciary relationship to the funds for which they have investment responsibility. Such a relationship, if it is present, imposes some legal standards regarding processes and decisions, which is reflected in the processes of the investment managers who serve that market segment.

Beginning in the second half of the 20th century, the tremendous growth of institutional investors, especially defined benefit pension plans, spurred a tremendous expansion in investment management firms or investment units of other entities (such as bank trust divisions) to service their needs.[2] As the potentially onerous financial responsibilities imposed on the sponsors by such plans became more evident, however, the 1980s and 1990s saw trends to other types of retirement schemes focused on participant responsibility for investment decisions and results. In addition, a long-lasting worldwide economic expansion created a great amount of individual wealth. As a result, investment advisors oriented to serving high-net-worth individuals as well as mutual funds (which serve the individual and, to a lesser extent, the smaller institutional market) gained in relative importance.

Such individual-investor-oriented advisors may incorporate a heavy personal financial planning emphasis in their services. Many wealthy families establish family offices to serve as trusted managers of their finances. **Family offices** are entities, typically organized and owned by a family, that assume responsibility for services such as financial planning, estate planning, and asset management, as well as a range of practical matters from tax return preparation to bill paying. Some family offices evolve such depth in professional staff that they open access to their services to other families (multi-family offices). In contrast to family offices, some investment management businesses service both individual and institutional markets, sometimes in separate divisions or corporate units, sometimes worldwide, and sometimes as part of a financial giant (American Express and Citigroup are examples of such financial supermarkets). In such cases, wrap-fee accounts packaging the services of outside investment managers may vie for the client's business with in-house, separately managed accounts, as well as in-house mutual funds, external mutual funds, and other offerings marketed by a brokerage arm of the business.

---

[1] These facts are based on statistics produced by the Investment Company Institute and the International Investment Funds Association.

[2] A defined benefit pension plan specifies the plan sponsor's obligations in terms of the benefit to plan participants. The plan sponsor bears the investment risk of such plans.

Investment management companies employ portfolio managers, analysts, and traders, as well as marketing and support personnel. Portfolio managers may use both outside research produced by **sell-side analysts** (analysts employed by brokerages) and research generated by in-house analysts—so-called **buy-side analysts** (analysts employed by an investment manager or institutional investor). The staffing of in-house research departments depends on the size of the investment management firm, the variety of investment offerings, and the investment disciplines employed. An example may illustrate the variety of talent employed: The research department of one money manager with $30 billion in assets under management employs 34 equity analysts, 23 credit analysts, 3 hedge fund analysts, 12 quantitative analysts, 4 risk management professionals, 1 economist, and 1 economic analyst. That same company has a trading department with 8 equity and 8 bond traders and many support personnel. CFA charterholders can be found in all of these functions.

3   THE PORTFOLIO PERSPECTIVE

The portfolio perspective is our focus on the aggregate of all the investor's holdings: the portfolio. Because economic fundamentals influence the average returns of many assets, the risk associated with one asset's returns is generally related to the risk associated with other assets' returns. If we evaluate the prospects of each asset in isolation and ignore their interrelationships, we will likely misunderstand the risk and return prospects of the investor's total investment position—our most basic concern.

The historical roots of this portfolio perspective date to the work of Nobel laureate Harry Markowitz (1952). Markowitz and subsequent researchers, such as Jack Treynor and Nobel laureate William Sharpe, established the field of **modern portfolio theory** (MPT)—the analysis of rational portfolio choices based on the efficient use of risk. Modern portfolio theory revolutionized investment management. First, professional investment practice began to recognize the importance of the portfolio perspective in achieving investment objectives. Second, MPT helped spread the knowledge and use of quantitative methods in portfolio management. Today, quantitative and qualitative concepts complement each other in investment management practice.

In developing his theory of portfolio choice, Markowitz began with the perspective of investing for a single period. Others, including Nobel laureate Robert Merton, explored the dynamics of portfolio choice in a multiperiod setting. These subsequent contributions have greatly enriched the content of MPT.

If Markowitz, Merton, and other researchers created the supply, three developments in the investment community created demand for the portfolio perspective. First, institutional investing emerged worldwide to play an increasingly dominant role in financial markets. Measuring and controlling the risk of large pools of money became imperative. The second development was the increasing availability of ever-cheaper computer processing power and communications possibilities. As a result, a broader range of techniques for implementing MPT portfolio concepts became feasible. The third related development was the professionalization of the investment management field. This professionalization has been reflected in the worldwide growth of the professional accreditation program leading to the Chartered Financial Analyst (CFA®) designation.

PORTFOLIO MANAGEMENT AS A PROCESS   4

The unified presentation of portfolio management as a process represented an important advance in the investment management literature. Prior to the introduction of this concept in the first edition of this book, much of the traditional literature reflected an approach of selecting individual securities without an overall plan. Through the eyes of the professional, however, portfolio management is a *process*, an integrated set of activities that combine in a logical, orderly manner to produce a desired product. The process view is a *dynamic* and *flexible* concept that applies to all types of portfolio investments—bonds, stocks, real estate, gold, collectibles; to various organizational types—trust company, investment counsel firm, insurance company, mutual fund; to a full range of investors—individuals, pension plans, endowments, foundations, insurance companies, banks; and is independent of manager, location, investment philosophy, style, or approach. Portfolio management is a continuous and systematic process complete with feedback loops for monitoring and rebalancing. The process can be as loose or as disciplined, as quantitative or as qualitative, and as simple or as complex as its operators desire.

The portfolio management process is the same in every application: an integrated set of steps undertaken in a consistent manner to create and maintain appropriate combinations of investment assets. In the next sections, we explore the main features of this process.

THE PORTFOLIO MANAGEMENT PROCESS LOGIC   5

Three elements in managing any business process are planning, execution, and feedback. These same elements form the basis for the portfolio management process as depicted in Figure 74-1.

5.1 The Planning Step

The planning step is described in the four leftmost boxes in Figure 74-1. The top two boxes represent investor-related input factors, while the bottom two factors represent economic and market input.

5.1.1 Identifying and Specifying the Investor's Objectives and Constraints

The first task in investment planning is to identify and specify the investor's objectives and constraints. **Investment objectives** are desired investment outcomes. In investments, objectives chiefly pertain to return and risk. **Constraints** are limitations on the investor's ability to take full or partial advantage of particular investments. For example, an investor may face constraints related to the concentration of holdings as a result of government regulation, or restrictions in a governing legal document. Constraints are either **internal**, such as a client's specific liquidity needs, time horizon, and unique circumstances, or **external**, such as tax issues and legal and regulatory requirements. In Section 6, we examine the objective and constraint specification process.

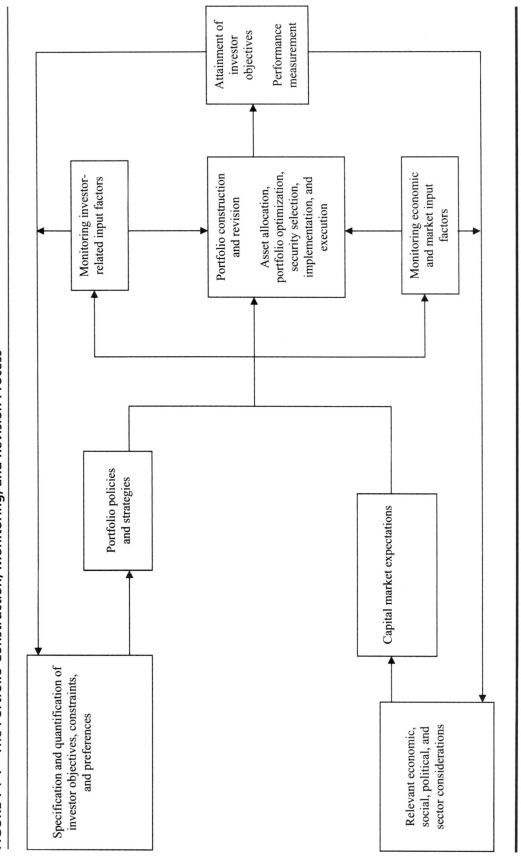

FIGURE 74-1   The Portfolio Construction, Monitoring, and Revision Process

5.1.2 Creating the Investment Policy Statement

Once a client has specified a set of objectives and constraints, the manager's next task is to formulate the investment policy statement. The IPS serves as the governing document for all investment decision-making. In addition to objectives and constraints, the IPS may also cover a variety of other issues. For example, the IPS generally details reporting requirements, rebalancing guidelines, frequency and format of investment communication, manager fees, investment strategy, and the desired investment style or styles of investment managers. A typical IPS includes the following elements:

► a brief client description;

► the purpose of establishing policies and guidelines;

► the duties and investment responsibilities of parties involved, particularly those relating to fiduciary duties, communication, operational efficiency, and accountability. Parties involved include the client, any investment committee, the investment manager, and the bank custodian;

► the statement of investment goals, objectives, and constraints;

► the schedule for review of investment performance as well as the IPS itself;

► performance measures and benchmarks to be used in performance evaluation;

► any considerations to be taken into account in developing the strategic asset allocation;

► investment strategies and investment style(s); and

► guidelines for rebalancing the portfolio based on feedback.

The IPS forms the basis for the strategic asset allocation, which reflects the interaction of objectives and constraints with the investor's long-run capital market expectations. When experienced professionals include the policy allocation as part of the IPS, they are implicitly forming capital market expectations and also examining the interaction of objectives and constraints with long-run capital market expectations. In practice, one may see IPSs that include strategic asset allocations, but we will maintain a distinction between the two types.

The planning process involves the concrete elaboration of an **investment strategy**—that is, the manager's approach to investment analysis and security selection. A clearly formulated investment strategy organizes and clarifies the basis for investment decisions. It also guides those decisions toward achieving investment objectives. In the broadest sense, investment strategies are passive, active, or semiactive.

► In a **passive investment approach**, portfolio composition does not react to changes in capital market expectations (*passive* means *not reacting*). For example, a portfolio indexed to the MSCI-Europe Index, an index representing European equity markets, might add or drop a holding in response to a change in the index composition but not in response to changes in capital market expectations concerning the security's investment value. **Indexing**, a common passive approach to investing, refers to holding a portfolio of securities designed to replicate the returns on a specified index of securities. A second type of passive investing is a strict **buy-and-hold strategy**, such as a fixed, but non-indexed, portfolio of bonds to be held to maturity.

► In contrast, with an **active investment approach**, a portfolio manager will respond to changing capital market expectations. Active management of a portfolio means that its holdings differ from the portfolio's **benchmark** or comparison portfolio in an attempt to produce positive excess risk-adjusted returns, also known as positive **alpha**. Securities held in different-from-benchmark weights reflect expectations of the portfolio manager that differ from consensus expectations. If the portfolio manager's differential expectations are also on average correct, active portfolio management may add value.

▶ A third category, the **semiactive**, **risk-controlled active**, or **enhanced index approach**, seeks positive alpha while keeping tight control over risk relative to the portfolio's benchmark. As an example, an index-tilt strategy seeks to track closely the risk of a securities index while adding a targeted amount of incremental value by tilting portfolio weightings in some direction that the manager expects to be profitable.

Active investment approaches encompass a very wide range of disciplines. To organize this diversity, investment analysts appeal to the concept of investment style. Following Brown and Goetzmann (1997), we can define an **investment style** (such as an emphasis on growth stocks or value stocks) as a natural grouping of investment disciplines that has some predictive power in explaining the future dispersion in returns across portfolios.

5.1.3 Forming Capital Market Expectations

The manager's third task in the planning process is to form capital market expectations. Long-run forecasts of risk and return characteristics for various asset classes form the basis for choosing portfolios that maximize expected return for given levels of risk, or minimize risk for given levels of expected return.

5.1.4 Creating the Strategic Asset Allocation

The fourth and final task in the planning process is determining the strategic asset allocation. Here the manager combines the IPS and capital market expectations to determine target asset class weights; maximum and minimum permissible asset class weights are often also specified as a risk-control mechanism. The investor may seek both single-period and multiperiod perspectives in the return and risk characteristics of asset allocations under consideration. A single-period perspective has the advantage of simplicity. A multiperiod perspective can address the liquidity and tax considerations that arise from rebalancing portfolios over time, as well as serial correlation (long- and short-term dependencies) in returns, but is more costly to implement.

This reading focuses on the creation of an IPS in the planning step and thereby lays the groundwork for the discussion in later chapters of tailoring the IPS to individual and institutional investors' needs. The execution and feedback steps in the portfolio management process are as important as the planning step. For now, we merely outline how these steps fit in the portfolio management process.

5.2 The Execution Step

The execution step is represented by the "portfolio construction and revision" box in Figure 74-1. In the execution step, the manager integrates investment strategies with capital market expectations to select the specific assets for the portfolio (the **portfolio selection/composition decision**). Portfolio managers initiate portfolio decisions based on analysts' inputs, and trading desks then implement these decisions (**portfolio implementation decision**). Subsequently, the portfolio is revised as investor circumstances or capital market expectations change; thus the execution step interacts constantly with the feedback step.

In making the portfolio selection/composition decision, portfolio managers may use the techniques of portfolio optimization. **Portfolio optimization**—quantitative tools for combining assets efficiently to achieve a set of return and risk objectives—plays a key role in the integration of strategies with expectations and appears in Figure 74-1 in the portfolio construction and revision box.

At times, a portfolio's actual asset allocation may purposefully and temporarily differ from the strategic asset allocation. For example, the asset allocation might change to reflect an investor's current circumstances that are different from normal. The temporary allocation may remain in place until circumstances return to those described in the IPS and reflected in the strategic asset allocation. If the changed circumstances become permanent, the manager must update the investor's IPS and the temporary asset allocation plan will effectively become the new strategic asset allocation. A strategy known as tactical asset allocation also results in differences from the strategic asset allocation. **Tactical asset allocation** responds to changes in short-term capital market expectations rather than to investor circumstances.

The portfolio implementation decision is as important as the portfolio selection/composition decision. Poorly managed executions result in transaction costs that reduce performance. Transaction costs include all costs of trading, including explicit transaction costs, implicit transaction costs, and missed trade opportunity costs. **Explicit transaction costs** include commissions paid to brokers, fees paid to exchanges, and taxes. **Implicit transaction costs** include bid–ask spreads and market price impacts of large trades. **Missed trade opportunity costs** can arise due to price changes that prevent trades from being filled.

In sum, in the execution step, plans are turned into reality—with all the attendant real-world challenges.

5.3 The Feedback Step

In any business endeavor, feedback and control are essential elements in reaching a goal. In portfolio management, this step has two components: monitoring and rebalancing, and performance evaluation.

5.3.1 Monitoring and Rebalancing

Monitoring and **rebalancing** involve the use of feedback to manage ongoing exposures to available investment opportunities so that the client's current objectives and constraints continue to be satisfied. Two types of factors are monitored: investor-related factors such as the investor's circumstances, and economic and market input factors.

One impetus for portfolio revision is a change in investment objectives or constraints because of changes in investor circumstances. Portfolio managers need a process in place to stay informed of changes in clients' circumstances. The termination of a pension plan or death of a spouse may trigger an abrupt change in a client's time horizon and tax concerns, and the IPS should list the occurrence of such changes as a basis for appropriate portfolio revision.

More predictably, changes in economic and market input factors give rise to the regular need for portfolio revision. Again, portfolio managers need to systematically review the risk attributes of assets as well as economic and capital market factors. A change in expectations may trigger portfolio revision. When asset price changes occur, however, revisions can be required even without changes in expectations. The actual timing and magnitude of rebalancing may be triggered by review periods or by specific rules governing the management of the portfolio and deviation from the tolerances or ranges specified in the strategic asset allocation, or the timing and magnitude may be at the discretion of the manager. For example, suppose the policy allocation calls for an initial portfolio with a 70 percent weighting to stocks and a 30 percent weighting to bonds. Suppose the value of the stock holdings then grows by 40 percent, while the value of the bond holdings grows by 10 percent. The new weighting is roughly 75 percent in stocks and 25 percent in bonds. To bring the portfolio back into compliance with investment policy, it must be rebalanced back to the long-term policy weights. In any event, the rebalancing decision is a crucial one that must take into account many factors, such as transaction costs and taxes (for taxable investors). Disciplined rebalancing will have a major impact on the attainment of investment objectives. Rebalancing takes us back to the issues of execution, as is appropriate in a feedback process.

5.3.2 Performance Evaluation

Investment performance must periodically be evaluated by the investor to assess progress toward the achievement of investment objectives as well as to assess portfolio management skill.

The assessment of portfolio management skill has three components. **Performance measurement** involves the calculation of the portfolio's rate of return. **Performance attribution** examines why the portfolio performed as it did and involves determining the sources of a portfolio's performance. **Performance appraisal** is the evaluation of whether or not the manager is doing a good job based on how the portfolio did relative to a benchmark (a comparison portfolio).

Often, we can examine a portfolio's performance, in terms of absolute returns, through three sources: decisions regarding the strategic asset allocation, **market timing** (returns attributable to shorter-term tactical deviations from the strategic asset allocation), and **security selection** (skill in selecting individual securities within an asset class). However, portfolio management is frequently conducted with reference to a benchmark, or for some entities, with reference to a stream of projected liabilities or a specified target rate of return. As a result, relative portfolio performance evaluation, in addition to absolute performance measurement, is often of key importance.

With respect to relative performance we may ask questions such as, "Relative to the investment manager's benchmark, what economic sectors were **underweighted** or **overweighted**?" or "What was the manager's rationale for these decisions and how successful were they?" Portfolio evaluation may also be conducted with respect to specific risk models, such as multifactor models, which attempt to explain asset returns in terms of exposures to a set of risk factors.

Concurrent with evaluation of the manager is the ongoing review of the benchmark to establish its continuing suitability. For some benchmarks, this review would include a thorough understanding of how economic sectors and subsectors are determined in the benchmark, the classification of securities within them, and how frequently the classifications change. For any benchmark, one would review whether the benchmark continues to be a fair measuring stick given the manager's mandate.

As with other parts of the portfolio management process, performance evaluation and performance presentation are critical. These topics play a central role in the portfolio management process.

5.4 A Definition of Portfolio Management

In sum, the process logic is incorporated in the following definition, which is the cornerstone for this book. **Portfolio management** is an ongoing process in which

- ▶ investment objectives and constraints are identified and specified,
- ▶ investment strategies are developed,
- ▶ portfolio composition is decided in detail,
- ▶ portfolio decisions are initiated by portfolio managers and implemented by traders,
- ▶ portfolio performance is measured and evaluated,
- ▶ investor and market conditions are monitored, and
- ▶ any necessary rebalancing is implemented.

Although we have provided general insights into the portfolio management process, we make no judgments and voice no opinions about how the process should be organized, who should make which decisions, or any other process-operating matter. How well the process works is a critical component of investment success. In a survey of pension fund chief operating officers, Ambachtsheer, Capelle, and Scheibelhut (1998) found that 98 percent of the respondents cited a poor portfolio management process as a barrier to achieving excellence in organizational performance. The organization of the portfolio management process of any investment management company should be the result of careful planning.

INVESTMENT OBJECTIVES AND CONSTRAINTS   6

As previously discussed, the IPS is the cornerstone of the portfolio management process. Because of the IPS's fundamental importance, we introduce its main components in this reading. In this section, we return to the tasks of identifying and specifying the investor's objectives and constraints that initiate the planning step.

Although we discuss objectives first and then constraints, the actual process of delineating these for any investor may appropriately start with an examination of investor constraints. For example, a short time horizon affects the investor's ability to take risk.

6.1 Objectives

The two objectives in this framework, risk and return, are interdependent—one cannot be discussed without reference to the other. The risk objective limits how high the investor can set the return objective.

6.1.1 Risk Objective

The first element of the risk–return framework is the **risk objective** because it will largely determine the return objective. A 10 percent standard deviation risk objective, for example, implies a different asset allocation than a 15 percent standard deviation risk objective, because expected asset risk is generally positively correlated with expected asset return. In formulating a risk objective, the investor must address the following five questions:

1. *How do I measure risk?* Risk measurement is a key issue in investments, and several approaches exist for measuring risk. In practice, risk may be measured in absolute terms or in relative terms with reference to various risk concepts. Examples of absolute risk objectives are a specified level of standard deviation or variance of total return. The **variance** of a random variable is the expected value of squared deviations from the random variable's mean. Variance is often referred to as volatility. **Standard deviation** is the positive square root of variance. An example of a relative risk objective is a specified level of tracking risk. **Tracking risk** is the standard deviation of the differences between a portfolio's and the benchmark's total returns.

    Downside risk concepts, such as **value at risk (VAR)**, may also be important to an investor. **Value at risk** is a probability-based measure of the loss that one anticipates will be exceeded only a specified small fraction of the time over a given horizon—for example, in 5 percent of all monthly holding periods. Besides statistical measures of risk, other risk exposures, such as exposures to specific economic sectors, or risk with respect to a factor model of returns, may be relevant as well.

2. *What is the investor's willingness to take risk?* The investor's stated willingness to take risk is often very different for institutional versus individual investors. Managers should try to understand the behavioral and, for individuals, the personality factors behind an investor's willingness to take risk. In the reading on individual investors, we explore behavioral issues in reference to the investor's willingness to take risk.

3. *What is the investor's ability to take risk?* Even if an investor is eager to bear risk, practical or financial limitations often limit the amount of risk that can be prudently assumed. For the sake of illustration, in the following discussion we talk about risk in terms of the volatility of asset values.

    ▶ In terms of spending needs, how much volatility would inconvenience an investor who depends on investments (such as a university in relationship to its endowment fund)? Or, how much volatility would inconvenience an investor who otherwise cannot afford to incur substantial short-term losses? Investors with high levels of wealth relative to probable worst-case short-term loss scenarios can take more risk.

    ▶ In terms of long-term wealth targets or obligations, how much volatility might prevent the investor from reaching these goals? Investors with high levels of wealth relative to long-term wealth targets or obligations can take more risk.

    ▶ What are the investor's liabilities or pseudo liabilities? An institution may face legally promised future payments to beneficiaries (liabilities) and an individual may face future retirement spending needs (pseudo liabilities).

    ▶ What is the investor's financial strength—that is, the ability to increase the savings/contribution level if the portfolio cannot support the planned spending? More financial strength means more risk can be taken.

4. *How much risk is the investor both willing and able to bear?* The answer to this question defines the investor's risk tolerance. **Risk tolerance**, the capacity to accept risk, is a function of both an investor's willingness and ability to do so. Risk tolerance can also be described in terms of **risk aversion**, the degree of an investor's inability and unwillingness to take risk. The investor's specific risk objectives are formulated with that investor's level of risk tolerance in mind. Importantly, any assessment of risk tolerance must

consider both an investor's willingness and that investor's ability to take risk. When a mismatch exists between the two, determining risk tolerance requires educating the client on the dangers of excess risk taking or of ignoring inflation risk, depending on the case. In our presentation in this book, we assume that such education has taken place and that we are providing an appropriate risk objective in the IPS proposed to the client. When an investor's willingness to accept risk exceeds ability to do so, ability prudently places a limit on the amount of risk the investor should assume. When ability exceeds willingness, the investor may fall short of the return objective because willingness would be the limiting factor. These interactions are shown in Table 74-1.

An investor with an above-average ability to assume risk may have legitimate reasons for choosing a lower risk strategy. As well, an investor may face the pleasant situation of having an excess of wealth to meet financial needs for a long period of time. In these cases, the investor needs to have a clear understanding of the eventual consequences of the decision to effectively spend down excess wealth over time. As with any strategy, such a decision must be reevaluated periodically. In the case of a high-net-worth investor who has earned substantial wealth from entrepreneurial risk taking, such an investor may now simply not want to lose wealth and may desire only liquidity to spend in order to maintain her current lifestyle.

5. *What are the specific risk objective(s)?* Just as risk may be measured either absolutely or relatively, we may specify both absolute risk and relative risk objectives. In practice, investors often find that quantitative risk objectives are easier to specify in relative than in absolute terms. Possibly as a consequence, absolute risk objectives in particular are frequently specified in qualitative rather than quantitative terms.

What distinguishes the risk objective from risk tolerance is the level of specificity. For example, the statement that a person has a "lower than average risk tolerance" might be converted operationally into "the loss in any one year is not to exceed x percent of portfolio value" or "annual volatility of the portfolio is not to exceed y percent." Often, clients—particularly individual investors—do not understand or appreciate this level of specificity, and more-general risk-tolerance statements substitute for a quantitative risk objective.

6. *How should the investor allocate risk?* This is how some investors frame **capital allocation decisions** today, particularly when active strategies will play a role in the portfolio. The question may concern the portfolio as a whole or some part of it. **Risk budgeting** disciplines address the above question most directly. After the investor has determined the *measure* of risk of concern to him (e.g., VAR or tracking risk) and the *desired total quantity of risk* (the

TABLE 74-1	Risk Tolerance	
Willingness to Take Risk	**Ability to Take Risk**	
	Below Average	**Above Average**
Below Average	Below-average risk tolerance	Resolution needed
Above Average	Resolution needed	Above-average risk tolerance

overall **risk budget**), an investor using **risk budgeting** would allocate the overall risk budget to specific investments so as to maximize expected overall risk-adjusted return. The resulting optimal risk budgets for the investments would translate to specific allocations of capital to them.

6.1.2 Return Objective

The second element of the investment policy framework is the **return objective**, which must be consistent with the risk objective. Just as tension may exist between willingness and ability in setting the risk objective, so the return objective requires a resolution of return desires versus the risk objective. In formulating a return objective, the investor must address the following four questions:

1. *How is return measured?* The usual measure is **total return**, the sum of the return from price appreciation and the return from investment income. Return may be stated as an absolute amount, such as 10 percent a year, or as a return relative to the benchmark's return, such as benchmark return plus 2 percent a year. Nominal returns must be distinguished from real returns. **Nominal** returns are unadjusted for inflation. **Real** returns are adjusted for inflation and sometimes simply called **inflation-adjusted returns**. Also, pretax returns must be distinguished from post-tax returns. **Pretax** returns are returns before taxes, and **post-tax** returns are returns after taxes are paid on investment income and realized capital gains.

2. *How much return does the investor say she wants?* This amount is the **stated return desire**. These wants or desires may be realistic or unrealistic. For example, an investor may have higher than average return desires to meet high consumption desires or a high ending wealth target: for instance, "I want a 20 percent annual return." The advisor or portfolio manager must continually evaluate the desire for high returns in light of the investor's ability to assume risk and the reasonableness of the stated return desire, especially relative to capital market expectations.

3. *How much return does the investor need to achieve, on average?* This amount is the **required return** or **return requirement**. Requirements are more stringent than desires because investors with requirements typically must achieve those returns, at least on average. An example of a return requirement is the average return a pension fund projects it must earn to fund liabilities to current and future pensioners, based on actuarial calculations. The compound rate of return that an individual investor must earn to attain the asset base needed for retirement is another example of a return requirement. A third example would be the return that a retired investor must earn on his investment portfolio to cover his annual living expenses. We illustrate these last two cases.

   Suppose that a married couple needs £2 million in 18 years to fund retirement. Their current investable assets total £1,200,000. The projected future need (£2 million) incorporates expected inflation. The couple would need to earn $(£2,000,000/£1,200,000)^{1/18} - 1.0 = 2.88$ percent per year after-tax to achieve their goal. Every cash flow needs to be accounted for in such calculations. If the couple needed to liquidate £25,000 from the portfolio at the end of each year (keeping all other facts unchanged), they would need to earn 4.55 percent per year on an after-tax basis to have £2 million in 18 years (a financial calculator is needed to confirm this result). If all investment returns were taxed at 35 percent, 4.55 percent after tax would correspond to a 7 percent pretax required return $[4.55/(1 - 0.35) = 7\%]$.

A retiree may depend on his investment portfolio for some or all of his living expenses. That need defines a return requirement. Suppose that a retiree must achieve a 4 percent after-tax return on his current investment portfolio to meet his current annual living expenses. Thus, his return requirement on a real, after-tax basis is 4 percent per year. If he expects inflation to be 2 percent per year and a 40 percent tax rate applies to investment returns from any source, we could estimate his pretax nominal return requirement as (After-tax real return requirement + Expected inflation rate)/(1 − Tax rate) = (4% + 2%)/(1 − 0.40) = 10 percent.

In contrast to desired returns, which can be reduced if incongruent with risk objectives, large required returns are an important source of potential conflict between return and risk objectives. Other required return issues that are relevant to specific situations include the following:

▶ What are the needs and desires for current spending versus ending wealth?

▶ How do nominal total return requirements relate to expected rates of price inflation? If assets fund obligations subject to inflation, the return requirements should reflect expected rates of inflation.

4. *What are the specific return objectives?* The return objective incorporates the required return, the stated return desire, and the risk objective into a measurable annual total return specification. For example, an investor with a 5 percent after-tax, required, inflation-adjusted annual rate of return but above-average risk tolerance might reasonably set a higher than 5 percent after-tax, inflation-adjusted annual rate of return objective to maximize expected wealth.

An investor's return objective should be consistent with that investor's risk objective. A high return objective may suggest an asset allocation with an expected level of risk that is too great in relation to the risk objective, for example. In addition, the anticipated return from the portfolio should be sufficient to meet wealth objectives or liabilities that the portfolio must fund.

For investors with current investment income needs, the return objective should be sufficient to meet spending needs from capital appreciation and investment income: When a well-considered return objective is not consistent with risk tolerance, other adjustments may need to take place, such as increasing savings or modifying wealth objectives.

An investor delegating portfolio management to an investment manager will communicate a **mandate**—a set of instructions detailing the investment manager's task and how his performance will be evaluated—that includes a specification of the manager's benchmark. Because the manager's performance will be evaluated against the benchmark, the benchmark's total return is an effective return objective for the investment manager. These instructions may be part of the investment policy statement or, in the case of a portfolio with multiple managers, outlined in separate instructions for each mandate to each manager.

Although an **absolute return objective** is sometimes set (e.g., 8 percent), the reality of the markets suggests that a relative return objective may be more plausible. A **relative return objective** is stated as a return relative to the portfolio benchmark's total return (e.g., 1 percent higher than the benchmark).

Table 74-2 illustrates the variation in return requirement and risk tolerance among various categories of investors.

TABLE 74-2   Return Requirements and Risk Tolerances of Various Investors

Type of Investor	Return Requirement	Risk Tolerance
Individual	Depends on stage of life, circumstances, and obligations	Varies
Pension Plans (Defined Benefit)	The return that will adequately fund liabilities on an inflation-adjusted basis	Depends on plan and sponsor characteristics, plan features, funding status, and workforce characteristics
Pension Plans (Defined Contribution)	Depends on stage of life of individual participants	Varies with the risk tolerance of individual participants
Foundations and Endowments	The return that will cover annual spending, investment expenses, and expected inflation	Determined by amount of assets relative to needs, but generally above-average or average
Life Insurance Companies	Determined by rates used to determine policyholder reserves	Below average due to factors such as regulatory constraints
Non-Life-Insurance Companies	Determined by the need to price policies competitively and by financial needs	Below average due to factors such as regulatory constraints
Banks	Determined by cost of funds	Varies

6.2 Constraints

The investor's risk and return objectives are set within the context of several constraints: liquidity, time horizon, tax concerns, legal and regulatory factors, and unique circumstances. Although all of these factors influence portfolio choice, the first two constraints bear directly on the investor's ability to take risk and thus constrain both risk and return objectives.

6.2.1 Liquidity

A **liquidity requirement** is a need for cash *in excess of new contributions* (for pension plans and endowments, for example) or *savings* (for individuals) at a specified point in time. Such needs may be anticipated or unanticipated, but either way they stem from **liquidity events**. An example of a liquidity event is planned construction of a building in one year.

The liquidity requirement may reflect nonrecurring needs or the desire to hold cash against unanticipated needs (a safety or reserve fund). This requirement may be met by holding cash or cash equivalents in the portfolio or by converting other assets into cash equivalents. Any risk of economic loss because of the need to sell relatively less liquid assets to meet liquidity requirements is **liquidity risk**. (An asset that can be converted into cash only at relatively high total cost is said to be relatively less liquid.) Liquidity risk, therefore, arises for two reasons: an asset-side reason (asset liquidity) and a liability-side reason (liquidity requirements). Portfolio managers control asset selection but not liquidity requirements; as a result, in practice, managers use asset selection to manage liquidity risk. If the portfolio's asset and income base are large relative to its potential liquidity requirements, relatively less liquid assets can be held. A distinct consideration is liquidity requirements in relation to **price risk** of the asset—the risk of fluctuations in market price.

Assets with high price risk are frequently less liquid, especially during market downturns. If the timing of an investor's liquidity requirements is significantly correlated with market downturns, these requirements can influence asset selection in favor of less risky assets. In many cases, therefore, consideration of both liquidity risk and price risk means that an investor will choose to hold some part of the portfolio in highly liquid and low-price-risk assets in anticipation of future liquidity requirements. Investors may also modify the payoff structure of a risky portfolio to address liquidity requirements using derivative strategies, although such modifications often incur costs. (**Derivatives** are contracts whose payoffs depend on the value of another asset, often called the underlying asset.)

6.2.2 Time Horizon

Time horizon most often refers to the time period associated with an investment objective. Investment objectives and associated time horizons may be short term, long term, or a combination of the two. (A time horizon of 10 years or more is often considered to be long term. Investment performance over the long term should average results over several market and business cycles.) A multistage horizon is a combination of shorter term and longer term horizons. An example of a multistage horizon is the case of funding children's education shorter term and the investor's retirement longer term.

Other constraints, such as a unique circumstance or a specific liquidity requirement, can also affect an investor's time horizon. For example, an individual investor's temporary family living arrangement can dictate that his time horizon constraint be stated in multistage terms. Similarly, an institutional investor's need to make an imminent substantial disbursement of funds for a capital project can necessitate a multistage approach to the time horizon constraint.

In general, relevant time horizon questions include the following:

▶ *How does the length of the time horizon modify the investor's ability to take risk?* The longer the time horizon the more risk the investor can take. The longer the time horizon, the greater the investor's ability to replenish investment resources by increasing savings. A long-term investor's labor income may also be an asset sufficiently stable to support a higher level of portfolio risk.[3] Cash may be safe for a short-term investor but risky for a long-term investor who will be faced with continuously reinvesting.

▶ *How does the length of the time horizon modify the investor's asset allocation?* Many investors allocate a greater proportion of funds to risky assets when they address long-term as opposed to short-term investment objectives. Decreased risk-taking ability with shorter horizons can thus constrain portfolio choice.

▶ *How does the investor's willingness and ability to bear fluctuations in portfolio value modify the asset allocation?* With a focus on risk, even an investor with a long-term objective may limit risk taking because of sensitivity to the possibility of substantial interim losses. The chance of unanticipated liquidity needs may increase during market downturns, for instance, because a market downturn may be linked to a decline in economic activity affecting income or other sources of wealth. An investor that often faces unanticipated short-term liquidity needs will usually favor investments with a shorter time horizon so as to limit the risk of loss of value.

---

[3] See Campbell and Viceira (2002) for a discussion of this and the following point.

► *How does a multistage time horizon constrain the investor's asset allocation?* The investment policy must be designed to accommodate all time horizons in a multistage horizon case. Such design will probably entail some compromise in the setting of objectives to attain short-, medium-, and long-term goals.

6.2.3 Tax Concerns

A country's tax policy can affect important aspects of investment decision-making for investors who reside there. **Tax concerns** arise for taxable investors because tax payments reduce the amount of the total return that can be used for current needs or reinvested for future growth. Differences between the tax rates applying to investment income and capital gains will influence taxable investors' choice of investments and their timing of sales. Estate taxes on wealth triggered by the investor's death can also affect investment decisions. Finally, tax policy changes that affect security prices affect both taxable and tax-exempt investors.

6.2.4 Legal and Regulatory Factors

Legal and **regulatory factors** are external factors imposed by governmental, regulatory, or oversight authorities to constrain investment decision-making. In the United Kingdom, for example, regulations issued by the Financial Services Authority (FSA) limit the concentration of holdings in debt and equity securities for U.K. mutual funds. Another example is the United States' Employee Retirement Income Security Act (ERISA) of 1974, as interpreted by regulatory agencies and the courts. ERISA limits the acquisition and holding of employer securities by certain pension plans. Some countries limit the use of certain asset classes in retirement accounts.

6.2.5 Unique Circumstances

Unique circumstances are internal factors (other than a liquidity requirement, time horizon, or tax concern) that may constrain portfolio choices. For example, a university endowment may be constrained to avoid certain investments against which there may be ethical objections or social responsibility considerations. Similarly, an individual investor's portfolio choices may be constrained by circumstances focusing on health needs, support of dependents, and other circumstances unique to the particular individual. Investors may specify avoidance of nondomestic shares or derivatives. Portfolio choices may also be constrained by investor capability in terms of both human resources and financial resources such as time, interest, background, and technical expertise.

7   THE DYNAMICS OF THE PROCESS

One of the truly satisfying aspects of portfolio management as a professional activity is the underlying logic and the dynamism of the portfolio process concept. In a broad sense, the work of analysts, economists, and market strategists is all a matter of "getting ready." The work of portfolio management is the action: taking the inputs and moving step by step through the orderly process of converting this raw material into a portfolio that maximizes expected return relative to the investor's ability to bear risk, that meets the investor's constraints and preferences, and that integrates portfolio policies with expectational factors and market uncertainties. Portfolio management is where the payoff is, because this is where it all comes together. Of course, it is the end result of this process that is judged: the performance of the portfolio relative to expectations and comparison standards.

Professionalism is enhanced and practice improved by managing portfolios as a process that

▶ consists of the steps outlined in this book,

▶ flows logically and systematically through an orderly sequence of decision-making, and

▶ is continuous once put into motion with respect to a given investor.

This view approaches portfolio management not as a set of separate elements operating by fits and starts as intuition or inspiration dictates but rather as an integrated whole in which every decision moves the portfolio down the process path and in which no decision can be skipped without sacrificing functional integrity.

THE FUTURE OF PORTFOLIO MANAGEMENT　　8

In the last few decades, portfolio management has become a more science-based discipline somewhat analogous to engineering and medicine. As in these other fields, advances in basic theory, technology, and market structure constantly translate into improvements in products and professional practices.

Among the most significant recent theoretical advances in investments is the recognition that the risk characteristics of the nontradable assets owned by an individual client, such as future earnings from a job, a business, or an expected inheritance, should be included in the definition of that client's portfolio. In the institutional area also, there is an increasing awareness and use of multifactor risk models and methods of managing risk.

Among the most significant market developments is the emergence of a broad range of new standardized derivative contracts—swaps, futures, and options. As active trading in these standardized products continues to develop, they make possible the creation of an infinite variety of customized investment products tailored to the needs of specific clients. As analysts continue to develop a more comprehensive view of risk, they also command a wider set of tools with which to manage it.[4]

THE ETHICAL RESPONSIBILITIES OF PORTFOLIO MANAGERS　　9

In this reading, we have initiated a course of study that we hope will further the reader in his or her career as an investment professional. We select the term investment *professional* advisedly. The dictionary defines professional as "conforming to the standards of a profession". Every thoughtful person who has explored the subject has concluded that professional standards are of two types: standards of competence and standards of conduct. Merely drawing a livelihood from managing or advising on the investment of client monies is insufficient in itself to make an investment professional.

---

[4] This section on the future of portfolio management was contributed by Dr. Zvi Bodie.

But verbal distinctions are not the most important point. The conduct of a portfolio manager affects the well-being of clients and many other people. The connection to individuals and their welfare is always present; it is no less important in those institutional contexts in which the portfolio manager may never meet the client. In the first years of the 21st century press attention focused on abuses in the U.S. mutual fund industry such as late trading, abusive market timing, selective disclosure of information on portfolio holdings, and undisclosed payments for "shelf space" to gain placement on brokers' preferred lists.[5] Certain fund executives facilitated or participated in these activities for personal enrichment, at the expense of the well-being of their clients, mutual fund shareholders. In truth, the docket of cases of professional misconduct is never empty, but the profession can and must work towards minimizing it. The portfolio manager must keep foremost in mind that he or she is in a position of trust, requiring ethical conduct towards the public, client, prospects, employers, employees, and fellow workers. For CFA Institute members, this position of trust is reflected in the Code of Ethics and Standards of Professional Conduct to which members subscribe, as well as in the Professional Conduct Statement they submit annually. Ethical conduct is the foundation requirement for managing investment portfolios.

---

[5] The listing follows the enumeration of William H. Donaldson, CFA, chair of the U.S. Securities and Exchange Commission, in a speech to the Mutual Fund Directors Forum on 7 January 2004.

SUMMARY

In this reading, we have presented the portfolio management process and the elements of the investment policy statement.

- According to the portfolio perspective, individual investments should be judged in the context of how much risk they add to a portfolio rather than on how risky they are on a stand-alone basis.

- The three steps in the portfolio management process are the planning step (objectives and constraint determination, investment policy statement creation, capital market expectation formation, and strategic asset allocation creation); the execution step (portfolio selection/composition and portfolio implementation); and the feedback step (performance evaluation and portfolio monitoring and rebalancing).

- Investment objectives are specific and measurable desired performance outcomes, and constraints are limitations on the ability to make use of particular investments. The two types of objectives are risk and return. The two types of constraints are internal (posed by the characteristics of the investor) and external (imposed by outside agencies).

- An investment policy statement is a written planning document that governs all investment decisions for the client. This document integrates a client's needs, preferences, and circumstances into a statement of that client's objectives and constraints.

- A policy or strategic asset allocation establishes exposures to IPS-permissible asset classes in a manner designed to satisfy the client's long-run objectives and constraints. The plan reflects the interaction of objectives and constraints with long-run capital market expectations.

- In a passive investment strategy approach, portfolio composition does not react to changes in expectations; an example is indexing, which involves a fixed portfolio designed to replicate the returns on an index. An active approach involves holding a portfolio different from a benchmark or comparison portfolio for the purpose of producing positive excess risk-adjusted returns. A semiactive approach refers to an indexing approach with controlled use of weights different from the benchmark.

- The portfolio selection/composition decision concerns portfolio construction and often uses portfolio optimization to combine assets efficiently to achieve return and risk objectives. The portfolio implementation decision concerns the trading desk function of implementing portfolio decisions and involves explicit and implicit transaction costs.

- The elements of performance evaluation are performance measurement, attribution, and appraisal. Performance measurement is the calculation of portfolio rates of return. Performance attribution is the analysis of those rates of return to determine the factors that explain how the return was achieved. Performance appraisal assesses how well the portfolio manager performed on a risk-adjusted basis, whether absolute or relative to a benchmark.

- Portfolio monitoring and rebalancing use feedback to manage ongoing exposures to available investment opportunities in order to continually satisfy the client's current objectives and constraints.

- Portfolio management is an ongoing process in which the investment objectives and constraints are identified and specified, investment policies and strategies are developed, the portfolio composition is decided in detail, portfolio decisions are initiated by portfolio managers and implemented by traders, portfolio performance is evaluated, investor and market conditions are monitored, and any necessary rebalancing is implemented.

▶ To determine a risk objective, there are several steps: specify a risk measure (or measures) such as standard deviation, determine the investor's willingness to take risk, determine the investor's ability to take risk, synthesize the investor's willingness and ability into the investor's risk tolerance, and specify an objective using the measure(s) in the first step above.

▶ To determine a return objective, there are several steps: specify a return measure such as total nominal return, determine the investor's stated return desire, determine the investor's required rate of return, and specify an objective in terms of the return measure in the first step above.

▶ A liquidity requirement is a need for cash in excess of the contribution rate or the savings rate at a specified point in time. This need may be either anticipated or unanticipated.

▶ A time horizon is the time period associated with an investment objective. Investment objectives and associated time horizons may be short term, long term, or a combination of these two. A multistage horizon is a combination of shorter term and longer term horizons. A time horizon can be considered a constraint because shorter time horizons generally indicate lower risk tolerance and hence constrain portfolio choice, making it more conservative.

▶ A tax concern is any issue arising from a tax structure that reduces the amount of the total return that can be used for current needs or reinvested for future growth. Tax concerns constrain portfolio choice. If differences exist between the tax rates applying to investment income and capital gains, tax considerations will influence the choice of investment.

▶ Legal and regulatory factors are external considerations that may constrain investment decision making. For example, a government agency may limit the use of certain asset classes in retirement portfolios.

▶ Unique circumstances are internal factors (other than a liquidity requirement, time horizon, or tax concerns) that may constrain portfolio choices. For example, an investor seeking to avoid investments in tobacco companies will place an internal constraint on portfolio choice.

PROBLEMS FOR READING 74

1. A. An individual expects to save €50,000 during the coming year from income from non-portfolio sources, such as salary. She will need €95,000 within the year to make a down payment for a house purchase. What is her liquidity requirement for the coming year?

B. Endowments are funds that are typically owned by non-profit institutions involved in educational, medical, cultural, and other charitable activities. Classified as institutional investors, endowments are almost always established with the intent of lasting into perpetuity.

The Wilson-Fowler Endowment was established in the United States to provide financial support to Wilson-Fowler College. An endowment's spending rate defines the fraction of endowment assets distributed to the supported institution. The Wilson-Fowler Endowment has established a spending rate of 4 percent a year; the endowment follows the simple rule of spending, in a given year, an amount equal to 4% × (Market value of the endowment at the end of the prior year). This amount is committed to the budgetary support of the college for the coming year. At the end of the prior year, the market value of the Wilson-Fowler Endowment's assets stood at $75,000,000. In addition, the Wilson-Fowler Endowment has committed to contribute $1,000,000 in the coming year to the construction of a new student dormitory. Planners at the endowment expect the endowment to receive contributions or gifts (from alumni and other sources) of $400,000 over the coming year. What is the anticipated liquidity requirement of the Wilson-Fowler Endowment for the coming year?

2. The Executive Director of the Judd University Endowment estimates that the capital markets will provide a 9 percent expected return for an endowment portfolio taking above-average risk, and a 7 percent expected return for an endowment portfolio taking average risk. The Judd Endowment provides tuition scholarships for Judd University students. The spending rate has been 4 percent, and the expected tuition inflation rate is 3 percent. Recently university officials have pressured the endowment to increase the spending rate to 6 percent. The endowment has an average to below-average ability to accept risk and only an average willingness to take risk, but a university official claims that the risk tolerance should be raised because higher returns are needed. Discuss an appropriate return objective and risk tolerance for the Judd Endowment.

3. Stux (1994) describes a country allocation strategy across five major equity markets: the United States, the United Kingdom, Germany, France, and Japan. In this strategy, a measure of relative attractiveness among the five equity markets is used as a factor in determining the weights of the five equity markets in the overall portfolio. The investment in each country, however, whatever the country's weight, is an indexed investment in the equity market of that country. The weights of the five equity markets in the overall portfolio generally are expected to differ from benchmark weights (the weights of the countries in an appropriate benchmark for the international equity market), within limits.

A. Characterize the two components (portfolio weights and within-country investments) of the country allocation strategy using the text's framework for classifying investment strategies.

B. Characterize the country allocation strategy overall.

4. Characterize each of the investment objectives given below as one of the following: an absolute risk objective, a relative risk objective, an absolute return objective, or a relative return objective.

   A. Achieve a rate of return of 8 percent a year.

   B. Limit the standard deviation of portfolio returns to 20 percent a year or less.

   C. Achieve returns in the top quartile of the portfolio's peer universe (the set of portfolios with similar investment objectives and characteristics).

   D. Maintain a 10 percent or smaller probability that the portfolio's return falls below the threshold level of 5 percent per annum over a one-year time horizon.

   E. Achieve a tracking risk of no more than 4 percent per annum with respect to the portfolio's benchmark.

Questions 5 through 10 relate to James Stephenson. Select and justify the best answer.

James Stephenson, age 55 and single, is a surgeon who has accumulated a substantial investment portfolio without a clear long-term strategy in mind. Two of his patients who work in financial markets comment as follows:

▶ James Hrdina: "My investment firm, based on its experience with investors, has standard investment policy statements in five categories. You would be better served to adopt one of these standard policy statements instead of spending time developing a policy based on your individual circumstances."

▶ Charles Gionta: "Developing a long-term policy can be unwise given the fluctuations of the market. You want your investment advisor to react continuously to changing conditions and not be limited by a set policy."

Stephenson hires a financial advisor, Caroline Coppa. At their initial meeting, Coppa compiles the following notes:

Stephenson currently has a $2.0 million portfolio that has a large concentration in small-capitalization U.S. equities. Over the past five years, the portfolio has averaged 20 percent annual total return on investment. Stephenson hopes that, over the long term, his portfolio will continue to earn 20 percent annually. When asked about his risk tolerance, he described it as "average." He was surprised when informed that U.S. small-cap portfolios have experienced extremely high volatility.

He does not expect to retire before age 70. His current income is more than sufficient to meet his expenses. Upon retirement, he plans to sell his surgical practice and use the proceeds to purchase an annuity to cover his post-retirement cash flow needs.

Both his income and realized capital gains are taxed at a 30 percent rate. No pertinent legal or regulatory issues apply. He has no pension or retirement plan but does have sufficient health insurance for post-retirement needs.

5. The comments about investment policy statements made by Stephenson's patients are *best* characterized as

	Hrdina	Gionta
A.	Correct	Correct
B.	Correct	Incorrect
C.	Incorrect	Correct
D.	Incorrect	Incorrect

6. In formulating the return objective for Stephenson's investment policy statement, the *most* appropriate determining factor for Coppa to focus on is

   A. Return desires

   B. Ability to take risk

   C. Return requirement

   D. Stephenson's returns over last five years

7. Stephenson's willingness and ability to accept risk can be *best* characterized as

	Willingness to accept risk	Ability to accept risk
A.	Below average	Below average
B.	Below average	Above average
C.	Above average	Below average
D.	Above average	Above average

8. Stephenson's tax and liquidity constraints can be *best* characterized as

	Tax constraint	Liquidity constraint
A.	Significant	Significant
B.	Significant	Insignificant
C.	Insignificant	Significant
D.	Insignificant	Insignificant

9. Stephenson's time horizon is best characterized as

   A. short-term and single-stage

   B. short-term and multistage

   C. long-term and single-stage

   D. long-term and multistage

10. Stephenson's return objective and risk tolerance are most appropriately described as

	Return Objective	Risk Tolerance
A.	Below average	Below average
B.	Below average	Above average
C.	Above average	Below average
D.	Above average	Above average

11. James Stephenson Investment Profile

Case Facts

Type of investor	Individual; surgeon, 55 years of age, in good health
Asset base	$2 million
Stated return desire *or* investment goal	10 percentage points above the average annual return on U.S. small-capitalization stocks
Annual spending needs	$150,000
Annual income from nonportfolio sources (before tax)	$350,000 from surgical practice
Other return factors	Inflation is 3%
Risk considerations	Owns large concentration in U.S. small-capitalization stocks
Specific liquidity requirements	$70,000 charitable donation in 10 months
Time specifications	Retirement at age 70
Tax concerns	Income and capital gains taxed at 30 percent

Questions:

1. Underline the word at right that best describes the client's:

A. *Willingness to accept risk*	Below average	Above average
B. *Ability to accept risk*	Below average	Above average
C. *Risk tolerance*	Below average	Above average
D. *Liquidity requirement*	Significant	Not significant
E. *Time horizon*	Single stage	Multistage
F. *Overall time horizon*	Short to intermediate term	Long term
G. *Tax concerns*	Significant	Not significant

2. Discuss appropriate client objectives:

A. *Risk*

B. *Return*

12. Foothill College Endowment Fund

Case Facts

Type of investor	Institutional; endowment
Purpose	Provide annual scholarships currently totaling $39.5 million
Asset base	$1 billion
Stated return desire	6 percent, calculated as spending rate of 4 percent plus previously expected college tuition inflation of 2 percent
Other return factors	Revised expectation of college tuition inflation is 3 percent
Tax concerns	Tax-exempt

Questions

1. Underline the word at right that best describes the client's:

A. *Risk tolerance*	Below average	Above average
B. *Liquidity requirement*	Significant	Not significant
C. *Time horizon*	Single stage	Multistage
D. *Overall time horizon*	Short to intermediate term	Long term
E. *Tax concerns*	Significant	Not significant

2. Discuss appropriate client objectives:

A. *Risk*

B. *Return*

13. Vincenzo Donadoni Investment Profile
(adapted from 1998 CFA Level III exam)

Case Facts

Type of investor	Individual; 56 year old male in good health
Asset base	13.0 million Swiss francs (CHF)
Stated return desire *or* investment goal	Leave a trust fund of CHF 15.0 million for three children
Annual spending needs	CHF 250,000 rising with inflation
Annual income from other sources (after tax)	CHF 125,000 consulting income for next two years only
Ability to generate additional income	No
Willingness to accept risk	Impulsive, opinionated, successful with large bets as a businessman, believes success depends on taking initiative

Specific liquidity requirements	CHF 1.5 million immediately to renovate house CHF 2.0 million in taxes due in nine months
Time specifications	Long term except for liquidity concerns
Legal and regulatory factors	None
Unique circumstances	None

Questions

1. Underline the word at right that best describes the client's:

A. *Willingness to accept risk*	Below average	Above average
B. *Ability to accept risk*	Below average	Above average
C. *Risk tolerance*	Below average	Above average
D. *Liquidity requirement*	Significant	Not significant
E. *Time horizon*	Single stage	Multistage
F. *Overall time horizon*	Short to intermediate term	Long term

2. Discuss appropriate client objectives:

A. *Risk*

B. *Return*

APPENDIX

Appendix A Solutions to Practice Questions, End-of-Reading Problems, and Concept Checks

SOLUTIONS FOR READING 64

1. A. $S_0 = \$1,000$

$F(0,T) = \$1,100$

$T = 1$

$V_0(0,T) = \$1,000 - \$1,100/(1.0675) = -\$30.44$

B. Because the value is negative, the payment is made by the short to the long.

2. A. $S_0 = \$500$

$T = 2/12 = 0.1667$

$r = 0.035$

$F(0,T) = \$500 \times (1.035)^{0.1667} = \$502.88$

B. Sell the security for \$500 and invest at 3.5 percent for two months. At the end of two months, you will have \$502.88. Enter into a forward contract now to buy the security at \$498 in two months.

Arbitrage profit = \$502.88 − \$498 = \$4.88

C. $S_t = \$490$

$t = 1/12 = 0.0833$

$T = 2/12 = 0.1667$

$T - t = 0.0834$

$r = 0.035$

$V_t(0,T) = \$490.00 - \$502.88/(1.035)^{0.0834} = -\$11.44$. This represents a gain to the short position.

3. A. $S_0 = \$100$

$T = 1$

$r = 0.05$

$F(0,T) = \$100(1.05) = \$105$

B. $S_t = \$90$

$t = 3/12 = 0.25$

$T = 1$

$T - t = 0.75$

$r = 0.05$

$V_t(0,T) = \$90 - \$105/(1.05)^{0.75} = -\$11.23$

The investor is short so this represents a gain.

C. $S_t = \$107$

$t = 5/12 = 0.4167$

$T = 1$

$T - t = 0.5834$

$r = 0.05$

$V_t(0,T) = \$107 - \$105/(1.05)^{0.5834} = \$4.95$

The investor is short, so this represents a loss to the short position.

D. $S_t = \$98$

F(0,T) = $105

$V_T(0,T) = \$98 - \$105 = -\$7$

Gain to short position $= \$7$

Loss on asset $\quad = -\$2$ (based on $100 − $98)

Net gain $\qquad = \$5$

This represents a return of 5 percent on an asset worth $100, the same as the risk-free rate.

E. $S_t = \$110$

F(0,T) = $105

$V_T(0,T) = 110 - 105 = \$5$

Loss to short position $= -\$5$

Gain on asset $\quad = \$10$ (based on $110 − $100)

Net gain $\qquad = \$5$

This represents a return of 5 percent on an asset worth $100, the same as the risk-free rate. The overall gain on the transaction is the same as in Part D because the forward contract was executed at the no-arbitrage price of $105.

4. A. $S_0 = \$225$

T = 1

r = 0.0475

$F(0,T) = \$225(1.0475) = \$235.69$

B. $S_t = \$250$

t = 4/12 = 0.3333

T = 1

T − t = 0.6667

r = 0.0475

$V_t(0,T) = \$250.00 - \$235.69/(1.0475)^{0.6667} = \$21.49$

The investor is long, so a positive value represents a gain.

C. $S_t = \$200$

t = 8/12 = 0.6667

T = 1

T − t = 0.3333

r = 0.0475

$V_t(0,T) = \$200.00 - \$235.69/(1.0475)^{0.3333} = -\$32.07$

The investor is long, so this represents a loss to the long position.

D. $S_t = \$190$

F(0,T) = $235.69

$V_T(0,T) = \$190.00 - \$235.69 = -\$45.69$

Loss to long position $= -\$45.69$

Gain on asset $\quad = \$35.00$ (based on $225 − $190)

Net loss $\qquad = -\$10.69$

E. $S_t = \$240$

$F(0,T) = \$235.69$

$V_T(0,T) = \$240.00 - \$235.69 = \$4.31$

Gain to long position $= \$4.31$

Loss on asset $= -\$15.00$ (based on $\$240 - \$225$)

Net loss $= -\$10.69$

This loss is the same as the loss in Part D. In fact, the loss would be the same for any other price as well, because the forward contract was executed at the no-arbitrage price of $235.69. The loss of $10.69 is the risk-free rate of 4.75 percent applied to the initial asset price of $225.

5. A. The no-arbitrage forward price is $F(0,T) = \$200(1.05)3/12 = \$202.45$.

Because the forward contract offered by the dealer is overpriced, sell the forward contract and buy the security now. Doing so will yield an arbitrage profit of $2.55.

Borrow $200 and buy security. At the end of three months, repay $202.45

At the end of three months, deliver the security for $205.00

Arbitrage profit $2.55

B. At a price of $198.00, the contract offered by the dealer is underpriced relative to the no-arbitrage forward price of $202.45. Enter into a forward contract to buy in three months at $198.00. Short the stock now, and invest the proceeds. Doing so will yield an arbitrage profit of $4.45.

Short security for $200 and invest proceeds for three months $202.45

At the end of three months, buy the security for $198.00

Arbitrage profit $4.45

6. A. $S_0 = \$150$

$T = 250/365$

$r = 0.0525$

$PV(D,0,T) = \$1.25/(1.0525)^{30/365} + \$1.25/(1.0525)^{120/365} +$
                $\$1.25/(1.0525)^{210/365}$

         $= \$3.69$

$F(0,T) = (\$150.00 - \$3.69)(1.0525)^{250/365} = \$151.53$

B. $S_t = \$115$

$F(0,T) = \$151.53$

$t = 100/365$

$T = 250/365$

$T - t = 150/365$

$r = 0.0525$

After 100 days, two dividends remain: the first one in 20 days, and the second one in 110 days.

$PV(D,t,T) = \$1.25/(1.0525)^{20/365} + \$1.25/(1.0525)^{110/365} = \$2.48$

$V_t(0,T) = \$115.00 - \$2.48 - \$151.53/(1.0525)^{150/365} = -\$35.86$

A negative value is a gain to the short.

C. $S_T = \$130$

$F(0,T) = \$151.53$

$V_T(0,T) = \$130.00 - \$151.53 = -\$21.53$

The contract expires with a value of negative $21.53, a gain to the short.

7. **A.** $S_0 = \$1,145$

   $T = 90/365 = 0.2466$

   $r = 0.0425$

   $r^c = \ln(1 + 0.0425) = 0.0416$

   $\delta^c = 0.0175$

   $F(0,T) = (\$1,145 \times e^{-0.0175(0.2466)})(e^{0.0416(0.2466)}) = \$1,151.83$

   B. $S_t = \$1,225$

   $T = 90/365 = 0.2466$

   $t = 28/365 = 0.0767$

   $T - t = 0.1699$

   $r = 0.0425$

   $r^c = \ln(1 + 0.0425) = 0.0416$

   $\delta^c = 0.0175$

   $V_t(0,T) = (\$1,225 \times e^{-0.0175(0.1699)}) - (1151.83e^{-0.0416(0.1699)}) = \$77.65$

   This is a gain to the long position.

   C. $S_T = \$1,235$

   $F(0,T) = \$1,151.83$

   $V_T(0,T) = \$1,235.00 - \$1,151.83 = \$83.17$

   The contract expires with a value of $83.17, a gain to the long.

8. **A.** The investor should enter into a short forward contract, locking in the price at which he can sell the bond in 365 days.

   $B_0^c(T + Y) = \$1,146.92$

   $T = 365/365 = 1$

   $r = 0.06$

   Between now (i.e., 200 days since the original purchase) and the next 365 days, the investor will receive two coupons, the first 165 days from now and the second 347 days from now.

   $PV(CI,0,T) = \$40/(1.06)^{165/365} + \$40/(1.06)^{347/365} = \$76.80$

   $F(0,T) = (\$1,146.92 - \$76.81)(1.06)^{365/365} = \$1,134.32$

   B. $B_t^c(T + Y) = \$1,302.26$

   $F(0,T) = \$1,134.32$

   $t = 180/365$

   $T = 365/365$

   $T - t = 185/365$

   $r = 0.04$

   We are now on the 380th day of the bond's life. One more coupon payment remains until the expiration of the forward contract. The coupon payment is in $547 - 380 = 167$ days.

   $PV(CI,0,T) = \$40/(1.04)^{167/365} = \$39.29$

   $V_t(0,T) = \$1,302.26 - \$39.29 - \$1,134.32/(1.04)^{185/365} = \$150.98$

   A positive value is a loss to the short position.

9. A. A 6×12 FRA expires in 180 days and is based on 180-day LIBOR.

   B. $h = 180$

      $m = 180$

      $h + m = 360$

      $L_0(h + m) = 0.0595$

      $L_0(h) = 0.057$

$$FRA(0,h,m) = \left[\frac{1 + 0.0595\left(\frac{360}{360}\right)}{1 + 0.0570\left(\frac{180}{360}\right)} - 1 \right]\left(\frac{360}{180}\right) = 0.0603$$

   C. $h = 180$

      $m = 180$

      $g = 45$

      $h - g = 135$

      $h + m - g = 315$

      $L_{45}(h - g) = 0.0590$

      $L_{45}(h + m - g) = 0.0615$

$$V_t(0,h,m) = \frac{1}{1 + 0.0590\left(\frac{135}{360}\right)} - \frac{1 + 0.0603\left(\frac{180}{360}\right)}{1 + 0.0615\left(\frac{315}{360}\right)} = 0.00081$$

      For \$10,000,000 notional principal, the value of the FRA would be $= 0.00081 \times 10,000,000 = \$8,100$.

   D. $h = 180$

      $m = 180$

      $L_{180}(h + m) = 0.0625$

      At expiration, the payoff is $\dfrac{(0.0625 - 0.0603)\left(\frac{180}{360}\right)}{1 + 0.0625\left(\frac{180}{360}\right)} = 0.001067$

      Based on a notional principal of \$10,000,000, the corporation, which is long, will receive $\$10,000,000 \times 0.001067 = \$10,670$ from the dealer.

10. A. A 3×6 FRA expires in 90 days and is based on 90-day LIBOR.

   B. $h = 90$

      $m = 90$

      $h + m = 180$

      $L_0(h) = 0.06$

      $L_0(h + m) = 0.0614$

$$FRA(0,h,m) = \left[\frac{1 + 0.0614\left(\frac{180}{360}\right)}{1 + 0.06\left(\frac{90}{360}\right)} - 1 \right]\left(\frac{360}{90}\right) = 0.0619$$

C. h = 90

m = 90

g = 30

h − g = 60

h + m − g = 150

$L_{30}(h - g) = 0.055$

$L_{30}(h + m - g) = 0.0562$

$$V_t(0,h,m) = \frac{1}{1 + 0.055\left(\frac{60}{360}\right)} - \frac{1 + 0.0619\left(\frac{90}{360}\right)}{1 + 0.0562\left(\frac{150}{360}\right)}$$

$$= -0.001323$$

For \$15,000,000 notional principal, the value of the FRA would be = −0.001323 × 15,000,000 = −\$19,845. Because the manager is short, this represents a gain to his company.

11. **A.** The risk to the U.S. company is that the value of the Swiss franc will decline and it will receive fewer U.S. dollars on conversion. To hedge this risk, the company should enter into a contract to sell Swiss francs forward.

B. $S_0 = \$0.5974$

T = 90/365

r = 0.02

$r^f = 0.05$

$$F(0,T) = \left[\frac{0.5974}{(1.05)^{90/365}}\right](1.02)^{90/365} = \$0.5931$$

C. $S_t = \$0.55$

T = 90/365

t = 30/365

T − t = 60/365

r = 0.02

$r^f = 0.05$

$$V_t(0,T) = \frac{\$0.55}{(1.05)^{60/365}} - \frac{\$0.5931}{(1.02)^{60/365}} = -\$0.0456$$

This represents a gain to the short position of \$0.0456 per Swiss franc. In this problem, the U.S. company holds the short forward position.

12. First calculate the fair value or arbitrage-free price of the forward contract:

$S_0 = \$1.0231$

T = 180/365

r = 0.04

$r^f = 0.05$

$$F(0,T) = \left[\frac{1.0231}{(1.05)^{180/365}}\right](1.04)^{180/365} = \$1.0183$$

The dealer quote for the forward contract is \$1.0225; thus, the forward contract is overpriced. To earn a risk-free profit, you should enter into a forward contract to sell euros forward in six months at \$1.0225. At the same time, buy euros now.

  i. Take $\dfrac{\$1.0231}{(1.05)^{180/365}} = \$0.9988$. Use it to buy $\dfrac{1}{(1.05)^{180/365}} = 0.9762$ euros.

  ii. Enter a forward contract to deliver €1.00 at $1.0225 in six months.

  iii. Invest €0.9762 for six months at 5 percent per year and receive €0.9762 × 1.05$^{180/365}$ = €1.00 at the end of six months.

  iv. At expiration, deliver the euro and receive $1.0225. Return over six months is $\dfrac{\$1.0225}{\$0.9988} - 1 = 0.0237$, or 4.74 percent a year.

This risk-free annual return of 4.74 percent exceeds the U.S. risk-free rate of 4 percent.

13. A. The risk to you is that the value of the British pound will rise over the next 30 days and it will require more U.S. dollars to buy the necessary pounds to make payment. To hedge this risk you should enter a forward contract to buy British pounds.

  B. $S_0 = \$1.50$

     $T = 30/365$

     $r = 0.055$

     $r^f = 0.045$

     $F(0,T) = \left[\dfrac{\$1.50}{(1.045)^{30/365}}\right](1.055)^{30/365} = \$1.5018$

  C. $S_t = \$1.53$

     $T = 30/365$

     $t = 10/365$

     $T - t = 20/365$

     $r = 0.055$

     $r^f = 0.045$

     $V_t(0,T) = \dfrac{\$1.53}{1.045^{20/365}} - \dfrac{\$1.5012}{1.055^{20/365}} = \$0.0295$

Because you are long, this is a gain of $0.0295 per British pound.

14. A. $r^{fc} = \ln(1.04) = 0.0392$

     $r^c = \ln(1.06) = 0.0583$

  B. $S_0 = \$0.6667$

     $T = 90/365$

     $r^{fc} = 0.0392$

     $r^c = 0.0583$

     $F(0,T) = (\$0.6667 \times e^{-0.0392(90/365)})(e^{0.0583(90/365)}) = \$0.6698$

  C. $S_t = \$0.65$

     $T = 90/365$

     $t = 25/365$

     $T - t = 65/365$

     $r^{fc} = 0.0392$

     $r^c = 0.0583$

     $V_t(0,T) = (\$0.65 \times e^{-0.0392(65/365)}) - (\$0.6698 \times e^{-0.0583(65/365)}) = -\$0.0174$

The value of the contract is −$0.0174 per Swiss franc.

15. First, calculate the fair value or arbitrage free price of the forward contract:

$S_0 = \$0.00812$ per yen

$T = 90/365$

$r = 0.045$

$r^f = 0.02$

$$F(0,T) = \left[\frac{\$0.00812}{(1.02)^{90/365}} \right](1.045)^{90/365} = \$0.00817$$

The dealer quote for the forward contract is $0.00813. Therefore, the forward contract is underpriced. To earn a risk-free profit, you should enter into a forward contract to buy yen in three months at $0.00813. At the same time, sell yen now.

   i. The spot rate of $0.00812 per yen is equivalent to ¥123.15 per U.S. dollar. Take $\dfrac{¥123.15}{(1.045)^{90/365}} = ¥121.82$. Use it to buy $\dfrac{1}{(1.045)^{90/365}} = 0.9892$ U.S. dollars.

   ii. Enter a forward contract to buy yen at $0.00813 in three months. One U.S. dollar will buy $\dfrac{1}{\$0.00813} = ¥123.00$

   iii. Invest $0.9892 for three months at 4.5 percent a year and receive $0.9892 \times 1.045^{90/365} = \$1.00$ at the end of three months.

   iv. At expiration, deliver the dollar and receive ¥123. The return over three months is $\dfrac{¥123.00}{¥121.82} - 1 = 0.00969$, or 3.88 percent a year.

Because we began our transactions in yen, the relevant comparison for the return from our transactions is the Japanese risk-free rate. The 3.88 percent return above exceeds the Japanese risk-free rate of 2 percent. Therefore, we could borrow yen at 2 percent and engage in the above transactions to earn a risk-free return of 3.88 percent that exceeds the rate of borrowing.

SOLUTIONS FOR READING 65

1. Her gain caused by the increase in the price of Dow Jones Industrial Average futures is $10(9,086 - 9,020) = 660. Because Craft had a short position in S&P Midcap 400 futures, her loss caused by the increase in the price of S&P Midcap 400 futures is $500(370.20 - 369.40) = 400. Craft's net gain is $660 - $400 = 260.

2. **A.** $T = 90/365 = 0.2466$. The futures price is

   $$f_0(T) = S_0(1 + r)^T$$
   $$f_0(0.2466) = 300(1.06)^{0.2466} = $304.34 \text{ per ounce}$$

   B. Do the following:

   ▶ Enter a short futures position—that is, sell the futures at $306.

   ▶ Buy gold at $300.

   ▶ At expiration, deliver an ounce of gold and receive $306.

   This amount is $1.66 more than $304.34, which is the sum of the cost of the asset ($300) and the loss of interest on this amount at the rate of 6 percent a year ($4.34). Thus, the overall strategy results in a riskless arbitrage profit of $1.66 per futures contract. You can also look at this scenario in terms of returns: Investing $300 and receiving $306 90 days later is an annual return of 8.36 percent, because $300(1.0836)^{(90/365)} = 306$. This return is clearly greater than the risk-free return of 6 percent.

   C. The steps in this case would be the reverse of the steps in Part B above. So, do the following:

   ▶ Enter a long futures position; that is, buy the futures at $303.

   ▶ Sell short the gold at $300.

   ▶ At expiration, take the delivery of an ounce of gold and pay $303.

   This amount paid is $1.34 less than $304.34, which is the sum of the funds received from the short sale of the asset ($300) and the interest earned on this at the rate of 6 percent per year ($4.34). Thus, the overall strategy results in a riskless arbitrage profit of $1.34 per futures contract. In terms of rates, receiving $300 up front and paying $303 90 days later represents an annual rate of 4.12 percent, because $300(1.0412)^{(90/365)} = 303$. This rate is clearly less than the risk-free rate of 6 percent. Thus, the overall transaction is equivalent to borrowing at a rate less than the risk-free rate.

3. **A.** $T = 75/365 = 0.2055$. The futures price is $f_0(0.2055) = 90(1.07)^{0.2055} = 91.26$.

   B. Storage costs must be covered in the futures price, so we add them:

   $$f_0(0.2055) = 91.26 + 3 = 94.26$$

   C. A positive cash flow, such as interest or dividends on the underlying, reduces the futures price:

   $$f_0(0.2055) = 91.26 - 0.50 = 90.76$$

D. We add the storage costs and subtract the positive cash flow:

$$f_0(0.2055) = 91.26 + 3 - 0.50 = 93.76$$

E. We would do the following:

▶ Sell the futures at $95.

▶ Buy the asset at $90.

▶ Because the asset price compounded at the interest rate is $91.26, the interest forgone is 1.26. So the asset price is effectively $91.26 by the time of the futures expiration.

▶ We have incurred storage costs of $3 on the asset. We have received $0.50 from the asset. At expiration, we deliver the asset and receive $95. The net investment in the asset is $91.26 + $3.00 − $0.50 = $93.76. If we sell it for $95, we make a net gain of $1.24. Thus, the overall strategy results in a riskless arbitrage profit of $1.24 per futures contract. One can also look at this profit in terms of returns. Investing $90 and receiving a net of $95.00 − $3.00 + $0.50 = $92.50 75 days later is an annual return of 14.26 percent, because $90(1.14264)^{(75/365)} = 92.50. This return is clearly greater than the risk-free return of 7 percent.

F. The last settlement price was $89.50, and the price in our answer in Part A is $91.26. The value of a long futures contract is the difference between these prices, or $1.76.

G. When the futures contact is marked to market, the holder of the futures contract receives a gain of $1.76, and the value of the futures contract goes back to a value of zero.

4. A. Because the futures contract expires in 18 months, T = 1.5. The risk-free rate, $r_0(T)$, is 0.05. When computing the accumulated value of the coupons on the bond and the interest on them until the futures contract expires, note that the first coupon is paid in exactly six months and reinvested for the one year remaining until expiration. Also, the second coupon is paid in exactly one year and reinvested for the six months remaining until expiration, and the third coupon is paid in exactly one and a half years and not reinvested. So, the accumulated value of the coupons on the bond and the interest on them is

$$0.04(1.05)^1 + 0.04(1.05)^{0.5} + 0.04 = 0.1230$$

Because the underlying bond is the only deliverable bond in this simplistic problem, the conversion factor is 1.0, so no adjustment is required. Now the futures price is easily obtained as

$$f_0(T) = B_0^c(T + Y)[1 + r_0(T)]^T - FV(CI,0,T)$$
$$f_0(1.5) = 1.1488(1.05)^{1.5} - 0.1230$$
$$= 1.1130$$

B. Buy the five-year bond for $1.1488 and sell the futures for $1.1130. Hold the position for one and a half years until the futures expiration. Collect and reinvest the coupons in the meantime. When the futures contract expires, deliver the bond and receive the futures price of $1.1130. In addition, you will have the coupons and interest on them of $0.1230 for a total of $1.1130 + $0.1230 = $1.2360. You invested $1.1488 and end up with $1.2360 a year and a half later, so the return per dollar invested is $1.2360/$1.1488 = 1.0759$. Because this amount is paid in 1.5 years, the annual equivalent of this is

$$1.0759^{1/1.5} = 1.05$$

This return is equivalent to the 5 percent risk-free rate.

5. **A.** Because the futures contract expires in 15 months, $T = 1.25$. The risk-free rate, $r_0(T)$, is 0.05. To compute the accumulated value of the coupons on the bond and the interest on them until the futures contract expires, we note that the first coupon is paid in exactly six months and reinvested for the nine months (0.75 years) remaining until expiration. Also, the second coupon is paid in exactly one year and reinvested for the three months (0.25 years) remaining until expiration. So, the accumulated value of the coupons on the bond and the interest on them is

$$0.03(1.05)^{0.75} + 0.03(1.05)^{0.25} = 0.0615$$

B. Because the underlying bond is the only deliverable bond in this part of the problem, the conversion factor is 1, and no adjustment is required. So, the futures price is

$$f_0(T) = B_0^c(T + Y)[1 + r_0(T)]^T - FV(CI,0,T)$$
$$f_0(1.25) = 1(1.05)^{1.25} - 0.0615$$
$$= 1.0014$$

C. The futures price now is the price computed in Part B above divided by the conversion factor. Because the conversion factor is 1.0567, the futures price is

$$\frac{1.0014}{1.0567} = 0.9477$$

6. **A.** $T = 73/365 = 0.20$. The futures price should be

$$f_0(T) = S_0(1 + r)^T - FV(D,0,T)$$
$$f_0(0.20) = 1{,}521.75(1.0610)^{0.20} - 5.36$$
$$= 1{,}534.52$$

Alternatively, we can find the present value of the dividends:

$$PV(D,0,T) = \frac{FV(D,0,T)}{(1 + r)^T}$$
$$PV(D,0,0.20) = \frac{5.36}{(1.0610)^{0.20}} = 5.30$$

Then the futures price would be

$$f_0(T) = [S_0 - PV(D,0,T)](1 + r)^T$$
$$f_0(0.20) = (1{,}521.75 - 5.30)(1.061)^{0.20}$$
$$= 1{,}534.52$$

B. One specification based on the yield δ is

$$\frac{1}{(1+\delta)^T} = 1 - \frac{FV(D,0,T)}{S_0(1+r)^T}$$
$$= 1 - \frac{5.36}{1,521.75(1.061)^{0.20}} = 0.9965$$

So, $(1+\delta)^T$ is $1/0.9965 = 1.0035$. Then the futures price is

$$f_0(T) = \left(\frac{S_0}{(1+\delta)^T}\right)(1+r)^T$$
$$f_0(0.20) = \left(\frac{1,521.75}{1.0035}\right)(1.061)^{0.20}$$
$$= 1,534.51$$

The difference comes from rounding.

Under the other specification, the yield would be found as

$$\delta* = \frac{PV(D,0,T)}{S_0}$$
$$= \frac{5.30}{1,521.75} = 0.0035$$

Then the futures price would be

$$f_0(T) = S_0(1 - \delta*)(1+r)^T$$
$$f_0(0.20) = 1,521.75(1 - 0.0035)(1.061)^{0.20}$$
$$= 1,534.49$$

The difference comes from rounding.

C. The continuously compounded risk-free rate is $r^c = \ln(1+r) = \ln(1.061) = 0.0592$. The continuously compounded dividend yield is $\delta^c = \ln(1+\delta) = (1/T)\ln[(1+\delta)^T] = (1/0.20)\ln(1.0035) = 0.0175$. The futures price is

$$f_0(T) = S_0 e^{(r^c - \delta^c)T}$$
$$f_0(0.20) = 1,521.75 e^{(0.0592 - 0.0175)0.20}$$
$$= 1,534.49$$

The difference comes from rounding.

7. A. $T = 201/365 = 0.5507$. The futures price should be

$$f_0(T) = S_0(1+r)^T - FV(D,0,T)$$
$$f_0(0.5507) = 443.35(1.0650)^{0.5507} - 5.0 = 454.0$$

Alternatively, we can find the present value of the dividends:

$$PV(D,0,T) = \frac{FV(D,0,T)}{(1+r)^T}$$
$$PV(D,0,0.5507) = \frac{5.0}{(1.0650)^{0.5507}} = 4.83$$

Then the futures price would be

$$f_0(T) = [S_0 - PV(D,0,T)](1 + r)^T$$
$$f_0(0.5507) = (443.35 - 4.83)(1.065)^{0.5507}$$
$$= 454.0$$

Because the futures contract is selling at 458.50, which is higher than the price computed above, the futures contract is overpriced.

B. The arbitrageur will buy the stocks underlying the index at their current price of $443.35. Also, the arbitrageur will sell the futures contract at the settlement price of $458.50. The arbitrageur will collect and reinvest the dividends, which would be worth $5 at the time of the futures expiration. At the time of expiration, the arbitrageur will get the settlement price of $458.50. So, the arbitrageur invests $443.35 at the beginning and receives $5.00 + $458.50 = $463.50 at the expiration 201 days later. The return per dollar invested over the 201-day period is

$$\frac{463.50}{443.35} = 1.0454$$

The annual risk-free rate is 6.5 percent, equivalent to a return per dollar invested of $(1.065)^{0.5507} = 1.0353$ over the 201-day period. Thus, the return to the arbitrageur from the transactions described above exceeds the risk-free return. Alternatively, one could see that to the arbitrageur, the return per dollar invested, over a year, is $1.0454^{365/201} = 1.0832$. This annualized return of 8.32 percent is clearly greater than the annual risk-free rate of 6.5 percent.

8. $T = 100/365 = 0.274$

A. The futures price is

$$f_0(T) = \left(\frac{S_0}{(1 + r^f)^T}\right)(1 + r)^T$$
$$f_0(0.274) = \left(\frac{1.4390}{1.058^{0.274}}\right)(1.063)^{0.274}$$
$$= 1.4409$$

B. The continuously compounded equivalent rates are

$$r^{fc} = \ln(1.058) = 0.0564$$
$$r^c = \ln(1.063) = 0.0611$$

The futures price is

$$f_0(T) = (S_0 e^{-r^{fc}T}) e^{r^c T}$$
$$f_0(T) = (1.4390 e^{-0.0564(0.274)}) e^{0.0611(0.274)}$$
$$= 1.4409$$

C. The actual futures price of $1.4650 is higher than the price computed above—the futures contract is overpriced. To take advantage, the arbitrageur needs to buy the foreign currency and sell the futures contract. First, however, we must determine how many units of the currency to buy. Because we need to have 1 unit of currency, including the interest, the number of units to buy is

$$\frac{1}{(1.058)^{0.274}} = 0.9847$$

So we buy 0.9847 units, which costs 0.9847($1.4390) = $1.417. We sell the futures at $1.4650 and hold until expiration. During that time, the accumulation of interest will make the 0.9847 units of the currency grow to one unit. Using the futures contract, at expiration we convert this unit at the futures rate of $1.4650. The return per dollar invested is

$$\frac{1.4650}{1.417} = 1.0339$$

or a return of 3.39 percent over 100 days. The U.S. annual risk-free rate is 6.3 percent, which is equivalent to a return per dollar invested of $(1.063)^{0.274} = 1.0169$, over the 100-day period. Thus, the return to the arbitrageur from the transactions described above exceeds the risk-free return. Alternatively, one could see that to the arbitrageur, the return per dollar invested, over a year, is $(1.0339)^{365/100} = 1.1294$. This annualized return of 12.94 percent is more than double the annual risk-free rate of 6.3 percent.

SOLUTIONS FOR READING 66

1. Call price, $c_0 = \$4.50$

Put price, $p_0 = \$6.80$

Exercise price, $X = \$70$

Risk-free rate, $r = 5$ percent

Time to expiration $= 139/365 = 0.3808$

Current stock price, $S_0 = \$67.32$

Bond price $= X/(1 + r)^T = 70/(1 + 0.05)^{0.3808} = \$68.71$

A. Synthetic call $= p_0 + S_0 - X/(1 + r)^T = 6.8 + 67.32 - 68.71 = \$5.41$

Synthetic put $= c_0 + X/(1 + r)^T - S_0 = 4.5 + 68.71 - 67.32 = \$5.89$

Synthetic bond $= p_0 + S_0 - c_0 = 6.8 + 67.32 - 4.5 = \$69.62$

Synthetic underlying $= c_0 + X/(1 + r)^T - p_0 = 4.5 + 68.71 - 6.8 = \$66.41$

B.

Instrument	Actual Price	Synthetic Price	Mispricing/Profit
Call	4.50	5.41	0.91
Put	6.80	5.89	0.91
Bond	68.71	69.62	0.91
Stock	67.32	66.41	0.91

Thus, the mispricing is the same regardless of the instrument used to look at it.

C. The actual call is cheaper than the synthetic call. Therefore, an arbitrage transaction where you buy the call (underpriced) and sell the synthetic call (overpriced) will yield a risk-free profit of $\$5.41 - \$4.50 = \$0.91$.

As shown below, at expiration no cash will be received or paid out.

	Value at Expiration	
Transaction	$S_T < 70$	$S_T > 70$
Buy call	0	$S_T - 70$
Sell synthetic call		
Short put	$-(70 - S_T)$	0
Short stock	$-S_T$	$-S_T$
Long bond	70	70
Total	0	0

D. The actual put is more expensive than the synthetic put. Therefore, an arbitrage transaction in which you buy the synthetic put (underpriced) and sell the put (overpriced) will yield a risk-free profit of $\$6.80 - \$5.89 = \$0.91$. As shown below, at expiration no cash will be received or paid out.

Value at Expiration

Transaction	$S_T < 70$	$S_T > 70$
Sell put	$-(70 - S_T)$	
Buy synthetic put		
Long call	0	$S_T - 70$
Long bond	70	70
Short stock	$-S_T$	$-S_T$
Total	0	0

2. Current stock price, S = $100

Up move, u = 1.1

Down move, d = 0.85

Exercise price, X = $90

Risk-free rate, r = 6.5 percent

A. Stock prices one period from now are

$$S^+ = Su = 100(1.1) = \$110$$
$$S^- = Sd = 100(0.85) = \$85$$

Call option values at expiration one period from now are

$$c^+ = Max(0,110 - 90) = \$20$$
$$c^- = Max(0,85 - 90) = \$0$$

The risk-neutral probability is

$$\pi = \frac{1.065 - 0.85}{1.1 - 0.85} = 0.86 \text{ and } 1 - \pi = 0.14$$

The call price today is

$$c = \frac{0.86(20) + 0.14(0)}{1.065} = 16.15$$

B. If the current call price is $17.50, it is overpriced. Therefore, we should sell the call and buy the underlying stock. The hedge ratio is

$$n = \frac{20 - 0}{110 - 85} = 0.8$$

For every option sold we should purchase 0.8 shares of stock. If we sell 100 calls we should buy 80 shares of stock.

Sell 100 calls at 17.50 =	1,750
Buy 80 shares at 100 =	−8,000
Net cash flow =	−6,250

At expiration the value of this combination will be

$$80(110) - 100(20) = \$6,800 \text{ if } S_T = 110$$
$$80(85) - 100(0) = \$6,800 \text{ if } S_T = 85$$

We invested $6,250 for a payoff of $6,800. The rate of return is $(6,800/6,250) - 1 = 0.088$. This rate is higher than the risk-free rate of 0.065.

C. If the current call price is $14, it is underpriced. Therefore, we should buy the call and sell the underlying stock. The hedge ratio is

$$n = \frac{20 - 0}{110 - 85} = 0.8$$

For every option purchased we should sell 0.8 shares of stock. If we buy 100 calls we should sell 80 shares of stock.

Buy 100 calls at 14	=	−1,400
Sell 80 shares at 100	=	8,000
Net cash flow	=	6,600

Thus, we generate $6,600 up front.

At expiration the value of this combination will be

$$100(20) - 80(110) = -\$6,800 \text{ if } S_T = 110$$
$$100(0) - 80(85) = -\$6,800 \text{ if } S_T = 85$$

We generated $6,600 up front and pay back $6,800. The rate of return is $(6,800/6,600) - 1 = 0.0303$. This borrowing rate is lower than the risk-free rate of 0.065.

3. Current stock price, $S = \$150$

Up move, $u = 1.33$

Down move, $d = 0.85$

Exercise price, $X = \$150$

Risk-free rate, $r = 4.5$ percent

A. Stock prices one period from now are

$$S^+ = Su = 150(1.33) = \$199.5$$
$$S^- = Sd = 150(0.85) = 127.5$$

Put option values at expiration one period from now are

$$p^+ = Max(0,150 - 199.5) = \$0$$
$$p^- = Max(0,150 - 127.5) = \$22.5$$

The risk-neutral probability is

$$\pi = \frac{1.045 - 0.85}{1.33 - 0.85} = 0.4063, \text{ and } 1 - \pi = 0.5937$$

The put price today is

$$\pi = \frac{0.4063(0) + 0.5937(22.50)}{1.045} = 12.78$$

B. If the current put price is $14, it is overpriced. In order to create a hedge portfolio, we should sell the put and short the underlying stock. The hedge ratio is

$$n = \frac{p^+ - p^-}{S^+ - S^-} = \frac{0 - 22.5}{199.5 - 127.5} = -0.3125$$

For every option sold, we should sell 0.3125 shares of stock. If we sell 10,000 puts, we should sell 3,125 shares of stock.

Sell 10,000 puts at 14   = 140,000
Sell 3,125 shares at 150 = 468,750
Net cash flow   = 608,750

Thus, we generate $608,750 up front.

At expiration, the value of this combination will be

$-3,125(199.5) - 10,000(0) = -\$623,437$ if $S_T = \$199.5$
$-3,125(127.5) - 10,000(22.5) = -\$623,437$ if $S_T = \$127.5$

We generated $608,750 up front and pay back $623,437. The rate of return is

$$\frac{623,437}{608,750} - 1 = 0.0241$$

This borrowing rate is lower than the risk-free rate of 0.045.

C. If the current put price is $11, it is underpriced. In order to create a hedge portfolio, we should buy the put and buy the underlying stock. The hedge ratio is

$$n = \frac{p^+ - p^-}{S^+ - S^-} = \frac{0 - 22.5}{199.5 - 127.5} = -0.3125$$

For every option purchased we should buy 0.3125 shares of stock. If we buy 10,000 puts we should buy 3,125 shares of stock.

Buy 10,000 puts at 11   = −110,000
Buy 3,125 shares at 150 = −468,750
Net cash flow   = −578,750

That is, we invest $578,750.

At expiration, the value of this combination will be

$3,125(199.5) + 10,000(0) = \$623,437$ if $S_T = \$199.5$
$3,125(127.5) + 10,000(22.5) = \$623,437$ if $S_T = \$127.5$

We invested \$578,750 for a payoff of \$623,437. The rate of return is $\frac{623,437}{578,750} - 1 = 0.0772$. This rate is higher than the risk-free rate of 0.045.

4. Current stock price, S = \$65

Up move, u = 1.20

Down move, d = 0.83

Risk-free rate, r = 5 percent

A. Exercise price, X = \$60

Stock prices in the binomial tree one and two periods from now are

$S^+ = Su = 65(1.20) = \$78$
$S^- = Sd = 65(0.83) = \$53.95$
$S^{++} = Su^2 = 65(1.20)(1.20) = \$93.60$
$S^{+-} = Sud = 65(1.20)(0.83) = \$64.74$
$S^{--} = Sd^2 = 65(0.83)(0.83) = \$44.78$

Call option values at expiration two periods from now are

$c^{++} = \text{Max}(0, 93.60 - 60) = \$33.6$
$c^{+-} = \text{Max}(0, 64.74 - 60) = \$4.74$
$c^{--} = \text{Max}(0, 44.78 - 60) = \$0$

The risk-neutral probability is

$$\pi = \frac{1.05 - 0.83}{1.20 - 0.83} - 0.5946, \text{ and } 1 - \pi = 0.4054$$

Now find the option prices at time 1:

$$c^+ = \frac{0.5946(33.6) + 0.4054(4.74)}{1.05} = \$20.86$$

$$c^- = \frac{0.5946(4.74) + 0.4054(0)}{1.05} = \$2.68$$

The call price today is

$$c = \frac{0.5946(20.86) + 0.4054(2.68)}{1.05} = \$12.85$$

B. The hedge ratios at each point in the binomial tree are calculated as follows:

At the current stock price of \$65,

$$n = \frac{c^+ - c^-}{S^+ - S^-} = \frac{20.86 - 2.68}{78 - 53.95} = 0.7559$$

Therefore, today at time 0, the risk-free hedge would consist of a short position in 10,000 calls and a long position in 7,559 shares of the underlying stock.

At a stock price of \$78,

$$n^+ = \frac{c^{++} - c^{+-}}{S^{++} - S^{+-}} = \frac{33.6 - 4.74}{93.6 - 64.74} = 1$$

Now the risk-free hedge would consist of a short position in 10,000 calls and a long position in 10,000 shares of the underlying stock.

At a stock price of $53.95,

$$\frac{n^- = c^{+-} - c^{--}}{S^{+-} - S^{--}} = \frac{4.74 - 0}{64.74 - 44.78} = 0.2375$$

Now the risk-free hedge would consist of a short position in 10,000 calls and a long position in 2,375 shares of the underlying stock.

C. Exercise price, X = $70

Stock prices in the binomial tree one and two periods from now are

$$S^+ = Su = 65(1.20) = \$78$$
$$S^- = Sd = 65(0.83) = \$53.95$$
$$S^{++} = Su^2 = 65(1.20)(1.20) = \$93.6$$
$$S^{+-} = Sud = 65(1.20)(0.83) = \$64.74$$
$$S^{--} = Sd^2 = 65(0.83)(0.83) = \$44.78$$

Call option values at expiration two periods from now are

$$c^{++} = \text{Max}(0, 93.6 - 70) = \$23.6$$
$$c^{+-} = \text{Max}(0, 64.74 - 70) = \$0$$
$$c^{--} = \text{Max}(0, 44.78 - 70) = \$0$$

The risk-neutral probability is

$$\pi = \frac{1.05 - 0.83}{1.20 - 0.83} = 0.5946, \text{ and } 1 - \pi = 0.4054$$

Now find the option prices at time 1:

$$c^+ = \frac{0.5946(23.6) + 0.4054(0)}{1.05} = \$13.36$$
$$c^- = \frac{0.5946(0) + 0.4054(0)}{1.05} = \$0$$

The call price today is

$$c = \frac{0.5946(13.36) + 0.4054(0)}{1.05} = \$7.57$$

D. The hedge ratios at each point in the binomial tree are calculated as follows.

At the current stock price of $65,

$$n = \frac{c^+ - c^-}{S^+ - S^-} = \frac{13.36 - 0}{78 - 53.95} = 0.5555$$

Therefore, today at time 0, the risk-free hedge would consist of a short position in 10,000 calls and a long position in 5,555 shares of the underlying stock.

At a stock price of $78,

$$n^+ = \frac{c^{++} - c^{+-}}{S^{++} - S^{+-}} = \frac{23.6 - 0}{93.6 - 64.74} = 0.8177$$

Now, the risk-free hedge would consist of a short position in 10,000 calls and a long position in 8,177 shares of the underlying stock.

At a stock price of $53.95,

$$n^- = \frac{c^{+-} - c^{--}}{S^{+-} - S^{--}} = \frac{0 - 0}{64.74 - 44.78} = 0$$

Zero shares of the underlying stock are needed for the short position in calls.

5. Current stock price, S_0 = $65

Up move, u = 1.20

Down move, d = 0.83

Risk-free rate, r = 5 percent

A. Exercise price, X = $60

Stock prices in the binomial tree one and two periods from now are

$$S^+ = Su = 65(1.20) = \$78$$
$$S^- = Sd = 65(0.83) = \$53.95$$
$$S^{++} = Su^2 = 65(1.20)(1.20) = \$93.6$$
$$S^{+-} = Sud = 65(1.20)(0.83) = \$64.74$$
$$S^{--} = Sd^2 = 65(0.83)(0.83) = \$44.78$$

Put option values at expiration two periods from now are

$$p^{++} = Max(0, 60 - 93.6) = \$0$$
$$p^{+-} = Max(0, 60 - 64.74) = \$0$$
$$p^{--} = Max(0, 60 - 44.78) = \$15.22$$

The risk-neutral probability is

$$\pi = \frac{1.05 - 0.83}{1.20 - 0.83} = 0.5946 \text{ and } 1 - \pi = 0.4054$$

Now find the option prices at time 1:

$$p^+ = \frac{0.5946(0) + 0.4054(0)}{1.05} = \$0$$

$$p^- = \frac{0.5946(0) + 0.4054(15.22)}{1.05} = \$5.88$$

The put price today is

$$p = \frac{0.5946(0) + 0.4054(5.88)}{1.05} = \$2.27$$

B. Unlike the hedge portfolio for calls, which has the opposite positions in the two instruments (calls and underlying stock), the hedge portfolio for puts has the same positions in the two instruments. Therefore, the current value of the hedge portfolio for puts is

$$H = nS + p$$

The possible values of the hedge portfolio one period later are

$$H^+ = nS^+ + p^+$$
$$H^- = nS^- + p^-$$

Setting H^+ equal to H^- and solving for n,

$$n = \frac{p^- - p^+}{S^+ - S^-}$$

Note that the above formula is the same as that for the hedge portfolio for calls, except that the p^+ and p^- have switched positions in the numerator. Similarly, the hedge ratios for the next time point are

$$n^+ = \frac{p^{+-} - p^{++}}{S^{++} - S^{+-}}$$
$$n^- = \frac{p^{--} - p^{+-}}{S^{+-} - S^{--}}$$

At the current stock price of $65,

$$n = \frac{p^- - p^+}{S^+ - S^-} = \frac{5.88 - 0}{78 - 53.95} = 0.2445$$

Therefore, today at time 0, the risk-free hedge would consist of a long position in 10,000 puts and a long position in 2,445 shares of the underlying stock.

At a stock price of $78,

$$n^+ = \frac{p^{+-} - p^{++}}{S^{++} - S^{+-}} = \frac{0 - 0}{93.6 - 64.74} = 0$$

Zero shares of the underlying stock are needed for the long position in puts.

At a stock price of $53.95,

$$n^- = \frac{p^{--} - p^{+-}}{S^{+-} - S^{--}} = \frac{15.22 - 0}{64.74 - 44.78} = 0.7625$$

Now the risk-free hedge would consist of a long position in 10,000 puts and a long position in 7,625 shares of the underlying stock.

C. Exercise price, X = $70

Stock prices in the binomial tree, one and two periods from now are

$$S^+ = Su = 65(1.20) = \$78$$
$$S^- = Sd = 65(0.83) = \$53.95$$

$$S^{++} = Su^2 = 65(1.20)(1.20) = \$93.6$$
$$S^{+-} = Sud = 65(1.20)(0.83) = \$64.74$$
$$S^{--} = Sd^2 = 65(0.83)(0.83) = \$44.78$$

Put option values at expiration two periods from now are

$$p^{++} = Max(0, 70 - 93.6) = \$0$$
$$p^{+-} = Max(0, 70 - 64.74) = \$5.26$$
$$p^{--} = Max(0, 70 - 44.78) = \$25.22$$

The risk-neutral probability is

$$\pi = \frac{1.05 - 0.83}{1.20 - 0.83} = 0.5946, \text{ and } 1 - \pi = 0.4054$$

Now find the option prices at time 1:

$$p^+ = \frac{0.5946(0) + 0.4054(5.26)}{1.05} = \$2.03$$

$$p^- = \frac{0.5946(5.26) + 0.4054(25.22)}{1.05} = \$12.72$$

The put price today is

$$p = \frac{0.5946(2.03) + 0.4054(12.72)}{1.05} = \$6.06$$

D. The hedge ratios at each point in the binomial tree are calculated as follows:

At the current stock price of $65,

$$n = \frac{p^- - p^+}{S^+ - S^-} = \frac{12.72 - 2.03}{78 - 53.95} = 0.4445$$

Therefore, today at time 0, the risk-free hedge would consist of a long position in 10,000 puts and a long position in 4,445 shares of the underlying stock.

At stock price $78,

$$n^+ = \frac{p^{+-} - p^{++}}{S^{++} - S^{+-}} = \frac{5.26 - 0}{93.6 - 64.74} = 0.1823$$

Therefore, at time 1, the risk-free hedge would consist of a long position in 10,000 puts and a long position in 1,823 shares of the underlying stock.

At stock price $53.95,

$$n^- = \frac{p^{--} - p^{+-}}{S^{+-} - S^{--}} = \frac{25.22 - 5.26}{64.74 - 44.78} = 1$$

Now, the risk-free hedge would consist of a long position in 10,000 puts and a long position in 10,000 shares of the underlying stock.

SOLUTIONS FOR READING 67

1. A. The present value factors for 180, 360, 540, and 720 days are as follows:

$$B_0(180) = \frac{1}{1 + 0.0585(180/360)} = 0.9716$$

$$B_0(360) = \frac{1}{1 + 0.0605(360/360)} = 0.9430$$

$$B_0(540) = \frac{1}{1 + 0.0624(540/360)} = 0.9144$$

$$B_0(720) = \frac{1}{1 + 0.0665(720/360)} = 0.8826$$

The semiannual fixed rate (or payment per \$1 of notional principal) is calculated as

$$FS(0, n, m) = FS(0,4,180) = \frac{1 - 0.8826}{0.9716 + 0.9430 + 0.9144 + 0.8826}$$
$$= 0.0316$$

The annualized fixed rate (or payment per \$1 of notional principal) is $0.0316(360/180) = 0.0632$. Because the notional principal is \$25,000,000, the semiannual fixed payment is $25,000,000(0.0316) = \$790,000$.

B. The new present value factors for 60, 240, 420, and 600 days are as follows:

$$B_{120}(180) = \frac{1}{1 + 0.0613(60/360)} = 0.9899$$

$$B_{120}(360) = \frac{1}{1 + 0.0629(240/360)} = 0.9598$$

$$B_{120}(540) = \frac{1}{1 + 0.0653(420/360)} = 0.9292$$

$$B_{120}(720) = \frac{1}{1 + 0.0697(600/360)} = 0.8959$$

The present value of the remaining fixed payments plus the \$1 hypothetical notional principal is $0.0316(0.9899 + 0.9598 + 0.9292 + 0.8959) + 1(0.8959) = 1.0152$.

The present value of the floating payments plus the hypothetical \$1 notional principal is $1.0293(0.9899) = 1.0189$, where

► 1.0293 is the first floating payment, $0.0585(180/360) + 1$, which is the market value of the remaining payments plus the \$1 notional principal, and

► 0.9899 is the discount factor.

Based on a notional principal of \$25,000,000, the market value of the swap to the pay-floating, receive-fixed party is $(1.0152 - 1.0189)$ $25,000,000 = -\$92,500$. Thus, the market value of the swap to opposite party that pays fixed and receives floating is \$92,500.

2. A. The present value factors for 90, 180, 270, and 360 days are as follows:

$$B_0(90) = \frac{1}{1 + 0.0656(90/360)} = 0.9839$$

$$B_0(180) = \frac{1}{1 + 0.0640(180/360)} = 0.9690$$

$$B_0(270) = \frac{1}{1 + 0.0621(270/360)} = 0.9555$$

$$B_0(360) = \frac{1}{1 + 0.0599(360/360)} = 0.9435$$

The quarterly fixed rate (or payment per \$1 of notional principal) is calculated as

$$FS(0, n, m) = FS(0,4,90) = \frac{1 - 0.9435}{0.9839 + 0.9690 + 0.9555 + 0.9435}$$
$$= 0.0147$$

The annualized fixed rate (or payment per \$1 of notional principal) is $0.0147(360/90) = 0.0588$. Because the notional principal is \$15,000,000, the quarterly fixed payment is $15,000,000(0.0147) = \$220,500$.

B. The new present value factors for 60, 150, 240, and 330 days are as follows:

$$B_{30}(90) = \frac{1}{1 + 0.0384(60/360)} = 0.9936$$

$$B_{30}(180) = \frac{1}{1 + 0.0379(150/360)} = 0.9845$$

$$B_{30}(270) = \frac{1}{1 + 0.0382(240/360)} = 0.9752$$

$$B_{30}(360) = \frac{1}{1 + 0.0406(330/360)} = 0.9641$$

The present value of the remaining fixed payments plus the \$1 notional principal is $0.0147(0.9936 + 0.9845 + 0.9752 + 0.9641) + 1(0.9641) = 1.0217$.

The present value of the floating payments plus hypothetical \$1 notional principal is $1.0164(0.9936) = 1.0099$, where

▶ 1.0164 is the first floating payment, $0.0656(90/360) + 1$, which is the market value of the remaining payments plus the \$1 notional principal, and

▶ 0.9936 is the discount factor.

Based on a notional principal of \$15,000,000, the market value of the swap to the pay-floating, receive-fixed party is $(1.0217 - 1.0099)15,000,000 = \$177,000$. Thus, the market value of the swap to the pay-fixed, receive-floating party is $-\$177,000$.

3. A. First calculate the fixed payment in dollars. The dollar present value factors for 180, 360, 540, and 720 days are as follows:

$$B_0(180) = \frac{1}{1 + 0.0585(180/360)} = 0.9716$$

$$B_0(360) = \frac{1}{1 + 0.0605\,(360/360)} = 0.9430$$

$$B_0(540) = \frac{1}{1 + 0.0624\,(540/360)} = 0.9144$$

$$B_0(720) = \frac{1}{1 + 0.0665\,(720/360)} = 0.8826$$

The semiannual fixed payment per $1 of notional principal is calculated as

$$FS(0,\,n,\,m) = FS(0,4,180) = \frac{1 - 0.8826}{0.9716 + 0.9430 + 0.9144 + 0.8826}$$

$$= 0.0316$$

The annualized fixed payment per $1 of notional principal is calculated as $0.0316(360/180) = 0.0632$.

Now calculate the fixed payment in pounds. The pound present value factors for 180, 360, 540, and 720 days are as follows:

$$B_0^{£}(180) = \frac{1}{1 + 0.0493\,(180/360)} = 0.9759$$

$$B_0^{£}(360) = \frac{1}{1 + 0.0505\,(360/360)} = 0.9519$$

$$B_0^{£}(540) = \frac{1}{1 + 0.0519\,(540/360)} = 0.9278$$

$$B_0^{£}(720) = \frac{1}{1 + 0.0551\,(720/360)} = 0.9007$$

The semiannual fixed payment per £1 of notional principal is calculated as

$$FS(0,\,n,\,m) = FS(0,4,180) = \frac{1 - 0.9007}{0.9759 + 0.9519 + 0.9278 + 0.9007}$$

$$= 0.0264$$

The annualized fixed payment per £1 of notional principal is calculated as $0.0264(360/180) = 0.0528$.

B. The new dollar discount factors for 60, 240, 420, and 600 days are as follows:

$$B_{120}(180) = \frac{1}{1 + 0.0613\,(60/360)} = 0.9899$$

$$B_{120}(360) = \frac{1}{1 + 0.0629\,(240/360)} = 0.9598$$

$$B_{120}(540) = \frac{1}{1 + 0.0653\,(420/360)} = 0.9292$$

$$B_{120}(720) = \frac{1}{1 + 0.0697\,(600/360)} = 0.8959$$

The present value of the remaining fixed payments plus the $1 notional principal is $0.0316(0.9899 + 0.9598 + 0.9292 + 0.8959) + 1(0.8959) = 1.0152$.

The present value of the floating payments plus hypothetical $1 notional principal discounted back 120 days is $1.0293(0.9899) = 1.0189$, where

▶ 1.0293 is the first floating payment, $0.0585(180/360) + 1$, which is the market value of the remaining payments plus the $1 notional principal, and

▶ 0.9899 is the discount factor.

The new pound discount factors for 60, 240, 420, and 600 days are as follows:

$$B_{120}^{£}(180) = \frac{1}{1 + 0.0517(60/360)} = 0.9915$$

$$B_{120}^{£}(360) = \frac{1}{1 + 0.0532(240/360)} = 0.9657$$

$$B_{120}^{£}(540) = \frac{1}{1 + 0.0568(420/360)} = 0.9379$$

$$B_{120}^{£}(720) = \frac{1}{1 + 0.0583(600/360)} = 0.9114$$

The present value of the remaining fixed payments plus the £1 notional principal is $0.0264(0.9915 + 0.9657 + 0.9379 + 0.9114) + 1(0.9114) = 1.0119$. Convert this amount to the equivalent of $1 notional principal; that is, $1/\$1.41$: $1.0119(1/1.41) = £0.7177$. Now convert to dollars at the current exchange rate $\$1.35/£$: $0.7177(1.35) = \$0.9688$.

The present value of the floating payments plus hypothetical £1 notional principal is $1.0247(0.9915) = 1.016$, where

▶ 1.0247 is the first floating payment, $0.0493(180/360) + 1$, which is the market value of the remaining payments plus the £1 notional principal, and

▶ 0.9915 is the discount factor.

Convert this amount to the equivalent of $1 notional principal; that is, $1/\$1.41$: $1.016(1/1.41) = £0.7206$. Now convert to dollars at the current exchange rate $\$1.35/£$: $0.7206(1.35) = \$0.9728$.

The market values based on notional principal of $1 are as follows:

i. Pay £ fixed and receive $ fixed = $\$0.0464 = 1.0152 - 0.9688$

ii. Pay £ floating and receive $ fixed = $\$0.0424 = 1.0152 - 0.9728$

iii. Pay £ floating and receive $ floating = $\$0.0461 = 1.0189 - 0.9728$

iv. Pay £ fixed and receive $ floating = $\$0.0501 = 1.0189 - 0.9688$

4. A. First calculate the fixed payment in dollars. The dollar present value factors for 90, 180, 270, and 360 days are as follows:

$$B_0(90) = \frac{1}{1 + 0.0656(90/360)} = 0.9839$$

$$B_0(180) = \frac{1}{1 + 0.0640(180/360)} = 0.9690$$

$$B_0(270) = \frac{1}{1 + 0.0621(270/360)} = 0.9555$$

$$B_0(360) = \frac{1}{1 + 0.0599(360/360)} = 0.9435$$

The quarterly fixed payment per \$1 of notional principal is calculated as

$$FS(0, n, m) = FS(0,4,90) = \frac{1 - 0.9435}{0.9839 + 0.9690 + 0.9555 + 0.9435}$$
$$= 0.0147$$

The annualized fixed payment per \$1 of notional principal is $0.0147(360/90) = 0.0588$.

Now calculate the fixed payment in euros. The euro present value factors for 90, 180, 270, and 360 days are as follows:

$$B_0^{€}(90) = \frac{1}{1 + 0.0682(90/360)} = 0.9832$$

$$B_0^{€}(180) = \frac{1}{1 + 0.0673(180/360)} = 0.9674$$

$$B_0^{€}(270) = \frac{1}{1 + 0.0661(270/360)} = 0.9528$$

$$B_0^{€}(360) = \frac{1}{1 + 0.0668(360/360)} = 0.9374$$

The quarterly fixed payment per €1 of notional principal is calculated as

$$FS(0, n, m) = FS(0,4,90) = \frac{1 - 0.9374}{0.9832 + 0.9674 + 0.9528 + 0.9374}$$
$$= 0.0163$$

The annualized fixed payment per €1 of notional principal is $0.0163(360/90) = 0.0652$.

B. The new dollar discount factors for 60, 150, 240, and 330 days are as follows:

$$B_{30}(90) = \frac{1}{1 + 0.0384(60/360)} = 0.9936$$

$$B_{30}(180) = \frac{1}{1 + 0.0379(150/360)} = 0.9845$$

$$B_{30}(270) = \frac{1}{1 + 0.0382(240/360)} = 0.9752$$

$$B_{30}(360) = \frac{1}{1 + 0.0406(330/360)} = 0.9641$$

The present value of the remaining fixed payments plus the \$1 notional principal is $0.0147(0.9936 + 0.9845 + 0.9752 + 0.9641) + 1(0.9641) = 1.0217$.

The present value of the floating payments plus hypothetical \$1 notional principal is $1.0164(0.9936) = 1.0099$, where

▶ 1.0164 is the first floating payment, $0.0656(90/360) + 1$, which is the market value of the remaining payments plus the $1 notional principal, and

▶ 0.9936 is the discount factor.

The new euro discount factors for 60, 150, 240, and 330 days are as follows:

$$B_{30}^{\text{€}}(90) = \frac{1}{1 + 0.0583(60/360)} = 0.9904$$

$$B_{30}^{\text{€}}(180) = \frac{1}{1 + 0.0605(150/360)} = 0.9754$$

$$B_{30}^{\text{€}}(270) = \frac{1}{1 + 0.0613(240/360)} = 0.9604$$

$$B_{30}^{\text{€}}(360) = \frac{1}{1 + 0.0651(330/360)} = 0.9437$$

The present value of the remaining fixed payments plus the €1 notional principal is $0.0163(0.9904 + 0.9754 + 0.9604 + 0.9437) + 1(0.9437) = 1.0068$. Convert this amount to the equivalent of $1 notional principal; that is, 1/$0.86: $1.0068(1/0.86) = €1.1707$. Now convert to dollars at the current exchange rate of $0.82 per euro: $1.1707(0.82) = \$0.96$.

The present value of the floating payments plus hypothetical €1 notional principal is $1.0171(0.9904) = 1.0073$, where

▶ 1.0171 is the first floating payment, $0.0682(90/360) + 1$, which is the market value of the remaining payments plus the €1 notional principal, and

▶ 0.9904 is the discount factor.

Convert this amount to the equivalent of $1 notional principal; that is, 1/$0.86: $1.0073(1/0.86) = €1.1713$. Now convert to dollars at the current exchange rate of $0.82 per euro: $1.1713(0.82) = \$0.9605$. The market values based on notional principal of $1 are

i. Pay € fixed and receive $ fixed $= \$0.0617 = 1.0217 - 0.96$

ii. Pay € floating and receive $ fixed $= \$0.0612 = 1.0217 - 0.9605$

iii. Pay € floating and receive $ floating $= \$0.0494 = 1.0099 - 0.9605$

iv. Pay € fixed and receive $ floating $= \$0.0499 = 1.0099 - 0.96$

5. A. First calculate the fixed payment in pounds. The pound present value factors for 180 and 360 days are as follows:

$$B_0^{\text{£}}(180) = \frac{1}{1 + 0.0623(180/360)} = 0.9698$$

$$B_0^{\text{£}}(360) = \frac{1}{1 + 0.0665(360/360)} = 0.9376$$

The semiannual fixed payment per £1 of notional principal is calculated as

$$FS(0, n, m) = FS(0,2,180) = \frac{1 - 0.9376}{0.9698 + 0.9376} = 0.0327$$

The annualized fixed payment per £1 of notional principal is calculated as $0.0327(360/180) = 0.0654$.

Now calculate the fixed payment in euros. The euro present value factors for 180 and 360 days are as follows:

$$B_0^{\euro}(180) = \frac{1}{1 + 0.0563(180/360)} = 0.9726$$

$$B_0^{\euro}(360) = \frac{1}{1 + 0.0580(360/360)} = 0.9452$$

The quarterly fixed payment per €1 of notional principal is calculated as

$$FS(0,\ n,\ m) = FS(0,2,180) = \frac{1 - 0.9452}{0.9726 + 0.9452} = 0.0286$$

The annualized fixed payment per €1 of notional principal is $0.0286(360/180) = 0.0572$.

B. The new pound present value factors for 120 and 300 days are as follows:

$$B_{60}^{\pounds}(180) = \frac{1}{1 + 0.0585(120/360)} = 0.9809$$

$$B_{60}^{\pounds}(360) = \frac{1}{1 + 0.0605(300/360)} = 0.9520$$

The present value of the remaining fixed payments plus the £1 notional principal is $0.0327(0.9809 + 0.9520) + 1(0.9520) = 1.0152$.

The present value of the floating payments plus hypothetical £1 notional principal is $1.0312(0.9809) = 1.0115$, where

▶ 1.0312 is the first floating payment, $0.0623(180/360) + 1$, which is the market value of the remaining payments plus the £1 notional principal, and

▶ 0.9809 is the discount factor.

The new euro discount factors for 120 and 300 days are as follows:

$$B_{60}^{\euro}(180) = \frac{1}{1 + 0.0493(120/360)} = 0.9838$$

$$B_{60}^{\euro}(360) = \frac{1}{1 + 0.0505(300/360)} = 0.9596$$

The present value of the remaining fixed payments plus the €1 notional principal is $0.0286(0.9838 + 0.9596) + 1(0.9596) = 1.0152$. Convert this to the equivalent of £1 notional principal; that is, $1/£0.61$: $1.0152(1/0.61) = €1.6643$.

Now convert to pounds at the current exchange rate of £0.57 per euro: $1.6643(0.57) = £0.9487$. The present value of the floating payments plus hypothetical €1 notional principal is $1.0282(0.9838) = 1.0115$, where

▶ 1.0282 is the first floating payment, $0.0563(180/360) + 1$, which is the market value of the remaining payments plus the €1 notional principal, and

▶ 0.9838 is the discount factor.

Convert this amount to the equivalent of £1 notional principal; that is, $1/£0.61$: $1.0115(1/0.61) = €1.6582$. Now convert to pounds at the current exchange rate of £0.57 per euro: $1.6582(0.57) = £0.9452$. The market values based on notional principal of £1 are:

    i. Pay £ fixed and receive € fixed $= -£0.0665 = 0.9487 - 1.0152$

   ii. Pay £ floating and receive € fixed $= -£0.0628 = 0.9487 - 1.0115$

  iii. Pay £ floating and receive € floating $= -£0.0663 = 0.9452 - 1.0115$

  iv. Pay £ fixed and receive € floating $= -£0.07 = 0.9452 - 1.0152$

6. A. The present value factors for 180, 360, 540, and 720 days are as follows:

$$B_0(180) = \frac{1}{1 + 0.0458(180/360)} = 0.9776$$

$$B_0(360) = \frac{1}{1 + 0.0528(360/360)} = 0.9499$$

$$B_0(540) = \frac{1}{1 + 0.0624(540/360)} = 0.9144$$

$$B_0(720) = \frac{1}{1 + 0.0665(720/360)} = 0.8826$$

The semiannual fixed payment per $1 of notional principal is calculated as

$$FS(0, n, m) = FS(0,4,180) = \frac{1 - 0.8826}{0.9776 + 0.9499 + 0.9144 + 0.8826}$$

$$= 0.0315$$

The annualized fixed payment per $1 of notional principal is $0.0315(360/180) = 0.0630$.

B. The new present value factors for 20, 200, 380, and 560 days are as follows:

$$B_{160}(180) = \frac{1}{1 + 0.0544(20/360)} = 0.9970$$

$$B_{160}(360) = \frac{1}{1 + 0.0629(200/360)} = 0.9662$$

$$B_{160}(540) = \frac{1}{1 + 0.0679(380/360)} = 0.9331$$

$$B_{160}(720) = \frac{1}{1 + 0.0697(560/360)} = 0.9022$$

The present value of the remaining fixed payments plus the $1 notional principal is $0.0315(0.9970 + 0.9662 + 0.9331 + 0.9022) + 1(0.9022) = 1.0219$. The value of the equity payment is

$$\left(\frac{1204.10}{1150.89}\right) = 1.0462$$

Based on a notional principal of $100,000,000, the market value of a swap to pay the fixed and receive the equity return is $(1.0462 - 1.0219)100,000,000 = \$2,430,000$.

7. A. The asset manager enters into the swap at time $t = 0$. After moving forward 100 days the next floating payment is due on day 180—that is, 80 days from now. Based on the rate in effect on day 100, the present value factor is

$$B_{100}(180) = \frac{1}{1 + 0.0427(80/360)} = 0.9906$$

The next floating payment, based on the rate in effect on day 90, will be $0.0432(90/360) = 0.0108$. The present value of the next floating payment plus the $1 market value of the remaining floating payments is $0.9906(1.0108) = 1.0013$. The value of the equity payment is

$$\left(\frac{1595.72}{1561.27}\right) = 1.0221$$

Based on a notional principal of $50 million, the market value of the swap to the party that pays floating and receives the equity return is $(1.0221 - 1.0013)50{,}000{,}000 = \$1{,}040{,}000$.

8. The value of the equity payment received on the Russell 2000 is

$$\left(\frac{524.29}{478.19}\right) = 1.0964$$

The value of the equity payment made on the DJIA is

$$\left(\frac{10016}{9867.33}\right) = 1.0151$$

Based on a notional principal of $15 million, the market value of the swap to the pay the return on the DJIA and receive the return on the Russell 2000 is $(1.0964 - 1.0151)15{,}000{,}000 = \$1{,}219{,}500$.

9. A. The present value factors for 180, 360, 540, and 720 days are as follows:

$$B_0(180) = \frac{1}{1 + 0.042(180/360)} = 0.9794$$

$$B_0(360) = \frac{1}{1 + 0.0474(360/360)} = 0.9547$$

$$B_0(540) = \frac{1}{1 + 0.0554(540/360)} = 0.9246$$

$$B_0(720) = \frac{1}{1 + 0.0661(720/360)} = 0.8832$$

The semiannual fixed payment per $1 of notional principal is calculated as

$$FS(0, n, m) = FS(0,4,180) = \frac{1 - 0.8832}{0.9794 + 0.9547 + 0.9246 + 0.8832}$$

$$= 0.0312$$

The annualized fixed payment per \$1 of notional principal is $0.0312(360/180) = 0.0624$. Based on a notional principal of \$50,000,000, the four possible ways to exercise this swaption are

  i. Exercise the swaption, entering into a receive-fixed, pay-floating swap. The fixed receipt is (based on the exercise rate of 7 percent) \$50,000,000$(0.07 \times 180/360)$ \$1,750,000.

  The first floating payment is (based on the 180-day rate of 4.20 percent in effect at the time the swap is initiated) \$50,000,000$(0.0420 \times 180/360) = $ \$1,050,000.

  ii. Exercise the swaption, entering into a receive-fixed, pay-floating swap *and* entering into a pay-fixed, receive-floating swap at the market rate.

  The fixed receipt is (based on the exercise rate of 7 percent) \$1,750,000.

  The fixed payment is (based on the rate of 6.24 percent) \$50,000,000 $(0.0624 \times 180/360) = $ \$1,560,000.

  The first floating payment and receipt of \$1,050,000 offset each other.

  iii. Exercise the swaption with offsetting swap netted.

  The holder would receive a net payment stream of \$1,750,000 $-$ \$1,560,000 $=$ \$190,000.

  iv. The holder can choose to receive an up-front cash payment now of \$190,000 $(0.9794 + 0.9547 + 0.9246 + 0.8832) = $ \$710,961.

B. At expiration, the market value of a bond with face (exercise price) of \$1 and annual coupon 7 percent $= (0.07 \times 180/360)(0.9794 + 0.9547 + 0.9246 + 0.8832) + 1(0.8832) = 1.0142$. The payoff on a call option on this bond with exercise price \$1 is Max $[0,(1.0142 - 1)] = 0.0142$. Based on notional principal of \$50,000,000, the payoff is \$50,000,000$(0.0142) = $ \$710,000. This amount is the same as the payoff on the swaption computed in Part A (iv) above (the difference comes from rounding).

10. A. The present value factors for 180, 360, 540, and 720 days are as follows:

$$B_0(180) = \frac{1}{1 + 0.0583(180/360)} = 0.9717$$

$$B_0(360) = \frac{1}{1 + 0.0605(360/360)} = 0.9430$$

$$B_0(540) = \frac{1}{1 + 0.0614(540/360)} = 0.9157$$

$$B_0(720) = \frac{1}{1 + 0.0651(720/360)} = 0.8848$$

The semiannual fixed payment per \$1 of notional principal is calculated as

$$FS(0, n, m) = FS(0,4,180) = \frac{1 - 0.8848}{0.9717 + 0.9430 + 0.9157 + 0.8848}$$
$$= 0.031$$

The annualized fixed payment per \$1 of notional principal is 0.031 $(360/180) = 0.062$.

Based on a notional principal of $10,000,000, the four possible ways to exercise this payer swaption are

i. Exercise the swaption, entering into pay-fixed and receive-floating swap.

The fixed payment is (based on the exercise rate of 5 percent) $10,000,000 (0.05 × 180/360) = $250,000.

The first floating receipt is (based on the 180-day rate in effect at the time the swap is initiated of 5.83 percent) $10,000,000(0.0583 × 180/360) = $291,500.

ii. Exercise the swaption, entering into pay-fixed and receive-floating swap, and entering into receive-fixed pay-floating swap at the market rate.

The fixed payment is (based on the exercise rate of 5 percent) $250,000.

The fixed receipt is (based on the rate of 6.2 percent) $10,000,000(0.062 × 180/360) = $310,000.

The first floating payment and receipt of $291,500 offset each other.

iii. Exercise the swaption with offsetting swap netted.

The holder would receive a net payment stream of $310,000 − $250,000 = $60,000

iv. The holder can choose to receive an up-front cash payment now of 60,000 (0.9717 + 0.9430 + 0.9157 + 0.8848) = $222,912.

B. At expiration, the market value of a bond with face (exercise price) of $1 and annual coupon 5 percent = (0.05 × 180/360) (0.9717 + 0.9430 + 0.9157 + 0.8848) + 1(0.8848) = 0.9777. The payoff on a put option on this bond with exercise price $1 is Max [0,(1 − 0.9777)] = 0.0223. The payoff based on a notional principal of $10,000,000 is 0.0223(10,000,000) = $223,000. This amount is the same as the payoff on the swaption as computed in Part A (iv) above (the difference comes from rounding).

11. **A.** The present value factors for 90, 180, 270, and 360 days are as follows:

$$B_0(180) = \frac{1}{1 + 0.0373(90/360)} = 0.9908$$

$$B_0(360) = \frac{1}{1 + 0.0429(180/360)} = 0.9790$$

$$B_0(540) = \frac{1}{1 + 0.0477(270/360)} = 0.9655$$

$$B_0(720) = \frac{1}{1 + 0.0538(360/360)} = 0.9489$$

The quarterly fixed payment per $1 of notional principal is calculated as

$$FS(0, n, m) = FS(0,4,180) = \frac{1 - 0.9489}{0.9908 + 0.9790 + 0.9655 + 0.9489}$$

$$= 0.0132$$

The annualized fixed payment per $1 of notional principal is 0.0132(360/90) = 0.0528. The market value at expiration of the receiver swaption is Max {0,[0.065 × (90/360) − 0.0132](0.9908 + 0.9790 + 0.9655 + 0.9489)} = 0.012. Based on notional principal of $100,000,000, the market value is 100,000,000(0.012) = $1,200,000.

B. At expiration, the market value of a bond with face (exercise price) of $1 and annual coupon of 6.5 percent is $(0.065 \times 90/360)(0.9908 + 0.9790 + 0.9655 + 0.9489) + 1(0.9489) = 1.012$. The payoff on a call option on this bond with exercise price $1 is Max $[0,(1.012 - 1)] = 0.012$. This is the same as the payoff on the swaption.

12. A. The present value factors for 180, 360, 540, and 720 days are as follows:

$$B_0(180) = \frac{1}{1 + 0.0583(180/360)} = 0.9717$$

$$B_0(360) = \frac{1}{1 + 0.0616(360/360)} = 0.9420$$

$$B_0(540) = \frac{1}{1 + 0.0680(540/360)} = 0.9074$$

$$B_0(720) = \frac{1}{1 + 0.0705(720/360)} = 0.8764$$

The semiannual fixed payment per $1 of notional principal is calculated as

$$FS(0, n, m) = FS(0,4,180) = \frac{1 - 0.8764}{0.9717 + 0.9420 + 0.9074 + 0.8764}$$

$$= 0.0334$$

The annualized fixed payment per $1 of notional principal is calculated as $0.0334(360/180) = 0.0668$.

The new present value factors for 180, 360, and 540 days are as follows:

$$B_{180}(180) = \frac{1}{1 + 0.0429(180/360)} = 0.9790$$

$$B_{180}(360) = \frac{1}{1 + 0.0583(360/360)} = 0.9489$$

$$B_{180}(540) = \frac{1}{1 + 0.0618(540/360)} = 0.9152$$

The present value of the remaining fixed payments plus the $1 notional principal is $0.0334(0.9790 + 0.9489 + 0.9152) + 1(0.9152) = 1.0102$.

Because we are on the payment date, the present value of the remaining floating payments plus hypothetical $1 notional principal is automatically 1.0.

The market value of the swap to the pay-floating, receive-fixed party is $(1.0102 - 1) = \$0.0102$. So the market value of the swap to the pay-fixed, receive-floating party is $-\$0.0102$. Because the swap is marked to market, the party that pays floating will now receive $0.0102 per $1 of notional principal from the party that pays fixed. The two parties would then reprice the swap.

B. The new fixed-rate payment per $1 of notional principal is

$$FS(r0, n, m) = FS(0,3,180) = \frac{1 - 0.9152}{0.9790 + 0.9489 + 0.9152 + 0.8764}$$

$$= 0.0298$$

13. A. The present value factors for 90, 180, 270, and 360 days are as follows:

$$B_0(90) = \frac{1}{1 + 0.0252\,(90/360)} = 0.9937$$

$$B_0(180) = \frac{1}{1 + 0.0305\,(180/360)} = 0.9850$$

$$B_0(270) = \frac{1}{1 + 0.0373\,(270/360)} = 0.9728$$

$$B_0(360) = \frac{1}{1 + 0.0406\,(360/360)} = 0.9610$$

The quarterly fixed payment per \$1 of notional principal is calculated as

$$FS(0, n, m) = FS(0,4,90) = \frac{1 - 0.9610}{0.9937 + 0.9850 + 0.9728 + 0.9610}$$

$$= 0.01$$

The annualized fixed payment per \$1 of notional principal is calculated as $0.01(360/90) = 0.04$.

The new present value factors for 90, 180, and 270 days are as follows:

$$B_{90}(90) = \frac{1}{1 + 0.0539\,(90/360)} = 0.9867$$

$$B_{90}(180) = \frac{1}{1 + 0.0608\,(180/360)} = 0.9705$$

$$B_{90}(270) = \frac{1}{1 + 0.0653\,(270/360)} = 0.9533$$

The present value of the remaining fixed payments plus the \$1 notional principal is $0.01(0.9867 + 0.9705 + 0.9533) + 1(0.9533) = 0.9824$.

Because we are on the payment date, the present value of the remaining floating payments plus hypothetical \$1 notional principal is automatically 1.0.

The market value of the swap to the pay-floating, receive-fixed party is $(0.9824 - 1) = -\$0.0176$. So, the market value of the swap to the pay-fixed, receive-floating party is \$0.0176. Because the swap is marked to market, the party that pays floating will now pay \$0.0176 per \$1 of notional principal to the party that pays fixed. The two parties would then reprice the swap.

B. The new fixed-rate payment per \$1 of notional principal is

$$FS(0, n, m) = FS(0,3,90) = \frac{1 - 0.9533}{0.9867 + 0.9705 + 0.9533} = 0.0160$$

SOLUTIONS FOR READING 68

Solutions are for Practice Questions found in Reading

1. The invoice price is equal to

> contract size × futures settlement price × conversion factor
> + accrued interest

The futures settlement price is 97-24 or 97.75 (= 97 + 24/32). The futures settlement price per \$1 of par value is therefore 0.9775. The invoice price is then:

> \$100,000 × 0.9775 × 1.17 + \$3,800 = \$118,167.50

2. The proceeds received are:

> converted price = futures price × conversion factor
> = \$97 × 0.9710 = \$94.1870

The term repo rate is 4.7%, so the interest from reinvesting the interim coupon payment is

> interest from reinvesting the interim coupon payment
> $= \$3.5 \times 0.047 \times \left(\dfrac{37}{360}\right) = \$0.0169$

Summary:

converted price	= \$94.1870
accrued interest received	= 0.7096
interim coupon payment	= 3.5000
interest from reinvesting the interim coupon payment	= 0.0169
proceeds received	= \$98.4135

The cost of the investment is the purchase price for the issue plus the accrued interest paid, as shown below:

> cost of the investment = \$95 + \$3.0110 = \$98.0110

The implied repo rate is then:

> $\text{implied repo rate} = \dfrac{\$98.4135 - \$98.0110}{\$98.0110} \times \dfrac{360}{62} = 0.0238 = 2.38\%$

3. **A.** The investor will exercise the call option because the price of the futures contract exceeds the strike price. By exercising the investor receives a long position in the Treasury bond futures contract and the call option writer receives the corresponding short position. The futures price for both parties is the strike price of \$98. The positions are then marked-to-market using the futures price of \$103 and the option

writer must pay the option buyer $5 (the difference between the futures price of $103 and the strike price of $98).

   After this, the positions look as follows:

▶ the investor (the buyer of the call option) has a long position in the Treasury bond futures contract at $103 and cash of $5

▶ the writer of the call option has a short position in the Treasury bond futures contract at $103 and has paid cash of $5

B. The investor will exercise the put option because the price of the futures contract is less than the strike price. By exercising the investor receives a short position in the Treasury bond futures contract and the put option writer receives the corresponding long position. The futures price for both parties is the strike price of $105. The positions are then marked-to-market using the futures price of $105 and the option writer must pay the option buyer $9 (the difference between the strike price of $105 and the futures price of $96).

   After this, the positions look as follows:

▶ the investor (the buyer of the put option) has a short position in the Treasury bond futures contract at $105 and cash of $9

▶ the writer of the call option has a long position in the Treasury bond futures contract at $105 and has paid cash of $9

4. Although the payments are quarterly rather than semiannual as illustrated in the text illustration, the concept is the same.

A. Since the swap rate is 4.4%, the fixed-rate payment each quarter will be:

$100 million $\times$ (0.044/4) = $1.1 million

(In the next reading, this number will be fine tuned to allow for the fact that not every quarter has the same number of days.)

B. Since 3-month LIBOR is 7.2%, the first quarterly payment will be:

$100 million $\times$ (0.072/4) = $1.8 million

5. There is a payoff to the cap if the cap rate exceeds 3-month LIBOR. For Periods 1 and 2, there is no payoff because the 3-month LIBOR is below the cap rate. For Periods 3 and 4, there is a payoff and the payoff is determined by:

$100 million $\times$ (3-month LIBOR − cap rate)/4

The payoffs are summarized below:

Period	3-month LIBOR (%)	Payoff ($)
1	6.7%	$ 0
2	7.0	0
3	7.4	100,000
4	7.6	150,000

SOLUTIONS FOR READING 68

Solutions for the End of Chapter Problems

1. The swap rate is the fixed rate that the fixed-rate payer agrees to pay over the life of the swap. The swap spread is the spread that is added to a benchmark Treasury security (from the Treasury yield curve) to obtain the swap rate.

2. **A.** The fixed-rate payer agrees to pay the swap rate (i.e., the fixed rate). Since Mr. Munson has agreed to pay the swap rate, he is the fixed-rate payer. The commercial bank is the fixed-rate receiver.

   B. Since the swap rate is 5.6%, the fixed-rate payment each quarter will be:

   $$\$40,000,000 \times (0.056/4) = \$560,000$$

   C. Since 3-month LIBOR is 3.6%, the first quarterly payment will be:

   $$\$40,000,000 \times (0.036/4) = \$360,000$$

3. A swap can be interpreted in the following two ways: (i) as a package of forward contracts and (ii) as a package of cash market instruments. It is a package of forward contracts because basically the fixed-rate payer is agreeing to pay a fixed amount for "something." That something is the reference rate and therefore the value of what the fixed-rate receiver is receiving in exchange for the fixed-rate payment at an exchange date will vary. This is equivalent to a forward contract where the underlying is the reference rate. There is not just one forward contract but one for each date at which an exchange of payments will be made over the life of the swap. Thus, it is a package of forward contracts.

   The second interpretation is that an interest rate swap is a package of cash market instruments. Specifically, from the perspective of the fixed-rate payer—the party paying fixed and receiving floating—it is equivalent to buying a floating-rate note (with the reference rate for the note being the reference rate for the swap) and funding (i.e., obtaining the funds to buy the floating-rate note) by issuing a fixed-rate bond (with the coupon rate for the bond being the swap rate). The par value of the floating-rate note and the fixed-rate bond is the notional amount of the swap. For the fixed-rate receiver, a swap is equivalent to purchasing a fixed-rate bond and funding it by issuing a floating-rate note.

4. **A.** If interest rates decrease, the fixed-rate payer will lose, as an appreciation in the value of the swap will cause an unrealized loss in value to the short position. This is because the swap rate (i.e., a fixed rate) is being paid but that rate is above the prevailing market rate necessary to receive the reference rate.

   B. If interest rates decrease, the fixed-rate receiver will realize an appreciation in the value of the swap. This is because the fixed-rate receiver is being paid a higher rate (i.e., the swap rate) than prevailing in the market in exchange for the reference rate.

5. An investor who is short the bond market benefits if interest rates increase. The party to an interest rate swap that benefits if interest rates increase is the fixed-rate payer. Thus, a fixed-rate payer is said to be short the bond market.

6. There is no payoff to the cap if the cap rate exceeds 3-month LIBOR. For Periods 2 and 3, there is no payoff because 3-month LIBOR is below the cap rate. For Periods 1 and 4, there is a payoff and the payoff is determined by:

$10 million $\times$ (3-month LIBOR $-$ cap rate)/4

The payoffs are summarized below:

Period	3-month LIBOR (%)	Payoff ($)
1	8.7%	17,500
2	8.0	0
3	7.8	0
4	8.2	5,000

7. There is a payoff to the floor if 3-month LIBOR is less than the floor rate. For Periods 1 and 2, there is no payoff because 3-month LIBOR is greater than the floor rate. For Periods 3 and 4, there is a payoff and the payoff is determined by:

$20 million $\times$ (floor rate $-$ 3-month LIBOR)/4

The payoffs are summarized below:

Period	3-month LIBOR (%)	Payoff ($)
1	4.7%	0
2	4.4	0
3	3.8	10,000
4	3.4	30,000

8. Once the fee for the interest rate floor is paid, the seller of an interest rate floor is not exposed to counterparty risk. Only the seller, not the buyer, must perform.

9. A. An interest rate cap or floor is equivalent to a package of interest rate options. So, for example, if an interest rate cap is for three years and payments are made quarterly, this is equivalent to 12 interest rate options.

   B. Since a cap is equivalent to a package of interest rate options, each option in the package is called a caplet. So, if an interest rate cap, for example, is for three years and makes quarterly payments, then there are 12 interest rate options and there are then 12 caplets. Similarly, since a floor is equivalent to a package of interest rate options, each interest rate option in the package is called a floorlet.

SOLUTIONS FOR READING 70

Solutions are for Concept Checks found in Reading

1. We can characterize the entire population by two representative investors. One is the "uninformed" investor, who does not engage in security analysis and holds the market portfolio, whereas the other optimizes using the Markowitz algorithm with input from security analysis. The uninformed investor does not know what input the informed investor uses to make portfolio purchases. The uninformed investor knows, however, that if the other investor is informed, the market portfolio proportions will be optimal. Therefore, to depart from these proportions would constitute an uninformed bet, which will, on average, reduce the efficiency of diversification with no compensating improvement in expected returns.

2. **a.** Substituting the historical mean and standard deviation in equation 70-2 yields a coefficient of risk aversion of

$$\overline{A} = \frac{E(r_M) - r_f}{.01 \times \sigma_M^2} = \frac{8.2}{.01 \times 20.6^2} = 1.93$$

   b. This relationship also tells us that for the historical standard deviation and a coefficient of risk aversion of 3.5 the risk premium would be

$$E(r_M) - r_f = .01 \times \overline{A}\sigma_M^2 = .01 \times 3.5 \times 20.6^2 = 14.9\%$$

3. For these investment proportions, w_{Ford}, w_{GM}, the portfolio β is

$$\beta_P = w_{Ford}\beta_{Ford} + w_{GM}\beta_{GM}$$
$$= (.75 \times 1.25) + (.25 \times 1.10) = 1.2125$$

   As the market risk premium, $E(r_M) - r_f$, is 8%, the portfolio risk premium will be

$$E(r_P) - r_f = \beta_P[E(r_M) - r_f]$$
$$= 1.2125 \times 8 = 9.7\%$$

4. The alpha of a stock is its expected return in excess of that required by the CAPM.

$$\alpha = E(r) - \{r_f + \beta[E(r_M) - r_f]\}$$
$$\alpha_{XYZ} = 12 - [5 + 1.0(11 - 5)] = 1\%$$
$$\alpha_{ABC} = 13 - [5 + 1.5(11 - 5)] = -1\%$$

ABC plots below the SML, while *XYZ* plots above.

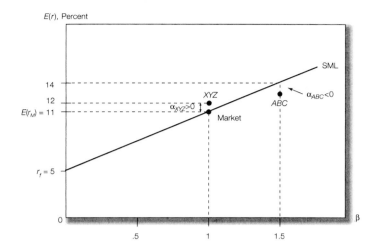

5. The project-specific required return is determined by the project beta cou-pled with the market risk premium and the risk-free rate. The CAPM tells us that an acceptable expected rate of return for the project is

$$r_f + \beta[E(r_M) - r_f] = 8 + 1.3(16 - 8) = 18.4\%$$

which becomes the project's hurdle rate. If the IRR of the project is 19%, then it is desirable. Any project with an IRR equal to or less than 18.4% should be rejected.

6. If the basic CAPM holds, any zero-beta asset must be expected to earn on average the risk-free rate. Hence the posited performance of the zero-beta portfolio violates the simple CAPM. It does not, however, violate the zero-beta CAPM. Since we know that borrowing restrictions do exist, we expect the zero-beta version of the model is more likely to hold, with the zero-beta rate differing from the virtually risk-free T-bill rate.

7. Consider investors with time horizon h_{IV} who will be indifferent between illiquid (I) and very illiquid (V) classes of stock. Call z the fraction of liqui-dation cost by which the gross return of class V stocks is increased. For these investors, the indifference condition is

$$[r + y\, c_I] - c_I/h_{LI} = [r + z\, c_V] - c_V/h_{IV}$$

This equation can be rearranged to show that

$$[r + z\, c_V] - [r + y\, c_I] = (c_I - c_V)/h_{IV}$$

SOLUTIONS FOR READING 71

Solutions are for Concept Checks Found in Reading

1. The variance of each stock is $\beta^2 \sigma_M^2 + \sigma^2(e)$.

   For stock A, we obtain

   $$\sigma_A^2 = .9^2(20)^2 + 30^2 = 1,224$$
   $$\sigma_A = 35$$

   For stock B,

   $$\sigma_B^2 = 1.1^2(20)^2 + 10^2 = 584$$
   $$\sigma_B = 24$$

   The covariance is

   $$\beta_A \beta_B \sigma_M^2 = .9 \times 1.1 \times 20^2 = 396$$

2. $\sigma^2(e_p) = (1/2)^2[\sigma^2(e_A) + \sigma^2(e_B)]$
   $$= (1/4)(30^2 + 10^2)$$
   $$= 250$$

   Therefore $\sigma(e_P) = 15.8$

3. **A.** Total market capitalization is $3,000 + 1,940 + 1,360 = 6,300$.
   Therefore, the mean excess return of the index portfolio is

   $$\frac{3,000}{6,300} \times 10 + \frac{1,940}{6,300} \times 2 + \frac{1,360}{6,300} \times 17 = 10$$

   B. The covariance between stock B and the index portfolio equals

   $$\text{Cov}(R_B, R_M) = \beta_B \sigma_M^2 = .2 \times 25^2 = 125$$

   C. The total variance of B equals

   $$\sigma_B^2 = \text{Var}(\beta_B, R_M + e_B) = \beta_B^2 \sigma_M^2 + \sigma^2(e_B)$$

   Systematic risk equals $\beta_B^2 \sigma_M^2 = .2^2 \times 25^2 = 25$.
   Thus the firm-specific variance of B equals

   $$\sigma^2(e_B) = \sigma_B^2 - \beta_B^2 \sigma_M^2 = 30^2 - .2^2 \times 25^2 = 875$$

4. The CAPM is a model that relates expected rates of return to risk. It results in the expected return–beta relationship, where the expected risk premium on any asset is proportional to the expected risk premium on the market portfolio with beta as the proportionality constant. As such the model is impractical for two reasons: (i) expectations are unobservable, and (ii) the theoretical market portfolio includes every risky asset and is in practice unobservable. The next three models incorporate additional assumptions to overcome these problems.

The single-factor model assumes that one economic factor, denoted F, exerts the only common influence on security returns. Beyond it, security returns are driven by independent, firm-specific factors. Thus for any security, i,

$$r_i = E(r_i) + \beta_i F + e_i$$

The single-index model assumes that in the single-factor model, the factor F can be replaced by a broad-based index of securities that can proxy for the CAPM's theoretical market portfolio. The index model can be stated as $R_i = \alpha_i + \beta_i R_M + e_i$.

At this point it should be said that many interchange the meaning of the index and market models. The concept of the market model is that rate of return *surprises* on a stock are proportional to corresponding surprises on the market index portfolio, again with proportionality constant β.

5. Merrill Lynch's alpha is related to the CAPM alpha by

$$\alpha_{\text{Merrill}} = \alpha_{\text{CAPM}} + (1 - \beta)r_f$$

For GM, $\alpha_{\text{Merrill}} = .14\%$, $\beta = .80$, and we are told that r_f was .6%. Thus

$$\alpha_{\text{CAPM}} = .14\% - (1 - .80).6\% = .02\%$$

GM still performed well relative to the market and the index model. It beat its "benchmark" return by an average of .02% per month.

6. The industries with positive adjustment factors are most sensitive to the economy. Their betas would be expected to be higher because the business risk of the firms is higher. In contrast, the industries with negative adjustment factors are in business fields with a lower sensitivity to the economy. Therefore, for any given financial profile, their betas are lower.

SOLUTIONS FOR READING 72

Solutions are for Concept Checks found in Reading

1. The GDP beta is 1.2 and GDP growth is 1% better than previously expected. So you will increase your forecast for the stock return by $1.2 \times 1\% = 1.2\%$. The revised forecast is for an 11.2% return.

2. With these lower risk premia, the expected return on the stock will be lower:

   $$E(r) = 4\% + 1.8 \times 4\% + .7 \times 2\% = 12.6\%$$

3. **A.** This portfolio is not well diversified. The weight on the first security does not decline as n increases. Regardless of how much diversification there is in the rest of the portfolio, you will not shed the firm-specific risk of this security.

   B. This portfolio is well diversified. Even though some stocks have three times the weight as other stocks ($1.5/n$ versus $.5/n$), the weight on all stocks approaches zero as n increases. The impact of any individual stock's firm-specific risk will approach zero as n becomes ever larger.

4. The SML says that the expected return on the portfolio should be $4\% + (\frac{1}{3})(10 - 4) = 6\%$. The return actually expected is only 5%, implying that the stock is overpriced and that there is an arbitrage opportunity. Buy \$1 of a portfolio that is $\frac{2}{3}$ invested in T-bills and $\frac{1}{3}$ in the market. The return on this portfolio is $\frac{2}{3}r_f + \frac{1}{3}r_M = \frac{2}{3} \times 4\% + \frac{1}{3}r_M$. Sell \$1 of Portfolio G. The net return on the combined position is:

$\$1 \times \left[\dfrac{2}{3} \times .04 + \dfrac{1}{3}r_M\right]$	Buy portfolio invested $\frac{2}{3}$ in T-bills and $\frac{1}{3}$ in the market index.
$-\$1 \times \left[.05 + \dfrac{1}{3}(r_M - .10)\right]$	Sell \$1 in portfolio G, with expected return of 5% and beta of $\frac{1}{3}$ on surprise in market return.
$\$1 \times .01$	Total

   The profit per dollar invested is risk-free and precisely equal to the deviation of expected return from the SML.

5. The equilibrium return is $E(r) = r_f + \beta_{P1}[E(r_1) - r_f] + \beta_{P2}[E(r_2) - r_f]$ Using the data in Example 11.5:

   $$E(r) = 4 + .2 \times (10 - 4) + 1.4 \times (12 - 4) = 16.4\%$$

6. **A.** For Louisiana residents, the stock is not a hedge. When their economy does poorly (low energy prices), the stock also does poorly, thereby aggravating their problems.

   B. For Massachusetts residents, the stock is a hedge. When energy prices increase, the stock will provide greater wealth with which to purchase energy.

C. If energy consumers (who are willing to bid up the price of the stock for its hedge value) dominate the economy, then high oil-beta stocks will have lower expected rates of return than would be predicted by the simple CAPM.

SOLUTIONS FOR READING 73

Solutions are for Concept Checks found in Reading

1. We show the answer for the annual compounded rate of return for each strategy and leave the monthly rate for you to compute. Beginning-of-period fund:

$$F_0 = \$1,000$$

End-of-period fund for each strategy:

$$F_1 = \begin{cases} \$3,600 & \text{Strategy} = \text{Bill only} \\ \$67,500 & \text{Strategy} = \text{Market only} \\ \$5,360,000,000 & \text{Strategy} = \text{Perfect timing} \end{cases}$$

Number of periods: $N = 52$ years
Annual compounded rate:

$$[1 + r_Z]^N = \frac{F_1}{F_0}$$

$$r_A = \left(\frac{F_1}{F_0}\right)^{1/N} - 1$$

$$r_A = \begin{cases} 2.49\% & \text{Strategy} = \text{Bills only} \\ 8.44\% & \text{Strategy} = \text{Market only} \\ 34.71\% & \text{Strategy} = \text{Perfect timing} \end{cases}$$

2. The timer will guess bear or bull markets completely randomly. One-half of all bull markets will be preceded by a correct forecast, and similarly for bear markets. Hence $P_1 + P_2 - 1 = \frac{1}{2} + \frac{1}{2} - 1 = 0$.

3. **A.** When short positions are prohibited, the analysis is identical except that negative-alpha stocks are dropped. In that case the sum of the ratios of alpha to residual variance for the remaining two stocks is .7895. This leads to the new composition of the active portfolio. If x denotes new portfolio weights, then

$$x_1 = .3457/.7895 = .4379$$
$$x_2 = .4438/.7895 = .5621$$

The alpha, beta, and residual standard deviation of the active portfolio are now

$$\alpha_A = .4379 \times .07 + .5621 \times .03 = .0475$$
$$\beta_A = .4379 \times 1.6 + .5621 \times .5 = .9817$$
$$\sigma(e_A) = [.4379^2 \times .45^2 + .5621^2 \times .26^2]^{\frac{1}{2}} = .2453$$

The cost of the short sale restriction is already apparent. The alpha has shrunk from 20.56% to 4.75%, while the reduction in the residual standard deviation is more moderate, from 82.62% to 24.53%. In fact, a negative-alpha stock is potentially more attractive than a positive-alpha one: Since most stocks are positively correlated, the negative position that is required for the negative-alpha stock creates a better diversified active portfolio.

The optimal allocation of the new active portfolio is

$$w_0 = \frac{.0475/.6019}{.08/.04} = .3946$$

$$w^* = \frac{.3946}{1 + (1 - .9817) \times .3946} = .3918$$

Here, too, the beta correction is essentially irrelevant because the portfolio beta is so close to 1.0.

Finally, the performance of the overall risky portfolio is estimated at

$$S_P^2 = .16 + \left[\frac{.0475}{.2453}\right]^2 = .1975; \; S_P = .44$$

It is clear that in this case we have lost about half of the original improvement in the Sharpe measure. Note, however, that this is an artifact of the limited coverage of the security analysis division. When more stocks are covered, then a good number of positive-alpha stocks will keep the residual risk of the active portfolio low. This is the key to extracting large gains from the active strategy.

We calculate the "Modigliani-square," or M^2 measure, as follows:

$$E(r_{P*}) = r_f + S_p\sigma_M = .07 + .44 \times .20 = .158, \text{ or } 15.8\%$$
$$M^2 = E(r_{P*}) - E(r_M) = 15.8\% - 15\% = 0.8\%$$

which is a bit less than half the M^2 value of the unconstrained portfolio.

B. When the forecast for the market-index portfolio is more optimistic, the position in the active portfolio will be smaller and the contribution of the active portfolio to the Sharpe measure of the risky portfolio also will be smaller. In the original example the allocation to the active portfolio would be

$$w_0 = \frac{.2056/.6826}{.12/.04} = .1004$$

$$w^* = \frac{.1004}{1 + (1 - .9519) \times .1004} = .0999$$

Although the Sharpe measure of the market is now better, the improvement derived from security analysis is smaller:

$$S_P^2 = \left(\frac{.12}{.20}\right)^2 + \left(\frac{.2056}{.8262}\right)^2 = .4219$$
$$S_P = .65; \qquad S_M = .60$$

SOLUTIONS FOR READING 74

1. **A.** The liquidity requirement for this individual is her need for cash in excess of her savings during the coming year. Therefore, her liquidity requirement is €95,000 − €50,000 = €45,000.

   B. The Wilson-Fowler Endowment's anticipated liquidity requirement is $600,000, calculated as $1,000,000 (the planned contribution to the construction of the new dormitory) minus $400,000 (the anticipated amount of new contributions to the endowment). Note that the amount of 4% × $75,000,000 = $3,000,000, as provided for in the spending rule, is fully committed to budgetary support; thus this amount is not available to help meet the endowment's planned contribution to the building project.

2. The Judd Endowment's risk tolerance is limited by its ability and willingness to accept risk. Risk tolerance is *not* a function of a need for higher returns. The return objective should be consistent with risk tolerance, so an appropriate return objective for the Judd Endowment is 7 percent. A spending rate of 6 percent is too high for this endowment; raising the return objective to 9 percent would only compound the problem created by a 6 percent spending rate, which is inappropriately high for this endowment.

3. **A.** The country allocation strategy as described mixes elements of active and passive investment approaches. The portfolio weights are actively determined and differ from benchmark weights, within limits. However, the investments in individual countries are passive, indexed investments.

   B. Overall, we can classify the country allocation strategy as a semiactive or controlled-active investment approach.

4. **A.** This is an absolute return objective because it does not reference a comparison to the performance of another portfolio but rather is stated in terms of a fixed number (an 8 percent annual return).

   B. This is an absolute risk objective because it does not reference a comparison to the performance of another portfolio but rather is stated in terms of a fixed number (a standard deviation of return of 20 percent a year).

   C. This is a relative return objective because it references a comparison to the performance of other portfolios.

   D. This is an absolute risk objective because it addresses the risk that a portfolio's return will fall below a minimum acceptable level over a stated time horizon.

   E. This is a relative risk objective because it references a comparison to the performance of another portfolio, the benchmark.

5. D is correct. The IPS identifies pertinent investment objectives and constraints for a *particular* investor. Clearly identified objectives and constraints ensure that the policy statement is accurate and relevant to the investor's specific situation and desires. The result should be an optimal balance between return and risk for that investor. The IPS provides a long-term plan for an investor and a basis for making disciplined investment decisions over time. The absence of an investment policy statement reduces decision making to an individual-event basis and often leads to pursuing short-term opportunities that may not contribute to, or may even detract from, reaching long-term goals.

Managing Investment Portfolios: A Dynamic Process, Third Edition, by John L. Maginn, Donald L. Tuttle, Dennis W. McLeavey, and Jerald E. Pinto. Copyright © CFA Institute. Reprinted with permission.

6. B is correct. An investor's ability to take risk puts an upper limit on a reasonable return objective.

7. D is correct. Even though Stephenson describes his risk tolerance as "average," his present investment portfolio and his desire for large returns indicate an above-average willingness to take risk. His financial situation (large asset base, ample income to cover expenses, lack of need for liquidity, and long time horizon) indicates an above-average ability to accept risk.

8. B is correct. Stephenson has adequate income to cover his living expenses and has no major outlays for which he needs cash, so his liquidity needs are minimal. He is not a tax-exempt investor (both income and capital gains are taxed at 30%), so taxes should play a considerable role in his investment decisions.

9. D is correct. Stephenson's time horizon is long—he is currently only 55 years old. The time horizon consists of two stages: the first stage extends to his retirement in 15 years; the second stage may last for 20 years or more and extends from retirement until his death.

10. D is correct.

Risk: Stephenson has an above-average risk tolerance based on both his ability and willingness to assume above-average risk. His large asset base, long time horizon, ample income to cover expenses, and lack of need for liquidity or cash flow indicate an above-average ability to assume risk. His concentration in U.S. small-capitalization stocks and his desire for high returns indicate substantial willingness to assume risk.

Return: Stephenson's financial circumstances (long time horizon, sizable asset base, ample income, and low liquidity needs) and his risk tolerance warrant an above-average total return objective. His expressed desire for a continued return of 20 percent, however, is unrealistic. Coppa should counsel Stephenson on what level of returns to reasonably expect from the financial markets over long periods of time and to define an achievable return objective.

11. James Stephenson

Underline the word at right that best describes the client's:

A. *Willingness to accept risk* Below average <u>Above average</u> Explanation in 2A below

B. *Ability to accept risk* Below average <u>Above average</u> Explanation in 2A below

C. *Risk tolerance* Below average <u>Above average</u> Explanation in 2A below

D. *Liquidity requirement* Significant <u>Not significant</u> $70,000 can be met by expected annual saving of $350,000 × (1 − 0.3) − $150,000 = $95,000

E. *Time horizon* Single stage <u>Multistage</u> Stage 1: Pre-retirement Stage 2: Retirement

F. *Overall time horizon* Short to intermediate term <u>Long term</u> Overall time horizon could be 20 to 30 years or more

G. *Tax concerns* <u>Significant</u> Taxed at 30% rate Not significant

Discuss appropriate client objectives:

A. *Risk:* Stephenson has an above-average risk tolerance based on both his ability and willingness to assume above-average risk. His large asset base, long time horizon, ample income to cover expenses, and lack of need for liquidity or cash flow indicate an above-average ability to assume risk. His concentration in U.S. small-capitalization stocks and his desire for high returns indicate substantial willingness to assume risk.

B. *Return:* Stephenson's financial circumstances (long time horizon, sizable asset base, ample income, and low liquidity needs) and his risk tolerance warrant an above-average total return objective. His expressed desire for a return 10 percentage points above the average return on U.S. small capitalization stocks, however, is unrealistic. The portfolio manager should counsel Stephenson on what level of returns to reasonably expect from the financial markets over long periods of time and to define an achievable return objective.

12. Foothill College Endowment Fund

Underline the word at right that best describes the client's:

A. *Risk tolerance*	Below average	<u>Above average</u> Explanation in 2A below	
B. *Liquidity requirement*	Significant	<u>Not significant</u> Budgeted support at 4% × $1 billion exceeds scholarship needs of $39.5 million	
C. *Time horizon*		<u>Single stage</u>	Multistage
D. *Overall time horizon*	Short to intermediate term	<u>Long term</u> Provide support in perpetuity	
E. *Tax concerns*	Significant	<u>Not significant</u> Tax-exempt	

Discuss appropriate client objectives:

A. *Risk:* The endowment fund, with a large asset base and very long time horizon, has an above-average risk tolerance.

B. *Return:* An estimate for the endowment's required annual return is the sum of the spending rate (4 percent) plus the expected annual college tuition inflation rate (3 percent) for a total of 7 percent.

The endowment's objective is to maintain the long-term purchasing power of its assets while providing a stable flow of funds for scholarships.

13. Vincenzo Donadoni

Underline the word at right that best describes the client's:

A. *Willingness to accept risk*	Below average	<u>Above average</u> Explanation in 2A below	
B. *Ability to accept risk*	Below average Explanation in 2A below	<u>Above average</u>	
C. *Risk tolerance*	Below average Explanation in 2A below	<u>Above average</u>	
D. *Liquidity requirement*	<u>Significant</u> CHF 1.5 million needed now CHF 2 million due in nine months	Not significant	

E. *Time horizon*	Single stage	<u>Multistage</u> *Three stages:* First nine months Next 20 to 30 years Life of trust
F. *Overall time horizon*	Short to intermediate term	<u>Long term</u> Overall time horizon is approximately 20 to 30 years

Discuss appropriate client objectives:

A. *Risk:* Donadoni has an above-average risk tolerance based on both his willingness and ability to accept above-average risk. He is a risk taker with a long time horizon, a relatively low need for income, and a large asset base.

B. *Return:* To meet his long-term goal of a leaving a CHF 15.0 million trust fund for his three children, Donadoni must also achieve growth of his current assets. In accordance with his above-average risk tolerance and his goal of leaving the trust, Donadoni should adopt an above-average total real return objective.

Donadoni has a minimal need for additional cash flow given his current expenses, income, and asset base: $(250,000 - 125,000)/(13 \text{ million} - 1.5 \text{ million}) = 1.1\%$. In nine months, his need will grow due to inflation of his expenses, his reduction in income, and his reduced asset base: $(250,000 - 0)/(13 \text{ million} - 1.5 \text{ million} - 2 \text{ million in taxes}) = 2.6\%$ return. As a long-run average, a 2.6 percent real return should be achievable.

4⅝ 4¹¹⁄₁₆ ⅝

5½ 5½ — ⅝

5½ 2¹³⁄₁₆ — ⅛

20⅝ 21³⁄₁₆ — ⅞

17⅜ 18⅛ + ⅞

6½ 6½ — ½

7¼ 3¹⁷⁄₃₂ — ⅛

15⁄16

1 9⁄16 ⅝

1¹⁵⁄₃₂ 9⁄16

7¹⁵⁄₁₆ 7¹³⁄₁₆ 7¹⁵⁄₁₆

2⅝ 2¹¹⁄₃₂ 2½ +

2¾ 2¼ 2¼

6⅛ 12¹⁄₁₆ 11³⁄₈ 11¾ +

87 33¾ 33 33¹⁄₁₆ —

502 25⅝ 24⁹⁄₁₆ 25⅜ +

833 12 11⅝ 11⁷⁄₈ +

16 10½ 10½ 10⅝ —

78 15⅞ 15¹³⁄₁₆ 15⅞

4608 9¹⁄₁₆ 8¼ 8⅞ +

430 11¼ 10⅝ 10⅝

GLOSSARY

Abnormal rate of return The amount by which a security's actual return differs from its expected rate of return which is based on the market's rate of return and the security's relationship with the market.

Abnormal return Return on a stock beyond what would be predicted by market movements alone. Cumulative abnormal return (CAR) is the total abnormal return for the period surrounding an announcement or the release of information.

Absolute priority rule The hierarchy whereby claims are satisfied in corporate liquidation.

Accounting A detailed report to the trust beneficiaries by a trustee of his stewardship, also used to discharge the trustee.

Accounting earnings Earnings of a firm as reported on its income statement.

Accounting profit Total revenues minus total explicit costs.

Accounting Standards Board (ASB) The Accounting Standards Board issues Financial Reporting Standards (FRSs) for the United Kingdom. It took over the task of setting accounting standards from the Accounting Standards Committee in 1990.

Accounts payable A liability that results from the purchase of goods or services on open account, that is, without a signed note payable.

Accounts receivable Amounts owed to a company by customers as a result of delivering goods or services and extending credit in the ordinary course of business. Also referred to as *trade receivables*.

Accrual accounting The system of recording financial transactions as they come into existence as a legally enforceable claim, rather than when they settle.

Accrued expenses payable Incurred costs or expenses that have not been paid. Also referred to as *accruals*.

Accrued interest Interest earned but not yet due and payable. This is equal to the next coupon to be paid on a bond multiplied by the time elapsed since the last payment date and divided by the total coupon period. Exact conventions differ across bond markets.

Accumulate Wall Street expression for buying on a large scale over time, typically by an institution. "Accumulation" of a stock is said to occur if a number of institutions are gradually adding to their holdings.

Accumulated other comprehensive income Cumulative gains or losses reported in shareholders' equity that arise from changes in the fair value of available-for-sale securities, from the effects of changes in foreign-currency exchange rates on consolidated foreign-currency financial statements, from certain gains and losses on financial derivatives and from adjustments for under-funded pension plans.

Acquisition The purchase of an entire company or a controlling interest in a company.

Active management Attempts to achieve portfolio returns more than commensurate with risk, either by forecasting broad market trends or by identifying particular mispriced sectors of a market or securities in a market.

Active portfolio In the context of the Treynor-Black model, the portfolio formed by mixing analyzed stocks of perceived nonzero alpha values. This portfolio is ultimately mixed with the passive market index portfolio.

Actual change in cash and equivalents A term used on the cash flow analysis statement that consists of the change in cash and cash equivalents between reporting periods.

Additional information Information that is required or recommended under the GIPS standards and is not considered as "supplemental information" for the purposes of compliance.

Additions Assets transferred to a trust after the initial funding.

Adjustable-rate mortgage A mortgage whose interest rate varies according to some specified measure of the current market interest rate.

Adjusted operating cash flow Reported operating cash flow adjusted for the reclassification of selected nonoperating items and for nonrecurring items of operating cash flow. See also *sustainable operating cash flow.*

Adjusted EBITDA Conventional earnings before interest, taxes, depreciation, and amortization (EBITDA) with additional adjustments for other noncash or nonrecurring items of revenue, expense, gain, and loss.

Administrative fees All fees other than the trading expenses and the investment management fee. Administrative fees include custody fees, accounting fees, consulting fees, legal fees, performance measurement fees, or other related fees. These administrative fees are typically outside the control of the investment management firm and are not included in either the gross-of-fees return or the net-of-fees return. However, there are some markets and investment vehicles where administrative fees are controlled by the firm.

Adverse selection The likelihood that individuals who seek to borrow money may use the funds that they receive for unworthy, high-risk projects.

Agency conflict An ethical problem that can arise any time one person (i.e., agent) is hired to perform a service or act in the interest of another (i.e., principal).

Agency problem Conflicts of interest among stockholders, bondholders, and managers.

Agency trade A trade in which a broker acts as an agent only, not taking a position on the opposite side of the trade.

Aggregate demand (1) The relationship between the quantity of real GDP demanded and the price level. (2) The total of all planned expenditures for the entire economy.

Aggregate production function The relationship between the quantity of real GDP supplied and the quantities of labor and capital and the state of technology.

Aggressive Implies a concentrated portfolio holding smaller capitalization stocks than the general market, often with higher price/earnings and lower yields, together with low reserves. Often implies unusual volatility.

Aggressive cost capitalization Cost capitalization that stretches the flexibility of generally accepted accounting principles beyond its intended limits, resulting in reporting as assets items that should have been expensed.

AICPA The American Institute of Certified Public Accountants. The AICPA is the national association of CPAs in the United States.

AIMR (1) The Association for Investment Management and Research (AIMR®) awards the CFA® certification and sets professional standards that must be applied by its members worldwide. (2) A standard performance presentation system. For information call 804-980-3547 or go to *http://www.aimr.org*.

Allocative efficiency A situation in which we cannot produce more of any good without giving up some of another good that we value more highly.

Alpha The abnormal rate of return on a security in excess of what would be predicted by an equilibrium model like CAPM or APT.

Alphabet stock *See tracking stock*.

Alternative investments Hedge funds, venture capital pools, options and other derivatives, real estate, and other non-stock or -bond market securities.

American Depositary Receipt (ADR) A certificate of ownership issued by a U.S. bank to promote local trading in a foreign stock. The U.S. bank holds the foreign shares and issues ADRs against them.

American option An option contract that can be exercised at any time until its expiration date.

American terms With reference to U.S. dollar exchange rate quotations, the U.S. dollar price of a unit of another currency.

Amortizing swap An interest rate swap with a decreasing notional principal amount.

Anomalies (1) Security price relationships that appear to contradict a well-regarded hypothesis; in this case, the efficient market hypothesis. (2) Patterns of returns that seem to contradict the efficient market hypothesis.

Antitrust law A law that regulates and prohibits certain kinds of market behavior, such as monopoly and monopolistic practices.

Antitrust legislation Laws that restrict the formation of monopolies and regulate certain anticompetitive business practices.

Appraisal ratio The signal-to-noise ratio of an analyst's forecasts. The ratio of alpha to residual standard deviation.

Appreciation An increase in the exchange value of one nation's currency in terms of the currency of another nation.

Arbitrage The simultaneous purchase of an undervalued asset or portfolio and sale of an overvalued but equivalent asset or portfolio, in order to obtain a riskless profit on the price differential. Taking advantage of a market inefficiency in a risk-free manner.

Arbitrage pricing theory An asset pricing theory that is derived from a factor model, using diversification and arbitrage arguments. The theory describes the relationship between expected returns on securities, given that there are no opportunities to create wealth through risk-free arbitrage investments.

Arbitrage pricing theory (APT) A theory that posits that the expected return to a financial asset can be described by its relationship with several common risk factors. The multifactor APT can be contrasted with the single-factor CAPM.

Arithmetic mean (AM) A measure of mean annual rates of return equal to the sum of annual holding period rates of return divided by the number of years.

Ask price The price at which a market maker is willing to sell a security (also called *offer price*).

Asset allocation Dividing of investment funds among several asset classes to achieve diversification.

Asset allocation decision Choosing among broad asset classes such as stocks versus bonds.

Asset class Securities that have similar characteristics, attributes, and risk/return relationships.

Assets Amounts owned; all items to which a business or household holds legal claim.

Assets under management (AUM) The total market value of the assets managed by an investment firm.

Asset turnover (ATO) The annual sales generated by each dollar of assets (sales/assets).

Asymmetric information Possession of information by one party in a financial transaction but not by the other party.

At-the-money option An option for which the strike (or exercise) price is close to (at) the current market price of the underlying asset.

Auction market A market where all traders in a good meet at one place to buy or sell an asset. The NYSE is an example.

Autonomous expenditure The sum of those components of aggregate planned expenditure that are not influenced by real GDP. Autonomous expenditure equals investment, government purchases, exports, and the autonomous parts of consumption expenditure and imports.

Available-for-sale security A default classification for an investment in a debt or equity security that is not classified as either a held-to-maturity security or a trading security.

Average cost pricing rule A rule that sets price to cover cost including normal profit, which means setting the price equal to average total cost.

Average tax rate The total tax payment divided by total income. It is the proportion of total income paid in taxes.

BA *Banker's acceptance.*

Backwardation Condition in which *spot price* of commodity exceeds price of *future* (cf. *contango*).

Balanced budget A government budget in which tax revenues and expenditures are equal.

Balanced fund A mutual fund with, generally, a three-part investment objective: (1) to conserve the investor's principal, (2) to pay current income, and (3) to increase both principal and income. The fund aims to achieve this by owning a mixture of bonds, preferred stocks, and common stocks.

Balance of payments A system of accounts that measures transactions of goods, services, income, and financial assets between domestic households, businesses, and governments and residents of the rest of the world during a specific time period.

Balance of payments accounts A country's record of international trading, borrowing, and lending.

Balance sheet A financial statement that shows what assets the firm controls at a fixed point in time and how it has financed these assets.

Balloon payment Large final payment (e.g., when a loan is repaid in installments).

Bank overdraft Checks presented for payment that exceed a company's bank balance. A book overdraft becomes a bank overdraft when outstanding checks are presented for payment.

Barriers to entry Legal or natural constraints that protect a firm from potential competitors.

Barter The direct exchange of goods and services for other goods and services without the use of money.

Base year The year that is chosen as the point of reference for comparison of prices in other years.

Basis point A hundredth of a percent; thus 75 basis points equals three-quarters of 1 percentage point.

Basis swap An interest rate swap involving two floating rates.

Bear market Widespread decline in security prices (cf. *bull market*).

Behavioral finance (1) Involves the analysis of various psychological traits of individuals and how these traits affect how they act as investors, analysts, and portfolio managers. (2) Branch of finance that stresses aspects of investor irrationality.

Benchmark A standard measurement used to evaluate the performance of a portfolio. The benchmark may be some passive index or the aggregate performance on a universe of comparable portfolios (see *composite*).

Benchmark bond A bond representative of current market conditions and used for performance comparison.

Benchmark portfolio A comparison standard of risk and assets included in the policy statement and similar to the investor's risk preference and investment needs, which can be used to evaluate the investment performance of the portfolio manager.

Beta A standardized measure of systematic risk based upon an asset's covariance with the market portfolio.

Bid–asked spread The difference between a dealer's bid and asked price.

Bid–ask spread The difference between the quoted ask and the bid prices.

Bidder The acquiring firm.

Bid price The price at which a dealer is willing to purchase a security.

Big Board Colloquial term for the New York Stock Exchange.

Bilateral arbitrage With reference to currencies, an arbitrage involving two currencies only.

Binomial model An option valuation model predicated on the assumption that stock prices can move to only two values over any short time period.

Black-Scholes formula   An equation to value a call option that uses the stock price, the exercise price, the risk-free interest rate, the time to maturity, and the standard deviation of the stock return.

Black-Scholes option pricing model   A valuation equation that assumes the price of the underlying asset changes continuously through the option's expiration date by a statistical process known as *geometric Brownian motion*.

Black-Scholes or Black-Scholes-Merton formula   A standard option pricing formula derived by F. Black and M. Scholes and also by R. Merton.

Block   A large stock transaction (e.g., ten thousand shares or more).

Blue chip   A large, stable, well-known, widely held, seasoned company with a strong financial position, usually paying a reasonable dividend.

Boilerplate   Standard terms and conditions, e.g., in a debt contract.

Bond   A security issued by a borrower that obligates the issuer to make specified payments to the holder over a specific period. A *coupon bond* obligates the issuer to make interest payments called coupon payments over the life of the bond, then to repay the *face value* at maturity.

Bond indenture   The contract between the issuer and the bondholder.

Bond rating   Rating of the likelihood of bond's default.

Book entry   Registered ownership of stock without issue of stock certificate.

Book overdraft   A negative cash balance for reporting purposes consisting of the excess of outstanding checks over a stated bank cash balance.

Books   A shorthand reference to shareholder as opposed to income tax financial information.

Book-to-market effect   The tendency for stocks of firms with high ratios of book-to-market value to generate abnormal returns.

Book value   An accounting measure describing the net worth of common equity according to a firm's balance sheet.

Bottom-up   Developing a portfolio by focusing on individual securities.

Bourse   A French term often used to refer to a stock market.

Broker   An agent who executes orders to buy or sell securities on behalf of a client in exchange for a commission.

Brokered market   A market where an intermediary (a broker) offers search services to buyers and sellers.

Budget constraint   All of the possible combinations of goods that can be purchased (at fixed prices) with a specific budget.

Budget deficit   The amount by which government spending exceeds government revenues.

Bullet payment   Single final payment, e.g., of a loan (in contrast to payment in installments).

Bull market   Widespread rise in security prices (cf. *bear market*).

Bund   Long-term German government *bond.*

Business cycle   The periodic but irregular up-and-down movement in production.

Business risk   The variability of operating income arising from the characteristics of the firm's industry. Two sources of business risk are sales variability and operating leverage.

Buy-and-hold strategy   A passive portfolio management strategy in which securities (bonds or stocks) are bought and held to maturity.

Buyback   Repurchase agreement.

Cable   The exchange rate between U.S. dollars and sterling.

Callable bond   A bond that the issuer may repurchase at a given price in some specified period.

Call auction   See *fixing*.

Call option   A contract that gives its holder the right to buy an asset, typically a financial instrument, at a specified price through a specified date.

Call protection   An initial period during which a callable bond may not be called.

Call provision   Provision that allows an issuer to buy back the *bond* issue at a stated price.

Call provisions   Specifies when and how a firm can issue a call for bonds outstanding prior to their maturity.

Cap agreement   A contract that on each settlement date pays the holder the greater of the difference between the reference rate and the cap rate or zero; it is equivalent to a series of call options at the reference rate.

Capital   The tools, equipment, buildings, and other constructions that businesses now use to produce goods and services.

Capital account   A component of the balance of payments that reflects unrequited (or unilateral) transfers corresponding to capital flows entailing no compensation (in the form of goods, services, or assets). Examples include investment capital given (without future repayment) in favor of poor countries, debt forgiveness, and expropriation losses.

Capital accumulation   The growth of capital resources.

Capital allocation decision   Allocation of invested funds between risk-free assets versus the risky portfolio.

Capital allocation line (CAL) A graph showing all feasible risk–return combinations of a risky and risk-free asset.

Capital appreciation A return objective in which the investor seeks to increase the portfolio value, primarily through capital gains, over time to meet a future need rather than dividend yield.

Capital asset pricing model (CAPM) An equilibrium theory that relates the expected return of an asset to its market risk (see *beta*).

Capital budget List of planned investment projects, usually prepared annually.

Capital budgeting A project analysis in which a project's receipts and outlays are valued over a project's life.

Capital consumption The decrease in the capital stock that results from wear and tear and obsolescence.

Capital controls Legal restrictions on the ability of a nation's residents to hold and trade assets denominated in foreign currencies.

Capital Employed (Real Estate) The denominator of the return expressions, defined as the "weighted-average equity" (weighted-average capital) during the measurement period. Capital employed should not include any income or capital return accrued *during* the measurement period. Beginning capital is adjusted by weighting the cash flows (contributions and distributions) that occurred during the period. Cash flows are typically weighted based on the actual days the flows are in or out of the portfolio. Other weighting methods are acceptable; however, once a methodology is chosen, it should be consistently applied.

Capital expenditures Expenditures made in the purchase of long-term productive assets, such as property, plant, and equipment, whose cost is amortized against income in future periods.

Capital gain The positive difference between the purchase price and the sale price of an asset. If a share of stock is bought for $5 and then sold for $15, the capital gain is $10.

Capital gains The amount by which the sale price of a security exceeds the purchase price.

Capital goods Producer durables; nonconsumable goods that firms use to make other goods.

Capitalization Long-term debt plus *preferred stock* plus *net worth*.

Capitalized interest Interest incurred during the construction period on monies invested in assets under construction that is added to the cost of the assets.

Capitalized operating cost Expenditure that is reported as an asset to be amortized against future revenue.

Capital lease A lease that transfers, in an economic sense, the risks and rewards of ownership to the lessee without transferring title. Lease payments made are comprised of interest and principal. Property held under a capital-lease agreement is accounted for as an asset. This cost is amortized over the relevant useful life.

Capital loss The negative difference between the purchase price and the sale price of an asset.

Capital market Financial market (particularly the market for long-term securities).

Capital market instruments Fixed-income or equity investments that trade in the secondary market.

Capital market line (CML) The line from the intercept point that represents the risk-free rate tangent to the original efficient frontier; it becomes the new efficient frontier since investments on this line dominate all the portfolios on the original Markowitz efficient frontier.

Capital markets Includes longer-term, relatively riskier securities.

Capital rationing Shortage of funds that forces a company to choose between worthwhile projects.

Capital stock The total quantity of plant, equipment, buildings, and inventories.

Capital structure Mix of different securities issued by a firm.

CAPM Capital asset pricing model.

Capture hypothesis A theory of regulatory behavior that predicts that the regulators will eventually be captured by the special interests of the industry being regulated.

Capture theory A theory of regulation that states that the regulations are supplied to satisfy the demand of producers to maximize producer surplus—to maximize economic profit.

Carve-out Public offering of shares in a subsidiary.

Cash Currency, coin, and funds on deposit that are available for immediate withdrawal without restriction. Money orders, certified checks, cashier's checks, personal checks, and bank drafts are also considered cash.

Cash after operations A Uniform Credit Analysis®– defined cash flow amount that consists of gross cash profit less cash operating expense.

Cash and carry Purchase of a security and simultaneous sale of a *future*, with the balance being financed with a loan or *repo*.

Cash cost of revenue A term used on the cash flow analysis statement that consists of cash payments to vendors and other suppliers, including employees, for the purchase of products and the procurement of services provided to customers.

Cash earnings Net income plus goodwill amortization.

Cash equivalents Short-term and highly liquid investments readily convertible into known amounts of cash and close enough to maturity that there is insignificant risk of changes in value from interest rate movements.

Cash flow An unspecified term that may refer to either total cash flow or operating cash flow. In most cases, use of the term refers to operating cash flow.

Cash flow after debt service A term used on the cash flow analysis statement that consists of cash flow from operations less required principal payments on long-term debt capital leases.

Cash flow after dividends A term used on the cash flow analysis statement that consists of cash flow after debt service less dividends paid.

Cash flow analysis The search for the fundamental drivers that underlie a company's cash flow stream and affect its sustainability.

Cash flow analysis statement A cash flow statement designed to facilitate analysis by creditors, equity investors, and analysts that provides multiple partitions of the overall change in cash and cash equivalents and highlights sustainable and nonrecurring sources and uses of cash. An example of the cash flow analysis statement is provided in Exhibit 9.4.

Cash flow available for debt service A term used on the cash flow analysis statement that consists of core operating cash flow plus other cash income minus other cash expense and minus income taxes paid. Cash flow available for debt service is cash flow available for the payment of interest and required principal payments on debt and capital leases.

Cash flow drivers The fundamental factors of growth and changes in profitability and efficiency that serve to increase and decrease core operating cash flow.

Cash flow from operations A term used on the cash flow analysis statement that consists of cash flow available for debt service less total interest paid. The term also is used to refer to cash provided or used by operating activities and operating cash flow as those terms are defined by generally accepted accounting principles.

Cash flow impact The measured effects of cash flow drivers of growth and changes in profitability and efficiency on core operating cash flow.

Cash flow tracking Determining whether cash flows are associated with nonrecurring items of revenue, gain, expense, and loss. The timing of the cash flows is also investigated.

Cash from revenue A term used on the cash flow analysis statement that consists of cash collections from customers for product sales and services provided.

Cash from sales A Uniform Credit Analysis®–defined cash flow amount that consists of gross collections from customers for sales made and services provided.

Cash gross margin A term used on the cash flow analysis statement that consists of cash from revenue minus cash cost of revenue.

Cash operating expense A Uniform Credit Analysis®–defined cash flow amount that consists of cash paid for sales and marketing, general and administrative, and research and development expenditures. The term is defined the same way on the cash flow analysis statement.

Cash production costs A Uniform Credit Analysis®–defined cash flow amount that consists of payments made for inventory purchased or manufactured and services provided.

Cash settlement A procedure for settling futures contracts in which the cash difference between the futures price and the spot price is paid instead of physical delivery.

Cash surrender value of life insurance That portion of a life insurance premium that will be returned to the policyholder in the event the policy is canceled.

Caution One of the three components of the standard of prudence governing trustees; avoidance of undue risk and attentiveness to the protection of trust property.

CD Certificate of deposit.

Central bank A bank's bank and a public authority that regulates a nation's depository institutions and controls the quantity of money.

CEO Chief executive officer.

Certificate of deposit An unsecured evidence of indebtedness of a bank, which may be sold to others. Usually with a face value of $100,000 or more and bearing interest below the prime rate.

Ceteris paribus Other things being equal—all other relevant things remaining the same.

CFTC Commodity Futures Trading Commission.

CFO Chief financial officer.

Chaebol A Korean conglomerate.

Change in accumulated other comprehensive income A term used on the cash flow analysis statement that refers to the change in accumulated other comprehensive income between reporting periods.

Change in cash and equivalents after external financing A term used on the cash flow analysis statement that refers to the change in cash before external financing plus cash provided from external financing minus cash used in external financing adjusted for the change in accumulated other comprehensive income.

Change in cash before external financing A term used on the cash flow analysis statement that consists of cash flow after dividends minus cash paid for investments, capital expenditures, and intangibles.

Chapter 11 Bankruptcy procedure designed to reorganize and rehabilitate defaulting firm.

Chapter 7 Bankruptcy procedure whereby a debtor's assets are sold and the proceeds are used to repay creditors.

Characteristic line Regression line that indicates the systematic risk (beta) of a risky asset.

CHIPS Clearinghouse Interbank Payments System.

Classical growth theory A theory of economic growth based on the view that real GDP growth is temporary and that when real GDP per person increases above subsistence level, a population explosion brings real GDP back to subsistence level.

Clayton Act A federal antitrust law passed in 1914. Section 7, which is most relevant to mergers and acquisitions, prohibits the acquisition of stock and assets of a company when the effect is to lessen competition.

Clearinghouse An organization that settles and guarantees trades in some financial markets.

Closed-end fund An investment company with a fixed number of shares. New shares cannot be issued and the old shares cannot be redeemed. Shares are traded in the marketplace, and their value may differ from the underlying net asset value of the fund.

CMOs Collateralized mortgage obligations.

COD Cash on delivery.

Coefficient of variation (CV) A measure of relative variability that indicates risk per unit of return. It is equal to: standard deviation divided by the mean value. When used in investments, it is equal to: standard deviation of returns divided by the expected rate of return.

Collar (1) An upper and lower limit on the interest rate on a floating-rate note. (2) An options strategy that brackets the value of a portfolio between two bounds.

Collateral A specific asset pledged against possible default on a bond. Mortgage bonds are backed by claims on property. Collateral trust bonds are backed by claims on other securities. Equipment obligation bonds are backed by claims on equipment.

Collateralized mortgage obligation (CMO) A mortgage pass-through security that partitions cash flows from underlying mortgages into classes called tranches that receive principal payments according to stipulated rules.

Collateral trust bonds A mortgage bond wherein the assets backing the bond are financial assets like stocks and bonds.

Commercial bank A firm that is licensed by the Comptroller of the Currency in the U.S. Treasury or by a state agency to receive deposits and make loans.

Commercial paper Short-term unsecured debt issued by large corporations.

Commingled fund Typically, an investment pool run by a bank, in which participation is represented by accounting units rather than shares.

Commission recapture Credit for brokerage generated is then applied to such services as custody and appraisal.

Commitment fee Fee charged by bank on an unused *line of credit.*

Common stock Equities, or equity securities, issued as ownership shares in a publicly held corporation. Shareholders have voting rights and may receive dividends based on their proportionate ownership.

Company cost of capital The expected return on a portfolio of all the firm's securities.

Comparative advantage The ability to produce a good or service at a lower opportunity cost than other producers.

Compensating balance Non-interest-bearing demand deposits to compensate banks for bank loans or services.

Competitive environment The level of intensity of competition among firms in an industry, determined by an examination of five competitive forces.

Competitive market A market that has many buyers and many sellers, so no single buyer or seller can influence the price.

Competitive strategy The search by a firm for a favorable competitive position within an industry within the known competitive environment.

Complete portfolio The entire portfolio, including risky and risk-free assets.

Composite A universe of portfolios with similar investment objectives.

Composition Voluntary agreement to reduce payments on a firm's debt.

Compound interest Reinvestment of each interest payment on money invested to earn more interest (cf. *simple interest*).

Concentration ratio   The percentage of all sales contributed by the leading four or leading eight firms in an industry; sometimes called the *industry concentration ratio.*

Concentration ratios   Measures of the percentage of total industry revenues accounted for by a certain number of firms, usually the top four or eight.

Conglomerate   A combination of unrelated firms.

Conglomerate merger   *Merger* between two companies in unrelated businesses (cf. *horizontal merger, vertical merger*).

Constant growth model   A form of the dividend discount model that assumes dividends will grow at a constant rate.

Consumer Price Index (CPI)   An index that measures the average of the prices paid by urban consumers for a fixed "basket" of the consumer goods and services.

Consumption   The use of goods and services for personal satisfaction. Can also be viewed as spending on new goods and services out of a household's current income. Whatever is not consumed is saved. Consumption includes such things as buying food and going to a concert.

Consumption expenditure   The total payment for consumer goods and services.

Consumption function   The relationship between amount consumed and disposable income. A consumption function tells us how much people plan to consume at various levels of disposable income.

Consumption goods   Goods bought by households to use up, such as food and movies.

Contango   A situation in a futures market where the current contract price is greater than the current spot price for the underlying asset.

Contestable market   A market in which firms can enter and leave so easily that firms in the market face competition from potential entrants.

Continuous compounding   Interest compounded continuously rather than at fixed intervals.

Contraction   A business fluctuation during which the pace of national economic activity is slowing down.

Contract price   The transaction price specified in a forward or futures contract.

Controller   Officer responsible for budgeting, accounting, and auditing in a firm (cf. *treasurer*).

Convenience yield   An adjustment made to the theoretical forward or futures contract delivery price to account for the preference that consumers have for holding spot positions in the underlying asset.

Conversion factors   The adjustments made to Treasury bond futures contract terms to allow for the delivery of an instrument other than the standardized underlying asset.

Conversion parity price   The price at which common stock can be obtained by surrendering the convertible instrument at par value.

Conversion premium   The excess of the market value of the convertible security over its equity value if immediately converted into common stock. Typically expressed as a percentage of the equity value.

Conversion price   *Par value* of a *convertible bond* divided by the number of shares into which it may be exchanged.

Conversion ratio   The number of shares of common stock for which a convertible security may be exchanged.

Conversion value   The value of the convertible security if converted into common stock at the stock's current market price.

Convertible   A bond or preferred stock that offers the investor the right to convert his holding into common stock under set terms.

Convertible bond   A bond with an option allowing the bondholder to exchange the bond for a specified number of shares of common stock in the firm. A *conversion ratio* specifies the number of shares. The *market conversion price* is the current value of the shares for which the bond may be exchanged. The *conversion premium* is the excess of the bond's value over the conversion price.

Convexity   A measure of the degree to which a bond's price-yield curve departs from a straight line. This characteristic affects estimates of a bond's price volatility for a given change in yields.

Core operating cash flow   A term used on the cash flow analysis statement that consists of cash gross margin minus cash operating expense. Core operating cash flow is cash flow generated by core or central operations, before income taxes, other cash income and interest paid.

Corporate bonds   Long-term debt issued by private corporations typically paying semiannual coupons and returning the face value of the bond at maturity.

Corporate trustee   A bank or trust company having federal or state authority to serve as a trustee.

Corporation   A legal entity that may conduct business in its own name just as an individual does; the owners of a corporation, called shareholders, own shares of the firm's profits and enjoy the protection of limited liability.

Correlation   See *covariance.*

Correlation coefficient A statistic in which the covariance is scaled to a value between minus one (perfect negative correlation) and plus one (perfect positive correlation).

Cost of capital Opportunity cost of capital.

Cost of carry The cost associated with holding some asset, including financing, storage, and insurance costs. Any yield received on the asset is treated as a negative carrying cost.

Cost-of-service regulation Regulation based on allowing prices to reflect only the actual cost of production and no monopoly profits.

Counterparty Party on the other side of a *derivative* contract.

Country risk Uncertainty due to the possibility of major political or economic change in the country where an investment is located. Also called *political risk*.

Coupon The interest rate on a bond, expressed as a percentage of its face (not market) value. At one time bonds (and indeed stocks) contained coupons resembling postage stamps, which one "clipped" or cut periodically and presented for payment of interest (or dividends).

Coupon rate A bond's interest payments per dollar of par value.

Covariance A measure of the degree to which returns on two risky assets move in tandem. A positive covariance means that asset returns move together. A negative covariance means they vary inversely.

Covenant Clause in a loan agreement.

Covered call A trading strategy in which a call option is sold as a supplement to a long position in an underlying asset or portfolio of assets.

Covered interest arbitrage A trading strategy involving borrowing money in one country and lending it to another designed to exploit price deviations from the interest rate parity model.

Covered option *Option* position with an offsetting position in the underlying asset.

Creative cash flow reporting Any and all steps used to alter operating cash flow and, in the process, provide a more positive signal about a firm's sustainable cash-generating ability. Creative cash flow reporting may entail steps taken within the boundaries of generally accepted accounting principles, beyond those boundaries, or by the inclusion of nonrecurring amounts in operating cash flow.

Creative response Behavior on the part of a firm that allows it to comply with the letter of the law but violates the spirit, significantly lessening the law's effects.

Credit analysis An active bond portfolio management strategy designed to identify bonds that are expected to experience changes in rating. This strategy is critical when investing in high-yield bonds.

Credit derivative Contract for *hedging* against loan default or changes in credit risk (see *default swap*).

Credit enhancement Contract for *hedging* against loan default or changes in credit risk (see *default swap*).

Credit risk See Default risk.

Credit scoring A procedure for assigning scores to borrowers on the basis of the risk of default.

Cross-rate The exchange rate between two currencies, derived from their exchange rates with a third currency.

Crowding-out effect The tendency for a government budget deficit to decrease in investment.

Cum dividend With dividend.

Cumulative abnormal return See *abnormal return*.

Cumulative preferred stock Stock that takes priority over *common stock* in regard to dividend payments. Dividends may not be paid on the common stock until all past *dividends* on the *preferred stock* have been paid.

Currency The bills and coins that we use today.

Currency appreciation The rise in the value of one currency in terms of another currency.

Currency depreciation The fall in the value of one currency in terms of another currency.

Currency exposure The sensitivity of the asset return, measured in the investor's domestic currency, to a movement in the exchange rate.

Currency swap A contract to exchange streams of fixed cash flows denominated in two different currencies.

Current account A category of balance of payments transactions that measures the exchange of merchandise, the exchange of services, and unilateral transfers.

Current asset Asset that will normally be turned into cash within a year.

Current income A return objective in which the investor seeks to generate income rather than capital gains; generally a goal of an investor who wants to supplement earnings with income to meet living expenses.

Current liability Liability that will normally be repaid within a year.

Current ratio A ratio representing the ability of the firm to pay off its current liabilities by liquidating current assets (current assets/current liabilities).

Current yield A bond's annual coupon payment divided by its price. Differs from yield to maturity.

Custodians Agents who hold property in safekeeping for others, usually without inherent investment management responsibility.

Customer acquisition costs Initial direct costs incurred in adding to a company's customer base, including direct-response advertising, commissions, and related administrative costs. When capitalized, prospective customer-related revenues must be expected to exceed amounts capitalized. Depending on the industry, such costs may have other names, including subscriber acquisition costs and policy acquisition costs.

Cyclical company A firm whose earnings rise and fall with general economic activity.

Cyclical developments Changes in business activity that are caused by moves in the overall economy between expansion and recession.

Cyclical industries Industries with above-average sensitivity to the state of the economy.

Cyclicals Some industries are perennially subject to the vagaries of the business cycle: mining, steel, construction, automobiles, chemicals, machine tools, and the like. It is impossible to get away from the cyclical effect in business, just as there is always alternation between good and bad weather, so a cyclical company will have an irregular earnings pattern, and usually an irregular stock price pattern too.

Cyclical stock A stock with a high beta; its gains typically exceed those of a rising market and its losses typically exceed those of a falling market.

Cyclical surplus or deficit The actual surplus or deficit minus the structural surplus or deficit.

Data mining (data snooping) Excessive search to find interesting (but probably coincidental) behavior in a body of data.

DCF Discounted cash flow.

DDM Dividend discount model.

Dealer An agent that buys and sells securities as a principal (for its own account) rather than as a broker for clients. A dealer may function, at different times, as a broker or as a dealer. Sometimes called a *market maker*.

Debenture Unsecured *bond*.

Debentures Bonds that promise payments of interest and principal but pledge no specific assets. Holders have first claim on the issuer's income and unpledged assets. Also known as *unsecured bonds*.

Debt issue costs The cost of issuing debt, including appraisal and recording fees, and commitment fees paid separately to a lender.

Decision tree Method of representing alternative sequential decisions and the possible outcomes from these decisions.

Decline stage The fourth and final stage of a company's life cycle during which revenue declines and earnings turn to losses. Depending on the amount of noncash expenses reported, such as depreciation and amortization expense, operating cash flow may remain positive until very late in the decline stage.

Default premium A differential in promised yield that compensates the investor for the risk inherent in purchasing a corporate bond that entails some risk of default.

Default risk The risk that an issuer will be unable to make interest and principal payments on time.

Default swap *Credit derivative* in which one party makes fixed payments while the payments by the other party depend on the occurrence of a loan default.

Defeasance Practice whereby the borrower sets aside cash or *bonds* sufficient to service the borrower's debt. Both the borrower's debt and the offsetting cash or bonds are removed from the balance sheet.

Defensive competitive strategy Positioning the firm so that its capabilities provide the best means to deflect the effect of the competitive forces in the industry.

Defensive industries Industries with little sensitivity to the state of the economy.

Defensive stock A stock whose return is not expected to decline as much as that of the overall market during a bear market (a beta less than one).

Deferred revenue Revenue that is collected in advance of being earned and is reported as a liability. Also known as *unearned revenue*.

Deferred tax assets Future tax benefits that result from (1) the origination of a deductible temporary difference, that is, a tax deduction that can be used in a future period, or (2) a loss or tax-credit carryover. These future tax benefits are realized upon the reversal of deductible temporary differences. In addition, realization can occur by the offsetting of a loss carryforward against taxable income or a tax credit carryforward against taxes currently payable.

Deferred tax liabilities Future tax obligations that result from the origination of taxable temporary differences. Upon origination, these temporary difference cause pretax financial income to exceed taxable income. These future tax obligations are paid later when temporary differences reverse, now causing taxable income to exceed pretax book income.

Defined benefit pension plan A pension plan to which the company contributes a certain amount each year and promises to pay employees a specified income after they retire. The benefit size is based on factors such as workers' salary and time of employment.

Defined benefit plan A retirement plan that specifies the amount an employee collects after different periods of employment.

Defined benefit plans Pension plans in which retirement benefits are set according to a fixed formula.

Defined contribution pension plan A pension plan in which worker benefits are determined by the size of employees' contributions to the plan and the returns earned on the fund's investments.

Defined contribution plan A retirement plan with benefits based on the earnings of the contributions made, taking account of the length of employment.

Defined contribution plans Pension plans in which the employer is committed to making contributions according to a fixed formula.

Deflation The situation in which the average of all prices of goods and services in an economy is falling.

Degree of operating leverage Percentage change in profits for a 1% change in sales.

Delta The change in the price of the option with respect to a $1 change in the price of the underlying asset; this is the option's *hedge ratio,* or the number of units of the underlying asset that can be hedged by a single option contract.

Delta hedge A dynamic hedging strategy using options with continuous adjustment of the number of options used, as a function of the delta of the option.

Demand The relationship between the quantity of a good that consumers plan to buy and the price of the good when all other influences on buyers' plans remain the same. It is described by a demand schedule and illustrated by a demand curve.

Demand curve A curve that shows the relationship between the quantity demanded of a good and its price when all other influences on consumers' planned purchases remain the same.

Demand for labor The relationship between the quantity of labor demanded and the real wage rate when all other influences on a firm's hiring plans remain the same.

Demand-pull inflation An inflation that results from an initial increase in aggregate demand.

Dependent variable A variable whose value changes according to changes in the value of one or more independent variables.

Depreciation Reduction in the value of capital goods over a one-year period due to physical wear and tear and also to obsolescence; also called *capital consumption allowance*. Can also be viewed as a decrease in the exchange value of one nation's currency in terms of the currency of another nation.

Depreciation proxy for replacement capital expenditures A term used on the cash flow analysis statement that consists of depreciation and amortization of property, plant, and equipment used in operations and serves as an approximation of the cost of replacing that portion of property, plant, and equipment consumed by operations during a reporting period.

Depression An extremely severe recession.

Deregulation The elimination or phasing out of regulations on economic activity.

Derivatives Securities bearing a contractual relation to some underlying asset or rate. Options, futures, forward, and swap contracts, as well as many forms of bonds, are derivative securities.

Descendants The direct parental line, including children, grandchildren, great-grandchildren, and so on.

Devaluation Deliberate downward adjustment of a currency against its fixed parity.

Diff Differential swap.

Dilution Reduction in shareholders' equity per share or earnings per share that arises from some changes among shareholders' proportionate interests.

Diminishing marginal returns The tendency for the marginal product of an additional unit of a factor of production is less than the marginal product of the previous unit of the factor.

Directed brokerage A manager is asked to direct business to a specified broker, usually to pay for services.

Direct exchange rate The amount of local or domestic currency required to purchase one unit of foreign currency.

Direct Investments (Private Equity) An investment made directly in venture capital or private equity assets (i.e., not via a partnership or fund).

Direct quote For foreign exchange, the number of U.S. dollars needed to buy one unit of a foreign currency (cf. *indirect quote*).

Direct-response advertising Advertising designed to elicit sales to customers who can be shown to have responded specifically to the advertising in the past. Such costs can be capitalized when persuasive historical evidence permits formulation of a reliable estimate of the future revenue that can be obtained from incremental advertising expenditures.

Discontinued operations   Net income and the gain or loss on disposal of a discontinued business segment or separately measured business unit.

Discount   A bond selling at a price below par value due to capital market conditions.

Discounted cash flow (DCF)   Future cash flows multiplied by *discount factors* to obtain *present value.*

Discount factor   *Present value* of $1 received at a stated future date.

Discounting   The conversion of a future amount of money to its present value.

Discount rate   (1) Rate used to calculate the present value of future cash flows. (2) The interest rate at which the Fed stands ready to lend reserves to depository institutions.

Discretionary account   An account of a customer who gives a broker the authority to make buy and sell decisions on the customer's behalf.

Disposable income   Aggregate income minus taxes plus transfer payments.

Dissident   A shareholder, or group of shareholders, who oppose current management and may try to use the proxy process to gain control of the company or to try to get the company to take certain actions, such as payment of certain dividends. Dissidents often try to have their representatives placed on the board of directors.

Diversifiable risk   Risk attributable to firm-specific risk, or nonmarket risk. *Nondiversifiable* risk refers to systematic or market risk.

Diversification   (1) Spreading a portfolio over many investments to avoid excessive exposure to any one source of risk. (2) In mergers and acquisitions, a term that refers to buying companies or assets outside the companies' current lines of business.

Divestiture   The sale of a component of the company, such as a division.

Dividend   Payment by a company to its stockholders.

Dividend discount model (DDM)   A formula stating that the intrinsic value of a firm is the present value of all expected future dividends.

Dividend payout ratio   Percentage of earnings paid out as dividends.

Dividend reinvestment plan (DRIP)   Plan that allows shareholders to reinvest dividends automatically.

Dividends   Portion of a corporation's profits paid to its owners (shareholders).

Dividends paid   A term used on the cash flow analysis statement that refers to cash disbursements for dividends on common and preferred stock.

Dividend yield   Annual dividend divided by share price.

Dow Jones Industrial Average (DJI or DJIA)   A price-weighted average of thirty industrial companies.

Duration   The average maturity of a bond. The longer the duration, the more sensitive will be the price to interest rate changes.

Dynamic hedging   Constant updating of hedge positions as market conditions change.

Early stage   With reference to venture capital financing, the stage associated with moving into operation and before commercial manufacturing and sales have occurred. Includes the start-up and first stages.

Earnings before interest, taxes, depreciation, and amortization (EBITDA)   An earnings-based measure that often serves as a surrogate for cash flow. The measure actually represents working capital provided by operations before interest and taxes.

Earnings before interest and taxes (EBIT)   Net income measured before interest expense and before income tax expense. EBIT has a long history of being used as a basis for measuring fixed-charge coverage.

Earnings management   The practice of using flexibility in accounting rules to improve the apparent profitability of the firm.

Earnings momentum   A strategy in which portfolios are constructed of stocks of firms with rising earnings.

Earnings multiplier model   A technique for estimating the value of a stock issue as a multiple of its future earnings per share.

Earnings retention ratio   Plowback ratio.

Earnings surprise   A company announcement of earnings that differs from analysts' prevailing expectations.

Earnings yield   The ratio of earnings to price, E/P.

EBIT   Earnings before interest and taxes.

EBITDA   Earnings before interest, taxes, depreciation, and amortization.

Economic depreciation   The change in the market value of capital over a given period.

Economic efficiency   A situation that occurs when the firm produces a given output at the least cost.

Economic exposure   Risk that arises from changes in real exchange rates (cf. *transaction exposure, translation exposure*).

Economic growth   (1) Increases in per capita real GDP measured by its rate of change per year. (2) The expansion of production possibilities that results from capital accumulation and technological change.

Economic growth rate   The percentage change in the quantity of goods and services produced from one year to the next.

Economic income Cash flow plus change in *present value*.

Economic model A description of some aspect of the economic world that includes only those features of the world that are needed for the purpose at hand.

Economic profit A firm's total revenue minus its opportunity cost.

Economic profits Total revenues minus total opportunity costs of all inputs used, or the total of all implicit and explicit costs.

Economic rent A payment for the use of any resource over and above its opportunity cost.

Economic rents Profits in excess of the competitive level.

Economic risk As used in currency risk management, the risk that arises when the foreign currency value of a foreign investment reacts systematically to an exchange rate movement.

Economics The social science that studies the choices that individuals, businesses, governments, and entire societies make and how they cope with scarcity and the incentives that influence and reconcile those choices.

Economic theory A generalization that summarizes what we think we understand about the economic choices that people make and the performance of industries and entire economies.

Economic value added (EVA) (1) The spread between ROA and cost of capital multiplied by the capital invested in the firm. It measures the dollar value of the firm's return in excess of its opportunity cost. (2) Internal management performance measure that compares net operating profit to total cost of capital. Indicates how profitable company projects are as a sign of management performance.

Economic welfare A comprehensive measure of the general state of economic well-being.

Economies of scale The reduction of a company's average costs due to increasing output and spreading out fixed costs over higher output levels.

Economies of scope The ability of a firm to utilize one set of inputs to provide a broader range of outputs or services.

Effective duration Direct measure of the interest rate sensitivity of a bond (or any financial instrument) based upon price changes derived from a pricing model.

Efficient frontier The set of all efficient portfolios for various levels of risk.

Efficient market A market in which any relevant information is immediately impounded in asset prices.

Efficient Market Hypothesis Crudely, the belief that since all information about stocks is available, their current market price represents their true value. If this were true, certain investors would not achieve consistently superior results, which they do, and since all information about a chess game is available to both opponents, there should not be consistently superior players. All information is never known, judgment is unevenly distributed, and decision making is imperfectly organized and moved by great tides of emotion.

Efficient portfolio A portfolio that provides the best expected return for a given level of risk.

Effective duration Percentage change in bond price per change in the level of market interest rates.

Effective tax rate The income tax provision divided by income before the income tax provision.

Efficiency The case in which a given level of inputs is used to produce the maximum output possible. Alternatively, the situation in which a given output is produced at minimum cost.

Efficient capital market A market in which security prices rapidly reflect all information about securities.

Efficient diversification The organizing principle of modern portfolio theory, which maintains that any risk-averse investor will search for the highest expected return for any level of portfolio risk.

Efficient frontier The set of portfolios that has the maximum rate of return for every given level of risk, or the minimum risk for every potential rate of return.

Efficient market Market in which security prices reflect information instantaneously.

Efficient portfolio Portfolio that offers the lowest risk (*standard deviation*) for its *expected return* and the highest expected return for its level of risk.

EFT Electronic funds transfer.

Electronic crossing networks Order-driven trading systems in which market orders are anonymously matched at prespecified times at prices determined in the primary market for the system.

Emerging Issues Task Force (EITF) The EITF assists the Financial Accounting Standards Board through the timely identification, discussion, and resolution of financial accounting issues based on existing authoritative literature.

Emerging markets Often, countries so defined by the International Finance Corporation (IFC), based on their per capita income.

Empirical Relying on real-world data in evaluating the usefulness of a model.

Empirical duration   Measures directly the interest rate sensitivity of an asset by examining the percentage price change for an asset in response to a change in yield during a specified period of time.

Employee Retirement Income Security Act (ERISA)   Governs most private pension and benefit plans.

Endogenous growth theory   A theory of economic growth that does not assume that the marginal productivity of capital declines as capital is added.

Endowment funds   Organizations chartered to invest money for specific purposes.

Endowments   The various resources in an economy, including both physical resources and such human resources as ingenuity and management skills.

Entrepreneurship   The human resource that organizes labor, land, and capital. Entrepreneurs come up with new ideas about what and how to produce, make business decisions, and bear the risk that arise from their decisions.

EPS   Earnings per share.

Equilibrium   The situation when quantity supplied equals quantity demanded at a particular price.

Equilibrium price   The price at which the quantity demanded equals the quantity supplied.

Equities   Another name for shares. The capitalization of a company consists of "equity"—or ownership—represented by common or preferred shares (stock), and debt, represented by bonds, notes, and the like. (In England, "corporation stock" means municipal bonds, incidentally.)

Equity   (1) *Common stock* and *preferred stock*. Often used to refer to common stock only. (2) *Net worth*.

Equity carve-out   The issuance of equity in a division or part of a parent company that then becomes a separate company.

Equity security   An ownership interest in an enterprise, including preferred and common stock.

Equity swap   A swap transaction in which one cash flow is tied to the return to an equity portfolio position, often an index such as the Standard and Poor's 500, while the other is based on a floating-rate index.

ESOP   Employee stock ownership plan.

Estimated rate of return   The rate of return an investor anticipates earning from a specific investment over a particular future holding period.

Euribor   Interbank offer rate for short-term deposits in euros. Euribor is determined by an association of European banks.

Euro   The common currency of many European countries.

Eurobond   A bond underwritten by a multinational syndicate of banks and placed mainly in countries other than the country of the issuer; sometimes called an *international bond*.

Eurocurrency market   Interbank market for short-term borrowing and lending in a currency outside of its home country. For example, borrowing and lending of U.S. dollars outside the United States. Thus, it is an offshore market escaping national regulations. This is the largest money market for several major currencies.

Eurodollar deposit   Dollar deposit with a bank outside the United States.

Eurodollar market   The U.S. dollar segment of the Eurocurrency market.

Eurodollars   Dollar-denominated deposits at foreign banks or foreign branches of American banks.

European option   A European option can be exercised only on the expiration date. Compare with an American option, which can be exercised before, up to, and on its expiration date.

European terms   With reference to U.S. dollar exchange rate quotations, the price of a U.S. dollar in terms of another currency.

European Union (EU)   A formal association of European countries founded by the Treaty of Rome in 1957. Formerly known as the EEC.

EVA   Economic value added.

Event study   Research methodology designed to measure the impact of an event of interest on stock returns.

Excess cash margin (ECM)   An interpretive ratio used to measure the relationship between adjusted operating cash flow and adjusted operating earnings. The ratio measures in percent terms the excess of cash margin (adjusted operating cash flow to revenue) over net margin (adjusted operating earnings to revenue). The ratio is calculated as ((Adjusted operating cash flow − Adjusted operating earnings)/Revenue) × 100). Increases in the ratio over time indicate that adjusted operating cash flow is growing faster or declining slower than adjusted operating earnings. Decreases in the ratio over time indicate that adjusted operating cash flow is growing slower or declining faster than adjusted operating earnings.

Excess return   Rate of return in excess of the risk-free rate.

Exchange of assets   Acquisition of another company by purchase of its assets in exchange for cash or shares.

Exchange rate   Price of a unit of one country's currency in terms of another country's currency.

Exchange rate risk   Uncertainty due to the denomination of an investment in a currency other than that of the investor's own country.

Exchange-traded funds (ETFs) A type of mutual fund traded like other shares on a stock market, having special characteristics particularly related to redemption, and generally designed to closely track the performance of a specified stock market index.

Exchanges National or regional auction markets providing a facility for members to trade securities. A seat is a membership on an exchange.

Executor The legal representative of a person who dies with a will.

Exercise price The transaction price specified in an option contract; also known as the *strike price*.

Exercise price (striking price) Price at which a call option or put option may be exercised.

Expansion A business cycle phase between a trough and a peak—phase in which real GDP increases.

Expectations theory Theory that forward interest rate (forward exchange rate) equals expected spot rate.

Expected rate of return The return that analysts' calculations suggest a security should provide, based on the market's rate of return during the period and the security's relationship to the market.

Expected return Average of possible returns weighted by their probabilities.

Expected return–beta relationship Implication of the CAPM that security risk premiums (expected excess returns) will be proportional to beta.

Expected utility The average utility arising from all possible outcomes.

Exports The goods and services that we sell to people in other countries.

Ex-Post After the fact.

Extended amortization period An amortization period that continues beyond a long-lived asset's economic useful life.

External financing A term used on the cash flow analysis statement that consists of net debt and equity capital raised from external sources.

Externality A consequence of an economic activity that spills over to affect third parties. Pollution is an externality. Can also be viewed as a situation in which a private cost (or benefit) diverges from a social cost (or benefit); a situation in which the costs (or benefits) of an action are not fully borne (or gained) by the two parties engaged in exchange or by an individual engaging in a scarce-resource-using activity.

Extra dividend *Dividend* that may or may not be repeated (cf. *regular dividend*).

Extraordinary item Gain or loss that is unusual and infrequent in occurrence.

Face value The amount paid on a bond at redemption and traditionally printed on the bond certificate. This face value excludes the final coupon payment. Sometimes referred to as *par value*.

Factor beta Sensitivity of security returns to changes in a systematic factor. Alternatively, factor loading; factor sensitivity.

Factoring Arrangement whereby a financial institution buys a company's *accounts receivable* and collects the debt.

Factor loading See *factor beta*.

Factor model A way of decomposing the factors that influence a security's rate of return into common and firm-specific influences.

Factor portfolio A well-diversified portfolio constructed to have a beta of 1.0 on one factor and a beta of zero on any other factor.

Factor sensitivity See *factor beta*.

Factors of production The productive resources that businesses use to produce goods and services.

Fair value (1) The amount at which an asset could be acquired or sold in a current transaction between willing parties in which the parties each acted knowledgeably, prudently, and without compulsion. (2) The theoretical value of a security based on current market conditions. The fair value is the value such that no arbitrage opportunities exist.

FASB Financial Accounting Standards Board.

Federal Deposit Insurance Corporation (FDIC) A government agency that insures the deposits held in banks and most other depository institutions; all U.S. banks are insured this way.

Federal funds Non-interest-bearing deposits by banks at the Federal Reserve. Excess reserves are lent by banks to each other.

Federal funds rate The interest rate that depository institutions pay to borrow reserves in the interbank federal funds market.

Fictitious revenue Revenue recognized on a nonexistent sale or service transaction.

Fiduciary A person who supervises or oversees the investment portfolio of a third party, such as in a trust account, and makes investment decisions in accordance with the owner's wishes.

Fiduciary relationship An arrangement under which a person (the fiduciary) has a duty to act for another's benefit (the beneficiary).

FIFO The first-in first-out accounting method of inventory valuation.

Film production costs Costs incurred in producing a motion picture, including costs to obtain a screenplay; compensation of cast members, directors, producers, extras and other staff; set construction and operations; wardrobe and accessories; sound synchronization; on-location costs; and postproduction costs such as music, special effects and editing.

Financial account A component of the balance of payments covering investments by residents abroad and investments by nonresidents in the home country. Examples include direct investment made by companies, portfolio investments in equity and bonds, and other investments and liabilities.

Financial Accounting Standards Board (FASB) The principal standard-setting body in the United States. Its primary standards are Statements of Financial Accounting Standards (SFASs).

Financial assets Financial assets such as stocks and bonds are claims to the income generated by real assets or claims on income from the government.

Financial capital Funds used to purchase physical capital goods such as buildings and equipment.

Financial engineering Combining or dividing existing instruments to create new financial products.

Financial innovation The development of new financial products—new ways of borrowing and lending.

Financial intermediaries Institutions that transfer funds between ultimate lenders (savers) and ultimate borrowers.

Financial intermediation The process by which financial institutions accept savings from businesses, households, and governments and lend the savings to other businesses, households, and governments.

Financial lease (capital lease, full-payout lease) Long-term, noncancelable lease (cf. *operating lease*).

Financial risk The variability of future income arising from the firm's fixed financing costs, for example, interest payments. The effect of fixed financial costs is to magnify the effect of changes in operating profit on net income or earnings per share.

Firm (1) An economic unit that hires factors of production and organizes those factors to produce and sell goods and services. (2) For purposes of the GIPS standards, the term "firm" refers to the entity defined for compliance with the GIPS standards.

Firm-specific risk See *diversifiable risk*.

Fiscal policy The government's attempt to achieve macroeconomic objectives such as full employment, sustained economic growth, and price level stability by setting and changing taxes, making transfer payments, and purchasing goods and services.

Fixed costs Costs that do not vary with output. Fixed costs include such things as rent on a building. These costs are fixed for a certain period of time; in the long run, they are variable.

Fixed-income security A security such as a bond that pays a specified cash flow over a specific period.

Fixed investment Purchases by businesses of newly produced producer durables, or capital goods, such as production machinery and office equipment.

Fixing A method for determining the market price of a security by finding the price that balances buyers and sellers. A fixing takes place periodically each day at defined times. Sometimes called a *call auction*.

Flexible exchange rates Exchange rates that are allowed to fluctuate in the open market in response to changes in supply and demand. Sometimes called *floating exchange rates*.

Flexible exchange rate system A system in which exchange rates are determined by supply and demand.

Floating-rate bond A bond whose interest rate is reset periodically according to a specified market rate.

Floating-rate note (FRN) Short- to intermediate-term bonds with regularly scheduled coupon payments linked to a variable interest rate, most often LIBOR.

Floor A contract on an interest rate, whereby the writer of the floor periodically pays the difference between a specified floor rate and the market interest rate if, and only if, this difference is positive. This is equivalent to a stream of put options on the interest rate.

Floor agreement A contract that on each settlement date pays the holder the greater of the difference between the floor rate and the reference rate or zero; it is equivalent to a series of put options on the reference rate.

Floor-plan financing A loan arrangement that is typically used to finance durable goods inventory such as automobiles, mobile homes, recreational vehicles, boats and motorcycles, where the underlying inventory is pledged as loan security. Any outstanding loan balance is linked directly to inventory levels, increasing as inventory levels increase and requiring repayment as inventory levels decline.

Flow A quantity measured per unit of time; something that occurs over time, such as the income you make per week or per year or the number of individuals who are fired every month.

Foreign bond   A bond issued on the domestic capital market of another country.

Foreign currency risk premium   The expected movement in the (direct) exchange rate minus the interest rate differential (domestic risk-free rate minus foreign risk-free rate).

Foreign direct investment   The acquisition of more than 10 percent of the shares of ownership in a company in another nation.

Foreign exchange   The purchase (sale) of a currency against the sale (purchase) of another.

Foreign exchange expectation   A relation that states that the forward exchange rate, quoted at time 0 for delivery at time 1, is equal to the expected value of the spot exchange rate at time 1. When stated relative to the current spot exchange rate, the relation states that the forward discount (premium) is equal to the expected exchange rate movement.

Foreign exchange market   A market in which households, firms, and governments buy and sell national currencies.

Foreign exchange rate   (1) The price of one currency in terms of another. (2) The possibility that changes in the value of a nation's currency will result in variations in the market value of assets.

Forex   Foreign exchange.

Forward contract   An agreement between two counterparties that requires the exchange of a commodity or security at a fixed time in the future at a predetermined price.

Forward discount   A situation where, from the perspective of the domestic country, the spot exchange rate is smaller than the forward exchange rate with a foreign country.

Forward discount or premium   Refers to the percentage difference between the forward exchange rate and the spot exchange rate (premium if positive, discount if negative).

Forward exchange rate   Exchange rate fixed today for exchanging currency at some future date (cf. *spot exchange rate*).

Forward interest rate   (1) Interest rate fixed today on a loan to be made at some future date (cf. *spot interest rate*). (2) Rate of interest for a future period that would equate the total return of a long-term bond with that of a strategy of rolling over shorter-term bonds. The forward rate is inferred from the term structure.

Forward premium   A situation where, from the perspective of the domestic country, the spot exchange rate is larger than the forward exchange rate with a foreign country.

Forward rate   A short-term yield for a future holding period implied by the spot rates of two securities with different maturities.

Forward rate agreement (FRA)   A transaction in which two counter-parties agree to a single exchange of cash flows based on a fixed and floating rate, respectively.

Franchise factor   A firm's unique competitive advantage that makes it possible for a firm to earn excess returns (rates of return above a firm's cost of capital) on its capital projects. In turn, these excess returns and the franchise factor cause the firm's stock price to have a *P/E* ratio above its base *P/E* ratio that is equal to $1/k$.

Franchise value   In P/E ratio analysis, the present value of growth opportunities divided by next year's expected earnings.

Free cash flow   Cash not required for operations or for reinvestment.

Free cash flow hypothesis   Theory put forward by Michael Jensen, which asserts that the assumption of debt used to finance leveraged takeovers will absorb discretionary cash flows and help eliminate the agency problem between management and shareholders. It is assumed that with the higher debt service obligations, management would apply the company's cash flows to activities that are in management's interest and not necessarily in shareholders' interests.

Free cash flow to equity   This cash flow measure equals cash flow from operations minus capital expenditures and debt payments.

Full price (or dirty price)   The total price of a bond, including accrued interest.

Funded debt   Debt maturing after more than one year (cf. *unfunded debt*).

Funds   Traditionally defined as working capital, that is, the excess of current assets over current liabilities.

Funds from operations (FFO)   A term used by real estate investment trusts (REITs) and defined as net income or loss excluding gains or losses from debt restructuring and sales of property, plus depreciation and amortization of real estate assets.

Futures contract   A standardized contract to buy (sell) an asset at a specified date and a specified price (futures price). The contract is traded on an organized exchange, and the potential gain/loss is realized each day (marking to market).

Futures option   The right to enter a specified futures contract at a futures price equal to the stipulated exercise price.

Futures price The price at which a futures trader commits to make or take delivery of the underlying asset.

GAAP Generally accepted accounting principles.

GAAP operating cash flow Cash flow from operating activities computed in accordance with generally accepted accounting principles. Also see *reported operating cash flow.*

Game theory A tool that economists use to analyze strategic behavior—behavior that takes into account the expected behavior of others and the mutual recognition of independence.

Gamma How a security's price changes affect an option's **delta** (*q.v.*). Low for small price changes and high for large ones.

GDP deflator One measure of the price level, which is the average of current-year prices as a percentage of base-year prices.

Gearing Financial leverage.

Generally accepted accounting principles (GAAP) A common set of standards and procedures for the preparation of general-purpose financial statements that either have been established by an authoritative accounting rule-making body, such as the Financial Accounting Standards Board (FASB), or have over time become common accepted practice.

General Partner (Private Equity) (GP) A class of partner in a partnership. The GP retains liability for the actions of the partnership. In the PRIVATE EQUITY world, the GP is the fund manager and the LIMITED PARTNERS (LPs) are the institutional and high-net-worth investors in the partnership. The GP earns a management fee and a percentage of profits.

General Utilities Doctrine A component of the Tax Code that provided tax benefits for the sale of assets or liquidating distributions. It was repealed by the Tax Reform Act of 1986.

Generic See *plain-vanilla.*

Geometric mean (GM) The nth root of the product of the annual holding period returns for n years minus 1.

Global Of a fund or portfolio, invested both in the United States and abroad.

Global Investment Performance Standards™ (GIPS®) A global industry standard for the ethical presentation of investment performance results promulgated by the Association for Investment Management and Research.

Globalization Tendency toward a worldwide investment environment, and the integration of national capital markets.

Golden parachute Employment contract of upper management that provides a larger payout upon the occurrence of certain control transactions, such as a certain percentage share purchase by an outside entity or when there is a tender offer for a certain percentage of the company's shares.

Gold standard An international monetary system in which the parity of a currency is fixed in terms of its gold content.

Goods All things from which individuals derive satisfaction or happiness.

Goods and services The objects that people value and produce to satisfy their wants.

Goodwill An intangible asset representing the amount paid in the acquisition of either significant influence or control of an entity over the fair value of the acquired entity's identifiable net assets.

Governance The oversight of a firm's management.

Government budget deficit The deficit that arises when federal government spends more than it collects in taxes.

Government debt The total amount of borrowing that the government has borrowed. It equals the sum of past budget deficits minus budget surpluses.

Great Depression A decade (1929–1939) of high unemployment and stagnant production throughout the world economy.

Greenmail Situation in which a large block of stock is held by an unfriendly company, forcing the target company to repurchase the stock at a substantial premium to prevent a takeover.

Gross capital expenditures Capital expenditures before subtraction for the proceeds derived from the disposal of productive assets.

Gross cash profit A Uniform Credit Analysis (UCA)®–defined cash flow amount that consists of cash collected from sales less cash paid to suppliers.

Gross domestic product (GDP) Total value of a country's output produced by residents within the country's physical borders.

Gross investment The total amount spent on purchases of new capital and on replacing depreciated capital.

Gross margin Revenue minus cost of goods sold. Also referred to as *gross profit.*

Gross national product (GNP) Total value of a country's output produced by residents both within the country's physical borders and abroad.

Growth accounting A method of calculating how much real GDP growth results from growth of labor and capital and how much is attributable to technological change.

Growth cash flow profile The capacity of a firm to generate core operating cash flow as it grows reflecting a combination of its operating cushion and operating working capital requirements.

Growth company A company that consistently has the opportunities and ability to invest in projects that provide rates of return that exceed the firm's cost of capital. Because of these investment opportunities, it retains a high proportion of earnings, and its earnings grow faster than those of average firms.

Growth investing Emphasizes the future over apparent immediate undervaluation. Thus, usually implies buying companies with higher than average price-earnings ratios and lower dividend yields.

Growth-related capital expenditures, net of dispositions A term used on the cash flow analysis statement that consists of capital expenditures required to replace productive capacity consumed during a reporting period and to add infrastructure needed to maintain revenue growth. It is computed as capital expenditures net of cash received for dispositions of property, plant, and equipment less the depreciation proxy for replacement capital expenditures.

Growth stage The second period in a company's life cycle during which operating earnings turn positive and revenue increases faster than the rate of growth in the overall economy. Operating cash flow may be negative during the early part of the growth stage of a company's life cycle and turn positive as the firm becomes more established.

Growth stock A stock issue that generates a higher rate of return than other stocks in the market with similar risk characteristics.

Hedge fund An investment vehicle designed to manage a private, unregistered portfolio of assets according to any of several strategies. The investment strategy often employs arbitrage trading and significant financial leverage (e.g., short selling, borrowing, derivatives) while the compensation arrangement for the manager typically specifies considerable profit participation.

Hedge ratio (1) The percentage of the position in an asset that is hedged with derivatives. (2) The number of derivative contracts that must be transacted to offset the price volatility of an underlying commodity or security position.

Hedging (1) Buying one security and selling another in order to reduce risk. A perfect hedge produces a riskless portfolio. (2) The process of reducing the uncertainty of the future value of a portfolio by taking positions in various derivatives (e.g., forward and futures contracts).

Hedging demands Demands for securities to hedge particular sources of consumption risk, beyond the usual mean-variance diversification motivation.

Herfindahl index A measure of industry concentration equal to the sum of the squared market shares of the firms in the industry.

Highly leveraged transaction (HLT) Bank loan to a highly leveraged firm (formerly needed to be separately reported to the Federal Reserve Board).

High-yield bond A bond rated below investment grade. Also referred to as *speculative-grade bonds* or *junk bonds.*

Holding company A company that owns the stock of other corporations. A holding company may not engage in actual operations of its own but merely manages various operating units that it owns an interest in.

Holding-period return The rate of return over a given period.

Horizontal merger The joining of firms that are producing or selling a similar product.

Hot issue A newly issued stock that is in strong demand; often it will go to a premium over its original issue price.

Human capital The knowledge and skill that people obtain from education, on-the-job training, and experience.

Hurdle rate Minimum acceptable rate of return on a project.

Illiquidity premium Extra expected return as compensation for limited liquidity.

IMM International monetary market.

Implicit costs Expenses that managers do not have to pay out of pocket and hence do not normally explicitly calculate, such as the opportunity cost of factors of production that are owned; examples are owner-provided capital and owner-provided labor.

Implied volatility The volatility of an asset that is implicit in the current market price of an option (using a standard Black-Scholes-Merton formula).

Imports The goods and services that we buy from people in other countries.

Imputation tax system Arrangement by which investors who receive a *dividend* also receive a tax credit for corporate taxes that the firm has paid.

Incentive A reward that encourages or a penalty that discourages an action.

Incentives Rewards for engaging in a particular activity.

Incentive system A method of organizing production that uses a market-like mechanism inside the firm.

Income approach   Measuring national income by adding up all components of national income, including wages, interest, rent, and profits.

Income beneficiary   A person entitled to all or a share of the income of a trust.

Income effect   The effect of a change in income on consumption, other things remaining the same.

Income elasticity of demand   The responsiveness of demand to a change in income, other things remaining the same. It is calculated as the percentage change in the quantity demanded divided by the percentage change in income.

Income from continuing operations   After-tax net income before discontinued operations, extraordinary items, and the cumulative effect of changes in accounting principle.

Income fund   A mutual fund providing for liberal current income from investments.

Income statement   A financial statement showing a firm's revenues and expenses during a specified period.

Income stock   *Common stock* with high *dividend yield* and few profitable investment opportunities (cf. *growth stock*).

Income tax provision   Income tax expense as computed on income before taxes and reported on the income statement.

Income taxes payable   Income taxes currently due and payable to a taxing authority.

Indenture   The legal agreement that lists the obligations of the issuer of a bond to the bondholder, including payment schedules, call provisions, and sinking funds.

Independent variable   A variable whose value is determined independently of, or outside, the equation under study.

Index fund   A portfolio designed to replicate the performance of an index.

Indexing   A passive bond portfolio management strategy that seeks to match the composition, and therefore the performance, of a selected market index.

Index model   A model of stock returns using a market index such as the SP 500 to represent common or systematic risk factors.

Index option   A call or put option based on a stock market index.

Indirect exchange rate   The amount of foreign currency required to purchase one unit of domestic currency.

Indirect-method format   A format for the operating section of the cash flow statement that presents the derivation from net income of cash flow provided by operating activities. The format starts with net income and adjusts for nonoperating items, noncash income and expense, and changes in operating-related working capital accounts.

Indirect quote   For foreign exchange, the number of units of a foreign currency needed to buy one U.S. dollar (cf. *direct quote*).

Industry life cycle   Stages through which firms typically pass as they mature.

Inflation   The rate at which the general level of prices for goods and services is rising.

Inflation-adjusted return   A rate of return that is measured in terms of real goods and services; that is, after the effects of inflation have been factored out.

Inflation rate   The percentage change in the price level from one year to the next.

Information   An attribute of a good market that includes providing buyers and sellers with timely, accurate information on the volume and prices of past transactions and on all currently outstanding bids and offers.

Information ratio   Statistic used to measure a portfolio's average return in excess of a comparison, benchmark portfolio divided by the standard deviation of this excess return.

Initial margin   The amount that an investor must deposit to open a position in futures and some other derivatives; also used to refer to the initial equity required when a stock is purchased using borrowed money.

Initial public offering (IPO)   A company's first public issue of *common stock*.

Innovation   Transforming an invention into something that is useful to humans.

In play   When the market believes that a company may be taken over. At this time, the stock becomes concentrated in the hands of arbitragers and the company becomes vulnerable to a takeover and the target of a bid.

Input list   List of parameters such as expected returns, variances, and covariances necessary to determine the optimal risky portfolio.

Inside information   Nonpublic knowledge about a corporation possessed by corporate officers, major owners, or other individuals with privileged access to information about a firm.

Insider trading   Trading by officers, directors, major stockholders, or others who hold private inside information allowing them to benefit from buying or selling stock.

Institution   A retirement fund, bank, investment company, investment advisor, insurance company, or other large pool of investment buying power.

Intangible asset   Nonmaterial asset, such as technical expertise, a trademark, or a patent (cf. *tangible asset*).

Interest The payment for current rather than future command over resources; the cost of obtaining credit. Also, the return paid to owners of capital.

Interest cover Times interest earned.

Interest rate The number of dollars earned per dollar invested per period.

Interest rate collar The combination of a long position in a cap agreement and a short position in a floor agreement, or vice versa; it is equivalent to a series of range forward positions.

Interest rate effect One of the reasons that the aggregate demand curve slopes downward: Higher price levels increase the interest rate, which in turn causes businesses and consumers to reduce desired spending due to the higher price of borrowing.

Interest rate parity An arbitrage process that ensures that the forward discount or premium equals the interest rate differential between two currencies.

Interest rate risk The uncertainty of returns on an investment due to possible changes in interest rates over time.

Interest rate swap An agreement calling for the periodic exchange of cash flows, one based on an interest rate that remains fixed for the life of the contract and the other that is linked to a variable-rate index.

Intermediate Of bonds, usually five to seven years' maturity.

Intermediate goods Goods used up entirely in the production of final goods.

Internal rate of return (IRR) Discount rate at which investment has zero net present value.

Internal-use software development costs Costs incurred in developing new software applications for a company's own use and not for licensing to customers. Internal-use software development costs are capitalized once the preliminary project stage is completed.

Internal Valuation (Real Estate) An INTERNAL VALUATION is an advisor's or underlying third-party manager's best estimate of MARKET VALUE based on the most current and accurate information available under the circumstances. An INTERNAL VALUATION could include industry practice techniques, such as discounted cash flow, sales comparison, replacement cost, or a review of all significant events (both general market and asset specific) that could have a material impact on the investment. Prudent assumptions and estimates MUST be used, and the process MUST be applied consistently from period to period, except where a change would result in better estimates of MARKET VALUE.

International Accounting Standard (IAS) An accounting standard issued by the International Accounting Standards Committee. This committee has been replaced by the International Accounting Standards Board (IASB). IAS standards have been adopted by the IASB.

International Accounting Standards Board (IASB) An international standard setting body. Its principal standard-setting products are International Financial Reporting Standards (IFRSs). The IASB assumed its duties from the International Accounting Standards Committee (IASC). Existing International Accounting Standards issued by the IASC were adopted by the IASB.

International CAPM An equilibrium theory that relates the expected return of an asset to its world market and foreign exchange risks.

International Financial Reporting Standard (IFRS) A financial reporting standard issued by the International Accounting Standards Board.

International Fisher relation The assertion that the interest rate differential between two countries should equal the expected inflation rate differential over the term of the interest rates.

International monetary market (IMM) The financial futures market within the Chicago Mercantile Exchange.

International Swaps and Derivatives Association (ISDA) An association of swap dealers formed in 1985 to promote uniform practices in the writing, trading, and settlement procedures of swaps and other derivatives.

In the money An option that has positive intrinsic value.

Intrinsic value The portion of a call option's total value equal to the greater of either zero or the difference between the current value of the underlying asset and the exercise price; for a put option, intrinsic value is the greater of either zero or the exercise price less the underlying asset price. For a stock, it is the value derived from fundamental analysis of the stock's expected returns or cash flows.

Inventory investment Changes in the stocks of finished goods and goods in process, as well as changes in the raw materials that businesses keep on hand. Whenever inventories are decreasing, inventory investment is negative; whenever they are increasing, inventory investment is positive.

Inventory turnover The number of times during a year that inventory is sold and replaced. Calculated by dividing cost of goods sold by ending inventory.

Inverse relationship A relationship between variables that move in opposite directions.

Invested Capital (Private Equity) The amount of paid-in capital that has been invested in portfolio companies.

Investing Buying an asset, such as a bond, corporate stock, rental property, or farm, with reasonably determinable underlying earnings.

Investment (1) Any use of today's resources to expand tomorrow's production or consumption. *Can also be viewed as* spending by businesses on things such as machines and buildings, which can be used to produce goods and services in the future. The investment part of total output is the portion that will be used in the process of producing goods in the future. (2) The current commitment of dollars for a period of time in order to derive future payments that will compensate the investor for the time the funds are committed, the expected rate of inflation, and the uncertainty of future payments.

Investment Advisor (Private Equity) Any individual or institution that supplies investment advice to clients on a per fee basis. The investment advisor inherently has no role in the management of the underlying portfolio companies of a partnership/fund.

Investment bankers Firms specializing in the sale of new securities to the public, typically by underwriting the issue.

Investment company A firm that issues (sells) shares, and uses the proceeds to invest in various financial instruments or other assets.

Investment Company Act of 1940 One of several pieces of federal legislation passed after the October 1929 stock market crash and the Great Depression. This law regulated the activities and reporting requirements of investment companies, which are firms whose principal business is the trading and management of securities.

Investment decision process Estimation of intrinsic value for comparison with market price to determine whether or not to invest.

Investment demand The relationship between investment and real interest rate, other things remaining the same.

Investment grade Bonds rated AAA to BBB.

Investment-grade bond Bond rated BBB and above or Baa and above. Lower-rated bonds are classified as speculative-grade or junk bonds.

Investment horizon The time period used for planning and forecasting purposes or the future time at which the investor requires the invested funds.

Investment management company A company separate from the investment company that manages the portfolio and performs administrative functions.

Investment Management Fee The fee payable to the investment management firm for the on-going management of a portfolio. Investment management fees are typically asset based (percentage of assets), performance based (based on performance relative to a benchmark), or a combination of the two but may take different forms as well.

Investment portfolio Set of securities chosen by an investor.

Investment strategy A decision by a portfolio manager regarding how he or she will manage the portfolio to meet the goals and objectives of the client. This will include either active or passive management and, if active, what style in terms of top-down or buttom-up or fundamental versus technical.

IPO Initial public offering.

IRR Internal rate of return.

IRS Internal Revenue Service.

Joint venture When companies jointly pursue a certain business activity.

Junior debt Subordinated debt.

Just-in-time System of inventory management that requires minimum inventories of materials and very frequent deliveries by suppliers.

Keiretsu A network of Japanese companies organized around a major bank.

Keynesian An economist who believes that left alone, the economy would rarely operate at full employment and that to achieve full employment, active help from fiscal policy and monetary policy is required.

Labor The work time and work effort that people devote to producing goods and services.

Labor force Individuals aged 16 years or older who either have jobs or are looking and available for jobs; the number of employed plus the number of unemployed.

Labor productivity Total real domestic output (real GDP) divided by the number of workers (output per worker).

Labor unions Worker organizations that seek to secure economic improvements for their members; they also seek to improve the safety, health, and other benefits (such as job security) of their members.

Land The natural resources that are available from nature. Land as a resource includes location, original fertility and mineral deposits, topography, climate, water, and vegetation.

Later stage   With respect to venture capital financing, the stage after commercial manufacturing and sales have begun. Later-stage financing includes second-stage, third-stage, and mezzanine financing.

Law of demand   The observation that there is a negative, or inverse, relationship between the price of any good or service and the quantity demanded, holding other factors constant.

Law of diminishing returns   As a firm uses more of a variable input, with a given quantity of other inputs (fixed inputs), the marginal product of the variable input eventually diminishes.

Law of one price   The rule stipulating that equivalent securities or bundles of securities must sell at equal prices to preclude arbitrage opportunities.

LBO   Leveraged buyout.

Lease   Long-term rental agreement.

Lease receivables   Amounts due from customers on long-term sales-type lease agreements.

Lessee   User of a leased asset (cf. *lessor*).

Lessor   Owner of a leased asset (cf. *lessee*).

Letter of credit   Letter from a bank stating that it has established a credit in the company's favor.

Letter stock   Privately placed *common stock*, so-called because the *SEC* requires a letter from the purchaser that the stock is not intended for resale.

Leverage   (1) The relation between the value of the asset position and the amount of equity invested. (2) Leverage (in England "gearing") is of two sorts: financial and sales. If a company is capitalized half in stock and half in bonds, for instance, a 10 percent change in profits will produce roughly a 20 percent change in earnings per share.

Leveraged buyout (LBO)   When an investor or group borrows money, usually on the security of a company's own assets, to take control of it, usually expecting to sell assets to reduce this debt.

Leverage ratio   Ratio of debt to total capitalization of a firm.

Liabilities   Amounts owed; the legal claims against a business or household by nonowners.

Life cycle   The progression of a firm through various stages of its organizational life, consisting of start-up, growth, maturity, and decline, during which earnings and operating cash flow have certain characteristic relationships.

LIFO   The last-in first-out accounting method of valuing inventories.

LIFO liquidation   A reduction in the physical quantity of an inventory that is accounted for using the LIFO method. A LIFO liquidation usually produces a nonrecurring increase in earnings because the older costs associated with the liquidated units are lower than current inventory costs.

Limit order   An order to buy or sell a security at a specific price or better (lower for a buy order and higher for a sell order).

Limited liability   A legal concept whereby the responsibility, or liability, of the owners of a corporation is limited to the value of the shares in the firm that they own.

Limited partnership   *Partnership* in which some partners have *limited liability* and general partners have unlimited liability.

Linear relationship   A relationship between two variables that is illustrated by a straight line.

Line of credit   Agreement by a bank that a company may borrow at any time up to an established limit.

Liquid   Term used to describe an asset that can be quickly converted to cash at a price close to fair market value.

Liquid asset   Asset that is easily and cheaply turned into cash—notably cash itself and short-term securities.

Liquidating dividend   *Dividend* that represents a return of capital.

Liquidation   The sale of all of a company's assets whereby the firm ceases to exist.

Liquidation value   Net amount that could be realized by selling the assets of a firm after paying the debt.

Liquidity   (1) The degree to which an asset can be acquired or disposed of without much danger of any intervening loss in nominal value and with small transaction costs. Money is the most liquid asset. (2) The extent to which a stock trades widely in the market, and can thus be purchased or sold without excessively influencing the price. Also, a company's net asset position, particularly in cash or cash equivalents.

Liquidity preference theory   Theory that the forward rate exceeds expected future interest rates.

Liquidity premium   (1) Additional return for investing in a security that cannot easily be turned into cash; (2) difference between the forward interest rate and the expected spot interest rate.

Liquidity risk   Uncertainty due to the ability to buy or sell an investment in the secondary market.

London Interbank offered rate (LIBOR)   The rate at which international banks lend on the Eurocurrency market. This is the rate quoted to a top-quality borrower. The most common maturities are one month, three months, and six months. There is a LIBOR for the U.S. dollar and a few other major currencies. LIBOR is determined by the British Banking Association in London. See also *Euribor.*

Long position   The buyer of a commodity or security or, for a forward contract, the counterparty who will be the eventual buyer of the underlying asset.

Long run   (1) The time period during which all factors of production can be varied. (2) A period of time in which the quantities of all resources can be varied.

Long-run average cost curve   The locus of points representing the minimum unit cost of producing any given rate of output, given current technology and resource prices.

Long-term receivables   Amounts due from customers, typically on an installment basis, which extend beyond one year.

LP   Linear programming.

LYON   Liquid yield option note.

Macroeconomics   The study of the behavior of the economy as a whole, including such economywide phenomena as changes in unemployment, the general price level, and national income.

MACRS   Modified accelerated cost recovery system.

Maintenance margin   The minimum margin that an investor must keep on deposit in a margin account at all times.

Management buyout   An **LBO** (*q.v.*), led by insiders.

Management fee   The compensation an investment company pays to the investment management company for its services. The average annual fee is about 0.5 percent of fund assets.

Mandatorily redeemable preferred stock   Preferred stock that carries an unconditional obligation to be repurchased at a specified or determinable date, making the shares a hybrid security between debt and equity.

Margin   (1) Cash or securities set aside by an investor as evidence that he or she can honor a commitment. (2) The percent of cost a buyer pays in cash for a security, borrowing the balance from the broker. This introduces leverage, which increases the risk of the transaction.

Margin account   The collateral posted with the futures exchange clearinghouse by an outside counterparty to insure its eventual performance; the *initial* margin is the deposit required at contract origination while the *maintenance* margin is the minimum collateral necessary at all times.

Margin call   A request by an investor's broker for additional capital for a security bought on margin if the investor's equity value declines below the required maintenance margin.

Margin deposit   The amount of cash or securities that must be deposited as guarantee on a futures position. The margin is a returnable deposit.

Marginal benefit   The benefit that a person receives from consuming one more unit of a good or service. It is measured as the maximum amount that a person is willing to pay for one more unit of the good or service.

Marginal cost   The opportunity cost of producing one more unit of a good or service. It is the best alternative forgone. It is calculated as the increase in total cost divided by the increase in output.

Marginal cost pricing   A system of pricing in which the price charged is equal to the opportunity cost to society of producing one more unit of the good or service in question. The opportunity cost is the marginal cost to society.

Marginal costs   The change in total costs due to a one-unit change in production rate.

Marginal product   The increase in total product that results from a one-unit increase in the variable input, with all other inputs remaining the same. It is calculated as the increase in total product divided by the increase in the variable input employed, when the quantities of all other inputs are constant.

Marginal revenue   The change in total revenue that results from a one-unit increase in the quantity sold. It is calculated as the change in total revenue divided by the change in quantity sold.

Marginal tax rate   The part of each additional dollar in income that is paid as tax.

Mark to market   Reflecting current market value changes in an appraisal.

Marked to market   The settlement process used to adjust the margin account of a futures contract for daily changes in the price of the underlying asset.

Market   All of the arrangements that individuals have for exchanging with one another. Thus, for example, we can speak of the labor market, the automobile market, and the credit market.

Market analysis   Great tides flow in the market, and an unemotional investor may be able to improve his odds by taking them into account. In the euphoric times when almost every new issue goes to a premium, and everybody you meet is bullish, the veteran cuts back. In the midst of gloom, when sound values are being jettisoned because they are "going lower," when many companies sell in the market for less than their cash in the bank, and when the subscription services are bearish, he reappears with his bushel basket and sweeps in the bargains.

Of course, euphoria can progress to a manic condition, and gloom degenerate into despair. Nevertheless, it is helpful to know the patient's current status, as measured by odd-lot short sales, mutual fund cash, brokers' credit balances, net advances, and the like. They can be studied in figures or shown in graphic form, like the graphs produced by a lie detector (heartbeat, breathing, sweating, etc.). This is quite different from the astrology of "double tops" and so forth that the **chartists** (*q.v.*) invoke.

Marketability discount　A discount applied to the value of some securities, such as securities in closely held companies, based on their comparatively lower liquidity.

Market capitalization (market cap)　The number of shares a company has outstanding times the price per share.

Market demand　The demand of all consumers in the marketplace for a particular good or service. The summation at each price of the quantity demanded by each individual.

Market failure　A state in which the market does not allocate resources efficiently.

Market impact　With reference to execution costs, the difference between the actual execution price and the market price that would have prevailed had the manager not sought to trade the security.

Market maker　An institution or individual quoting firm bid and ask prices for a security and standing ready to buy or sell the security at those quoted prices. Also called a *dealer*.

Market model　(1) Model suggesting a linear relationship between actual returns on a stock and on the market portfolio. (2) A method that is used in event studies. Regression analysis is used to compute the return that is attributable to market forces. It is used to compute "excess returns" that may be attributable to the occurrence of an event.

Market order　An order to buy or sell a security immediately at the best price available.

Market portfolio　The portfolio that includes all risky assets with relative weights equal to their proportional market values.

Market power　The ability to influence the market, and in particular the market price, by influencing the total quantity offered for sale.

Market price of risk　A measure of the extra return, or risk premium, that investors demand to bear risk. The reward-to-risk ratio of the market portfolio.

Market risk premium　The amount of return above the risk-free rate that investors expect from the market in general as compensation for systematic risk.

Market risk (systematic risk)　Risk that cannot be diversified away.

Market return　The standard (typically the SP 500) against which stock portfolio performance can be measured.

Market share test　The percentage of a market that a particular firm supplies, used as the primary measure of monopoly power.

Market timer　An investor who speculates on broad market moves rather than on specific securities.

Market timing　Trying to catch short-term market movements. Extremely difficult.

Market Value　The current listed price at which investors buy or sell securities at a given time.

Market value added (MVA)　External management performance measure to compare the market value of the company's debt and equity with the total capital invested in the firm.

Marking to market　Procedure whereby potential profits and losses on a futures position are realized daily. The daily futures price variation is debited (credited) in cash to the loser (winner) at the end of the day.

Master limited partnership (MLP)　A limited partnership whose shares are publicly traded. Its key advantage is that it eliminates the layer of corporate taxation because MLPs are taxed like partnerships, not corporations.

Maturity strategy　A portfolio management strategy employed to reduce the interest rate risk of a bond portfolio by matching the maturity of the portfolio with its investment horizon. For example, if the investment horizon is 10 years, the portfolio manager would construct a portfolio that will mature in 10 years.

MBO　Management buyout.

MDA　Multiple-discriminant analysis.

Means of payment　A method of settling a debt.

Mean-variance analysis　Evaluation of risky prospects based on the expected value and variance of possible outcomes.

Measurement error　Errors in measuring an explanatory variable in a regression that leads to biases in estimated parameters.

Merger　(1) Acquisition in which all assets and liabilities are absorbed by the buyer (cf. *exchange of assets, exchange of stock*); (2) more generally, any combination of two companies.

Mezzanine section　A middle section on the balance sheet positioned between liabilities and shareholders' equity, where claims that have elements of both, including minority interests, typically are reported.

Microcap　Refers to companies with a market capitalization in the $100 million to $300 million range.

Microeconomics   The study of the choices that individuals and businesses make, the way those choices interact, and the influence governments exert on them.

Midcap   Companies with a market capitalization in the $3 billion to $4 billion range.

Minimum-variance frontier   Graph of the lowest possible portfolio variance that is attainable for a given portfolio expected return.

Minority interest in equity   The interest in the equity of an entity that reflects the portion of shareholders' equity owned by noncontrolling or third-party investors, or investors outside the consolidated entity.

MLP   See *master limited partnership.*

Modern portfolio theory (MPT)   Principles underlying analysis and evaluation of rational portfolio choices based on risk–return trade-offs and efficient diversification.

Modified accelerated cost recovery system (MACRS)   Schedule of *depreciation* deductions allowed for tax purposes.

Modified duration   Measure of a bond's price sensitivity to interest rate movements. Equal to the duration of a bond divided by one plus its yield to maturity.

Monetarist   An economist who believes that the economy is self-regulating and that it will normally operate at full employment, provided that monetary policy is not erratic and that the pace of money growth is kept steady.

Monetarists   Macroeconomists who believe that inflation in the long run is always caused by excessive monetary growth and that changes in the money supply affect aggregate demand both directly and indirectly.

Monetary policy   The Fed conducts the nation's monetary policy by changing in interest rates and adjusting the quantity of money.

Money   Any medium that is universally accepted in an economy both by sellers of goods and services as payment for those goods and services and by creditors as payment for debts.

Money illusion   Reacting to changes in money prices rather than relative prices. If a worker whose wages double when the price level also doubles thinks he or she is better off, that worker is suffering from money illusion.

Money market   (1) The market for short-term debt securities with maturities of less than one year. (2) Includes short-term, highly liquid, and relatively low-risk debt instruments.

Money supply   The amount of money in circulation.

Monopolist   The single supplier of a good or service for which there is no close substitute. The monopolist therefore constitutes its entire industry.

Monopolization   The possession of monopoly power in the relevant market and the willful acquisition or maintenance of that power, as distinguished from growth or development as a consequence of a superior product, business acumen, or historical accident.

Monopoly   A market structure in which there is one firm, which produces a good or service that has no close substitute and in which the firm is protected from competition by a barrier preventing the entry of new firms.

Monte Carlo simulation   Method for calculating the probability distribution of possible outcomes, e.g., from a project.

Mortgage-backed security   Ownership claim in a pool of mortgages or an obligation that is secured by such a pool. Also called a *pass-through*, because payments are passed along from the mortgage originator to the purchaser of the mortgage-backed security.

Moving average   The continually recalculating average of security prices for a period, often 200 days, to serve as an indication of the general trend of prices and also as a benchmark price.

Multifactor CAPM   Generalization of the basic CAPM that accounts for extra-market hedging demands.

Multifactor model   An empirical version of the APT where the investor chooses the exact number and identity of the common risk factors used to describe an asset's risk-return relationship. Risk factors are often designated as *macroeconomic* variables (e.g., inflation, changes in gross domestic product) or *microeconomic* variables (e.g., security-specific characteristics like firm size or book-to-market ratios).

Multifactor models   Model of security returns positing that returns respond to several systematic factors.

Multiple   Short for price-earnings multiple.

Multiplier   The amount by which a change in autonomous expenditure is magnified or multiplied to determine the change in equilibrium expenditure and real GDP.

Municipal bonds   Tax-exempt bonds issued by state and local governments, generally to finance capital improvement projects. General obligation bonds are backed by the general taxing power of the issuer. Revenue bonds are backed by the proceeds from the project or agency they are issued to finance.

Must   A required provision for claiming compliance with the GIPS standards.

Mutual fund An investment company that pools money from shareholders and invests in a variety of securities, including stocks, bonds, and money market securities. A mutual fund ordinarily stands ready to buy back (redeem) its shares at their current net asset value, which depends on the market value of the fund's portfolio of securities at the time. Mutual funds generally continuously offer new shares to investors.

Mutual fund theorem A result associated with the CAPM, asserting that investors will choose to invest their entire risky portfolio in a market-index mutual fund.

Mutually exclusive projects Two projects that cannot both be undertaken.

NASDAQ National Association of Securities Dealers Automated Quotations. It is the trading system for the over-the-counter market.

Nash equilibrium The outcome of a game that occurs when player A takes the best possible action given the action of player B and player B takes the best possible action given the action of player A.

National income (NI) The total of all factor payments to resource owners. It can be obtained by subtracting indirect business taxes from NDP.

Natural monopoly A monopoly that arises from the peculiar production characteristics in an industry. It usually arises when there are large economies of scale relative to the industry's demand such that one firm can produce at a lower average cost than can be achieved by multiple firms.

Negative relationship A relationship between variables that move in opposite directions.

Neoclassical growth theory A theory of economic growth that proposes that real GDP grows because technological change induces a level of saving and investment that makes capital per hour of labor grow.

Net asset value (NAV) (1) The market value of the assets owned by a fund. (2) The value of each share expressed as assets minus liabilities on a per-share basis.

Net capital expenditures Gross capital expenditures minus proceeds from the disposal of productive assets.

Net cash after operations A Uniform Credit Analysis®–defined cash flow amount that consists of cash after operations plus other cash income minus other cash expense and minus income taxes paid.

Net debt Total debt minus cash on hand.

Net exports The value of exports minus the value of imports.

Net income plus depreciation Often referred to as traditional cash flow, its calculation removes an important noncash expense from net income.

Net investment Net increase in the capital stock—gross investment minus depreciation.

Net operating loss carryover Tax benefits that allow companies to use net operating losses in certain years to offset taxable income in other years.

Net present value (NPV) A measure of the excess cash flows expected from an investment proposal. It is equal to the present value of the cash inflows from an investment proposal, discounted at the required rate of return for the investment, minus the present value of the cash outflows required by the investment, also discounted at the investment's required rate of return. If the derived net present value is a positive value (i.e., there is an excess net present value), the investment should be acquired since it will provide a rate of return above its required returns.

Net public debt Gross public debt minus all government interagency borrowing.

Net working capital Current assets minus current liabilities.

Net worth (1) The difference between assets and liabilities. (2) Book value of a company's *common stock*, surplus, and *retained earnings*.

Network effect A situation in which a consumer's willingness to purchase a good or service is influenced by how many others also buy the item.

New entrant An individual who has never held a full-time job lasting two weeks or longer but is now seeking employment.

New growth theory A theory of economic growth based on the idea that real GDP per person grows because of the choices that people make in the pursuit of ever greater profit and that growth can persist indefinitely.

New issue Common stocks or bonds offered by companies for public sale.

Nominal GDP The value of the final goods and services produced in a given year valued at the prices that prevailed in that same year. It is a more precise name for GDP.

Nominal interest rate The interest rate in terms of nominal (not adjusted for purchasing power) dollars.

Nominal values The values of variables such as GDP and investment expressed in current dollars, also called money values; measurement in terms of the actual market prices at which goods and services are sold.

Nominal yield   A bond's yield as measured by its coupon rate.

Noncontrolling interest   Generally, minority interest. However, the term is used to reflect a minority shareholder interest when the definition of control is extended beyond a simple majority share ownership interest. Any interest in an entity besides that of a controlling shareholder.

Nondiversifiable risk   See *systematic risk.*

Nonqualified stock option   An option to purchase stock that requires payment of ordinary income taxes by the option holder on the date of exercise on income equal to the excess of the market price of the purchased stock over the exercise price of the option. The company issuing the option receives an expense deduction equal to the ordinary income of the option holder.

Nonrecurring cash flow   Operating cash flow that appears infrequently or that may appear with some regularity but is very irregular in amount. In addition, even though included in operating cash flow, nonrecurring cash flow often is not closely tied to the core operating activities of the firm.

Nonsystematic risk   Nonmarket or firm-specific risk factors that can be eliminated by diversification. Also called *unique risk* or *diversifiable risk.* Systematic risk refers to risk factors common to the entire economy.

Normal distribution   Symmetric bell-shaped distribution that can be completely defined by its mean and *standard deviation.*

Normal rate of return   The amount that must be paid to an investor to induce investment in a business; also known as the *opportunity cost of capital.*

Note   Unsecured debt with a maturity of up to 10 years.

Notes   Intermediate-term debt securities with maturities longer than 1 year but less than 10 years.

Notes payable   Promissory notes that are evidence of a debt and state the terms of interest and principal payment.

Notional principal   (1) Principal amount used to calculate swap payments. (2) The principal value of a swap transaction, which is not exchanged but is used as a scale factor to translate interest rate differentials into cash settlement payments.

NPV   Net present value.

NYSE   New York Stock Exchange.

Objectives   The investor's goals expressed in terms of risk and return and included in the policy statement.

Off-balance-sheet financing   Financing that is not shown as a liability in a company's balance sheet.

Offensive competitive strategy   A strategy whereby a firm attempts to use its strengths to affect the competitive forces in the industry and, in so doing, improves the firm's relative position in the industry.

Offer price   The price at which a market maker is willing to sell a security (also called *ask price*).

Official reserves   The amount of reserves owned by the central bank of a government in the form of gold, Special Drawing Rights, and foreign cash or marketable securities.

One third rule   The rule that, with no change in technology, a 1 percent increase in capital per hour of labor brings, on the average, a one third of 1 percent increase in real GDP per hour of labor.

Open account   Arrangement whereby sales are made with no formal debt contract. The buyer signs a receipt, and the seller records the sale in the sales ledger.

Open-end fund   An investment company that continuously offers to sell new shares, or redeem them, at prices based on the market value of the assets owned by the fund (net asset value).

Open interest   The number of futures contracts outstanding.

Operating cash flow   Cash flow from operating activities computed in accordance with generally accepted accounting principles.

Operating cushion   Operating profit before depreciation and amortization expense.

Operating earnings   An earnings measure that excludes selected items of nonrecurring gain, revenue, loss, and expense. This is not a GAAP measure, and its determination may vary widely among different companies.

Operating income   See *operating profit.*

Operating lease   A lease that does not transfer the risks and rewards of ownership to the lessee. Operating lease payments are expensed as incurred.

Operating leverage   The use of fixed-production costs in the firm's operating cost structure. The effect of fixed costs is to magnify the effect of a change in sales on operating profits.

Operating loss carryforward   For tax purposes only, losses are first carried back for 2 years, eliminating previous profits and producing a tax refund. If losses remain, then these may be carried forward for as long as 20 years. These losses will shield future profits from taxation. Corporations also may elect to forgo the loss carryback and only carry the loss forward for 20 years.

Operating payables Amounts due vendors, including accounts payable and notes payable for purchases made.

Operating profit Core pretax profit from central operations calculated as revenue minus cost of goods sold, selling, general and administrative expense, and research and development expense.

Operating receivables Customer-related receivables including accounts receivable, notes receivable, and, for contractors, cost plus profit recognized in excess of amounts billed customers.

Operating working capital Current assets, including operating receivables, inventory, and prepaid expenses, that are used in operations minus current liabilities, including operating payables and accrued expenses payable that are incurred in operations.

Opportunity cost (1) The highest-valued, next-best alternative that must be sacrificed to obtain something or to satisfy a want. (2) With reference to execution costs, the loss (or gain) incurred as the result of failure or delay in the execution of a trade, or failure to complete a trade in full.

Opportunity cost of capital The normal rate of return, or the available return on the next-best alternative investment. Economists consider this a cost of production, and it is included in our cost examples.

Optimal portfolio The portfolio on the efficient frontier that has the highest utility for a given investor. It lies at the point of tangency between the efficient frontier and the curve with the investor's highest possible utility.

Optimal risky portfolio An investor's best combination of risky assets to be mixed with safe assets to form the complete portfolio.

Option See *call option, put option.*

Option-adjusted spread A type of yield spread that considers changes in the term structure and alternative estimates of the volatility of interest rates. It is spread after adjusting for embedded options.

Option contract An agreement that grants the owner the right, but not the obligation, to make a future transaction in an underlying commodity or security at a fixed price and within a predetermined time in the future.

Option delta Hedge ratio.

Option premium The purchase price of a call option or put option that reflects both an intrinsic value for the option represented by the difference between the option's exercise price and the market price of the asset covered by the option and the time value of money.

Options Clearing Corporation (OCC) A company designed to guarantee, monitor margin accounts, and settle exchange-traded option transactions.

Order-driven market A market without active market makers in which buy-and-sell orders directly confront each other; an auction market.

Origin The intersection of the *y* axis and the *x* axis in a graph.

OTC Over-the-counter.

Other cash income (expense) A Uniform Credit Analysis®–defined cash flow amount that consists of cash receipts and disbursements that are not part of core operations. The term is defined the same way on the cash flow analysis statement. Other cash income examples include collections for interest, dividends, rents, royalties, and miscellaneous collections. Other cash expense examples include payments for corporate restructuring, severance, and litigation.

Out-of-the-money option An option that has no intrinsic value.

Overdraft A negative cash balance.

Overnight A deal from today to the next business day.

Over-the-counter (OTC) Informal market that does not involve a securities exchange. Specifically used to refer to the Nasdaq dealer market for *common stocks.*

Overweighted A condition in which a portfolio, for whatever reason, includes more of a class of securities than the relative market value alone would justify.

Paid-In Capital (Private Equity) The amount of committed capital a limited partner has actually transferred to a venture fund. Also known as the *cumulative drawdown amount.*

Partnership A business owned by two or more joint owners, or partners, who share the responsibilities and the profits of the firm and are individually liable for all the debts of the partnership.

Par value (1) The principal amount repaid at maturity of a bond. Also called *face value.* (2) The officially determined value of a currency.

Par yield curve The yield curve drawn for government coupon bonds of different maturities that trade at, or around, par.

Passive investment strategy See *passive management.*

Passive management Buying a well-diversified portfolio to represent a broad-based market index without attempting to search out mispriced securities.

Passive portfolio A market index portfolio.

Passive strategy See *passive management.*

Pass-through security Pools of loans (such as home mortgage loans) sold in one package. Owners of pass-throughs receive all principal and interest payments made by the borrowers.

Pass-through securities   *Notes* or *bonds* backed by a package of assets (e.g., mortgage pass-throughs, *CARs, CARDs*).

Patent   A government-sanctioned exclusive right granted to the inventor of a good, service, or productive process to produce, use, and sell the invention for a given number of years.

Payables   Accounts payable.

Payables turnover   The number of times during a year that operating payables are repaid and reincurred. Calculated by dividing cost of goods sold by ending operating payables.

Payback   The time required for the added income from the convertible security relative to the stock to offset the conversion premium.

Payout ratio   *Dividend* as a proportion of earnings per share.

Peak   The point at which a business cycle turns from expansion into recession.

Peer group comparison   A method of measuring portfolio performance by collecting the returns produced by a representative universe of investors over a specific period of time.

P/E ratio   Share price divided by earnings per share.

Per capita   Latin, meaning "by the head." Distributing to "issue per capita" means to distribute trust property to persons who take, in their own right, an equal portion of the property.

Perfect competition   An industry structure characterized by certain conditions, including many buyers and sellers, homogeneous products, perfect information, easy entry and exit, and no barriers to entry. The existence of these conditions implies that each seller is a price taker.

Performance appraisal   The assessment of an investment record for evidence of investment skill.

Performance attribution   The attribution of investment performance to specific investment decisions (such as asset allocation and country weighting).

Performance presentation standards (PPS)   A comprehensive set of reporting guidelines created by the Association for Investment Management and Research (AIMR) (now the CFA Institute), in an effort to fulfill the call for uniform, accurate, and consistent performance reporting.

Perpetuity   An investment without any maturity date. It provides returns to its owner indefinitely.

Personal income (PI)   The amount of income that households actually receive before they pay personal income taxes.

Personal trust   An amount of money set aside by a grantor and often managed by a third party, the trustee. Often constructed so one party receives income from the trust's investments and another party receives the residual value of the trust after the income beneficiaries' death.

Physical capital   All manufactured resources, including buildings, equipment, machines, and improvements to land that is used for production.

PIK   Pay-in-kind bond.

Plain-vanilla   Refers to a security, especially a bond or a swap, issued with standard features. Sometimes called *generic*.

Planning horizon   The long run, during which all inputs are variable.

Point   One percent (1%).

Poison pill   A right issued by a corporation as a preventative antitakeover defense. It allows right holders to purchase shares in either their own company or the combined target and bidder companies at a discount, usually 50%. This discount may make the takeover prohibitively expensive.

Poison put   A *covenant* allowing the *bond*holder to demand repayment in the event of a hostile *merger.*

Policy acquisition costs   See *customer acquisition costs.*

Policy statement   A statement in which the investor specifies investment goals, constraints, and risk preferences.

Political risk   Possibility of the expropriation of assets, changes in tax policy, restrictions on the exchange of foreign currency for domestic currency, or other changes in the business climate of a country.

Pooling of interest   Method of accounting for *mergers* (no longer available in the USA). The consolidated balance sheet of the merged firm is obtained by combining the balance sheets of the separate firms (cf. *purchase accounting*).

Portfolio   A group of investments. Ideally, the investments should have different patterns of returns over time.

Portfolio investment   The purchase of less than 10 percent of the shares of ownership in a company in another nation.

Portfolio management   Process of combining securities in a portfolio tailored to the investor's preferences and needs, monitoring that portfolio, and evaluating its performance.

Positive market feedback   A tendency for a good or service to come into favor with additional consumers because other consumers have chosen to buy the item.

Positive relationship   A relationship between two variables that move in the same direction.

Poverty A situation in which a household's income is too low to be able to buy the quantities of food, shelter, and clothing that are deemed necessary.

Preferences A description of a person's likes and dislikes.

Preferred habitat theory Holds that investors prefer specific maturity ranges but can be induced to switch if risk premiums are sufficient.

Preferred stock A class of stock with priority rights, both as to dividends and in liquidation, over the common stock of the same company. Corporations pay a much lower income tax on dividends from their investments in other corporations (where it has already been taxed) than on direct business earnings. Preferred stock is usually priced at the level that makes it attractive to a corporation, taking account of this tax exemption, and as a result is rarely tax-efficient for individuals.

Premature revenue Revenue recognized for a confirmed sale or service transaction in a period prior to that called for by generally accepted accounting principles.

Premium (1) A bond selling at a price above par value due to capital market conditions. (2) The purchase price of an option.

Prepaid expenses Costs or expenses that have been paid in advance of being incurred. Also referred to as *prepaids*.

Present value The value of a future amount expressed in today's dollars; the most that someone would pay today to receive a certain sum at some point in the future.

Present value of growth opportunities (PVGO) *Net present value* of investments the firm is expected to make in the future.

Presumptive remaindermen Those persons who, if a trust were to terminate at any given time, are entitled to take the then trust corpus.

Price controls Government-mandated minimum or maximum prices that may be charged for goods and services.

Price discrimination Selling a given product at more than one price, with the price difference being unrelated to differences in cost.

Price-driven market A market in which dealers (market makers) adjust their quotes continuously to reflect supply and demand; also known as a *dealer market*.

Price–earnings multiple See *price–earnings ratio*.

Price–earnings ratio The ratio of a stock's price to its earnings per share. Also referred to as the *P/E multiple*.

Price effect The effect of a change in the price on the quantity of a good consumed, other things remaining the same.

Price level The average level of prices as measured by a price index.

Price momentum A portfolio strategy in which you acquire stocks that have enjoyed above-market stock price increases.

Price risk The component of interest rate risk due to the uncertainty of the market price of a bond caused by changes in market interest rates.

Price war A pricing campaign designed to capture additional market share by repeatedly cutting prices.

Primary market The market in which newly issued securities are sold by their issuers, who receive the proceeds.

Prime rate Benchmark lending rate set by U.S. banks.

Principal (1) The outstanding balance on a loan. (2) The corpus or capital of a trust, as distinguished from the income produced.

Principal-agent problem The problem of devising compensation rules that induce an agent to act in the best interest of a principal.

Principal trade A trade through a broker who guarantees full execution at specified discount/premium to the prevailing price.

Private equity *Equity* that is not publicly traded and that is used to finance business start-ups, *leveraged buy-outs*, etc.

Private information Information that is available to one person but is too costly for anyone else to obtain.

Private placement A new issue sold directly to a small group of investors, usually institutions.

Private trusts A term used to identify trusts created by individuals for individuals, either during life or under will.

Producer Price Index (PPI) A statistical measure of a weighted average of prices of goods and services that firms produce and sell.

Product differentiation The distinguishing of products by brand name, color, and other minor attributes. Product differentiation occurs in other than perfectly competitive markets in which products are, in theory, homogeneous, such as wheat or corn.

Production Any activity that results in the conversion of resources into products that can be used in consumption.

Productivity curve A relationship that shows how real GDP per hour of labor changes as the amount of capital per hour of labor changes with a given state of technology.

Productivity growth slowdown A slowdown in the growth rate of output per person.

Profit The income earned by entrepreneurship.

Profitability index Ratio of a project's *NPV* to the initial investment.

Profit margin See *return on sales.*

Pro forma Projected.

Pro-forma earnings A measure of earnings performance that selectively excludes nonrecurring as well as some noncash items.

Program trading Coordinated buy orders and sell orders of entire portfolios, usually with the aid of computers, often to achieve index arbitrage objectives.

Property rights Social arrangements that govern the ownership, use, and disposal of resources or factors of production, goods, and services that are enforceable in the courts.

Proprietorship A business owned by one individual who makes the business decisions, receives all the profits, and is legally responsible for the debts of the firm.

Prospectus Summary of the *registration* statement providing information on an issue of securities.

Protective put A trading strategy in which a put option is purchased as a supplement to a long position in an underlying asset or portfolio of assets; the most straightforward form of *portfolio insurance.*

Proxy An instrument empowering an agent to vote in the name of the shareholder.

Proxy contest When a dissident shareholder or group of shareholders try to take control of the board of directors or use the process to enact certain changes in the activities of the company.

Proxy vote Vote cast by one person on behalf of another.

Prudent investor rule An investment manager must act in accord with the actions of a hypothetical prudent investor.

Public good A good or service that is both nonrival and nonexcludable—it can be consumed simultaneously by everyone and from which no one can be excluded.

Purchase accounting Method of accounting for *mergers.* The assets of the acquired firm are shown at market value on the balance sheet of the acquirer (cf. *pooling of interest*).

Purchasing power The value of money for buying goods and services. If your money income stays the same but the price of one good that you are buying goes up, your effective purchasing power falls, and vice versa.

Purchasing power parity (PPP) A theory stating that the exchange rate between two currencies will exactly reflect the purchasing power of the two currencies.

Pure plays Companies that operate within clearly defined market boundaries.

Put option A contract that gives its holder the right to sell an asset, typically a financial instrument, at a specified price through a specified date.

Put options Options to sell a security (stock or bond) within a certain period at a specified price.

q Ratio of the market value of an asset to its replacement cost.

Qualified Institutional buyers (QIBs) Institutions that are allowed to trade unregistered stock among themselves.

Quality of earnings The realism and conservatism of the earnings number and the extent to which we might expect the reported level of earnings to be sustained.

Quantity demanded The amount of a good or service that consumers plan to buy during a given time period at a particular price.

Quick ratio A measure of liquidity similar to the current ratio except for exclusion of inventories (cash plus receivables divided by current liabilities).

Quota A quantitative restriction on the import of a particular good, which specifies the maximum amount that can be imported in a given time period.

Random walk Describes the notion that stock price changes are random and unpredictable.

Rate of return The future financial benefit to making a current investment.

Rational expectation The most accurate forecast possible, a forecast that uses all the available information, including knowledge of the relevant economic forces that influence the variable being forecasted.

Real assets Tangible assets and intangible assets used to carry on business (cf. financial assets).

Real Estate Real estate investments include:
- Wholly owned or partially owned properties,
- Commingled funds, property unit trusts, and insurance company separate accounts,
- Unlisted, private placement securities issued by private real estate investment trusts (REITs) and real estate operating companies (REOCs), and
- Equity-oriented debt, such as participating mortgage loans or any private interest in a property where some portion of return to the investor at the time of investment is related to the performance of the underlying real estate.

Real Estate Investment Trust (REIT) An entity that may invest in real estate or mortgages on real estate and whose earnings are exempt from federal taxation. REITs must meet certain strict requirements contained in the Internal Revenue Code including distribution of at least 90 percent of their earnings to shareholders to avoid taxation of profit at the corporate level.

Real exchange rate The exchange rate adjusted by the inflation differential between the two countries.

Real foreign currency risk The risk that real prices of consumption goods might not be identical in different countries. Also known as *real exchange rate risk*, or *purchasing power risk*.

Real Gross Domestic Product (real GDP) The value of final goods and services produced in a given year when valued at constant prices.

Real income A household's income expressed as a quantity of goods that the household can afford to buy.

Real interest rate The nominal interest rate adjusted for inflation; the nominal interest rate minus the inflation rate.

Real option The flexibility to modify, postpone, expand or abandon a project.

Real options Options embedded in a firm's real assets that give managers valuable decision-making flexibility, such as the right to either undertake or abandon an investment project.

Real rate of interest The nominal rate of interest minus the anticipated rate of inflation.

Realized capital gains Capital gains that result when an appreciated asset is sold; realized capital gains are taxable.

Real values Measurement of economic values after adjustments have been made for changes in the average of prices between years.

Real wage rate The quantity of goods and services that an hour's work can buy. It is equal to the money wage rate divided by the price level.

Rebalancing Realigning the proportions of assets in a portfolio as needed.

Receivables Accounts receivable.

Receivables days The number of days it would take to collect the ending balance in operating receivables at the year's average rate of revenue per day. Calculated by dividing 365 by receivables turnover.

Receivables turnover The number of times during a year that operating receivables are collected and replaced with new revenue transactions. Calculated by dividing revenue by ending operating receivables.

Receiver A bankruptcy practitioner appointed by secured creditors in the United Kingdom to oversee the repayment of debts.

Recession There are two common definitions of recession. They are: (1) A business cycle phase in which real GDP decreases for at least two successive quarters. (2) A significant decline in activity spread across the economy, lasting for more than a few months, visible in industrial production, employment, real income, and wholesale-retail trade.

Reclassification adjustment An adjustment to reported operating cash flow that moves a cash flow item from one classification to another, such as from operating cash flow to investing cash flow or from financing cash flow to operating cash flow. An example would be the reclassification of a tax benefit from stock options from operating cash flow to financing cash flow. The goal of these reclassifications is to produce a more sustainable measure of operating cash flow.

Record date Date set by directors when making dividend payment. *Dividends* are sent to stockholders who are registered on the record date.

Recycling The reuse of raw materials derived from manufactured products.

Registration Process of obtaining *SEC* approval for a public issue of securities.

Registration statement Required to be filed with the SEC to describe the issue of a new security.

Regression analysis In statistics, a technique for finding the line of best fit.

Regression equation An equation that describes the average relatinship between a dependent variable and a set of explanatory variables.

Regular dividend *Dividend* that the company expects to maintain in the future.

Regulation Rules administrated by a government agency to influence economic activity by determining prices, product standards and types, and conditions under which new firms may enter an industry.

Reinvestment Profits (or depreciation reserves) used to purchase new capital equipment.

Relative price The ratio of the price of one good or service to the price of another good or service. A relative price is an opportunity cost.

Relative return A portfolio's return compared with its benchmark.

Remainder The trust corpus existing at the termination of the life beneficiary's interest.

Rent The income that land earns.

Replacement capital expenditures Capital expenditures required to replace productive capacity consumed during a reporting period.

Replacement cost Cost to replace a firm's assets. "Reproduction" cost.

Repo Repurchase agreement.

Reported operating cash flow Cash flow from operating activities computed in accordance with generally accepted accounting principles. Also see *operating cash flow*.

Repurchase agreement (RP, repo, buy-back) Purchase of Treasury securities from a securities dealer with an agreement that the dealer will repurchase them at a specified price.

Required principal payments on long-term debt and capital lease obligations A term used on the cash flow analysis statement that consists of the current portion of long-term debt and capital lease obligations at the beginning of the year.

Required rate of return The return that compensates investors for their time, the expected rate of inflation, and the uncertainty of the return.

Reserves (1) Cash in a bank's vault plus the bank's deposits at Federal Reserve banks. (2) The fixed-income component of a portfolio, notably shorter-term highly liquid instruments.

Residual claim Refers to the fact that shareholders are at the bottom of the list of claimants to assets of a corporation in the event of failure or bankruptcy.

Residual income After-tax profit less the *opportunity cost of capital* employed by the business (see also *economic value added*).

Residual risk The **specific risk** contained in a security, as distinct from the general market risk.

Residuals Parts of stock returns not explained by the explanatory variable (the market-index return). They measure the impact of firm-specific events during a particular period.

Residual Value (Private Equity) The remaining equity that a limited partner has in the fund. (The value of the investments within the fund.) Also can be referred to as *ending market value* or *net asset value*.

Resources Things used to produce other things to satisfy people's wants.

Restatement of the Law Third, Trusts A book of rules and principles promulgated by the American Law Institute, concerning the conduct of a trustee in the management of a trust. It serves as a guide for lawyers, trustees, and investment advisors.

Restricted cash Cash set aside for a particular purpose either through a legal restriction related to a third party or through a more informal internal company restriction.

Restructuring charge Costs associated with restructuring activities, including the consolidation and/or relocation of operations or the disposition or abandonment of operations or productive assets. Such charges may be incurred in connection with a business combination, a change in an enterprise's strategic plan, or a managerial response to declines in demand, increasing costs, or other environmental factors.

Restructuring charges Also referred to as *big bath write-offs*. In a merger context it refers to a company's taking large write-offs following an acquisition, which lowers current income but may carry the implication that future income may be higher.

Restructuring reserve A liability reflecting restructuring costs to be paid or realized in future periods.

Retained earnings Earnings that a corporation saves, or retains, for investment in other productive activities; earnings that are not distributed to stockholders.

Return on assets (ROA) A profitability ratio; earnings before interest and taxes dividend by total assets.

Return on equity (ROE) (1) An accounting ratio of net profits divided by equity. (2) An excellent definition is profit margin × turnover × leverage, where profit margin is sales ÷ profits, turnover is sales ÷ assets, and leverage is assets ÷ equity. It is extremely high in industries with high RD that is expensed rather than capitalized and added to equity, such as pharmaceuticals.

Return on investment (ROI) Generally, book income as a proportion of net book value.

Return on sales (ROS), or profit margin The ratio of operating profits per dollar of sales (EBIT divided by sales).

Revenue bond A bond that is serviced by the income generated from specific revenue-producing projects of the municipality such as toll roads or athletic stadiums.

Reverse synergy 4 − 1 = 5; where, following a sell-off, the remaining parts of a company are more valuable than the original parent business.

Revolving credit Legally assured *line of credit* with a bank.

Reward-to-variability ratio Ratio of a portfolio's risk premium to its standard deviation.

Risk A situation in which more than one outcome might occur and the probability of each possible outcome can be estimated.

Risk arbitrage Speculation on perceived mispriced securities, usually in connection with merger and acquisition targets.

Risk averse The assumption about investors that they will choose the least risky alternative, all else being equal.

Risk aversion Describes the fact that investors want to minimize risk for the same level of expected return. To take more risk, they require compensation by a risk premium.

Risk budgeting In a portfolio management context, the setting of risk limits for individual managers.

Risk-free asset An asset with a certain rate of return; often taken to be short-term T-bills.

Risk-free rate The interest rate that can be earned with certainty.

Risk-neutral See *risk-averse.*

Risk premium An expected return in excess of that on risk-free securities. The premium provides compensation for the risk of an investment.

Risk–return trade-off If an investor is willing to take on risk, there is the reward of higher expected returns.

Risky asset An asset with uncertain future returns.

Rival A good or service or a resource is rival if its use by one person decreases the quantity available for someone else.

ROI Return on investment.

RP Repurchase agreement.

Rule 144a *SEC* rule allowing *qualified institutional buyers* to buy and trade unregistered securities.

Russell 1000 Index The 1000 largest companies in the Russell 3000 index.

Russell 3000 Index The 3000 largest U.S. companies, capital-weighted, which represent about 98 percent of the investible equity market.

Russell 2000 Index The 2000 smallest companies in the Russell 3000 index.

Safe harbor Practices that satisfy such requirements as the Prudent Investor Rule.

Sale and leaseback A sale followed by the immediate leaseback of the asset sold by its previous owner.

Salvage value Scrap value of plant and equipment.

Sampling A technique for constructing a passive index portfolio in which the portfolio manager buys a representative sample of stocks that comprise the benchmark index.

Sarbanes-Oxley Act An act of Congress signed into law on July 30, 2002, that tightened the oversight of firms that audit public companies, added criminal penalties for earnings management activities, and took steps generally to improve company internal controls and corporate governance.

Saving The act of not consuming all of one's current income. Whatever is not consumed out of spendable income is, by definition, saved. Saving is an action measured over time (a flow), whereas savings are a stock, an accumulation resulting from the act of saving in the past.

Scatter diagram (1) A diagram that plots the value of one economic variable against the value of another. (2) Plot of returns of one security versus returns of another security. Each point represents one pair of returns for a given holding period.

Scenario analysis Analysis of the profitability of a project under alternative economic scenarios.

Seasonal factors Natural ebbs and flows in business activity occurring annually that are caused by changes in the seasons.

Seasoned issue Issue of a security for which there is an existing market (cf. *unseasoned issue*).

SEC Securities and Exchange Commission.

Secondary boycott A boycott of companies or products sold by companies that are dealing with a company being struck.

Secondary issue (1) Procedure for selling blocks of *seasoned issues* of stock; (2) more generally, sale of already issued stock.

Secondary market The market in which outstanding securities are bought and sold by owners other than the issuers. Purpose is to provide liquidity for investors.

Sector rotation An investment strategy which entails shifting the portfolio into industry sectors that are forecast to outperform others based on macro-economic forecasts.

Sector rotation strategy An active strategy that involves purchasing stocks in specific industries or stocks with specific characteristics (low *P/E*, growth, value) that are anticipated to rise in value more than the overall market.

Securities Stocks and bonds.

Securities Exchange Act of 1934 The federal law that established the Securities and Exchange Commission. It also added further regulations for securities markets. The law has been amended several times since its initial passage. One of the amendments that is relevant to mergers is the Williams Act of 1968.

Securitization Substitution of tradable securities for privately negotiated instruments.

Securitized accounts receivable A financing arrangement where accounts receivable are pooled and an undivided interest in the receivables pool, which represents a claim on the entire pool of receivables, is sold, effectively creating a security that is backed by the receivables. It is accounted for as a sale of accounts receivable.

Security analysis Determining correct value of a security in the marketplace.

Security characteristic line A plot of the excess return on a security over the risk-free rate as a function of the excess return on the market.

Security market line (SML) The line that reflects the combination of risk and return of alternative investments. In CAPM, risk is measured by systematic risk (beta).

Self-interest The choices that you think are the best for you.

Sell-off A general term describing a sale of a part of a company. It also includes other more specific transactions, such as divestitures or spin-offs.

Senior debt Debt that, in the event of bankruptcy, must be repaid before *subordinated debt* receives any payment.

Sensitivity analysis Analysis of the effect on project profitability of possible changes in sales, costs, and so on.

Separation property The property that portfolio choice can be separated into two independent tasks: (1) determination of the optimal risky portfolio, which is a purely technical problem, and (2) the personal choice of the best mix of the risky portfolio and the risk-free asset.

Services Mental or physical labor or help purchased by consumers. Examples are the assistance of physicians, lawyers, dentists, repair personnel, housecleaners, educators, retailers, and wholesalers; things purchased or used by consumers that do not have physical characteristics.

Settlement price The official closing price of a futures contract set by the clearinghouse at the end of the day and used for marking to market.

Settlor The creator of an inter vivos trust; also same as *grantor, trustor*, or *creator*.

Share of stock A legal claim to a share of a corporation's future profits; if it is common stock, it incorporates certain voting rights regarding major policy decisions of the corporation; if it is preferred stock, its owners are accorded preferential treatment in the payment of dividends.

Share-the-gains, share-the-pains theory A theory of regulatory behavior in which the regulators must take account of the demands of three groups: legislators, who established and who oversee the regulatory agency; members of the regulated industry; and consumers of the regulated industry's products or services.

Sharpe measure A relative measure of a portfolio's benefit-to-risk ratio, calculated as its average return in excess of the risk-free rate divided by the standard deviation of portfolio returns.

Sharpe ratio The ratio of mean excess return (return minus the risk-free rate) to standard deviation of returns (or excess returns).

Shortage A situation in which quantity demanded is greater than quantity supplied at a price below the market clearing price.

Short hedge A hedge involving the sale of forward or futures contracts to cover the risk of a long position in the spot market.

Short interest rate A one-period interest rate.

Short position The seller of a commodity or security or, for a forward contract, the counterparty who will be the eventual seller of the underlying asset.

Short run The short run in microeconomics has two meanings. (1) For the firm, it is the period of time in which the quantity of at least one input is fixed and the quantities of the other inputs can be varied. The fixed input is usually capital—that is, the firm has a given plant size. (2) For the industry, the short run is the period of time in which each firm has a given plant size and the number of firms in the industry is fixed.

Short sale The sale of shares not owned by the investor but borrowed through a broker and later repurchased to replace the loan. Profit is earned if the initial sale is at a higher price than the repurchase price.

Should Encouraged (recommended) to follow the recommendation of the GIPS standards but not required.

Signal (1) Action that demonstrates an individual's unobservable characteristics (because it would be unduly costly for someone without those characteristics to take the action). (2) An action taken by an informed person (or firm) to send a message to uninformed people or an action taken outside a market that conveys information that can be used by that market.

Simulation Monte Carlo simulation.

Single-factor model A model of security returns that acknowledges only one common factor. See *factor model*.

Sinking fund Bond provision that requires the issuer to redeem some or all of the bond systematically over the term of the bond rather than in full at maturity.

Skill One of the three components of the standard of prudence governing trustees; familiarity with business matters.

Slope The change in the value of the variable measured on the y-axis divided by the change in the value of the variable measured on the x-axis.

Yield to maturity   The total yield on a bond obtained by equating the bond's current market value to the discounted cash flows promised by the bond. Also called *actuarial yield*.

Yield spread   The difference between the promised yields of alternative bond issues or market segments at a given time relative to yields on Treasury issues of equal maturity.

Zero-beta portfolio   The minimum-variance portfolio uncorrelated with a chosen efficient portfolio.

Zero-coupon bond   A bond that pays its par value at maturity but no periodic interest payments. Its yield is determined by the difference between its par value and its discounted purchase price. Also called *original issue discount (OID) bonds*.

Z-score   Measure of the likelihood of bankruptcy.

INDEX

Page numbers followed by n refer to footnootes.

A

Aaker, David, V4: 227
AAR. *See* average accounting rate of return (AAR)
Aaron Rents, Inc., V2: 235–236
Aastrom Biosciences, Inc., V2: 375–376
abandonment options as real options, V3: 54, 56–57
Abate, James A., V4: 611
Abbey National (U.K.), V3: 269
Abbott Laboratories, V3: 189–190
ABG Gas Supply, LLC, V2: 195–197
abnormal earnings, V4: 572, 575
abnormal return, V4: 23; V6: 420
ABO. *See* accumulated benefit obligation (ABO)
ABS. *See* asset-backed sector (ABS) bonds
absolute prepayment speed (ABS), V5: 240
absolute priori rule, V5: 19
absolute return objective, V6: 447
absolute valuation model, V4: 27–29
Acacia Research Corp., V2: 252
accountability, V3: 133, 169
accounting conventions, V1: 571–572
accounting estimates, V4: 495n5
accounting income
  capital budgeting cash flows and, V3: 8–9
  project analysis/evaluation, V3: 61–64
accounting information, equity analysis and, V4: 18–14, 22
accounting methods, V4: 62. *See also* national accounting standards
  aggressive practices, V4: 595–596
  balance sheet adjustments for fair value, V4: 591–592
  cash flow and, V4: 536
  changes in, V4: 595
  clean surplus relationship, V4: 588–589
  earnings per share (EPS), V4: 498
  global differences in, V4: 135–147, 327
  goodwill, V4: 594
  intangible assets, V4: 592–495
  international considerations, V4: 551, 596–597

international harmonization of, V4: 137–139
nonrecurring items, V4: 595
residual income valuation model, V4: 588–596
Accounting Principles Board (APB)
  Opinion No. 16, V2: 102
  Opinion No. 18, V2: 22
accounting rate of return, V3: 26–27
accounting risk, V3: 169
Accounting Trends and Techniques (AICPA), V2: 87
accounts payable
  on cash flow analysis statement, V2: 410
  cash flow and, V2: 321–322, 329
  extending payment terms on, V2: 284–285
accounts receivable, classification of, V2: 290–295, 328
accreting swaps, V6: 256
accrual accounting, V2: 25, 441
accruals to revenue ratio, V2: 423
accumulated benefit obligation (ABO), V2: 67. *See also* pensions
accumulated postretirement benefit obligation (APBO), V2: 83
accumulation period, V5: 244
acid-test ratio, V5: 13–14
Acme Boot, V5: 31
acquisitions, V4: 11, 11n3. *See also* business combinations; mergers
  affecting earnings analysis, V2: 459–460
  cash flow and, V2: 213–214, 259–263
  defined, V2: 99
  standards for, V2: 100
Acree Products, V3: 249
active investment approach, V6: 439–440
active investment managers/styles, V4: 13, 17n10
active portfolio
  in construction of optimal risky portfolio, V6: 424–426
  in Treynor-Black portfolio construction, V6: 420
active portfolio management, V6: 411–432
  introduction, V6: 411–413
  alpha forecasts, V6: 427–429
  lure of, V6: 411–413
  market timing, V6: 414–418

multifactor models, V6: 426–427
objectives of active portfolios, V6: 413–414
security selection, V6: 418–426
summary, V6: 430–431
active risk management, in trusts, V1: 187
active strategy, V4: 23, 67
Activision, Inc., V2: 247
activity ratios, V2: 3, 468–469
actual returns
  above required returns, V4: 310–311
  vs. expected returns, V6: 374
A.D.A.M., Inc., V2: 248
ADC. *See* All Digital Component Corporation (ADC)
add-on interest, V6: 15
additional compensation arrangements, V1: 15, 76–77
Adelphia, V3: 139–140
adjusted beta, V6: 380
adjusted book value per common shares, V2: 450–451
adjusted coefficient of variation, V1: 279–280, 280n26
adjusted operating cash flow. *See* sustainable operating cash flow (SOCF)
adjusted present value (APV), V3: 26–27; V4: 432n2
administrative prudence, V1: 181
Adolf Coors Co., V2: 428
ADR. *See* American Depository Receipts (ADRs)
ADS (American depository shares), V3: 246
Advanced Power Technology, Inc., V2: 259, 260–261, 262
Advanta Mortgage Loan Trust, V5: 233–234
advertising, capitalizing cost of, V2: 239
Aerotechnique S.A., V3: 108
Africa, economic growth trends in, V1: 399
after-tax cost of debt, V4: 259–260
age, demographics of, V1: 581–589
agency costs, V3: 209
agency costs of equity, V3: 209
agency note futures contracts, V6: 289
agency problem, V3: 136
agency relationships, V3: 136–141; V5: 22–26

I-1

I-4   Index

individual, and arbitrage pricing
    theory, V6: 401–402
overvalued, V2: 386
of rental companies, V2: 235–237
selling and leasing back, V2:
    298–302
tangible/intangible, V3: 285
value of, V6: 23
Association for Investment Manage-
    ment and Research (AIMR),
    V4: 33–34, 38; V5: 29
code of ethics, V4: 34, 38
Professional Conduct Statement,
    V4: 34
research reports, V4: 38
Standards of Practice Handbook, V4: 38
asymmetric information, V3: 209,
    282–283
at-the-money, V6: 131, 133
Atlantic option, V6: 289, 295
AT&T Corp., V2: 310, 311, 327;
    V3: 268, 313–315
Wireless Services, V3: 269
auction market, V4: 48–49
auctions, calls, V5: 230
*Auditor's Responsibility to Consider Fraud
    and Error in an Audit of Financial
    Statements*, V4: 19n13
Australia, mortgage-backed securities,
    V5: 238–239
authorized participants, V4: 78
auto loans
    overview, V5: 239–241
    amortization, V5: 223–224
automated trading systems, V4: 48–50
AutoNation, Inc., V2: 214, 259
autoregressive conditional
    heteroskedasticity (ARCH),
    V5: 89–90
Avado Brands, Inc., V2: 276
available-for-sale securities
    classification and reporting of, V2:
        16, 111–112, 211
    international reporting of, V2: 14
    unrealized value changes in,
        V2: 10n6
    U.S. guidelines on, V2: 11–12, 13–14
Avaya, Inc., V2: 287
Avenaugh, Miles, V3: 111
Aventis (France/Germany), V3: 269
average accounting rate of return
    (AAR), V3: 10, 16
average cost pricing, V1: 422
average inventory processing period,
    V2: 3
average life
    overview, V5: 169
    contraction/expansion risks,
        V5: 173

home equity loans (HEL),
    V5: 234–235
PAC collars, V5: 195
prepayment stability, V5: 190
tranches, V5: 179, 189
variability, V5: 179
zero-volatility spread, V5: 268
average payables payment period,
    V2: 3
average receivable collection period,
    V2: 3
Aviall, Inc., V2: 280, 281, 284
Avis Rent a Car, V3: 330
Avon Products, Inc., V2: 313–315
AXA, V2: 44

B
backward induction, V5: 112
backwardation, V6: 91
backwardation, normal, V6: 92
Baker Hughes, Inc., V2: 285
balance of payments, V1: 485–486,
    511–518
balance of payments analysis, V1: 488
balance sheet
    adjusted book value per share,
        V2: 450–451
    adjustment checklist, V2: 444
    adjustments for fair value,
        V4: 591–592
    asset adjustments, V2: 441–442, 443,
        445–447
    book value analysis, V2: 441
    capital structure analysis,
        V2: 451–452
    consolidated *vs.* equity method,
        V2: 31–32, 33
    equity adjustments, V2: 445,
        449–450
    exchange rate disclosure on,
        V2: 167–169
    foreign currency translation
        methods affecting, V2: 152
    functional currency choice
        affecting, V2: 160
    liability adjustments, V2: 442–443,
        445, 447–449
    non-U.S. company adjustments to,
        V2: 452–453
    problems with, V2: 440–441
    purchase *vs.* pooling method, V2:
        105–106
    quality of earnings indicators, V4: 20
    securities reporting on, V2: 11, 12,
        14
balance sheet management, V4: 18
Ball Corporation, V2: 309
balloon maturity, V5: 205
Bancel, Franck, V3: 118

Banco Santander Central Hispano
    (Spain), V3: 269
Bank Boston, V3: 274
Bank for International Settlements,
    V6: 220
bank loans, V5: 29–31
Bank of America, V3: 269, 273–274
    equity-index linked notes,
        V6: 313–315
    interest rate swap example, V6: 229,
        231
Bank of New England, V3: 274
Bank of Nova Scotia, V3: 246; V4: 517
Bank of Scotland, V3: 274n11
Bank One, V3: 268, 269
bankers' bourses, V4: 47
banking
    innovation in, V4: 88–89
    interstate bank banking, V4: 89
banking sector
    leverage and, V3: 217–219
    mergers and, V3: 268, 270, 273–274,
        273n9, 273n10
    and restrictions on dividend
        payments, V3: 243
bankruptcy, V3: 201, 208–209
    predictions, V5: 41–42
    swaps and credit risk, V6: 263
BankSouth, V3: 274
barbell portfolios, V5: 80–81
Barclay's Bank (U.K.), V3: 243, 245
Barnett Banks, V3: 274
barriers, entrance/exit, V4: 160; V5: 12
Barron's, V2: 62
basic earnings per share, V4: 498
basic model of capital budgeting,
    V3: 60–61
basic prices, V1: 572–573
basis points, and standard deviations,
    V5: 85, 87
basis swaps, V6: 229n5, 255
Bavishi, Vinod, V4: 146
Baycorp, V3: 286
Bayer AG (Germany), V3: 226, 313
Bayern Chemicals KgaA, V3: 109–110
BCP (Portugal), V3: 269
bear markets, and forecasting, V6: 418
bear tranche, V6: 317
The Beard Co., V2: 309, 320–321
Beasley, M., V5: 25–26
Beazer Homes USA, Inc., V2: 276–277,
    370–372
Behner, Thomas, V3: 115
Belgium, intercompany investment
    reporting in, V2: 44
bell-shaped curve, in Black-Scholes-
    Merton model, V6: 187
benchmark value of the multiple,
    V4: 506

put-call-forward parity, V6: 203
put-call parity, V6: 157–163
    arbitrage opportunity, V6: 161–163
    defined, V6: 158–159
    fiduciary call, V6: 157–158
    options on forwards, V6: 202–205
    protective put, V6: 158
    synthetics, V6: 159–161
put option, V6: 289
puts on LIBOR, V4: 110
PVCF (present value of cash flows)
    model, V4: 276, 432–434
PVGO (present value of growth
    opportunities), V4: 172–173,
    390–391

Q

QIBs (qualified institutional buyers),
    V4: 72
QSPE (qualifying special purpose
    entity), V2: 129
quadratic relationship, V1: 207–208,
    208n4
Qualcomm, Inc., V2: 254, 255, 385
qualified institutional buyers (QIBs),
    V4: 72
qualifying special purpose entity
    (QSPE), V2: 129
qualitative dependent variables,
    V1: 315–317
quality of earnings, V2: 461–462.
    See also earnings
quality of earnings analysis, V4: 18–22
quality option, V6: 288
quality tests, V5: 251
Quanex (NX), V2: 46
quantitative equity strategies,
    V4: 32n27
quantitative methods, V1: 199–200
quarterly estimates, V4: 297
Quebec Securities Act (1986), V4: 71
Questar, V1: 380
quick ratio, V2: 3; V5: 14
Quicksilver Resources, V1: 382
quiet period, V1: 144
quote-driven market, V4: 48
quoted depth, V6: 351
quoted spreads, V6: 351
quotes
    on exchange rates, V6: 38
    on futures options, V6: 294
    on futures prices, V6: 281
QVC, V3: 290
Qwest Corp., V2: 239

R

R-square statistic, V6: 379
ramp-up periods, V5: 250
Ramsey, Frank, V1: 412

random walks, V1: 315
rapid accelerating growth, V4: 154
rate-of-return regulation, V1: 423
rates of return
    to investors, V6: 352
    on *i*th security, V6: 419
    in market timing, V6: 414–416
    using factor models, V6: 390–391
    well-diversified portfolios, V6: 395
rating agencies
    covenants, V5: 38
    credit enhancements, V5: 225–226
    duration, V5: 78–81
    notches, V5: 10n6
    outlook, V5: 9
    portfolio diversity, V5: 251n24
    process, V5: 8–9
    securitization, V5: 220
    watches, V5: 9
rating system, for investment decision
    making, V1: 147, 153
ratio analysis. *See also* financial ratios
    international analysis, V4: 135
rational efficient markets formulation,
    V4: 26
rational expectations hypothesis, V4: 88
Raychem Corp., V2: 262
Rayonier, V3: 330
real estate investment trusts (REITs),
    V2: 207
real exchange rate movements,
    V1: 537, 551–553
real exchange rate risk, V1: 539
real foreign currency risk, V1: 539
real interest rate(s), V1: 490, 518–519
real money supply, V1: 519n21
real options, V6: 143, 321–325
    capital budgeting, V3: 53–57
    defined, V6: 322
    international frequency of use,
        V3: 26–27
real returns, V6: 446
realized returns, and index model,
    V6: 374–375
realized value of alpha, V6: 376
reasonable and adequate basis.
    See diligence and reasonable basis
rebalancing function, V4: 13
rebalancing portfolios, V6: 441–442
receivables
    in cash flow analysis, V2: 410, 412,
        443, 446
    classification of, V2: 222, 214,
        253–256, 290–295, 328
    securitized, V2: 290–295, 409
receivables days, V2: 422
receivables to revenue ratio, V2: 423
receivables turnover ratio, V2: 3, 161,
    421–422

receiver swaption, V6: 257, 261
recession phase, V4: 149, 157
recognition
    GAAP on, V2: 384
    of impairments, V2: 112–113
    of losses, V2: 23n21
    of pension obligations, V2: 72,
        73–74. *See also* pensions
    of price changes, V2: 9–10
record date of dividend payment,
    V3: 237
record keeping, in soft dollar context,
    V1: 130, 140
records retention, V1: 16, 89–90
recovery phase, V4: 149, 157
reduced form models, V5: 43, 43n59
reference assets/rates, V5: 66, 251–252
referral fees, V1: 16, 100–102
refinancing
    auto loans, V5: 240
    burnout, V5: 172
    incentives, V5: 172, 271
registered investment advisors, V6: 434
regression analysis, V1: 201–202,
    248–249
    analysis of variance in, with one
        independent variable,
        V1: 241–244
    assumptions of linear regression in,
        V1: 225–228
    coefficient of determination in,
        V1: 230–232, 279–280
    hypothesis testing in, V1: 232–240
    limitations of, V1: 247
    linear regression in, V1: 222–225
    multiple regression in, V1: 263–318.
        See also multiple linear regression
    prediction intervals in, V1: 244–246
    standard error of estimate in,
        V1: 228–230
    yield curve changes, V5: 63
regression coefficients, V1: 222, 265,
    277–279
regression equation, V6: 369–370
regression error, V1: 222, 226, 226n25
regression residual, V1: 223
regression sum of squares, V1: 277, 278
regressors, V1: 264n1
regular dividends, V3: 226–227
regulations, V1: 419–420, 431; V4: 220.
    See also antitrust laws
    changes/risks, V5: 12
    and cost-benefit analysis, V1: 430
    cost of, V1: 427–428
    and deregulation, V1: 428–430
    economic, objectives of, V1: 423
    enforcement costs, V5: 24
    of futures contracts, V6: 59
    in global economy, V1: 419–420